Society for Post-M

Exploring N... ions

from Seasonal Presence to Perma... ttlement

St John's, Newfoundland 16-20 June 2010

An international conference on the occasion of the 400th anniversary of the founding of the first English settlement in Canada at Cupers Cove, Newfoundland, in 1610

CALL FOR PAPERS & SESSIONS

The Society for Post Medieval Archaeology, Memorial University of Newfoundland, and Bournemouth University are pleased to announce a conference which will reconsider early phases of colonisation of the New World in the context of wider processes of settlement and sedentism, in both northeastern North America and Europe. We invite researchers working on relevant themes to propose papers or sessions. The conference will be held in St John's, Newfoundland, one of the first places exploited by Europeans in the New World. The conference language will be English.

Conference Theme People move all the time. The 16th-18th centuries were a turbulent time around the North Atlantic, with a great deal of population movement on every scale: national, regional; rural, urban, suburban; international, transjurisdictional, and especially transatlantic. The focus of this conference is the tail end of those processes: sedentism. How/why/when do people turn temporary use of a place into permanent occupation?

Suggested Sessions Seasonal camps: potters' kilns, mining camps, fishing stations
Transatlantic exploration and tentative settlement: e.g. Cartier-Roberval in Quebec, 1542
Artifacts: How do they reflect sedentism ? Ecofacts: Scientific study of mobility and sedentism
Environmental resource attractions & Environmental impacts
Environmental adjustments: settlement of new environments, e.g. at new elevations or latitudes
Displacement: emigrants, immigrants & dispossession, e.g. of Native Peoples
Demographics: seasonal populations: male-dominated, youth-dominated ?

We invite proposals for sessions and papers on these or similar themes. Presentations will be 20 minutes, followed by a brief discussion. The Society for Post-Medieval Archaeology plans to publish selected contributions as a monograph. We expect to be able to offer financial support to some overseas speakers and students, details depending on our funding.

Please send paper or session titles with abstracts of up to 200 words by 1 September 2009 to:

Peter Pope <ppope@mun.ca> OR **Mark Brisbane <mbrisbane@bmth.ac.uk>**

POST-MEDIEVAL ARCHAEOLOGY

VOLUME 43 PART 1

The Recent Archaeology of the Early Modern Period in Québec City

Guest Editor: William Moss

THE JOURNAL OF THE SOCIETY FOR POST-MEDIEVAL ARCHAEOLOGY

2009

Post-Medieval Archaeology (ISSN 0079-4236 (print); 1745-8137 (online)) is published biannually by Maney Publishing; Volume 43 is the volume for 2009.

Subscriptions are entered by the volume and include postage (air-speeded overseas). Subscriptions must be prepaid at the rate appropriate to the location of the subscriber.

Volume 43 (2009) 2 issues:
Institutional rate (including online access): £150; North America: US$304
Individual rate: £42*; North America: US$84

* Subscriptions are welcomed from individuals who do not wish to join the Society for Post-Medieval Archaeology if prepaid by personal cheque or credit card and if the journal is to be sent to a private address.

All orders must be sent to Customer Sales and Services, Maney Publishing, Suite 1C, Joseph's Well, Hanover Walk, Leeds LS3 1AB, UK (fax: +44 (0) 113 386 8178; email: subscriptions@maney.co.uk) or to Maney Publishing North America, 875 Massachusetts Avenue, 7th Floor, Cambridge, MA 02139, USA (fax: 617 354 6875; email: maney@maneyusa.com). All cheques must be payable to Maney Publishing.

Back issues Maney Publishing holds journals from the current and previous year. Older volumes are held by our official stockists, Periodicals Service Company, to whom all orders and enquiries should be addressed. Periodicals Service Company, 11 Main Street, Germantown, NY 12525, USA. Tel: +1 5185 374 700; fax: +1 5185 375 899; email: psc@periodicals.com

Advertising and general enquiries should be sent to Maney Publishing.

Maney Publishing is the trading name of W. S. Maney & Son Ltd, Suite 1C, Joseph's Well, Hanover Walk, Leeds LS3 1AB, UK.

***Post-Medieval Archaeology* is indexed or abstracted in**: *Abstracts in Anthropology*, *Academic Search*, *America: History and Life*, *Art and Archaeology Technical Abstracts*, *British and Irish Archaeological Abstracts*, *British Humanities Index*, *Current Abstracts*, *Getty Conservation Institute Project Bibliographies*, *Historical Abstracts*, *International Bibliography of Periodicals Literature (IBZ)*, *MLA*, *Numismatic Literature*, *Periodicals Index Online*, *Repertoire International de la Littérature de l'Art*, *Royal Historical Society Bibliography*, *Scopus*, and *TOC Premier*.

Summaries translated by Sophie Blain, Friederike Hammer, Marta Caroscio and Alejandra Gutiérrez

The European Reference Index for the Humanities (ERIH), published by the European Science Foundation in 2007, places *Post-Medieval Archaeology* in its category 'A': high-ranking international publications with a very strong reputation among researchers of the field in different countries, regularly cited all over the world.

Front Cover Illustration
Quebec vers le sud-ouest, 1992 (courtesy of Pierre Lahoud)

Back Cover & Title Page Design
The drawing by P. Brears is of a miner, from a 15th-century brass in All Saints' Church, Newland, Gloucestershire.

Contents

Introduction: the archaeology of a North American city and the early modern period in Québec
By William Moss 1

Before New France

The natural environment of the Québec City region during the Holocene
By Louise Filion, Martin Lavoie *and* Lydia Querrec 13

A universe under strain: Amerindian nations in north-eastern North America in the 16th century
By Marcel Moussette 30

An aborted attempt at settling New France in the 16th century: Cartier and Roberval's Charlesbourg Royal

Charlesbourg-Royal and France-Roi (1541–43): France's first colonization attempt in the Americas
By Richard Fiset *and* Gilles Samson 48

The archaeological collection from the Cartier-Roberval site (1541–43): a remarkable testimony to French colonization efforts in the Americas
By Hélène Côté 71

From myth to reality: archaeobotany at the Cartier-Roberval Upper Fort site
By Julie-Anne Bouchard-Perron *and* Allison Bain 87

Governing New France from the Château Saint-Louis

The Saint-Louis forts and chateaux site: archaeology in the heart of New France
By Pierre Cloutier *and* Paul-Gaston L'Anglais 106

The origins of the Château Saint-Louis, the residence of the Governor of New France
By Manon Goyette 125

Fort Saint-Louis and other 17th-century fortification works discovered recently in Québec City
By Jacques Guimont 140

Administering New France from the Intendant's Palace

The Intendant's Palace site: urbanization of Québec City's Lower Town
By Réginald Auger, Daniel Simoneau *and* Allison Bain 156

The Intendant's Palace site: new insight into its physical evolution and initial occupation
By Daniel Simoneau 171

Bugs, seeds and weeds at the Intendant's Palace: a study of an evolving landscape
By Allison Bain, Julie-Anne Bouchard-Perron, Réginald Auger *and* Daniel Simoneau . 183

Inhabiting New France

Québec in the time of Champlain
By Françoise Niellon 198

The Seminary of Québec site: from New France's earliest farm to its first religious institution
By Daniel Simoneau. 213

An archaeological view of the French colonial port of Québec
By Serge Rouleau 229

The foreshore of the St Lawrence at the Îlot Hunt site in the 17th and 18th centuries: an open dump?
By Céline Cloutier 245

Credits

Guest Editor: William Moss

Text Editing: François D.-Girard, Alison McGain, Jane Macauley, Christian Roy and Hélène Côté

Translation: Alison McGain and Jane Macaulay assisted by Donald Kellough, Kathryn Lawson, Abigail Ratcliffe, Anne-Hélène Kerbiriou and Jean-Paul Salaün

Entente de développement culturel
Ville de Québec
Culture, Communications et Condition féminine Québec
Parks Canada Parcs Canada
Canada
CELAT
AAQ
Commission de la Capitale Nationale Québec

Post-Medieval Archaeology **43/1** (2009), 1–12

Introduction: the archaeology of a North American city and the early modern period in Québec

By WILLIAM MOSS

SUMMARY: Over the years, an impressive number of research programmes have been conducted on major archaeological sites in Québec City. These programmes have been implemented by large research teams affiliated to several institutions. Both individually and collectively, these initiatives have generated considerable new knowledge on the early modern period in the New World. They have also created a research context which is unique in Canada, not only because of the number of individuals involved but also the scale and quality of the results. This introduction gives a brief overview of these programmes, whose findings are generally published only in French.

INTRODUCTION

This volume of *Post-Medieval Archaeology*, published by the Society for Post-Medieval Archaeology (SPMA), is the result of collaboration between the SPMA and the Association des archéologues du Québec (AAQ). It contains fifteen papers translated into English from French, the language of Québec City and of the different researchers who participated in this cooperative venture. French versions of thirteen of the papers will appear in the 2009 edition of *Archéologiques*, a journal published annually by the AAQ.

Two of the papers selected for publication under this joint project appear exclusively in English in this volume of *Post-Medieval Archaeology*, as they have already appeared in French in other journals. Marcel Moussette's text, 'A universe under strain: Amerindian nations in north-eastern North America in the 16th century', was first published in *Les cahiers des dix* in 2005,[1] while Françoise Niellon's paper 'Québec in the time of Champlain' was published in *Archéologiques* in 2008.[2] They have been included in *Post-Medieval Archaeology* for the benefit of English-language readers because of their importance for providing a comprehensive view of the subjects presented in the other papers, all of which are first-time publications.

All the sites examined in the present volume, excepting the Cartier-Roberval site, are located within the limits of the Historic District of Old Québec, which has been inscribed on UNESCO's World Heritage List. As a whole, they present a vision of this heritage city that differs from the classical perception, which is limited to its built heritage and town plan — both readily perceptible to the passer-by. Including archaeological sites in the definition of cultural heritage in Québec City has broadened this term to encompass a wealth of new knowledge and material evidence in the form of artefacts and collections.

The sites discussed in this volume of *Post-Medieval Archaeology* can easily be described by superlatives, not only because of their archaeological interest, which stems from the quality of the artefacts and architectural features comprising them, but also because of their contribution to a renewed and profound understanding of regional, national and even international history. These sites are also of considerable symbolic importance to Canadian and Québécois cultural heritage.

 DOI: 10.1179/007942309X12457508843801

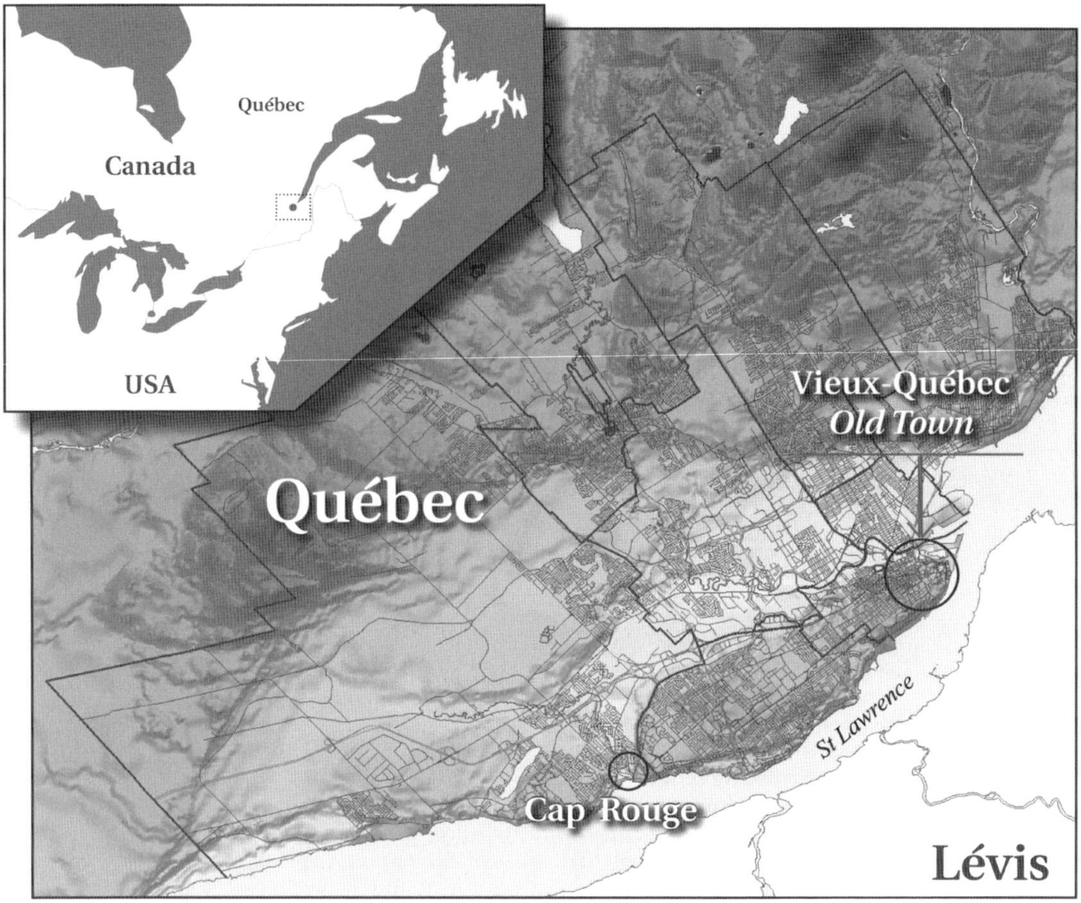

FIG. 1
Map of Québec City showing the old town and Cap Rouge (drawn by D. Bussières).

QUÉBEC IN 2008

In 2008, Québec City celebrated the 400th anniversary of its founding by Samuel de Champlain. The celebration was an occasion to commemorate events that took place in 1608, as well as those that happened in the decades preceding and following this key date. Indeed, the year 1608 can be seen as a point in a process of transition rather than as a beginning or an end. It is important to remember that Native Americans had already been living in the region of Québec for nearly ten millennia when Champlain landed here, and that contacts between Aboriginals and different European actors in the north-eastern part of the continent were already well established at the time. For its first years, Québec was no more than a trading post and could not claim the status of town or city.

The manner in which this volume of *Post-Medieval Archaeology* looks at the years before and after 1608 is specific to the context of commemorating the rich history of Québec. It presents the vision of a community of researchers working for a series of important institutions: the City of Québec; the Ministère de la Culture, des Communications et de la Condition feminine (MCCCF) and the Commission de la capitale nationale du Québec (CCNQ), both of which are affiliated with the Québec provincial government; Parks Canada, a federal government agency; and Université Laval. Each organization has its own mission and mandates, but their researchers have several things in common. Apart from their appreciation of their city, they share the knowledge and the know-how of their discipline as well as the expertise they have developed during their research over the years. The results presented here are the legacy of several generations of researchers, and they represent a new sum of knowledge, an assessment of the gains made thus far and a reminder of the questions that remain to be addressed in order to complete the general portrait. Several archaeological projects are still under way and, in some cases, still in their early stages. Some of the interpretations presented in this volume will thus evolve and mature in the future. Interested readers are therefore invited to take a look at these projects again in the coming years.

Québec's 400th anniversary celebrations provided an excellent opportunity to present the results of the various archaeological research programmes conducted in the city. First, many of the programmes were still active, making it relatively easy to compile new information on them. In addition, the commemoration activities gave momentum to the projects and, accordingly, to the development of the archaeological sites. Indeed, there was a firm desire to communicate the results of this research to the general public.

The portrait of Québec's urban fabric produced by these projects has thus been woven by different institutions, each working in its own corporate environment and telling its own story. The material and intellectual synergy that has been created in the process is representative of the practice of archaeology in Québec and in Canada.

The federal government, represented by the Parks Canada Agency, has spearheaded numerous projects on Québec City's fortifications, of which it is the principal owner. One of these projects has centred on the Saint-Louis Forts and Châteaux National Historic Site, which is not only part of the fortification network but also a major tourist attraction. The government of the Province of Québec has also implemented several initiatives, focused, for example, on Champlain's Habitation and the Place Royale sector as a whole. In some instances, the provincial government works in partnership with other organizations such as the CCNQ and the City of Québec. The City, for its part, has undertaken research on a number of major sites in the old town, such as the Seminary of Québec, Îlot Hunt and the Intendant's Palace. As for Université Laval, it has carried out research on several sites, including the Intendant's Palace, in the context of its field school. The university's researchers and students are also involved in a number of the other projects described here.

The present volume thus required the collaboration of several actors who pooled their efforts in order to publish the results of their current research for the benefit of the scientific community.

QUÉBEC IN SPACE AND IN TIME

Québec is located at the meeting point of three of the major geological regions of north-eastern North America. Therefore, the region has physical diversity, the origins of which can be traced to its post-glacial past, particularly the events of the Holocene.[3] This diversity is also due to the different ecological zones that can be reached by the St Lawrence River and its numerous tributaries. Unlike the central latitudes of Europe, the Québec City area has been habitable for only the past 10,000 years, as prior to that time it was covered by the Wisconsinian continental ice sheet and the post-glacial seas that formed in the wake of the glacier's retreat. However, since human populations first penetrated the area, it has been occupied continuously. Nevertheless, relatively few sites have been associated with the region's prehistoric period, which concludes with the arrival of Europeans in the 16th century.

The strategic geopolitical position of the site where Québec City now stands was rapidly recognized by the first Europeans to venture into the region in search of a passage to China and the wealth of this *terra incognita*. Indeed, this site is situated at the entry point to the Great Lakes Basin, the heart of the North American continent and of all the riches therein. Moreover, for these early explorers, the site occupied an eminently defensible position, being located at a narrowing of the St Lawrence River and encompassing the Cap Diamant promontory. Québec maintained strategic military importance until the end of the 19th century.[4]

Canadian readers will be familiar with the temporal subdivisions used by the authors of the papers in this volume: the period of first contacts between Native Americans and Europeans during the 16th century; the French regime, running from the beginning of the 17th century until the Treaty of Paris in 1763; and the subsequent British regime, which ends with the creation of the Dominion of Canada in 1867. They will also be familiar with the different events punctuating this time scale: the first voyages of discovery, such as those of Jacques Cartier in the 1530s; the founding of Québec by Samuel de Champlain in 1608; its brief occupation by the Kirke brothers, corsairs of the English Crown, from 1629 to 1632; the imposition of royal government in 1663; the fall of Québec to British arms at the Battle of the Plains of Abraham in 1759, made official by the Treaty of Paris, which brought an end to the Seven Years War in 1763;[5] and the unsuccessful siege of Québec by the American revolutionary army under the command of General Benedict Arnold in 1775.

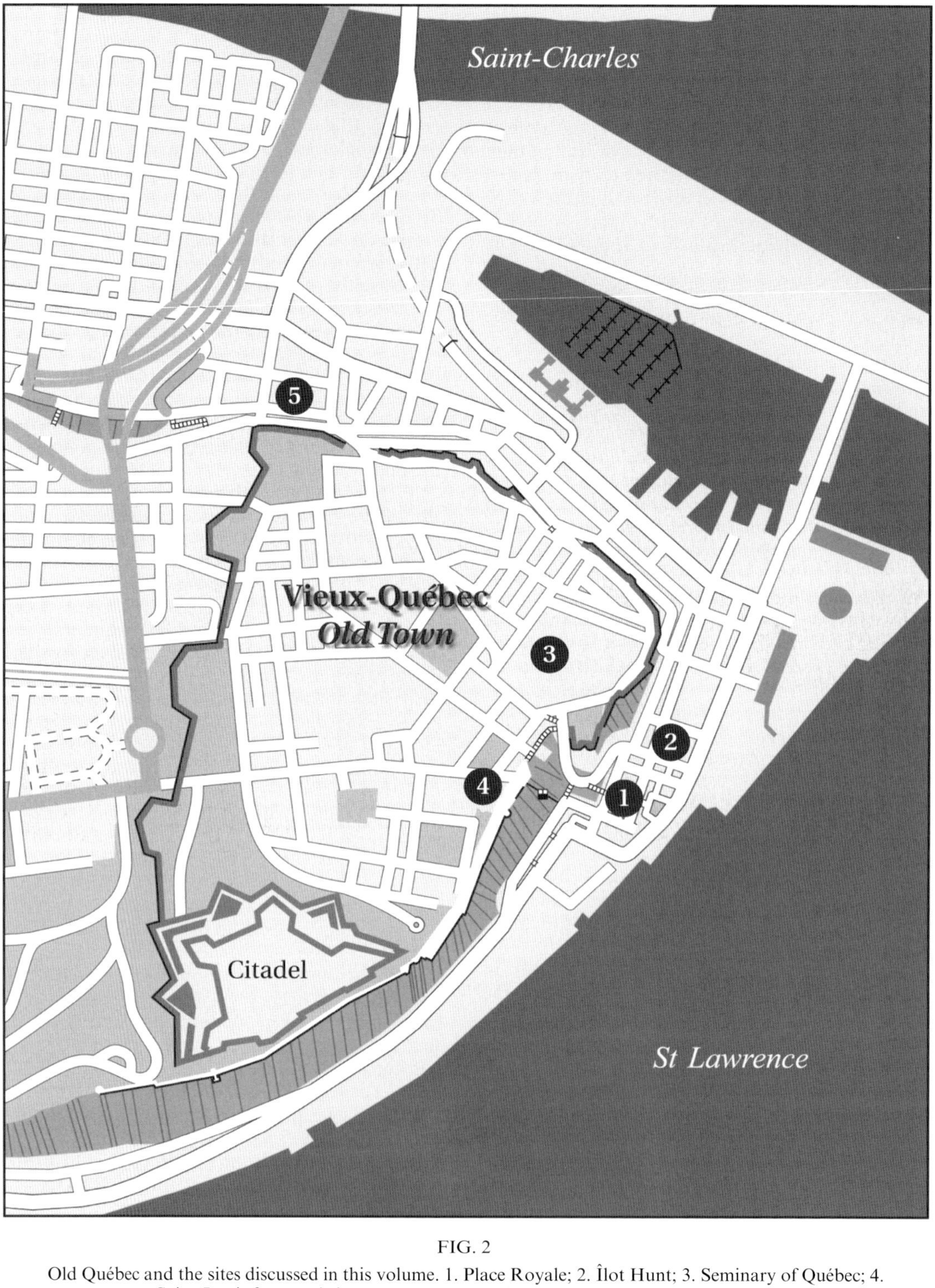

FIG. 2

Old Québec and the sites discussed in this volume. 1. Place Royale; 2. Îlot Hunt; 3. Seminary of Québec; 4. Saint-Louis forts and chateaux; 5. Intendant's Palace (drawn by D. Bussières).

FIG. 3
Aerial photograph of Old Québec. 1. Place Royale; 2. Îlot Hunt; 3. Seminary of Québec; 4. Saint-Louis forts and chateaux; 5. Intendant's Palace (photograph, P. Lahoud).

All of these crucial events took place in the context of the early modern period in the New World colonies, which began with European expansion into new continents and ended with three revolutions, two of which were political (those of the British colonies in North America and of France) and one of which was social (the industrial revolution). British readers must thus recast their vision of this early modern period in terms of the history of North America if they are properly to understand the papers in this volume.

In recounting the history of Québec, the occupation of this territory by Native American peoples over a 10,000-year period should of course be taken into account. However, since this would go beyond the reach of this volume, it is worth noting, for readers who would like to continue on this line of enquiry, that a new synthesis on the prehistory of the Québec region is now available.[6] For our present purposes, the historical focus of this volume of *Post-Medieval Archaeology* begins in the 16th century, when Europeans first entered the Gulf of St Lawrence in pursuit of whales and cod. They soon came into contact with Aboriginal groups, and multiple exchanges ensued. Obtaining furs for the European market in exchange for symbolic and utilitarian objects in metal, glass and other exotic materials that were immediately prized by Amerindians rapidly constituted the basis of this trade economy. The French and the English were also in search of gold, diamonds and other precious objects, as can be seen through recent discoveries made on the Cartier-Roberval and the Intendant's Palace sites.

Before the founding of New France and during the decades following the colonization efforts of Cartier and Roberval, the site now occupied by Québec City did not play a preponderant role in relations between Native nations and the different groups of Europeans who were increasingly present in North America. According to recent interpretations, newly developing exchange networks may have bypassed the Strait of Québec by following rivers flowing to the eastern seaboard of the mid-Atlantic Ocean or by following the northern route extending from Lake Saint-Jean to Georgian Bay. It was not until the 17th century, when France decided to establish a permanent foothold near Native American fur suppliers, that a permanent post was created at Québec, giving birth to both the city and the colony of New France.

Once created, the new colony had to be populated, protected, managed and provisioned, processes that required uniting the colony's principal functions in a single locale, the city of Québec. Notwithstanding its status as a city and as the capital of New France, Québec was never a large urban centre during the French regime. Only 31 people stayed with Samuel de Champlain during his first winter at the new outpost in 1608. A century later, in 1707, the population attained only 1,939 souls. At the beginning of the Seven Years War in 1755, 7,215 people lived in the city, but that number fell to 3,497 by 1762, shortly before the end of the conflict. Immigration increased following the cessation of hostilities, and the population reached 7,162 inhabitants in 1795.[7]

In 1650, the Jesuit Raguenau described the town as a miserable hamlet of 30 houses distributed with no apparent order.[8] Raguenau's evaluation was probably too severe, as a town plan had been implanted in 1635 by Charles Huault de Montmagny, New France's first governor. Also, the construction of defensive systems under military engineers at the end of the 17th and the beginning of the 18th century imposed a well-defined town plan.[9] Even today it is obvious that Québec was planned from the 17th century onwards.

The evolution of the French colony's political organization can be broken down into two main periods. During the first 50 years, the colony was administered by private companies that exercised monopolies or pursued free trade. However, their inability to combine commerce with populating the new territory led the king to accord New France the status of a royal colony in 1663. For all intents and purposes, the territory was then administered like a metropolitan province, under the direction of two official representatives of the king, namely, the governor and the intendant.[10] It is necessary to understand fully this colonial administration shared by two high-ranking figures in order to appreciate the contribution of research on two of the sites discussed in this volume: the Saint-Louis forts and chateaux site and the Intendant's Palace site.

A number of archaeological sites, among the richest in Québec City, illustrate the evolution of this urban centre. Large-scale research programmes, designed to be carried out over several years while being adapted to the day-to-day functioning of a living city, have been undertaken over the past quarter-century by several organizations. In the process, understanding of the city has evolved and been enlarged. More complete knowledge of the French presence during the first third of the 16th century and of the presence of French merchants and adventurers during the last third of that century have led us to reconsider the significance of the year 1608. Although the general public perceives it as the year New France was founded, 1608 can no longer really be seen as a founding date but rather as the point when the French presence shifted from transitory to permanent. It is thus a crucial date in the evolution of the relations that had begun nearly a full century earlier between Native Americans and the French.

As for the year 2008, with its powerful symbolic charge for commemorating Québec's history, it offered an opportunity to reassess our knowledge of the city, to initiate syntheses of existing data and to envisage new directions thanks to the synergy developed between researchers and various public organizations. It can be hoped that this new understanding, through its richness and depth, will generate a new vision of the full potential of Québec's archaeological heritage.

AN ARCHAEOLOGICAL PERSPECTIVE ON THE CITY

This section provides a summary of the main results of the various archaeological research projects in Québec City. It begins with a brief overview of the sites on which these results were obtained and the manner in which these findings are presented in this volume of *Post-Medieval Archaeology*. It will then discuss the new knowledge acquired through the projects and the different research approaches applied. The aim of the section is to underscore the complementary nature of the interpretations yielded by the different sites and highlight the new portrait of the city that has emerged in the course of this archaeological research.

THE ARCHAEOLOGICAL SITES

The archaeological sites discussed in the volume are presented according to five main themes that reflect key phases in the history of Québec. Other factors, such as the nature of the research conducted on the sites, the institutional context in which the work has been carried out and the internal coherence of the subjects concerned, have also had an impact on the volume's general organization.

In the first section, 'Before New France', two papers describe the situation on the north-eastern part of the continent before the arrival of Europeans. The first, by L. Filion, M. Lavoie and L. Querrec, presents the environmental context since the end of the most recent glacial period with a view to providing a better understanding of the environmental data from the different sites dealt with in this volume. The second, by M. Moussette, describes encounters between Native Americans and Europeans during the 16th century, a time when each group was defining the nature of its relations with the other.

The papers in the second chapter, 'An aborted attempt at settling New France in the 16th century: Cartier and Roberval's Charlesbourg-Royal', describe research currently underway on a major new site attesting to the presence of Europeans in North America. The site was occupied for only two short years, yet it fully illustrates the will of European powers to establish themselves in the Americas. Despite the failure of this effort, the site has definite symbolic importance in the pantheon of colonization attempts in Post-Columbian America. Finds from this site are particularly important for our understanding of material culture and the changing environment during this very early period of European presence in the New World.

The next two chapters examine two sites of fundamental importance for the administration of the colony of New France. These sites are particularly rich in material remains — structural features, artefacts and ecofacts — and are also of clear symbolic importance for the French colony. Furthermore, they are particularly rich, given the intense urban development in their vicinity. The titles of these two chapters — 'Governing New France from the Château Saint-Louis' and 'Administering New France from the Intendant's Palace' — aptly describe the subject matter of the three papers each chapter contains.

The final chapter — 'Inhabiting New France' — comprises four papers presenting the results of investigations on a series of sites in Old Québec. The papers describe different aspects of the life of the city's inhabitants, as well as of the city itself, which, during the French Regime and especially the 17th century, represented only a minute portion of the territory of the present-day urban agglomeration.

NEW KNOWLEDGE

All the papers in this volume present new knowledge about the city and the colony, garnered for the most part during major projects carried out over the past ten years.[11] Three papers are an exception, however, insofar as they provide syntheses of large corpora of data acquired over a much longer period of time. The first, by L. Filion, M. Lavoie and L. Querrec and second, by M. Moussette have been described above. A third paper, 'Québec in the time of Champlain', by F. Niellon, assembles existing information concerning the early years of the city. Niellon describes the main archaeological sites containing information about the first three decades of the city's history: Champlain's Habitation, the Hébert and Couillard homesteads on the Seminary of Québec site and, lastly, Cap Tourmente, located 40km downstream from Québec. Her examination of the principal structural remains and collections discovered on these sites represents the most exhaustive portrait yet drawn of this crucial period.

A fourth paper in this volume also looks at data amassed over a long period, although in relation to a single site. In 'The Seminary of Québec site: from New France's earliest farm to its first religious institution', D. Simoneau follows the evolution of archaeological research on a site in the heart of Old Québec from the middle of the 19th century up to today. Through in-depth analysis of over 100 years of investigation on this site, where the first private dwellings in New France have been discovered, Simoneau recounts the lives of the first settlers in the colony.

Although still relatively unexplored, certain new sites uncovered recently in Québec bear witness to some of the most significant moments of European settlement in North America. In their article 'Charlesbourg-Royal and France-Roi (1541–43): France's first colonization attempt in the Americas', R. Fiset and G. Samson recount recent discoveries made on the Cartier-Roberval site starting in 2006, after more than half a century of unsuccessful efforts to locate remains of this early French colonization initiative. Though it was occupied for only two years, the Cartier-Roberval site harbours quite a sizeable set of archaeological remains. Research has only just begun here, but traces of the French feudal system have already been identified, including artefacts associated with the nobility, possibly even with the Viceroy, Sieur de Roberval. The collection from the site is very rich despite its fragmentary condition and the limited area excavated to date. Jewellery, fine glassware and Italian maiolica all bear witness to the opulence of the first settlers, while crucibles, lead pellets, sulphur nodules and fragments of a scorifier speak to the explorers' attempts to locate precious metals. The collection is analysed by H. Côté in the paper 'The archaeological collection from the Cartier-Roberval site (1541–43): a remarkable testimony to French colonization efforts in the Americas'. According to her analysis, the collection exhibits similarities to the material culture of certain regions in France and other parts of Europe, as shown, for example, by a comparison of the Cartier-Roberval material with artefacts from the *Mary Rose*. In the article 'From myth to reality: archaeobotany at the Cartier-Roberval Upper Fort site', J.-A. Bouchard-Perron and A. Bain describe oats, grapes, olives, dates, peas and lentils unearthed at the site. They also recount the discovery of Iroquoian pottery, kernels of corn and sunflower seeds, all resulting from contacts between Native Americans and Europeans.

A number of sites in Québec City have been the focus of archaeological research for the past 30 years. Investigations on some of them intensified, however, in the years leading up to the 400th anniversary of the city's founding. For example, the Saint-Louis Forts and Châteaux National Historic Site, which was studied intensively in the 1980s during the reconstruction of Dufferin Terrace,[12] has recently been the scene of renewed research. The new programme, which is described by P. Cloutier and P.-G. L'Anglais in 'The Saint-Louis forts and chateaux site: archaeology in the heart of New France', has brought to light important new information on this fortified complex. Some of this data pertains to the residence of the representative of the king of France in North America and is the focus of a paper by M. Goyette entitled 'The origins of the Château Saint-Louis, the residence of the governor of New France'. Since the Saint-Louis forts and chateaux site played host to the first organized fortifications in the colony, the paper by J. Guimont, 'Fort Saint-Louis and other 17th-century fortification works discovered recently in Québec City', uses this location as a starting point for reflection on the construction of defensive works, initially under the administration of trading companies and, from 1663, under the administration of the French Crown. Although the fundamental importance of fortifications to Québec City has already been well documented by historians using the abundant archaeological data at their disposal,[13] recent work on the Saint-Louis forts and chateaux site has unveiled new aspects of the defence of the town during the 17th century.

The case of the Intendant's Palace site is similar to that of the Saint-Louis forts and chateaux site. One of its components, the first Intendant's Palace, was the scene of intensive research by Université Laval's field school from 1982 to 1988.[14] The field school returned to the site in 2000, using an environmental approach aimed at exploring the wealth of information on this urban site. As described by R. Auger, D. Simoneau and A. Bain in 'The Intendant's Palace site: urbanization of Québec City's Lower Town', this new approach has revealed the ways in which this urban space, which served a range of functions in the course of its history, was restructured after each change in vocation. Initially serving as an industrial complex that integrated shipbuilding, beer making and potash production, this site — which was, incidentally, the city's first industrial park — was transformed into an administrative complex. According to D. Simoneau in his paper 'The Intendant's Palace site: new insight into its physical evolution and initial occupation', this process involved more than a simple change of function or a mere accumulation of occupation levels, but entailed a physical and symbolic reorganization of this space in a wider urban environment that was itself constantly changing. Lastly, through an analysis of arthropods and plant remains in 'Bugs, seeds and weeds at the Intendant's Palace site: a study of an evolving landscape', A. Bain, J.-A. Bouchard-Perron, R. Auger and D. Simoneau examine the manner in which the site's natural environment was modified during these periods of reorganization.

No history of Québec would be complete without an examination of its port. Indeed, this aspect of the city's development is just as important for recent historical syntheses[15] as it is for new archaeological research. Québec was the only seaport located in the interior of the continent during the French regime, for neither Trois-Rivières nor Montréal was accessible to sea-going vessels until the 19th century. S. Rouleau analyses structural remains of Québec's port infrastructures in 'An archaeological view of the French colonial port of Québec' in order to ascertain their impact on the urban landscape. The city's wharves were largely private constructions, but they could be commandeered by the Crown in time of war in order to install cannon batteries for protecting the port. They were erected in riverine and estuarine settings with high tidal ranges, whose amplitude varied from 4 to 7m depending on the season and made for an extreme environment to which the port's builders constantly had to adapt. Thanks to recent archaeological research, our understanding of this adaptation process has gone beyond that which would have been achieved using iconographic and written sources alone.

A second paper on the port, written by C. Cloutier, examines the physical conditions of this part of the urban environment. Entitled 'The foreshore of the St Lawrence at the Îlot Hunt site in the 17th and 18th centuries: an open dump?', it questions the exact nature of the riverbank. Cloutier's description of this environment as seen through the archaeological data differs from the picture provided by official documents of the time.

RENEWED APPROACHES

New information about Québec City has resulted in part from renewed research approaches adopted specifically for archaeology in this urban setting. These approaches have two focuses, one being interdisciplinary studies in general, the other environmental reconstruction. Interest in the latter stems in part from a research design developed by Université Laval for its field school at the Îlot Hunt site.[16] Laval is an important partner in many of the projects described in this volume because of the specialized analyses its researchers perform as part of these projects or through the university's own research programmes and its training initiative for new archaeologists. Its constant efforts to interpret data in long-term contexts put into perspective the changes caused to the environment by the arrival of Europeans in the St Lawrence Valley. The changes that occurred over the last 10,000 years are due to natural processes following the retreat of the continental ice sheet, while those that have taken place over the last 400 years are due to human intervention. As stated by Filion *et al.*,

> Although geological and geomorphological events and the climatic characteristics of the Holocene were a determining factor in the long-term dynamics of ecosystems, environmental changes of the last few centuries were essentially anthropogenic . . . Species introduction has diversified current flora and greatly differentiated it with respect to native flora. Although quite lush from a bird's-eye view, the current vegetation of the Québec region is quite different from the way it was in the days of Cartier and Champlain, in the 16th and 17th centuries, and even of Pehr Kalm, in 1749.

Work on the Cartier-Roberval and Intendant's Palace sites offers concrete examples of changes brought about since the arrival of Europeans. For instance, seeds of non-native species such as common corncockle (*Agrostemma githago* L.), spurge (*Euphorbia* sp.) and mustard (*Brassica* sp.) discovered on the Cartier-Roberval site point to the impact of the newcomers on the local vegetation. In addition, analysis of archaeobotanical, archaeoentomological, zooarchaeological and dendrochronological data from the Intendant's Palace site, in conjunction with the abundant historical information, has led to a better understanding of the spatial organization of activities in the King's Stores, as well as a precise picture of the site's physical environment. As shown by the presence of ectoparasites such as lice and bedbugs, hygienic conditions within this prestigious complex were little better than elsewhere in the city. The study of contexts associated with Jean Talon's brewery during the 1660s have also made it possible to document the rapidity with which European weeds replaced domestic species. Indeed, prickly lettuce (*Lactuca serriola* L.) is now known to have been present 200 years earlier than previously thought.

Recent archaeological research has also documented hygiene in other parts of the urban environment. Céline Cloutier's analysis of the foreshore of the St Lawrence at the end of the 17th century indicates that the banks of the river were used for disposing of different sorts of refuse. Objects associated with trade between Europeans and Native Americans were also among the items found on the foreshore. Nonetheless, pollution of human and animal origin next to the river during the 17th and 18th centuries was less than would be expected from official documents describing the colony or from historical sources describing French cities during the Middle Ages.

CONCLUSION

Knowledge of the city of Québec has been greatly enriched by recent archaeological research programmes. Nevertheless, the portrait of the city remains fragmentary. It can only be hoped that these programmes will continue and that the research described in this volume will be completed. It can also be hoped that the new approaches developed for these projects and tested by them will be applied to other sites in this urban centre and the surrounding region — particularly in less affluent parts of the city and in rural zones — in order to develop a more complete picture of colonial society during the Euro-Québécois period. Finally, it can be hoped that diffusion of the results of these programmes will encourage the exchange of information amongst colleagues sharing common interests.

ACKNOWLEDGEMENTS

Several people contributed in different ways to preparing this volume of *Post-Medieval Archaeology*, which proved to be a complex endeavour involving several institutional partners on both sides of the Atlantic. I would first like to thank the authors who participated with enthusiasm in writing the various papers. In addition, the external evaluators — Marc-André Bernier, Christian Bélanger, François Bélanger, Andrée Bolduc, Michel Brassard, Pierre Drouin, Patrick Eid, Michelle Garneau, Dominique Lalande, Robert Larocque, Brad Loewen, Steven Pendery, Peter Pope, Louise Roy, Martin Royer — merit special thanks for their comments on the papers. The project would not have been possible without the collaboration and support of the editor of *Archéologiques* — Christian Roy — and editors of *Post-Medieval Archaeology* — John Allan, Hugo Blake and Jacqui Pearce. François Girard did a masterful job of revising and formatting the texts whereas Alison McGain and Jane McCauley, assisted by Donald Kellough, Kathryn Lawson and Abigail Ratcliffe, translated and revised the texts swiftly and with rigour. Lastly, Pierre Drouin of the AAQ, Réginald Auger of Université Laval's Centre interuniversitaire d'études sur les lettres, les arts et les traditions (CÉLAT), Robert Gauvin of Parks Canada and Nicolas Giroux of the CCNQ facilitated the production of this volume, as did the City of Québec and the MCCCF according to the terms of a cultural development agreement concluded between these two bodies.

NOTES

[1] Moussette 2005.

[2] Niellon 2008.

[3] See Filion *et al.* in this volume.

[4] Moussette & Moss 2008; Drouin & Caulier 2001; Parent & Allard 2001.

[5] Known as the War of Conquest in French Canada and as the French and Indian Wars in the United States. To each his own reading of history!

[6] Auger 2008.

[7] Hare *et al.* 1987, 324.

[8] Quoted in Hare *et al.* 1987, 17.

[9] See Moussette & Moss 2008; Desloges 2001.

[10] Desloges 2008a; Havard & Vidal 2008, 152–9; Moogk 2000, 53–86.

[11] The research programme undertaken in Place Royale by the government of the Province of Québec in the 1970s and 1980s has not been discussed in this volume even though it is extremely interesting for historical archaeology in Canada. This decision was motivated by the fact that no research teams are currently working on this site or its collections. R. Côté (2000) provides the best overview of this body of research.

[12] Beaudet 1990.

[13] Charbonneau *et al.* 1982.

[14] Moussette 1994.

[15] Desloges 2008b.

[16] L'Anglais 1994.

BIBLIOGRAPHY

PUBLISHED SOURCES

Charbonneau, A., Desloges, Y. & Lafrance, M. 1982, *Québec, the Fortified City: from the 17th to the 19th Century*, Ottawa: Parks Canada.

Auger, R. 2008, 'L'Espace amérindien avant l'arrivée des Européens à Québec', in Vallières *et al.* 2008, **1**, 57–100.

Auger, R. & Moss, W. 2002, 'The archaeology of physical and social transformation: high times, low tides and tourist floods on Québec City's waterfront', in Mayne & Murray 2002, 132–44.

Beaudet, P. (ed.) 1990, *Under the Boardwalk in Québec City: Archaeology in the Courtyard and Gardens of the Château Saint-Louis*, Montréal: Guernica.

Côté, R. 2000, *Place-Royale: quatre siècles d'histoire*, Québec: Musée de la civilisation.

Courville, S. & Garon, R. (eds) 2001, *Québec, ville et capitale*, Sainte-Foy (Québec): Les Presses de l'Université Laval.

Desloges, Y. 2001, 'Quand fortification rime avec planification urbaine', in Courville & Garon 2001, 72–7.

Desloges, Y. 2008a, 'Québec, capitale coloniale française', in Vallières *et al.* 2008, **1**, 199–289.

Desloges, Y. 2008b, 'Au rythme des marées: Québec et son économie, 1608–1791', in Vallières *et al.* 2008, **1**, 101–98.

Drouin, S. & Caulier, B. 2001, 'Une tête de pont vers l'intérieur du continent', in Courville & Garon 2001, 56–64.

Hare, J., Lafrance, M. & Ruddel, D.-T. 1987, *Histoire de la ville de Québec, 1608–1871*, Montréal: Boréal.

Havard, G. & Vidal, C. 2008, *Histoire de l'Amérique française*, Paris: Flammarion.

L'Anglais, P.-G. 1994, *La Recherche archéologique en milieu urbain: d'une archéologie dans la ville vers une archéologie de la ville*, Les Cahiers du CÉLAT, hors série **6**.

Mayne, A. & Murray, T. (eds) 1993, *The Archaeology of Urban Landscapes, Explorations in Slumland*: Cambridge: University Press.

Moogk, P. 2000, *La Nouvelle-France: the Making of French Canada — a Cultural History*, East Lansing: Michigan State University Press.

Moussette, M. 1994, *Le Site du Palais de l'intendant à Québec: genèse et structuration d'un lieu urbain*, Sillery: Septentrion.

Moussette, M. 2005, 'Un univers sous tension: les nations amérindiennes du Nord-Est de l'Amérique du nord au XVIe siècle', *Les Cahiers des Dix* **59**, 149–77.

Moussette, M. & Moss, W. 2008, 'Québec, ville coloniale et porte atlantique du nouveau monde: un point de vue archéologique', in Roy & Côté 2008, 18–37.

Niellon, F. 2008, 'Québec au temps de Champlain', in Roy & Côté 2008, 1–17.

Parent, A. & Allard, M. 2001, 'Le lieu le mieux situé', in Courville & Garon 2001, 8–19.

Roy, C. & Côté, H. (eds) 2008, *Rêves d'Amériques: regard sur l'archéologie de la Nouvelle-France — Dreams of the Americas: Overview of New France Archaeology*, Archéologiques, hors série **2**.

Vallières, M. *et al.* 2008, *Histoire de Québec et de sa région*, Québec: Les Presses de l'Université Laval.

ABBREVIATIONS

AAQ	Association des archéologues du Québec
CCNQ	Commission de la capitale nationale du Québec
CÉLAT	Centre interuniversitaire d'études sur les lettres, les arts et les traditions
MCCCF	Ministère de la Culture, des Communications et de la Condition feminine

SUMMARY IN FRENCH, GERMAN, ITALIAN AND SPANISH

RÉSUMÉ

Introduction: l'archéologie d'une ville en Amérique du Nord, les débuts de Québec

Ces dernières années, un grand nombre de programmes de recherche ont été conduits sur des sites archéologiques majeurs dans la ville de Québec. Ces programmes ont été appliqués par de grandes équipes de recherche affiliées à plusieurs institutions. Ces initiatives ont généré à la fois individuellement et collectivement une connaissance considérable sur le début de la période moderne dans le Nouveau Monde. Elles ont également créé un contexte de recherche qui est unique au Canada, à cause non seulement du nombre d'individus sollicités, mais aussi de l'échelle et de la qualité des résultats. Cette présentation donne un bref aperçu de ces programmes, dont les découvertes sont généralement publiées uniquement en français.

ZUSAMMENFASSUNG

Einführung: Archäologie einer nordamerikanischen Stadt und der früh-moderne Zeitabschnitt in Quebec

Über die Jahre wurde eine beeindruckende Anzahl von Forschungsprojekten bedeutender archäologischer Ausgrabungen in der Stadt Quebec unternommen. Diese Untersuchungen wurden von größeren Forschungsteams verschiedener Institutionen durchgeführt. Im Einzelnen wie auch im Gesamtausmaß haben die verschiedenen Unterfangen beträchtliche neue Erkenntnisse über die früh-moderne Zeit in der Neuen Welt geschaffen. Sie haben einen für Canada einzigartig neuen Untersuchungszusammenhang geschaffen, nicht nur durch die Anzahl der involvierten Personen, sondern auch im Hinblick auf den Umfang und die Güte der Ergebnisse. Diese Einführung liefert einen kurzen Überblick über diese Programme, deren Ergebnisse im Allgemeinen nur auf Französisch publiziert sind.

RIASSUNTO

Introduzione: archeologia di una città nord-Americana e la prima età moderna in Quebec

Nel corso del tempo, un imponente numero di progetti di ricerca è stato condotto in importanti siti archeologici nella città di Quebec. Questi progetti sono stati portati avanti da gruppi di ricerca formati da numerosi studiosi afferenti a istituzioni diverse. Sia come singole iniziative, sia nel loro complesso, queste ricerche hanno incrementato notevolmente la conoscenza della prima età moderna nel Nuovo Mondo. Hanno inoltre creato un contesto di ricerca unico in Canada, non solo per il numero di persone coinvolte, ma anche per la quantità e la qualità dei risultati raggiunti. Questa introduzione fornisce una breve panoramica su questi progetti, i cui risultati sono generalmente pubblicati solo in francese.

RESUMEN

Introducción: la arqueología de una ciudad norteamericana y los comienzos del período moderno en Quebec

A lo largo de los años se ha llevado a cabo un número impresionante de programas de investigación en yacimientos arqueológicos de la ciudad de Quebec. Tales programas han sido realizados por grandes equipos afiliados a varias instituciones y han generado nuevos datos, tanto a nivel individual como colectivo, sobre los comienzos del período moderno en el Nuevo Mundo. También han creado un marco de investigación único en Canadá, no sólo por el número de individuos que han tomado parte sino también por la escala y la calidad de los resultados. Esta introducción presenta brevemente dichos programas cuyos resultados se suelen publicar por lo general sólo en francés.

Ville de Québec, Service de l'aménagement du territoire, Division du design, de l'architecture et du patrimoine, 295 boulevard Charest Est, Québec (Québec), Canada G1K 3G8
[william.moss@ville.quebec.qc.ca]

Post-Medieval Archaeology **43/1** (2009), 13–29

The natural environment of the Québec City region during the Holocene

By LOUISE FILION, MARTIN LAVOIE *and* LYDIA QUERREC

SUMMARY: In the St Lawrence River valley the 10,000-year period following the Wisconsinian glaciation was marked by major geographic and climatic changes which influenced the development of plant communities. In this paper the Holocene environments in the Québec City region have been reconstructed on the basis of palaeogeographic and palaeoecological data. Fluctuations in relative sea level, particularly in recent millennia, are of particular interest in light of Québec's situation as a marine gateway on the St Lawrence. Changes in plant cover since Euro-American settlement some 400 years ago are principally due to forest clearing for agriculture and more recently to urban development.

INTRODUCTION

The Holocene, which has lasted about 10,000 years to date, has been marked by major geographic and climatic changes in the St Lawrence River valley (Fig. 1). The organization of plant communities followed the postglacial migration of flora and fauna from their southernmost position at the glacial maximum of the Wisconsinian (18,000 BP, conventional age). This transformation of the natural environment took place through the slow development of ecosystems, as characterized by their vegetation and soils, under the influence of natural and anthropogenic disturbances. Human impacts were originally of the nomadic type, in the form of Palaeo-Indian habitation, and then gave way to more permanent settlement as European populations moved into the continent. Environments evolved in a geographic and climatic context that has varied greatly over these past ten millennia.

Given its location in the St Lawrence Lowlands, between the Canadian Shield to the north and the Appalachians to the south, the Québec City region has undergone a complex sequence of glaciation/deglaciation events, as well as changes in relative sea level (RSL). In the light of Québec's situation as a marine gateway on the St Lawrence, particular attention will be paid in this paper to RSL fluctuations. The city's environs feature a true estuarine façade downstream of the Québec sound and a fluvial configuration upstream (Fig. 2). Moreover, the region lies at the confluence of several major tributaries, the Montmorency and Saint-Charles rivers on the north shore, and the Etchemin and Chaudière rivers on the south. Québec City's famed promontory rises to an altitude of 110m and is outlined by rocky escarpments, which have earned the city its designation as a natural fortress; the promontory has hosted a series of fortifications, made initially of wood and later stone. A. Painchaud, M. Parent and M. Allard, and M. Moussette and W. Moss have described the determining factors of the landscape which, along with the proximity to neighbouring river valleys, favoured the establishment of the first settlers in the region, who were markedly dependent on the river system.[1] This paper will focus on the natural environment of the Québec City region during the Holocene, as reconstructed primarily on the basis of palaeogeographic and palaeoecological data. Environments in the latter part of this epoch were reconstructed using a number of studies on the region's vegetation and flora.

DOI: 10.1179/007942309X12457508843847

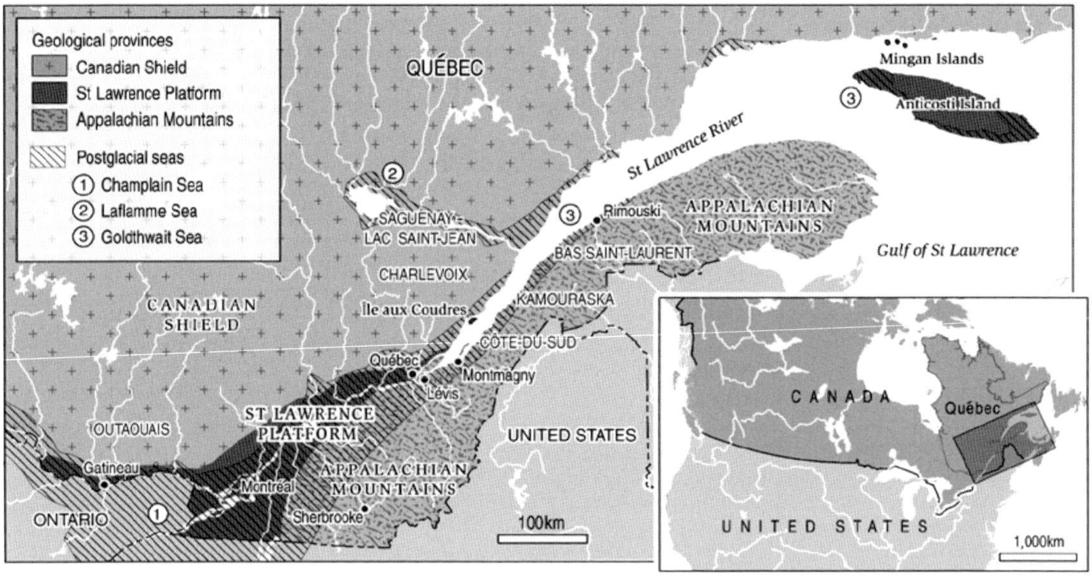

FIG. 1
Geological provinces and postglacial seas in southern Québec and location of geographical regions mentioned in the text.

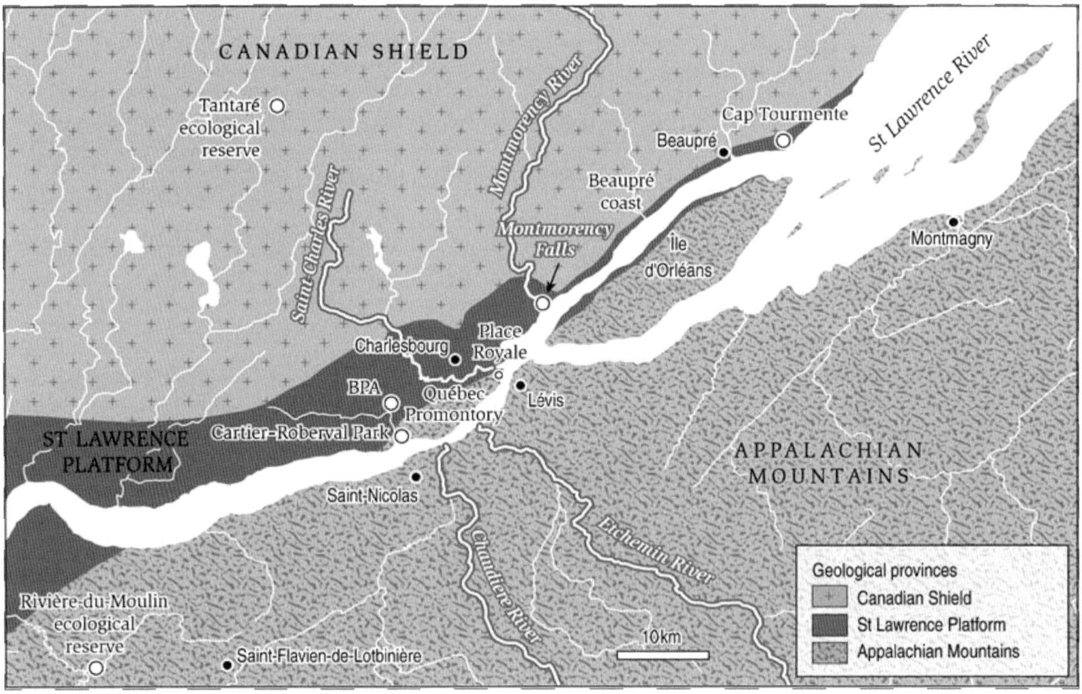

FIG. 2
Location of sites studied and places mentioned in the text.

GEOLOGY AND GEOMORPHOLOGY OF THE QUÉBEC CITY REGION

The Québec City region borders on three geological districts (Fig. 1): the Canadian Shield (Grenville Province), the St Lawrence Platform and the Appalachians.[2] The Shield is an assemblage of very old — in fact, Pre-Cambrian — igneous and metamorphic rocks. The Grenville Province extension of this Pre-Cambrian Shield is estimated to be 950 million years old. The southern edge of the Shield, where it meets the St Lawrence Platform, is a rift that formed some 600 million years ago. This abrupt edge effect is particularly evidenced by the St Lawrence fault zone, notably the imposing cliff face (83m) where one can see Montmorency Falls, a few kilometres north-east of Québec (Fig. 2). Until some 460 million years ago, i.e. during the Cambro-Ordovician period of the Lower Palaeozoic, sediments deposited along the periphery of emerged land on the continental shelf of the former Iapetus Ocean. The rocks forming the St Lawrence Platform are accordingly sedimentary (calcareous and dolomitic), although not folded like those of the Appalachian Province. They are typically composed of Trenton limestones, and Utica and Lorraine schists. The Appalachian range formed between 460 and 380 million years ago. Over the course of several orogenic phases the sediments were folded, deformed and even transported in the form of basal thrust sheets often enclosing flysches (i.e. turbidite deposits frequently observed on continental platforms); they eventually covered part of the St Lawrence Platform. The northern limit of the Appalachian zone (Logan Fault) is defined by the Québec City promontory, and by Île aux Coudres and almost all of Île d'Orléans, both in the St Lawrence Estuary. Anticosti Island and the Mingan Islands in the Gulf of St Lawrence are formed of non-folded sedimentary rocks and belong to the St Lawrence Platform (Fig. 1).

A description of the Quaternary events predating the Last Glacial Maximum and the subsequent glaciation/deglaciation of Québec and Labrador can be found in the synoptic studies conducted by S. Occhietti and his colleagues, and by P. Pagé.[3] The last two million years have been characterized by several Quaternary glaciations during which continental glaciers covered the top half of the northern hemisphere. The latest glacial period was the Wisconsinian (the Würm, in Europe), which peaked some 18,000 years ago. At the time the edge of the Laurentide Ice Sheet in eastern North America extended down to the latitude of New York City.[4] Under the weight of the ice, which was several kilometres thick (up to 3–3.5km over Hudson Bay), the continent was pressed down; it stayed depressed for several thousand years after the continental ice sheet retreated.[5]

The Québec City region was covered by the Laurentide Ice Sheet until about 12,500 BP. Once it started, the withdrawal of the ice sheet was swift, although the ice front did stall for a time, as evidenced by a number of sandy-gravelly ridges associated with the Saint-Narcisse Moraine in the Laurentian foothills.[6] Deposited between 10,700 and 10,500 BP (at the beginning of the Younger Dryas), this moraine extends 750km through the province of Québec, from the Charlevoix region to the Ottawa River valley, where it has been associated with the moraines of Ontario's Algonquin Park, thus forming one of the world's longest moraine systems.[7]

Once the ice retreated from the St Lawrence River valley, an arm of the Atlantic Ocean reached into the lowlands between 11,500 and 9800–9750 BP, forming the epicontinental seas: the Laflamme Sea in the Saguenay–Lac Saint-Jean Lowlands, the Goldthwait Sea downstream of Québec and the Champlain Sea upstream of the Québec sound (Fig. 1). Both during and after the retreat of the continental ice masses, the RSL rose rapidly in response to a massive inflow of meltwater and subglacial water into the seawaters submerging the St Lawrence Valley.[8] This influx of cold water at the southern margin of the ice sheet may have influenced the climate at the Pleistocene/Holocene boundary (around 11,000–10,000 BP). The result was that cold conditions remained in the St Lawrence River valley despite the continuing retreat of the ice front.[9] However, it appears these conditions changed drastically with the glacio-isostatic rebound and rapid land emergence, and with the development of drainage basins and rivers cutting through the unconsolidated sediments. Trees established in the Laurentian foothills north of Québec between 9400 and 9000 BP,[10] which means that the non-arboreal phase in the Québec City area was probably quite short.[11]

The post-glacial marine limit stood at about 225m in the Kamouraska region[12] and at 210–35m in Charlesbourg,[13] on the south and north shore of the St Lawrence River respectively (Figs 1–2). When the post-glacial seas reached their limit, the Québec Sound was an estimated 40km wide, as opposed to barely 1km today. The penetration of seawaters upstream from the Québec Sound appears to have taken place about 11,200–11,100 BP.[14] A detailed study of the Saint-Nicolas site (Fig. 2) revealed that between 11,300 and 9750 BP, the palaeoenvironments of the Champlain Sea featured heavy marine currents, tides 5–10m high and wide variations in water temperature and salinity as a result of the proximity of the glacial front.[15] The sedimentary sequence comprises glacial, glacio-marine and marine deposits. Although the transgression facies is marked by strong heterogeneity in sediment granulometry, the deposit corresponding to the submersion phase consists of massive clay and loam, as deposited in deep water (> 100m).[16] Towards 9800–9750 BP the Champlain Sea gave way to Lampsilis Lake, a large body of fresh water upstream of Québec.[17]

Although isostasis and eustasis are based on complex calculations still open to interpretation, J.-C. Dionne indicates that the rate of land emergence was very rapid,[18] from 50–100mm/year when the Goldthwait Sea was at its limit, i.e. 12,000–11,000 BP, to roughly 10mm/year after 11,000 BP, several millimetres/year after 2000 BP, some 3–4mm/year from about 500 years ago, and finally 0.8–1mm/year at present. During the Lower Holocene, the quickly emerging surfaces were first colonized by low vegetation, which comprised plants of both arctic type (e.g. *Arctostaphyllos*) and boreal type (e.g. *Kalmia, Vaccinium*), including conifers (*Picea*) which formed the first post-glacial forests.[19] The only site in the St Lawrence Lowlands evidencing the initial plant establishment and forest development from 9800 BP is at Saint-Flavien-de-Lotbinière (Fig. 2), where spruce stumps were found *in situ* over marine sands, although buried under several metres of aeolian sands.[20] In that respect, a vast dune system was in fact deposited in the central St Lawrence Lowlands at the very beginning of the Holocene, between 9850 and 9050 BP, under the influence still being exerted by the retreating ice mass, the front of which stood at the southern edge of the Canadian Shield.[21] Prevailing high-pressure winds shaped these parabolic dunes, which extend in a NE–SW direction, enabling fossilization of the remains of the first land plants to colonize the area and of the primeval forests of the lowlands.

The land emergence curve proposed by Dionne for the St Lawrence Estuary reveals a fairly low RSL (approximately 10m below current RSL) between 7000 and 6400 BP (Fig. 3).[22] During this time on the south shore of the St Lawrence Estuary the moist vegetation dominated by *Typha* and *Cyperaceae* shifted to white pine (*Pinus strobus* L.)/eastern hemlock (*Tsuga canadensis* (L.) Carr.) mixed forests, as attested by numerous large stumps found in the current intertidal zone near Montmagny (Fig. 2).[23] This forest formation characteristic of well-drained soils lasted only a few centuries. Towards 6500–6400 BP eastern larch (*Larix laricina* (Du Roi) K. Koch), a hygrophilous tree species, was established on this riparian site.[24] Between 5800 and 4500 BP the RSL may have risen 10–12m above the current level (Fig. 3). This

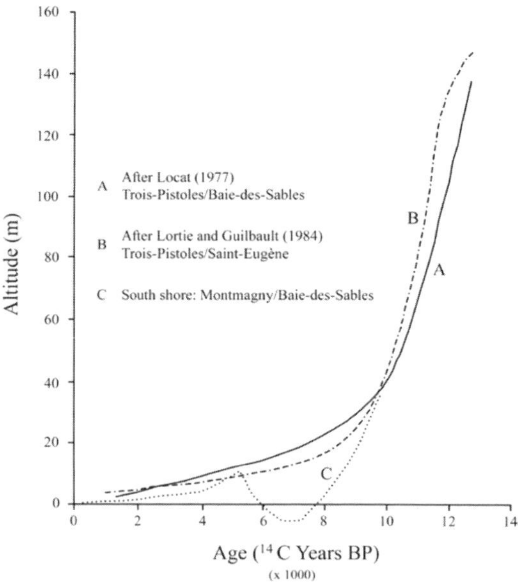

FIG. 3

Land emergence curve along the south shore of the St Lawrence Estuary (after Dionne 1988a, 241).

second Holocene marine transgression, the Laurentian Transgression, led to the deposition of several beaches and terraces.[25] In short, the estuarine regions of the St Lawrence downstream from Québec underwent a double transgression (post-glacial and Laurentian) as well as a double marine regression during the Holocene rather than a single, postglacial, marine transgression. This model belies the classic models that show continuous glacio-isostatic uplift of continents to their present level; they were based on an insufficient number of ^{14}C dates.

Towards 3000 BP RSL seems to have dropped to its current position. Although of lesser amplitude, its fluctuations of the last few thousand years had a major impact in that they helped shape raised beaches and low marine or fluvial terraces along the St Lawrence and some of its tributaries. Towards 2000 BP the RSL was roughly 4m higher on the beach of the Mitis terrace (Mitis Transgression), according to estimates made by Allard and Séguin at the foot of the Québec promontory in Place Royale (Fig. 2)[26] and more recently by Dionne on the basis of observations throughout the St Lawrence Estuary.[27] This low terrace, which is 3.5 to 8m high, often abuts the Micmac Cliff, an escarpment measuring at least 10–20m high and reaching 45m in many places in and around the Québec City area.[28] The width of the Mitis terrace varies just as much. On the Beaupré coast (Fig. 2), for instance, it measures 150–800m across.[29] This low terrace played a major role in the human settlement of a number of coastal sites, in particular Cap Tourmente (Fig. 2), where settlers established the Petite-Ferme at the time of Champlain (AD 1608–35).[30] Conversely the rising RSL around 2000 BP may have had a hand in erasing all traces of Archaic and Palaeo-Indian occupation at altitudes below 4m.[31] Recent fluctuations in the RSL, although minor and difficult to quantify, have accelerated the erosion of coastal areas,[32] affecting human settlement on the Gulf of St Lawrence and socio-economic activities like marine transport on the St Lawrence.[33]

As already described, unconsolidated deposits in the Québec City region are of glacial, marine and fluvial origin. They are represented in the area by glacial deposits, particularly the compact calcareous Québec till, glacio-fluvial deposits (>90m) and aeolian sands (107–30m) deposited in the early Holocene (Saint-Flavien-de-Lotbinière sector), as well as littoral and alluvial deposits, i.e. strands, beaches, and marine or fluvial terraces.[34] On the Québec promontory superficial deposits are rather thin (<2–3m) and most often attributable to the weathering (alteration) of the schistose substrate. The soils dominating well-drained sites are orthic dystric brunisols (diagnostic horizon: Ah < 100mm) or orthic sombric brunisols (Ah > 100mm).[35] In the depression bordering the north side of the Québec promontory (Cap-Rouge–Limoilou depression), superficial deposits are up to 60m deep.[36] Because massive clay deposits impeded drainage, the dominant soils are gleysols or organic soils where natural depressions filled with peat occur.[37]

ESTABLISHMENT OF PLANT COMMUNITIES DURING THE HOLOCENE

Although the pollen records for the Québec region indicate that arctic-type plants were present at the beginning of the Holocene,[38] it appears that forest establishment on the newly emerged lands was rapid. Spruce (*Picea*) preceded or was accompanied by balsam fir (*Abies balsamea* (L.) Mill.) as shown by the pollen curve for the two species in the Lower Holocene.[39] However, based on pedoanthracological studies and ^{14}C dating (AMS) of macroscopic charcoal fragments in the well-drained soil of a maple forest north of Québec (Fig. 2, Tantaré site), B. Talon and her colleagues showed that fir and sugar maple (*Acer saccharum* Marsh.) were already found north of the St Lawrence between 9400 and 9000 BP, i.e. immediately after the Champlain Sea withdrew *c.* 9800–9750 BP.[40] This indicates that the sea was not an obstacle to the dispersal of seeds and the migration of trees in the study area, in contrast with the findings of S.D. Muller and P.J.H. Richard for the region of Montréal, where the Champlain Sea shorelines were further apart.[41]

At the Tantaré site, which belongs to the sugar maple/yellow birch domain, charcoal particles were buried by windfall trees, typical of mature deciduous forests.[42] The presence of charcoal enabled Talon and her colleagues to posit a drier climate at the beginning of the Holocene.[43] This corroborates the findings of C. Carcaillet and P. J.H. Richard who used microscopic charcoal from lake sediments to conclude that the climate was drier and more conducive to fire until about 8000–7500 BP.[44] These interpretations are in agreement with Richard,[45] who used fire to explain the high pollen percentages of jack pine (*Pinus divaricata* (Ait.) Dumont) and possibly green alder (*Alnus crispa* (Ait.) Pursh). In the latter case, however, the plant's successional status, i.e. a pioneer species, makes it difficult to distinguish between fire and cold climate as the determining factor, especially in the Lower Holocene, when all these factors may have combined at the same time and in varying intensity.

Several ^{14}C dates obtained from the lowermost peat deposits in the St Lawrence Valley indicate that paludification (i.e. the accumulation of peat on well-drained soils) was accelerated in the Mid-Holocene (after 7000 BP) and that it was postponed after land emergence.[46] At the FLAV site in Saint-Flavien-de-Lotbinière, for example (described later, Fig. 2), paludification of sandy surfaces did not start until about 7000 BP, whereas land emergence took place as early as 9800 BP.[47] In the same vein S. Laliberté reported on a ^{14}C date going back to 6000 BP in the Beaupré area (Fig. 2) from the lowermost peat of a bog that had developed on a marine terrace (108m), which itself had been established between 10,000 and 11,000 BP.[48] This millennia-long delay seems to indicate that the relatively dry climate of the Lower Holocene did not favour peat accumulation. After 7500 BP the climate was milder, warmer and more humid during the Hypsithermal period of the Mid-Holocene until 4000–3000 BP.[49] This reduced the influence of forest fire,[50] at least in the St Lawrence Valley, which was then dominated by deciduous forests and therefore less susceptible to this type of disturbance.

In order to draw an accurate picture of plant community establishment in the Québec area over the last 6,000–7,000 years, we have used pollen diagrams (unpublished data) from two sites: Saint-Flavien-de-Lotbinière (FLAV) and the Sainte-Foy outdoor recreation centre (Base de plein air: BPA)

(Fig. 2). The pollen analysis was conducted every 4cm at the FLAV site on a peat core that was 4m thick, and every 2cm at the BPA site on a peat core that was 1m thick.

The FLAV site is characterized by a stabilized dune system, with interdune depressed areas filled in by woody peat. Detailed macrofossil analysis helped document the forest succession during the Mid- and Late Holocene in the central St Lawrence Lowlands,[51] as the site combines characteristics of well-drained and poorly drained sites (dune ridges and interdune depressions, respectively). The BPA, at the heart of the Québec City region, is in a depression north of the Québec promontory. This small, ombrotrophic bog whose basal peat was dated 5500 BP was first studied by A. Larouche.[52] The top metre, covering the last 4,540 years, was subsequently analysed in high resolution by Lavoie and her colleagues,[53] with the prime objective of documenting environmental changes that occurred during the past few centuries.

SAINT-FLAVIEN-DE-LOTBINIÈRE SITE (FLAV)

The pollen data of the FLAV site (Fig. 4) show that forest communities were already well established about 7000 BP, which confirms the palaeoenvironmental reconstruction at this site conducted by N. Bhiry and L. Filion on the basis of plant macrofossils.[54]

The history of the vegetation was subdivided into five pollen zones (FLAV-I to FLAV-V). A total of 77 pollen taxa were identified. Zone FLAV-II had the greatest diversity of taxa (66) and zone FLAV-I the lowest (52).

FLAV-I ZONE (400–357cm; 6800–c. 4720 BP)

The pollen spectra are clearly dominated by white pine at the base of the diagram (400cm), where this species reaches its maximum (54%) for the last 7,000 years. The dominance of pine then gives way to a rapid increase in hemlock representation, which attains 45% at 375cm. Birch percentages are also substantial (mean: 32%), reaching a maximum of 42% at the top of this zone. The analysis of plant macro-remains revealed that the type of birch present in FLAV-1 was yellow birch (*Betula alleghaniensis* Britton).[55] Sugar maple, elm (*Ulmus*) and black ash (*Fraxinus nigra* Marsh.) were also present. Pollen concentrations in this zone were higher than in the other pollen zones (mean: 1,884,400 grains/cm^3).

Our pollen data corroborate the palaeodendroecological findings of L. Filion and F. Quinty,[56] who used tree trunks preserved in the interdune peat to demonstrate the simultaneous presence of white pine and hemlock over approximately two millennia. However, their data also indicate that white pine preceded hemlock. According to G. Magnan's pollen data from Beaupré (Fig. 2),[57] i.e. at the north-easternmost limit of the hemlock's range in North America, the hemlock pollen percentage increased about 5700 BP (interpolated age). This date matches that of the oldest fossil tree trunk found in the peat of the Saint-Flavien-de-Lotbinière site.[58] The high representation of these two tree species attests to the abundance of gymnosperms in the forest environments of the Mid-Holocene. White pine and hemlock may have formed mixed stands, as is currently the case at the Rivière-du-Moulin ecological reserve in Lotbinière (Fig. 2). In all likelihood, these two species were particularly abundant as companion species in the region's maple forest.

FLAV-II ZONE (357–197.5cm; c. 4720–c. 3070 BP)

This zone was subdivided into four subzones, based principally on the fluctuations in pollen representation of hemlock, but also that of oak (*Quercus*) and beech (*Fagus grandifolia* Ehrh.).

FLAV-IIa subzone (357–270cm)

The FLAV-IIa subzone is characterized by the drastic drop in hemlock representation — from 42% near the end of zone I at 359cm to a low of 3% at 335cm. Offsetting this decrease is a marked increase in the percentage of oak from 345cm (mean: 12%). Its maximum representation of 19% occurs at 338cm, at which depth N. Bhiry and L. Filion identified macro-remains (acorns, wood) of red oak (*Quercus rubra* L.).[59] With maximum representation of 59% at 310cm, *Betula* is more common in this subzone than in FLAV-I (mean: 42%).

The decline in hemlock pollen count is a biotic and biostratigraphic event of the Mid-Holocene, which has been attributed to insect defoliation on the basis of direct evidence of phytophagous activity, i.e. conifer needles browsed by the hemlock looper (*Lambdina fiscellaria fiscellaria* (Guen.)).[60] Our pollen data, which reflect extra-local and even regional vegetation, seem to indicate that two angiosperms — red oak and yellow birch — took advantage of the hemlock decline and temporarily modified the relative proportion of gymnosperms (temperate conifers) in their favour.

FLAV-IIb subzone (270–242.5cm)

For the *c.* 3900–3800 BP period, the pollen representation of hemlock remains low, indicating that its decline was still ongoing, whereas that of beech

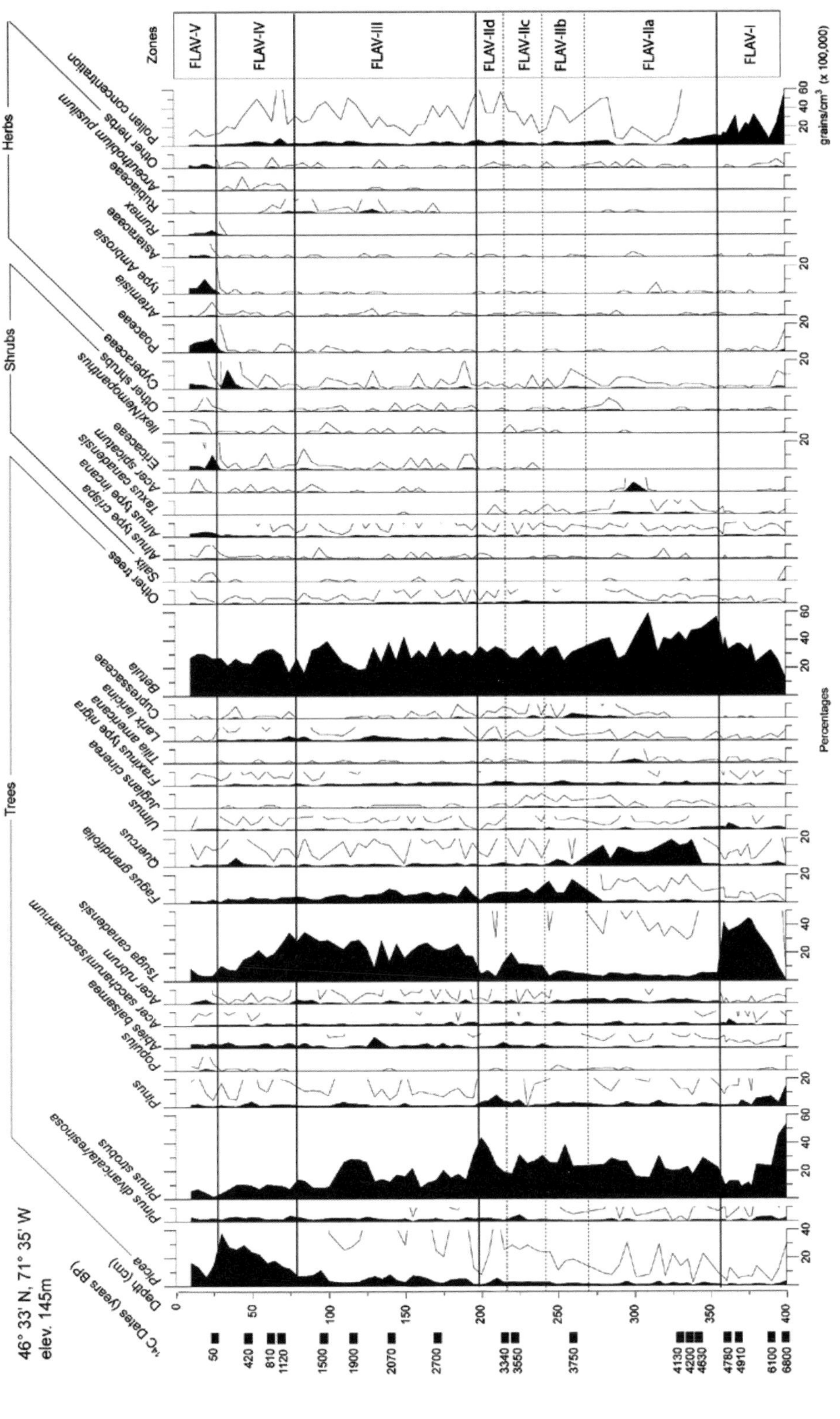

FIG. 4

Simplified pollen diagram of Saint-Flavien-de-Lotbinière (FLAV). The unshaded curves reflect pollen percentages with a 10x exaggeration. Only taxa with a minimum representation of 1% are represented on the diagram. Curves identified as Other trees, Other shrubs or Other herbs include taxa with representation ≤1%. Non-vascular taxa are not represented. Radiocarbon dates are from Bhiry & Filion 1996b (analysts, M. Lavoie and N. Morasse).

starts to increase (mean: 12.5%). The figure for oak also decreases and then remains fairly stable with a mean of 1.6% until the top of the diagram, which contrasts with the peak (19%) reached in subzone FLAV-IIa. The average percentage of birch drops from 42% to 32%, but also stabilizes thereafter until the top of the diagram. Beech was a relative latecomer to this assemblage,[61] but did take over from oak as the hemlock dominance declined.

FLAV-IIc (242.5–212cm) and FLAV-IId (212–197.5cm) subzones

These two subzones show an increase in hemlock representation (3.6% to 20%), followed by a drop (minimum: 3%). This second minimum reflects a greatly increased representation of white pine (44%), the only tree species that seems to have taken advantage of hemlock's second decline.

The fluctuations in the pollen representation of hemlock, notably the peak about 3650 BP in the FLAV-IIc zone, agree with the data obtained from hemlock wood megafossils.[62]

FLAV-III ZONE (197.5–77.5cm; c. 3070–c. 1250 BP)

The FLAV-III zone features elevated hemlock pollen percentages attaining 35% (mean: 24%). The pollen curves for beech and birch remain relatively stable, as do those of sugar maple, ash and elm. The mean representation of white pine drops to 17% (not counting the peak between 110 and 125cm) in favour of the boreal conifers: spruce, balsam fir and eastern larch.

FLAV-IV ZONE (77.5–27.5cm; c. 1250 BP–c. 90 BP) AND FLAV-V ZONE (<27.5cm; <c. 90 BP)

In the FLAV-IV zone, spruce and hemlock percentages show an inverse trend. Spruce rises gradually to a maximum of 37%, while hemlock decreases just as gradually to a minimum of 8%. This replacement of temperate by boreal conifers points to a cooling of the climate, which started around 2,800–2,500 years ago,[63] when the ombrotrophication of peat bogs and paludification of well-drained sites such as dune crests occurred.[64]

The FLAV-V zone (~90 last years) corresponds to a period of human activity that translated into a net decrease in tree species and the concomitant appearance of ruderal species (Poaceae, *Ambrosia*, Tubuliflorae, *Rumex*). A total of 61 pollen taxa were identified in this zone. Pollen concentrations were lower in FLAV-V than in preceding zones (mean: 127,000 grains/cm^3).

PEAT BOG AT THE SAINTE-FOY OUTDOOR RECREATION CENTRE (BPA)

The diagram of the peat bog at the Sainte-Foy outdoor recreation centre (BPA) covers the last 4,540 years (Fig. 5). As the spore and pollen analysis of the peat's uppermost metre was done with high stratigraphic resolution, the resulting data shed much light on the deforestation that took place during historical times. The pollen diagram was divided into two zones (BPA-I and BPA-II), each of which was divided into subzones. A total of 82 pollen taxa were identified. Zone II had a greater diversity of taxa (78) than zone I (61). The increase over the past few centuries is essentially attributed to the increase in herbaceous plants during Euro-American settlement.

BPA-I ZONE (100–36cm; 4540–c. 580 BP)

In this zone, the arboreal pollen (mean: 95%) and the high pollen concentrations (mean: 334,775 grains/cm^3) correspond to a forest environment. The pollen assemblages indicate that maple forests have been present in Québec for at least 4,540 years. They include several thermophilous species characteristic of maple forests in southern Québec, such as sugar maple, elm, black ash, walnut (*Juglans*), beech, basswood and hickory (*Carya* sp.), as well as hemlock. Although maple characterizes pollen spectra in the entire diagram, several changes in the relative abundance of certain tree species justified dividing BPA-1 into three subzones.

BPA-Ia subzone (100–90cm)

The BPA-Ia subzone marks the beginning of the hemlock decline. Pollen percentages of 10–15% for this species are clearly lower than in the FLAV-I zone (before the decline) in Saint-Flavien-de-Lotbinière (maximum: 40–5%). On the other hand, birch percentages in the BPA-Ia subzone are higher (mean: 54%) than in the FLAV-I zone (mean: 32%).

BPA-Ib subzone (90–62cm)

The BPA-Ib subzone reflects the hemlock decline, as determined in the preceding diagram. Indeed, the pollen representation of hemlock in this subzone averages only 1.2%. Birch percentages are very high (mean: 64%), exceeding those of the BPA-Ia subzone (mean: 54%). The equatorial diameters of *Betula* pollen indicate a dominance of large-diameter grains associated with yellow birch, which corroborates the botanical identifications of macro-remains conducted by Bhiry and Filion at Saint-Flavien-de-Lotbinière.[65] The

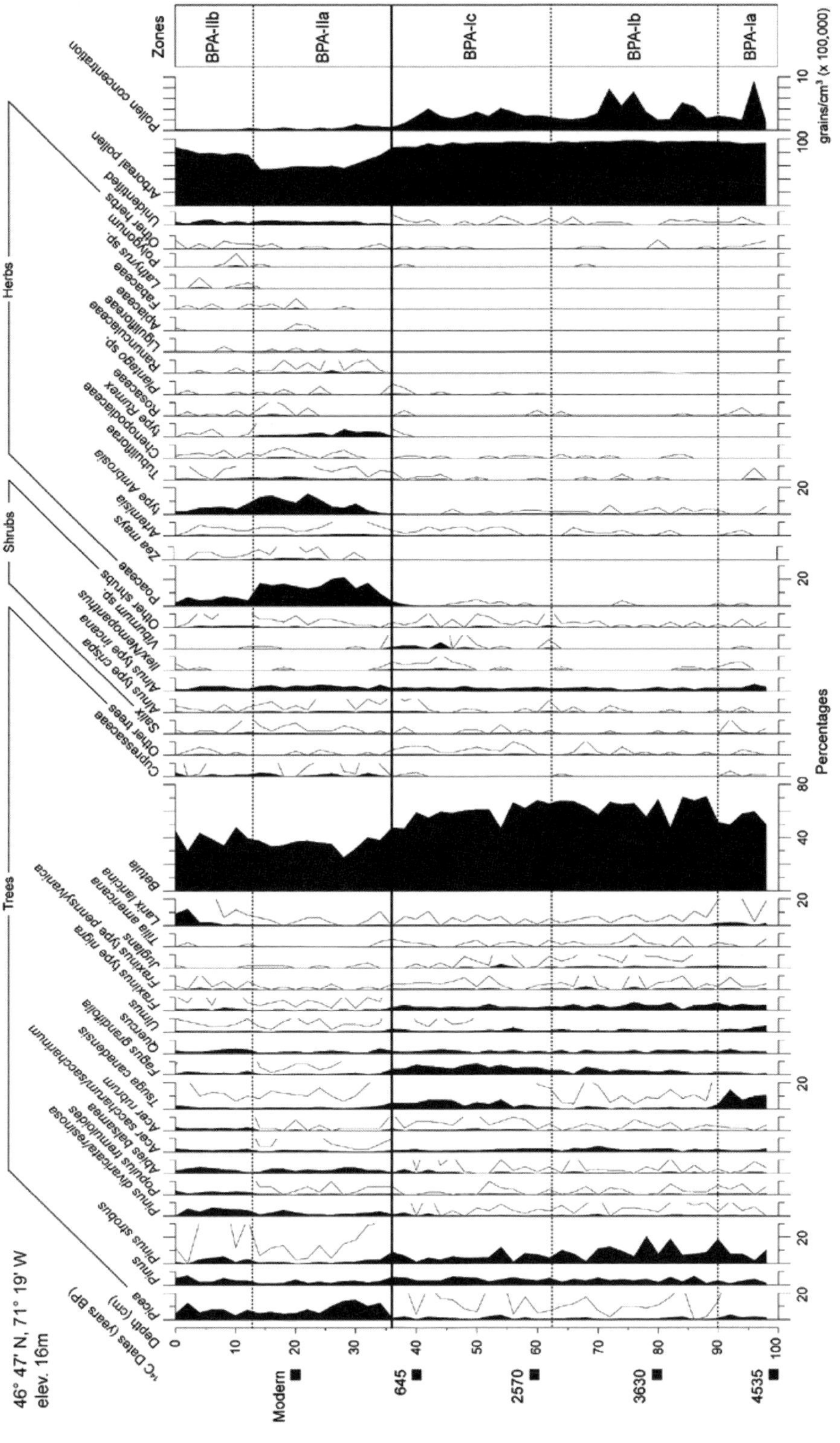

FIG. 5

Simplified pollen diagram of the Sainte-Foy outdoor recreation centre (Base de plein air: BPA). The unshaded curves reflect pollen percentages with a 10x exaggeration. Only taxa with a minimum representation of 1% are represented on the diagram. Curves identified as Other trees, Other shrubs or Other herbs include taxa with representation ≤1%. Non-vascular taxa are not represented. Radiocarbon dates are from Lavoie *et al.* 2008 (analysts, C. Laframboise, É.C. Robert and M. Lavoie).

pollen representation of beech increases a little in this subzone (mean: 3%), whereas that of other deciduous thermophilous tree species remains fairly constant.

BPA-Ic subzone (62–36cm)

The BPA-Ic subzone reveals a slight increase in hemlock pollen, as was observed in the FLAV-IIc subzone in the previous diagram. The beech representation is greater (5–10%) in this subzone than in BPA-Ib. The pollen percentages of *Betula* remain elevated (mean: 58%) and relatively stable. Equatorial diameters of *Betula* grains at two levels correspond to those of yellow birch.

BPA-II ZONE (36 to 0cm; c. *580* BP *to present day)*

BPA-IIa subzone (36–13cm)

In the BPA-IIa subzone there is a clear increase in the representation of ruderal herbaceous plants, particularly the true grasses (Poaceae) (maximum of 22% at 28cm), ragweed (type *Ambrosia*; maximum of 15% at 22cm) and various sorrels (*Rumex*). The influx of herbaceous plants also includes maize (*Zea mays* L.), the first pollen grains of which were identified at 30cm, and rye (*Secale cereale* L.), which was found at 22cm. Among the other herbaceous plants either appearing or increasing are sagebrush (*Artemisia*), Tubuliflorae (sub-family Compositaea), Chenopodiaceae, Rosaceae, plantain (*Plantago*), Ranunculaceae, Ligulifloreae (sub-family Compositaea), Apiaceae and Fabaceae.

As well subzone IIa shows a clear decrease in the pollen representation of most thermophilous tree species, both temperate conifers (white pine and hemlock) and deciduous species (beech, sugar maple, elm, oak, ash). This drop reflects the clearing of forests for agricultural purposes (mean tree pollen: 60%). The clearing is also evident in lowered total pollen concentrations (mean: 51,000 grains/cm^3). Spruce and balsam fir alone increased in this period. Micro- and macroscopic charcoal particles were found at several levels (14, 16, 18, 22, 26 and 36cm), an indication that fires of either human or natural origin occurred in the area.

Subzone IIb (13 to 0cm)

In subzone IIb, there is a slight increase in the representation of deciduous trees (mean tree pollen: 80%), including trembling aspen (*Populus tremuloides* Michx.), a shade-intolerant pioneer species that establishes at early stages of plant succession. Other trees include jack pine and red pine (*Pinus divaricata*/*resinosa*), sugar maple, red maple (*Acer rubrum* L.), beech, oak and black ash. The greater percentages of eastern larch at the top of the diagram reflect its presence within the bog, which is further attested to by numerous stomata on the pollen slides. The increase in pollen percentages of deciduous trees results from the decrease in certain ruderal plants (Poaceae, type *Ambrosia*, *Rumex*) due to the decline of agriculture and probably the incursion of urban development on arable land. Among the new pollen taxa appearing in subzone IIb are *Lathyrus* sp. and *Polygonum* sp. The *Lathyrus* genus belongs to the Fabaceae family (formerly Leguminoseae). This could be the result of the proliferation of the meadow peavine (*Lathyrus pratensis* L.), a ruderal plant introduced from Europe, starting in Québec and moving eastward.[66] In the same vein, several species of *Polygonum* (smartweed) have naturalized in Québec.[67]

TRANSFORMATIONS OVER RECENT CENTURIES AND CURRENT ENVIRONMENTS

The Québec City area belongs to the Great Lakes–St Lawrence forest zone of eastern Canada, subregion L3 of the mid-St Lawrence,[68] and more specifically to the maple/basswood bioclimatic domain,[69] also known as the *érablière laurentienne*.[70] The regional climate is of the continental temperate type, but humid owing to the proximity of the St Lawrence Estuary. Mean annual temperature is 4.04°C. Total annual precipitation is 1.23m, 26% of which falls as snow. The average temperatures of the warmest and coldest months are 19.2°C in July and −12.8°C in January.[71]

In the early days of the colony the environment around the Québec City region may have been dominated by different types of maple forest. Sugar maple probably predominated on the well-drained sites of the promontory, associating with hardwoods like basswood, white ash (*Fraxinus americana* L.) and beech. Maple stands in the area feature a number of associated tree species; ten or so different species can easily be identified.[72] Variants depend primarily on the topography and drainage (Fig. 6). Red oak and white pine, two xero-mesophytic species, are more abundant on the thin, well-drained soils of the promontory, as can be observed in wooded residential neighbourhoods. The Cartier-Roberval Park at the western end of the Québec promontory (Fig. 2) is representative of such maple forest on well-drained sites, although white pine is currently under-represented there. The wood of that species has been in great

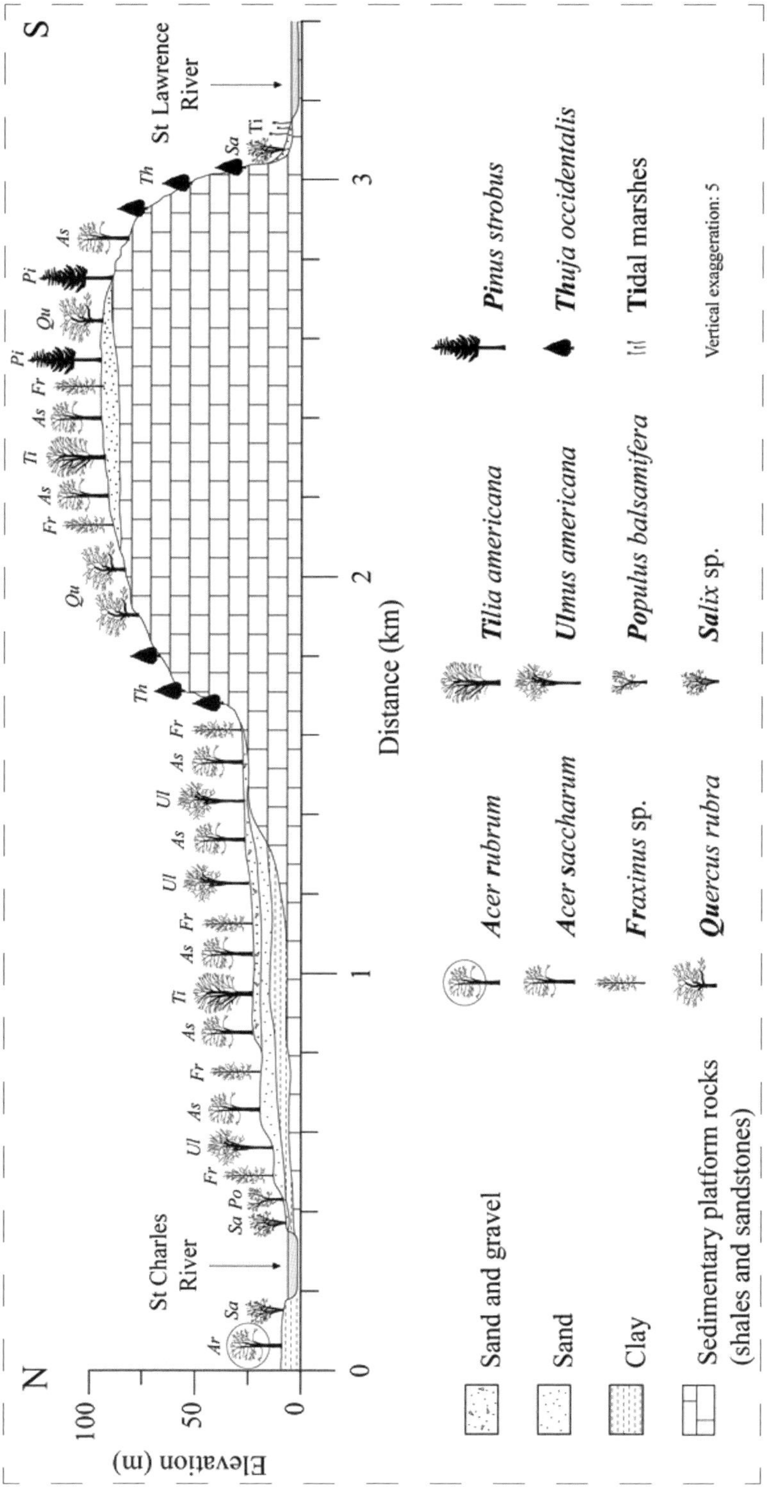

FIG. 6

North–south topographic profile showing the potential vegetation south of the Saint-Charles River and on the Québec promontory.

demand since the founding of the colony, especially as lumber, but it was also massively exported to Europe in the early 19th century, notably to build the British naval fleet.[73]

As the Québec City region marks the northeastern limit of the maple/basswood domain, it is very close to the maple/yellow birch domain, the most cold-hardy variant of deciduous temperate forests. Yellow birch may once have grown on some north-facing slopes of the Québec promontory, especially on the lower surfaces which are well supplied in runoff water by the rocky cliff.

White cedar (*Thuja occidentalis* L.) is very abundant on all rocky escarpments defining the perimeter of the Québec promontory (Fig. 6), and on the rocky cliffs along the Beaupré coast (Fig. 2). As this species can withstand poor drainage and moist soils, it must also have been plentiful on lowlands and flat terrains. Wood cedar is rot-resistant and has been abundantly used since colonial days for the construction of infrastructure in moist conditions, such as docks, palisades, foundations and fences.[74]

On the clayey soils in natural depressions with impeded drainage, deciduous forest dominated by red maple must have been abundant before agricultural clearing of the lowlands. Red maple and balsam fir possibly formed mixed stands since Pehr Kalm, the Swedish botanist who sailed up the St Lawrence in 1749, reported on the abundance of both species north of Québec City.[75] Coniferous forests dominated by eastern larch and black spruce are found at the periphery of peatlands,[76] like those of site BPA, whose development has already been described (Fig. 2).

Given the extent of the marine and fluvial shorelines in the region, the plant cover also includes a number of hydrophytic plant associations, which have been described in detail by M. Cauboue.[77] The tidal marshes of the St Lawrence dominated by bulrushes (*Scirpus* sp.) and spartina (*Spartina* sp.) are yielding to various shrub associations of alder (*Alnus* sp.) and willow (*Salix* sp.), including tree-sized willows as in the Les Saules area by the Saint-Charles River, then to riparian forests of ash (*Fraxinus* sp.), poplar (*Populus* sp.) and elm (*Ulmus* sp.), which foreshadow the transition to well-drained forests. These riparian forests are sporadically subjected to high tides along the St Lawrence, and to flooding due to springtime breakup or torrential rains along the smaller rivers. Today riparian forests are found only as residual groves, having been overtaken by agricultural or urban development.

In brief, when the first European settlers arrived some 400 years ago, the natural environment of the Québec City region was clearly dominated by deciduous forests, with conifers as companion species in well-drained sites (white pine and possibly eastern hemlock on the promontory, white cedar on cliffs) as well as poorly drained sites (white cedar, balsam fir, spruces and eastern larch). Non-forested areas were either open water surfaces (the St Lawrence Estuary and that of its main tributaries) and tidal marshes, which may have been the sole herbaceous sites in the absence of cultivated land.[78] Although geological and geomorphological events and the climatic characteristics of the Holocene were a determining factor in the long-term dynamics of ecosystems, environmental changes of the last few centuries were essentially anthropogenic. Since the first attempts at Euro-American settlement, initially by Jacques Cartier at the mouth of the Saint-Charles River (then called the Sainte-Croix) in 1535, later by both Cartier and Roberval at the mouth of the Cap Rouge River in 1541–43,[79] and the establishment of a trading post (the Habitation) by Champlain on the point of Québec in 1608,[80] the forest component of the area never ceased diminishing from the 17th century and was transformed over the years.

Baillargeon summarized the various stages of urban development, which took place from east to west, and analysed the influence of urbanization on the vegetation of the Québec promontory.[81] The first stage was the early deforestation of the lowlands from Place Royale to Côte d'Abraham and of the eastern end of the Québec promontory inside the fortifications during the 17th and 18th centuries.[82] This was followed by the clearing of the eastern half of the Québec promontory during the first half of the 19th century, agricultural development of the northern part of the promontory, the enlargement of Lower Town through landfilling, residential development towards the west of the Québec promontory during the 20th century, especially after the Second World War, the disappearance of farmland throughout the promontory and finally residential and port development in Lower Town and along the St Lawrence. The result was that all natural forests gave way to residual woodlots or transitional plant communities, notably fallow land peripheral to greater Québec or within urbanized spaces, or were replaced by man-made environments like lawns, empty lots, industrial land or portside development.[83] Despite the human influence, some relatively natural forests have survived like those of Cartier-Roberval Park or Domaine Cataracoui. Situated on the south side of the Québec promontory, they testify to its forested past.

The plant inventory and analysis of the Québec promontory conducted by Baillargeon lists 1,148 taxa, 645 (56%) of which are native and

503 (44%) introduced.[84] Roughly a quarter of the endemic taxa and many exotic but naturalized (i.e. ephemeral) taxa have disappeared since the beginning of the colony, so that only 867 remain. The main transformations of the flora in response to the European influence over the last 400 years were the disappearance of numerous native taxa and the introduction of plants from other regions of eastern Canada, America or Eurasia. Gains were particularly important among Compositeae, Poaceae and Brassicaceae (formerly Cruciferae).[85] Species introduction has diversified current flora and greatly differentiated it with respect to native flora. Although quite lush from a bird's-eye view, the current vegetation of the Québec region is quite different from the way it was in the days of Cartier and Champlain in the 16th and 17th centuries and even of Pehr Kalm in 1749.

ACKNOWLEDGEMENTS

The authors are grateful to the following persons for their thoughtful comments on an earlier version of the manuscript: Andrée Bolduc, scientist at the Geological Survey of Canada (Québec Office); Michelle Garneau, professor at the Geography Department of the Université du Québec à Montréal (UQAM); Réginald Auger, professor at the Department of History and director of the Centre interuniversitaire d'études sur les lettres, les arts et les traditions (CÉLAT) of Université Laval; and Patrick Lajeunesse, professor at the Geography Department of Université Laval. Maps were drawn in the cartography laboratory of Laval's Geography Department by Sylvie Saint-Jacques and Serge Duchesneau.

NOTES

1 Painchaud 1993; Parent & Allard 2001; Moussette & Moss 2008.
2 Saint-Julien & Hubert 1975; Landry & Mercier 1984; Bourque 2008.
3 Occhietti 1989; Pagé 1999; Occhietti *et al.* 2001a; Occhietti *et al.* 2004.
4 Dyke & Prest 1987; Occhietti *et al.* 2001a.
5 Marshall *et al.* 2001; Tarasov & Peltier 2004.
6 LaSalle & Elson 1975; LaSalle *et al.* 1977; Parent *et al.* 1985; Occhietti *et al.* 2001a.
7 Simard *et al.* 2003; Daigneault & Occhietti 2006.
8 Cummings & Occhietti 2001.
9 Occhietti *et al.* 2001b.
10 Talon *et al.* 2005.
11 Richard 1994.
12 Dionne & Pfalzgraf 2001; Dionne 2003.
13 Dionne 1977; 1997; Cummings & Occhietti 2001; Bolduc 2003; Bolduc *et al.* 2003; Laliberté 2006.
14 Occhietti & Richard 2003; Richard & Occhietti 2005.
15 Occhietti *et al.* 2001b.
16 Parent & Occhietti 1988.
17 Parent & Occhietti 1988; Occhietti 1989; Occhietti *et al.* 2004.
18 Dionne 1988a; 1988b; 2001a; 2001b.
19 Filion 1987.
20 Filion 1987; Filion & Quinty 1993.
21 Filion 1987.
22 Dionne 1988a; 1988b.
23 Dionne 1988a.
24 Bhiry *et al.* 2000.
25 Dionne 1988a; 1997; 2001a.
26 Allard & Séguin 1992.
27 Dionne 2002.
28 Dionne 2002.
29 Dionne 2002.
30 Niellon 2008.
31 Allard & Séguin 1992; Garneau 1997.
32 Bernatchez & Dubois 2004.
33 D'Arcy *et al.* 2005.
34 Filion 1987; Morneau 1989; Occhietti 1989; Dionne 2001a.
35 Soil Classification Working Group 1998; Auger & Payette 2008.
36 Morneau 1989.
37 Morneau 1989; Soil Classification Working Group 1998.
38 Richard 1973.
39 Richard 1993.
40 Talon *et al.* 2005.
41 Muller & Richard 2001.
42 Payette *et al.* 1990.
43 Talon *et al.* 2005.
44 Carcaillet & Richard 2000.
45 Richard 1993.
46 Payette 2001.
47 Filion 1987.
48 Laliberté 2006.
49 Richard 1994 ; 1995; Lavoie *et al.* 1995; Bhiry & Filion 1996a.
50 Richard 1995.
51 Bhiry & Filion 1996b.
52 Larouche 1979.
53 Lavoie *et al.* 2008.
54 Bhiry & Filion 1996b.
55 Bhiry & Filion 1996b.
56 Filion & Quinty 1993.
57 Magnan 2006.
58 Filion & Quinty 1993.
59 Bhiry & Filion 1996b.
60 Bhiry & Filion 1996c.
61 Bennett 1985.
62 Filion & Quinty 1993.
63 Richard 1994.
64 Bhiry & Filion 1996b.

[65] Bhiry & Filion 1996b.
[66] Marie-Victorin 1995.
[67] Marie-Victorin 1995.
[68] Rowe 1972.
[69] Ansseau *et al.* 1996.
[70] Grandtner 1966.
[71] Environment Canada 2008.
[72] Grandtner 1966; Ansseau *et al.* 1996.
[73] Hardy & Séguin 1984, 5.
[74] Rousseau *et al.* 1977, 254, 279, 312.
[75] Rousseau *et al.* 1977, 309.
[76] Morneau 1989.
[77] Cauboue 1972.
[78] Baillargeon 1981.
[79] Samson *et al.* 2007.
[80] Niellon 2008.
[81] Baillargeon 1981.
[82] Moussette & Moss 2008.
[83] Baillargeon 1981.
[84] Baillargeon 1981.
[85] Baillargeon 1981.

BIBLIOGRAPHY

PUBLISHED SOURCES

Allard, M. & Séguin, J. 1992, 'Le niveau du Saint Laurent de 2000 BP et l'occupation amérindienne préhistorique de la Place Royale, à Québec', *Géogr. Phys. Quat.* **46**, 181–8.

Ansseau, C., Gagnon, G. & Vasseur, L. 1996, 'Domaine de l'érablière à tilleul', in Bérard 1996, 171–84.

Bennett, K.D. 1985, 'The spread of *Fagus grandifolia* across eastern North America during the last 18,000 years', *J. Biogeogr.* **12**, 147–64.

Bérard, J.A. 1996, *Manuel de foresterie*, Québec: Presses de l'Université Laval.

Bernatchez, P. & Dubois, J.-M. 2004, 'Bilan des connaissances de la dynamique de l'érosion des côtes du Québec maritime Laurentidien', *Géog. Phys. Quat.* **58**, 45–71.

Bhiry, N. & Filion, L. 1996a, 'Characterization of the soil hydromorphic conditions in a paludified dunefield during the Mid-Holocene hemlock decline near Québec City, Québec', *Quat. Res.* **46**, 281–97.

Bhiry, N. & Filion, L. 1996b, 'Holocene plant succession in a dune-swale environment of southern Québec: a macrofossil analysis', *Ecoscience* **3**, 330–42.

Bhiry, N. & Filion, L. 1996c, 'The Mid-Holocene hemlock decline linked with phytophagous insect activity', *Quat. Res.* **45**, 312–20.

Bhiry, N., Garneau, M. & Filion, L. 2000, 'Macrofossil record of a Middle Holocene drop in relative sea level at the St. Lawrence Estuary, Québec', *Quat. Res.* **54**, 228–37.

Bolduc, A. 2003, *Géologie des formations superficielles, Charny, Québec*, open file 1776, 1:50,000, Geological Survey of Canada.

Bolduc, A. *et al.* 2003, *Géologie des formations superficielles, région de Québec, Québec*, open file 3835, 1:50,000 (rev.), Geological Survey of Canada.

Bourque, P.-A. 2008, *Planète Terre: le Québec géologique*, <http://www.ggl.ulaval.ca/personnel/bourque/s5/plan.section.5.html> [accessed 4 July 2008].

Carcaillet, C. & Richard, P.J.H. 2000, 'Holocene changes in seasonal precipitation highlighted by fire incidence in eastern Canada', *Clim. Dyn.* **16**, 549–59.

Courville, S. & Garon, R. (eds) 2001, *Québec: ville et capitale*, Québec: Presses de l'Université Laval.

Cummings, D. & Occhietti, S. 2001, 'Late Wisconsinian sedimentation in the Québec City region: evidence for energetic subaqueous fan deposition during initial deglaciation', *Géog. Phys. Quat.* **55**, 257–73.

Daigneault, R.-A. & Occhietti, S. 2006, 'Les moraines du massif Algonquin, Ontario, au début du Dryas récent, et corrélation avec la Moraine de Saint-Narcisse', *Géog. Phys. Quat.* **60**, 103–18.

Dionne, J.-C. 1977, 'La mer de Goldthwait au Québec', *Géog. Phys. Quat.* **31**, 61–80.

Dionne, J.-C. 1988a, 'Holocene relative sea-level fluctuations in the St. Lawrence estuary, Québec, Canada', *Quat. Res.* **29**, 233–44.

Dionne, J.-C. 1988b, 'Évidence d'un bas niveau marin durant l'Holocène à Saint-Fabien-sur-Mer, estuaire maritime du Saint-Laurent', *Norois* **35**, 19–34.

Dionne, J.-C. 1997, 'Bilan vicennal des connaissances sur la mer de Goldthwait au Québec', *Bull. Ass. Québécoise Étude Quat.* **23**, 6–20.

Dionne, J.-C. 2001a, 'Relative sea-level changes in the St. Lawrence Estuary from deglaciation to present day', in Weddle & Retelle 2001, 271–84.

Dionne, J.-C. 2001b, 'Troncs d'arbres fossiles sur la batture de l'anse de Bellechasse (Québec): indice d'une fluctuation mineure du niveau marin relatif à l'Holocène supérieur', *Géog. Phys. Quat.* **55**, 301–6.

Dionne, J.-C. 2002, 'État des connaissances sur la ligne de rivage Micmac de J. W. Goldthwait (estuaire du Saint-Laurent)', *Géog. Phys. Quat.* **56**, 97–121.

Dionne, J.-C. 2003, 'Événements holocènes mis en évidence dans une coupe de la terrasse Mitis à l'embouchure de la rivière Fouquette, sur la rive sud du Moyen Estuaire du Saint-Laurent', *Géog. Phys. Quat.* **57**, 241–7.

Dionne, J.-C. & Pfalzgraf, F. 2001, 'Fluctuations holocènes du niveau marin relatif à Rivière-Ouelle, côte sud du moyen estuaire du Saint-Laurent: données complémentaires', *Géog. Phys. Quat.* **55**, 289–300.

Dyke, A.S. & Prest, V.K. 1987, 'Late Wisconsinan and Holocene history of the Laurentide Ice Sheet', *Géogr. Phys. Quat.* **41**, 237–63.

Ehlers, J. & Gibbard, P.L. (eds) 2004, *Quaternary Glaciations: Extent and Chronology*, **2**. *North America*, New York: Elsevier.

Environment Canada 2008, *Climate Normals*, <http://www.climate.weatheroffice.ec.gc.ca/climate_normals/index_e.html> [accessed 4 July 2008).

Filion, L. 1987, 'Holocene development of parabolic dunes in the Central St Lawrence Lowland, Québec, Canada', *Quat. Res.* **28**, 196–209.

Filion, L. & Quinty, F. 1993, 'Macrofossil and tree-ring evidence for long-term forest succession and mid-Holocene hemlock decline', *Quat. Res.* **40**, 89–97.

Fulton, R.J. 1989 (ed.), *Quaternary Geology of Canada and Greenland*, Ottawa: Supply and Services Canada.

Garneau, M. 1997, 'Paléoécologie d'un secteur riverain de la rivière Saint-Charles: analyse macrofossile du site archéologique de la Grande Place à Québec', *Géogr. Phys. Quat.* **51**, 211–20.

Grandtner, M.M. 1966, *La Végétation forestière du Québec méridional*, Québec: Presses de l'Université Laval.

Hardy, R. & Séguin, N. 1984, *Forêt et société en Mauricie*, Montréal: Boréal Express.

Landry, B. & Mercier, M. 1984, *Notions de géologie avec exemples du Québec*, Outremont: Modulo Éditeur.

LaSalle, P. & Elson, J.A. 1975, 'Emplacement of the St-Narcisse moraine as a climatic event in Eastern Canada', *Quat. Res.* **5**, 621–5.

Lavoie, M., Larouche, A. & Richard, P.J.H. 1995, 'Conditions du développement de la tourbière de Farnham, Québec', *Géog. Phys. Quat.* **49**, 305–16.

Marie-Victorin, F. 1995, *Flore laurentienne*, 3rd edn, Montréal: Presses de l'Université de Montréal.

Marshall, S.J., James, T.S. & Clarke, G.K.C. 2001, 'North American Ice Sheet reconstructions at the Last Glacial Maximum', *Quat. Sci. Rev.* **21**, 175–92.

Morneau, F. 1989, 'Contribution à une méthodologie de caractérisation et de cartographie écologique en milieu urbain: le cas de la Basse-Ville de Québec', *Les Cahiers du CRAD* **12**, 1–113.

Moussette, M. & Moss, W. 2008, 'Québec, ville coloniale et porte atlantique du nouveau monde: un point de vue archéologique', in Roy & Côté 2008, 18–37.

Muller, S.D. & Richard, P.J.H. 2001, 'Post-glacial vegetation migration in conterminous Montréal Lowlands, southern Québec', *J. Biogeogr.* **28**, 1169–93.

Niellon, F. 2008, 'Québec au temps de Champlain', in Roy & Côté 2008, 1–17.

Occhietti, S. 1989, 'Géologie quaternaire de la sous-région de la vallée du Saint-Laurent et des Appalaches', in Fulton 1989, 374–417.

Occhietti, S. *et al.* 2001a, 'Late Wisconsinan glacial dynamics, deglaciation, and marine invasion in southern Québec', in Weddle & Retelle 2001, 243–70.

Occhietti, S. *et al.* 2001b, 'Paléoenvironnements de la Mer de Champlain dans la région de Québec, entre 11,300 et 9750 BP: le site de Saint-Nicolas', *Géog. Phys. Quat.* **55**, 23–46.

Occhietti, S. *et al.* 2004, 'Late Wisconsinan-Early Holocene deglaciation of Québec-Labrador', in Ehlers & Gibbard 2004, 243–73.

Occhietti, S. & Richard, P.J.H. 2003, 'Effet réservoir sur les âges ^{14}C de la Mer de Champlain à la transition Pléistocène-Holocène: révision de la chronologie de la déglaciation au Québec méridional', *Géog. Phys. Quat.* **57**, 115–38.

Pagé, P. 1999, *Les Grandes Glaciations*, Montréal: Guérin.

Painchaud, A. 1993, *Paléogéographie de la Pointe de Québec (Place Royale)*, Québec: Publications du Québec.

Parent, A. & Allard, M. 2001, 'Le lieu le mieux situé', in Courville & Garon 2001, 8–19.

Parent, M. *et al.* 1985, 'Paléogéographie du Québec méridional entre 12 500 et 8000 ans BP', *Recherches Amérindiennes au Québec* **15**, 17–34.

Parent, M. & Occhietti, S. 1988, 'Late Wisconsinan deglaciation and Champlain sea invasion in the St. Lawrence valley, Québec', *Géog. Phys. Quat.* **42**, 215–46.

Payette, S. 2001, 'L'évolution des tourbières à l'Holocène: la stratigraphie', in Payette & Rochefort 2001, 345–70.

Payette, S., Filion, L. & Delwaide, A. 1990, 'Disturbance regime of a cold-temperate forest as deduced from tree-ring patterns', *Can. J. For. Res.* **20**, 1228–41.

Payette, S. & Rochefort, L. (eds) 2001, *Écologie des tourbières du Québec-Labrador*, Québec: Presses de l'Université Laval.

Richard, P.J.H. 1973, 'Histoire postglaciaire comparée de la végétation dans deux localités au sud de la région de Québec', *Nat. Can.* **100**, 591–603.

Richard, P.J.H. 1993, 'Origine et dynamique postglaciaire de la forêt mixte au Québec', *Rev. Palaeobot. Palynol.* **79**, 31–68.

Richard, P.J.H. 1994, 'Postglacial palaeophytogeography of the eastern St. Lawrence River watershed and the climatic signal of the pollen record', *Palaeogeogr. Palaeoclim. Palaeoecol.* **109**, 137–61.

Richard, P.J.H. 1995, 'Le couvert végétal du Québec-Labrador il y a 6000 ans BP: essai', *Géog. Phys. Quat.* **49**, 117–40.

Richard, P.J.H. & Occhietti, S. 2005, '^{14}C chronology for ice retreat and inception of Champlain sea in the St. Lawrence lowlands, Canada', *Quat. Res.* **63**, 353–8.

Rousseau, J., Béthune, G. & Morisset, P. 1977, *Voyage de Pehr Kalm au Canada en 1749*, Montréal: Pierre Tisseyre.

Rowe, J.S. 1972, *Forest Regions of Canada*, Ottawa: Information Canada.

Roy, C. & Côté, H. (eds) 2008, *Rêves d'Amériques: regard sur l'archéologie de la Nouvelle-France — Dreams of the Americas: Overview of New France Archaeology*, Archéologiques, hors série **2**.

Saint-Julien, P. & Hubert, C. 1975, 'Evolution of the Taconian Orogen in the Québec Appalachian', *Amer. J. Sci.* **275-A**, 337–62.

Simard, J., Occhietti, S. & Robert, F. 2003, 'Retrait de l'inlandsis sur les Laurentides au début de l'Holocène: transect de 600 km entre le Saint-Maurice et le Témiscamingue (Québec)', *Géog. Phys. Quat.* **57**, 189–204.

Soil Classification Working Group 1998, *The Canadian System of Soil Classification*, 3rd edn, Ottawa: Canadian Department of Agriculture and Agri-food.

Talon, B. *et al.* 2005, 'Reconstruction of the long-term fire history of an old-growth deciduous forest in Southern Québec, Canada, from charred wood in mineral soils', *Quat. Res.* **64**, 36–43.

Tarasov, L. & Peltier, R. W. 2004, 'A geophysically constrained large ensemble analysis of the deglacial history of the North American ice-sheet complex', *Quat. Sci. Rev.* **23**, 359–88.

Weddle, T.K. & Retelle, M.J. (eds) 2001, *Deglaciation History and Relative Sea-Level Changes: Northern New England and Adjacent Canada*, Geol. Soc. Amer. Spec. Pap. **351**.

UNPUBLISHED SOURCES

Auger, S. & Payette, S. 2008, 'Le site archéologique Cartier-Roberval à Québec: cadre géographique et écologique, volet pédologique', final rep. to CCNQ.

Baillargeon, G. 1981, 'Zonation et modification de la composition de la flore vasculaire dans une région urbaine: la Colline de Québec', Université Laval MA thesis.

Cauboue M. 1972, 'Étude écologique des forêts ripariennes du Saint-Laurent aux environs de Québec', Université Laval MA thesis.

D'Arcy, P., Bibeault, J.-F. & Raffa, R. 2005, 'Changements climatiques et transport maritime sur le Saint-Laurent', Ouranos: Étude exploratoire d'options d'adaptation réalisée pour le Comité de concertation navigation du Plan d'action Saint-Laurent.

Laliberté, S. 2006, 'Sédimentologie et stratigraphie d'un delta édifié dans un contexte de régression forcée: exemple du delta de la rivière Sainte-Anne, Québec, Canada', Université Laval MA thesis.

Larouche, A. 1979, 'Histoire postglaciaire comparée de la végétation à Sainte-Foy et au mont des Éboulements, Québec, par l'analyse macrofossile et l'analyse pollinique', Université Laval MA thesis.

LaSalle, P., Martineau, G. & Chauvin, L. 1977, 'Morphologie, stratigraphie et déglaciation de la région de Beauce, Notre-Dame, Parc des Laurentides', Québec: Ministère des Richesses Naturelles DPV-516.

Lavoie, M., Laframboise, C. & Robert, É.C. 2008, 'Histoire postglaciaire de la végétation dans la région du site archéologique Cartier-Roberval', activity rep. to CCNQ.

Magnan, G. 2006, 'Dynamique holocène de la végétation régionale à Beaupré, Québec, par l'analyse sporopollinique', Université Laval Bachelor's thesis.

Samson, G., Fiset, R. & Chrétien, Y. 2007, 'Programme de recherche archéologique. Projet archéologique Cartier-Roberval', CCNQ.

ABBREVIATIONS

AAQ	Association des archéologues du Québec
BPA	Base de plein air
CCNQ	Commission de la Capitale-Nationale du Québec
CRAD	Centre de recherche en amenagement et développement
FLAV	Saint-Flavien-de-Lotbinière
RSL	Relative sea level

SUMMARY IN FRENCH, GERMAN, ITALIAN AND SPANISH

RÉSUMÉ

Les environnements naturels de la région de Québec durant l'Holocène

Dans la vallée du fleuve du Saint-Laurent, la période de 10 000 ans suivant la glaciation du Wisconsinien a été marquée par des changements géographiques et climatiques qui ont influencé le développement des paysages végétaux. Dans cet article, les environnements de l'Holocène dans la région de Québec ont été reconstruits à partir de données paléogéographiques et paléoécologiques. Les fluctuations du niveau relatif de la mer, particulièrement au cours des derniers millénaires, sont d'un intérêt particulier compte tenu de la situation de Québec comme portail maritime sur le Saint-Laurent. Des changements dans la couverture végétale depuis l'implantation euro-américaine il y a 400 ans environ sont principalement dus à des déboisements forestiers pour l'agriculture et plus récemment pour le développement urbain.

ZUSAMMENFASSUNG

Die Umweltbedingungen im Gelände der Stadt Quebec während des Alluviums

Im St Lawrence-Flußtal war der 10,000 Jahre währende Zeitabschnitt nach der Wisconsin-Eiszeit durch größere geographische und klimatische Veränderungen gekennzeichnet, die besonders die Pflanzenwelt beeinflußten. In diesem Bericht wird die alluviale Umwelt in der Gegend der Stadt Quebec auf Grund paläographischer und paläoökologischer Daten rekonstruiert. Schwankungen des relativen Wasserstandes, besonders in jüngsten Jahrtausenden, sind angesichts der Lage von Quebec als Tor zum Meer und zum St Lawrence Fluß von besonderem Interesse. Der Wechsel der Pflanzendecke seit der euroamerikanischen Besiedlung vor ungefähr vierhundert Jahren beruht im Wesentlichen auf Rodungen für die Landwirtschaft und in jüngerer Zeit für städtische Besiedlung.

RIASSUNTO

L'ambiente naturale nella regione della città di Quebec durante l'Olocene

Nella valle del fiume San Lorenzo, il periodo di 10.000 anni che seguì la glaciazione Wisconsiniana, fu contraddistinto da importanti cambiamenti geografici e climatici che influenzarono lo sviluppo di associazioni vegetali. Basandosi sui dati paleogeografici e paleoecologici, in questo contributo sono stati ricostruiti i paleoambienti olocenici nella regione della città di Quebec. Le fluttuazioni del livello medio del mare, specialmente quelle degli ultimi millenni, sono di particolare interesse alla luce della situazione del Quebec come sbocco marittimo sul fiume San Lorenzo. I cambiamenti nella vegetazione, che seguirono l'insediamento degli Europei in America del nord circa 400 anni fa, sono principalmente riconducibili alla deforestazione per l'agricoltura e più recentemente all'urbanizzazione.

RESUMEN

El medioambiente natural de la ciudad de Quebec durante el Holoceno

El período de 10,000 años que siguió a la glaciación Wisconsiana estuvo marcado en el valle del río St Lawrence por grandes cambios geográficos y climáticos que tuvieron una gran influencia en el desarrollo de las comunidades de plantas. En el presente artículo se reconstruyen los medioambientes del Holoceno en la región de la ciudad de Quebec según datos paleogeográficos y paleoecológicos. Las fluctuaciones relativas en el nivel del mar, sobre todo en los milenios recientes, son de interés especial por la situación de Quebec como salida marina al St Lawrence. Los cambios producidos en la cubierta de flora desde el asentamiento euro-americano de hace unos 400 años son debidos principalmente al talado de bosques para la agricultura y más recientemente al desarrollo urbano.

Département de géographie, 2405, rue de la Terrasse, Université Laval, Québec (Québec), Canada G1V 0A6

[Louise.Filion@cen.ulaval.ca; martin.lavoie@cen.ulaval.ca; lydia.querrec.1@ulaval.ca]

Post-Medieval Archaeology **43/1** (2009), 30–47

A universe under strain: Amerindian nations in north-eastern North America in the 16th century

By MARCEL MOUSSETTE

SUMMARY: Archival and archaeological research has improved understanding of the 16th-century European presence in north-eastern North America. Links may now be established between assemblages of European objects uncovered on Amerindian sites in the continent's interior, providing insights into how the newcomers' arrival and encounter with Aboriginal people affected local populations. Despite their limitations, the material remains provide an Amerindian-generated viewpoint that, when considered in conjunction with archival evidence, can be related to European narratives. This paper attempts to measure the intensity and scope of early contacts and establish the main events surrounding them.

INTRODUCTION

It is generally acknowledged by historians that Bristol merchants, excluded from Icelandic fishing grounds, undertook foreign voyages as early as the 1480s, seeking cod and the mythical island of Brazil, and eventually reached the shores of present-day Newfoundland. These expeditions left only a few vague documentary traces concerning the lands visited by the seafarers, but it was in their wake that the Venetian Giovanni Caboto sailed from Bristol on 2 May 1497, and, crossing the Atlantic, navigated the coast of the North American continent from Labrador to New England. On his return Cabot declared that he had sailed all the way to Asia and that his discovery would give England access to the riches of the Orient, without having to take the long sea route around the southern tip of Africa. The true situation turned out to be quite different and, denied spices and silks, Europeans had to make do with the country's other natural resources — cod and furs in great abundance.[1]

In the conclusion of Bernard G. Hoffman's book, *Cabot to Cartier: Sources for a Historical Ethnography of Northeastern North America, 1497–1550*, published in 1961, the author asked a series of pertinent questions for which he had no answers:

> One large and important category of sources deals with the Newfoundland fishery and with associated aspects of fur trade and Indian–European contacts. These documents, however, leave much to be desired. We do not have any clear idea of the composition of the fleet at different times; of the national backgrounds and characteristics of the sailors involved; of the different fishing practices and equipment, ports, harbours, and fishing grounds; of the nature of the trade goods, and what items were transferred in barter with the natives; of the philosophical and religious viewpoints of the fishermen and their attitudes towards the natives. The discovery of new sources may possibly answer some of these points, but most will have to be resolved only through the painstaking study of the existing archival materials. Until that is done, the European fishing fleet must remain one of the little known factors in early culture contact in the north-east.[2]

 DOI: 10.1179/007942309X12457508843883

The questions raised by Hoffman were certainly taken seriously, for in the 1970s and early 1980s historians succeeded in determining the size of the European fleet and, most notably, established the presence of Basque cod fishermen and whalers in the Gulf of St Lawrence and Newfoundland during the 16th century. This type of research is exemplified by the work carried out by Selma H. Barkham in the archives of the Spanish Basque Country, by Laurier Turgeon in Bordeaux, by René Bélanger in the Basque Country and, more recently, by Peter Pope in his study of the presence of Breton and English cod fishermen in Newfoundland in the 1500s.[3]

COD FISHERMEN, WHALERS AND AMERINDIANS

The research carried out by the historians mentioned above is significant for the fact that it goes beyond ancient maps and accounts written by the 15th- and 16th-century explorers and merchants who investigated the coastal regions of the North-East and the tributaries of rivers flowing into the Atlantic. René Bélanger's study of place names clearly demonstrates the presence of Basque fishermen on the south and west coasts of Newfoundland, on the North Shore and along the coasts of the Gulf of St Lawrence, the Strait of Belle Isle and the St Lawrence Estuary. Turgeon's study presents a number of interesting points, in particular the impressive size of the mid-16th-century fishing fleet:

> The tally the English navigator Anthony Parkhurst made in the course of a reconnaissance mission in 1578 set the number of European ships around the 'new found land' between 350 and 380: 150 French cod-fishing vessels, 100 Spanish, 50 Portuguese, 30 to 50 English, and 20 to 30 Basque whalers. Although some historians deem these figures to be exaggerated, they are, if anything, lower than the actual ones, based on evidence in the notarial archives of Bordeaux, La Rochelle and Rouen, which by themselves point to more than 150 French ships for certain years around the mid-century. Parkhurst was probably unable to count the ships plying the Grand Banks at various times of the year and at the same time all the inshore fishing boats scattered along several thousand miles of coastline.[4]

Like Innis before him, Turgeon also argued that the cod fishery in France had developed as sedentary fishing before becoming mobile.[5] This aspect will be seen to have been of considerable importance when I deal later with contacts between the French and the Amerindians. Turgeon's intensive archival research also enabled him to demonstrate that fishermen were already involved in fur trading with the Amerindians in the mid-16th century and that 'in the latter half of the century this trade took on considerable importance in Bordeaux', although fishing remained the primary economic activity.[6]

The outstanding merit of historian Barkham's work resides not only in her archival research demonstrating the concentration of Basque whalers in Grand Bay (Strait of Belle Isle) in the second half of the 16th century, but also in her decision to pursue fieldwork in search of material traces of these former activities. Thus it was that she organized the first archaeological survey in the Strait of Belle Isle in 1977, accompanied by two experienced archaeologists, Walter Kenyon and James Tuck. At the village of Red Bay, on the shores of the bay bearing the same name, they found thousands of fragments of coarse red earthenware roof tiles, like those seen on the houses in the milder climatic regions of southern Europe. Similar tiles were also found on Saddle Island, located in the bay. On this site the researchers also came across the remains of stone walls, covered with a solidified black substance which was subsequently analysed and found to be charred animal fat. Given these indicators alone, the site's archaeological potential, combined with the archaeological data previously collected by Barkham, was so promising that the next year, in 1978, a vast land and underwater excavation project was undertaken. This continued for a decade and led to discoveries that have been extremely important for reconstructing the whale-hunting activities of the Basque seamen. Excavations revealed a common dwelling, associated with a rich assemblage of artefacts;[7] a cooper's workshop; various types of tryworks for rendering whale blubber into oil; a cemetery holding the remains of 125 individuals; a few traces of contact with Aboriginals, in particular a piece of St Lawrence Iroquoian-type pottery left in a structure before its roof collapsed; and the remains of four galleons, one of which was the object of a systematic excavation that enabled researchers to deduce the techniques used for building the vessel and to study its rigging and cargo, including a collection of 10,000 casks providing first-hand information on cooperage.[8]

The Red Bay project has made a significant contribution to our knowledge of the 16th century in a number of ways. First, the material remains give a very clear picture of the Europeans in action as they sought to set up and run a truly proto-industrial establishment in a natural and cultural context that was unfamiliar to them. These remains are also concrete evidence of the scale on which market capitalism deployed its efforts when it began to expand in the 16th century. As researchers reconstructed the enterprise's primary chain of operations, centred on whale oil production, and the related secondary chains of operation, such as shipbuilding and manufacturing casks to transport the oil, a clearer picture emerged of how an Atlantic zone was being established, stretching from the coasts of France to North America. Finally, simply from a methodological point of view, the finds made at Red Bay provided a powerful catalyst for subsequent excavations on the sites of Middle Bay, Île Nue de Mingan, Bon-Désir and Île aux Basques.

The originality of Peter Pope's approach lies in his use of material remains uncovered by archaeologists alongside archives to demonstrate the dominant presence of Bretons on the shores of Newfoundland until around 1580, after which time they faced stiff competition from English fishermen for the same fishing grounds.[9] While the English presence had already received archaeological support from the excavation of fishing establishments such as Ferryland and the discovery of ceramics from North Devon, South Devon and South Somerset at these sites, it was Pope who identified coarse earthenware cooking pots and storage jars as having forms and compositions that linked them unquestionably to pottery sites identified in Brittany. Given that the Breton presence in 16th-century North America has not been documented very extensively, this finding is very important since it provides researchers with a tool to follow the traces of Bretons who came here to fish or trade.

Now that archaeological evidence of the early European presence has been brought to light, it is possible to establish links between these material remains and European objects uncovered on Amerindian sites in the continent's interior and thereby attempt to gain a better understanding of how the newcomers' arrival and their encounter with the Aboriginals affected local populations. Despite their limitations, these objects can provide us with a viewpoint generated by the Amerindians themselves and one that, when considered in conjunction with travel accounts and other archives, can be compared with the perspective provided by European texts.

THE FRENCH ON THE NORTH-EAST COASTS OF NORTH AMERICA

In the 16th century, despite the expansion of the English fishery in Newfoundland towards the end of the 1500s, cod fishing in the north-east waters of North America continued to be dominated by the French. It should also be mentioned that the Breton, Norman and Basque fishermen initially engaged in sedentary cod fishing.[10] Since Newfoundland and the Gulf of St Lawrence offered the right climatic conditions in summer, the Europeans set up their installations on beaches, where they could salt and dry the cod that abounded not far from shore.[11] It seems likely that such protracted stays on dry land would have presented opportunities for the fishermen and the Aboriginals to meet and exchange with one another.

It is known that contacts between the Europeans and the Amerindians varied in tenor. For example, the Beothuks in Newfoundland eventually adopted an inward-turning attitude that contrasted with the openness to trade generally shown by other groups. Rather than obtaining metal objects and other goods in exchange for the pelts of animals they had trapped, the Beothuks helped themselves to whatever the Europeans left behind at their fishing camps when they returned home for the winter. The Beothuks' strategy is reflected in the vast assemblage of reused metal items uncovered by Ralph Pastore on the Boyd's Cove site, located on the east coast of Newfoundland in a vaguely defined area visited by French fishermen to the north and English fishermen to the south:

> Indeed, an examination of Boyd's Cove collection makes it clear that it was the site of a well-developed iron industry. Fish hooks were straightened out and shaped into awls and the tips of spikes were flattened, producing a spatulate-shaped edge that would have been ideal for scraping the fat from hides. But it was in the production of arrow and lance points that the Beothuk iron-workers really demonstrated their skills.[12]

It goes without saying that although scavenging gave the Beothuks the advantage of avoiding violent confrontation with the newcomers when they met, and although it helped them maintain their traditional way of life to a great extent, such activities also provoked hostile reactions from Europeans who occupied the shore. The Beothuks' retreat inland also seems eventually to have cut them off from the maritime resources that constituted a considerable part of their diet. These factors no doubt contributed to the Beothuks' disappearance in the 19th century.

The shores south of Nova Scotia were also visited, in particular by Norman fishermen who came to fish for cod and exchange goods for furs in the second half of the 16th century. Since cod is not found to the south of Cap Cod, Turgeon rightly concluded that the Norman fishermen would have focused their activities on the southern shores of Acadia, which began to form an identity in the 17th century, and the vast region further south known at the time as Florida or Norumbega (Fig. 1). From an archaeological viewpoint, the presence of these fishermen is supported by the discovery of European trade goods on a series of 16th-century Algonquian sites scattered between Passaquamody Bay in New Brunswick and Rhode Island.[13]

FIG. 1

Map of north-eastern North America showing the location of the main place names and Aboriginal populations mentioned in this paper. Plain arrows represent possible itineraries followed by the Basques, Bretons and Normans, while dotted arrows indicate some of the trade routes used by Amerindians in the 16th century (drawn by A. Héroux).

It is therefore clear that the French presence could be felt along thousands of kilometres of coastline north of Cap Cod right up to the shores of Labrador on the Gulf of St Lawrence. If we take into consideration the well-documented activities of the Basques at the mouth of the Saguenay[14] and the voyages of discovery undertaken by Cartier, and by the merchants of St Malo from 1581 onwards,[15] this presence could have been felt as far as the Lachine Rapids near Montréal and perhaps even further up the St Lawrence River. It follows that the expansion of France's Atlantic zone, effected to a great degree by Basques, Bretons and Normans, touched numerous Aboriginal groups: the Beothuks of Newfoundland and the Strait of Belle Isle; the Mi'kmaqs of the Gaspé Peninsula and Acadia; the Maliseets of Acadia; the St Lawrence Iroquoians of Canada; and the Almouchiquois and other nations of Norumbega. This list includes only those groups with which the Europeans came into direct contact. However, several of the Amerindian nations that were in a position to exchange furs for goods directly with French fishermen or merchants took on the role of middlemen and transported European objects further inland, where they could be bartered or traded among the other nations living there. It has been possible to reconstruct some of the paths by which the European goods penetrated the interior of the continent. These paths offer insights into a few of the changes and events that marked Aboriginal populations at the time. It is this complex story that I will attempt to tell, using discoveries made by archaeologists on 16th-century Amerindian sites in north-east North America.

PATHS INLAND THROUGH NORUMBEGA AND ACADIA

The place name Norumbega, as it appears on old maps, designated both a region roughly equivalent to present-day New England, vaguely situated between Acadia to the north and Florida to the south, and an exact location, the estuary of the Penobscot River and its islands.[16] The coast of the region was inhabited by nations that spoke Algonquian languages and dwelt at the mouths of rivers flowing into the Atlantic. It is believed that during the 16th century European material came to this region from two different sources, the Normans and the Basques. As indicated above, Norman fishermen were probably the first Europeans to engage in fur trade on this coast.[17] The trade goods they brought with them consisted generally of small objects that were often decorative or sewing-related. They included bells, bracelets, rings, ear pendants, pins, needles, scissors, knives, mirrors, chain links, axes and kettles. The chain links, bells and ear pendants were probably made of copper or brass. There are fewer mentions of copper kettles in documents related to Norman trade than in those related to the Basques.[18]

The second source of European material — trade with Basque cod fishermen and whalers — is better documented, and there are records of large quantities of material brought to sites along the shores of the Gulf of St Lawrence and to coastal Newfoundland, Labrador and Acadia. While several types of objects were traded, it is metal and glass items that have survived on 16th-century Mi'kmaq sites in Nova Scotia and New Brunswick, where they are found in abundance.[19]

For the protohistoric period, Whitehead has identified no fewer than nine such sites, all of which are 'copper kettle burials'. However, only two, the Northport and Pictou sites on the north shore of the Northumberland Strait, have been systematically excavated. The list of grave goods of European origin found at the two sites is revealing, for it represents in large part the array of objects that would continue to be exchanged for decades to come. They include, naturally enough, the red copper kettles typical of the period, with their bails attached to an iron band under the rim; glass beads; iron knives, daggers and swords; iron axes, adzes and caulking knives; a copper-alloy saw blade; iron arrowheads, spearheads, awls and fishhooks; an iron hinge and a sherd of green-glazed Saintonge pottery. This rich material, consisting mainly of utilitarian metal objects, is evidence of the close relationship maintained by the Mi'kmaqs with the Europeans and, being found in grave sites, shows the value that was attributed to these objects.

It is well known that the Mi'kmaqs engaged in maritime navigation, sometimes over considerable distances.[20] In a recent article, Charles Martijn has demonstrated from ethnohistoric and archaeological sources that the Mi'kmaqs had a vast maritime domain extending over the Gulf of St Lawrence, where they travelled in large sea canoes between islands to harvest the resources found in this zone.[21] It was in such a context that the Mi'kmaqs came into contact with European fishermen in the 16th century and began to trade furs with them. These Aboriginals were quick to borrow cultural elements from the newcomers, and several early 17th-century documents describe them dressed in European-style clothing and sailing the coastal waters of Nova Scotia and the Gulf of Main in shallops and pinnaces equipped with one or more masts.[22] Whitehead believes that the Mi'kmaqs' theft of a pinnace belonging to Étienne Bellanger, who came from Normandy to trade for furs on the east coast of Nova Scotia in 1583, is the first recorded incident showing the Mi'kmaqs' skill in handling European boats.[23] This implies that the Mi'kmaqs were capable of navigating long distances at an earlier date than previously thought; they could have travelled along the coast of New England with goods obtained from the Basques and exchanged them there for furs and shell beads.[24] It is hardly surprising that the Mi'kmaqs should act as middlemen between the Basques and Algonquian language groups living along the shores of Nova Scotia and New England, given that they had been in close contact with the Basques since the mid-16th century – so close in fact that the two groups communicated in a jargon that was a mix of Basque and Algonquian words:

> Communication between the Basques (and the early French) and Algonquian happened by means of a trade language that was a mixture of Basque and Algonquian. This language was used from southern Labrador to New England and to a lesser extent along the shores of the St Lawrence Gulf, probably with local varieties. Some 40 words and phrases that have been written down in the early contact period by missionaries and travellers as being uttered by the Micmac and the Montagnais are without any doubt Basque phrases and words.[25]

This linguistic adaptation is another aspect of the interaction evidenced by the large quantities of diverse European objects discovered in Mi'kmaq graves dating from the protohistoric period in Nova Scotia.

There is another potential source for the Basque goods that arrived in the Gulf of Maine area near the end of the 16th century, that is, through Etchemin or Maliseet middlemen, who also spoke an Algonquian language. When the St Lawrence Iroquoians disappeared, these Amerindian groups had direct access, via the river system, to the region of the St Lawrence River at the mouth of the Saguenay, where the Basques were already very active in the fur trade. However, all existing documentary evidence for such contact dates only from the beginning of the 17th century.[26]

To the south of present-day New England, another route for distributing European goods from the Atlantic seaboard to the inland regions developed in the 16th century. This southern route followed part of a prehistoric trade network along which native copper, seashells and non-local lithic material was moved. It went northward, following the Susquehanna River upstream towards Iroquoia. Our knowledge of this network comes from archaeologist James W. Bradley, who reconstructed it on the basis of his study of relations between the Onondagas, who were members of the Five Nations Iroquois confederacy, and the Susquehannocks.[27] The arrival of European objects and materials on the Atlantic seaboard had a profound influence on the material culture of the Onondagas, who at the time occupied highlands in the river system emptying into Lake Ontario via Lake Oneida, and that of the Susquehannocks, who lived in the upper regions of the Susquehanna River, which flowed toward the sea.

During the initial phase of the period, which may be termed protohistoric, the Susquehannocks were merely one of the links in a trade network based on sea shells, often shaped into beads or simply pierced with a hole, a few objects in non-local stone and European goods made of smelted copper, copper alloys, iron and glass. The seashell beads came from species found along the mid-Atlantic seaboard or further south, beyond North Carolina, but the European material is similar to that associated with well-documented historic sources. It consists mainly of small non-utilitarian objects — copper ornaments in the shape of tubes, disks, spirals and hoops suitable for use as necklace pendants, ear pendants and bracelets. According to the sources cited above, this type of archaeological assemblage corresponds to the trade goods used by the Normans. Furthermore, chemical and metallographic analyses of two categories of these objects — the spirals that could be used as pendants and the hoops, or bracelets, found particularly on protohistoric sites in Iroquoia — demonstrated that they were made of sheet metal, possibly by Amerindians, using flat pieces of copper or brass seemingly cut from the sides of kettles brought from Europe. Thus there seem to have been two sources of European metal supplies; the red copper no doubt came from copper kettles traded in great numbers by the Basques in Mi'kmaq territory, while the brass, an alloy of copper and zinc, most probably came from Norman traders, who preferred this metal.[28] Although the results of this study are based on the detailed analysis of only two types of object, they nonetheless point in the same direction as the historic sources, corroborating what is known about how the Normans traded on the coast of Norumbega and the intermediary role played by the Mi'kmaqs in their relations with the Basques. The study also sheds more light on the intersection of Aboriginal and European trade routes. Returning to the Susquehannock–Onondaga network, there is a strong correlation between the distribution of seashells and that of European material, indicating that these two categories of object followed the same routes. There is also contemporary evidence of contact between the Onondagas and the Susquehannocks. This is reflected mainly in the Susquehanna-type pottery (Schultz Incised) adopted by the Onondagas with almost no modification, found in archaeological assemblages along with seashells from the Atlantic seaboard and European objects. It is thus clear that the Susquehannocks and Onondagas were part of a protohistoric trade network. In the mid-16th century, trade took on such important dimensions that the Susquehannocks abandoned the territory they had been living in around the northern branch of the Susquehanna River and moved downstream to a location 300km to the south. This migration took them closer to the sea and no doubt gave them better control over access to European goods. Radical changes in the Susquehannocks' lifestyle suggest that they were dealing with new tensions: instead of establishing small, unfortified hamlets as they had previously, they built a single large village with a palisade around it. By this time the trading system had been profoundly transformed from its early protohistoric predecessor:

> By the end of the century, the character of the exchange system was nearly the opposite of what it had been a century earlier. Instead of small quantities of material circulating widely through an extended series of networks, large quantities now followed increasingly specific routes to a more limited number of destinations.[29]

The growing importance of trade and the increased presence of Europeans were signs of things to come. Even greater changes would occur in the following century, when the Europeans established permanent settlements in north-east North America. In the 17th century, the Susquehannocks became powerful middlemen in the fur trade. However, through rivalry with the Iroquois, they became involved in a drawn-out conflict that began in 1660 and ended with their dispersal in 1675.[30]

In contrast, archaeological research shows that the Onondagas living further north did not experience cultural change to the degree that the Susquehannocks did. Onondaga sites reveal European objects that arrived from the south through trade with the Susquehannocks. But these objects are generally made of materials like copper alloy (used mostly for ornaments in the shape of tubes, disks, hoops and spirals) and glass (used for two types of beads) that the Onondagas might have associated with exotic materials that were already known to them, such as native copper and seashells or crystals.[31] The new materials and objects could thus be integrated into Onondaga culture without producing acculturation with negative effects.

Another outside influence on 16th-century Onondaga culture can be seen in the groups' pottery, as elements of Huron and St Lawrence Iroquoian ceramic traditions were incorporated into Onondaga vessels (changes in the shape and height of the neck on certain vessels and increased variety in decorations on recipients).[32] Such northern influences also show up in other objects found on Onondaga sites; they include effigy pipes with features associated with the pipes of the St Lawrence Iroquoians, native copper presumably coming from the Great Lakes region, and an incised walrus ivory dagger which probably originated further north.[33] Like the European materials, these exogenous objects do not seem to have affected Onondaga culture in any profound way.

According to Bradley,[34] the Onondagas and their St Lawrence Iroquoian neighbours living in present-day Jefferson County began to engage in hostilities near the end of the prehistoric period. Archaeological research shows that the communities lived in fortified villages at this time; human skeletal remains have also been found in waste pits and St Lawrence Iroquoian cultural elements occasionally turn up on Onondaga sites. At the beginning of the protohistoric period, when European material started to arrive around 1500, there was a dramatic increase in the presence of St Lawrence Iroquoian cultural features, as mentioned in the previous paragraph. By the end of the century, these features became less evident and were integrated into the Onondaga culture. Bradley interprets these changes as indicating that a significant number of St Lawrence Iroquoians arrived among the Onondagas and were assimilated into their culture. Were they refugees or captives? Bradley's position on the question seems ambiguous. At one point he talks about St Lawrence Iroquoian refugees, while at another he refers to hostilities between the two groups and in his conclusion favours the idea that the Onondagas were instrumental in the dispersal of the St Lawrence Iroquoians. However that might be, St Lawrence Iroquoian cultural features show a marked increase on Onondaga sites dating from the time that these Iroquoians were dispersed from their villages in Jefferson County, an event that must be related to the dispersal of all the St Lawrence Iroquoians in the St Lawrence Valley shortly after Jacques Cartier visited Hochelaga.

Even as north–south trade grew more intense and diversified, the Onondagas were able to integrate the new cultural features that came their way and even take advantage of them, as is shown by their reuse of iron objects and fragments.[35] At the end of the protohistoric period, in the early 17th century, Onondaga villages were still laid out in a pattern that had changed little from that of the prehistoric period, which suggests a certain continuity.[36] However, despite the Onondaga culture's capacity for integration, its openness to outside influences meant that at the end of the protohistoric period it was not exactly the same as it had been at the beginning. With the stability the Onondagas were able to maintain, their culture enjoyed a certain continuity as it underwent changes. Even the arrival of the St Lawrence Iroquoians in their midst did not have a disintegrating effect, but rather resulted in an assimilation process that was a catalyst for a redefinition of Onondaga identity.[37] However, this was before the establishment of European settlements in the North-East.

PATHS INLAND VIA THE ST LAWRENCE

The state of archaeological research on early contact between Europeans and Amerindians in the St Lawrence Valley is peculiar, if not downright bizarre. For, despite incontestable 16th-century documentary evidence, it was only about ten years ago that archaeologists were able to gather solid material proof of such encounters in the land between the Atlantic regions and the Great Lakes:

> Relations written in both the 16th and 17th centuries attest that Europeans encountered different Amerindian groups as the newcomers' settlement expanded from east to west along the St Lawrence from the Atlantic to the Great Lakes. To the north of the Great Lakes region, the last two decades of archaeological work, in Huron and Neutral territory at least, have uncovered material evidence of the 'first contacts' documented by ethnographic texts, complementing the picture they provide. However, in the region between the Great Lakes and the Atlantic coast, no site has yet been recognized as illustrating this period.[38]

The gaping hole in our knowledge for the early contact period, a crucial time for both the Europeans and the Aboriginals, is no doubt the result of both historical and methodological factors. It is possible that the number of European objects exchanged with the Amerindians was very limited in the 16th century, or that trade goods were passed from one middleman to another and thus ended up being used on sites much further inland. The sudden disappearance of the St Lawrence Iroquoians in the second half of the 16th century may also have helped to create a sort of vacuum, or no man's land, in the St Lawrence Valley. In any case, when Québec sites were excavated in the 1970s and 1980s, it was normal practice for archaeologists to separate European from Aboriginal material; European finds were analysed by material culture specialists for the historic period whilst Amerindian artefacts were studied by specialists for the prehistoric period, but there was no provision for a subsequent reconsideration of the results to see how they might be interrelated. This methodological compartmentalization, combined with the historic factors just outlined, could easily make it difficult or even impossible to recognize a transitional period between prehistory and European settlement, when European objects were integrated into Aboriginal material culture, presaging the advent of cultural changes.

Of course, the whole question of naming periods becomes of secondary importance at one point, since protohistory and early contact are actually phases in a continuous process of cultural transformation engendered by the 'gradual intrusion' of the European world into that of the Amerindians.[39] This 'gradual intrusion' gathered pace with time, as contacts intensified, leading to an ever greater number of European objects, particularly trade goods, on Amerindian sites. At the same time, traditional techniques for making things like pottery and stone tools continued to be used up to the end of the 17th century and even into the 18th century.[40]

According to Moreau, European objects took two different east–west paths as they moved inland from the St Lawrence estuary.[41] The first route followed the vast St Lawrence waterway itself, along which European objects could travel westward to the middle estuary, and perhaps even to Montréal. The second was much more complicated and used the river systems of the three main tributaries of the St Lawrence, located on its northern shores. These tributaries were the Ottawa River, furthest to the west, the Saguenay River in the east, and the Saint-Maurice River between them. They all sprang from sources deep in the boreal forest to the south-east of James Bay, making it possible for travellers to transfer from one to another quite easily.[42] This second route was an ancient one that had been used for the native copper trade since the Archaic period and continued to be used right up to the early historic period.[43] On the basis of archaeological evidence, it appears that goods found west of Montréal came via the northern route much more often than by the St Lawrence route.[44]

Archaeological work to date on sites along the St Lawrence corridor from the Strait of Belle Isle to Montréal supports the idea that European objects were conveyed along this route. In the 16th century, the period that Moreau and Langevin identify with the 'earliest signs of European presence', there is good evidence for what might be termed a 'Basque ripple effect' in this area. Most excavated Basque whaling stations have yielded objects related to the Amerindians, indicating that contacts had taken place. At the same time, certain items of Basque origin are found on Amerindian sites. For example, a specific type of ceramic ware turns up on several of the Basque sites, indicating that they were clearly related, and perhaps even contemporary. These coarse earthenware cooking pots — with green-glazed exteriors, decorated with vertical appliqué bands bearing a relief pattern of little lozenges — have been unearthed on the sites of Red Bay and Middle Bay, both of which are on the Lower North Shore, and at Anse à la Cave and Île aux Basques, near the mouth of the Saguenay. The same type of pottery has also been found on an Amerindian site known as EiBg-9, located on the western shore of the Blanc-Sablon River, which flows into the Strait of Belle Isle at about 50km from Red Bay. The fragmented remains of three Basque cooking pots were discovered in association with a central hearth containing a large quantity of charred bones (indicating that it was probably a Beothuk occupation) along with forged nails, two keys, a copper wire, a core and flakes made of ballast flint, whalebone and fragments of dyed fabric.[45] On another more recent site on the shore of the Blanc-Sablon River, Pintal uncovered an assemblage of flakes and stone tools testifying to a rich Amerindian material culture, as well as some artefacts of European origin — forged nails, a faceted black glass bead and a sherd of coarse earthenware with a chemical composition similar to that of Domfront ceramics from Normandy.[46] This exogenous material no doubt dates from the period identified by Moreau with the 'earliest signs of European presence', when 16th-century Norman fishermen and Basque whalers visited the St Lawrence Estuary and travelled as far as the mouth of the Saguenay. However, the objects they brought did not stay where they left them.

At the Anse à la Baleine site, on Île aux Basques, Auger and Lalande uncovered a Late Woodland Iroquoian vessel, characteristic of the period 1550–1650, in the same layer as a European-made cooking pot of the same type as the one found by Pintal at the EiBg-9 Amerindian site at Blanc-Sablon.[47] Further upstream, on the Rocher de la Chapelle site (CgEo-2) on Île aux Oies, a few vessels of the types made by St Lawrence Iroquoians were also found in association with European material such as nails, scraps of copper, metal bands, cast-iron and copper kettles and, more significantly, sherds of a green-glazed pan, similar to the fragments uncovered on Basque sites and the Amerindian Blanc-Sablon site, but which had in some cases been shaped into circular game pieces with one glazed face.[48] Such pieces, traditionally made of bone, were used by the Iroquoians and Algonquians to play a sort of game of chance, quite like European dice-throwing. On the Place Royale site in Québec City, archaeologists identified a group of hearths, beneath which lay an assemblage of glass beads that could date from a little before Champlain's arrival at this spot in 1608. One of these beads — oval-shaped with opaque green and white stripes — has been identified by William Fiztgerald as dating from the last quarter of the 16th century and usually related to the presence of Basques.[49] Still further upstream, the Dawson site on the Island of Montréal has revealed a few European artefacts in association with ceramic containers, some of which represented types produced by the St Lawrence Iroquoians.[50] This site, discovered by geologist William Dawson at the end of the 19th century, has been the subject of several publications and debates, but it has never been possible to establish with certainty whether the European objects were actually related to a St Lawrence Iroquoian occupation of the place.

On 16th-century sites in the region to the north of Lake Ontario, pre-1580 archaeological assemblages indicate that not very many European goods reached the other Iroquoians, that is, the Hurons and Neutrals living much further inland. On Huron sites from this period, Ramsden found only a few types of metal object: little cylinders rolled out of scraps of copper and a scattering of iron items in the shape of awls and small axes.[51] Similarly, on Neutral sites dating from the period 1500–80 (before the fur trade really commenced), Fitzgerald reported only a negligible quantity of European objects – a single glass bead in both the McPherson and Zap sites and a little iron axe in the Sapher ossuary.[52] It is perhaps noteworthy that these assemblages of European objects associated with Neutral and Huron sites are quite similar to the assemblage found on the Dawson St Lawrence Iroquoian site, which continues to raise questions as to whether it was a protohistoric site.

It is intriguing that the vast area between the St Lawrence Iroquoians on the Island of Montréal and the Hurons living in Huronia, north of Lake Ontario, has revealed no sign of European objects on sites dating from the protohistoric period. It is difficult to explain this hiatus, for the area was occupied by St Lawrence Iroquoian villages as far west as the eastern end of Lake Ontario (Jefferson County). Bruce Trigger has proposed that this absence resulted from the fact that, in the early to mid-16th century, the main path by which European objects were conveyed was not along the Upper St Lawrence, leading to eastern Ontario, but rather via the northern river systems, which led to Huronia.[53] If this were the case, the Hurons would have had no reason to attack the St Lawrence Iroquoians, since they would already have controlled trade with Europeans via the northern route; the disappearance of the St Lawrence Iroquoians would then have been more probably caused by an invasion of their territory by Iroquois coming from south of Lake Ontario. At first glance, this explanation seems very plausible, since the Hurons could quite easily have bypassed the St Lawrence Iroquoians by obtaining European objects from the Algonquins via the old native copper trade route that followed a northerly path and led all the way to Tadoussac.

The absence of European artefacts in this region leads to the question of how and why the St Lawrence Iroquoians disappeared in the second half of the 16th century. To address this question, one cannot simply establish a scenario based on the lack of European objects in these Amerindians' territory; it is also necessary to ask how their disappearance might be linked to relations between them and the Hurons-Petuns, to the degree that such relations can be determined from archaeological data. The latter approach has been taken by James Pendergast.[54] First, he noticed a gradual increase in the quantity of ceramics made by St Lawrence Iroquoian women potters on Huron sites from 1500, when such artefacts made up no more than 10% of the assemblages, to 1580 and thereafter, when they accounted for 35% of the assemblage on the Trent site and 16% of that on the Dawn site. By 1580, the St Lawrence Iroquoian sites west of Montréal were no longer occupied; documentary evidence suggests that the sites at Montréal and further east were also abandoned around 1600. After 1615, St Lawrence Iroquoian women potters continued to produce their characteristic ceramics on Huron sites, but by that point the St Lawrence Iroquoians had disappeared as a distinct group. By then, the Hurons were at war with the Iroquois, and their territory, Huronia, had shrunk considerably.

The presence of St Lawrence Iroquoian women potters on Huron sites — Pendergast reports 26 of them — can be explained in two ways: either they were taken there by force by the Hurons following raids on St Lawrence Iroquoian villages along the St Lawrence River, or they sought refuge there for some reason (invasion by the Iroquois, epidemics brought by Europeans, climate change resulting from the Little Ice Age).[55] The two alternatives were examined by Peter Ramsden and Bruce Jamieson.[56] The presence of pottery produced by St Lawrence Iroquoian women on Huron sites contrasts with a lack of pipes made by men from the same nation, and this suggests that the women were kept as captives while the men had been eliminated. This hypothesis is supported by the fact that human bones are frequently found in both St Lawrence Iroquoian and Huron villages. On the other hand, it is possible that the Iroquois had dispersed the St Lawrence Iroquoians and that the women potters were simply refugees who had married into Huron families.

Pendergast favours the first of these two hypotheses.[57] Like Ramsden, he finds that the absence of pipes indicates that St Lawrence Iroquoian men were eliminated and the women taken captive. Another sign of confrontation between the two groups is that more males than females are represented in the remains of cannibalized individuals on Huron sites. A climate of hostility developed after 1450 throughout the Iroquoian lands. The Iroquois began to consolidate their position in fortified villages separated by buffer zones, indicating that they were protecting themselves from enemies coming from beyond their territory.[58] Similarly, the Hurons-Petuns and St Lawrence Iroquoians also enclosed their villages with palisades.[59] It was in this widespread climate of conflict that the buffer zone between the St Lawrence Iroquoians and the Hurons-Petuns developed after 1450, reaching its maximum size after 1550, when the Hurons migrated northward to Georgian Bay.

Pendergast's thesis is especially interesting in that it argues that the Hurons' motivation for eliminating the St Lawrence Iroquoians cannot be attributed entirely to a desire to secure their role as intermediaries with the Europeans, since the conflict between the two Amerindian groups can be traced to a much earlier time than the protohistoric period.[60] Indeed, Pendergast believes that the whole question is best understood if it is considered in its broader context, taking into account the central role Iroquoian culture gave to war, which was seen as a necessary exercise to replace the community's dead.[61] In the end, the Hurons' appropriation of the role of middlemen with the Europeans, to the detriment of the St Lawrence Iroquoians, may be seen as one of the final expressions of an endemic atmosphere of hostility among the Iroquoians that began at the end of the prehistoric period.

The dramatic disappearance of the St Lawrence Iroquoians in the late 16th century was no doubt also the outcome of two other factors related to their encountering Europeans: the introduction of microbes to which Amerindians had not built up immunity, and the increased use of pelts in exchange, marking the beginning of an organized fur trade.[62] While it is impossible to produce direct evidence of the effects of epidemics in the 16th century, it may be presumed, on the basis of what is known about the catastrophic consequences they had on the Hurons in the second quarter of the 17th century, that they caused similar havoc among the St Lawrence Iroquoians, who had been in contact with Europeans since at least 1534. As for the influence of increased trade in furs, archaeological evidence offers plausible, if not indisputable, support for this factor:

> With historical and archival evidence indicating that it was not until the last quarter of the 16th century that substantial amounts of European goods were being injected into coastal Aboriginal societies and ultimately into inland exchange networks, such a sudden increase should be observable archaeologically. This phenomenon could presumably be recognized from a series of temporally sequential archaeological sites that span the 16th and 17th centuries.[63]

Indeed, Lennox and Fitzgerald have identified two successive archaeological assemblages on Iroquois, Neutral and Huron sites for the period they associated with the beginning of the fur trade (1580–1630).[64] The first, dating from 1580–1600, is characterized by black and white glass beads with a ceramic core, copper kettles with handles attached to an iron band encircling the body of the vessel, large iron axe-heads and long-bladed straight knives, as well as bracelets, rings and projectile points cut out of copper kettle fragments. The second assemblage, dating from 1600–30, is much more varied. It contains many types of glass bead, including tubular white and blue examples and several oval ones, similar to those unearthed on the Place Royale site in Québec City.[65] The axes and kettles of the earlier assemblage are still present, but they are of poorer quality: the axes are lighter and contain less iron, while the kettles, many of which are now made of brass, have handles attached to outer lugs fashioned near the rim. The later assemblage is also distinguished by a greater number of utilitarian items, such as copper-alloy ladles and a new type of knife made in one piece with a thick iron handle. For Fitzgerald, the significant changes reflected in the two assemblages are signs of a major event, which could be the Basques' departure, no doubt for new whaling grounds, and their replacement by the French.[66]

Having examined the trade route via the St Lawrence, let us now turn our attention to the other, more northerly route, which led from the Saguenay River to the Great Lakes region. This was described to Jacques Cartier by the Amerindians of Stadacona as early of 1535:

> And we were told by the chief Donnaconna, Taiguragni, and Domagaya and others, that the said river, called the river of Saguenay, extends to the said Saguenay, which is distant from the mouth of the river more than one moon to the west-north-west, and that after eight or nine days' journey, it is deep enough for boats only; but that the best and most direct route and the safest is by the great river to a point beyond Hochelaga, where a stream flows from the said Saguenay, and enters the river, as we ourselves saw, and that thence it is a journey of one moon. And they gave us to understand that in that country the people are clad in woollens as we are, that there are many towns and tribes, and friendly people, and that they have much gold and red copper. They also told us that the whole country from the said first river to Hochelaga and Saguenay is an island surrounded and bordered by streams and by the great river, and that above the said Saguenay the stream enters two or three very large and broad lakes, and that thereafter one comes upon a freshwater sea, of which there is no record of the end having been seen, as they have been told by those of the Saguenay, for they themselves, they said, had never been there.[67]

This description of the mysterious Saguenay and its gold has been viewed by historians as pure fabrication on the part of the Amerindians to lure the French into trading with them. Nonetheless, the report contains quite accurate topographical information, such as the location of rapids where Lake Saint-Jean empties into the Saguenay, the confluence of the Ottawa River with the St Lawrence near Hochelaga, and the existence of the Great Lakes. Gold is mentioned — although one could suspect that Cartier added this element to the report in order to justify his expedition to the king — as is copper, a metal the Amerindians knew well, since for centuries they had collected it in its native state around Lake Superior and traded it. Furthermore, the notion that an island was formed by the area bordered by the Saguenay to the east, the Ottawa to the west, the St Lawrence to the south, and the series of little rivers to the north between the Saguenay and the Great Lakes was not simply the product of a fevered imagination. One must put oneself in the skin of the French explorer, who knew very little about the way Amerindians travelled inland with their light birch-bark canoes, which could be portaged from one river system to another. For him, the fact that a traveller could go from the Saguenay River to a freshwater sea by boat implied a direct water route between the two places, which meant that the immense region to the north of the St Lawrence between the Ottawa and the Saguenay would have to be a sort of island surrounded by rivers. Whatever the case, the archaeology of this second route, leading north-westward to the continent's interior, remains relatively undeveloped. What is known so far comes from research carried out under the direction of Jean-François Moreau at the Université du Québec à Chicoutimi over the past 20 years or so.

According to written documents, it was not until 1647 that a European, the Jesuit Father Dequen, used this route to reach at least one of its principal stopover points, at Lake Saint-Jean.[68] Since neither Cartier nor even Champlain, both of whom knew of the route's existence, used it to go to meet the Amerindians living further inland, it seems possible that these groups had no direct contact with Europeans engaged in the fur trade in the 16th century and first half of the 17th. If this were the case, the period known as protohistory would have lasted a little over 100 years in this region. Consequently, during this time, Amerindians living in the hinterland could have obtained European goods from Aboriginal middlemen, who acquired them from the Europeans coming to trade at Tadoussac, at the mouth of the Saguenay. These middlemen would have transported the objects via the northern trade route that followed lakes, rivers and portage trails to Lake Huron and Huronia.

Although the archaeology of the northern route has not been fully developed, it nonetheless provides evidence that can be used to verify or modify the scenario sketched above. Of the many sites excavated in the Saguenay–Lac-Saint-Jean river system, the one that contains the best material for illuminating questions about the protohistoric period is the DhFk-7 site, a place used by Amerindians at the outlet of Lake Ashuapmushuan (or Chamouhouane), where it flows into the Ashuapmushuan (or Ashaupmouchouane) River. Discovered in 1985, the site was dug by Moreau and his team between 1987 and 1990.[69] They uncovered a dozen small hearths, no doubt the remains of temporary camps set up by nomadic Algonquian groups as they visited the site at different times.[70] The objects associated with these occupations fall into four general categories: lithic material, Amerindian pottery, copper-alloy items and glass beads. Eighty per cent of the 5,700 flakes and tools, 'of fairly recent manufacture', were made of locally available materials, that is, local quartzite and Mistassini quartzite; this suggests that the population that made them had been established in the region for a long time.[71] Six of the seven Amerindian pottery vessels unearthed are similar in shape and style to pottery produced by Hurons in the Georgian Bay area. Two of these Huron-style vessels are of a type found only on 17th-century sites. The pottery thus testifies to the existence of relations between Huronia and the DhFk-7 site.[72] The few copper articles, consisting mainly of scrap pieces (five), along with a stemmed projectile point and two artefacts of uncertain identification (needle and pendant?), had all been cut out of a European copper-alloy kettle. The fact that the DhFk-7 site's occupants used copper this way links them with Huronia, where, as explained above, such artefacts are found in assemblages from the period. However, the copper stemmed projectile point from the DhFk-7 site copies the shape of Algonquian points made of stone, while Hurons cut out their copper points in the shape of an isosceles triangle; this leads Moreau to believe that, like the lithic material, the copper objects found on the site were made by nomadic Amerindians living in the boreal forest.[73] The glass beads, numbering 91 in all, are comparable to those found on Huron sites dating from the first half of the 17th century, with the majority corresponding to beads typical of the period 1600–25.[74]

Moreau's research is particularly interesting in that it helps to fill in a gap in our knowledge of protohistory. The group of temporary camps occupied by nomadic Algonquians 250km from the mouth of the Saguenay at the beginning of the 17th century show influences coming from two different directions along the old copper trade route linking the Great Lakes and the Saguenay River. Arriving from the south-west, the influence of the Hurons can be seen in the Algonquians' pottery. In the opposite direction, arriving from the south-east, the influence of the Basques and French in the St Lawrence Valley is reflected in the presence of European goods in the form of glass beads and copper-alloy kettles. The Algonquians' strong cultural cohesion is evidenced by the archaeological assemblages on their sites; they vigorously maintained their traditional stone tool-making technology and integrated a new material in the form of copper alloy in producing stemmed points similar to their stone points. Despite this cohesion, the nomadic hunters had unknowingly already become part of an immense economic network that linked them with humans they had not yet met and with a continent they never dreamed existed.

CONCLUSION

From an archaeological perspective, relations between Europeans and the Amerindians of the North-East in the 16th century were marked by what I have termed a Basque 'ripple effect' and, to a certain degree, by trade with Breton and Norman voyagers, who obtained furs in exchange for a fairly limited quantity of goods that eventually reached Huronia and Iroquoia. Assemblages of European objects on Beothuk, Iroquoian, Onondaga, Huron and Neutral sites dating from before 1580 contain only a few iron and copper items and perhaps the odd glass bead. On sites dating from 1580 to 1600, assemblages of European objects become much richer and more diversified in Onondaga, Huron and Neutral country, suggesting that the fur trade had begun to intensify, as is corroborated by contemporary documents. This period was also marked by the disappearance of the St Lawrence Iroquoians, an event of major significance, since this people had previously occupied the entire region between the present-day Québec City area and the Upper St Lawrence. It appears that this destruction of an entire society was carried out by the Hurons, whose relations with the St Lawrence Iroquoians had been belligerent for some time; they seem to have been prompted to take such an extreme action by the hope that closer contact with Europeans would give them the advantages promised by control of the fur trade. It is also very likely that disease played a role in weakening the St Lawrence Iroquoians, who were in direct contact with new germs to which they had no immunity. However, this aspect of European contact, which was to have a disastrous effect in the second quarter of the 17th century, has left no archaeological or historical traces dating from the protohistoric period.[75]

Looking beyond the economic aspect of trade, it may be wondered what significance was attributed by the Amerindians of the North-East to the materials and objects introduced by the Europeans. Archaeologists agree that, during the protohistoric period, a large proportion of these materials and objects were human ornaments, which are often found in burials along with utilitarian items such as copper kettles and iron knives, which, with the ornaments, represented grave goods to accompany the deceased in the next world. These practices and the fact that the decorative objects were frequently made by Amerindians out of exogenous material — European copper and glass — has led archaeologists to posit that the objects had an ideological significance. It is proposed that Amerindians to some degree appropriated new materials and things coming from another world by letting them replace or simply join objects made of local materials like clay, stone, native copper and seashells. This interpretation is supported by the fact that the Amerindians decorated their bodies with such ornaments while they were alive and placed them in graves to accompany the dead. It may be imagined that during their lifetimes these ornaments had a variety of meanings for the Amerindians who wore them. They may have had a playful or aesthetic role related to appearance; or they may have been symbols of status, since the number of individuals who had them must have been quite limited; and they could have offered protection against the Other, disease and evils in general, given the virtues attributed to the new materials, particularly copper. Is it possible that some of these meanings continued to be attributed to the objects that accompanied Amerindians in the afterlife? If so, it was probably the objects' protective function that mattered most, for that is what would best serve the needs of the deceased in their new life.

It may be objected that this exercise in interpretation boils down to mere speculation. Researchers venture into vague and uncharted territory when they attempt to discover the deeper significance of objects found on archaeological sites. But risky as this attempt may be, the sites used by the Onondagas, Neutrals, Hurons and nomads of the boreal forest during the last phase of the protohistoric period show a significant increase in European materials related to the intensification of the fur trade; at the same time, they display no signs of any cultural disintegration. An exception to this observation is, of course, the dispersal of the St Lawrence Iroquoians through an act of aggression that was no doubt catalysed by the new advantages offered by trade with Europeans.

What explanation can be given for this relative stability in the face of the impact of the newly introduced European goods and materials in the 16th century? Few people have reflected on the question.[76] For the protohistoric period in the North-East, I believe the research by James W. Bradley on the Onondagas comes closest to satisfying the question. Asking 'What was the motivation for acquiring European goods?', Bradley replies: 'The answer, to put it most succinctly, is that the initial Iroquois response to Europeans and their materials was not an economic one, it was ideological. The reason one sought European goods was not for material gain, but to obtain their "power".'[77]

Bradley considers the Iroquois' quest for power through the acquisition of more European goods as analogous to a cargo cult,[78] at least in its earliest phase, when the Aboriginals saw a correspondence between the power they attributed to the strangers who had come from another world and the power of the goods they obtained from the newcomers in exchange for simple animal pelts. Although an analogous situation may have existed, the fact remains that it cannot be demonstrated by archaeological evidence. Furthermore, during the protohistoric period, the Onondagas continued to show such cultural stability that it is impossible to find signs of any major transformation provoked by the acquisition of European goods, or of the state of crisis which generally results in societies where the cargo cult phenomenon has been observed.

However, evidence that European goods were thought to offer protection and power may be found not just in an increase in the number of European objects, but also in other traces of material culture from the time of early contacts. For Bradley, one such trace is represented by the spiral ear pendants mentioned in a previous section of this paper; they are found throughout Iroquoia, on sites dating from the protohistoric period.[79] These pendants, probably made by Amerindian middlemen using copper or brass sheet metal obtained from the Basques and Normans, could well have been charms with great power to protect the wearer from the new diseases that appeared after the first contact with Europeans. Bradley draws a parallel between the power of these charms and the Algonquian myth of the great Underwater Panther, who guarded the native copper of the Great Lakes and whose tail was covered with copper scales. 'Those fortunate enough to find or possess a piece of copper from the Panther's tail had a charm of great healing power.'[80]

A clear reference to the power attributed by the Amerindians to Great Lakes native copper can be found fairly late in the 17th century, in the Jesuit Relations of 1666 and 1667:

> One often finds at the bottom of the water pieces of pure copper, often to twenty livres weight. I have several times seen such pieces in the savages' hands; and, since they are superstitious, they keep them as so many divinities, or as presents which the gods dwelling beneath the water have given them, and on which their welfare is to depend. For this reason they preserve these pieces of copper, wrapped up, among their most precious possessions. Some have kept them for more than 50 years; others have had them in their families from time immemorial, and cherish them as household gods.[81]

The notion that copper is an underwater gift of the gods seems to fit well with the myth of the great Underwater Panther reported by Bradley. If native copper was already revered, the availability of European materials would have acted as a potent catalyst in the quest for strength and power. This would explain the heightened aggressiveness shown to their neighbours by Iroquois and Hurons, since they lived far inland and had to use middlemen to obtain European goods.

Another important aspect on which the present study sheds light is the scope of existing trade networks: from one end to the other, the trade routes form an immense quadrilateral enclosing over 2,000,000km^2, or 3.7 times the area of France. If one considers that it was only in the second half of the 16th century — and even, it could be said, in the last quarter of that century — that considerable amounts of European material were transported throughout the vast North-East interior from the Atlantic coast, it must be concluded that this transfer of goods occurred at an astonishingly rapid pace. This speedy transfer is a strong argument in support of the hypothesis that, far from being a completely wild region practically untouched by human presence, north-eastern North America was in fact at this time a place that was inhabited and travelled through by people whose cultures may have sometimes been very different but who were constantly interacting with one another and faced novelty with openness.

At the end of the protohistoric period, it seems that Amerindian societies, despite the relative stability of their cultural systems when in direct or indirect contact with the Basque, Breton and Norman newcomers, had become increasingly involved in the world economy through the capitalist expansion of the Atlantic zone and through the fur trade. As a result, they were probably already affected by changes that presaged the enormous upheavals they would undergo in the 17th century, when permanent settlements were established in the North-East by the French, Dutch and English.

ACKNOWLEDGEMENTS

I wish to thank Gilles Gallichan for editing the French version of this paper (published in *Les Cahiers des Dix*, 2005, Québec: Les Éditions La Liberté), Denys Delâge for fruitful discussions, Clara Marceau for keyboarding, and Greg Waselkov and Marc Lavoie for providing me with articles and reports that were difficult to obtain through libraries. Financial assistance for the translation of this paper came from the Centre interuniversitaire sur les lettres, les arts et les traditions (CÉLAT).

NOTES

[1] Trudel 1963, 20.

[2] Hoffman 1961, 213.

[3] Barkham 1982, 42–63; Turgeon 1986, 523–49; Bélanger 1971; Pope 2003, 122–33.

[4] Turgeon 1998, 590–1.
[5] Turgeon 1986, 533–4.
[6] Turgeon 1986, 537 [translation]; Pope 2004, 13–19; Allaire 2004, 50–1. Allaire's research led him to determine that North American furs did not arrive on the European market until the second half of the 16th century and that the Peace of Cateau-Cambrésis, in 1559, between France and Spain was what made it possible for the French to make regular trips to North America to obtain furs.
[7] Tuck & Grenier 1981, 180–8; Tuck 1985a, 224–47; Tuck 1985b, 50–7; Grenier 1985, 58–68.
[8] Chapdelaine & Kennedy 1990, 41–3; Loewen 1999; Grenier *et al.* 2007.
[9] Pope 2003; 2008.
[10] Pope 2004, 15–19.
[11] Pope 2004, 14.
[12] Pastore 1995, 6.
[13] Turgeon 1998, 585–610; Turgeon 2004, 98–112.
[14] Thevet 1986, 250–1.
[15] Trudel 1963.
[16] Trudel 1963, 61; D'Abate 1994, 61–88; Morison 1971, 488–91.
[17] Turgeon 1998, 596–7; Turgeon 2004, 98–112.
[18] Turgeon 1990; Fitzgerald *et al.* 1993, 48.
[19] Whitehead 1993, 23–70; Fitzgerald *et al.* 1993, 48; Harper 1957, 11–36.
[20] Martijn 1986.
[21] Martijn 2003, 44–102.
[22] Bourque & Whitehead 1994, 136–40.
[23] Whitehead 1986, 229.
[24] Bourque & Whitehead 1994, 140–5.
[25] Bakker 1990, 90.
[26] Bourque & Whitehead 1994, 136.
[27] Bradley 1987.
[28] Bradley & Childs 1991, 7–17; Turgeon 1990, 86. With respect to the Basques' supplying red copper, see Turgeon (1990, 86). It must be taken into consideration that this account of the situation, although offering a good avenue of investigation, remains conjectural and deserves to be studied in more detail.
[29] Bradley 1987, 89.
[30] Hunt 1967, 131–44.
[31] Bradley 1987, 66–7.
[32] Bradley 1987, 64–9.
[33] Bradley 1987, 54–64.
[34] Bradley 1987, 83–8.
[35] Bradley 1987, 12.
[36] Bradley 1987, 53.
[37] Bradley 1987, 87.
[38] Moreau & Langevin 1992, 37. [Translation.]
[39] Moreau & Langevin 1992, 39.
[40] Moreau & Langevin 1992, 44.
[41] Moreau 1992, 105–10.
[42] Moreau 1992, 106.
[43] Trigger 1986, 148; Moreau 1992, 106.
[44] Trigger 1986, 145.
[45] Pintal 1998, 241.
[46] Pintal 1998, 234–40.
[47] Auger *et al.* 1992, 65, 69.
[48] Moussette 1994, 12–15; Moussette 1995, 10–11.
[49] Clermont *et al.* 1992, 336, 422.
[50] Pendergast & Trigger 1972; Jamieson 1990, 401.
[51] Ramsden 1990, 373.
[52] Lennox & Fitzgerald 1990, 429.
[53] Trigger 1986, 145–8.
[54] Pendergast 1993, 9–47.
[55] Pendergast 1993, 15.
[56] Ramsden 1988, 47–8; Jamieson 1990, 402–3.
[57] Pendergast 1993, 10.
[58] Pendergast 1993, 15.
[59] Pendergast 1993, 15–21. It is also possible, as James W. Bradley notes, that the creation of this buffer zone resulted in the influx of St Lawrence Iroquoians among the Onondagas.
[60] Pendergast 1993, 10–11.
[61] Pendergast 1993, 22.
[62] Lennox & Fitzgerald 1990, 437.
[63] Fitzgerald 1995, 32.
[64] Lennox & Fitzgerald 1990, 431.
[65] Clermont *et al.* 1992, 336, 422.
[66] Fitzgerald 1995, 37.
[67] Biggar 1914, 145. [Translation.]
[68] Moreau 1992, 107.
[69] Moreau 1992, 110–12.
[70] Moreau 1992, 115.
[71] Moreau 1992, 117.
[72] Moreau 1992, 118.
[73] Moreau 1992, 119, 122.
[74] Moreau 1992, 122–3.
[75] Moussette 2008.
[76] Such researchers include, among others, James W. Bradley, William R. Fitzgerald and Jean-François Moreau, whose work has been of great use in writing this paper.
[77] Bradley 1987, 111.
[78] According to Honigmann (1959, 264–6), the cargo cult developed in Melanesia in recent times, when the Aboriginals of this land formed a belief that a cargo of European goods, on which they had become very dependent, would be delivered to them by ship or airplane, in the shape of presents from their ancestors or other spirits. The cargo cult is described as a nativist movement that arises in societies gripped by crisis as they attempt to break with ancient ways and replace them with new forms.
[79] Bradley & Childs 1991.
[80] Bradley & Childs 1991, 16.
[81] Thwaites 1959, 265–7. In a previous paper, I proposed that the value attributed to copper by the Amerindians could have been an important factor in their accepting the religious medals representing God and the saints given to them by missionaries in the 17th century (Moussette 2001, 327). In the context of

the present paper, it might be suggested that the connection made between the Underwater Panther's copper and European copper in the 16th century represented a first step towards this acceptance or a form of syncretism.

BIBLIOGRAPHY

PUBLISHED SOURCES

Allaire, B. 2004, 'Le commerce européen de la fourrure avant Champlain', in Litalien & Vaugeois 2004, 50–1.

Baker, E.A. *et al.* (eds) 1994, *American Beginnings: Exploration, Culture and Cartography in the Land of Norumbega*, Lincoln: University of Nebraska.

Bakker, P. 1990, 'A Basque etymology for the word "Iroquois"', *Man in the Northeast* **40**, 89–93.

Barkham, S.H. 1982, 'Documentary evidence for 16th-century whaling ships in the Strait of Belle Isle', in Story 1982, 42–63.

Bélanger, R. 1971, *Les Basques dans l'estuaire du Saint-Laurent*, Montréal: Université du Québec.

Biggar, H.P. 1914, *The History of New France* **2**, Toronto: Champlain Soc.

Bourque, B.J. & Whitehead, R.H. 1994, 'Trade and alliances in the contact period', in Baker *et al.* 1994, 136–40.

Bradley, J.W. 1987, *Evolution of the Onondaga Iroquois: Accommodating Change, 1500–1655*, Syracuse: University Press.

Bradley, J.W. & Childs, T.S. 1991, 'Basque earrings and panther's tails: the forms of cross-cultural contact in sixteenth-century Iroquoia', in Ehrenreich 1991, 7–17.

Chapdelaine, C. & Kennedy, G.G. 1990, 'The origin of the Iroquoian rim sherd from Red Bay', *Man in the Northeast* **40**, 41–3.

Clermont, N., Chapdelaine, C. & Guimont, C. 1992, *L'Occupation historique et préhistorique de Place-Royale*, Collection Patrimoines, Dossiers **76**.

D'Abate, R. 1994, 'On the meaning of a name: "Norumbega" and the representation of North America', in Baker *et al.* 1994, 61–88.

De Waele, M. & Pâquet, M. (eds) 2008, *Québec, Champlain, le monde*, Québec: Université Laval.

Ehrenreich, R. (ed.) 1991, *Metals in Society: Theory beyond Analysis*, Masca Res. Pap. Sci. Archaeol. **8**:2.

Ellis, C.J. & Ferris, N. (eds) 1990, *The Archaeology of Southern Ontario to A.D. 1650*, London: Ontario Archaeol. Soc.

Fitzgerald, W.R. 1995, 'A late sixteenth-century European trade assemblage from north-eastern North America', in Hook & Gaimster 1995, 29–44.

Fitzgerald, W.R., Turgeon, L. & Whitehead, R.H. 1993, 'Late sixteenth-century Basque banded copper kettle', *Hist. Archaeol.* **27**:1, 44–57.

Fortin, M. (ed.) 1992, *L'Archéologie et la rencontre de deux mondes*, Québec: Musée de la Civilisation.

Grenier, R. 1985, 'Excavating a 400-year-old Basque galleon', *Nat. Geog.* **168**:1, 158–68.

Grenier, R., Bernier, M.-A. & Stevens, W. (eds) 2007, *The Underwater Archaeology of Red Bay: Basque Shipbuilding and Whaling in the 16th Century*, Ottawa: Parks Canada.

Harper, J.R. 1957, 'Two seventeenth-century Micmac copper kettle burials', *Anthropologica* **4**, 11–36.

Hoffman, B.G. 1961, *Cabot to Cartier: Sources for a Historical Ethnography of Northeastern North America, 1497–1550*, Toronto: University Press.

Honigmann, J.J. 1959, *The World of Man*, New York: Harper.

Hook, D.R. & Gaimster, D.R.M. (eds) 1995, *The Scientific Study of Artifacts from Post-Medieval America*, Brit. Mus. Occ. Pap. **109**.

Hunt, G.T. 1967, *The Wars of the Iroquois: a Study of Intertribal Trade Relations*, Madison: University of Wisconsin.

Jamieson, J.B. 1990, 'The archaeology of the St Lawrence Iroquoians', in Ellis & Ferris 1990, 385–404.

Lennox, P.A. & Fitzgerald, W.R. 1990, 'The culture, history and archaeology of the Neutral Iroquoians', in Ellis & Ferris 1990, 405–56.

Litalien, R. & Vaugeois, D. (eds) 2004, *Champlain: la naissance de l'Amérique française*, Québec: Septentrion.

Martijn, C.A. (ed.) 1986, *Les Micmacs et la mer*, Montréal: Recherches amérindiennes au Québec.

Martijn, C.A. 2003, 'Early Mi'kmaq presence in Southern Newfoundland: an historical perspective, *c.* 1500–1763', *Newfoundland Stud.* **19**:1, 44–102.

Moreau, J.-F. 1992, 'Objets amérindiens et européens au Saguenay–Lac-Saint-Jean: la portée des transferts culturels en forêt boréale', in Fortin 1992, 105–10.

Moreau, J.-F. & Langevin, E. 1992, 'Premières manifestations européennes en pays amérindien: le cas de la frange méridionale du Subarctique oriental', *Recherches amérindiennes au Québec* **22**:4, 37–48.

Morison, S.E. 1971, *The European Discovery of North America: the Northern Voyages, A.D. 1500–1600*, New York: Oxford University.

Moussette, M. 2001, 'Les médailles religieuses: une forme de l'imagerie baroque en Nouvelle-France', *Les Cahiers des Dix* **55**, 294–329.

Moussette, M. 2008, 'L'Amérique du Nord avant Champlain', in De Waele & Pâquet 2008, 25–44.

Pendergast, J.F. 1993, 'More on when and why the St Lawrence Iroquoians disappeared', in Pendergast & Chapdelaine 1993, 9–47.

Pendergast, J.F. & Chapdelaine, C. (eds) 1993, *Essays in Northeastern Archaeology* **8**, Dundas: Copetown.

Pendergast, J.F. & Trigger, B.C. (eds) 1972, *Cartier's Hochelaga and the Dawson Site*, Montréal: McGill-Queen's University.

Pintal, J.-Y. 1998, *Aux Frontières de la mer: la préhistoire de Blanc-Sablon*, Québec: Collection Patrimoines, Dossiers **68**.

Pope, P. 2003, 'The European occupation of southeast Newfoundland: archaeological perspectives on competition for fishing rooms, 1530–1680', in Roy *et al.* 2003, 122–33.

Pope, P. 2004, *Fish into Wine: the Newfoundland Plantation in the Seventeenth Century*, Chapel Hill: University of North Carolina.

Pope, P. 2008, 'Post-medieval Breton earthenwares in Newfoundland', *Post-Medieval Archaeol.* **42**:2, 48–74.

Ramsden, P.G. 1988, 'A society transformed', *Rotunda* **20**:4, 45–8.

Ramsden, P.G. 1990, 'The Hurons: archaeology and culture history', in Ellis & Ferris 1990, 361–84.

Roy, C. *et al.* (eds) 2003, *Mer et monde: questions d'archéologie maritime*, Archéologiques, hors série **1**.

Schlesinger, R. & Schlesinger, A.P. (eds) 1986, *André Thevet's North America: a Sixteenth-Century View*, Montréal: McGill-Queen's University.

Sproul Thomson, J.S. & Thomson, C. (eds) 1985, *Archaeology in Newfoundland and Labrador, 1984*, St John's: Newfoundland Museum.

Story, M. (ed.) 1982, *Early European Settlement and Exploitation in Atlantic Canada*, St John's: Memorial University of Newfoundland.

Thevet, A. 1986, 'Grand insulaire', in Schlesinger & Schlesinger 1986, 250–1.

Thwaites, R.G. (ed.) 1959, *The Jesuit Relations and Allied Documents* **50**, New York: Pageant Book.

Trigger, B.G. 1986, *Natives and Newcomers*, Montréal: McGill-Queen's University.

Trudel, M. 1963, *Histoire de la Nouvelle-France: les vaines tentatives, 1524–1603*, Montréal: Fides.

Tuck, J.A. 1985a, '1984 excavations at Red Bay Labrador', in Sproul Thomson & Thomson 1985, 224–47.

Tuck, J.A. 1985b, 'Unearthing Red Bay's whaling history', *National Geog.* **168**:1, 50–7.

Tuck, J.A. & Grenier, R. 1981, 'A 16th-century Basque whaling station in Labrador', *Sci. Amer.* **245**:5, 180–8.

Turgeon, L. 1986, 'Pour redécouvrir notre 16e siècle: les pêches à Terre-Neuve d'après les archives notariales de Terre-Neuve', *Revue d'histoire de l'Amérique française* **39**:4, 523–49.

Turgeon, L. 1990, 'Basque-Amerindian trade in the Saint Lawrence during the sixteenth century: new documents, new perspectives', *Man in the Northeast* **40**, 81–7.

Turgeon, L. 1998, 'French fishers, fur traders, and Amerindians during the sixteenth century: history and archaeology', *William Mary Quart.* **54**:4, 585–610.

Turgeon, L. 2004, 'Les Français en Nouvelle-Angleterre avant Champlain', in Litalien & Vaugeois 2004, 98–112.

Whitehead, R.H. 1986, 'Navigation des Micmacs le long de la côte de l'Atlantique', in Martijn 1986, 225–32.

Whitehead, R.H. 1993, *Nova Scotia: the Protohistoric Period, 1500–1630*, Curatorial Rep. **75**, Halifax: Nova Scotia Museum.

UNPUBLISHED SOURCES

Auger, R., Fitzgerald, W. & Turgeon, L. 1992, 'Île aux Basques 1991: fouilles archéologiques et reconnaissances', Québec: CÉLAT, Université Laval.

Loewen, B. 1999, 'Les Barriques de Red Bay et l'espace atlantique septentrional vers 1565', Université Laval PhD thesis.

Moussette, M. 1994, 'Île aux Oies: intervention archéologique de 1993', Québec: CÉLAT, Université Laval.

Moussette, M. 1995, 'Île aux Oies: intervention archéologique de 1994', Québec: CÉLAT, Université Laval.

Pastore, R.T. 1995, 'Boyd's Cove', Ottawa: Parks Canada Historic Sites and Monuments Board of Canada Agenda Papers.

ABBREVIATIONS

AAQ	Association des archéologues du Québec
CÉLAT	Centre interuniversitaire de recherche sur les lettres, les arts et les traditions

SUMMARY IN FRENCH, GERMAN, ITALIAN AND SPANISH

RÉSUMÉ

Un univers sous tension : les nations amérindiennes du Nord-Est de l'Amérique du nord au XVIe siècle

Les recherches archivistiques et archéologiques ont amélioré notre compréhension de la présence européenne au XVIe siècle dans le nord-est de l'Amérique du Nord. Les liens entre les assemblages des objets européens découverts sur des sites amérindiens à l'intérieur du continent peuvent désormais être établis, ce qui fournit un aperçu de la manière dont l'entrée des nouveaux arrivants et la rencontre avec les populations aborigènes ont affecté les populations locales. Malgré leurs limites, les vestiges matériels fournissent un point de vue engendré par les Amérindiens qui, lorsque pris en considération avec les indices archivistiques, peuvent être rattachés aux récits européens. Cet article cherche à mesurer l'intensité et la portée des contacts anciens et à apprécier les principaux événements les entourant.

ZUSAMMENFASSUNG

Die Umweltbelastung: amero-indianische Nationen im Nordosten Nordamerikas im 16. Jh.

Archivare und archäologische Untersuchungen haben das Verständnis für die europäische Präsenz in Nordostamerika vertieft. Man kann jetzt Verbindungen herstellen zwischen europäischen Gegenständen, die auf amero-indianischem Gelände im Inneren des Kontinents gefunden wurden, und der Wirkung, die die Ankunft der Neuankömmlinge und die Begegnung mit den Ureinwohnern gehabt hat. Trotz ihrer Begrenztheit können die materiellen Überreste einen Beitrag zum Verständnis der amero-indianischen Entwicklung leisten, insbesondere, wenn man sie in Verbindung mit archivierten Hinweisen und überlieferten europäischen Erzählungen betrachtet. Dieser Bericht ist ein Versuch, die Intensität und den Umfang der frühen Kontakte in Zusammenhang mit den Hauptereignissen zu setzen.

RIASSUNTO

Un universo sotto pressione: le nazioni amerindiane nell'America del nord-est durante il XVI secolo

La ricerca archivistica e archeologica hanno migliorato la conoscenza della presenza europea nel nord-est del nord America durante il XVI secolo. È adesso possibile stabilire delle relazioni fra i contesti che hanno restituito oggetti europei in siti amerindiani nell'interno del continente, fornendo altresì un quadro su come il sopraggiungere dei nuovi arrivati e l'incontro con le popolazioni indigene abbia influito sulla popolazione locale. Nonostante le loro limitazioni, i resti materiali forniscono un punto di vista amerindiano che, quando considerato unitamente ai documenti d'archivio, può essere ricollegato ai racconti europei. Quest'articolo cerca di valutare l'intensità e lo scopo dei primi contatti, delineando gli avvenimenti principali che fecero da sfondo.

RESUMEN

Un universo bajo tensión: las naciones amerindias en el noreste de Norte América en el siglo XVI

La investigación de archivos y arqueológica ha mejorado considerablemente nuestro conocimiento de la presencia europea en el siglo XVI en el noreste de Norte América. Ahora es posible interrelacionar grupos de objetos europeos encontrados en yacimientos amerindios en el interior del continente para informarnos de cómo la llegada de los europeos y su encuentro con los aborígenes afectó a las poblaciones locales. A pesar de sus limitaciones, los restos materiales proporcionan el punto de vista amerindio que, cuando considerado junto al material de los archivos, se puede relacionar con las narrativas europeas. Este artículo intenta medir la intensidad y extensión de los primeros contactos a la vez que establece los principales acontecimientos que los rodearon.

CÉLAT, Faculté des lettres, Université Laval, Québec, Canada G1V 0A6
[Marcel.Moussette@celat.ulaval.ca]

Post-Medieval Archaeology **43/1** (2009), 48–70

Charlesbourg-Royal and France-Roy (1541–43): France's first colonization attempt in the Americas

By RICHARD FISET *and* GILLES SAMSON

SUMMARY: The site of the first French attempt to establish a colony in North America, by Jacques Cartier and Sieur de Roberval in 1541–43, was discovered on the Cap Rouge headland of Québec in 2005. A major multidisciplinary research programme has followed. Buildings on the cliff edge and possible traces of defences were identified as parts of the Upper Fort described by Roberval. Some construction techniques are paralleled in northern France. Finds and botanical evidence suggest that the area was used by people of high status and indicate contact with the St Lawrence Iroquoians. The site was destroyed by fire.

INTRODUCTION

The discovery in 2005 of part of the site where Jacques Cartier and Sieur de Roberval unsuccessfully attempted to found a colony in 1541–43 has rekindled interest in Canada in this aborted colonization effort. The settlement, now in Québec City's Cap Rouge district, was first called Charlesbourg-Royal by Cartier (1541–June 1542) and then France-Roy by Sieur de Roberval (July 1542–43). The portion discovered corresponds to what Roberval described as the Upper Fort; the part of the settlement known as Lower Fort has not yet been found.

A number of interpretations and hypotheses can now be put forward regarding the 16th-century settlement; they relate to aspects of its architecture and spatial organization, its defences including the presence of towers, and its occupation by an elite group who evidently had contacts with Amerindians. The interpretation stems from a comparative analysis of archaeological, historical and architectural data from France and the New World.

HISTORICAL BACKGROUND

France's exploration and settlement of the Gulf of St Lawrence in the 16th century were hesitant and inconsistent. French colonial endeavours in Canada were hampered by her engagement in the Italian Wars (1494–1559), in which repeated efforts to make territorial gains in Italy monopolized military resources.

When François I visited Mont Saint Michel in 1532, Abbot Jean Le Veneur, Grand Almoner of France, introduced the king to Jacques Cartier, who offered his services to discover a north-west passage to Asia. The king was interested in Cartier's proposal, but in order to circumvent restrictions imposed by previous agreements, he first secured the support of Pope Clement VII.

A compromise was worked out, paving the way for Cartier's first voyage to the New World. On 18 March 1534 he was given 6,000 *livres tournois* and a mandate to explore the kingdom of Newfoundland 'to discover certain islands and countries where it is said that a great abundance of gold and other precious things is to be found'.[1] Soon after his return to France in September, he

 DOI: 10.1179/007942309X12457508843928

was entrusted with leading a second expedition to the New World, despite the fact that his country had been preparing for war since the summer. This time he was granted 3,000 *livres tournois*[2] for a voyage that was to last fifteen months, including a stay on the Sainte-Croix River (later known as the Saint-Charles), which flows through present-day Québec City, and an expedition up the St Lawrence to Hochelaga, on what is now the Island of Montréal, to determine whether the river was navigable above the Lachine Rapids.[3]

While Cartier overwintered in Canada a large army was raised in Lyon in France; in June 1536 war broke out again with Spain. Thus, on Cartier's return to France, he had to delay his explorations in the New World until the Peace of Aigues Mortes was concluded in July 1538. In September of that year Cartier and François I settled the accounts for the previous voyages and no doubt reached agreement on another expedition, for it was at this time that Cartier drew up his 'Mémoire de 1538', which details the men and supplies required to found a colony in Canada.[4]

Protests by the French over the allocation of territory in the New World led to diplomatic negotiations with Spain and Portugal. Concern among the Spanish was such that they took to spying on their rivals; several reports show that they viewed Canada as the gateway to the 'New Indies', and therefore as Spanish territory.[5] An armada under the command of the Marques del Valle or of Don Alonso de Lugo, Adelantado of the Canary Islands, was instructed to intercept and sink Cartier's ships.[6] Fortunately, the Spanish did not find the vessels and the expedition launched by Cartier in May 1541 was able to proceed. Roberval left for Canada a year later, entrusted, even though he was a Protestant, with full authority over a colony which was largely Catholic.

When Roberval reached Newfoundland he met Cartier, who was on his way back to Saint-Malo. Roberval continued on to the Cap Rouge fort, which he renamed France-Roy, and made preparations to reoccupy the site. Meanwhile, France and Spain declared war again in July 1542. In September, once Roberval was settled at Cap Rouge, he sent two ships back to France bearing two men instructed to 'come backe againe unto him the yeere next ensuing, furnished with victuals and other things, as it should please the King: and also to bring newes out of France how the King accepted certaine Diamants which were sent him'.[7] François I seems to have followed up these requests for, in January 1543, he commissioned Paul d'Aussillon to set sail for Canada with two ships laden with provisions for Roberval.[8]

During the winter of 1543, Charles V of Spain forged an alliance with Henry VIII of England. An ultimatum was delivered to François I, who responded by officially reopening hostilities in June.[9] Later supply ships leaving France for Canada may have been ordered to repatriate Roberval and his soldiers.[10] The conflict did not end until September 1544.

Meanwhile, Roberval continued to fulfil his responsibilities in Canada despite a difficult winter. In spring he followed in Cartier's footsteps and travelled to Hochelaga in the hope of discovering a navigable route to Asia. In a message sent to Cap Rouge on 19 June 1543, he instructed the 30 settlers to stay until 22 July, and if he was not back by then, to return to France.[11] No further details can be gleaned from documents about the end of the Cap Rouge colony.

In 1608 Champlain came to the place where Québec City stands today and built his first Habitation, thereby beginning the region's permanent occupation. This settlement, which was situated in Place Royale and on the Québec promontory, soon expanded westward. By 1637, pioneer families were already occupying the banks of the St Lawrence River in the area of modern-day Cap Rouge, which was then part of the Gaudarville seigneury, a strip of land measuring 44 arpents (2.5km) along the river and 12 leagues (60km) deep.

Villeneuve's map of 1685[12] shows that, unlike the surrounding area, the Cap Rouge headland was wooded in the late 17th century. This suggests that it had not been cleared, farmed or inhabited during the early occupation of the Gaudarville seigneury (1637–*c.* 1685). Murray's map of 1760–62[13] and a drawing of 1759 by a soldier in Wolfe's army[14] show that it was still tree-covered in the 18th century and was bordered by steep slopes.

In 1823 the timber merchants William and Henry Atkinson acquired a roughly 40 acre (16ha) property from the last seigneur of the Gaudarville seigneury, Michel Louis Juchereau Duchesnay. The land, including the Cartier-Roberval site, would be used for building the 'Carouge' or 'Redclyffe' villa,[15] whose construction marked the first known occupation of the site since 1541–43. In 1846, William Atkinson sold the property; it continued to be called 'Cap Rouge Hill'.[16]

In the second half of the 19th century the lot changed hands on several occasions, the last involving its sale to the Transcontinental Railway. The transaction was not finalized until 1911, although a railway bridge had been built in 1906–08; its eastern side overlies part of the Cartier-Roberval site. Although the railway inevitably impacted on the site, it also prevented the neighbourhood from being used for residential or other purposes and thus helped to protect the remains of the Upper Fort. The Cartier-Roberval Park lies to the north of the railway.

ARCHAEOLOGICAL RESEARCH

DESCRIPTION OF THE SITE

The Cartier-Roberval site (CeEu-4) is on the Cap Rouge headland, which is part of the Québec promontory, at the confluence of the Cap Rouge and St Lawrence rivers. Its altitude on the cliff edge varies from about 35m above sea level on the western side to 45m at its highest point to the south (Fig. 1).

The area set aside for archaeological investigation covers 22,830m^2. It includes the estimated area of the Upper Fort and land outside the enceinte that could have been used for activities such as farming. For the purposes of the archaeological fieldwork, the site was divided into nine zones named A to J (Fig. 1). Excavations have concentrated on zones A, B and C — a roughly 2,000m^2 sector south of the bridge that would have been occupied by at least a portion of the 16th-century colony. The site slopes upward from west to east, with a gradient of 13% between zones A and C and 6% between zones C and E.

At least four overlying fill deposits have been identified. The largest was laid down in the 20th century to support the railway and one of its bridge abutments (Fig. 2); the second can be associated with excavations to erect the bridge trestles. The third may result from digging a recent drainage ditch; the fourth can be linked to 19th- and 20th-century activities to level the ground along the cliff on the site's west side.

The railway bridge is a massive 52m-high steel structure, towering over the site. Two of its 30 trestles stand in the northern part of zones B and D. The deep (3–4m thick) fill in this sector has prevented exploration of parts of the colonial settlement. When a pathway was laid out beneath the bridge, foundations of the 19th-century villa were found below the fill; it is possible, therefore, that 16th-century remains also survive nearby.

A few 19th-century pictorial sources shed light on the site's former appearance. A painting by J.P. Cockburn of 1831 shows the Atkinson property with a tree- and shrub-lined driveway leading up from the Cap Rouge River to the villa, an 'L'-shaped building whose Greek pediment was supported on four columns, with a low building to its west which may have been a stable. The artist seems to have been looking from the foot of the cliff near the river.

In 1834 Alfred Hawkins published an account of two discoveries made on the villa property. First, workers levelling ground in front of the house, on the side towards the point of the headland, uncovered a drystone feature with metal balls of various diameters lying among its stones. This was identified as the foundation of a fortification or building; the balls were said to be a type of shot used in the ship-mounted artillery of Cartier's era. Second, features interpreted as old furrows were brought to light when land was cleared for a bowling green behind the villa garden. These discoveries provide useful clues for estimating the size of the 16th-century colonial establishment.

Many remains of the Upper Fort seem to have been left undisturbed. Those uncovered so far lie mainly on the southern part of the headland, which is now owned by the Commission de la capitale nationale du Québec (CCNQ). Other parts are believed to survive in Cartier-Roberval Park, which belongs to the City of Québec, and on the land owned by Canadian National Railway.

OBJECTIVES

The main aim of the first phase of the multidisciplinary research undertaken in 2006–08 was to determine and record the limits of the 16th-century French occupation and its structural features and artefacts.[17] At the core of the settlement effort was made to locate buildings and establish their dimensions and internal layout; outside this zone the goal was to establish the approximate location of areas used for subsistence and other activities. The programme also aimed to find components of the defences, such as a palisade or ditch, presumed to be necessary for a colonial establishment.

More specifically, the project sought to understand the settlement's spatial organization and way of life, and to assess the extent to which it reflected the architectural and military traditions of 16th-century France, as well as the presence of a governing elite. Lastly, it aimed to examine whether the establishment revealed by archaeological work matched Roberval's description of the fort and was in keeping with his status of viceroy of the new territory.

METHODOLOGY

Test pits were first dug over an area of about 22,000m^2 to determine the extent of the Upper Fort. They measured 0.50 × 0.50m or 1 × 1m, and were placed at regular intervals of 5m or 10m. When positive evidence was found, excavation continued along the same axes until the limits of the occupied area were reached; digging stopped within each pit when promising levels were found.

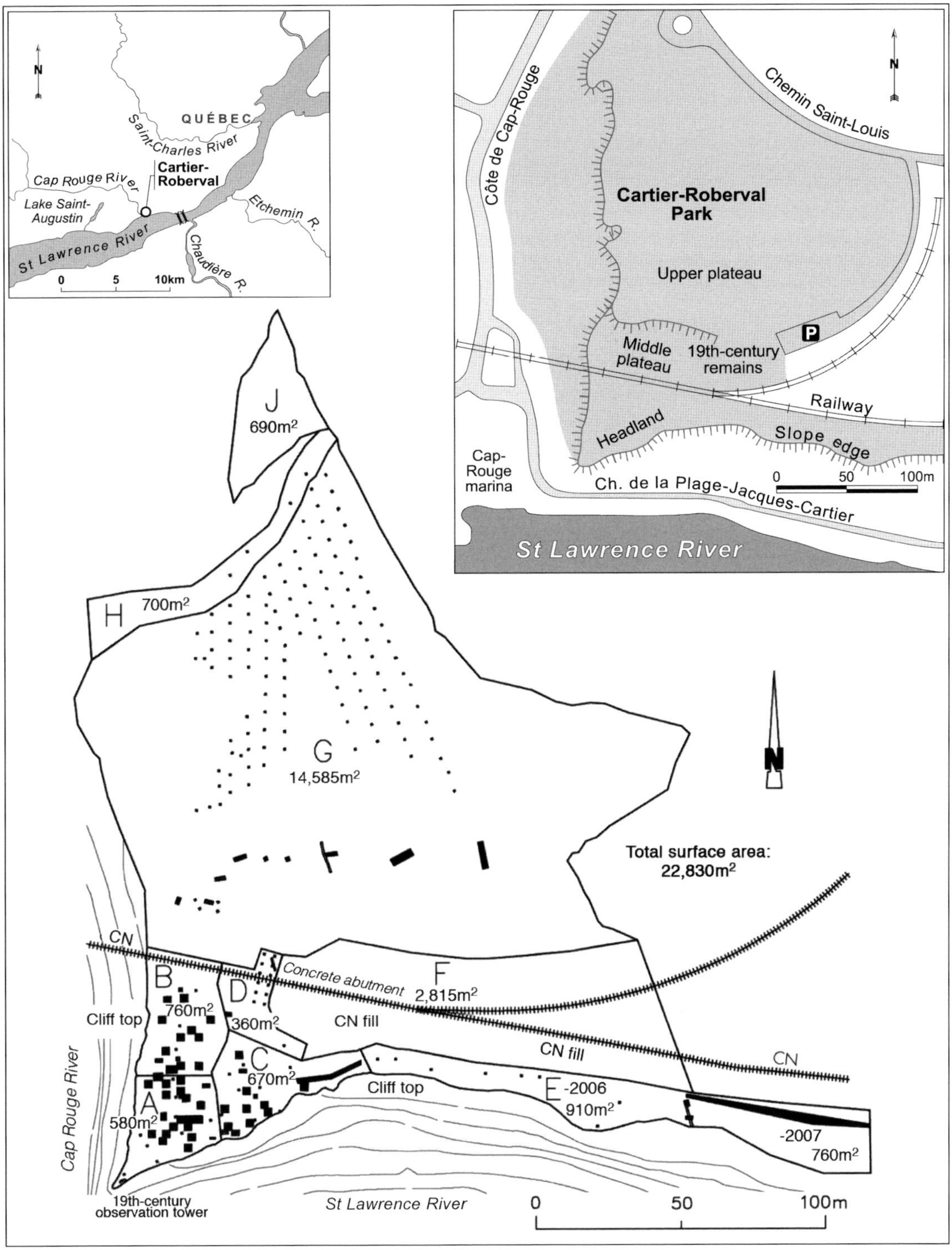

FIG. 1

Cartier-Roberval site, Cap Rouge (CeEu-4): surface area of excavation zones (A. Forget, CCNQ).

FIG. 2
Cartier-Roberval site (CeEu-4): 20th-century fill deposited to support the railway (photograph, R. Fiset).

In the main part of the site, detailed excavations were generally carried out within 2 × 2m areas or 'units'. At first they were positioned to sample as large an area as possible, taking into account any surface features with archaeological potential. The location and size of subsequent excavation units were based on the discoveries made in the initial ones.

Soil processing was an important part of the fieldwork. After a series of trials it was decided that, in order to recover small finds, soil from chosen layers would be sieved. Charcoal for archaeobotanical study was collected in flotation tanks designed specifically for the project.[18]

COMPLEMENTARY ANALYSES

A number of complementary analyses are being carried out by specialists in dendroecology, botany, soil morphology, pedology, palynology, charcoal analysis, palaeotopography and geoarchaeology. They have shed new light on the site's physical environment, palaeoenvironmental history and habitability, and on the varied geological resources (sandstone, clay, mineral deposits, etc.) of the vicinity.[19]

Study of the human environment has focused on the material culture (artefacts, ecofacts and architecture) associated with the French colonists and their Amerindian hosts. Conventional observation has been accompanied by comparison with collections from Europe. Some more specialized techniques have also been employed, including C14 dating of charcoal, neutron activation of glass and microscopic analysis of soil.

In archival research, the corpus compiled by Henry Percival Biggar in 1930 has provided the bulk of the material consulted for the programme. In 2007 project historian Bernard Allaire started investigating the archives of coastal cities in France that played a role in the expeditions of Cartier and Roberval, namely Rouen, Honfleur, Le Havre, Saint-Malo, La Rochelle and Bordeaux.[20] Research is also underway in the Château Roberval archives and in Lyon and Paris. This work may lead to discoveries like the one made in the late 19th century by Émile Morel,[21] who found a receipt dated 18 July 1545 in the archives at Roberval's chateau. It recorded that Roberval had purchased a wheel-lock pistol, 500 pike irons and seven syringes (four brass and three pewter), which were taken to Cap Rouge or were intended for a forthcoming expedition.

RESULTS

The site's soil is of lacustrine origin and began to form more than 8,000 years ago. When the first Europeans set foot on the headland it was thus almost in a virgin state and was covered with maple forest established some 5,000 years earlier. Cartier described the main species growing in the forest in his travel log.[22]

Generally speaking, soil profiles at the western limit of the site comprise six layers, four of which are of human origin. At the surface is a thin layer of compacted recent humus less than 0.01m thick. Beneath this are mineral horizons containing less than 17% organic carbon. The first, encountered almost everywhere on the site, consists of clayey shaly loam deposited during the construction of the railway; it contains ceramics of *c.* 1860–90. Underneath it are traces of another humic layer 0.028–0.18m thick (on average 0.08m) that formed during the roughly 300-year period between the departure of the early European settlers and the arrival of the Atkinson brothers. It covers a 16th-century burnt layer consisting of dark grey to black clayey loam containing a large amount of shale mixed with charcoal and fired clay, with artefacts and ecofacts (seeds, pits, etc.) usually showing signs of carbonization caused by exposure to the fire. The burnt remains have deteriorated over time due to erosion and seasonal variation in ambient conditions.

A third humic layer 0.058–0.14m thick (on average 99mm) corresponds to the surface soil that existed when Cartier arrived. This layer, which is very clayey and compact, formed over a period of several thousand years and was observed in various parts of the site beneath 16th-century debris. It covers the original undisturbed soil, which consists of several dozen centimetres of red shale gravel overlying bedrock. This gravel dates back more than 7,500 years, to the period when the site was in contact with the waters of an ancient lake.

This stratigraphic sequence is not found throughout the site. For example, in the southern portion, the humic layer above the 16th-century debris is very thin, suggesting that the upper part of this horizon has been removed. The clayey humic layer that the settlers would have walked on in the 16th century is absent from the eastern part of the site, but lies at a depth of over 1.0m in the northern part.

The different soil layers described above can be associated with five phases of the history of the site: Phase I, the period prior to the 16th century; Phase II, the 16th-century European occupation; Phase III, an intermediate period dating from 1543 to 1823; Phase IV, the occupation of the villa between 1823 and 1906; and Phase V, the period from 1906 to 2006, associated with the construction of the railroad and subsequent use of the site.

BUILDING AREAS

The researchers have identified structural components of wood, earth or stone, as well as stratigraphic layers and artefacts dating from the 16th century. They have also defined six areas containing construction materials, each of which seems to be associated with a structure in which wood was a major component. These areas point to the presence of a building complex along the cliff on the west side of the site and along part of the cliff to the south (Fig. 3).

The building areas also reflect a range of building methods, particularly as far as the structures' foundations are concerned. At least four different construction techniques are represented: a) sandstone masonry bonded with local clay; b) upright posts with sandstone packing; c) upright posts wedged in place with sandstone and resting on a base of flat sandstone fragments; and d) timber framing with earth infill.

Building area 1

The first building area was identified along the edge of the cliff on the south side of the site in zone C. It contained a wall that extended over a distance of about 3.60m (Fig. 4). At its eastern end it turned south, forming a 90° corner, and then continued for slightly less than 2m to the edge of the cliff. Charcoal and 16th-century artefacts were found in association with this feature. Radiocarbon dating of a charcoal sample taken from burnt wood lying on top of the wall provided a date of 380 ± 60 BP (Beta-234906),[23] for a calibrated age range of 1430 to 1650 (96%).

This masonry feature was of fairly rough construction and measured 0.55m wide by an average of 0.13m high. It consisted of no more than two irregular courses of stone and, as indicated by a study of the area's mineral resources,[24] was built, for the most part, with greenish sandstone

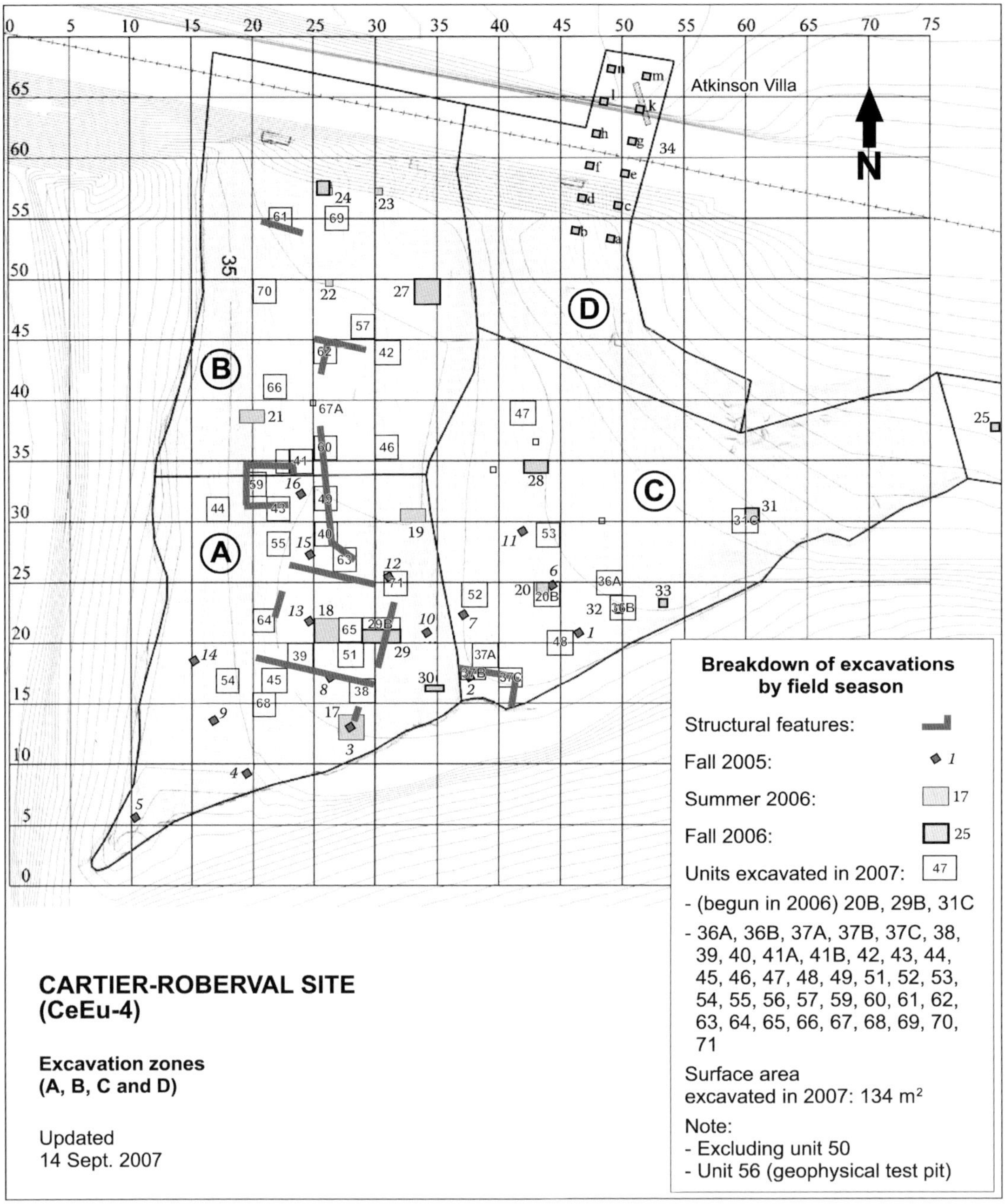

FIG. 3

Cartier-Roberval site (CeEu-4): Cap Rouge headland (A. Forget, CCNQ).

extracted near the site; a few pieces of shaly stone were also used; the masonry was bonded with local clay.

This feature is believed to have supported a wooden structure, carbonized traces of which were found on top of the stonework. The traces were too limited, however, to determine how the structure was made. Nevertheless the discovery of this wall points to the presence of a building in the southern part of the site, part of which seems to

FIG. 4
Cartier-Roberval site (CeEu-4): wall remains, building area 1 (photograph, R. Fiset).

have disappeared over the cliff due to erosion. The structure was orientated south-east/north-west; its south side would thus have faced the mouth of the Cap Rouge River and up the St Lawrence.

Building area 2

The second building area is situated in zone A at the tip of the headland, to the west of building area 1. It is the most impressive of the six building areas because of the large number of construction materials (charcoal, pieces of wood (Fig. 5) and baked clay) found, and also due to its artefact and archaeobotanical content. The baked clay covered an area of about 100m^2 within this building area, suggesting that clay was used abundantly for building walls and other major structural components. Traces of fire extended beyond the limits of the area, but became less concentrated towards the south. They disappeared completely further north, in building areas 3 and 4, as well as towards the east and west.

Only a limited number of structural elements survived in this area. They included pieces of burnt wood and impressions left in the clayey soil by timbers that had disintegrated with age or through changes in environmental conditions. These impressions created small depressions, the largest of which formed narrow trenches measuring about 0.30m wide and containing burnt earth; other impressions were found around postholes.

Even though the wood components were heavily damaged by fire, analysis of these remains with the trench-shaped impressions left by disintegrated timbers made it possible to identify alignments that may point to the location of the outside walls of a building. One of these alignments lies to the south and another to the west. However, archaeological evidence for these exterior walls is still limited, making it difficult to define the entire perimeter of the structure. Despite the discovery of traces of wood to the east, it is impossible to establish clearly the limit on this side. The location of the northern limit also remains uncertain,

FIG. 5
Cartier-Roberval site (CeEu-4): building area 2 (photograph, R. Fiset).

although it may coincide with an alignment of stones parallel to the proposed southern limit. If so, it is suggested that the building measured at least 9.00 × 9.50m.

Some smaller pieces of burnt wood were uncovered inside the building limits; the smallest pieces were very fragmented. These remains were generally in a very fragile state; the wood disintegrated easily when touched. To preserve them, their structure was solidified with epoxy; in fact every major timber discovered on the site was also treated in this way. Judging by the alignment of the smaller pieces of wood, the structure seems to have been orientated north-west/south-east.

Two large timbers were also found near the centre of the building. The one to the south measured 1.21m long, 0.13m wide and about 0.10m thick, and was parallel to the structure's southern limit. It was perpendicular to the other large timber, which was unearthed further north and measured over 1.60m long, 0.10m wide and *c.* 0.08m thick. These timbers were found at more or less the same level, which tends to confirm that they were in their original position. Perhaps they indicate the location of dividing walls or correspond to the joists of a wood floor.

In addition to these wood remains, which were a major feature of this part of the site, the fieldwork uncovered postholes for large round timbers in the southern portion of building area 2. One was packed around the rim and on the bottom with small stones; the others, further south, had diameters of 0.60–0.80m. Although the exact function of the posts that would have stood in these holes remains to be determined, it is highly likely that they supported components that rose high above the ground.

The presence of the large posthole with its surrounding stone packing inside the building area (Fig. 6) sheds some light on what the structure in this sector may have looked like. This posthole, in conjunction with the 0.20–0.70m-thick fire layer found in this area, points to the presence of a fairly tall structure, such as a tower — perhaps one of the two towers described by Roberval. Once the limits and orientation of the structure in building area 2 are better defined, it may be possible to determine whether and how it was related to the structure in building area 3.

FIG. 6
Cartier-Roberval site (CeEu-4): posthole with surrounding stone packing, building area 2 (photograph, R. Fiset).

Building area 3

A third building area was identified just north of building area 2. It contained two sections of stone wall, one longer than the other. The long section ran north–south over a length of about 10.50m, while the short one ran diagonally toward the south-east, from the southern end of the long section, over a distance of *c.* 2.20m (Fig. 7). There were upright posts at regular intervals in the long section of walling (Fig. 8).

The long north–south section was made of unbonded masonry set in a trench with a maximum width of around 0.40m. It was built with roughly cut pieces of green sandstone of varying size placed flat or on edge. The walling measured 0.25–0.35m wide by 0.49–0.73m high and, as shown in places where its base was reached, consisted of four to five courses of stone. The base lay on shale gravel, only a few centimetres above the bedrock. Soil found in gaps between the stones of this feature could represent the intentional infilling of the holes in which the vertical posts were set, or the natural processes of erosion or freeze-thaw action.

The shorter wall section running diagonally towards the south-east was made of pieces of undressed sandstone under 0.30m in size. It measured *c.* 0.20m wide and consisted of a single 0.11m-high course of stone. The stones were placed in a 0.20–0.30m-wide trench and criss-crossed one another in places.

Two post emplacements 6.74m apart were found 0.21m and 0.22m to the west of the long north–south section of wall. They were delimited by pieces of uncut or roughly hewn green sandstone of varying size surrounding a more or less circular hole which could have held a small post with a diameter of just over 0.15m. The post emplacement to the south was the more complete; the stones around it formed an oval with a diameter of 0.27–0.50m. From its base, dug into the natural soil, the hole was up to 0.24m deep.

The features uncovered in this sector may be the remains of a defence work erected between

FIG. 7
Cartier-Roberval site (CeEu-4): junction between two sections of walling uncovered in building area 3 (photograph, R. Fiset).

building area 2 and building areas 5 and 6. They are believed to represent a continuous structure running from south to north and thus to indicate a possible structural link, in the form of an enceinte, between the various building components, completely enclosing the east side of this part of the site. The different construction methods in the two wall sections suggest that the enceinte could have taken different forms. It is also conceivable that it extended to and encompassed the masonry feature found in building area 1. Another masonry structure uncovered in 2008, which is more or less parallel to this enceinte, could be associated with this defence work.

Building area 4

A fourth building area was identified to the west of building area 3. It was bordered to the east by the long north–south wall section uncovered in building area 3 and contained, for the most part, a solid mass of shale masonry measuring *c.* 4.0 × 4.50m. Two unburnt timbers lay parallel to one another beside this structure, one on its north side and the other on its south (Fig. 9). There were at least two notches in the one to the north, into which another horizontal timber or upright pieces of wood may have been fitted.

This masonry feature was not excavated completely but simply cleaned so that it could be studied more easily. It was built mainly of undressed or splintered pieces of shale of varying size, mixed here and there with uncut pieces of sandstone. No specific construction pattern could be defined.

This solid mass of masonry covered part of a feature that may date from the 16th century. Although it was unearthed only partially, the feature was identified as a section of stone walling laid out on a north-west/south-east axis. It was built with roughly hewn 0.20–0.30m blocks of sandstone and measured 0.57m wide at the most; there were two to three courses of stone standing 0.24–0.30m high. It measured over 1.15m in length between the south wall of the excavation unit and an overlying timber, and appeared to continue beyond the timber, towards the north-west.

Areas 5 and 6

Other features, consisting mainly of burnt wood, were uncovered to the north of building area 4. They belong to at least two building areas, as shown by differences in their alignments, construction methods and materials. Nonetheless, the overall orientation of the features seems to be similar to that of the structure identified in building area 1.

Area 5, the more southerly of the two building areas, contained a burnt piece of wood with stones arranged on either side. North-east of this, next to two excavation units with numerous traces of wood, were the remains of two large pieces of burnt wood that may once have been superimposed. A small ball-shaped projectile of a calibre compatible with projectiles used with perriers was also unearthed. Scattered pieces of stone and a trench in area 5 probably also attest the presence of structural features.

Another piece of burnt wood and a few stones uncovered in building area 6, to the north of building area 5, also point to the presence of a structure. Lastly, an east–west trench containing many small fragments of burnt wood may be associated with a formwork.

Overall, it is difficult to interpret how building areas 5 and 6 were organized. Together they covered an area of over 300m^2.

FIG. 8
Cartier-Roberval site (CeEu-4): regularly spaced postholes in one of the wall sections uncovered in building area 3 (photograph, R. Fiset).

CONTACT WITH AMERINDIANS

The fieldwork has also yielded the earliest evidence in Québec of contact between Europeans and Amerindians. These finds (Fig. 10) hold great potential for advancing our knowledge about the period, and studies (for example, clay analysis and neutron activation of the pottery) have been undertaken to understand how best to integrate these new data with what is already known about the Amerindian world in the 16th century.

The Amerindian material consists mainly of Iroquoian pottery and plant macroremains, including corn kernels and sunflower seeds, which are associated with indigenous foodways. A total of over 100 sherds have been found at different levels throughout the site; most were recovered from the fire layer containing 16th-century European material, where they were distributed from the surface to a depth of some 0.40m. Since the site has not yielded traces of Amerindian occupation prior to the 16th-century European settlement, the Amerindian pottery may be considered to be contemporary with the colony of Cartier and Roberval.

Only two examples of the lithics — a quartz flake and a chert biface preform — can be identified as Amerindian with any certainty; the rest are not sufficiently diagnostic to be attributed to a specific origin. It should be remembered that in this period Europeans also worked stone for such purposes as building, making gunflints or strike-a-lights, and extracting samples for mineral testing. Some of the lithics, such as the chert, could even have been traded by the Europeans with Amerindians.

Nearly all the indigenous macroremains and much of the Amerindian pottery were uncovered in the layer related to the burning of the colonial occupation, but the pottery was also found in other contexts — for example, in 19th- and 20th-century deposits. The largest collection of Amerindian sherds was found in building area 2 of zone A,

FIG. 9
Cartier-Roberval site (CeEu-4): masonry mass, building area 4 (photograph, R. Fiset).

suggesting that they were deposited inside the fort buildings and thus may have been used to redistribute food obtained from the Amerindians.

INTERPRETATION

BUILDING A FORTIFIED COLONY

The organization of the building areas and some of the artefacts found suggest that these structures were intended not only for shelter but also for defence. The presence of what appears to be a defensive enceinte, along with the remains of at least two buildings and the discovery of a small-calibre cannonball, perhaps from a perrier, support the hypothesis that the site is that of the Upper Fort erected by Cartier and Roberval on the headland of Cap Rouge between 1541 and 1543.

The other excavated features are difficult to interpret. Although no contemporary plans or drawings of the colony are known, Roberval's description[25] helps us picture the Upper Fort, at least hypothetically:

> wherein there were two courtes of buyldings, a great Towre, and another of fortie or fiftie foote long: wherein there were divers chambers, an Hall, a Kitchine, houses of office, Sellers high and lowe, and neere unto it were an Oven and Milles, and a stoove to warme men in, and a Well before the house.

Roberval's account also sheds some light on the colony's Lower Fort, describing it as lying at the foot of the headland and having at least one defensive feature:

> part whereof was a great Towre of two stories high, two courtes of good buylding, where at the first all our victuals, and whatsoever was brought with us was sent to be kept: and neere unto that Towre there is another small river. In these two places above and beneath, all the meaner sort was lodged.

FIG. 10
Cartier-Roberval site (CeEu-4): Amerindian pottery (photograph, R. Fiset).

These descriptions, which suggest avenues for future research, are complemented by that given by Cartier, which alludes to the defensive nature of the establishment:

> toward the East there is a high and steepe cliff, where we made a way in maner of a payre of staires, and aloft we made a Fort to keepe the nether Fort and the ships, and all things that might passe as well by the great as by this small river ... And upon that high cliffe wee found a faire fountaine very neere the sayd Fort: adionying whereunto we found good store of stones, which we esteemed to be Diamants.[26]

In the 16th century the Cap Rouge headland would have offered a strategic commanding position, ideal for a stronghold, protecting the Lower Fort and the vessels anchored in a meander of the Cap Rouge River and providing a vantage point for keeping an eye on movement along the St Lawrence River and its tributary. In France heights had long been considered the best sites for forts; in choosing locations for their fortresses, French colonists in the New World sought the same sort of topography. An example is the description of Fort Coligny (1555–60), built on Coligny Island off the coast of Brazil:

> Since there were mountains at either end, Villegagnon had a small building put up on each of them: as well, on a hill rising 50 or 60 feet in the middle of the island, he had his residence built. On either side of this hill, we levelled the ground and made a few small places for constructions, including the hall where we assembled for worship and to eat,

and other buildings which lodged the some 80 persons we were (including all Villegagnon's people).[27]

SPATIAL ORGANIZATION

The two main stone foundations uncovered evidently represent different buildings, since they were constructed in very different ways and were differently orientated. At present the construction methods, alignments and functions of the other building areas are unknown.

The distribution of building remains suggests that activities at the Upper Fort were concentrated at the western edge of the cliff, which may have had a continuous line of structures along its entire length. The excavation team looked for signs that there had been a gateway in this area, but none was found; nor were traces of a palisade or ditch discovered on this side of the site. Since the area to the east of the six building areas yielded no structural evidence, it appears that the western part of the site represents an occupation zone covering an area of 1,500m^2. This zone may have been surrounded by a wall; it would have been occupied by nobility and gentlemen.

However, according to our research hypothesis,[28] the Upper Fort should have covered a much greater area of the Cap Rouge headland. It is very likely that it included another inhabited zone for ordinary people, as mentioned in Roberval's description, with living quarters for women and some of the military under Roberval's command. There must also have been designated areas for specific purposes; for example, land could have been set aside for farming. Unfortunately, the spatial organization of the fort and the area it covered are not mentioned directly in any historical document, except for a letter sent from Nantes to the Portuguese ambassador in France.[29] This mentions that the fort's palisade had a circumference of one league (more than 3km). Although this seems over-large, the writer may have referred to walls enclosing a field for livestock, as well as both the Upper and Lower Forts.

It is estimated that the inhabited and cultivated sectors of the colony would have covered an area of 10,000–22,000m^2; it would therefore have extended into what is now Cartier-Roberval Park. These figures are based on various considerations, including a study of the site's defensive needs, the historical description of the Upper Fort, and comparisons with other colonial establishments.

For defence, the area under the fort's control must have extended towards the north and east, where the upper plateau overlooked the colony (Fig. 1) and could have offered a vantage point for any attackers. A stream north of the excavated site would have been a suitable spot for a watermill; the upper settlement's defences would no doubt have protected this source of fresh water.

Roberval's description of the Upper Fort leads us to envisage an area spacious enough to hold a 'great Towre', a second tower 12–15m high, and two buildings with a kitchen, hall, cellars and offices; the yard would have been large enough to enclose an oven, mills, a stove and a well. Various necessary features are not mentioned in the description; the colonists would certainly have required a smithy, warehouses and a covered way for the movement of soldiers, as well as buildings for testing minerals, storing cereals and sheltering animals. They may have stood in the area between the upper and lower forts. The animals would also have needed pasture, which may have been found in the natural grasslands along the rivers' shores.

Cartier also set aside 1½ acres (the equivalent of 7,500m^2) for cultivation, and an area for a cemetery with about 85 burials. It is possible that the cultivated area formed a strip of cleared land that would have created a buffer zone between the fortifications and the forest to the north and east. In all, the space that was occupied, inhabited and fortified on the cliff top could have covered about 17,500m^2 of the 22,335m^2 area that is the subject of archaeological research (excavation zones A to J).

Another factor that would have affected the settlement's size and spatial organization was the number of people accompanying Cartier and Roberval. The original plans called for about 550 people to found the colony, a number considered sufficient to occupy, exploit and control the land. It would have been necessary to house this population in buildings put up by Cartier in 1541–42 or added by Roberval in 1542–43. However, the true number of colonists was merely a fraction of that planned: under Cartier's command there were only around 350 to 400 people living in either the Upper Fort or the Lower Fort, while under Roberval the colony had no more than 150 inhabitants. It is to be supposed that the military commanders and most of the defensive forces would have been housed at the Upper Fort, which may thus have had a population of some 75 to 100. Comparative data for the Cartier-Roberval colony and other establishments are presented in Table 1 and will be discussed in more detail below.

TRACES OF FIRE

When excavations were undertaken, it was soon apparent that the colony could well have been destroyed by fire. Evidence for this came from the south-west part of the site, which was characterized

TABLE 1

Surface area, population and number of people/m² in colonial settlements similar to the Upper Fort at Cap Rouge.

Settlement	Surface area	Population	People/m²
Charlesfort (Sc)	687.39m² 16 × 13 *toises* (29.09 × 23.63m)	28	0.04
Martin's Hundred (Va)	1,074.16m² 130 × 90ft (39.39 × 27.2m)	140	0.13
James Fort (Va)	11,568.84m² 420 × 300ft (127.27 × 90.90m)	104	0.0089
Sainte-Croix Island (Me)	4,544.87m² 225 × 220ft (68.18 × 66.66m)	76	0.01
Upper Fort, Cap Rouge (Qc)	**1,500m²**	**90**	**0.06**

Sources: Bassanier 1853; Noël Hume 2001; Kelso & Straube 2004; Biggar 1971.

by a layer containing large quantities of charcoal and fired clay mixed with soil. This layer varied in depth from 0.20 to 0.70m and extended from east to west over a distance of at least 9m. Further to the north, a shallower layer of similar material covered an area of nearly 1,500m². The depth of the layer probably depended on the size of the building that burned and the intensity of the fire, as well as subsequent disturbance and erosion. Fire affected not only the structural features, but also left its mark on several glass and wood artefacts and on archaeobotanical remains, which owe their preservation to their being carbonized.

Since no mention of a fire is made in the documents, the archaeological evidence of burning does not have an immediate explanation. Since the area excavated so far corresponds to a settlement which may have been built and occupied solely by Roberval, or only by Cartier, a number of hypotheses can be put forward. Cartier may have burnt his buildings before departing, or Amerindians may have done so after he left. In that case, Roberval would have had to rebuild the colony when he arrived. Alternatively, the viceroy could have set fire to the buildings before returning to France, or Amerindians could have burnt them after his departure.

At present the authors favour the explanation that Roberval, a soldier, would have followed the military custom of burning installations so that they could not fall into enemy hands. This military practice was carried out at Fort Carolina in 1565[30] and at General Wolfe's encampment in 1759.[31] If the Upper Fort was burnt deliberately, it could well have been Roberval who ordered it, since, unlike Cartier, he came from a military background.

Cartier's previous behaviour suggests it is unlikely that he would have envisaged burning the Cap Rouge colony. When he left the post on the Saint-Charles River where he spent the winter of 1535–36, he apparently did not destroy it, for when Champlain visited the ruins of these quarters in 1608 he noted worm-eaten lumber rather than charred remains. Moreover, Cartier was under Roberval's command and had been given responsibility for preparing the colony until the latter joined him; Cartier would have had little motivation for destroying his work. Finally, in Roberval's account of his arrival at Cap Rouge, there is no mention of evidence of a fire; if the colony had been burned down, it seems highly improbable that he would not have recorded this fact.

CONSTRUCTION TRADITIONS AND TECHNIQUES

The buildings erected on Cap Rouge from September 1541 were no doubt the work of masons and carpenters brought by Cartier as part of the crew of his five ships. It seems likely that Cartier and Roberval had previously arranged that Cartier, with his larger crew, would prepare the site of the new colony for the imminent arrival of a second group under Roberval. Cartier was probably supposed to erect the necessary buildings, including living quarters for Roberval and his gentlemen. In fact Roberval landed at Cap Rouge only in the summer of 1542; Cartier may not have been aware of this change of plan. It is possible that Cartier had orders to construct a stronghold with two forts capable of sheltering about 450–500 people — about 350 who would have arrived on the first ships and 150 who would come soon afterwards with Roberval.

In studying the remains at Cap Rouge, it is helpful to keep in mind the origins of the fort's builders. Both Cartier and Roberval came from northern France. The crew's carpenters and masons would also have come from this region, particularly Brittany, Normandy and Picardy. We may presume that the construction methods used at the fort would have followed the building traditions of these regions. The craftsmen's traditions would normally have had an effect on the choice of materials, the internal layout and the spatial organization of the buildings. As the designers of the forts, the builders must necessarily have applied what they knew about military architecture. Finally, they were no doubt influenced by the availability of local materials and any knowledge of the climate they had.

The excavations have provided a range of evidence for the construction techniques used in the Upper Fort. The presence of charcoal, alongside some stone and lumps of fired clay in the fire layer, suggests that use was made of *pisé* (unbaked earth), and especially of *colombage bousillé*.

Colombage bousillé was widely employed in northern France, and particularly in Upper Normandy.[32] It is a construction technique used in timber-framed buildings in which the panels between the vertical studs are infilled with cob, or with clay mixed with plant matter (for example straw or grass) or animal fibre (such as horsehair).[33] This building technique is characteristic of the part of France from which the Cap Rouge colonists would have come.[34]

Support for the idea that some of the Upper Fort structures were built using *colombage bousillé* comes from presence of pieces of wood which show signs of having been pressed against earth, and of lumps of clay containing charcoal or even bearing the imprint of wood on their surfaces. However, whereas wood is found throughout the building area, there is less clay than one would expect. It is possible that there was once more clay on the site, but that it has been carried off through erosion. This could easily have happened if the fire had been less intense in certain areas and the clay had not been baked; the raw clay would soon have disintegrated. It could also have been removed during subsequent ground-levelling operations.

Other remains, including traces of thin strips of wood in the clay, suggest that *colombage bousillé* was used at Cap Rouge. They could represent criss-crossed laths traditionally fixed between the upright timbers of a wall to secure the clay infilling the panels between them. The numerous fragments of sandstone found with the charred wood and fired clay could also have come from the filling; such materials were sometimes added to the clay to stiffen it. In France, a thin coat of limewash might be applied to the finished wall,[35] but there is no evidence of this practice at Cap Rouge.

As for the technique used for joining the timbers, the only clue yielded by the site is the size of the nails. Since they are less than 0.12m long, it is likely that the larger beams were held together with joints and pegs.[36] Although the size of the timbers and the way they were prepared are unknown, there are signs of squaring on one or more faces of the pieces of wood uncovered.

DISCUSSION

One of the most striking aspects of the initial excavation was the discovery of artefacts and botanical evidence associated with a privileged socio-economic lifestyle, including sherds of Italian maiolica, fine glassware and stained glass, and food remains such as olive and date stones and grape seeds.[37] It would have been normal for the colony's leaders to live in the fort high on the headland of Cap Rouge; according to normal practice in the 16th-century French seigneurial system, the governing classes, represented here by Sieur de Roberval and his gentlemen, would have occupied higher ground.

Evidence for the presence of the nobility at Cap Rouge is also found in a mandate for the appointment of Roberval as the leader of the colonial enterprise. Issued from Fontainebleau on 15 January 1541, it emphasized his status and the powers he obtained:

> to depute and constitute some excellent personage, of great loyalty and integrity to us and who is of good judgment, worth, and experience, to be head and leader of that enterprise, and to whom is given by us such power and authority as such a matter requires . . . as we might do if we were there in person . . . because of the great and entire confidence that we have from long experience in the person of our beloved and faithful Jean-François de La Roque, knight, seigneur of Roberval, and in his good judgment.[38]

Thus Roberval was entrusted with the very powers that the king would have wielded had he gone to Canada himself. Roberval's high social rank as viceroy and his weighty responsibilities are repeated in the same document. The king chose to:

> make, constitute, commission, and establish him by these presents our lieutenant general, head, leader, and captain of the said enterprise, and of all the ships and sea-going vessels, and likewise of all the persons, both soldiers, seamen, and others commisioned by Us and who will go on the said enterprise, expedition, and army going on the said voyage.[39]

Roberval was also to govern the new territory, distribute wages, administer justice and acquire lands by fair means or by force; he was to build cities, forts, churches and temples and to distribute fiefdoms to his companions, free of any rent for six years, dividing among them one third of the profits as compensation.[40]

François I may have been influenced in his choice of Roberval by their youthful friendship and by bonds between noble families. Roberval was a member of the 'nobility of the sword' in his own right, with a military career as a knight.[41] In 1534 he was honoured with the titles of the King's Man-at-Arms and Standard Bearer for the Company of Marshal Robert III de La Marck, Lord of Fleuranges.[42] On his return from North America, he continued to work in the service of the king. As a high-profile military engineer, he was entrusted with modernizing the fortifications of Paris and of Senlis (1544). He was also known for his skill in hydraulic engineering and his ability to capture cities.[43] The leader of the Cap Rouge colony thus had all the experience and knowledge required for building fortifications.

Apart from Roberval's description of the site, two 19th-century documents support the hypothesis that the colony was fortified. The first is the account of the historian Alfred Hawkins following his visit in 1834;[44] he noted a hillock which he proposed could contain the remains of the fortifications described by Cartier and Roberval. The other is a plan of 1846 by the notary Archibald Campbell (Fig. 11) which indicates the position of two ancient mounds, one on the point of the headland and the other a little further north, in what is now Cartier-Roberval Park, near a dried-up stream.

The southern mound is no longer visible, but excavations have been carried out at its presumed site at the tip of the headland. A thick layer of burnt 16th-century material was found. However, the humic layer seen elsewhere, representing the period between the colonists' departure and the arrival of the Atkinson family in 1823, was absent. It thus seems likely that the humic layer and the mound, perhaps containing evidence for one of Roberval's towers, were removed when landscaping was carried out in this area. The recorded position of the mound would have been an ideal spot for the 'great Towre'; in this position it would have dominated the surrounding countryside.

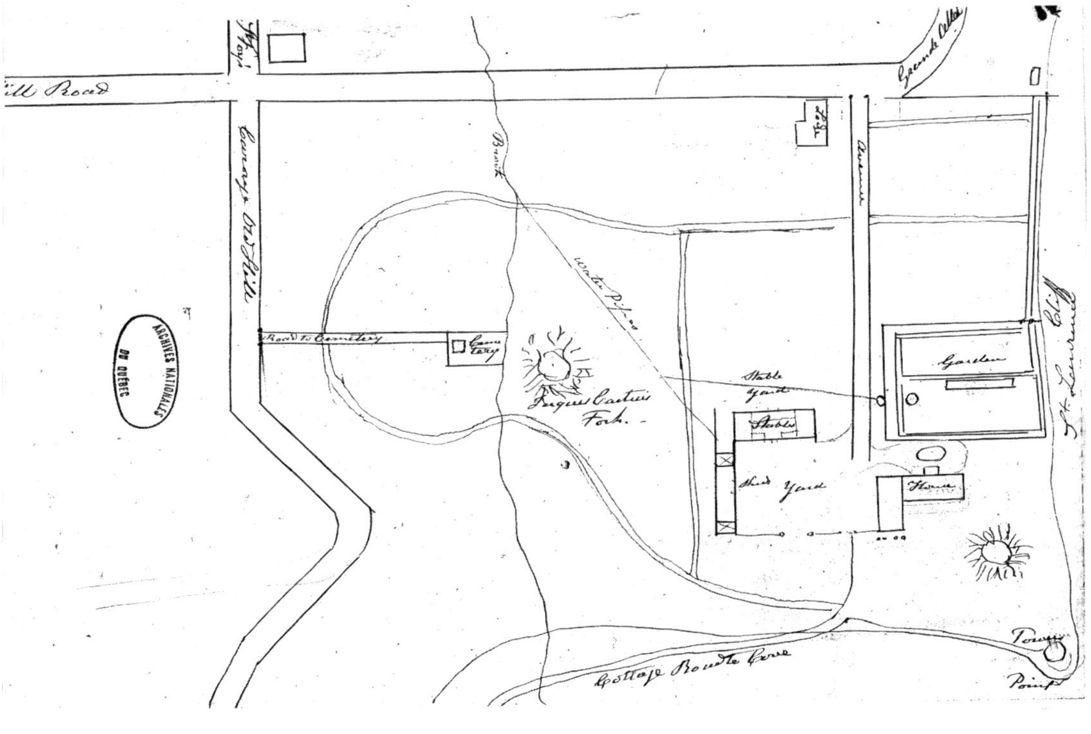

FIG. 11

Cartier-Roberval site (CeEu-4): sketch by the notary Archibald Campbell, 1846 (Greffe du notaire Archibald Campbell, le 4 décembre 1846, no. 10503-B, Cartographie, Bibliothèque et Archives Nationales du Québec).

The other mound, marked 'Jacques Cartier's fort' on the 1846 plan, is shown about 80m to the north. Excavations have not produced any clues about its location. The mound seems to correspond to the 'hillock of artificial construction' described by Alfred Hawkins on his visit to the property in 1834. He estimated that it was about one acre (63.6m) north of the Atkinson Villa and noted that very old trees were growing on it. The mound could have been formed by the remains of a tall structure built on one of the points overlooking the Cap Rouge River near the dried-up stream. If this structure was less strategically important than the rest of the fortifications, including the great tower, it may not have been burnt when the colonists departed, and this would explain why traces of it are hard to find.

In studying the Cap Rouge establishment, the authors have turned to information about other early colonial forts in the Americas to see if comparable remains have been recorded elsewhere. It is clear that settlements were fortified according to the precepts of military architecture that prevailed in the colonists' home countries. They generally had quadrangular layouts with salient angles at the corners, although Fort Carolina (1564–65) and James Fort (1607–99) were distinguished by their triangular plans. While forts in the New World sometimes had a simple banquette along the inside of the enceinte, they were generally built with earthworks that formed raised bastions, retained by timber walls.

Pictorial and archaeological evidence shows that this form of fort was much in vogue in North America in the 16th, 17th and 18th centuries. Examples are Port-Royal in Nova Scotia (1604–13), Fort St George at Popham, Maine (1607–08), Martin's Hundred in Virginia (1619–22) and Fort Louis at Mobile, Alabama (1702–11). None of hese forts had towers like those described by Roberval. The rare examples of strongholds with towers come from Navidad in Hispaniola (1492), La Isabella in Haiti (1493–98), as well as Charlesbourg-Royal and France-Roy at Cap Rouge (1541–43). It may be noted that towers were also built at Champlain's second Habitation[45] and at the Jesuits' fortified mission at Sillery (1650).

Although the forts erected in the New World displayed many aspects of military architecture that had been transposed from Europe and adapted to a new situation, their building materials were quite different. Instead of being largely of stone, they were usually constructed from locally available wood, earth and stone. In rare cases, such as the Frobisher fort (1576–78), Sainte-Croix Island and Port-Royal, prefabricated framing was brought from Europe.[46] These early North American forts, constructed of less durable material than their counterparts in Europe, have left archaeological remains that are quite different from those in Europe; they may offer clues that will help researchers decipher the remains at Cap Rouge.

When the Cap Rouge colony was established, French military architecture had been undergoing a long process of transition from the High Middle Ages to the Renaissance. The arrival of cannon required engineers to build thicker fortifications and add salient angles and cannon batteries to medieval enceintes. Towers were provided with chambers, wider loopholes and gun platforms at their tops.[47] When the first true bastions made their appearance around 1530, they represented a major innovation. Constructed with great quantities of earth to absorb enemy cannon shot, they supported open-air gun platforms and were protected by a ditch with a scarp and counterscarp.[48] The requirements of defensive flanking fire led to the development of the five-sided bastion as the norm, although bastions with orillons were constructed from 1524 in strongholds under the command of François I.

It might be wondered whether any of these innovations were used at Cap Rouge. Is it possible that some of the new features added to medieval stone castles were incorporated into the colonial fortifications? Roberval's description of the Upper and Lower Forts as having towers suggests that they followed a traditional model. Furthermore, the architecture of the Upper Fort would have had to be adapted to its uneven topography, which would not have been suitable for the classic quadrangular layout. The fact that the Upper Fort had only two towers instead of four probably reflects this.

Innovations that could have been adapted to the colonial setting include a predecessor of the bastion known as a *fausse-bray* — a form of external terrace following the contours of an enceinte and forming polygonal extensions at the corner towers.[49] The Cap Rouge forts might also have incorporated a boulevard, or bulwark — the predecessor of the bastion, consisting of a massive circular earthwork, sometimes with masonry retaining walls, erected in front of fortification walls.

The towers at Cap Rouge would not have been anachronisms, even though they were not in the forefront of military engineering. They were probably an expression of the French monarchy's desire to claim new land and display its power in a colonial establishment, symbolizing its territorial ambitions in North America. The leaders of the new colonial enterprise may have preferred to build their fortifications with the towers of a traditional medieval stronghold, whose 'mission was to protect the community's property and its population'.[50]

Furthermore, the nobility of 16th-century France would have found it unthinkable that they should live in a residence which did not reflect their prestige. Castles built in the provinces normally boasted towers as signs of seigneurial power.[51] Being of high rank, Sieur de Roberval and his gentlemen may naturally have wished to live within the complex of structures where the great tower apparently stood.

The forts were of course not merely expressions of power; they had to possess the features needed to defend the colony, especially since Spain had been alerted to France's plans in North America and threatened to put an end to them. For Roberval, the military scope and political importance of the Canadian mission probably justified putting off his voyage until he had sufficient arms; without them, there was a risk that he would not conquer and control the country, and that the colonial project would fail.

With an estimated area of around 1,500m^2 and about 90 people, the density of population in the Upper Fort was roughly 0.06 people per square metre. Table 1 compares this figure with that for some other North American colonial establishments. It can be seen that the settlements with the most space per person are James Fort and Sainte-Croix Island, while the most crowded was Martin's Hundred. The Cap Rouge colony and Charlesfort, which both belonged to France, show similar ratios.

It is conceivable that Roberval and Cartier agreed on a number of points about the new colony before they left France. These may have included the settlement layout, the number and types of buildings, the kind of defences, the roles of the two forts, and the number, skills and social status of the colonists. They may have sought the services of a French architect or, considering that Roberval was a military engineer, relied on their own experience. Some form of coordination seems to be implied by the 'Mémoire de 1538', a document that amounts to a form of preliminary plan listing the human and material resources required for the expedition. The two men must also have planned and shared preparatory work such as purchasing supplies and hiring workers.

It may be supposed that most of the buildings at Cap Rouge were constructed by Cartier's men before the winter of 1541–42. Various explanations for their different construction techniques may be suggested. It is possible that they were all put up at the same time but that stone was used for some buildings, wood and earth for others. Alternatively, they may have been erected in two stages — first in wood and clay (since these materials were readily to hand), then, after initial needs had been met, in stone. The secondary structures may also represent efforts to resolve problems such as water infiltration that had been observed in the first ones. It is also possible that some buildings were erected by Roberval before the winter of 1542–43.

Some authors have raised the question of the number of forts at Cap Rouge,[52] wondering whether Roberval could have built two different ones from the initial two built by Cartier. It seems improbable that Cartier would have burned his forts before leaving the colony, especially since no archaeological evidence of this has been found. He would not have had the right to destroy the forts he had built, given that he had received his mandate from Roberval and was under his orders.

CONCLUSIONS

Documentary and archaeological evidence indicate that the Cap Rouge headland was the site of a colonial establishment fortified with towers, and that the part closest to the cliff was occupied by members of the governing class — presumably Roberval and his gentlemen.

Archaeological excavations have shown that the settlement was burned, preserving artefacts and architectural remains. The discoveries made to November 2007 have led to the conclusion that part of the site occupied by French colonists between 1541 and 1543 has been found and that, within this sector, a number of building features belong to the Upper Fort, associated mainly with Roberval's stay in 1542–43.

Many of the artefacts recovered, notably the Italian maiolica, fine glassware and stained glass, are associated with privileged social status, suggesting that the buildings in which they were found were occupied by the fort's rulers. A colony's population would of course consist mainly of humbler people. Roberval records that the 'meaner sort' were lodged in both the upper and lower parts of the colony. Future archaeological work in the Upper Fort area may therefore identify their houses, as well as the other structures described by Roberval, such as the mills, the stove and the bread oven. Various features which were not mentioned in the documentary record may also be expected, such as powder magazines, smithies, stables, barns and other secondary buildings. If the Upper Fort site contains their remains, it may well extend beyond the limits proposed initially on the property of the CCNQ.

Although still at an early stage, research suggests that France's first colonization attempt in North America was greatly influenced by the feudal system and the notion of royal authority, which was stronger in France than in other European nations at the time,[53] and that these influences were reflected both in the king's choice of a viceroy and in buildings whose architecture was worthy of the monarch's prestige and ambition. Unfortunately for the colony, 'François I's desire for glory was embodied in the Italian dream'.[54] European wars drained France of human and material resources and repeatedly interrupted efforts to colonize and explore Canada. Combined with the disappointing results of mineral tests and the failure to find a passage to the Orient, this led to the abandonment of the colonization enterprise.

ACKNOWLEDGEMENTS

Our gratitude goes to all the team members and the many collaborators who have contributed to the Cartier-Roberval archaeological project. We also wish to thank the anonymous readers whose comments helped us to clarify the arguments presented in this article.

NOTES

[1] Biggar 1930, 42. [Translation, Cook 1993, 117.]
[2] Biggar 1930, 53.
[3] Bideaux 1986, 139.
[4] Biggar 1930, 70–4.
[5] Biggar 1930, 136, 170.
[6] Biggar 1930, 195–6, 240.
[7] Julien *et al.* 1984, 266 [Translation, Cook 1993, 110.] Hakluyt's English translation of the accounts of Cartier's third voyage and the voyage by Roberval have been quoted here to avoid erroneous interpretations that may have slipped into the 19th-century French versions of the text. The latter are translations of Hakluyt's English version; no original French accounts of the two voyages survive.
[8] Biggar 1930, 471.
[9] Knecht 1996, 484–5.
[10] Biggar 1901, 16–17.
[11] Bideaux 1986.
[12] Robert de Villeneuve 1685, *Carte des Environs De Quebec, En La Nouvelle France Mezuré Sur Le Lieu Très-Exactement, En 1685, Et 86, Par Le Sr Devillenevve, Injénieur du Roy*, APC, NMC 16690, map 2.
[13] James Murray 1760–62, *Carte de Murray*, ANQ, FM(1) P/300-1760-1-2, 2 sections – 1 – carte 4.
[14] *A View of Cape Rouge or Carouge, Nine Miles Above the City of Québec*, print by Peter Mazell after a drawing by Hervey Smith (McCord Museum, M2477) in Pownall 1768.
[15] Gaumond 2007.
[16] Minutes de notaires, Archibald Campbell, 1846, BAnQ-Q, cote CN301, S49 (microfilm 1-1550), 4 Dec. 1846, nos 10499, 10500.
[17] Samson *et al.* 2007.
[18] J.-A. Bouchard-Perron & A. Bain in this volume.
[19] Filion & Lafond Desrosiers 2008; Garneau 2008; Bhiry 2007; Auger & Payette 2008; Lavoie *et al.* 2008; Godbout *et al.* 2008; Côté 2008; Duval 2008.
[20] Allaire 2007, 4.
[21] Morel 1893, 20.
[22] Julien *et al.* 1984, 252.
[23] Duval 2008.
[24] Samson 2008.
[25] Cook 1993.
[26] Cook 1993, 101.
[27] De Léry 1594, 87. [Translation.]
[28] Samson *et al.* 2007.
[29] Biggar 1930, 408.
[30] Gaffarel 1875.
[31] Fiset 2005, 17.
[32] Fréal 1973, 5; Doyon & Hubrecht 1969, 208–14.
[33] Fréal 1973, 19.
[34] Fischer 1966, 88–95; Fréal 1973, 30.
[35] Fréal 1973, 19.
[36] Fréal 1973, 14.
[37] H. Côté in this volume.
[38] Biggar 1930, 179. [Translation, Cook 1993, 145.]
[39] Biggar 1930, 179. [Translation, Cook 1993, 145.]
[40] Biggar 1930, 156–7.
[41] Morel 1893, 5.
[42] Jacquart 1981, 16–17.
[43] Blanchard 1979, 8.
[44] Hawkins 1834, 63, 469.
[45] Niellon & Moussette 1985.
[46] Auger 1992; Fitzhugh & Olin 1991.
[47] Faucherre 1991; Rocolle 1973.
[48] Rocolle 1973, 166, 181.
[49] Hautecoeur 1965, 463.
[50] Faucherre 1991, 9. [Translation.]
[51] Charton-Le Clech 1991, 56–7.
[52] Trudel 1963.
[53] Jacquart 1981, 403.
[54] Jacquart 1981, 404. [Translation.]

BIBLIOGRAPHY

PUBLISHED SOURCES

Auger, R. 1992, 'Le premier établissement anglais au Nouveau Monde: les expéditions de Martin Frobisher (1576–1578) chez les Inuit de la terre de Baffin', in Fortin 1992, 133–70.

Bassanier, M. (ed.) 1853 [1586], *L'Histoire Notable de la Floride*, Paris: P. Jannet Libraire.

Bideaux, M. 1986, *Jacques Cartier: relations*, Montréal: Presses de l'Université de Montréal.
Biggar, H.P. 1901, *Early Trading Companies to New France*, New York: Argonaut Press.
Biggar, H.P. 1930, *A Collection of Documents relating to Jacques Cartier and the Sieur de Roberval*, Pub. APC **14**.
Biggar, H.P. (ed.) 1971 [1922–36], *The Works of Samuel de Champlain*, facs. edn, Toronto: University of Toronto Press.
Blanchard, A. 1979, *Les Ingénieurs du 'Roy' de Louis XIV à Louis XVI: étude du corps des fortifications*, Montpellier: Université Paul-Valéry.
Charton-Le Clech, S. 1991, *Chancellerie et culture au XVIe siècle (les notaires et secrétaires du roi de 1515 à 1547)*, Toulouse: Presses Universitaires du Mirail.
Cook, R. (ed.) 1993, *The Voyages of Jacques Cartier*, Toronto: University of Toronto Press.
De Léry, J. 1594, *Histoire d'un voyage fait en la terre du Brésil, autrement dite Amérique*, Genève: Eustache Vignon.
Doyon, G. & Hubrecht, R. 1969, *L'Architecture rurale & bourgeoise en France*, Paris: Vincent Fréal.
Faucherre, N. 1991, *Places fortes: bastion du pouvoir*, Paris: Desclée de Brouwer.
Fischer, R. 1966, *L'Art de restaurer une maison paysanne*, Paris: Hachette.
Fitzhugh, W. & Olin, J. 1991, *Archaeology of the Frobisher Voyages*, Washington: Smithsonian Institution Press.
Fortin, M. (ed.) 1992, *L'Archéologie et la rencontre de deux mondes: présence européenne sur des sites amérindiens*, Québec: Musée de la civilisation.
Fréal, J. 1973, *Maisons de Normandie*, Paris: Hachette Littérature.
Gaffarel, P. 1875, *Histoire de la Floride française*, Paris: Firmin-Didot.
Hautecoeur, L. 1965, *Histoire de l'architecture classique en France*, **1**. *La formation de l'idéal classique, la renaissance des humanistes (1535–1540 à 1589)*, Paris: Éditions Picard.
Hawkins, A. 1834, *Picture of Quebec*, Québec: Neilson & Cowan.
Jacquart, J. 1981, *François Ier*, Paris: Fayart.
Julien, C.A., Herval, R. & Beauchesne, T. (eds) 1984, *Jacques Cartier: voyages au Canada: avec les relations des voyages en Amérique de Gonneville, Verrazano et Roberval*, Paris: Éditions la Découverte.
Kelso, W.M. & Straube, B. 2004, *Jamestown Rediscovery 1994–2004*, Richmond, Va: Association for the Preservation of Virginia Antiquities.
Knecht, R.J. 1996, *Un Prince de la Renaissance, François 1er et son royaume*, Paris: Fayard.
Morel, É. 1893, 'Jean-François de la Roque, seigneur de Roberval, vice-roi du Canada', *Bull. de Géographie Historique et Descriptive*.
Niellon, F. & Moussette, M. 1985, *L'Habitation de Champlain*, Collection Patrimoines, Dossiers **58**, Québec: ministère de la Culture et des Communications.
Noël Hume, I. 2001, *Martin's Hundred*, Charlottesville, Va.: University Press of Virginia.
Pownall, T. 1768, *Scenographia Americana: or a Collection of Views of North America and the West Indies ... From Drawings Taken on the Spot by Several Officers of the British Army and Navy*, London: Thomas Jeffreys.
Rocolle, P. 1973, *2000 Ans de fortification française*, Paris: Charles-Lavauzelle.
Trudel, M. 1963, *Histoire de la Nouvelle-France*, **1**. *Les vaines tentatives, 1524–1603*, Montréal: Fides.
Bassanier, M. (ed.) 1853, *L'histoire notable de la Floride* [Laudonnière, R. G. 1586], Paris: P. Jannet Libraire.

UNPUBLISHED SOURCES

Allaire, B. 2007, 'Les voyages de Jacques Cartier et de Jehan François de La Roque de Roberval: pistes de recherche dans les sources françaises et sondages dans les archives parisiennes', Québec: CCNQ.
Auger, S. & Payette, S. 2008, 'Le site archéologique Cartier-Roberval à Québec: Cadre géologique et écologique, volet pédologique', Québec: CCNQ.
Bhiry, N. 2007, 'Reconstitution paléo-environnementale du site Cartier-Roberval (CeEu-4), Cap-Rouge, Québec', Québec: CCNQ.
Côté, R. 2008, 'Cap-Rouge: l'occupation de pied en cap. Morphologie historique du site Cartier-Roberval', Québec: CCNQ.
Duval, I. 2008, 'Caractérisations géochimique et pétrographique des matériaux lithiques du site archéologique Cartier-Roberval', Québec: CCNQ.
Filion, L. & Lafond Desrosiers, M. 2008, 'Le site archéologique Cartier-Roberval à Québec: Cadre géographique et écologique, volet dendroécologique', Québec: CCNQ.
Fiset, R. 2005, 'Archéologie des sites du campement de Wolfe (CfEs-22) et de la maison Vézina (CfEs-27), à Boischâtel', Association culturelle et artistique de la maison Vézina.
Garneau, M. 2008, 'Cadre géographique et écologique, volet floristique', Québec: CCNQ.
Gaumond, M. 2007, 'L'occupation du promontoire de Cap-Rouge: de Jacques Cartier et Roberval au "Transcontinental Railway system"', Québec: CCNQ.
Godbout, B., Filion, L. & Lavoie, M. 2008, 'Le site archéologique Cartier-Roberval à Québec: Cadre géographique et écologique, volet anthracologique', Québec: CCNQ.
Lavoie, M., Laframboise, C. & Robert, E.C. 2008, 'Histoire postglaciaire de la végétation dans la

région du site archéologique Cartier-Roberval: rapport d'activité final', Québec: CCNQ.

Samson, G. 2008, 'Dix-huit datations au carbone-14 pour le site archéologique Cartier-Roberval: tableau', Québec: CCNQ.

Samson, G., Fiset, R. & Chrétien, Y. 2007, 'Programme de recherche archéologique: projet archéologique Cartier-Roberval', Québec: CCNQ.

ABBREVIATIONS

ANQ	Archives nationales du Québec
APC	Public Archives of Canada
BAnQ-Q	Bibliothèque et Archives nationales du Québec à Québec
CCNQ	Commission de la capitale nationale du Québec

SUMMARY IN FRENCH, GERMAN, ITALIAN AND SPANISH

RÉSUMÉ

Charlesbourg-Royal et France-Roy (1541–43): la première tentative de colonisation française en Amérique

Le site de la première tentative française d'établir une colonie en Amérique par Jacques Cartier et le Sieur de Roberval en 1541–43 a été découvert sur le promontoire du Cap-Rouge à Québec en 2005. Un grand programme de recherche pluridisciplinaire a fait suite. Des constructions sur la falaise et de possibles traces de défense ont été identifiées comme faisant parties du fort d'en Haut décrit par Roberval. Certaines techniques de construction peuvent être comparées à celles du nord de la France. Des artefacts et des indices botaniques suggèrent que la zone était utilisée par des notables et suggèrent un contact avec les Iroquoïens du Saint-Laurent. Le site fut détruit par le feu.

ZUSAMMENFASSUNG

Charlesbourg-Royal und France-Roy (1541–43): Frankreichs erste Kolonisierungsversuche in Amerika

Der erste französische Versuch, in Amerika eine Niederlassung zu etablieren (Jacques Cartier und Sieur de Roberval, 1541–43), wurde 2005 auf der Landzunge Cap-Rouge bei Quebec gefunden. Eine größere multidisziplinarische Untersuchung folgte. Gebäude am Rande der Klippe und möglicherweise Spuren einer Verteidigungsanlage wurden, wie von Roberval beschrieben, als Teil des oberen Forts gefunden. Einige der Bautechniken haben Parallelen in Nordfrankreich. Funde und botanische Proben lassen auf Bewohner mit hohem Status schließen und weisen auch auf Kontakte mit den St Lawrence Iroquoianern hin. Die Anlage wurde durch Feuer zerstört.

RIASSUNTO

Charlesbourg-Royal e France-Roy (1541–43): i primi tentativi di colonizzazione francese in America

Nel 2005 fu scoperto nel promontorio di Cap Rouge, in Quebec, il sito del primo tentativo francese di fondare una colonia in America da parte di Jacques Cartier e Sieur de Roberval fra il 1541 e il 1543. Al rinvenimento seguì un importante progetto di ricerca multi-disciplinare. Gli edifici sulla sommità della rupe e alcune probabili tracce di strutture difensive furono identificati come parte della fortezza sommitale descritto da Roberval. Alcune tecniche costruttive trovano un parallelo nel nord della Francia. I ritrovamenti e i reperti botanici suggeriscono che l'area fosse usata da persone di alto rango e indicano contatti con gli Irochesi del San Lorenzo. Il sito fu distrutto da un incendio.

RESUMEN

Charlesbourg-Royal y France-Roy (1541–43): el primer intento francés de colonización en América

El lugar donde tuvo lugar el primer intento de colonización francés en América, por Jacques Cartier y Sieur de Roberval en 1541-43, fue descubierto en el 2005 en lo alto del Cap Rouge de Quebec. A tal descubrimiento siguió un gran programa multidisciplinar de investigación, por el que se localizaron edificios al borde del acantilado y posibles restos del sistema defensivo pertenecientes al fuerto alto descrito por Roberval. Algunas de las técnicas de construcción encontradas tienen paralelos en el norte de Francia. Los objetos materiales y restos botánicos sugieren que esta zona fue ocupada por gente de alta clase social y constatan contactos con los iroqueses del St Lawrence. El yacimiento fue destruido por un incendio.

Commission de la capitale nationale du Québec, Édifice Hector-Fabre, 525 boulevard René-Lévesque Est, Québec (Québec) Canada G1R 5S9 [richard.fiset@ccnq.org]; Commission de la capitale nationale du Québec, Édifice Hector-Fabre, 525 boulevard René-Lévesque Est, Québec (Québec), Canada G1R 5S9 [gsamson@ccnq.org]

Post-Medieval Archaeology **43/1** (2009), 71–86

The archaeological collection from the Cartier-Roberval site (1541–43): a remarkable testimony to French colonization efforts in the Americas

By HÉLÈNE CÔTÉ

SUMMARY: Excavations at the Cartier-Roberval site have discovered artefacts related to every-day activities and mineral exploration. They offer a picture of an extremely hierarchical society that transferred European social order and means of subsistence to North America. Preliminary study of the ceramics suggests the existence of a trade route with branches stretching from south-west France to Normandy, along which goods were conveyed to vessels outfitted for commercial, exploratory and colonizing missions.

INTRODUCTION

In 1541 François I commissioned Jean-François de La Rocque, Sieur de Roberval, to sail to North America to establish a colony and explore the riches of the new continent. In the same year, under Roberval's command, Jacques Cartier undertook his third voyage to North America. He left Saint-Malo on 23 May to found the first French colony in the Americas.

Until 2005 the settlement established by Cartier and Roberval on the heights of the headland later known as Cap Rouge seemed almost to belong to the realm of legend, for, despite numerous clues, researchers had failed to locate the site of its two forts.[1] The description of the Upper Fort given by Cartier and Roberval in their respective accounts,[2] and chance discoveries made in the 19th century, when construction work was carried out on the headland's upper plateau, had been insufficient to guide archaeologists.

In 2005, the Commission de la capitale nationale du Québec undertook an archaeological survey of land in Cap Rouge, on the outskirts of Québec City, as part of a programme to lay out pathways and lookouts in Cartier-Roberval Park. The archaeologist who carried out this task came across finds normally associated with early historic occupation.[3] After over 460 years of abandonment, the remains of the first French colony in North America had finally come to light.

Since numerous artefacts have now been recovered from the Upper Fort, it seems appropriate to present the archaeological collection assembled to date and present some hypotheses about the Cap Rouge colonists' lifestyle and means of subsistence. The following brief account will describe some of the activities of Cartier and Roberval before their departure, and introduce the archaeological collection recovered in the three excavation campaigns carried out so far. It will then look at specific aspects of the early assemblage — in particular those related to activities in the Upper Fort. It will close with a discussion of the origin of the objects, the social status of the fort's inhabitants, and the place of the Cap Rouge colony in the development of New France.

DOI: 10.1179/007942309X12457508843964

ANCHORS AWEIGH: EASY FOR SOME, HARDER FOR OTHERS

The navigators did not depart at the same time. Cartier was the first to set sail for North America. He left Saint-Malo on 23 May 1541 with five vessels carrying a cargo intended to provide for several hundred people for two years. Given the proximity of commercial centres like Rouen and the fact that trade routes passed through Saint-Malo, it seems likely that Cartier's ships would have held a broad range of consumer goods from many different places. It is known that in Rouen Cartier acquired munitions and provisions believed sufficient for two years. Since the city was then an international financial hub with links to the principal regions of Europe (Spain, Flanders, England, etc.) and overseas (Africa, America, Newfoundland, etc.), it would be expected that Cartier's cargo would have reflected this diversity of supply sources.[4] Some of his cargo may also have been obtained from the warehouses of Bordeaux, where merchants from Saint-Malo and Normandy often acquired goods;[5] the port was a particularly good source of merchandise from a wide range of production centres, since it was open both to the sea and to the largest hinterland in France.[6]

Our knowledge of the events that occurred between the departure of Cartier and that of Roberval is hazy. Roberval is known to have been in the process of acquiring his three vessels and completing work on the artillery when Cartier raised anchor in May 1541. For some reason, Roberval decided to stay in Europe. He sailed along the coast of Brittany and engaged in piracy off Finistère. These activities no doubt enabled him to appropriate all sorts of goods from diverse places. Finally, in the spring of 1542, he moored at La Rochelle to prepare his expedition to North America.[7]

The port of La Rochelle, unlike Bordeaux, does not have a large hinterland, but goods could easily have been shipped there from Nantes and Bordeaux.[8] It was also the adopted home of merchants from many different backgrounds (Italian, Portuguese, Spanish, Flemish, etc.), from whom Roberval could have acquired a wide variety of goods and food supplies.[9]

This brief look at Roberval's peregrinations and the commercial activity centred in Saint-Malo, La Rochelle and Bordeaux highlights the cosmopolitan nature of the transactions in these ports and suggests that their diversity should be reflected in the material culture from the Cartier-Roberval Upper Fort.

THE COLLECTION FROM THE CARTIER-ROBERVAL SITE

OVERVIEW OF THE EARLY HISTORIC ASSEMBLAGE

Charlesbourg-Royal, or France-Roy, as the colony perched on the heights of Cap Rouge was known, was active for such a short period that it might well have left few traces; all the remains could have easily been eradicated. However the archaeological work carried out since 2005 on the southern extremity of the headland[10] (Fig. 1) has shown that the colony left a long-lasting mark in the subsoil. The contexts associated with the early historic occupation have produced over 2,600 artefacts and 401 ecofacts (Table 1); most of them were found in 2007.

Of the different contexts associated with the occupation of the site,[11] those related to the occupation of the 16th-century fort provided the second largest assemblage — 26.5% of the total number of objects (Table 1). Metal accounts for the highest percentage of artefacts in the early historic collection, with 1,294 objects and fragments of objects (Table 2). The next largest category consists of 638 artefacts of materials other than metal, ceramic or glass — for example, wood or stone — and represents 23.81% of the total. Ceramics come third, with 624 sherds (23.28%), while glass is last, with 124 reference objects, accounting for 4.63% of all artefacts (Table 2).

This paper will not offer detailed descriptions of the material, but rather will deal with the salient features of the assemblage. The metal objects consist mainly of 770 wrought nails with flat, circular heads, along with some pieces of architectural hardware. A few items for personal use, such as jewellery and brass chest keys, have also been uncovered. With respect to pottery, there is quite a range of fabrics, which must have come from different production centres,[12] although these remain to be identified. The quantity of glass artefacts found is significant. Even though the number of beads and fragments of glass vessels and stained glass may seem relatively small, with only 124 objects, it must be remembered that at the time such material would have been difficult to transport and had special value as a marker of socio-economic status.

THE MAIN FUNCTIONS REPRESENTED IN THE COLLECTION

It is hardly surprising that the function best represented in the artefact collection is consumption in its various aspects.[13] Artefacts reflecting this function represent 83.21% of the total early assemblage

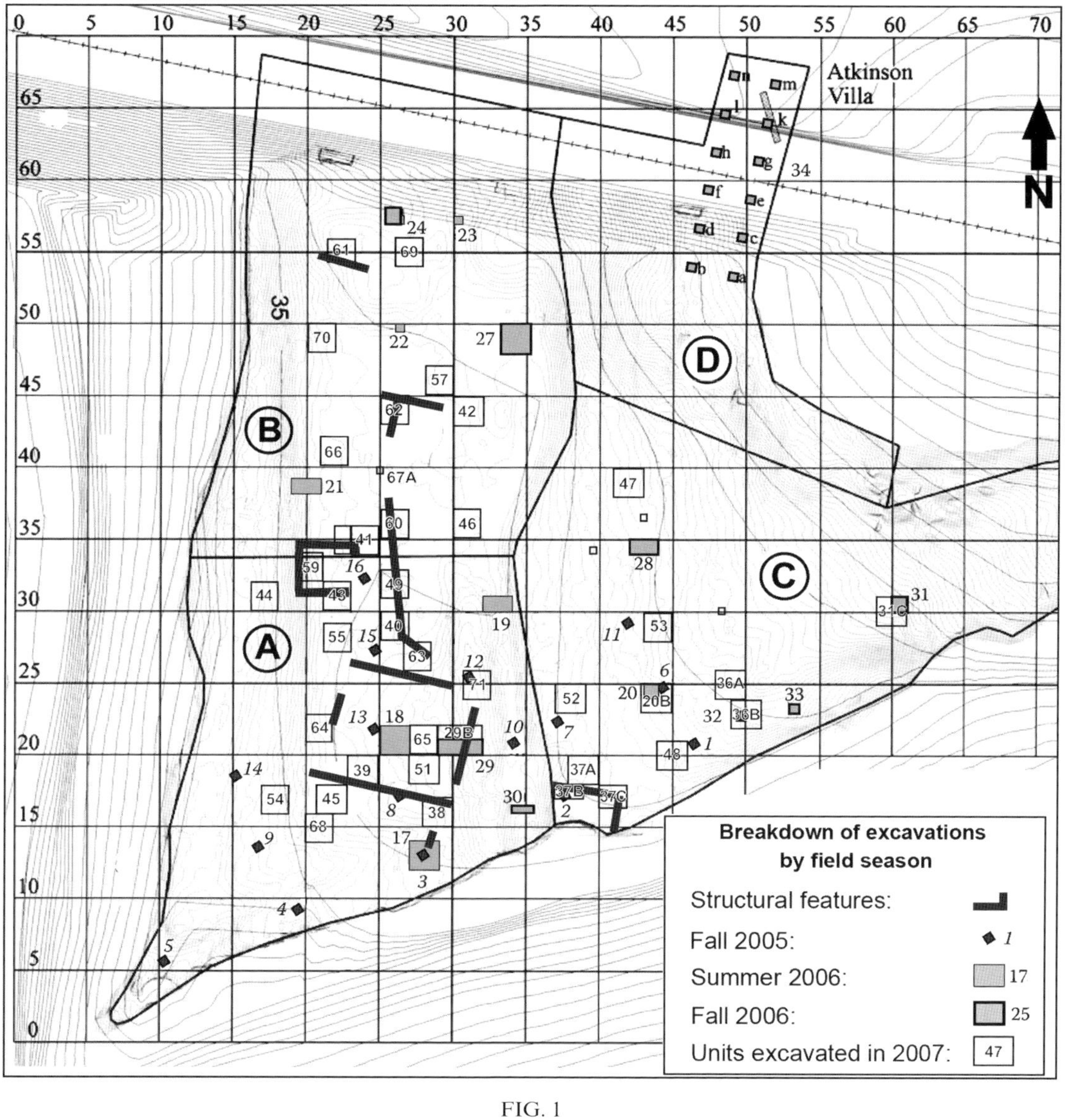

FIG. 1

Cartier-Roberval site (CeEu-4): location of excavation units south of the railway bridge (A. Forget, CCNQ).

TABLE 1

CeEu-4, Cartier-Roberval site: distribution of assemblages according to period of deposition.

Period	No. of artefacts	No. of ecofacts	Total	%
Amerindian presence	125	0	125	**1.07**
Early historic period (Cartier-Roberval)	2,680	401	3,081	**26.48**
Other (historic)	5,363	857	6,220	**53.47**
Undetermined	586	1,621	2,207	**18.98**
Total	**8,754**	**2,879**	**11,633**	**100**

TABLE 2

CeEu-4, Cartier-Roberval site: distribution of artefacts from the early historic occupation according to material.

Material	No. of artefacts	%
Metal	1,294	48.28
Other	638	23.81
Ceramic	624	23.28
Glass	124	4.63
Total	**2,680**	**100**

TABLE 3

CeEu-4, Cartier-Roberval site: distribution of artefacts from the early historic occupation according to functional category.

Function	No. of artefacts	%
Consumption	2,230	83.21
Variable function	267	9.96
Work on material	141	5.26
Acquisition of material	32	1.19
Sociotechnic and ideotechnic	10	0.38
Total artefacts	**2,680**	**100**

(Table 3). Objects that cannot be associated with any major function account for 9.96% of the collection; many have been burnt, including glass fragments rendered unrecognizable through exposure to extreme heat. Artefacts related to the working of materials make up 5.26% of the assemblage, many of them being related to the working of raw materials to produce items for consumption (Table 3). The number of artefacts belonging to other functions is very limited, with objects classified as having an acquisition function accounting for only 1.19% of the total and those with a sociotechnic or ideotechnic function[14] representing a mere 0.38% (Table 3).

The large number of consumption-related artefacts that could not be classified further (under 'undetermined consumption' in Table 4) is a consequence of their very fragmented state. The ceramics are a good example: vessels whose use could not be identified account for 34% of the total. Nevertheless, the collection is sufficiently rich to provide clues to the ways in which the inhabitants of the Upper Fort spent their days.

TABLE 4

CeEu-4, Cartier-Roberval site: distribution of artefacts according to various aspects of 'Consumption'.

Aspect	No. of artefacts	% total 'Consumption'
Undetermined consumption	947	42.47
Construction	916	41.08
Food	199	8.92
Other	108	4.85
Clothing	52	2.33
Medication	5	0.22
Beverages	3	0.13
Total	**2,230**	**100**

WORK AND DAYS, PART ONE: THE QUEST FOR GOLD AND DIAMONDS

The study of the artefacts associated with working raw materials was a priority in this case, since one of the colony's fundamental goals was to appropriate the natural resources that Amerindians had described to Cartier on his previous voyages. The navigator had returned from his second expedition with stones that he mistook for diamonds and gold. The question thus arises: to what degree is the quest for precious materials reflected in the archaeological collection found to date?

The excavations have brought to light a considerable number of artefacts and ecofacts testifying to various steps in the processing of precious materials. The most obvious items related to such activities are 38 crucible fragments (Fig. 2), most of which were found in excavation units in the southern third of the headland, near its point (Fig. 1).

These small, unglazed, coarse earthenware vessels have a dense buff fabric displaying tiny vesicles (air bubbles) and containing fine sand, tiny quartz crystals and a little very fine gravel. All the crucibles found so far have the same shape, with a generally cylindrical body and an average height of 35mm. The walls are straight but flare slightly at the rim and have a little external bulge just above the foot, probably to improve the stability of the flat base. The surface often shows traces of scraping and a few soot marks. The crucibles are not symmetrical.

The discovery of two cross-fitting fragments of a scorifier (a shallow vessel in which ore was first heated before being reheated with lead) offers an explanation for the many sulphur nodules found.

FIG. 2
Cartier-Roberval site (CeEu-4): coarse earthenware crucibles, average height 35mm (photograph, CCNQ).

Initial heating was intended to 'rough' the ore before it was amalgamated with lead; in this process sulphur was separated from the rest of the ore, becoming a waste product. The vessels used for this purpose can be identified by the glassy residue coating their surfaces; it results from the heating procedure. Since scorifiers did not need to have any particular shape or fabric composition, metallurgists often recycled vessels intended for some other use. This happened in the case of the Cap Rouge scorifier, which came from the bottom of a deep vessel whose fabric contained the kind of inclusions found in Breton pottery of the period; this possible origin will be discussed in more depth below. While the scorifier's fabric is not, properly speaking, refractory, it would probably have resisted heat well, given the high proportion of large quartz grains in it.

A lump of lead was also found with the crucibles, the scorifier and the sulphur. This would have been the residue left in the bottom of a crucible after metallurgical tests were carried out by heating prepared ore with lead to separate the desired elements from gangue.

On the basis of the remains brought to light so far, it seems certain that metallurgical tests were conducted on the Cartier-Roberval site. The location in which many crucibles were found along with the nodules of sulphur clearly indicates that these tests were carried out in one of the dwelling areas. The fact that such activities took place within the fort is not surprising when it is recalled that one of the reasons behind the attempt to establish a colony was the discovery and mining of precious metals.

WORK AND DAYS, PART TWO: COLONISTS GOING ABOUT THEIR DAILY BUSINESS

Like the artefacts described above, other finds provide evidence for activities that were related to acquiring and transforming materials, but in this case the goal was to tend to the needs of everyday life — for even avid metallurgists must eat and see to supplies.

The most notable example of a group of objects testifying to everyday activities comes in the form of fragments of paper, brass pins with wound wire heads and a thimble (Fig. 3). The instance is all the more remarkable since the paper into which the pins were inserted somehow survived the centuries without much damage. The fact that the pins were still in their original packaging indicates that they had not been used when the fort was abandoned and destroyed.

1 2

FIG. 3

Cartier-Roberval site (CeEu-4): 1. thimble; 2. paper of pins with wound-wire heads (photographs, S. Tremblay).

Looking for food was also part of daily activities. It may be imagined that the environment of the St Lawrence and Cap Rouge rivers supplied some of the food eaten by the fort's inhabitants. This idea is supported by the discovery of two hooks, as well as by a few pieces of lead which could have been used as gun shot, both for the outpost's defence and for hunting. While the fragmentation of the artefacts complicates any attempt to associate them with food preparation, it has been possible to identify sherds of ceramic cooking pots and a piece of cast iron from a kettle.

AT THE COLONISTS' TABLE

The fragmented condition of the ceramic assemblage has made it difficult to identify the vessel forms represented and thus to assign specific functions to them. However, it may be stated without much hesitation that most of the ceramics are associated with the main aspects of food consumption — intake, service and preservation. In a few cases it has been possible to link a vessel to one or other of these aspects of food use.

It is often hard to identify objects as being intended exclusively for food intake, at least until the 18th century, since people normally ate in a communal manner and few vessels were used specifically for serving or holding single portions. Those that did exist were usually made of pewter, a material rarely found on archaeological sites. The artefacts from the Upper Fort site nevertheless include a few items related to individual food intake. The most remarkable are the remains of the handles of at least three table knives belonging to the same set (Fig. 4), represented by the upper parts of wrought-iron handle frames surmounted by small spheres. Table knives, a luxury in the 16th century, were sold in sets of six. The handles were made of some noble material such as precious wood or ivory and set in a wrought-iron frame, which was coated with pewter before being plated with gold or silver.[15]

A few ceramic objects may also be associated with individual food intake; examples are a soup cup[16] and a porringer, both of which are made of glazed coarse earthenware, probably of Breton origin.[17] The most intriguing dining-related finds are the numerous sherds of green-tinted glassware, some specimens of which have very delicate rims. Could they belong to drinking glasses? This question cannot be answered unless more fragments of the same type come to light. However, another find offers support for the hypothesis that beverages — perhaps alcoholic ones — were enjoyed at mealtime by the colony's leaders. Evidence for this comes from the neck and mouth of a bottle or carafe of French blue-green glass (Fig. 4). Although the collection holds several other food-related objects, I will limit myself to mentioning two earthenware chafing dishes, probably made in Beauvaisis.

Study of the artefacts provides a good idea of what the table looked like when the colony's leaders sat down to eat, but it does not tell us what was simmering in the kettles, cooking pots and other heat-resistant vessels. Oddly enough, the excavations have revealed only 182 blanched animal bones, most of them from mammals. The explanation for this may lie in the location of the excavation units, which were generally inside structures (Fig. 1). If their interiors were kept clean, it is obvious that kitchen waste would have been removed from the buildings and perhaps even thrown over the cliff.

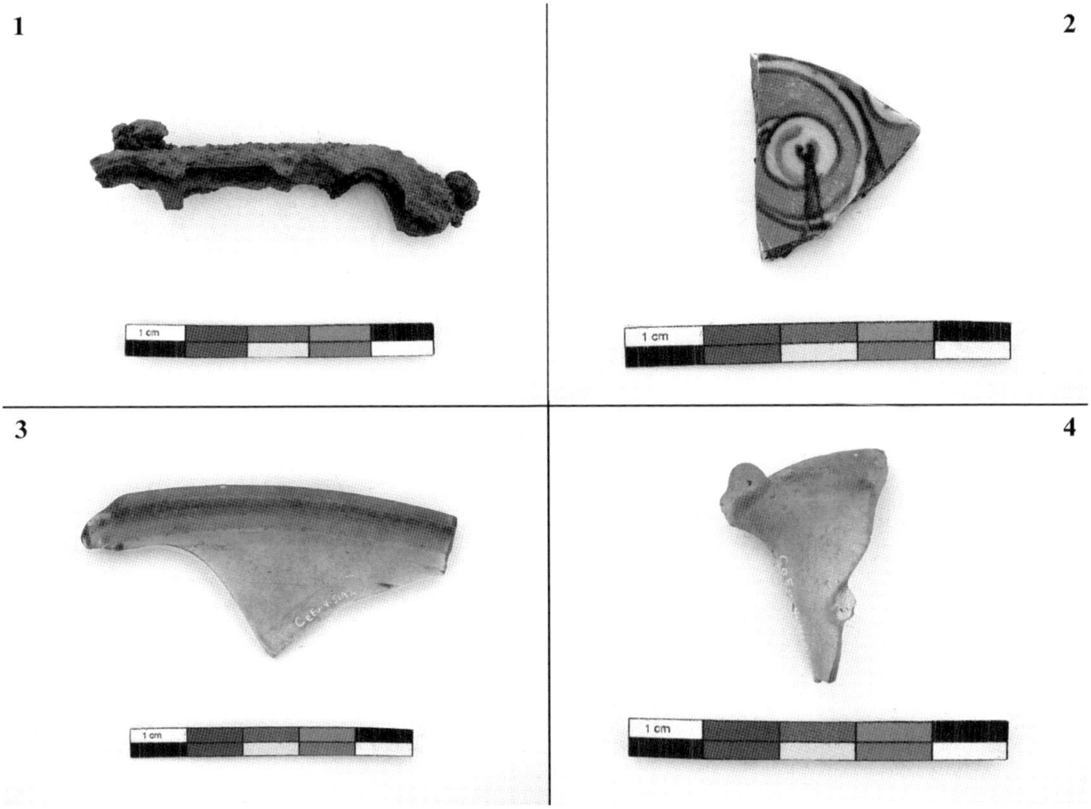

FIG. 4

Cartier-Roberval site (CeEu-4): 1. table knife handle; 2. sherd of a fluted bowl-like vessel (*saladier* or *coupe*) in Faenza maiolica; 3. rim sherd of a green glass *tazza*; 4. glass carafe neck (photographs, S. Tremblay; layout, H. Côté).

On the other hand, information about the plants eaten at the site is not lacking. The flotation of soil samples from 16th-century occupation contexts recovered a wide range of plant remains, including specimens of wheat, barley, grapes and olives, as well as corn kernels and sunflower seeds. From an archaeological viewpoint, it is difficult to know from what source the inhabitants of Cap Rouge derived their protein,[18] but there is no doubt that they depended greatly on European foods, despite a possible attempt to adapt to local resources (in the form of corn and sunflower seeds). Could this attempt have been prompted by contact with Amerindians who visited the vicinity? I will return to this question below.

OTHER ACTIVITIES

Artefacts associated with other aspects of the functional category of consumption add detail to our picture of daily life in the Cap Rouge colony, for people do not spend every hour working and eating. First, the colonists dressed before attending to the day's business. The site revealed a few objects related to this activity, including a brass clasp and the head of a pewter brooch, similar to examples brought to light in the excavation of the *Mary Rose*.[19] Another sartorial object is a coppery metal hoop that would have been inserted into a purse hem to reinforce it and make it more resistant to the knives of robbers.[20]

The inhabitants of the Upper Fort no doubt wore some of the jewellery in the collection. These include four brass rings. Three of them are of the same type, and each would have been set with a stone that has since disappeared (Fig. 5.2);[21] they are identical to a specimen uncovered in a 16th-century context from Southwark, London.[22] The fourth ring, which consists of a metal band with a thin, heart-shaped metal plate soldered to

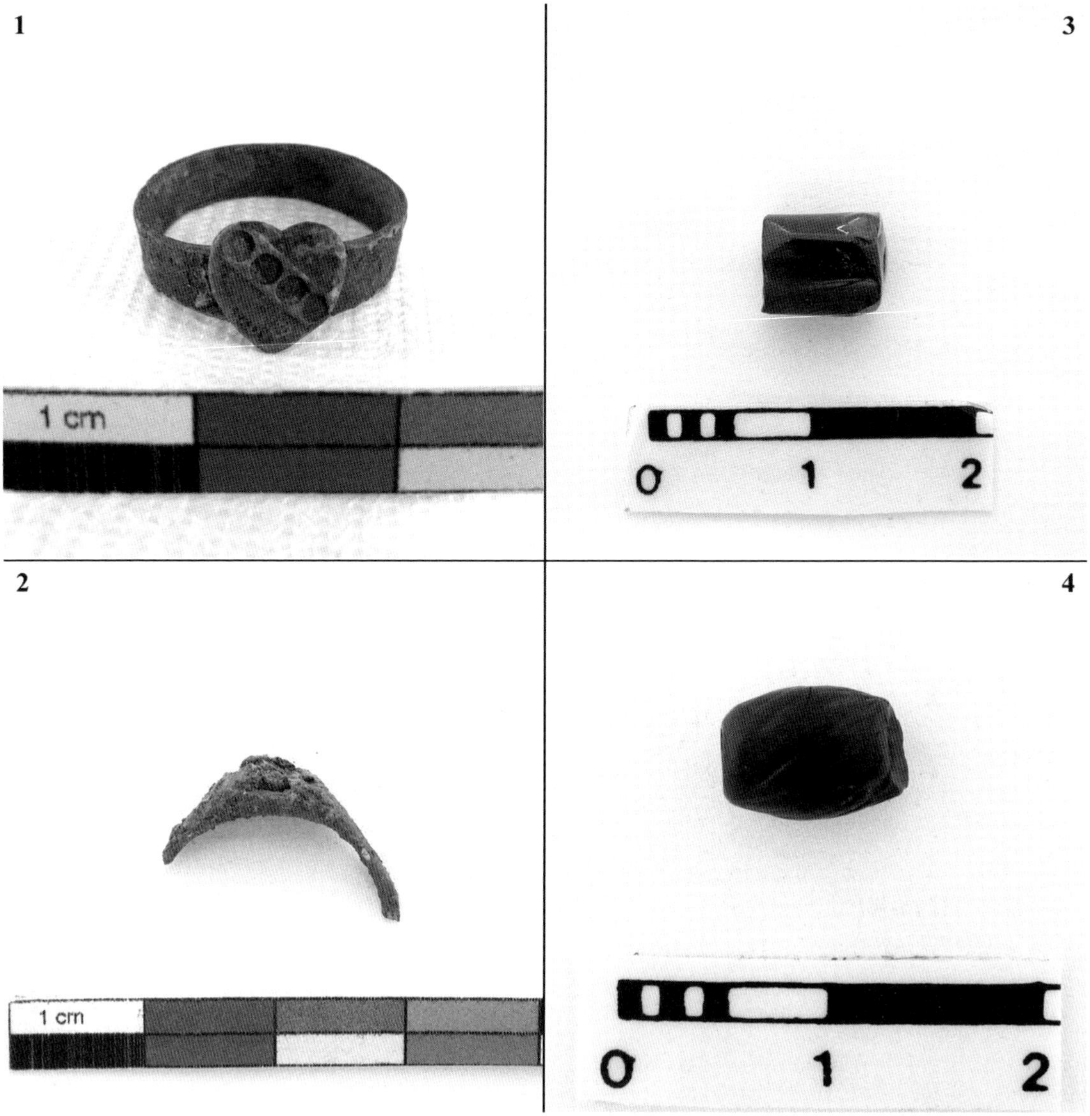

FIG. 5
Cartier-Roberval site (CeEu-4): 1. finger ring with heart-shaped plate; 2. one-piece finger ring; 3. facetted tubular bead; 4. jet bead (photograph, S. Tremblay; layout, H. Côté).

it (Fig. 5.1), has no equivalent that I am aware of. Beads can also add style to an outfit. The colonists may have worn some of the beads found, such as the five deep-blue tubular drawn-glass beads with four facets and bevelled corners (Fig. 5.3), or the several jet beads, three of which are of the melon type,[23] while another is ribbed and barrel-shaped (Fig. 5.4).[24]

Once dressed and adorned, the colonists were ready to start the day's work. For some of them, this meant trying to discover the new land's resources, while for others it meant going fishing or engaging in some similar activity that would make the colony's food supplies more reliable. For still others, the day's occupation involved tasks requiring complicated calculations. This is evidenced by the presence of two copper alloy jetons or tokens, one discovered in the south-west area of the site and the other at the northern end. Neither is in good condition, despite the conservation they have undergone, but on one of them it is possible to make out a motif similar to the cusped trefoil pattern typical of Nuremberg jetons.[25]

Finally, at day's end, when work was done and supper eaten, the fort's inhabitants enjoyed a little well-deserved leisure, during which they might play games, as is shown by an earthenware marble and a circular wooden game piece or token marked with an 'X'.

MULTI-PURPOSE OBJECTS?

Although the artefact collection associated with the 16th-century occupation of the Cartier-Roberval site is relatively large, considering the short lifetime of the occupation, most of the objects are so fragmented that they can be identified in only a very hypothetical manner. Therefore, assigning them an exact function is particularly difficult. In some cases, this problem is linked to the context in which an artefact was unearthed, for this factor can influence our understanding of a find. For example, the context may be revealing when one is trying to determine whether a ceramic vessel with a blackened surface was used for cooking food or for carrying out metallurgical tests. In the following section, I will look at a few enigmas of a similar nature.

Several fragments of a Montelupo maiolica syrup jar[26] and a north Italian maiolica pharmaceutical jar[27] were found in the south-west area of the site — the sector that yielded most of the crucibles and sulphur nodules (Fig. 1). Their context raises the possibility that the maiolica vessels were not actually used to hold pharmaceutical ingredients, since they may well have contained chemical substances intended for metallurgical work. The same sort of question arises in the case of a glass flask decorated with mould-blown vertical ribs, the remains of which were discovered in the sector bordering the northern end of the excavated area (Fig. 1). A flask of this type was identified in the barber-surgeon's chest on the *Mary Rose*, the English warship that sank off Portsmouth in 1545. Although this container could have held organic matter ready for examination, glass vessels were more commonly used by barber-surgeons to store corrosive or unstable products. Such ingredients were sometimes added to mixtures intended to cure diseases, but in the case of the Cartier-Roberval artefacts it is possible that the vessel's contents were acids used in various stages of the separation of metals. The question arises, 'should the two types of object be assigned a medicinal function, as is tempting at first sight, or rather a function related to the metallurgical testing carried out nearby?'. At present the question remains unanswerable.

The true functions of other artefacts are similarly puzzling. For example, several fragments of enamelled red glass testify to the presence of stained glass. Spontaneously one would tend to think that they came from an object with a sacred function; they might have decorated the windows of a chapel or belonged to a portable triptych illustrated with religious scenes. It is tempting, therefore, to hypothesize on the basis of these artefacts that the fort housed a place of worship. However, it should be borne in mind that the glass may have graced some small object such as an ornamental box, and thus have had far less cultural value.

In contrast, the discovery of tinted green glass fragments, probably from a *tazza* (or low-stemmed cup, Fig. 4.3), and pieces of a gadrooned bowl-like vessel (*coupe* or *saladier*) of Faenza maiolica (Fig. 4.2) seem at first simply to reflect the use of luxurious furnishings by members of the colony's ruling class, who seem to have lived in the south-west sector of the site (Fig. 1). However, these princely objects, intended more for show than for practical use, may well have taken the place of consecrated vessels: the *tazza* could have been used as a ciborium, while the Italian maiolica 'bowl' may have served as a chalice, especially since 16th-century Faenza goods were frequently decorated with religious scenes such as the death of St Sebastian.

It is thus difficult to determine the function of the large glass vessel and the gadrooned maiolica container. On the other hand, associating the enamelled red glass with the presence of religious-themed stained glass on the site is less equivocal, given the fact that it would almost have been obligatory for the fort to contain a place of worship. Despite uncertainties about the two vessels' functions, they and similar artefacts offer fairly strong evidence about the lifestyle of the colonists, and particularly the socioeconomic status of the occupants of the Upper Fort.

MEETING ANOTHER CULTURE

Nearly 100 sherds of Amerindian pottery were uncovered in contexts associated with the 16th-century occupation. It is almost certain that the vessels from which they came were inside the buildings when the settlement was destroyed, although a few fragments were probably deposited there later. It is not yet known why these artefacts, which are culturally related to the St Lawrence Iroquoians of the Terminal Late Woodland period (AD 1400–1600), were found in occupation levels associated with the 16th-century European colonists. One might hypothesize from these sherds that some form of commercial exchange existed between the two cultures; I will return to this below.

DISCUSSION

This brief presentation of the collection from the excavations of 2005–07 shows how informative the finds are. For example, the forms and fabrics of some ceramic types are quite unfamiliar to Québec archaeologists; these objects were manufactured and used at a very early date for Europeans in the Americas. Since the occupation of the site (1541–43) took place during the Renaissance, the collection reflects the transition between the Middle Ages and the modern era, a time of great cultural, political and scientific upheaval. The collection from this site presents researchers with very fragmented artefacts and with materials, forms and functions that straddle two eras.

The collection also opens a window onto a microcosm of human society, a small group of people who were prepared to take on the challenge of the unknown. Those who participated in this colonization attempt had to survive in a foreign, even hostile, environment, despite the fact that they did not have all the tools they needed at their disposal. Although the analysis of the collection is still in the early stages, the data obtained so far give some idea of the solutions tried by the occupants of the Upper Fort. As the future would show, these did not all turn out to be appropriate, but they no doubt enabled the colonists to acquire better knowledge of North America, and this must have contributed to the success of future French colonization efforts along the shores of the St Lawrence.

This brief look at the early historic assemblage from the site provides insights into some aspects of the lives of the inhabitants of the Upper Fort. However, it also raises numerous questions, which will be discussed below. The first has to do with the colonists' metallurgical research. This will be followed by a discussion of how the colony may have obtained its movable goods and foodstuffs. Finally, I will look at the social structure of the microcosm represented by the colony led by Cartier and Roberval.

THE CRUCIBLES — A QUESTION OF POLITICS OR INCOMPETENCE?

The sample of archaeological collections from the earliest North American colonial sites makes it clear that, from the time Europeans first tried to settle on the continent, a thirst for gold and other precious materials motivated metallurgical experiments similar to those conducted on the Cartier-Roberval site. The archaeological work carried out at La Isabela in the Dominican Republic provides ample proof of this. Founded by Christopher Columbus in 1493, the fortified settlement was occupied for only five years before being abandoned for Santo Domingo in 1496–97.[28] Excavations at La Isabela between 1989 and 1999 yielded many artefacts, including 100 triangular crucibles. The analysis of these objects led to the identification of graphite particles added to the fabric to improve its refractory properties, a technique associated with Bavarian pottery.[29] Similarly, excavations at Puerto Real, a Spanish settlement founded in 1503 on the Haitian side of the same Caribbean island, yielded a few crucibles in domestic contexts.[30]

Further north, investigations at James Fort in Virginia also brought to light artefacts related to metallurgy. When Jamestown was established in 1607, the ambitions of its founders were very much like those of the French at the Cartier-Roberval colony: the Virginia Company, which was in charge of this colonization effort, sought to convert the Aboriginals to Christianity,[31] discover a route to the Orient and seek precious materials, although the English settlement was also meant to export raw material or transform it into manufactured goods.[32] Documents relating to the Virginian establishment reveal that the Society of Mines Royal and the Society of Mineral and Battery Works supported the colonization effort because they were in dire need of new sources of zinc (this metal, which is indispensable in the production of brass, is virtually non-existent in England), and of new outlets for their copper reserves.[33] With time, these hopes of riches were disappointed, just as they were at the Cap Rouge colony.

Excavations at Jamestown recovered various pieces of distilling equipment used in metallurgy, such as fragments of a London-made coarse earthenware cucurbit (boiling vessel), a glass alembic (still)[34] and, above all, a number of triangular crucibles.[35] Chemical analyses determined that these objects were made with clay containing mullite or aluminium silicate. The most highly regarded crucibles of the time were produced in the Hesse region of Germany,[36] and their exceptional resistance to heat and thermal shock derived from their mullite-rich fabrics with relatively few other inclusions, such as iron oxide. The fact that the English colonizers purchased equipment of this quality shows how ambitious they were. The

Jamestown collection does not contain any circular crucibles similar to those found at Cap Rouge (Fig. 2).

Since the results of physico-chemical analyses carried out on the circular crucibles from the Cartier-Roberval site are not yet available, it is difficult to state anything about these containers with certainty, particularly with regard to their provenance. However, it may be stated fairly safely that these crucibles did not come from the same production centres as those found at La Isabela and Jamestown, given the differences in their formal characteristics. The Cap Rouge crucibles are distinguished by their circular shape and their buff fabric (Fig. 2), which is dense, but not to the point of making them practically indestructible, as Hessian ware is. Contemporary documents consulted to date have offered few clues to the objects' origins, for only Duhamel du Monceau, writing in the mid-18th century, mentions the existence of circular crucibles.[37] He also mentions the location of some production centres, including Picardy, the area around Paris and the Limousin and Auvergne regions.[38]

With these comments in mind — and even though the results of physico-chemical analyses of the Cartier-Roberval items remain to be seen — one can be reasonably sure that these crucibles did not come from German production centres such as Bavaria and Hesse, given their distinctive shape and fabric. Since the end of the Middle Ages German crucibles had been renowned throughout Europe for their remarkable technical qualities,[39] and the colonists who founded La Isabela and Jamestown placed great hope in the discovery of precious materials — which is why they acquired what was considered the very best equipment to achieve their ambitions. It must be asked why Cartier and Roberval, who shared the dreams of the Spanish and English colonists, did not judge it necessary to provide themselves with Hessian crucibles, with their superior reputation, for their metallurgical tests. Did they obtain their crucibles in France or elsewhere in Europe? Was their choice a result of negligence or incompetence on the part of the Cap Rouge colony's leaders, a lack of funds, favouritism towards certain suppliers, political pressure resulting from trade blockades, or some other factor that remains unknown? There are numerous possibilities, and only further research will narrow them down.

It seems clear that the Cap Rouge colonists included diamonds in their quest for precious materials, judging by the quartz crystals brought to light on the site, along with shale layers that had been split lengthwise to expose veins of quartz. At present it is uncertain whether the stones were worked by Europeans or by the Amerindian groups that visited the vicinity in the 16th century. However, associating these remains with the colonists is quite plausible, since the search for precious stones, like that for noble metals, was one of the important goals of the colonization enterprise.

The finds show quite clearly that tests for precious materials took place in the residence of one of the colony's leaders, and thus probably under his close supervision. This hypothesis took shape when a study of artefact distribution revealed that most of the crucible fragments were concentrated at the south-west end of the site (Fig. 1); this is where the sulphur nodes, lead residue and two scorifier sherds were also unearthed. The same general area yielded artefacts like jewellery and fragments of glass, fine vessels and Italian maiolica pharmaceutical jars, all of which indicate high socioeconomic status. Almost all the Italian maiolica has been found in this sector; only five fragments of this ware have appeared elsewhere. It appears, then, that metallurgical testing was carried out intensively in the place where some at least of the colony's ruling class resided.

ENSURING THE COLONY'S PROVISIONS

The difficulty of determining the provenance of the Cartier-Roberval crucibles illustrates the kind of puzzle encountered in studying the collection. Careful visual examination of the fabrics of the ceramics led to the identification of sixteen distinct types of coarse earthenware not encountered previously in Québec. A few specimens of known coarse earthenware types (Mérida, Biot and Beauvaisis) were also identified, as were some coarse stoneware varieties typical of production centres in the Loire region, Normandy and Germany.

Several of the unfamiliar types of coarse earthenware show characteristics usually associated with known pottery-producing regions but lack distinctive features that would identify them as coming from a specific production centre. An example is provided by objects whose hard white fabric with few inclusions visible to the naked eye is very much like the fabrics displayed by pottery from around Beauvais, north-east of Paris. Similarly, some sherds with a dark pink fabric and a translucent green glaze may have come from south-west France.

In other cases, identifying the provenance of the material is more problematic, although some headway has been made in this respect. For example, sherds of coarse earthenware with a fabric full of large fragments of quartz, sometimes reaching 1.88mm in diameter, bear a remarkable resemblance to vessels uncovered in excavations of fishing stations on the Atlantic shore of Newfoundland's Great Northern Peninsula (or Petit Nord Peninsula), some of which date to the 16th century. Chemical and petrological analyses of these vessels and comparison with Breton material established that the Newfoundland objects must have come from various small production centres in Brittany.[40] According to Pope, these centres would have produced wares for local consumption rather than for a wider market, given the multitude of little workshops scattered throughout Brittany.[41] Although the results of physico-chemical analyses of the heavily quartz-tempered Cap Rouge pottery are not yet available, it would make sense if they should turn out to be of Breton origin, considering that Jacques Cartier and some of his crew came from Brittany and his expedition set off from Saint-Malo.

Other ceramic types remain enigmatic. This is the case for a few objects displaying a dark orange fabric fired in a reducing atmosphere. Preliminary research points to a Dutch origin, but more evidence is needed before this can be confirmed.

A brief look at published literature, particularly from Britain, shows that English ship owners and those who outfitted Cartier and Roberval's vessels used a number of common supply points. For instance, the ceramics excavated on the *Mary Rose* contain several items produced in France. Both coarse earthenware and stoneware from Beauvaisis, Normandy, Brittany, the Loire Valley and Saintonge have been identified, as well as wares from Germany, the Low Countries and southern Europe (Portugal and Spain).[42] Likewise, it has been determined that the ceramics discovered in excavations at Southampton have French, German, Dutch and Iberian origins.[43]

The similarity between the ceramic assemblage from the Cartier-Roberval site and pottery collections from England highlights the importance of distribution centres like La Rochelle and Saint-Malo, which were visited by merchants and shipowners from both sides of the English Channel. It is not far-fetched to see the seeds of globalization in this interaction, especially when it is considered that the consumer goods in question were found not only on either side of the Channel, but also on either side of the Atlantic Ocean.

When we come to the question of the food contained in the ceramic vessels at Cap Rouge, the archaeological evidence demonstrates that some at least of the colonists (probably those of higher rank) were extremely dependent on provisions brought from Europe. This shows up clearly in the macroremains collection from the 2007 campaign; the plant remains include olive pits, grape seeds and European cereals. The presence of corn kernels and sunflower seeds in the site's archaeobotanical corpus raises the possibility that there was some form of exchange between the Europeans and Amerindians, and this idea is supported by the Amerindian sherds in the Iroquoian tradition discovered in layers associated with the 16th-century colonists. For it must be asked what the vessels held when they were brought into the buildings where they were found. It seems highly unlikely that these objects were acquired and kept by the colonists for their aesthetic value, and much more probable that the vessels were considered useful because of what they contained.

The question of the vessels' function may in part be answered by the results of the analyses of macroremains. For how could the corn kernels and sunflower seeds have entered the fort, if not because Aboriginals brought them there or gave them to the French? It is reasonable to think that Amerindian food would have been held in Iroquoian containers. This does not necessarily mean that the Amerindians had access to the interior of the fort, since the vessels and their contents could have been obtained by the French through an exchange of goods conducted outside the walls.

The possibility of this kind of exchange seems all the more likely in the light of the accounts of Cartier's third voyage and Roberval's wintering over at Cap Rouge, which record serious difficulties in food supplies. When his ships returned to France in September 1542, Roberval was obliged to impose food rationing in order to get through the winter at the colony. From then on, each 'mess' (a small group of people who shared a meal) had a daily limit of only two one-pound loaves of bread and half a pound of beef; there was salt pork for lunch and beef with beans for supper, while on fast days these meats were replaced by dried cod and porpoise.[44] Fortunately, the Amerindians could offer the colony's inhabitants some relief, if we are to go by the same accounts, which imply that relations between Roberval's people and the Aboriginals in the area had improved: 'About that time the Savages brought us great store of Aloses, which is a fish somewhat redde like a Salmon, to get knives and other small trifles for them.'[45] Although the Iroquoian vessels in the Terminal Late Woodland tradition and the remains of plants (corn and sunflower) used for food by the Aboriginals do not provide proof of trade activities between the Europeans and Amerindians, they offer clues that give us a clearer notion of the relationship between the two cultures, at least during the period that Roberval led the colony.

The evidence presented above strongly suggests that, at the start of the colonization project, the organizers adopted subsistence strategies based entirely on European foodstuffs. For the colony to survive, however, it was necessary to change these strategies very early on and make use of the possibilities offered by the new environment, with the help of the Aboriginal population.

MASTERS AND SERVANTS: THE SOCIAL HIERARCHY AT CAP ROUGE

A study of the archaeological collection from the Cartier-Roberval site casts light on an important feature which was probably central to the fabric of the colony: a social hierarchy that marked both its spatial organization (the layout of the buildings, the distinction between the two forts, etc.) and its organization of labour.

It has been seen that numerous artefacts indicating high socio-economic status were excavated. The fragments represent objects like gadrooned vessels (Fig. 4.2), syrup jars and a pharmaceutical jar in Italian maiolica, decorative table knives and an ornamental glass container (Fig. 4.3). The literature consulted leaves no doubt about the monetary and social value of these objects, particularly in the case of the Italian ceramics and the presumed *tazza*. For, although maiolica vessels could be used for dining, they were above all meant for show and, in the first half of the16th century, noble families and members of the wealthy bourgeoisie displayed them on dressers in banqueting halls.[46] Documentary evidence makes it clear that great value was attached to this type of pottery in the early 16th century. Great Italian families were often patrons of maiolica producers and commissioned complete dinner services from them. Elsewhere in Europe, nobles also acquired services decorated with their coats of arms. In France, for example, Constable Anne de Montmorency bought such items in 1535, and it is also known that an order was made for a service bearing the arms of Cardinal Antoine Duprat. Further examples exist in Bavaria (Albert V), Austria (Augsbourg, the Meuting family, 1520) and other Europe countries.[47]

The fragment of the glass container, which at this point in the research is believed to come from a *tazza* or low-footed cup (Fig. 4.3), is one of several glass artefacts. The discovery of a relatively large quantity of glass items on such an early site is of course exceptional, especially since they represent objects intended for table use, whether they actually held beverages (intake and service) or were displayed for show (like the Italian maiolica). Certain glass objects in museum collections have been clearly linked to social status; good examples are the Venetian glass goblets decorated with the arms of France and Brittany in the collection of the Musée national de la Renaissance in Écouen, France, and the similar goblet in the Metropolitan Museum of Art in New York. These vessels, which once all belonged to the same set, were probably commissioned by Anne of Brittany between 1498 and 1514.[48] The Cartier-Roberval site has also yielded a few fragments of Venetian-style dark blue glass with white trails, discovered in contexts associated with the 16th-century occupation of the fort. Among the many other artefacts indicative of high social status are rings, some of which are finely worked (Fig. 5.1–2), various clothing attachments, olive pits and grape seeds.

As mentioned previously, most of this household material was uncovered in excavation units in the south-west sector of the site (Fig. 1), and this suggests that the structural remains brought to light in the sector were related to a domestic building. However, the same space also yielded a few objects, in particular the stained glass fragments, which seem best explained as being connected to worship; it was also here that material for conducting metallurgical tests was found. With respect to the latter material, it seems very probable that tests for precious metals would have been carried out under the supervision of a member of the colony's governing class.

The stained glass fragments may be evidence that the building in question housed a consecrated place of worship. Since religious rites, unlike the metallurgical tests, did not require the supervision of a lay person, the reasons for having a chapel in the building are rather less obvious.

It is most likely that mineralogical and religious activities were carried out under the same roof because both were considered vital to the colony and thus had to take place where the elite lived and where they could oversee exactly what was happening. The presence of a place of worship seems all the more plausible when it is recalled that 17th- and 18th-century seigniories in isolated regions, far from any church, commonly had a chapel inside the manor house for the use of the *censitaires* (tenants). In addition, the leaders of the Cap Rouge enterprise may have wanted a chapel in their residence not only for practical reasons, but also as a symbol of their centralizing role in controlling activities that were essential to the colony's cohesion.

This leads us to the question of the establishment's other occupants — those on a lower rung of the social ladder. Where were they? The excavations seem to have uncovered only part of the colony's finer quarters along the cliff above the Cap Rouge River. The material discovered so far is more closely associated with the wealthy classes than with the common people. The absence of workaday objects is another indication of the hierarchical social organization that prevailed over this microcosm, for it is clear that the sector explored to date was occupied by a relatively uniform social group consisting of 'chemists', men of the cloth and other members of the colonial elite. Perhaps the settlement followed the pattern of cities with an upper and a lower town, each with its own role; the upper area would have sheltered the colony's leaders, the military, the clergy and specialized workers assigned to the search for precious metals, while the Lower Fort, where ships were anchored and goods were unloaded, would have housed immigrants of the lower classes. Appealing as this hypothesis might be, only further archaeological research can prove that it is right or wrong.

In short, the archaeological collection from the Cartier-Roberval site reflects a desire to transplant an ancient social order to an entirely new situation, in which a micro-society was taking shape and searching for points of reference that would enable it to put down roots. What followed would show that such an endeavour was doomed to fail.

CONCLUSION

The attempt to establish a colony under de Roberval between 1541 and 1543 ended in unmitigated failure, disappointing the aspirations of the settlement's leaders and the French king, François I. The venture was certainly a fiasco for the people involved, but in the long term it was surely not all in vain. The attempt can be seen in a more positive light when it is understood that the expeditions paved the way for 17th-century explorers, who were no doubt better prepared than their predecessors for what lay beyond the Gulf of St Lawrence. In the light of the earlier experience, the latter perhaps understood even before setting out that they would not be able to transplant European lifestyles directly to New France and that they would instead have to make changes adapted to North American conditions. Was the Cap Rouge colony a failure? It was indeed for its promoters but, for those who succeeded Cartier and Roberval, it was far from futile.

ACKNOWLEDGEMENTS

I wish to thank Fabienne Ravoire, a researcher at the INRAP and Peter Pope, Professor of Archaeology at Memorial University, for kindly sharing their expertise in 16th-century French ceramics with me. I am also grateful to Jean Rosen of the Université de Bourgogne for having examined the maiolica from the Cartier-Roberval site. My thanks also go to Marcos Martinón-Torres, lecturer at the Institute of Archaeology, University College London, for the interest he has shown in our collection and for giving us access to unpublished data.

NOTES

[1] According to the account of the third voyage, the Cap Rouge settlement comprised two distinct areas — the Upper Fort, with its two dwellings and various facilities, and the Lower Fort, which held buildings for lodging colonists and storing provisions.
[2] Bideaux 1986.
[3] Chrétien 2006.
[4] Allaire 2008a, 8.
[5] Allaire 2008b, 11.
[6] Allaire 2008b, 1.
[7] Allaire 2008c, 1.
[8] Allaire 2008c, 2–3.
[9] Allaire 2008c, 6.
[10] Fiset *et al.* 2008; Chrétien 2006.
[11] Although evidence of later occupation was uncovered in the course of the fieldwork, this article deals solely with the assemblage related to the 16th-century occupation of the headland.
[12] Sixteen types of ceramic not encountered previously in Québec were identified in the preliminary study of the collection.
[13] Consumption is used here in its larger sense. This functional category includes various aspects of consumption related to such things as food, clothing, ornaments, buildings and architecture.
[14] The sociotechnic and ideotechnic functions apply to artefacts used for trade, games, ritual, etc.
[15] Phillip Dunning, Parks Canada, pers. comm. (15 Dec. 2007).
[16] This object could have also been used as a butter pot.
[17] Peter Pope, Memorial University, pers. comm. (10 Apr. 2008).
[18] Nevertheless, animals including cows, sheep and pigs were reportedly brought on board by the crew for Cartier's third voyage (Bideaux 1986, 195).
[19] Gardiner & Allen 2005, fig. 2:78.
[20] Egan 2005, fig. 52.
[21] Since the three rings are for all practical purposes identical, they may have been intended as trade goods, but this is not the only possible explanation.
[22] Egan 2005, figs 39, 233.
[23] Turgeon 2001, 61: pl. 1, bb.
[24] Although it is almost certain that trade goods were brought on the 1541 voyage, the number of glass and jet beads discovered so far is too limited to justify

identifying them with trading activities at the Upper Fort.

[25] Nuremberg jetons were used to make calculations on counting boards. They were very common in the 16th century.

[26] Pharmaceutical jar with a spout.

[27] Jean Rosen, Université de Bourgogne, pers. comm. (9 Apr. 2008).

[28] <http://www.flmnh.ufl.edu/histarch/Isabela.htm> [accessed 12 Mar. 2008].

[29] Martinón-Torres 2008.

[30] McEwan 1995, 217.

[31] In the case of the Cap Rouge colony, invoking religious motives for undertaking the project was not exactly truthful.

[32] Kelso 2006, 1–2.

[33] Martinón-Torres & Rehren forthcoming, 1.

[34] Kelso & Straube 2004, figs 135–6.

[35] Kelso & Straube 2004, fig. 137; Kelso 2006, 182.

[36] Martinón-Torres & Rehren forthcoming, 4.

[37] Du Monceau 1777, 345, pl. 1.

[38] Du Monceau 1777, 342–7.

[39] Martinón-Torres & Rehren forthcoming, 4.

[40] Pope 2008, 49–51.

[41] Peter Pope, Memorial University, pers. comm. (10 Apr. 2008).

[42] Brown & Thomson 2005, 467–74.

[43] Platt & Coleman-Smith 1975, 149–79.

[44] Bideaux 1986, 208.

[45] Cook 1993, 110.

[46] Cassan & Vendé-Lobert 2002, 3.

[47] Cassan & Vendé-Lobert 2002, 4.

[48] <http://www.musee-renaissance.fr/homes/home_id20463_u1l2.htm> [accessed 3 Sept. 2007].

BIBLIOGRAPHY

PUBLISHED SOURCES

Bideaux, M. 1986, *Jacques Cartier: relations*, Montréal: Presses de l'Université de Montréal.

Brown, D.H. & Thomson, R. 2005, 'Pottery vessels', in Gardiner & Allen 2005, 462–78.

Cook, R. (ed.) 1993, *The Voyages of Jacques Cartier*, Toronto: University Press.

Deagan, K. 1995, *Puerto Real: the Archaeology of a Sixteenth-Century Spanish Town in Hispaniola*, Gainesville: University Press of Florida.

Du Monceau, D. 1777, *Descriptions des arts et métiers, faites ou approuvées par Messieurs de l'Académie royale des sciences de Paris*, **8**.

Egan, G. 2005, *Material Culture in London in an Age of Transition: Tudor and Stuart Period Finds* c. *1450*–c. *1700 from Excavations at Riverside Sites in Southwark*, MoLAS Monogr. **19**.

Gardiner, J. & Allen, M.J. (eds) 2005, *Before the Mast: Life and Death Aboard the Mary Rose*, Portsmouth: Mary Rose Trust.

Kelso, W.M. 2006, *Jamestown: the Buried Truth*, Charlottesville: University of Virginia Press.

Kelso, W.M. & Straube, B. 2004, *Jamestown Rediscovery*, Richmond, Va.: Association for the Preservation of Virginia Antiquities.

McEwan, B.G. 1995, 'Spanish precedents and domestic life at Puerto Real: the archaeology of two Spanish homesites', in Deagan 1995, 197–229.

Platt, C. & Coleman-Smith, R. 1975, *Excavations in Medieval Southampton 1953–1969*, **2** *The Finds*, Leicester: University Press.

Pope, P.E. 2008, 'The archaeology of France's migratory fishery on Newfoundland's Petit Nord', in Roy & Côté 2008, 38–54.

Roy, C. & Côté, H. (eds) 2008, *Rêves d'Amériques: Regard sur l'archéologie de la Nouvelle-France — Dreams of the Americas: Overview of New France Archaeology*, Archéologiques, hors série **2**, Québec: AAQ.

Turgeon, L. 2001, 'French beads in France and northeastern North America during the sixteenth century', *Hist. Archaeol.* **35**:4, 58–82.

UNPUBLISHED SOURCES

Allaire, B. 2008a, 'La logique normande: Recherches exploratoires sur l'expédition de J-F de La Rocque de Roberval aux Archives départementales de Seine Maritime à Rouen', Québec: CCNQ.

Allaire, B. 2008b, 'L'arrière-pays aquitain: Recherches exploratoires sur l'expédition de J-F de La Rocque de Roberval aux Archives départementales de Gironde et municipales de Bordeaux', Québec: CCNQ.

Allaire, B. 2008c, 'Le refuge rochelais: Recherches exploratoires sur l'expédition de J-F de La Rocque de Roberval aux Archives départementales de Charente-Maritime à La Rochelle', Québec: CCNQ.

Cassan, M. & Vendé-Lobert, G. 2002, 'La majolique italienne', Dossier pédagogique, Limoges: Musée national Adrien Dubouche, service culturel.

Chrétien, Y. *et al.* 2006, 'Inventaire archéologique au Parc Cartier-Roberval à Cap-Rouge (CeEu-4), automne 2005', Québec: MCCQ.

Fiset, R., Samson, G. & Chrétien, Y. 2008, 'Chantier archéologique Cartier-Roberval. Interventions 2006. Promontoire du cap Rouge (CeEu-4), Québec, rapport archéologique', Québec: CCNQ.

Martinon-Torres, M. 2008, 'Great Ambition, Little Profit: European Metallurgy in Early Colonial America', Québec: Journée d'étude (11 mai) du Groupe de recherche en Archéométrie, CÉLAT, conference paper.

Martinón-Torres, M. & Rehren, T. forthcoming, 'Trials and Errors in Search of Mineral Wealth:

Metallurgical Experiments in Early Colonial Jamestown', *J. Amer. Sci. Instrument Enterprise.*

ABBREVIATIONS

AAQ	Association des archéologues du Québec
CCNQ	Commission de la capitale nationale du Québec
CÉLAT	Centre interuniversitaire de recherche sur les lettres, les arts et les traditions
INRAP	Institut national de recherches archéologiques préventives
MCCQ	Ministère de la Culture et des Communications du Québec
MoLAS	Museum of London Archaeology Service

SUMMARY IN FRENCH, GERMAN, ITALIAN AND SPANISH

RÉSUMÉ

La collection archéologique du site Cartier-Roberval (1541–44) : témoignage unique d'un projet colonial français en Amérique

Les fouilles sur le site Cartier-Roberval ont permis la mise au jour des artefacts liés aux activités quotidiennes et à l'exploration minérale. Elles offrent une image d'une société extrêmement hiérarchisée qui a transféré l'ordre social et les moyens de subsistance européens à l'Amérique du nord. Les études préliminaires des céramiques suggèrent l'existence d'une route commerciale avec des branches s'étirant du sud-ouest de la France à la Normandie, à partir desquels les marchandises étaient transportées par bateaux équipés pour des missions commerciales, exploratrices et colonisatrices.

ZUSAMMENFASSUNG

Die archäologischen Funde der Cartier-Roberval (1541–43) Grabung: ein bemerkenswertes Zeugnis französischer Kolonisationsbemühungen in den Amerikas

Ausgrabungen an der Cartier-Roberval-Fundstelle brachten Gegenstände des täglichen Gebrauchs und der Mineralförderung zutage. Sie vermitteln das Bild einer extrem hierarchischen Gesellschaft, wie sie die europäische Gesellschaftsordnung und deren Mittel der Beschaffung des Lebensunterhalts nach Nordamerika exportiert hatte. Erste Ergebnisse der Keramikstudien weisen auf eine Handelsstraße mit Niederlassungen von Südwestfrankreich bis in die Normandie hin, deren Güter auf Schiffe verladen wurden, die für kommerzielle, Erkundungs- und Kolonisationsmissionen ausgestattet waren.

RIASSUNTO

La collezione archeologica del sito di Cartier-Roberval (1541–43): una testimonianza unica degli sforzi di colonizzazione francese nelle Americhe

Gli scavi nel sito di Cartier-Roberval hanno portato alla luce manufatti correlati alle attività quotidiane e all'esplorazione mineraria. Questi ritrovamenti offrono l'immagine di una società estremamente gerarchizzata, che trasferì l'ordine sociale e i modelli di sussistenza europei in nord America. Lo studio preliminare dei reperti ceramici suggerisce l'esistenza di una rotta commerciale con diramazioni che si protendevano dal sud-ovest della Francia fino alla Normandia, e lungo le quali le merci erano trasportate su imbarcazioni equipaggiate per scopi commerciali, di esplorazione e per missioni di colonizzazione.

RESUMEN

La colección arqueológica del yacimiento Cartier-Roberval (1541–43): un importante testimonio de los esfuerzos colonizadores franceses en las Américas

Las excavaciones en el yacimiento Cartier-Roberval han descubierto objetos relacionados con las actividades de la vida cotidiana y exploración mineral. La imagen que dichos objetos nos ofrecen es de una sociedad extremadamente jerarquizada que transfirió el orden social europeo y sus medios de subsistencia a Norte América. El estudio preliminar de la cerámica apunta a la existencia de una ruta comercial con varias ramas que abarcaban desde el suroeste francés a Normandía, por medio de las cuales se surtían de mercancías las naves destinadas al comercio, exploración y colonización.

Commission de la capitale nationale du Québec, Édifice Hector-Fabre, 525 boulevard René-Lévesque Est, Québec (Québec), Canada G1R 5S9 [helene-cote@ccnq.org]

Post-Medieval Archaeology **43/1** (2009), 87–105

From myth to reality: archaeobotany at the Cartier-Roberval Upper Fort site

By JULIE-ANNE BOUCHARD-PERRON *and* ALLISON BAIN

SUMMARY: The first official attempt at settlement in the St Lawrence Valley is recounted in a number of historical documents. These accounts were aimed at justifying the colonization project of Jacques Cartier and Sieur de Roberval in Canada; they provide little information on many aspects of the colonists' daily life. The recent discovery of the site where these two explorers settled in 1541–43 and the archaeological excavations carried out there provide an excellent opportunity to re-examine their colonization project. It is from that perspective that this paper presents some of the results of an archaeobotanical analysis conducted at the site.

INTRODUCTION

On 23 May 1541, five ships set sail from Saint-Malo, France, under the command of Jacques Cartier. They carried mariners, military men, craftsmen, gentlemen and prisoners who had only their native land and the promise of new horizons in common. Their venture would last just one year, after which they were joined and subsequently replaced by new crew members under the command of Sieur de Roberval. While the new recruits had similar aspirations to those of the men who had sailed with Cartier, they did not stay any longer than the previous group of colonists, but left the New World and the first official French settlement in North America in late 1543. This first very brief colonization effort inspired many writings beginning in the 19th century, and rapidly became the source of a genuine myth for Quebecers.[1] As underlined by three of the papers in this volume, the discovery of the Cartier-Roberval Upper Fort site provides a unique opportunity to put this colonial myth into perspective. Archaeobotanical data collected at the site in the summer of 2007 suggest that the activities of and choices made by these explorers during their time in Québec reflect their perception of their experience in their new natural and social environments. Researchers were able to achieve this degree of interpretation through the use of rigorous methodology and a thorough understanding of the processes affecting the representativeness of plant assemblages following their formation.

METHODOLOGY

Owing to the unique character of the Cartier-Roberval Upper Fort site, a series of tests were conducted in 2006 for the purpose of developing a suitable archaeobotanical strategy for the fieldwork and collecting a maximum of data. Despite the presence of a 19th-century occupation on the site, the test results led researchers to limit sampling in 2007 to layers associated with the 16th-century settlement, as they were the only layers to show traces of fire (Fig. 1) and, consequently, to potentially harbour carbonized plant remains. Samples for archaeobotanical analysis were collected in every 16th-century layer encountered with the expectation of obtaining a comprehensive picture of the distribution of plant remains on the site. For the sake of efficiency, archaeobotanical samples were taken differentially, based on the characteristics of the fire traces encountered during

DOI: 10.1179/007942309X12457508844008

the excavations and according to three strategies. The strategies and the samples obtained with them were assigned to three classes.

Class 1. The strategy and samples in this class are associated with layers containing multiple, marked signs of carbonization (abundance of charred wood, baked clay and fire-reddened elements). In such layers, all the sediment was collected for archaeobotanical analysis. Furthermore, operations,[2] or excavation units, where layers of this type were encountered were further divided for sampling into 1 × 1m quadrants (north-east, north-west, south-east, south-west) and by depth (0–10cm, 10–20cm, 20–30cm from the surface layer). Forty-five samples were taken in five excavation units (45, 51, 65, 68 and 70) according to the class 1 strategy. It is important to point out that the samples from unit 70 were not divided according to depth as the 16th-century layer was wrongly assumed to be too shallow for depth-based sampling.

Class 2. The strategy and samples in this class are associated with 'intermediate' excavation units with layers containing fewer signs of carbonization (smaller quantities of charred wood, baked clay and fire-reddened elements). These units were divided in half along an east–west axis, and around 20 litres of soil were collected from each half (north and south) in every 10cm level. As only a fraction of the sediment was collected, average samples were taken across the surface of each level — i.e. soil was collected from various spots — so as to ensure the results were representative.[3] Two different excavation units were sampled using this strategy (64 and 71) for a total of 10 samples.

Class 3. The strategy and samples in this class are associated with excavation units where the 16th-century layers contained very few signs of carbonization (no or almost no charred elements). In these cases, around 20 litres of sediment were collected from each 16th-entury layer to test its archaeobotanical potential. Like the class 2 samples, the samples in class 3 were average samples. Twenty-four samples were collected from five different excavation units (55, 57, 61, 63 and 69) using the class 3 strategy.

All of the samples were processed using a mechanical flotation device with a 0.25mm mesh. The device was derived from the Modified York Flotation Machine and experimentally designed for the needs of the site.[4] The purpose of flotation is to separate organic matter — the light fraction[5] — from inorganic matter — the heavy fraction[6] — in samples so as to reduce the amount of material to be sorted. To facilitate observation, the light fraction is divided into smaller groups using geological sieves with mesh openings of 5.6mm, 1mm and 0.5mm. In the case of the Cartier-Roberval samples, the choice made with regard to the smallest mesh aperture to be used was motivated by budgetary and time constraints, as well as by the fact that the deposits contained large amounts of clay and roots; however, this decision may have affected the composition of assemblages by limiting the possibility of recovering seeds under 500μm in size.[7]

Once the flotation process was complete, the heavy fraction from samples was water-sieved in home-made screens with an aperture of around 2mm to facilitate the removal of artefacts and ecofacts that had not floated. The light fraction was viewed under a low-power binocular microscope to isolate the plant remains. The remains were identified by comparing them against the reference collection of Université Laval's environmental archaeology laboratory, which contains modern specimens. Published photographs, drawings and descriptions[8] were also used. The botanical nomenclature follows that of Marie-Victorin (2002).[9] At the same time as the plant remains were identified, they were quantified for statistical analysis purposes. They were counted using the total count method, where each complete specimen equals '1' and where fragments are grouped to form the equivalent of one complete specimen.[10] There was nevertheless an exception in the case of mustard (*Brassica* sp.) as remains of this taxa were present in very high quantities in the samples from excavation unit 70. It was therefore decided that the number of remains counted for mustard would be limited to 500, i.e. the point after which they would represent over 80% of the botanical remains in the sample. This was an effective sorting technique and did not affect the statistical analyses insofar as all the other species were present in much smaller quantities (fewer than 50 specimens per sample).

RESULTS

Using the methodology described above, over 2,000 plant remains were identified in the floated samples, while none were found in the screened heavy fractions. Most of the remains identified were seeds, but they also included several fragments of fruit and flowers that could not be assigned to specific taxons.[11] Generally speaking, the samples from three excavation units (51, 65 and 70) stood out in that they contained much higher densities and wider diversities of remains than the samples from the other units. Moreover, during the excavations, the 16th-century layers from these three units had been identified as having excellent potential, as they contained marked signs of carbonization and seemed to be *in situ*. As the analysis is still preliminary, it was decided that this paper would focus solely on the results obtained in these three excavation units. Due to the low numbers of remains contained in the other units, the results derived therein cannot yet be interpreted in a meaningful manner without more contextual information or comparative data.

The excavation units selected for discussion were located in two building areas identified by the archaeologists (Fig. 1). Units 51 and 65 abutted each other in a building area in the southern part of the site and were both sampled using the class 1 strategy. Tables 1 and 2 present the raw counts obtained for every sample in these units. Unit 70 was located in a building area further north and was also to be sampled following the

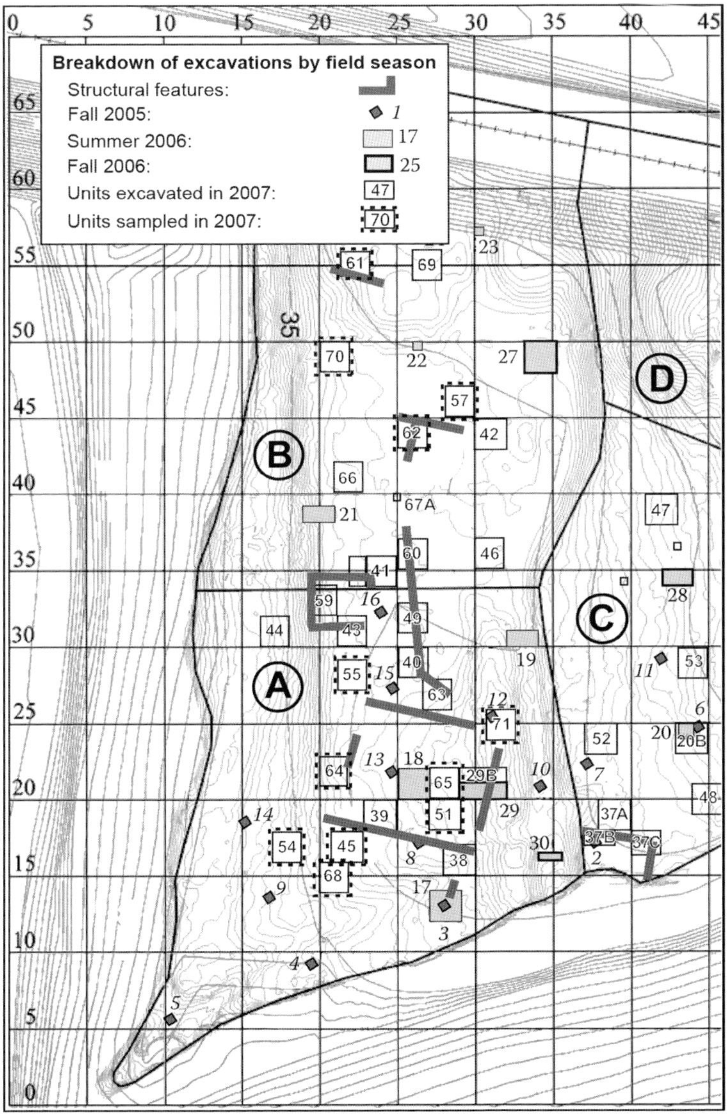

FIG. 1

Cartier-Roberval site (CeEu-4): location of excavated trenches, showing those sampled for archaeobotanical analysis in 2007 (scale: grid of 5 × 5m squares).

TABLE 1

Botanical species identified in lot [51A2]. Complete specimen counted as one; group of fragments forming the equivalent of a complete specimen counted as one.

	[51A2]											
	0–10cm				10–20cm				20–30cm			
	NE	NW	SE	SW	NE	NW	SE	SW	NE	NW	SE	SW
Quercus rubra L.~Red oak	1	2			1	1	1	1	1	2		
Quercus sp.~Oak		1										
Fagus grandifolia Ehrh. ~American beech						1						
Agrostemma Githago L. ~Common corncockle									1		1	
Euphorbia sp.~Spurge												
Crataegus sp.~Hawthorn							1					
cf. *Crataegus*~Hawthorn												
cf. *Sorbus*~Ash									1			
Prunus pensylvanica L.f. ~Small cherry								2				
Prunus cf. *virginiana* L. ~Small cherry		2										
Prunus sp.~Cherry												
Prunus sp.~Raspberry												
cf. *Fragaria*~Strawberry					1							
cf. *Pisum* sp.~Pea						1				1		
cf. *Lens* sp.~Lentil		1										
Vitis sp.~Grape	5	16	3	4	8	5	9	5	9	3	5	8
Olea europaea L. ~Cultivated olive					1	1						
Sambucus L.~Elder						1					1	
Asteraceae~Dandelion fam.						1						
Hordeum vulgare~Common hulled barley		8						7			3	1
Hordeum vulgare L. ~Common barley	2		3				3					
Hordeum sp.~Barley				1	4	2			1	3		
cf. *Hordeum*~Barley												
Triticum aestivum/ compactum~ Common/Clubed wheat		5								5		
Triticum sp.~Wheat			5	2	1	5	5	1	3		1	2
Zea mays L.~Maize							2					
cf. *Zea*~Maize												
Cereal	2	11	2	4	5	5	8	7	6	5	4	7
Small cereal		6				3	1			2		1
Unknown seed	4	5			4				5	1	2	
Unknown plant part		1	3	8	9		9	9		3		10
TOTAL	**14**	**57**	**13**	**11**	**25**	**26**	**30**	**23**	**27**	**22**	**17**	**19**

class 1 strategy. Nevertheless, as mentioned earlier, the samples were not divided according to depth. Table 3 presents the raw counts obtained for each quadrant in excavation unit 70 compared with the results obtained for each quadrant in units 51 and 65.

Tables 1–3 show that the samples contained as many indigenous as imported species (Table 3),

TABLE 2

Botanical species identified in lot [65B2]. Complete specimen counted as one; group of fragments forming the equivalent of a complete specimen counted as one.

	[65B2]											
	0–10cm				**10–20cm**				**20–30cm**			
	NE	NW	SE	SW	NE	NW	SE	SW	NE	NW	SE	SW
Quercus rubra L.~Red oak	2	2						1	0	2	1	1
Quercus sp.~Oak					1					1		
Fagus grandifolia Ehrh. ~American beech												
Agrostemma Githago L. ~Common corncockle												
Euphorbia sp.~Spurge												1
Crataegus sp.~Hawthorn					1							
cf. *Crataegus*~Hawthorn							1					
cf. *Sorbus*~Ash												
Prunus pensylvanica L.f. ~Small cherry							1					
Prunus cf. *virginiana* L. ~Small cherry												
Prunus sp.~Cherry							1					
Prunus sp.~Raspberry					1			1	1			
cf. *Fragaria*~Strawberry												
cf. *Pisum* sp.~Pea	1											
cf. *Lens* sp.~Lentil												
Vitis sp.~Grape	14	6	11	2	7	7	16	7	2	2	11	5
Olea europaea L. ~Cultivated olive												
Sambucus L.~Elder												
Asteraceae~Dandelion fam.												1
Hordeum vulgare~Common hulled barley												5
Hordeum vulgare L. ~Common barley			3					3	1			
Hordeum sp.~Barley	1						2					
cf. *Hordeum*~Barley						3					4	
Triticum aestivum/ compactum~ Common/Clubed wheat												
Triticum sp.~Wheat							1					1
Zea mays L.~Maize	1	1			1			1				
cf. *Zea*~Maize		1			1		1					
Cereal	2	3	2	1		1	5				5	6
Small cereal			1							1		
Unknown seed				2				1				2
Unknown plant part	2				1		3			1		
TOTAL	**21**	**13**	**17**	**5**	**12**	**11**	**28**	**14**	**4**	**6**	**21**	**22**

although imported species largely dominate the assemblages in terms of numbers. The general composition of plant remains for a given excavation unit and each of its quadrants is thus fairly similar, although the proportions for each species differ. Wheat, barley, grape[12] and red oak are the plants most commonly inventoried (Fig. 2). Generally speaking, almost all of the botanical

TABLE 3

Botanical species identified in each quadrant of lots [51A2], [65B2] and [70A6]. Complete specimen counted as one; group of fragments forming the equivalent of a complete specimen counted as one.

	[51A2]				[65B2]				[70A6]			
	NE	NW	SE	SW	NE	NW	SE	SW	NE	NW	SE	SW
Quercus rubra L. ~Red Oak	3	5	1	1	2	4	1	2				
Quercus sp.~Oak		1			1	1						
Fagus grandifolia Ehrh. ~American beech		1										
Chenopodium sp. ~Goosefoot										17		
Agrostemma Githago L. ~Common corncockle	1		1						1	1		
Euphorbia sp.~Spurge								1				
Brassica sp.~Mustard									>500	>500	>500	74
Crataegus sp. ~Hawthorn			1		1							
cf. *Crataegus*~Hawthorn							1					
cf. *Sorbus*~Ash	1											
Prunus pensylvanica L.f.~Small cherry				2			1					
Prunus cf. *virginiana* L. ~Small cherry		2								1		
Prunus sp.~Cherry							1					
Prunus sp.~Raspberry					2			1		1	2	
Fragaria sp. ~Strawberry	1											
cf. *Pisum* sp.~Pea		2			1							
cf. *Lens* sp.~Lentil		1										
Vitis sp.~Grape	22	24	17	17	23	15	38	14	5		4	
Olea europaea L. ~Cultivated olive	1	1									3	
Sambucus L.~Elder		1	1						1		1	
Asteraceae ~Dandelion fam.		1						1				
Hordeum vulgare ~Common hulled barley		8	3	8				5	1		9	
Hordeum vulgare L. ~Common barley	2		6		1		3	3	6	1		
Hordeum sp.~Barley	5	5		1	1		2					
cf. *Hordeum*~Barley						3	4					
Triticum aestivum /*compactum*~Common/ Clubed wheat		10							14	2	66	
Triticum sp.~Wheat	4	5	11	5			1	1	59	12		2
Zea mays L.~Maize			2		2	1		1	1			
cf. *Zea*~Maize					1	1	1					
Cereal	13	21	14	18	2	4	12	7	35	13	38	3
Small cereal		11	1	1		1	1		17	13	20	5
Unknown seed	13	6	2					5	1	2	24	25
Unknown plant part	9	4	12	27	3	1	3		2			2
TOTAL	**66**	**105**	**60**	**53**	**37**	**30**	**66**	**41**	**>641**	**>563**	**>667**	**109**

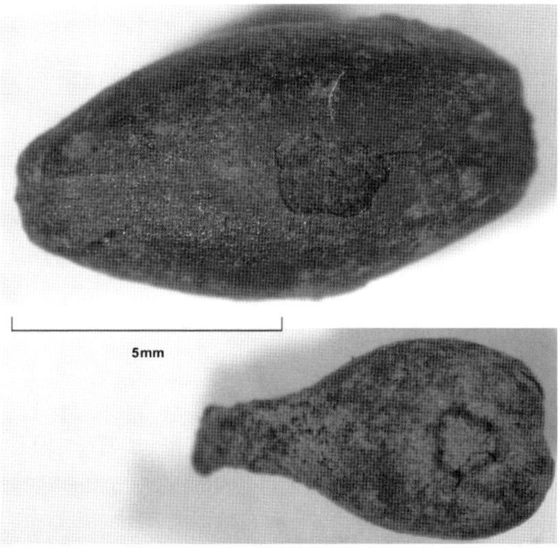

FIG. 2
Cartier-Roberval site (CeEu 4): charred covered-barley grain and grape seed (photograph, A. Allard).

remains contained in the samples were complete and displayed very little distortion.

The plant remains identified in excavation units 51, 65 and 70 can be divided into four groups according to their source (Table 3).[13] The first group is made up of remains of indigenous plants: red oak (*Quercus rubra* L.), strawberry (*Fragaria* sp.), ash (*Sorbus* sp.), cherry (*Prunus* cf. *virginiana* L. and *Prunus pensylvanica* L.f.), hawthorn (*Crataegus* sp.) and elder (*Sambucus* sp.). While plants from this group were found in all of the samples studied on the site, the density of each species was low. The second group consists of the remains of an American plant that required human intervention in order to grow at Québec latitudes, i.e. maize (*Zea mays* L.).[14] Very few remains of this plant were uncovered on the site (fewer than ten in all). As for the third group, it comprises the remains of European plants expressly imported by the colonists for their economic value: wheat (*Triticum aestivum/compactum*), barley (*Hordeum vulgare* L.), grape (*Vitis* sp.), olive (*Olea europaea* L.), cherry (*Prunus* sp.), pea (*Pisum* sp.), lentil (*Lens* sp.) and mustard (*Brassica* sp.). This group occurred in high densities in the various building areas. The fourth and last group of remains is associated with Old World plants that were probably introduced unintentionally: common corncockle (*Agrostemma githago* L.) and spurge (*Euphorbia* sp.). Indeed, there is no documentary evidence for any particular use of these plants and they were actually considered weeds. Only a small number of remains from these plants were found and they were in areas with concentrations of remains of economically important European plants.

FROM DEPOSITION TO EXCAVATION: CAUSES OF ALTERATION OF ASSEMBLAGES

Nearly half a millennium passed between the time when the site where Cartier and Roberval stayed was abandoned and the time when it was discovered. During that period, several processes are liable to have altered the archaeobotanical assemblages and skewed their representativeness. It is crucial that the effect of these taphonomic processes be taken into account in trying to recreate the environmental phenomena and human activities associated with the deposition of plant remains on the site.

After the plant remains were deposited in the 16th century, a number of phenomena, referred to as 'taphonomic processes' or post-depositional processes, may have altered the composition and quality of the archaeobotanical assemblages. Although further analysis is required to identify and assess the impact of these processes, it is possible that they did not significantly affect the excavation units discussed in this paper. They may have simply caused fragmentation and more or less random movement of some remains. If, on the other hand, post-depositional processes had a major impact on the units sampled, it would be reasonable to assume that no strong correlation would be observed between the content of samples from adjacent quadrants. Similarly, no strong correlation would be found between the content of samples collected from the same spot but at different depths. However, such correlations did exist between the samples studied, suggesting that the layers sampled were little affected by taphonomic processes. Moreover, this view is supported by the correspondence analysis[15] performed using the results obtained for samples from excavation units 51 and 65.[16] As shown in the correspondence analysis figure, there are no major differences between samples collected at varying depths in the same quadrant and between samples collected from nearby quadrants (Fig. 3).

A fire on a portion of the site burned the organic components of certain parts of plants, leaving a carbon skeleton not liable to decompose.[17] By preserving some plant remains, the fire therefore played a key role in the formation of the plant assemblages. However, the action of the fire distorted the remains in ways that vary with the

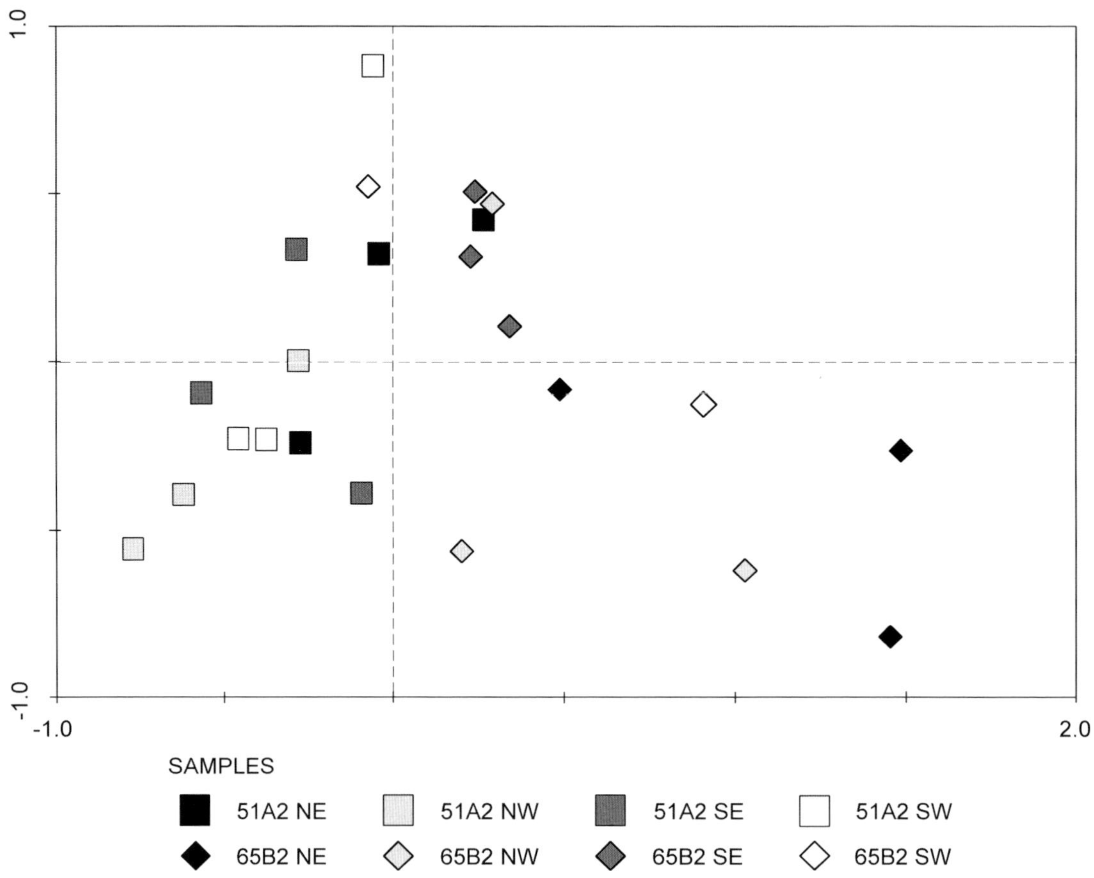

FIG. 3

Cartier-Roberval site (CeEu 4): correspondence analysis of samples from lots [51A2] and [65B2].

species and characteristics of the plants and their components, notably their density and morphology.[18] For example, the temperature and time required to char and break down a seed increases with the thickness of its outer seed coat. From that perspective, it is no surprise that cereals and legumes, which both have very thin outer coats, showed the highest rates of distortion. It can therefore be concluded that the assemblages studied represent only a fraction of the original assemblages. Numerous and varying factors influence the preservation of seeds by carbonization and, in most cases, their exact effects are not quantifiable. In order to account for the differential action of these factors, the criteria used to study assemblages are not directly related to plant characteristics liable to be affected by carbonization. For example, all plant remains will respond to fire in the same way, regardless of their geographic origin.

The physical conditions under which the fire occurred on the Cartier-Roberval site also influenced the preservation and general condition of the plant remains, which are discussed here in terms of distortion. For example, high moisture content can promote rapid carbonization of plant remains, but will cause greater distortion. Relatively little distortion was found in the 16th-century assemblages studied, suggesting that the fire occurred under fairly dry conditions or that the remains were not in direct contact with the fire. The former idea is supported by the absence of germinating cereal seeds, since seeds frequently germinate under somewhat wet conditions. Furthermore, distortion can indicate the average temperature and duration of a fire. Indeed, plant remains tend not to char and thus not to be preserved at temperatures below 250°C.[19] The higher the temperature above 250°C, the more likely the remains will become distorted and disintegrate. Margaritis and Jones[20] estimated that different plant parts can be preserved and identified after being subjected to a maximum temperature of 450°C. Also, the higher the temperature, the less time it will take for plant remains to char. Although the assemblages studied showed relatively little distortion, their distortion differed according to the area in which the assemblages were found. Generally speaking, more distortion was found in the remains from excavation unit 70 than in those from units 51 and 65, which suggests that the remains collected in unit 70 were probably exposed to higher average temperatures or were exposed to fire for a longer time. The discrepancy may be due to differences in the materials that fuelled the fire or in the building methods used in the two areas; the respective distances of the areas from the fire could also have played a role. Whatever the case, further testing is needed to validate this hypothesis.

Like taphonomic and preservation processes, the location of deposits also helps to understand archaeobotanical assemblages. However, even though all the samples analysed in this study were collected in two building areas dating to the 16th century,[21] the limits of the buildings in these areas were still uncertain in the summer of 2007. Nevertheless, the archaeobotanical contents of the class 1 samples shed light on the archaeological context of some of the excavation units (51, 65 and 70).[22] Indeed, edible taxa of European origin represent over 85% of all archaeobotanical remains in each sample from these units. This suggests intense human activity linked to food, and more specifically, to cooking, storage and consumption. Cooking and storage and some consumption may have occurred indoors, creating a higher potential for finding botanical remains around these locations. These observations suggest that excavation units 51, 65 and 70 were situated inside some of the 16th-century buildings. This hypothesis is further supported by the low rate of distortion and absence of germinating cereal seeds, which indicates that the remains were being maintained under dry conditions at the time when the fire occurred.

In short, to a certain extent, post-depositional and preservation processes affected the representativeness of the samples studied. In most cases, however, they do not seem to have had a marked impact. Sample representativeness may also have been affected by the context of sampling areas, which, as demonstrated here, seem to have been located inside buildings.

INDIGENOUS PLANTS . . . AND THE LOCAL ENVIRONMENT

After taking into account the probable effect of the taphonomy, preservation and location of deposits, one group of plant remains seemed to stand apart, namely the indigenous plants (Table 4). As previously indicated, this group contains the remains of nearly a dozen species found in small numbers in deposits throughout the site (both within and outside building areas). The plants to which the remains belong also have similar ecological preferences,[23] and therefore can occur in the same physical environment. As well, a number of phytosociological data suggest that these native species tend to grow in association with each other.[24] Therefore, this group of remains likely share a common geographical origin. It

TABLE 4

Classification of the identified species into groups based on geographical origin and edibility.

Local plants		Imported plants	
Edible	**Inedible**	**Edible**	**Inedible**
Hawthorn berry	Red oak (acorn cup)	Wheat	Common corncockle
Strawberry		Lentil	Spurge
Maize (cultivated)		Mustard	
Cherry		Olive	
Ash (fruit)		Barley	
Elder (fruit)		Pea	
		Prune	
		Grape	

is interesting to note that these species all grow under the site's current environmental conditions, suggesting that the local plants found in the assemblages come from the site's immediate surroundings.

The fact that these native plants come from the site's immediate environment does not explain why they were found within building areas or inside buildings *per se*. It does not seem plausible that such distribution was actually caused by environmental processes; rather, it is more likely attributable to human activities on the site. Such activities could be related to the fact that several of the plants identified (strawberry, ash, chokecherry, hawthorn, pin cherry and elder) produce edible fruit. Indeed, seeds of these species have been found in abundance (several thousand seeds per litre) in a number of privies in the Québec City area dating from the 17th century onward.[25] On the other hand, an abundance of seeds is generally deposited where local fruits are eaten, stored, thrown away or used.[26] For example, a single strawberry can contain hundreds of seeds. However, the assemblages studied on the Cartier-Roberval site contained only a small quantity of local plant remains. Furthermore, if the indigenous plant remains found on the site were the result of refuse accumulation, they would have been concentrated on the surface of the occupation layer. But that was not the case, as the remains of indigenous plants were present in all the samples taken in excavation units 51 and 65, regardless of depth. The relatively small number and the distribution of remains of local edible plants present in the assemblages therefore suggest that these plants were introduced accidentally into the building area where units 51 and 65 were located. The same goes for the oak remains, which comprise only the cup-shaped cupules, or the top, non-edible part of the acorn (Fig. 4), for which there is no documented use.

Although plant remains from the site's immediate surroundings could have been accidentally deposited inside building areas as a result of any number of activities, the size of the oak acorn cups, which makes them easy to spot, coupled with the presence of the plant remains throughout the 0.30m fire layer, limit the ways in which these remains could have been incidentally introduced. These elements suggest that the native plant remains may have been brought into the buildings with construction material. This hypothesis is consistent with the archaeologists' suggestion that local clay was used to build certain walls in the building areas.[27] Consequently, local plant remains were seemingly introduced into the buildings by chance, being mixed in with the clay used in construction;[28] at least, the fragmentation and number of acorn cups would seem to indicate this. And this would also explain why the native plant group is the only one to include partially charred remains: clay would have limited the effects of carbonization.

Analysis of the local plant remains collected from the sampled excavation units sheds new light on a number of aspects of the Cartier-Roberval settlement. First, there is no indication that these plants were knowingly used by the French colonists. Second, they probably reflect the site's immediate environment, which bears several similarities to the current physical environment and vegetation. Third, the remains appear to have been carried into the buildings in the local clay used for walls.

NATIVE CONTRIBUTIONS?

In addition to the indigenous plants previously mentioned, another American plant was identified on the site: maize (*Zea mays* L.) (Fig. 5). Maize remains differed from the other plant remains, though, in regard to their distribution within the building areas and to their density, which was very low. Maize was introduced to the Québec City area by Amerindians:[29] it cannot grow in Québec without human intervention. Also, its ecological preferences differ so sharply from those of the species in the local-plant group discussed above that it is not very likely that maize could have been cultivated in the site's immediate environment. Thus, the maize remains were in all likelihood deposited as a result of other activities. And even though all of the maize remains were found inside buildings, their presence is hard to explain without further analyses. With kernels being the only part of the ear found on the site, the maize could just as well have been introduced accidentally as be the result of the inhabitants' diet. However, the presence of maize is nevertheless significant in that it testifies to trade or at least contact between the settlers and local Amerindian populations.

EUROPEAN PLANTS ON THE MENU?

In addition to maize, food remains of European plants were found within the building areas sampled. However, they were present in larger numbers than all of the other plant types in the archaeobotanical assemblages. In fact, they dominated all of the assemblages and represented over 85% of the identified remains. Moreover, in excavation units 51 and 65, where samples were collected at various depths, they were found in similar quantities throughout the 30cm sampled. This suggests that European domesticated plants were intentionally brought onto the site and into

FIG. 4
Cartier-Roberval site (CeEu 4): charred red-oak acorn cup (photograph, A. Allard).

FIG. 5
Cartier-Roberval site (CeEu 4): charred maize grain (photograph, A. Allard).

buildings. This observation is in line with the fact that these plants were probably intended for dietary use since this was their principal use in the 16th century. Furthermore, given their high nutritional value and easy preservation in dry form, these plants were often favoured for long journeys, as attested by their presence on sites around the waterfront in London, England.[30] These qualities are also why the Spanish chose to bring these goods with them during their first attempts to settle North America.[31]

Plants destined for consumption frequently come into contact with flames during cooking accidents or the intentional burning of refuse.[32] However, a catastrophic fire, such as the one that occurred on the Cartier-Roberval site, can preserve food plants at various stages of their use: storage, preparation, consumption or disposal as refuse.[33] Several characteristics of the assemblages studied favour rejecting the possibility that the plant remains were deposited as a result of refuse accumulation. First, as previously mentioned, an accumulation of refuse would have led to higher concentrations of remains on the surface of the occupation layer, which is not the case here. Second, piles of refuse inside buildings would undoubtedly have been trampled on, causing greater fragmentation of remains, which was not observed in this study. Therefore, the plants must have been in protected areas.

The presence of wheat grains is significant in determining what dietary practices may have led to the formation of the assemblages. After harvesting, wheat is processed to separate the grains from chaff and weeds incidentally collected with the crop.[34] Considering that no chaff and only a small amount of weeds were found in the buildings, the wheat had probably already undergone this processing when the fire occurred. However, the processing was obviously not complete, since wheat was used primarily, during the period concerned here, for making flour and bread.[35] It is thus possible that the presence of wheat grains in the assemblages testifies to a latent phase in the flour-making process. The advantage of storing grains instead of flour is that grains keep longer and under more diverse conditions. A similar reasoning holds for the presence of barley (*Hordeum vulgare* L.) grains in a form other than that in which barley is generally eaten. However, it is harder to determine whether the barley grains were destined for human or animal consumption, since the use of barley as food declined in the 16th century in western Europe, and this cereal, especially covered barley, was then reserved for animal feed.[36] The transitional form in which the cereals were found on the Cartier-Roberval site, coupled with their density and distribution, suggests they were in storage when the fire occurred. Given that the distribution of olive (Fig. 6), grape, plum, pea, lentil and mustard remains was similar to that of the cereal remains, it is conceivable that they too were in storage when the fire occurred. While it is true that the remains of some of these species occurred in lower densities than did the remains of the cereals, the differences may be attributable to the following factors: only a fraction of the storage areas were excavated;

FIG. 6
Cartier-Roberval site (CeEu 4): charred olive stone (photograph, A. Allard).

the specific morphology of these species may have affected their charring potential; and, at the time, cereals were a staple of the European diet.

The results yielded by depth-based sampling in excavation units 51 and 65 may clarify certain aspects of the structures and methods used to store foodstuffs. Indeed, the majority of identified remains did not occur at the surface of the occupation layers, but rather were scattered throughout the 0.30m fire layer. This distribution indicates that the remains were not lying directly on the occupation layer at the time of the fire, but were located a certain height above ground when the fire occurred. Moreover, this contention is supported by the fact that only small grains were observed in the lower portion of the deposits, indicating that the remains spread to lower levels during the fire or were carried by water flowing through the deposits after the fire. This hypothesis is also consistent with historical data according to which, in the wetter and colder parts of France, foodstuffs were stored in attics to keep them dry and well ventilated so that they would not go mouldy.[37] Storage of these commodities in a high place, such as an attic,[38] is also consistent with Roberval's reports of both a high and a low storeroom on the site.[39]

In short, the majority of the archaeobotanical assemblages were made up of the remains of European plants that could easily have been brought into the site for storage and consumption. These foodstuffs were still edible and stored in a high, dry place, such as an attic, when the fire occurred. A number of similarities can be observed between the food plants brought into the Cartier-Roberval site and those found in early Spanish colonies at Puerto Real and La Isabela.[40]

UNDESIRABLE SPECIES

In addition to plants of economic value, other plants from the Old World were present in the assemblages. These plants have no historically recorded common use and were considered weeds in Europe. They were found in small numbers in the samples with higher cereal concentrations, suggesting that they were not intentionally brought into the site but accompanied European domesticates. In other words, common corncockle (*Agrostemma githago* L.) and spurge (*Euphorbia* sp.) would have crossed the Atlantic Ocean accidentally, mixed in with cereal grains, most likely wheat, after being harvested with these crops, whose fields they infested, in Europe. Their presence would therefore be attributable to inefficiency in the final stages of cereal processing, i.e. fine sieving and visual sorting. While the presence of these few Old World weed seeds on the site may seem insignificant, it was enough to alter the regional landscape and cause the settlers some definite discomfort. Corncockle seeds, for example, are particularly toxic. Incidences of poisoning are rare today, but the ingestion of seeds, even in small doses, can cause stomach cramps, diarrhoea, dizziness and weakness.[41]

Through their choice of supplies and, consequently, the accidental introduction of weeds, the settlers unwittingly changed the landscape around the Cartier-Roberval Upper Fort site and in the Québec City area in general. In fact, the oldest remains of several weeds carried in from Europe and still infesting fields in Québec were identified on the site. In addition to the species mentioned above, a number of imported plants may have had a similar impact, including mustard (*Brassica* sp.), of which an abundance of seeds (over 80% of the remains) were found in excavation unit 70.

DISCUSSION: FOOD CHOICES?

Several edible, economically important, plants were found in large numbers at the Cartier-Roberval Upper Fort site. The discovery of these plants is significant, especially since most of them are not mentioned in the historical documents (Table 5), which tended to focus on the local, indigenous flora around the fort. The presence of these plants sheds new light on the expedition's supplies. As mentioned earlier, most of the species found in the archaeobotanical assemblages were carried into inhabited zones unintentionally. Although they have made it possible to reconstruct a number of specific human activities, these species will not be discussed any further in this paper. Rather, the argumentation will now focus on the plants that

TABLE 5

Comparison between species found on the site and species mentioned in the historical documents (X = present).

	Archaeobotanical analysis	Historical documents
Sagebrush	X	
Hawthorn	X	X
Birch		X
Cedar		X
Chokecherry	X	
Hemp		X
Oak	X	
Chenopodium	X	
Cabbage		X
Date	X	
Spruce	X	
Maple		X
Bean		X
Strawberry	X	
Raspberry	X	
Wheat	X	X
Geranium	X	
Beech	X	
Lettuce		X
Lentil	X	
Maize	X	X
Pin cherry	X	
Mustard	X	X
Turnip		X
Common corncockle	X	
Hazelnut	X	
Olive tree	X	
Barley	X	
Small cherry	X	
Pea	X	
Plum tree	X	
Spurge	X	
Ash	X	
Elder	X	
Sunflower	X	
Vine	X	X

were intentionally brought into the site's buildings; the food the settlers ate — given that the plants were intended for food consumption; and the possible significance of the presence of these plants vis-à-vis the settlers' values.

The interpretation of the archaeobotanical assemblages revealed that only imported plant species were consciously brought onto the site. They were also the only plants that could be firmly associated with food-related activities, although this may simply be due to the type of activity that led to their deposition, namely, storage. Various means of food storage used in the 17th century have been inventoried in the Québec City area. During that period, 'dry' foods were stored in attics, separately from fresh fruit and vegetables, which were kept in cool places underground, such as basements or root cellars.[42] These different methods for preserving food could explain the predominance of dry and European foods in the excavated building areas. In all likelihood, the food plants identified at the site do not represent the entire plant-based diet of the settlers; whereas European foodstuffs would have been stored in a dry place, local products would have been stored and eaten fresh. Therefore, the archaeological fieldwork could have led to over-representation of Old World plants merely by unintentionally focusing on areas where plants were stored in raised structures exposed to the 16th-century fire. Further excavations are needed to validate this hypothesis.

Even though the use of different storage techniques very likely explains the high proportion of European plants found on the site, the predominance of these plants can, to a certain extent, still be considered significant. Indeed, a number of local plants that had a known equivalent in Europe at the time and were accessible to the settlers could have been stored for food consumption in a dry place instead of the imported species. It is worth noting in this regard that the travel logs of both Cartier and Roberval frequently refer to local foods in a negative light. While the distribution of maize was the same as that of the European plants, it is conceivable that the presence of maize merely reflects friendly trade between the settlers and Indigenous people. It is common for two groups who do not speak the same language to exchange food as a way of forging ties.[43] And, according to Cartier's and Roberval's travel logs, such exchanges frequently occurred with local Native groups. However, despite the fact that the settlers marvelled at the flora in the New World, they apparently turned their noses up at the food constantly offered by the Amerindians.[44] The clear predominance of Old World plants in the settlers' diet may simply reflect that disgust.

Therefore, even though the Cartier-Roberval and Spanish colonization missions resembled one another in terms of the foodstuffs they brought along, they differed with regard to the incorporation of local flora into the daily diet: local plants were clearly not part of the foodstuffs eaten by settlers on the Cartier-Roberval site. However, the numerical importance of Old World plants observed on the site could also be directly related to the very short settlement of the fort. Indeed, the inhabitants of the Spanish and British settlements being established during the same period further south had more time to adapt their eating habits gradually. Initially, they too tried to maintain a European diet[45] and displayed a strong reluctance to incorporate new food into the regular fare of the day.[46] However, the Spanish settlers were rapidly faced with food shortages, partly because of problems in obtaining fresh supplies and growing desired species.[47] This situation gave rise to a diet inspired by the food eaten by local Amerindian groups and the gradual creolization of European dietary habits, resulting in the creation of several new dishes and recipes.[48]

Generally speaking, in newly established colonies, as soon as there was a shortage in food normally eaten by the settlers, they accepted other available food sources. The more severe the food shortage, the more the settlers pushed the limits of what they considered edible.[49] In such instances, Amerindians often acted as intermediaries between the newcomers and the unfamiliar local flora.[50] As colonies became more firmly established, local flora was intentionally incorporated into foodways with a view to appropriating new geography. For example, the archaeobotanical assemblages of Jamestown dating from a few years after it was founded testify to experimentation with indigenous plants.[51] This general adaptation model would seem to indicate that the observed differences between the diet of the Cartier-Roberval settlers and that of other colonies are primarily attributable to the short duration of the settlers' stay. Also noteworthy is the fact that the role played by Amerindian groups on the Cartier-Roberval site is similar to the one they are described as having played in other colonization attempts. Indeed, they were linked to the presence on the site of the only plants that would have been exotic to the settlers.

CONCLUSION

Archaeobotanical analysis of the deposits on the Cartier-Roberval Upper Fort site has nuanced the understanding of the natural environment around the site, the diet of the colonists and the buildings they inhabited — information that could not have been obtained using historical documents alone. It has also made it possible to put names to plants not mentioned in the documents and whose presence on the site was purely accidental, but significant in terms of interpretation.

With regard to the fort's local environment, the historical literature essentially focuses on species that had significant value to the settlers. Although the archaeobotanical analysis identified some of these species, it also revealed the presence of other local plants that appear to have been of less interest to the settlers, such as strawberry, ash, cherry and elder. The discovery of these plant remains enhances the portrait of the local landscape as described in the historical documents. Several European weeds, most of which were imported accidentally, were identified as well on the site. This finding has provided the oldest evidence of the occurrence of these weeds in the region and is all the more important in that these plants irreversibly altered the site's immediate landscape and surrounding area.

The archaeobotanical data have also helped to flesh out the portrait of the site's buildings as gleaned from the historical documents — which contain only lists of the structures erected — by shedding light on some of the functions these buildings may have served. For example, these data have made it easier to delineate storage areas, particularly since the analysis of deposits in those areas suggests that the deposits were *in situ* and had been affected only slightly by taphonomic processes. In addition, the differences in the distortion of plant remains in excavation units 51 and 65, on the one hand, and unit 70, on the other, indicate a higher average temperature in unit 70. This may be due to differences in the respective distances of these units from the fire's origins or in the construction materials used in the two buildings where these units were located. Moreover, it is probable that local plant remains were carried into the buildings with construction materials, which is consistent with the suggestion that local clay may have been used to build walls. As for the function of the buildings, they seem to have been used, at least in part, for storing foodstuffs, even though they apparently did not contain a large quantity of plant refuse when the fire occurred. The distribution of plant remains in excavation units 51 and 65 suggests that the remains were in an above-ground structure, such as an attic, at the time of the fire.

In addition to confirming that the settlers imported wheat and mustard, as recorded in the historical documents, the archaeobotanical analysis showed that barley, grapes, olives, dates, peas and lentils were imported and kept on the site as well. Also, the discovery of weeds in association with cereals indicates that the latter were in all likelihood grown in Europe. Indeed, no evidence was found to confirm Cartier's and Roberval's reports that foodstuffs were grown around the settlement. Local plants made a minimal contribution to the settlers' diet; however, the presence of a small amount of maize highlights contact between the settlers and local Amerindian populations.

The identification and distribution of food plants not mentioned in the historical documents has made it possible to draw parallels with other colonization efforts that were contemporary with those of Cartier and Roberval. The foods these two explorers chose to bring with them on their expeditions seem to have been dictated by imperatives that were similar to those heeded by the Spanish and British during their first attempts at settlement in North America. However, in contrast with what occurred in Spanish and British settlements, the diet of the French colonists on the Cartier-Roberval site consisted primarily of European food, which might be explained by the short time the site was occupied. The small amount of indigenous and Amerindian plant remains shows that the settlers made little effort to incorporate new elements into their regular fare and thus testifies to their desire to maintain a European diet.

This archaeobotanical analysis has shed light on the environment in which Cartier and Roberval established their settlement, as well as on several aspects of their daily life during this aborted colonization attempt. Continued analysis of the samples collected in the summer of 2008 will further round out this portrait and, eventually, enable the study of social stratification on the site.

ACKNOWLEDGEMENTS

The archaeobotanical analysis of the samples collected on the Cartier-Roberval site was made possible through the collaboration and support of the Commission de la capitale nationale du Québec. We wish to thank the technical assistants Amélie Allard, Céline Dupont-Hébert, Geneviève Lachance, Geneviève Meunier and Stéphanie Wicha for their meticulous and diligent work. We would also like to thank our fellow archaeobotanists — Steve Archer, Ksenja Borejevic, Tonya Largy, Virginia Popper and, in particular, Heather Trigg — for giving us access to their reference collections as well as confirming or clarifying the identification of certain remains. Our thanks go as well to Jessica Bowes, Maryse Cloutier-Gélinas and various proofreaders whose comments helped to polish this paper. Finally, we are especially grateful to Dr Christine Hastorf, whose advice greatly improved the text.

NOTES

[1] Robert 1984.

[2] The system used to designate the excavation units on the site was modelled after the Tikal system (Swannack 1974). Under this system, each trench is assigned an operation number (e.g. 51, 65, 70) and each subdivision or extension of the trench is assigned a letter (e.g. 51A, 65B, 70A). A lot number is then assigned to each soil layer and each structural feature, so that each lot number corresponds to a single depositional episode (e.g. 51A1, 65B1, 70A1). For the purposes of this paper, the archaeobotanical analysis focused primarily on lots 51A2, 65B2 and 70A6.

[3] Lennstrom & Hastorf 1992.

[4] Bouchard-Perron 2008a.

[5] The light fraction includes, among other things, charred wood, preserved plant parts, insects and small bones.

[6] The heavy fraction generally consists of sediment, stones and artefacts.

[7] Wagner 1989, 22.

[8] Butler 1991; Cappers *et al.* 2006; Castner 2004; Davis 1993; Jones *et al.* 2004; Kühn 1991; Hillman *et al.* 1996; Hubbard 1992; Martin & Barkley 2000; Mangafa & Kotsakis 1996; Miller 1999; Renfrew 1973; Zohary & Hopf 2000.

[9] Marie-Victorin 2002.

[10] Jones 1991; Hubbard & Clapman 1992.

[11] The most specific taxonomic group to which an archaeological specimen can be assigned.

[12] For purposes of clarity, both the tables and the text refer to the grape in general. However, it should be noted that only two-thirds of the grape plants identified could be associated with cultivated grape (*Vitis vinifera* L.). It was impossible to identify the other specimens in that they had no features allowing them to be formally associated with a particular species. Thus, although it can be affirmed that the remains were largely cultivated grape, it is impossible to determine if a portion of them were local wild grape. It is important to underline, however, that the spatial distribution of cultivated grape remains and that of non-identified grape remains were exactly the same and corresponded to that of imported foodstuffs.

[13] Pearsall 1989.

[14] Boyd *et al.* 2008.

[15] This factorial technique makes it possible to highlight the biggest mathematical differences between results. On the basis of these differences, samples and taxa are then represented in a chart (e.g. Fig. 3) that expresses their divergences and similarities (absence of marked differences). The bigger the divergence between samples and taxa, the farther apart they will be in the chart. Conversely, the fewer factors of divergence between samples and taxa, the closer they will be in the chart. Since the divergence is expressed in

mathematical terms, it must be associated, once it has been represented in chart form, with the characteristics of the samples and taxa from which it likely derives. If a characteristic correlates with the position of samples or taxa in the chart, it means that it is one of the causes of divergence or similarity between them.

[16] Brinkkemper 1993, 83; Jones 1991, 70.

[17] Dincauze 2000, 334; Greig 1989, 14.

[18] Braadbaart & van Bergen 2005, 74; Minnis 1981, 149; Munson *et al.* 1971, 422.

[19] Boardman & Jones 1990, 1; Braadbaart & van Bergen 2005, 67; Wilson 1984.

[20] Margaritis & Jones forthcoming.

[21] See R. Fiset and G. Samson in this volume.

[22] Asch & Asch Sidell 1989.

[23] Dumont 2005a; 2005b.

[24] Burns & Honkala 1990.

[25] On the Intendant's Palace site (Bouchard-Perron 2008b) and the Aubert-de-la-Chesnaye site (Fortin 1995).

[26] The words seed and fruit are used here in their usual sense rather than their botanical sense.

[27] See R. Fiset and G. Samson in this volume.

[28] van der Veen 2007, 972.

[29] Cutler & Blake 2001.

[30] Given the lack of archaeobotanical studies of modern-day assemblages in France, we referred to the analyses conducted by Giorgi (1997) in England, and London in particular.

[31] Deagan & Cruxent 2002a, 137; 2002b, 140–1; Reitz & Scarry 1985.

[32] van der Veen 2007.

[33] van der Veen 2007.

[34] Hillman 1984; Jones 1984.

[35] Kiple & Ornelas 2000, 1878–80.

[36] Prance & Nesbitt 2005, 49; Vaughan & Geissler 1999, 4–5.

[37] Laurioux 2002, 78.

[38] Note that the archaeobotanical results are as yet the only findings supporting such a hypothesis.

[39] Cook 1993, 110.

[40] Deagan & Cruxent 2002a, 137; 2002b, 140–1; Reitz & Scarry 1985.

[41] Hardin & Arena 1969; Munroe 2008.

[42] Audet 2001, 142; Provencher 1996, 310–15.

[43] Preiswerk 1984, 250.

[44] Cook 1993.

[45] Deagan & Cruxent 2002a, 132; 2002b, 167, 185.

[46] Ferrières 2002, 115.

[47] Deagan & Cruxent 2002b, 182; Reitz & Cumbaa 1983, 152; Reitz & Scarry 1985, 55.

[48] Gremillon 2002; Mrozowski 1999; Scarry & Reitz 1990, 351–2.

[49] Huss-Ashmore & Johnston 1994.

[50] Reitz & McEwan 1995.

[51] Mrozowski 1999.

BIBLIOGRAPHY

PUBLISHED SOURCES

Anderson, P. 1999, *Prehistory of Agriculture: New Experimental and Ethnographic Approaches*, Los Angeles: University of California Press.

Asch, D. & Asch Sidell, N. 1989, 'Archaeological plant remains: applications to stratigraphic analysis', in Hastorf & Popper 1989, 86–96.

Audet, B. 2001, *Se nourrir au quotidien en Nouvelle-France*, Sainte-Foy (Québec): Éditions GID.

Blake, L. & Cutler, H. 2001, *Plants from the Past*, Tuscaloosa: University of Alabama Press.

Boardman, S. & Jones, G. 1990, 'Experiments on the effects of charring on cereal plant components', *J. Archaeol. Sci.* **17**, 1–11.

Boyd, M., Varney, T., Surette, C. & Surette, J. 2008, 'Reassessing the northern limit of maize consumption in North America: stable isotope, plant microfossil, and trace element content of carbonized food residue', *J. Archaeol. Sci.* **35**, 2545–56.

Braudel, F. (ed.) 1984, *Le Monde de Jacques Cartier: L'aventure au XVIe siècle*, Montréal: Libre-Expression.

Braadbaart, F. & van Bergen, P. 2005, 'Digital imaging analysis of size and shape of wheat and pea upon heating under anoxic conditions as a function of the temperature', *Veg. Hist. Archaeobot.* **14**, 67–75.

Brinkkemper, O. 1993. 'Indirect correspondence analysis and botanical macroremains: a case study', *Analecta Praehistorica Leidensia* **26**, 83–91.

Burns, R. & Honkala, B. 1990, *Silvics of North America*, 2 vols, Washington: US Department of Agriculture.

Butler, A. 1991, 'The Vicieae: problems of identification', in Renfrew 1991, 61–73.

Cappers, R.T.J., Bekker, R.M. & Jans, J.E.A. 2006, *Digital Seed Atlas of the Netherlands*, Groningen: Barkhuis Publishing.

Castner, J.L. 2004, *Photographic Atlas of Botany and Guide to Plant Identification*, Gainesville (Fl.): Feline Press.

Cook, R. (ed.) 1993, *The Voyages of Jacques Cartier*, Toronto: University of Toronto Press.

Cutler, H. & Blake, L. 2001, 'North American Indian corn', in Blake & Cutler 2001, 1–18.

Davis, L.W. 1993, *Weed Seeds of the Great Plains: A Handbook for Identification*, Lawrence: University Press of Kansas.

Deagan, K. 1983, *Spanish St. Augustine: The Archaeology of a Colonial Creole Community*, New York & London: Academic Press.

Deagan, K. 1995, *The Archaeology of a Sixteenth-Century Spanish Town in Hispaniola: Puerto Real*, Gainesville: University Press of Florida.

Deagan, K. & Cruxent, J.M. 2002a, *Colombus's Outpost among the Taínos: Spain and America at La Isabela 1493–1498*, New Haven & London: Yale University Press.

Deagan, K. & Cruxent, J.M. 2002b, *Archaeology at La Isabela: America's First European Town*, New Haven & London: Yale University Press.

Dincauze, D. 2000, *Environmental Archaeology: Principles and Practice*, Cambridge: University Press.

Dumont, B. 2005a, *Les Niches écologiques des arbres, arbustes et conifères*, Boucherville: Éditions Bertrand Dumond.

Dumont, B. 2005b, *Les Niches écologiques des vivaces et plantes herbacées*, Boucherville: Éditions Bertrand Dumond.

Etkin, N.L. (ed.) 1994, *Eating on the Wild Side. The Pharmacologic, Ecologic, and Social Implications of Using Noncultigens*, Tucson & London: University of Arizona Press.

Ferrières, M. 2002, *Histoire des peurs alimentaires du Moyen-Âge à l'aube du XXe siècle*, Paris: Éditions du Seuil.

Gaimster, D. & Stamper, P. (eds) 1997, *The Age of Transition: the Archaeology of English Culture 1400–1600*, Oxford: Oxbow.

Giorgi, J. 1997, 'Diet in late medieval and early modern London: the archaeobotanical evidence', in Gaimster & Stamper 1997, 197–213.

Greig, J. 1989, *Archaeobotany*, Strasbourg: European Science Foundation.

Gremillon, K., 2002, 'Archaeobotany at Old Mobile', *Hist. Archaeol.* **361**, 117–28.

Hardin, J.W. & Arena, J.M. 1969, *Human Poisoning from Native and Cultivated Plants*, Durham: Duke University Press.

Hastorf, C. & Popper, V. 1989, *Current Paleoethnobotany: Analytical Methods and Cultural Interpretations of Archaeological Plant Remains*, Chicago: University Press.

Hillman, G. 1984. 'Interpretation of archaeological plant remains: the application of ethnographic models from Turkey', in van Zeist & Casparie 1984, 1–41.

Hillman, G., Mason, S., De Moulins, D. & Nesbitt, M. 1996, 'Identification of archaeological remains of wheat: the 1992 London workshop', *Circaea, J. Ass. Environmental Archaeol.* **12**, 195–209.

Hubbard, R. 1992. 'Dichotomous keys for the identification of the major Old World crops', *Rev. Palaeobot. Palyn.* **73**, 105–15.

Hubbard, R. & Clapham, A. 1992, 'Quantifying macroscopic plant remains', *Rev. Palaeobotany and Palynology* **73**, 117–32.

Huss-Ashmore, R. & Johnston, S.L. 1994, 'Wild plants as cultural adaptations to food stress', in Etkin 1994, 62–82.

Jones, G. 1984, 'Interpretation of archaeological plant remains: Ethnographic models from Greece', in van Zeist & Casparie 1984, 43–61.

Jones, G. 1991, 'Numerical analysis in archaeobotany', in van Zeist, Wasylikowa & Behre 1991, 63–80.

Jones, S., Taylor, J. & Ash, F. 2004, *Seed Identification Handbook. Agriculture, Horticulture & Weeds*, Cambridge: NIAB.

Kiple, K. & Ornelas, K. (eds) 2000, *The Cambridge World History of Food*, Cambridge: University Press.

Kühn, F. 1991, 'Problems of identification of seeds and fruits of spelt wheat, oats and legumes', in Renfrew 1991, 59–60.

Laurioux, B. 2002, *Manger au Moyen Âge: pratiques et discours alimentaires en Europe aux XIVe et XVe siècles*, Paris: Hachette.

Lennstrom, H. & Hastorf, C. 1992, 'Testing old wives' tales in paleoethnobotany: a comparison of bulk and scatter sampling schemes from Pacan, Peru', *J. Archaeol. Sci.* **19**, 205–29.

Mangafa, M. & Kotsakis, K. 1996, 'A new method for the identification of wild and cultivated charred grape seeds', *J. Archaeol. Sci.* **23**, 409–18.

Marie-Victorin (Bro.) 2002, *Flore Laurentienne*, Montréal: Gaëtan Morin.

Martin, A. & Barkley, W. 2000, *Seed Identification Manual*, Caldwell: Blackburn Press.

Miller, T.E. 1999, 'A cautionary note on the use of morphological characters for recognizing taxa in wheat genus Triticum', in Anderson 1999, 169–72.

Minnis, P. 1981, 'Seeds in archaeological sites: sources and some interpretive problems', *Amer. Antiq.* **46**, 143–52.

Mrozowski, S. 1999, 'Colonization and the commodification of nature', *Int. J. Hist. Archaeol.* **33**, 153–66.

Munroe, D.B. 2008, *Canadian Poisonous Plants Information System*, <http://www.cbif.gc.ca/pls/pp/poison?p_x=px> [updated 18 March 2008].

Munson, P., Parmalee, P. & Yarnell, R. 1971, 'Subsistence ecology of Scovill, a Terminal Middle Woodland village', *Amer. Antiq.* **36**, 410–31.

Neuchatel (Institut d'ethnologie de l'université de) 1984, *Identité alimentaire et altérité culturelle*, Neuchatel: Institut d'ethnologie de l'université de Neuchatel.

Pearsall, D. 1989, 'Interpreting the meaning of macroremain abundance: the impact of source and context', in Hastorf & Popper 1989, 97–118.

Prance, G. & Nesbitt, M. 2005, *The Cultural History of Plants*, New York & London: Routledge.

Preiswerk, Y. 1984, 'Des nourritures pour dire une vision du monde?', in Neuchatel 1984, 249–57.

Provencher, J. 1996, *Les Quatre Saisons dans la vallée du Saint-Laurent*, Montréal: Boréal.

Reitz, E & Cumbaa, S. 1983, 'Diet and foodways of eighteenth-century Spanish St. Augustine', in Deagan 1983, 151–85.

Reitz, E. & Scarry, M. 1985, *Reconstructing Historic Subsistence with an Example from Sixteenth-Century Spanish Florida*, Soc. Hist. Archaeol. Special Pub. ser. **3**.

Reitz, E. & McEwan, B. 1995, 'Animals, environment, and the Spanish diet at Puerto Real', in Deagan 1995, 287–334.

Renfrew, J. 1973, *Palaeoethnobotany: the Prehistoric Food Plants of the Near East and Europe*, New York: Columbia University Press.

Renfrew, J. (ed.) 1991, *New Light on Early Farming: Recent Developments in Palaeoethnobotany*, Edinburgh: University Press.

Robert, J. 1984, 'L'invention d'un héros', in Braudel 1984, 295–302.

Scarry, M. & Reitz, E. 1990, 'Herbs, fish, scum, and vermin: subsistence strategies in sixteenth-century Spanish Florida', in Thomas 1990, 343–56.

Swannack, J. 1974, *Manuel de fouilles archéologiques*, Ottawa: Parcs Canada.

Thomas, D.H. (ed.) 1990, *Columbian Consequences*, **2**. *Archaeological and Historical Perspectives on the Spanish Borderlands East*, Washington: Smithsonian Press.

van der Veen, M. 2007, 'Formation processes of dessicated and carbonized plant remains — the identification of routine practice', *J. Archaeol. Sci.* **34**, 968–90.

van Zeist, W. & Casparie, W.A. (eds) 1984, *Plants and Ancient Man: Studies in Paleoethnobotany*, Rotterdam & Boston: Balkema.

van Zeist, W., Wasylikowa, K. & Behre, K.-E. 1991, *Progress in Old World Palaeoethnobotany*, Rotterdam: Balkema.

Vaughan, J.G. & Geissler, C. 1999, *The New Oxford Book of Food Plants*, Oxford: University Press.

Wagner, G. 1989, 'Comparability among recovery techniques', in Hastorf & Popper 1989, 17–35.

Wilson, D.G. 1984, 'The carbonisation of weed seeds and their representation in macrofossil assemblages', in van Zeist & Casparie 1984, 201–6.

Zohary, D. & Hopf, M. 2000, *Domestication of Plants in the Old World*, Oxford: University Press.

UNPUBLISHED SOURCES

Bouchard-Perron, J.-A. 2008a, 'D'un continent à l'autre: les restes végétaux sur le site Cartier-Roberval: Résultats de l'analyse archéobotanique de 2007', Québec: CCNQ.

Bouchard-Perron, J.-A. 2008b, 'L'Îlot des Palais: l'évolution d'un site à travers les restes végétaux: Résultats de l'analyse archéobotanique des dépôts des opérations 47 à 60 — Partie I', Québec: Ville de Québec.

Fortin, C. 1995, 'Analyse paléoethnobotanique du site Aubert-de-la-Chesnaye (Site CeEt-46, Québec)', Québec: Ville de Québec and MCCQ.

Margaritis, E. & Jones, M. forthcoming, 'Crop processing of *Olea europaea* L.: an experimental approach for the interpretation of archaeobotanical olive remains', *Veg. Hist. Archaeobot.*

ABBREVIATIONS

CCNQ Commission de la capitale nationale du Québec

CÉLAT Centre interuniversitaire d'Etudes de recherche sur les lettres, les arts et les traditions

MCCQ Ministère de la Culture et des Communications du Québec

SUMMARY IN FRENCH, GERMAN, ITALIAN AND SPANISH

RÉSUMÉ

Du mythe vers la réalité : l'archéobotanique sur le site du fort d'en Haut Cartier-Roberval

La première tentative d'implantation dans la vallée du Saint-Laurent est rapportée dans plusieurs sources historiques. Le but de ces comptes étaient de justifier le projet de colonisation de Jacques Cartier et le Sieur de Roberval au Canada; ils fournissent quelques informations sur les nombreux aspects de la vie quotidienne des colons. La récente découverte du site où ces deux explorateurs s'implantèrent en 1541–43 et les fouilles archéologiques qui y ont été menées fournissent une excellente opportunité pour réexaminer le projet de colonisation. Cet article présente les résultats de l'analyse archéobotanique menée sur le site.

ZUSAMMENFASSUNG

Von Mythos zu Tatsachen: Archäobotanik im oberen Cartier-Roberval-Fort

Die ersten offiziellen Versuche, eine Siedlung im St Lawrence-Tal zu gründen, findet man in einer Reihe von historischen Dokumenten. Die Berichte zielen auf eine Rechtfertigung des Kolonisationsvorhabens von Jacques Cartier and Sieur de Roberval in Canada hin, geben jedoch wenig Einzelheiten über verschiedene Aspekte des täglichen Lebens der Siedler. Die jüngsten Funde der Ausgrabung, wo die beiden Forscher 1541–43 siedelten, zusammen mit den archäologischen Grabungen, die dort durchgeführt wurden, bieten eine ausgezeichnete Gelegenheit, dieses Kolonisationsvorhaben neu zu untersuchen. Unter diesem Gesichtspunkt bringt der Bericht einige Ergebnisse der archäobotanischen Analyse dieser Grabung.

RIASSUNTO

Dal mito alla realtà: archeobotanica nel sito della fortezza superiore di Cartier-Roberval

Il primo tentativo ufficiale di insediamento nella valle del San Lorenzo è narrato in vari documenti storici. Questi racconti avevano l'intento di giustificare i progetti di colonizzazione di Jacques Cartier e Sieur de Roberval in Canada, ma forniscono poche informazioni su una varietà di aspetti della vita quotidiana dei colonizzatori. La recente scoperta del sito dove questi due esploratori si stabilirono fra il 1541 e il 1543, e gli scavi archeologici condotti nel medesimo forniscono un'eccellente opportunità per ri-esaminare i loro progetti di colonizzazione. Quest'articolo presenta in quest'ottica alcuni dei risultati di un'analisi archeobotanica condotta in questo sito.

RESUMEN

Del mito a la realidad: arqueobotánica en el yacimiento del fuerte alto Cartier-Roberval

El primer intento oficial para crear un asentamiento en el Valle St Lawrence ha quedado plasmado en la documentación histórica. Estos relatos intentan justificar el proyecto de colonización de Jacques Cartier y Sieur de Roberval en Canadá, pero carecen de detalle alguno sobre muchos aspectos de la vida cotidiana de los colonizadores. El hallazgo reciente del lugar donde se asentaron estos dos exploradores en 1541–43 y las excavaciones arqueológicas allí desarrolladas han proporcionado una oportunidad única para re-examinar su proyecto de colonización. Dentro de este panorama, el presente artículo presenta algunos de los resultados de un análisis arqueobotánico de dicho yacimiento.

CÉLAT and Department of History, 1030 Avenue des Sciences-humaines, Université Laval, Québec (Québec), Canada G1V 0A6 (JABP)
[julie-anne.bouchard-perron.1@ulaval.ca]

CÉLAT and Department of History, 1030 Avenue des Sciences-humaines, Université Laval, Québec (Québec), Canada G1V 0A6 (AB)
[Allison.bain@hst.ulaval.ca]

Post-Medieval Archaeology **43/1** (2009), 106–124

The Saint-Louis forts and chateaux site: archaeology in the heart of New France

By PIERRE CLOUTIER *and* PAUL-GASTON L'ANGLAIS

SUMMARY: The first of four forts called Fort Saint-Louis was built by Champlain in 1620. Since 1975 archaeological fieldwork has been undertaken in the forts, which housed the residence of the governors of New France, and in the governor's gardens. From 2005 to 2007 Parks Canada excavated 1,500m² of the Saint-Louis forts and chateaux, unearthing the chateaux's foundations and large sections of the fortifications. The excavations showed that the chateaux rested on Champlain's dwelling, confirming the significance of this spot, and that the defences were adapted to the topography. The artefacts reflect the site's residential and governance roles.

INTRODUCTION

Québec, the first permanent European settlement in Canada, became the capital of New France.[1] Fort Saint-Louis, which had been built at Québec in 1620 by the city's founder, Samuel de Champlain, emerged as the seat of executive power in New France and as the governor's place of residence. It came to constitute the heart of the colony. In 2001 the site was declared the Saint-Louis Forts and Châteaux National Historic Site of Canada (NHSC). Fieldwork conducted by Parks Canada from 2005 to 2007 revealed many structural remains associated with the first fort built by Champlain and with its three successors, the dwelling occupied by Champlain, the two governors' residences known as Château Saint-Louis, and the garden laid out nearby for the governor's private use. The archaeological excavations also yielded an artefact collection that is unique in many respects. These archaeological resources have reinforced the prime importance of the site.

This paper begins with a brief description of the location of the site and the reasons for its commemorative designation, and follows with a history of its occupation, placing particular emphasis on the French regime.[2] To enable the reader to grasp fully the site's historic significance, the paper then outlines the role of the governor and lists the individuals who held this position during the 150-year period of French colonial rule. As for more than 30 years what is now the Saint-Louis Forts and Châteaux NHSC has been the scene of major archaeological work and is deemed one of Canada's foremost archaeological sites, the bulk of the paper summarizes the principal discoveries made in the course of these investigations, focusing on the 2005–07 fieldwork.

Although the recent excavations generated a substantial amount of information, which has not yet been fully analysed, a comprehensive report of our conclusions will be published this year. Hitherto historical information gathered in the 1980s on the site's structural development has often overshadowed other aspects of the archaeological remains.[3] Since the fieldwork ended in 2007, Parks Canada researchers have concentrated on interpreting two important aspects of the site's history: the 17th-century evolution of the defences of the four forts, and the development and spatial organization of the buildings inside these fortifications before the second chateau was built in 1694.[4]

DOI: 10.1179/007942309X12457508844044

THE SITE, ITS COMMEMORATION AND HISTORY

Dufferin Terrace, a promenade which attracts over 2,000,000 visitors a year, overlooks the Cap Diamant cliff and the St Lawrence River (Fig. 1). Situated in front of Québec City's landmark Château Frontenac Hotel at an average altitude of 50m above sea level, the terrace has for over 150 years covered the remains of the Saint-Louis forts and chateaux. These lie at the eastern end of the Québec promontory, which provides a commanding view of the navigation channel constituting the gateway to Canada from the Atlantic Ocean. At Québec City the St Lawrence is no more than 1km wide. However, downstream from Île d'Orléans slightly further east, it broadens to over 13km and then continues to widen gradually as it flows to the Gulf of St Lawrence and then to the Atlantic, more than 1,000km away.

In 2001 the Historic Sites and Monuments Board of Canada recognized the historic significance of the Saint-Louis forts and chateaux on the grounds that they were an integral part of Québec's fortifications, served as the seat of executive power in the colony for over 200 years, and housed the residence of most of Canada's governors during the colonial era.[5] The NHSC encompasses not only the archaeological remains of the Saint-Louis forts and chateaux, but also the site of the governor's gardens. Since 1838 the older section of the gardens has served as an urban park, situated in the south-west part of the site.

The settlement of Québec developed initially by the river at the foot of the Cap Diamant cliff, where Samuel de Champlain erected his Habitation in 1608. In 1620 Champlain built a fort on top of the cliff, overlooking his settlement. Champlain sought to protect the commerce between France and its North American colony from other European competitors and to provide the population of Québec with a reduit, or refuge, in the event of attack by the native Iroquois.[6] This first fort, which Champlain named Fort Saint-Louis in honour of the French King Louis XIII, consisted of a simple wooden palisade around a dwelling. No illustrations of this work have been found.

FIG. 1

The Saint-Louis forts and chateaux archaeological site is situated at the foot of the Château Frontenac Hotel, which overlooks the Cap Diamant cliff. The area designated for commemorating the governors' presence in Québec City also includes the Governor's Garden, located in the wooded zone to the left of the hotel. North is to the right (© 2007 Ron Garnett, <http://www.Airspaces.ca>).

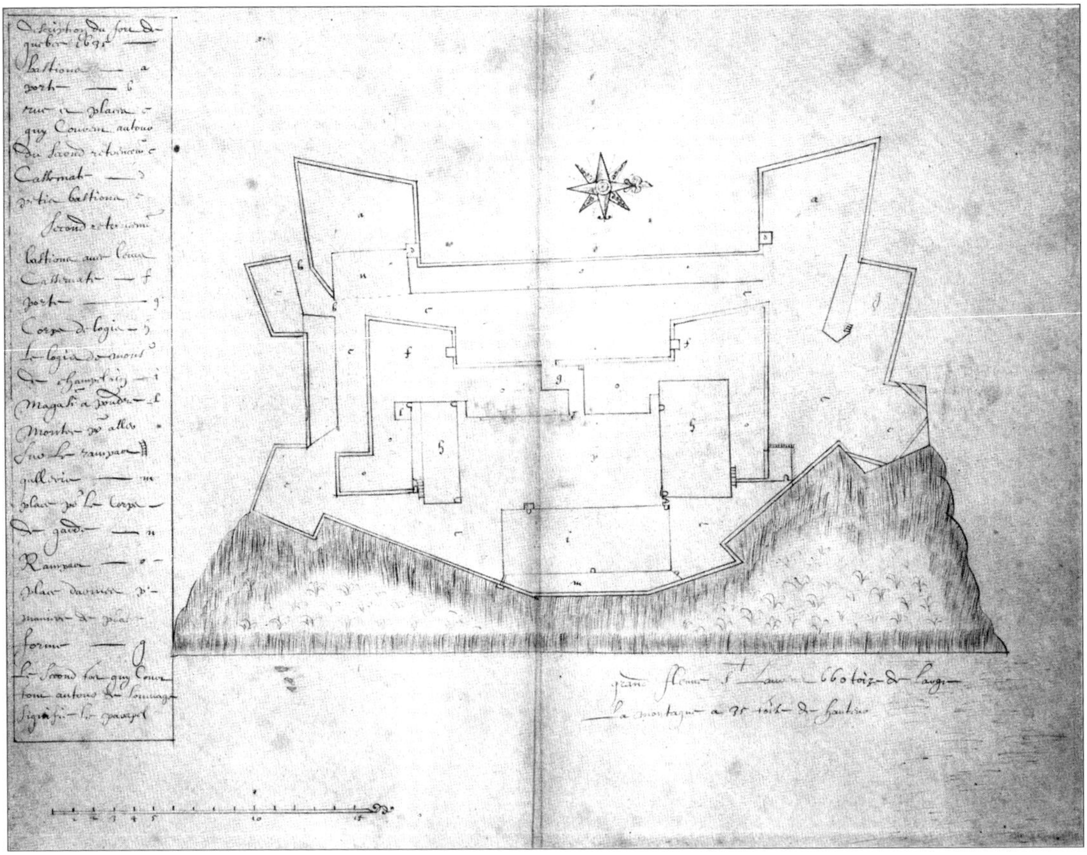

FIG. 2

Plan of the second Fort Saint-Louis in 1635 attributed to Jean Bourdon. The fort had a double enceinte and enclosed three buildings as well as other structures related to the site's defence (Department of Rare Books and Special Collections of the McGill University Libraries; facsimile held at the Cartothèque de l'Université Laval).

As by 1626 the fort was still unfinished and was already too small to serve as a reduit for the 60 or so people who then lived in Québec, Champlain ordered its demolition and began building another fort on the same spot. The new work had a double enceinte of earth ramparts faced with wood (Fig. 2). Two buildings, including the house where Champlain would live, were put up within the inner enceinte.[7] In 1644 Champlain's dwelling was described as made of stone. When the founder of Québec died there on 25 December 1635, the fort was still incomplete.

Charles Huault de Montmagny, the colony's first official governor, arrived in Québec from France in the summer of 1636. He immediately began improving the fort. After his departure, the renovation work he had planned continued under a succession of governors until the 1680s, changing the appearance and layout of the defensive installations and leading to the emergence of the third Fort Saint-Louis. Montmagny, who served as governor for about a dozen years, initially lived in the dwelling erected by Champlain; however, he had it demolished in 1647–48 and commissioned another residence, the first to be known as Château Saint-Louis. The building was a single-storey stone structure and, like its predecessor, boasted a wide private terrace along its river façade, affording a splendid view of the surrounding area. Montmagny also inaugurated a garden for the private use of the governor. This garden, which was one of the first ornamental gardens in North America, survives behind the Château Frontenac Hotel.[8]

Over the 25 years following Montmagny's term of office, six successive governors eventually completed Montmagny's plans for the fort enceinte,

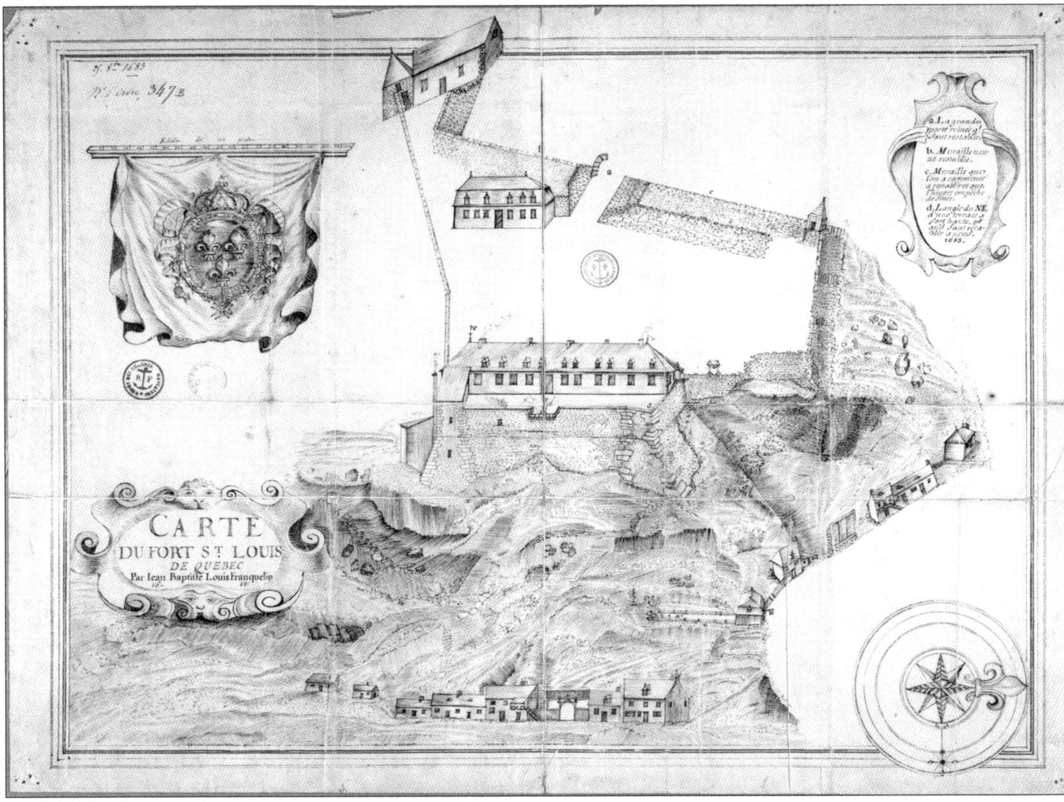

FIG. 3
Plan of Fort Saint-Louis in 1683 by Jean-Baptiste-Louis Franquelin. This perspective view of the third Fort Saint-Louis distorts the fort's layout. It shows the chateau with its terrace from the rear (ANOM, FR CAOM 3DFC347B).

but no changes were made to their residence (Fig. 3). The first major renovation was undertaken during Governor de La Barre's tenure. He enlarged the chateau by adding a private chamber, or closet, at the north end of the building in 1683 and a kitchen at the south end in 1684. He also restored large sections of the surrounding fortification wall that were at risk of collapsing. In 1685 his successor Denonville built a powder magazine outside the fort's south-west corner.

The celebrated Comte de Frontenac et de Palluau, who had already served as governor from 1672 to 1682, returned to the helm of the colony in 1689, barely a year before a fleet from Boston under the command of Admiral Phipps laid siege to Québec. Thanks to a palisade hastily erected around the city in the spring of 1690, as well as a few cannon batteries and Fort Saint-Louis, Québec withstood the attack and the colony was saved. However, the siege underscored the urgent need for a review of the colonial capital's fortifications. As early as 1691 Frontenac convinced Louis XIV to invest in building a permanent cannon battery on top of Cap Diamant. A year later the northern half of the battery was incorporated into the new enceinte of the fourth Fort Saint-Louis (Fig. 4). This stone enceinte became part of Québec's first permanent fortifications, built the following year. Much larger than its predecessor, it was equipped with Vauban-style bastions. From 1694 it protected the governor's brand new residence, modelled after the classical-style chateaux built in France at the time. However, only the northern two-thirds of the residence were completed, as Frontenac was unable to obtain sufficient funding for the rest.

His successor Callière resumed work on the chateau in 1700; but he was able to erect only a small section of the building between the part begun in 1694 and the old kitchen constructed in

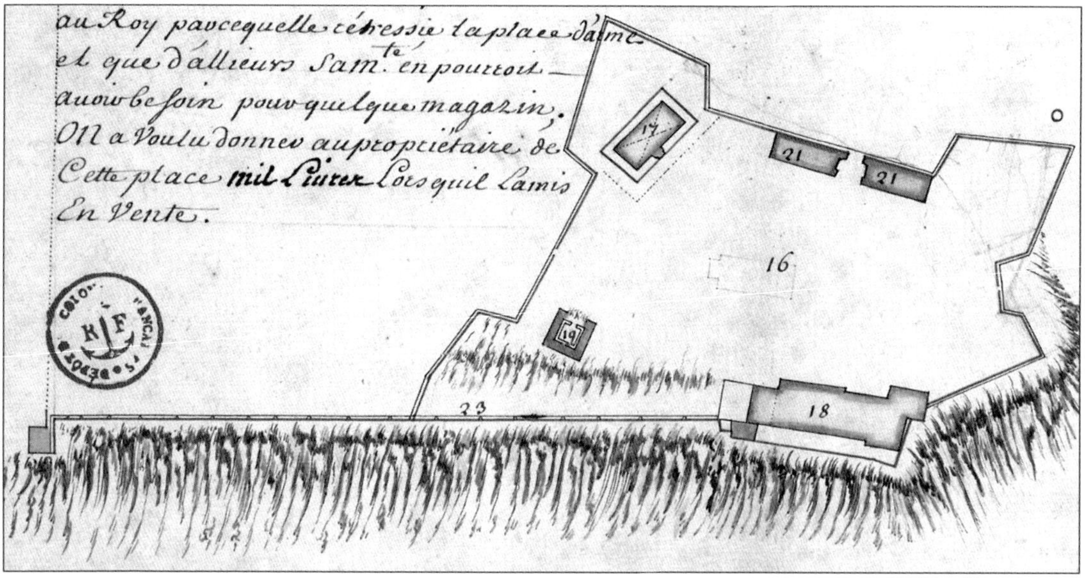

FIG. 4

Detail of a plan of Fort Saint-Louis and the Place d'Armes in 1700, probably drawn by Levasseur de Neré. It is an accurate depiction of the fourth Fort Saint-Louis with its cannon battery (23) to the south of the chateau. The governor's residence (18) is shown exactly as it appeared at the time. North to the right (ANOM, FR CAOM 3DFC369C).

1684, which Frontenac had not demolished. The result was a heterogeneous structure consisting of a two-storey hipped-roof classical-style section to the north attached to a modest single-storey section to the south. The governor's residence remained in this state for more than 20 years, as it was not until the 1720s that the chateau started in 1694 was finally completed, thanks to the efforts of Vaudreuil, who governed the colony from 1703 to 1725 (Fig. 5). The construction work undertaken by the military engineer and architect Chaussegros de Léry involved extending the south wing in order to provide apartments for the governor's wife, adding a privy wing at either end of the building and erecting a stairway on the façade. The structure was no doubt attractive, but the fact that neither its balcony could be completed nor a second stairway added to the façade meant that the building was not yet an architecturally harmonious whole. After 1723 the vaulted cellar, which had since 1694 served for storage, housed the chateau's kitchen and auxiliary services.

Vaudreuil's successor Beauharnois was, however, the first to live in a finished building which reflected fully the rank of governor. During his long and peaceful tenure Fort Saint-Louis became merely an enclosure that separated the governor's residence from the rest of the city. The fort's defensive role declined to such an extent that the old cannon battery, or at least the part within the enceinte, was abandoned in 1742. Château Saint-Louis did not undergo any further alterations during the French regime and continued to serve as the governor's residence until the British laid siege to Québec in the summer of 1759. Eight weeks of bombardment wrought considerable damage to the building, as it lay in the enemy's line of fire.

Although Québec surrendered in September and Montréal followed suit a year later, the colony did not become an official British possession until the signing of the Treaty of Paris in 1763. A few years later the British authorities restored Château Saint-Louis, except for its north end which had suffered so much damage during the bombardment that it had to be demolished. The governors continued to live there until 1784, when a new chateau was commissioned by one who had tired of residing in such a small dilapidated building. The new structure, still within the Fort Saint-Louis enceinte, stood in front of its predecessor near the 1685 powder magazine, which was now converted into a kitchen. The new residence, called Château Haldimand after the governor responsible for its

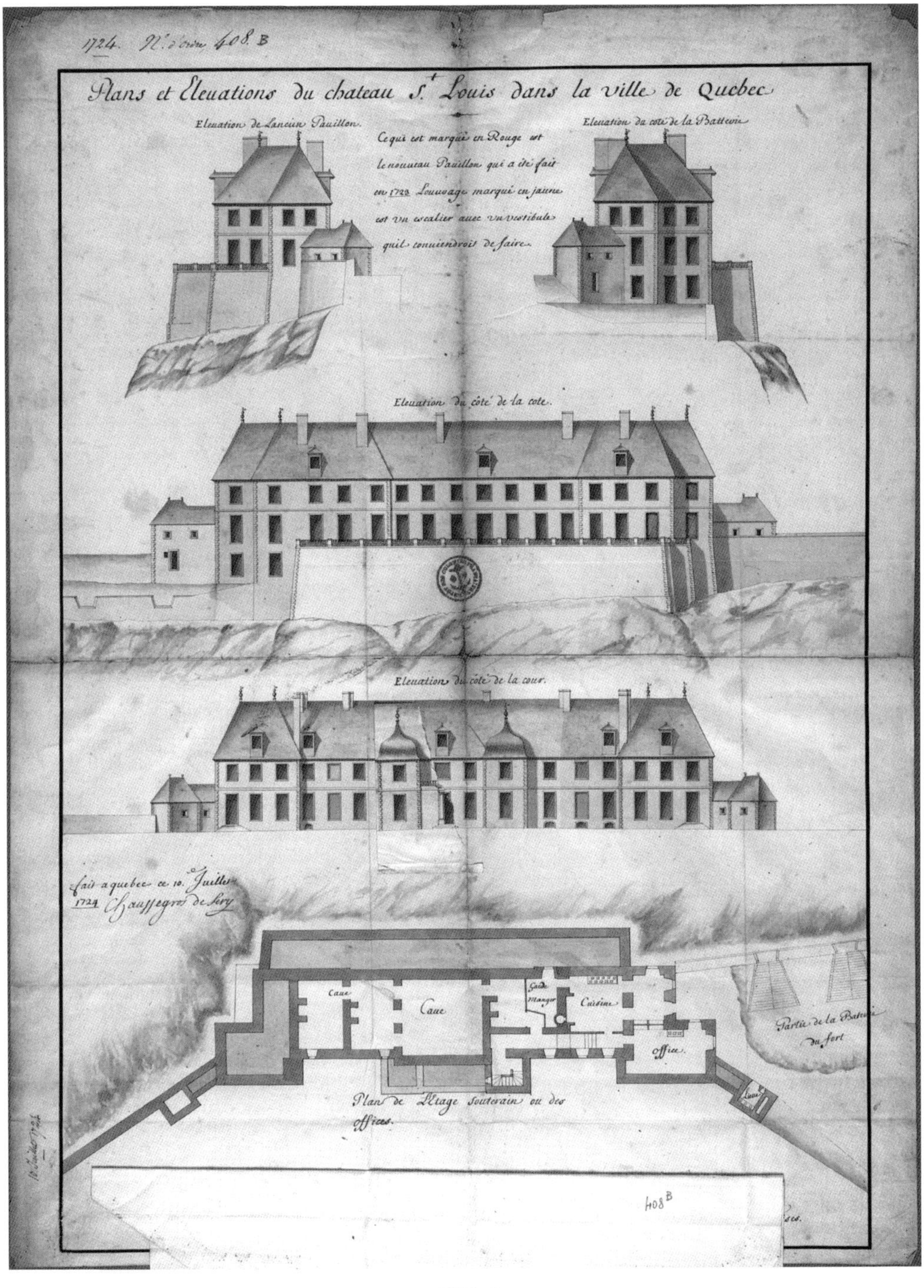

FIG. 5

Plans and elevations of Château Saint-Louis in 1724 by Chaussegros de Léry. At the bottom is the plan of the cellar, which was used for laying out the archaeological excavation units inside the chateau. Above the plan, from bottom to top, are elevations of the chateau's west courtyard façade, its east river façade and the façades of its north (left) and south (right) ends (ANOM, FR CAOM 3DFC408B).

construction, was occupied for a quarter of a century.[9] However, in 1811 the British governors returned to live in Château Saint-Louis, which had been equipped with a third storey and enlarged in front. During the British regime many secondary buildings were erected in the chateau's courtyard, including a kitchen, washhouse, greenhouse and icehouse. After an immense and accidental fire destroyed Château Saint-Louis in January 1834, the governors left the city for the healthier suburbs. In 1838, after Québec had lost its capital status and the governors resided elsewhere, the colonial administration opened the governor's former private spaces, including his gardens, to the public, and a terrace was built on the foundations of the old chateau. This promenade was later enlarged on two separate occasions, taking its current form and name, Dufferin Terrace, in 1879.

THE PEOPLE WHO SERVED AS GOVERNOR AND THEIR ROLE (Table 1)

Before 1663 New France was administered by merchant trading companies granted by the king of France a monopoly of the fur trade in exchange for populating the colony.[10] Champlain and the governors who succeeded him had almost total authority, being in charge of military, civil and judicial matters. They administered the colony with the help of a council made up of civilians and a few members of the clergy. Only the management

TABLE 1

The governors of New France. *died in office.

Date	Name	Comments
1612–35	Samuel de Champlain*	Commander in the absence of the viceroy.
1635–36	Marc-Antoine Bras-de-Fer de Châteaufort	Acting commander.
1636–48	Charles Huault de Montmagny	First official governor.
1648–51	Louis d'Ailleboust de Coulonge et d'Argentenay	
1651–56	Jean de Lauson	Left for France in 1656.
1656–57	Charles de Lauson de Charny	Acting governor, then governor. Son of the previous governor.
1657–58	Louis d'Ailleboust de Coulonge et d'Argentenay	Acting governor at the request of Charles de Lauson.
1657–61	Pierre de Voyer d'Argenson	Arrived 18 months after his appointment.
1661–63	Pierre Dubois, Baron d'Avaugour	
1663–65	Augustin de Saffray de Mézy*	First governor under royal administration.
1665	Jacques Leneuf de La Poterie	Acting governor following the death of Mézy.
1665–72	Daniel de Rémy de Courcelles	Defeated the Iroquois.
1672–82	Louis de Buade, Comte de Frontenac et de Palluau	First term of office.
1682–85	Joseph-Antoine Le Febvre de La Barre	
1685–89	Jacques-René de Brisay de Denonville	
1689–98	Louis de Buade, Comte de Frontenac et de Palluau*	Second term of office. Withstood the siege of 1690.
1698–1703	Louis Hector de Callière*	Signed the Great Peace of Montréal in 1701.
1703–25	Philippe de Rigaud, Marquis de Vaudreuil*	Lived in France from 1714 to 1716.
1714–16	Claude de Ramezay	Acting governor in the absence of Vaudreuil.
1725–26	Charles Le Moyne de Longueuil, Baron de Longueuil	Acting governor following the death of Vaudreuil.
1726–47	Charles de Beauharnois de La Boische, Marquis de Beauharnois	
1747–49	Roland-Michel Barrin, Marquis de La Galissonière	Acting governor in the absence of La Jonquière.
1749–52	Jacques-Pierre de Taffanel, Marquis de La Jonquière*	
1752	Charles Le Moyne de Longueuil, Baron de Longueuil	Acting governor following the death of La Jonquière.
1752–55	Ange Duquesne Demenneville, Marquis de Duquesne	
1755–60	Pierre de Rigaud de Vaudreuil de Cavagnial, Marquis de Vaudreuil	Last governor of New France.

of the colony's finances fell directly on the fur-trading companies. Following their failure to colonize, in 1663 Louis XIV took control of New France; for the following 100 years the colony was the equivalent of a French province under royal administration with civil rule entrusted to an intendant. A council, known as the Sovereign Council, was created; its members included the intendant, the bishop and a few representatives of the colonial elite, generally associated with the fur trade. It was, however, led by the governor, who was still the king's representative in the colony. He also remained head of the armed forces and was responsible for diplomacy with the Amerindian nations — a role of prime importance in maintaining the colony.[11] From 1626 the governor exercised power from his base in Fort Saint-Louis.

Those chosen as governors came from the French nobility, sometimes of very ancient lineage. With the exception of Lauson, they had all embraced a military career. Their appointment was often the result of ties to members of the fur-trading companies or to the royal court; in some cases, it was the crowning achievement of a brilliant army career. Governors were generally appointed for three years, although occasionally their term was renewed. Of the eighteen governors who held office under the French regime, only five had their tenure prolonged for more than ten years: Champlain, Montmagny, Frontenac, Vaudreuil and Beauharnois.

Champlain cannot be considered a governor in the strict sense of the word, for he never received a commission from the king; his powers, rights and privileges were granted to him by the viceroy.[12] And, unlike his successors, he was not a career member of the military nor was he of noble birth.[13] Nonetheless, Champlain remained the most important person in the colony until his death in 1635. The first official governor of New France was Montmagny, a knight of the Order of Malta, who was commissioned while Champlain was still in office, although he did not reach Québec until six months after the founder's death. Montmagny's successor, a military engineer by the name of d'Ailleboust, was the first in a series of short-lived governor appointees.

Frontenac, the third governor under royal administration, served from 1672 to 1682, and was the first since Montmagny to remain in office for such a long time. Seven years later he was reappointed and died in post in 1698. Vaudreuil, the next long-serving governor, lived in Château Saint-Louis with his wife, who was born in the colony, and some of their nine children, from 1703 until his death in 1725. The last governor of New France, his son Vaudreuil-Cavagnial, was the only person born in the colony to hold the position. Following the siege of Québec and the Battle of the Plains of Abraham in 1759, a year later he surrendered Montréal in order to spare his compatriots further suffering.

ARCHAEOLOGICAL FIELDWORK PRIOR TO 2005

The Saint-Louis Forts and Châteaux NHSC is owned by Parks Canada, a federal government agency responsible for administering Canada's national parks and national historic sites. For over 30 years it has carried out archaeological investigations within the area designated to commemorate the Saint-Louis forts and chateaux.[14] The fieldwork has involved intensive excavations, as well as test pitting and trenching, and the monitoring of mechanical digging. It has focused on the fort, a number of secondary buildings dating from the British regime and the governor's gardens. Apart from the 1997 excavations in the Governor's Garden, the archaeological investigations were mitigation projects. Although the discoveries made can be associated with all of the site's occupation periods from 1620 to 1834, only finds dating from the French regime are discussed here. They are presented according to their location, beginning with those unearthed in the garden sector to the south and ending with those found at the north end of the fourth fort (Fig. 6).

THE GOVERNOR'S GARDEN

In 1997 about 30 test pits and trenches were dug in the still-surviving Governor's Garden to the south of the Château Frontenac Hotel. The aims were to examine former landscaping features and structures: an enceinte, a well and a gardener's house.[15] The garden still has the same regular, quadrilateral shape it had when first laid out in the second quarter of the 17th century and the same orientation following the natural topography, which slopes gently downward towards the cliff to the east.[16] Although the site is still enclosed on three sides by a stone wall, the landscaping has changed and now corresponds to that of an urban park with paved pathways serving as pedestrian links between the surrounding streets. The Governor's Garden is the only part of the site designated to commemorate the presence of the colonial governors in Québec City which can still be identified in the urban landscape; virtually all the other components only survive below ground as archaeological traces.

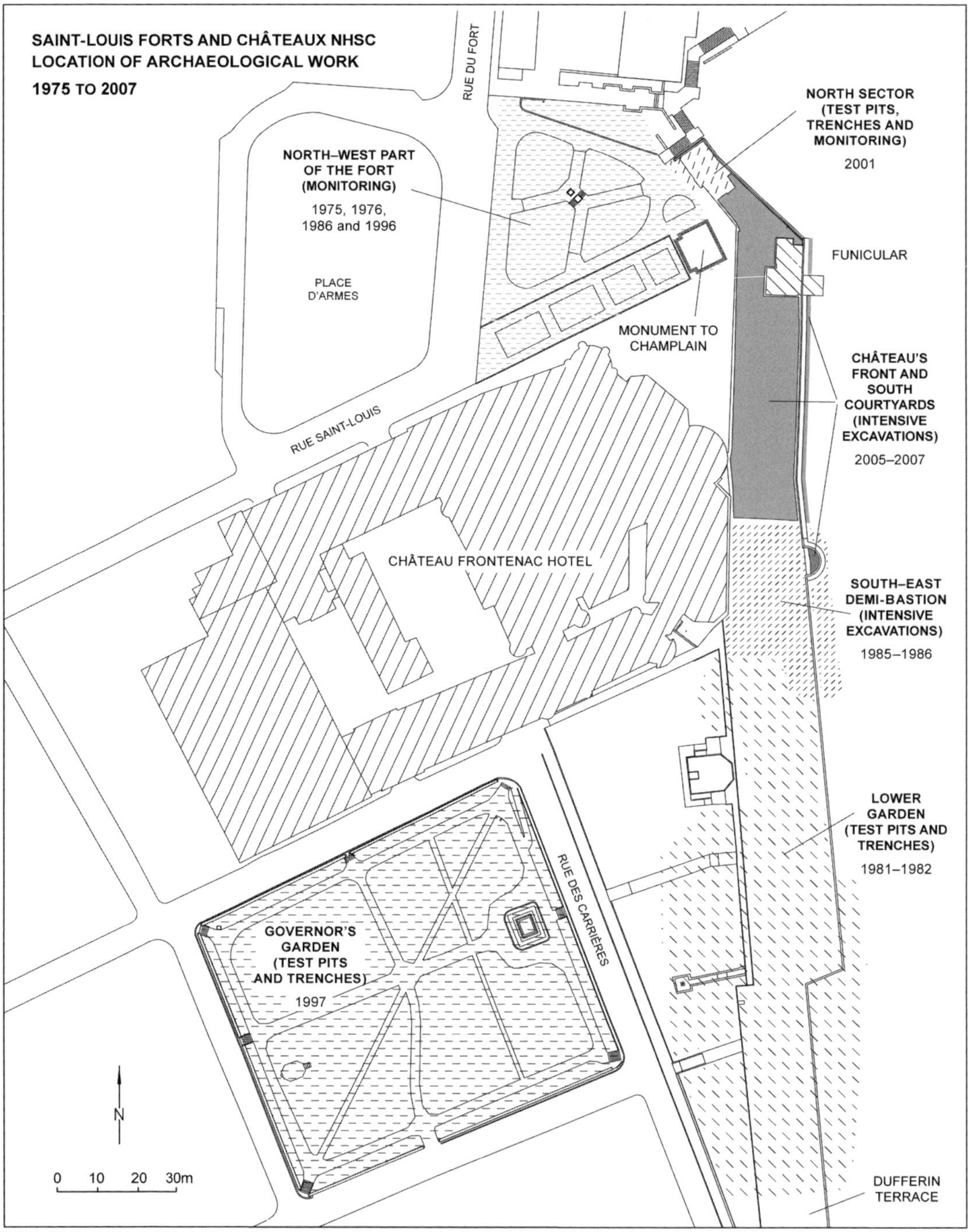

FIG. 6

Plan of the Saint-Louis Forts and Châteaux NHSC showing the location of archaeological work from 1975 to 2007 (drawn by L. Gagnon, Parks Canada, 2008-38G-05).

The excavations in the garden shed light on a number of its historic characteristics. The stratigraphy showed that the garden was laid out without the addition of soil from elsewhere, even though the bedrock lay at less than 0.80m, and sometimes at barely 0.30m, beneath the original ground surface. It is known that there was a vegetable garden, but this does not exclude the possibility that it also had ornamental plants and trees and thus served as a pleasure garden as well. Illustrations show cultivated zones laid out in a regular, rectilinear fashion, confirmed by the discovery of a pre-1753 pathway parallel to the northern boundary of the garden and of two perpendicular drains that were probably connected.

From the outset the garden seems to have been surrounded by a fence. As it was also equipped in 1660 with four small bastions, it could have served as a reduit for the population in the event of an Iroquois attack. Its defensive role was further bolstered in 1690, when a redoubt was built at each corner of the garden and a palisade was erected to protect the city's western side. Both remained in place for many years, disappearing only shortly before 1753, when a house was built for the gardener in charge of tending the vegetables. The site's private character was nonetheless retained, since a large stone wall was built in place of the palisade. It now constitutes the foundation of the park's enclosure wall. Structural remains associated with the gardener's house were unearthed by the garden's north wall, while a cistern dug into the bedrock was found beside the house. A well was also uncovered next to the eastern boundary of the garden. Both the well and the cistern were divided in two by the garden wall; the inside part of each was reserved for the gardener's use, while the outside parts were available to the public.

LOWER GARDEN SECTOR

The sector once occupied by the Lower Garden is further down from the Governor's Garden and to the south of the 1692 fort. Probably laid out at the beginning of the British regime, it remained in use right up to the construction of Dufferin Terrace in 1879. Under the French government this area was part of the city's defences. Archaeological excavations in this sector in the early 1980s brought to light several components of these defensive installations.[17]

According to the historical documents, a cannon battery was first built here before 1685. However, no traces of this work have yet been found. A new seventeen-piece battery was constructed in 1691, and eight of its cannon were later incorporated into the enceinte of the 1692 fort. Trenches dug outside the fort revealed rectangular cannon platforms, along with sections of the parapet wall belonging to the 1691 battery. A drystone wall erected to retain the higher ground behind the platforms was also discovered.

A second generation of cannon platforms, which were trapezoidal in shape, and a parapet wall were also found in this sector. They belong to a new battery constructed around 1740, when the eight cannon located inside the fort since 1692 were abandoned. Other mid-18th-century defence works brought to light comprise a cannon ramp, a low wall associated with a second tier of fire parallel to the escarp of Fort Saint-Louis's south-east bastion, and the parapet of a barbette battery mounted behind the 1740 battery in order to fire over it.

THE SOUTH-EAST DEMI-BASTION AND THE FOURTH FORT SAINT-LOUIS

Archaeological excavations in 1985–86 unearthed the entire south-east demi-bastion of the fourth Fort Saint-Louis.[18] It originally housed part of the 1691 battery. The left wall of the demi-bastion was reused to support the front wall of Dufferin Terrace, while part of its right face and flank were levelled during the British regime to make way for outbuildings of the governor's chateau, including a greenhouse and a large icehouse.[19] The plan of this demi-bastion confirms that the 1692 fortification was a Vauban-style work (Fig. 4). The discovery of a postern near the capital of the demi-bastion shows that the batteries inside and outside the enceinte were linked before the inner section was abandoned and infilled in the 1740s.

The fourth fort's enceinte was founded on bedrock and was between 1.0 and 1.40m wide at its base. The right face of the demi-bastion survived to a height of more than 4m at the capital. No information was gleaned, however, on the layout of a banquette on the demi-bastion's right face and flank from which muskets could be fired. Cannon platforms found to the left of the demi-bastion and outside the fort were rectangular in shape, showing they were part of the battery installed in 1691. The one within the fort was higher than the one outside, confirming the illustrations which depict two sections of the battery on different levels. The stratigraphy shows, as did the old plans, that the inner section of the battery was abandoned in the 1740s; but there was no archaeological evidence of its function thereafter.[20] The numerous artillery projectiles found in this sector demonstrate that this cannon battery located by the chateau was a prime target for British artillerymen during the 1759 siege.[21]

NORTH SECTOR OF THE FOURTH FORT SAINT-LOUIS

The north curtain wall and terminal bastions of the fourth Fort Saint-Louis were identified during the monitoring of landscaping and of the installation and maintenance of utilities.[22] As well, much new information was gathered in 2001 during an emergency excavation and related monitoring in the area of the fourth fort's north demi-bastion.[23]

For example, a layer of wood fragments was uncovered at the bottom of a barely 1m^2 mechanically excavated trench. The dendrochronological date suggests they may have been associated with one of the cannon platforms of the second Fort Saint-Louis erected by Champlain in 1626.[24] Two other trenches revealed the top of the revetment wall of the left rampart of the third Fort Saint-Louis' north redan, whose construction began in 1636, or perhaps 1648, and continued until 1660. The fourth fort's north-east demi-bastion was also clearly identified and its left flank completely uncovered. Further excavation showed that the retaining walls of Dufferin Terrace in this sector rest on remnants of the left face and right flank of this demi-bastion.

INTENSIVE ARCHAEOLOGICAL FIELDWORK, 2005–07

The 2005–07 fieldwork was undertaken as part of construction work aimed at stabilizing the northern part of Dufferin Terrace for public safety reasons. However, since previous research had shown the high archaeological potential of this sector, it was possible to define ambitious objectives and methodology for the fieldwork. Manual excavations were conducted in the 1,500m^2 area exposed by the removal of Dufferin Terrace's deck (Fig. 7).[25] Spread over three field seasons lasting about 20 weeks each, these investigations were carried out under the direction of a project manager in collaboration with two archaeologists, four assistant archaeologists and 20 diggers. Many other specialists, particularly in material culture and conservation, were also involved in the project.[26]

The area examined was once occupied by the second chateau and part of the fourth Fort Saint-Louis. The superimposition of historic plans also located here the eastern part of the three earlier forts and the dwelling inhabited by Champlain.[27] The fieldwork was intended to achieve two main objectives: locate structural and other remains of the historic occupation to enable architects and engineers to design the terrace's new structure so that it would not damage the cultural resources in place; and document, both diachronically and synchronically the archaeological data for the structures associated with the governor's residence, including Champlain's dwelling, and with the forts that housed this residence from 1620 to 1834. The choice of open-area excavations as the field methodology was motivated largely by information derived from maps, plans and other illustrations. The site was divided into five excavation zones according to the presumed location of these historic features: the chateau's south courtyard, its front courtyard, the building's interior, the northern part of the site, and the sector in front of Dufferin Terrace's façade wall.[28] They were subdivided further on the basis of the presumed location of structural remains. For example, the excavation trenches inside the chateau were delimited according to the anticipated location of the inner partition walls. In several instances this complicated the recording of the stratigraphy, since masonry remains rather than soil sections bounded the trenches. However, stratigraphic profiles running both east–west and north–south were left standing in the chateau's front and south courtyards.

During the fieldwork, excavation and recording of the stratigraphy were hampered by the gradual installation of a system of supports to shore the sides of trenches and to ensure the conservation of structural remains that rested on unstable fill, which also threatened the diggers' safety. Most of the structural remains related to the Saint-Louis forts and chateaux, and Champlain's dwelling were left *in situ*.[29] The area that could be excavated was reduced by the many secondary buildings erected in the south courtyard of Château Saint-Louis by the British regime. In some sectors earlier levels were explored only in restricted trenches. Inside the chateau digging stopped when the floor of each room was reached, with the result that only the cellar storage areas dating from 1694 and the cellar offices dating from 1723 were excavated. The decision to leave structural features in place was made in order to preserve remains related directly to the site's commemorative objectives testifying its defensive role and the presence of the colony's governors. An exception was made, however, where the flagstone floor of the larder in the second chateau had been damaged by the installation of a cement pillar in 1914. Here a trench dug to the level of the bedrock about 2m below revealed the foundations of a building erected by Champlain.

The front courtyard of the chateau and the north part of the fort were excavated to bedrock. Inside Château Saint-Louis and in the south courtyard sterile deposits were reached in less than

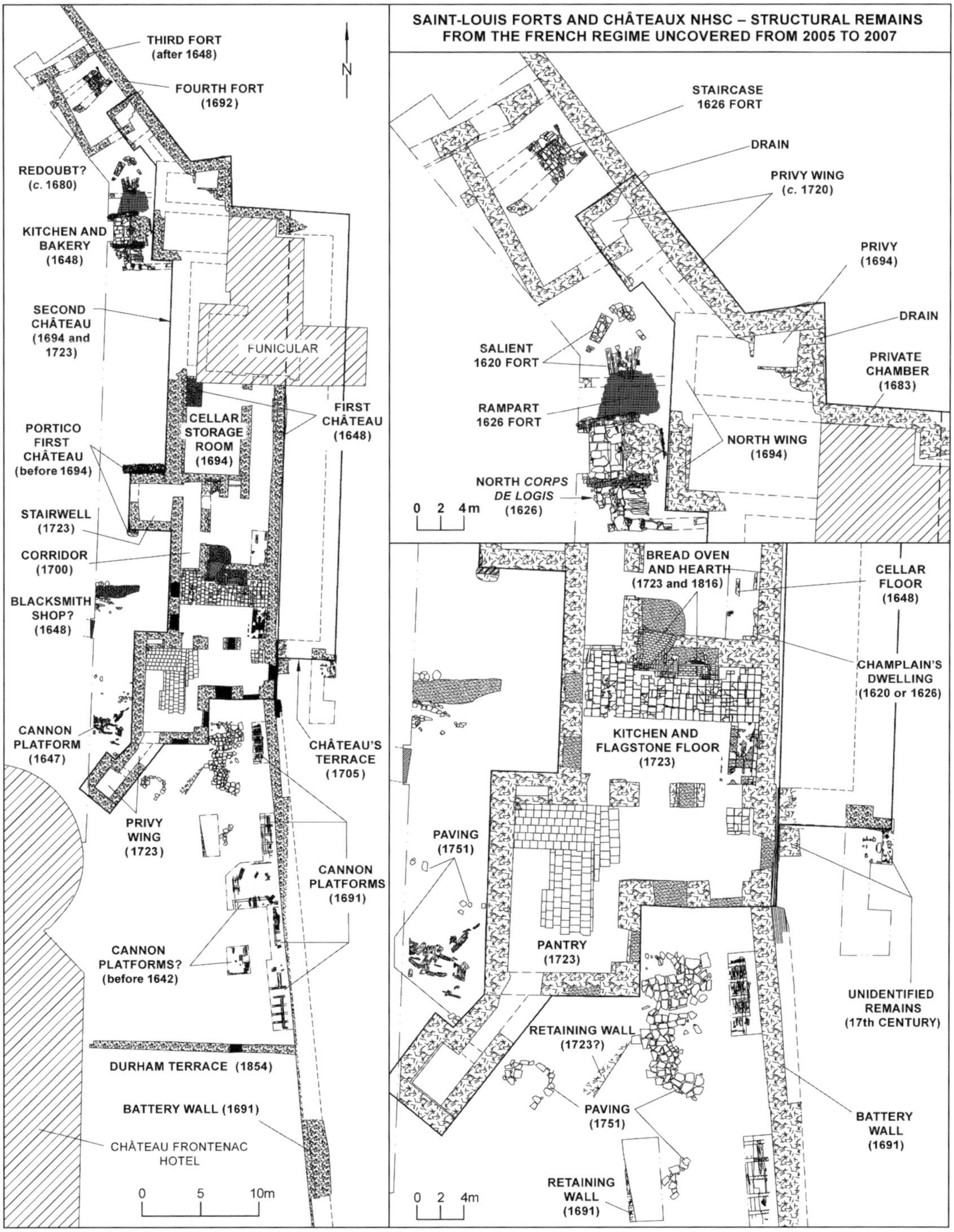

FIG. 7

Saint-Louis Forts and Châteaux NHSC: plan of structural remains dating from the French regime uncovered during the 2005–07 fieldwork (drawn by L. Gagnon, Parks Canada, 2008-38G-06).

10% of the area excavated.[30] The depth of soil excavated was 1.5m on average in the chateau's front courtyard, up to 3m in the north part of the fort and inside the chateau, over 6m behind the chateau's east wall, and as much as 8.5m to the south of the building. These differences are due to the site's natural topography, which slopes downward from the chateau's front courtyard to the north, east and south.[31]

In spite of the operational constraints, the objectives of the fieldwork were achieved with outstanding results. Not only was substantially new information gathered on each of the four forts, but the survival to their full height of the storage rooms and offices in the cellar of the governor's residence was spectacular. The aim of this part of the paper is not to describe each archaeological discovery in detail, but to summarize the significance of these finds in increasing our knowledge of the 17th-century history of the NHSC.

The remains of the four Saint-Louis forts shed new light on this period's defensive methods, which had hardly been documented.[32] For example, the discovery of a stone salient suggests that the first 1620 wooden fort was a pre-bastioned, almost medieval-style fortress. The field data, analysed in conjunction with historical documents, have now made it possible to reconstruct the second 1626 fort. Its builders seem to have taken full advantage of the local topography, using the variations in level to ensure that all of its components were properly commanded and that the angles of fire would make it possible to defend the fort adequately. By abandoning some of the previous work's outer components, the third 1636 fort occupied a somewhat smaller area on top of the cliff, although it still commanded the neighbourhood. As the late 17th-century Vauban-style bastioned work covered four times the area, it could have served as a reduit for the garrison. It also had twice as much fire power to protect Québec's harbour. This fourth fort was clearly designed to protect Québec not only from the indigenous Iroquois, but also against the European-style warfare practised by the English enemy.

Just as the four forts reused the same site and angles of defence, so the governor's residences were rebuilt on top of each other within the fort.[33] Even the south-east corner of Champlain's dwelling, the only part so far found *in situ*, was used in 1647–48 to support the south-east corner of Montmagny's chateau. Similarly, in 1694 Frontenac based part of the second chateau on the preceding structure. The Montmagny-era foundations were still an integral part of the building when it burned down in 1834. They later served to support the first two public terraces constructed in the 19th century.

Visitors to the first fort, whether Amerindian or European, would have been quite impressed by its interior, where the main dwelling and other buildings were laid out around a rectangular courtyard. As the complex was gradually transformed in the middle of the 17th century, this stately plan was preserved. The spatial organization was based on the use of different buildings for different functions, a feature highlighted by the archaeological fieldwork. The excavations revealed a bread oven in a building to the north of the courtyard and an area used for iron working to the south.

This layout, related to both the function and aesthetics of the chateau's front courtyard, changed somewhat from the mid-1680s, when the buildings to the north and south of the courtyard were demolished to make way for additions to the chateau. Apparently aesthetics were now the overriding concern. The trend continued from 1694, when the chateau was completely rebuilt in a more elaborate architectural style. Following the addition of a south wing (Fig. 5) and privy wings at each end of the building in 1723, the structure was longer than its predecessors and even more sumptuous than ever. The remains of the chateau are the most extensive of all those so far uncovered on the site. They testify to the governor's importance in the colony, not only by the quality of the construction material (regular limestone flagstones for flooring, stone for semicircular arches and brick for cross-ribbed vaults), but also by its physical organization (the storage rooms, kitchen and auxiliary service rooms in the cellar).

After the battery was erected south of the chateau in 1691, this area became part of the city's defences. The portion of the battery inside the enceinte was abandoned in the 1740s and incorporated into the chateau complex. Limestone paving was laid down to ease the delivery of merchandise to the cellar. The two generations of cannon platforms behind the masonry wall associated with the battery, the first rectangular in shape and the second trapezoidal, reflect the fort's defensive role prior to 1742, whereas the paving leading to the cellar clearly emphasizes that afterwards the Fort Saint-Louis enceinte played a domestic role enclosing the chateau.

The strategic character of the site chosen by Champlain for building his fort is borne out by the fact that its successor forts were also erected there. Similarly, the advantages of this location are underscored by the presence in each of these forts of the residence of the most important person in the colony. Situated atop Cap Diamant, both the fort and the chateau took advantage of the natural defence offered by the steep cliff and the over-200 degree view it afforded of the St Lawrence. Away from the riverbanks, the only spot that would have allowed an enemy to overlook the fort lay several hundred metres to the south-west.[34] The splendid view from the terrace of Champlain's dwelling and the two chateaux also erected on this spot was so appreciated by the British governors that they twice chose to renovate substantially Château Saint-Louis instead of residing in a more recent structure which did not offer the same view. After the 1834 fire, the city's poor sanitation prompted the governors to move to the suburbs. A larger terrace, raised on the ruins of the old chateau, was then opened to the public so that they too could admire the magnificent view.

MATERIAL CULTURE[35]

The artefact archive from the 2005–07 fieldwork covers the entire French regime, although rather unequally. It can be divided into five main periods: the first ten years of the site's occupation from 1620 to 1630; most of the 17th century from 1630 to 1690; the last decade of 17th century; the first half of the 18th century; and the late French occupation, from 1750 and to 1759, the year the city of Québec and the Saint-Louis fort and chateau were bombarded by British troops. Four periods are well represented in the collection because the fieldwork uncovered zones where refuse produced by the occupants of the forts and chateaux at those times had been discarded, namely a rubbish dumping zone, a privy pit and a few areas that had required substantial infilling.

During the first decade of the site's occupation, the cliff located behind the main dwelling occupied by Champlain and a few others was used for disposing rubbish. Although the resulting midden was small, it yielded a large number of pottery sherds and bone fragments. This assemblage is characterized by the presence of everyday stoneware imported from Normandy, in particular small pots for holding various solids, water jugs and jars for salted butter, a foodstuff typical of northern France. A few deep dishes made of coarse French earthenware bear witness to the tableware used by Champlain's companions.[36] The small lead projectiles reflect the crucial role of hunting in ensuring the survival of the early occupants, who derived one-third of their meat diet from wildfowl, particularly ducks and geese, with fish and mammals making up the rest.[37]

The finds also include a number of axe blades, some converted into wood-splitting wedges after being broken. They underscore the daily need for firewood and construction timber. The presence of floor tiles, which were of two different shapes, suggests that one of the buildings in the fort, probably Champlain's dwelling, was slightly more comfortable than the others. As none were found *in situ*, it is not possible to determine whether they were laid directly on the ground or on wood planking.[38] The glass beads and the Dutch or English pipes served initially as currency in the trade with the native people. However, it is also possible that the pipes were smoked by the Europeans.[39] Remarkably, the entire assemblage for the 1620–30 period is comparable to that found on the site of the Habitation, established at the foot of the cliff in 1608.[40]

Traces of the site's occupation from 1630 to 1690 are much more limited, consisting only of a few soil layers excavated in the fort's central courtyard and dated by the European tobacco pipes. Nonetheless, one of the fort's accessory buildings was brought to light in this zone. Its identification as a bakery may explain the concentration of Normandy stoneware water jugs in the courtyard, along with a few flat roof tiles, perhaps intended to diminish the risk of it catching fire. The recovery of iron slag, bars and offcuts from this zone indicates that a craftsman worked iron here, probably sporadically. The arquebus and musket barrels,[41] lock springs from firearms and the lock plate of a wheel-lock arquebus show that he may have worked as a gunsmith. Other artefacts from the fort's courtyard indicate that trade with Amerindians continued during the 1630–90 period. It now involved wampum, or small cylindrical beads made from shell and woven together in necklaces or wide bands, which was was used by the French and the aboriginals in concluding treaties and alliances.[42]

Infilling for the construction of a cannon battery along the edge of the cliff to the south of the chateau started in 1691. It yielded an impressive amount of food remains which have not yet been identified. The artefact assemblage is distinguished by one- and two-handled cooking pots, suitable for simmering milk-based recipes. It also contains a few pieces of tableware, different from and more refined varieties than those associated with the previous period: an early 17th-century delftware plate imitating Kraak porcelain[43] and small decorative goblets from Nevers. The delftware wall tiles, decorated with a blue hand-painted design representing a shepherdess, and the remnants of a coarse earthenware stove, which was a less costly version of the magnificent faïence models found in Europe at this time, testify to the embellishment of one of the rooms in the chateau in the late 17th century.

The period covering the first 50 years of the 18th century is the one best represented by the material culture. This is due in part to the discovery of a privy pit abandoned around 1720 which contained some complete items — a wine bottle and two wine glasses, a porcelain goblet from China and a one-handled earthenware pot from Saintonge, which may all have belonged to Governor Vaudreuil. Numerous fragmentary objects of this period were also unearthed in the south-east part of the chateau's front courtyard. The tableware is remarkable for its rich ornamentation inspired by Chinese porcelain and includes dishes imported from Delft, as well as a few faïence plates from Rouen, all with hand-painted blue decoration on a white ground; it also includes a knife with a magnificent handle embellished with silver and mother-of-pearl.[45] The well-worn hexagonal tiles with a green-glazed upper surface must have served as floor covering in the most commonly used rooms in the chateau during this period.[46] Interestingly, accounts of work undertaken in 1730 and 1733 mention repair to tiles in the chateau's apartments.[47]

The area to the south of the chateau also yielded a large amount of refuse, mostly tableware and glass, dating from the first half of the 18th century and associated with Governor Charles de La Boische de Beauharnois, the Marquis de Vaudreuil's successor. This group is distinguished by magnificent faïence plates from southern France and a dozen or so wine bottles, all bearing Beauharnois' coat of arms (Fig. 8).[48] Of the eighteen French governors, only Beauharnois can be associated with specific objects.

Excavations in the area directly in front of the chateau, where the courtyard was paved in 1750 and lowered in the 19th century, yielded very few artefacts which can be associated with the first half of the 18th century. The material retrieved includes various sword parts, the hook of a bayonet sheath and several gun flints, indicating the constant presence of the military on the site.[49] It also contains a heterogeneous assortment of objects, such as a horseshoe, an ice crampon and,

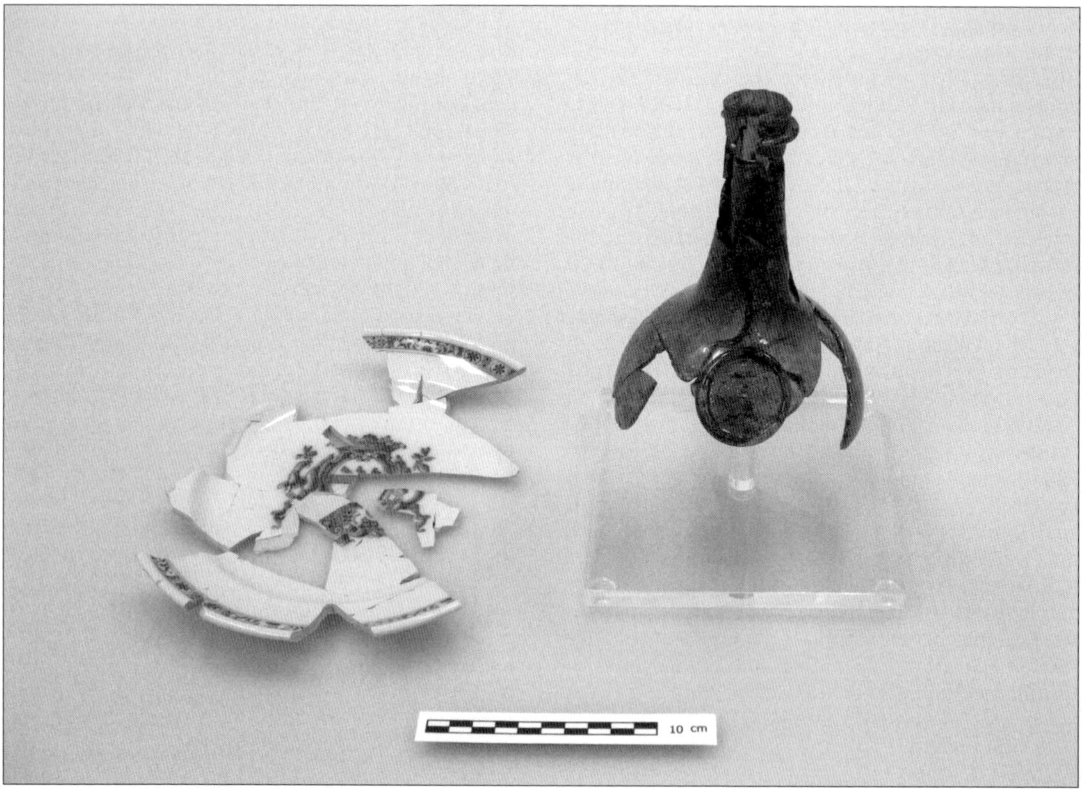

FIG. 8

Saint-Louis Forts and Châteaux NHSC: faïence plate and wine bottle bearing the coat of arms of Governor Beauharnois deposited in the south courtyard in the early 1740s when part of the cannon battery erected in 1691 was abandoned (Parks Canada, 38G08R2E001).

somewhat surprisingly, considering the non-commercial nature of the site, a large number of coins of low value, such as *deniers* and *douzains*.

Domestic objects from the last decade of the French regime are limited, amounting to only a few sherds of Moustiers faïence with hand-painted polychrome decoration and an equally small number of pieces of crizzled glass, both typical of the period.[50] There are, however, a large number of artillery projectiles derived from the British bombardment of the chateau during the long siege of the city in the summer of 1759. They include many 3 to 32lb (1.36 to 14.5kg) balls, shells with a diameter of 4.3 to 10in (0.11 to 0.25m), and 13in (0.33m) bombs — two of which were found in the crater produced when they exploded, attesting the intensity of the attack.[51]

CONCLUSION

Although large-scale archaeological excavations have been conducted in the Saint-Louis Forts and Châteaux NHSC, a great deal remains to be discovered. Even in the sectors investigated in 2005–07 extensive French-period deposits have yet to be explored, particularly in the chateau's south courtyard and underneath its cellars. Elsewhere three-quarters of the surface area of the forts have still not been excavated. As well the archaeological collections amassed in the last 25 years, which have the potential to shed considerable light on the governors' lifestyle and standards of living, need to be studied in depth. So far, only their basic characteristics have been described.

Since the late 1970s this site has aroused the interest of archaeologists. The intensive fieldwork undertaken between 2005 and 2007 has shown that this interest was well founded. Within the context of Canadian archaeology the place is exceptionally rich. Not only has it been occupied continuously since 1620, but the forts erected here, which overlooked and protected the city for 200 years, have left structural and other remains testifying to a defence system unique in Canada. And last but not least, the NHSC bears eloquent witness to the presence of the individuals who charted the colony's destiny for almost the whole colonial period, including the entire French regime, namely the governors of New France.

NOTES

[1] Québec was Canada's capital city until 1841, after which the capital alternated between Montréal, Kingston and York (Toronto). Québec City obtained the status again for a short period from 1859 to 1865. Subsequently the nation's capital was established permanently in Ottawa.

[2] Canada's colonial period extends from the founding of Québec on 3 July 1608 to the coming into force of the British North America Act on 1 July 1867. The period is divided into two phases: the French regime (1608–1763), when Canada was a colony of France, and the British regime (1763–1867), when Canada was a colony of Great Britain.

[3] Laurent & Saint-Pierre 1982.

[4] See papers by Guimont and Goyette in this volume.

[5] Québec lost its status as capital in 1840 with the signing of the Act of Union. The governor then moved to the new capital, Kingston.

[6] The historical data on the development of the Saint-Louis Forts and Châteaux NHSC come from Laurent & Saint-Pierre 1982.

[7] A third building may have been built by the Kirke brothers on the south side of the inner courtyard between 1629 and 1632 (Guimont and Goyette in this volume).

[8] Gauvin 2003, 9, 14.

[9] The old Château Saint-Louis housed the public administration during the period when the governor lived in Château Haldimand.

[10] Furs were Canada's main export throughout the French colonial period. Gaining control of the sources of their supply was the fundamental objective of France's colonial policy and one of the main reasons for conflicts between European colonies in North America.

[11] Desloges 2008.

[12] Lanctot 1929, 15–17.

[13] The founder of Québec served as a quartermaster under Henri IV in 1598 and later became a naval captain like his father; however, Champlain's military service was not a hallmark of his career. He may have acceded to the nobility in 1612 when he was named lieutenant to the viceroy of New France, the Prince de Condé (Trudel 2003).

[14] Small-scale archaeological monitoring was conducted on a few occasions by City of Québec archaeologists (Simoneau 1997, 2–12).

[15] Gauvin 2003.

[16] The Governor's Garden was laid out before 1648. During the French regime the garden was maintained and improved for the exclusive needs of the governors. At the beginning of the British administration its surface area was doubled and, following the natural topography, the old part was named the Upper Garden and the new part the Lower Garden.

[17] Moss 1994, 15–28.

[18] Renaud 1990.

[19] Renaud, *et al.* in Beaudet 1990.

[20] The 2005–07 fieldwork provided new information on the enceinte wall, the part of the battery inside the

wall and the use of this sector after the early 1740s (Guimont in this volume; later in the present paper).

[21] The projectiles are described later in this paper.

[22] For a synthesis of the archaeological work done in this sector in 1975, 1977, 1986 and 1996, see Simoneau 1997.

[23] Fieldwork carried out by Parks Canada archaeologist Robert Gauvin, whose results will be incorporated into the final report on the 2005–07 project to be tabled in spring 2009.

[24] The dendrochronology report indicates that the tree from which this wood came would have lived during the 1525 to 1636 period (38G27E9-1Q).

[25] The few trenches also dug on top of the cliff outside the front wall of Dufferin Terrace confirm the information gathered on the other side of this imposing retaining wall.

[26] When a project is large enough to warrant it, the standard practice in Euro-Québec archaeology is to place assistant archaeologists in charge of teams of about five diggers in separate sections of the site and to entrust them with recording the archaeological data they excavate. In such cases, the archaeologist in charge of the project is responsible for staff management, organizational logistics, field methods, the attainment of the excavation's objectives, and the site's interpretation. During the 2005–07 fieldwork, the role of head archaeologist was shared by two people: J. Guimont and P. Cloutier for the first two years and J. Guimont and M. Goyette for the last year. All three are now preparing the final field report under the direction of the project manager, R. Gauvin. In addition to the field team, the 2005–07 project involved laboratory staff and material culture experts, with three people in each category being assigned, respectively, to cleaning, numbering and inventorying the artefacts over the three-year period. Two of the material culture specialists, M. Brassard and P.-G. L'Anglais, are also involved in writing the final report. The project also required the assistance of three archaeological collections managers and eight conservators. Specialists in various fields were called on to identify the species and age of wood remains, the materials used to finish the chateau's interior and exterior, the type of stone used for construction purposes, the prehistoric material, plant macroremains, bone fragments and archaeometallurgical finds.

[27] See Laurent & Saint-Pierre 1982; also Parcs Canada 2004, 40–4. For the past 100 years historical studies have invariably located Château Saint-Louis in this area, the obvious conclusion to be drawn from the large body of historical documents and iconography (Gagnon 1925).

[28] The last sector was investigated solely by trenches rather than by open-area excavations.

[29] Some drains and wooden floors were dismantled.

[30] Archaeological excavation was not undertaken in the chateau's former cellars, which have since 1879 been occupied by the funicular linking Lower Town to Upper Town.

[31] The logistics of excavating were complicated by the layout of the site, which is accessible from only one end, and the overhead walkways which were erected to enable the public to access the southern part of Dufferin Terrace during the fieldwork (Fig. 1).

[32] For more detailed discussion, see Guimont in this volume.

[33] Goyette in this volume examines the development of the governors' residences before 1694.

[34] After the Cape Diamond Redoubt was built in 1693 as part of the first rampart along the city's western side, the fort could no longer be taken from the rear. The redoubt was located on the site where the Québec Citadel now stands.

[35] By Paul-Gaston L'Anglais.

[36] Dishes of exactly the same type were found at Cap Tourmente, the farm built by Champlain in 1626 and burned down by the Kirke brothers in 1628 (Guimont 1996, 31, 62). The Kirkes went on to capture Québec in 1629. These dishes may have been made in the Dieppe region (Geneviève Duguay, pers. comm., 2005).

[37] Ostéothèque de Montréal 2008, 20.

[38] Identical tiles were found near Champlain's Habitation in Lower Town, where the contexts do, however, span the entire 17th century (Niellon & Moussette 1981, 191–2, 528; also Niellon in this volume).

[39] Ayto 1994, 4–8. Even though the pipes were from countries other than France, they are thought to be associated with trade between the French and the Amerindians. A large number of identical pipes were uncovered in one of the turrets of Champlain's Habitation, beneath a layer containing traces of the fire that the Kirkes apparently set when they left the premises in 1632 (Niellon & Moussette 1981, 172; also Niellon in this volume).

[40] Niellon & Moussette 1981; also Niellon in this volume.

[41] Michel Brassard, pers. comm., 2008 (preliminary analysis).

[42] Billings 1980, 118.

[43] Late 17th-century contexts are rare in Québec City. A similar plate found in the privy of a house belonging to Charles-Aubert de La Chesnaye, then one of the city's wealthiest merchants, testifies to the interest of the ruling classes in this type of pottery (Cloutier 2004, 112).

[44] van der Pijl-Ketel 1982.

[45] These apparently luxurious items are only a small reflection of the wealth of the governors posted to Québec. The notary entrusted with drawing up an inventory of Vaudreuil's property, when the latter

died in 1726, valued the governor's silverware at close to 6,000 *livres*. The stone-built chateau almost 125 French feet (40.6m) long, two storeys high including the attic, and with vaulted cellars cost the tidy sum of 50,000 *livres* (Laurent & Saint-Pierre 1982, 133, 193).

[46] Tiles of the same type were dumped in the stairwell of the King's Stores at Québec (Moussette 1994, 111–13). Like Château Saint-Louis, this building put up in 1716 was funded by the king. Since the stores were also the work of engineer Gaspard Chaussegros de Léry, some of its construction material was similar to that used in the chateau.

[47] Laurent & Saint-Pierre 1982, 235, 237.

[48] Cardinal 1992, 55.

[49] Michel Brassard, pers. comm., 2008.

[50] L'Anglais 1994, 211–15.

[51] Brassard 2004, 6.

BIBLIOGRAPHY

PUBLISHED SOURCES

Ayto, E.G. 1994, *Clay Tobacco Pipes*, Princes Risborough: Shire.

Beaudet, P. (ed.) 1990, *Les Dessous de la terrasse à Québec: archéologie dans la cour et les jardins du château Saint-Louis*, Sillery: Septentrion. [Published in English as *Under the Boardwalk in Québec City: Archaeology in the Courtyard and Gardens of the Château Saint-Louis*, Montréal: Guernica Editions.]

Billings, C. 1980, 'Beads of shell and glass', in Gibson 1980, 118–27.

Brassard, M. 2004, 'Québec, ville bombardée à l'été 1759', *Archéologiques* **17**, 62–73.

Cardinal, P. 1992, 'Les armoiries du gouverneur Charles de Beauharnois', *Mémoires vives* **1–2**, 55.

Cloutier, C. 2004. *De la Stratification archéologique à la stratification social: hygiène urbaine et conditions de vie de six familles ouvrières du Faubourg Saint-Roch à Québec au XIXe siècle*, Cahiers d'archéologie du CÉLAT **16**.

Desloges, Y. 2008, *Saint-Louis Forts and Châteaux National Historic Site of Canada: Natural Wonders & Cultural Treasures*, <http://www.pc.gc.ca/lhn-nhs/qc/saintlouisforts/natcul/index_e.asp> [last modified 28 August 2008].

Gagnon, E. 1925 [1908], *Le Fort et le château Saint-Louis (Québec): étude archéologique et historique*, Montréal: Beauchemin.

Gibson, S.G. (ed.) 1980, *Burr's Hill: a 17th Century Wampanoag Burial Ground in Warren, Rhode Island*, Haffenreffer Museum of Anthropology, Studies in Anthropology and Material Culture **2**.

Guimont, J. 1996, *La Petite Ferme du Cap Tourmente: de la ferme de Champlain aux grandes volées d'oies*, Sillery: Septentrion.

Lanctot, G. 1929, *L'Administration de la Nouvelle-France: l'administration générale*, Paris: H. Champion.

L'Anglais, P.-G. 1994, *Les Modes de vie à Québec et à Louisbourg au milieu du XVIIIe siècle à partir de collections archéologiques*, **1**. *Place-Royale*, Québec: Collection Patrimoines, Publications du Québec.

Moussette, M. 1994, *Le Site du Palais de l'intendant à Québec: genèse et structuration d'un lieu urbain*, Sillery: Septentrion.

Moss, W. 1994, *Une Archéologie du paysage urbain à la terrasse Dufferin à Québec*, Rapports et mémoires de recherche du CÉLAT **23**.

Niellon, F. & Moussette, M. 1981, *L'Habitation de Champlain*, Québec: Publications du Québec.

Renaud, R. 1990, 'Par la bouche de mes canons', in Beaudet 1990, 21–9.

Trudel, M. 2003, 'Champlain, Samuel de', *Dictionary of Canadian Biography Online* <http://www.biographi.ca> [accessed in 2005 and 2006].

van der Pijl-Ketel, C.L. (ed.) 1982, *The Ceramic Load of the 'Witte Leeuw' (1613)*, Amsterdam: Rijksmuseum.

UNPUBLISHED SOURCES

Gauvin, R. 2003. 'Le Jardin des Gouverneurs à Québec: histoire, aménagements et archéologie', Parcs Canada.

Laurent, J. & Saint-Pierre, J. 1982, 'Les Forts et châteaux Saint-Louis, 1620–1760', Québec: Parcs Canada.

Ostéothèque de Montréal 2008, 'Analyse zooarchéologique de restes osseux du site 38G — LHNC des Forts-et-Châteaux–Saint-Louis (CeEt-40, Terrasse Dufferin), époque Champlain-Kirke, Ville de Québec', Montréal.

Parcs Canada 2004, 'Énoncé d'intégrité commémorative Lieu historique national du Canada des Forts-et-Châteaux–Saint-Louis', Parcs Canada, Unité de Gestion de Québec.

Simoneau, D. 1997, 'Rapport d'activités archéologiques: interventions ponctuelles 1996', Ville de Québec.

ABBREVIATIONS

ANOM	Archives nationales Outre-mer
CÉLAT	Centre interuniversitaire d'Études de recherche sur les lettres, les arts et les traditions
LHNC	Lieu historique national du Canada — NHSC National Historic Site of Canada
NHSC	National Historic Site of Canada

SUMMARY IN FRENCH, GERMAN, ITALIAN AND SPANISH

RÉSUMÉ

Le fort et le château Saint-Louis à Québec: fouilles au cœur de la Nouvelle-France

Le premier des quatre forts appelés Fort Saint-Louis a été construit par Champlain en 1620. Depuis 1975, des fouilles archéologiques ont été menées dans les forts qui ont abrité la résidence des gouverneurs de la Nouvelle-France et dans les jardins du gouverneur. De 2005 à 2007, Parcs Canada a fouillé 1 500 m² des forts Saint-Louis et des châteaux, mettant au jour les fondations des châteaux et de larges sections des fortifications. Les fouilles ont montré que les châteaux reposaient sur le logis de Champlain, confirmant l'importance de ce lieu, et que les défenses étaient adaptées à la topographie. Les artefacts reflètent les rôles résidentiel et de gouvernance du site.

ZUSAMMENFASSUNG

Die Saint Louis-Forts und das Schloß: Archäologie im Herzen Neufrankreichs

Das erste der vier Forts mit dem Namen Fort Saint Louis wurde von Champlain 1620 errichtet. Seit 1975 wurden archäologische Grabungen in den Forts durchgeführt, die auch die Residenz des Gouverneurs von Neufrankreich und seine Gärten einschlossen. Von 2005-07 grub Parcs Canada 1500 m² in den Forts und dem Schloß aus und förderten die Fundamente des Schlosses und große Teile der Befestigungsanlage zutage. Die Ausgrabungen zeigten, daß das Schloß auf dem Gebäude Champlains errichtet wurden, es bestätigt damit die Bedeutung des Ortes und daß die Verteidigungsanlagen der Topographie angepaßt waren. Die Artefakte der Grabung spiegeln den Wohn- und die Regierungsrolle der Anlage wieder.

RIASSUNTO

Le fortezze e il sito dei castelli di Saint-Louis: archeologia nel cuore della nuova Francia

Il primo delle quattro fortezze chiamati Fort Saint-Louis fu costruita da Champlain nel 1620. Fin dal 1975 sono state condotte ricerche archeologiche in queste strutture fortificate che ospitavano la residenza dei governatori della Nuova Francia, e nei giardini dei governatori. Fra il 2005 e il 2007 Parcs Canada ha scavato 1.500m² nelle fortezze e nei castelli di Saint-Louis, portando alla luce le fondamenta dei castelli e un largo tratto delle fortificazioni. Gli scavi mostrano che i castelli insistevano sulla dimora di Champlain, confermando il significato di quest'area, e che le strutture difensive si adattavano alla topografia. I manufatti riflettono il ruolo residenziale e di potere del sito.

RESUMEN

El yacimiento de los fuertes y castillos de Saint-Louis: arqueología en el corazón de Nueva Francia

El primero de los cuatro fuertes llamado Fort Saint-Louis fue construido por Champlain en 1620. Desde 1975 se han llevado a cabo diversas investigaciones arqueológicas en los fuertes, donde se hallaba la residencia de los gobernadores de Nueva Francia, y en los jardines del gobernador. Entre 2005 y 2007 Parcs Canada excavó 1,500m² de los fuertes y castillos de Saint-Louis descubriendo los cimientos del castillo junto con largas secciones de las fortificaciones. Las excavaciones demuestran que el castillo se fundó sobre la casa de Champlain, confirmando la importancia de este emplazamiento, y que las defensas se adaptaron a la topografía. Los materiales encontrados reflejan la función residencial y de gobierno que tuvo el yacimiento.

Parcs Canada, 3 Passage du Chien d'Or, C.P. 6060 Haute-Ville, Québec, Québec, Canada G1R 4V7
[pierre.cloutier@pc.gc.ca; paul-gaston.l'anglais@pc.gc.ca]

Post-Medieval Archaeology **43/1** (2009), 125–139

The origins of the Château Saint-Louis, the residence of the Governor of New France

By MANON GOYETTE

SUMMARY: Archaeological excavations from 2005 to 2007 on the site of the Château Saint-Louis uncovered evidence for the official residence of Canada's Governors General during the colonial era. The chateau underwent several changes in the course of its existence, and by the end of the French regime had become one of the colony's most prestigious buildings. The archaeological evidence shows that the layout of the chateau and its secondary buildings followed from an earlier spatial organization model applied by Champlain in 1626, apparently derived from an architectural tradition of north-west France.

INTRODUCTION

Archaeological excavations were conducted by Parks Canada at the Saint-Louis Forts and Châteaux National Historic Site of Canada (NHSC) from 2005 to 2007. In the course of this fieldwork, the foundations of the building that once served as the official residence of the Governor General of New France were uncovered almost in their entirety. The site on the heights of Cap Diamant had previously been occupied by a dwelling which formed part of the first Fort Saint-Louis, erected in 1620 by Samuel de Champlain, the founder of the country's first permanent colony.[1]

Founded in 1626, the fort at the top of Cap Diamant was designed to protect the small colony against attack. It included three buildings, one of which housed the living quarters of the colony's commander; their layout seems to have defined the spatial organization of later structures within the fort, in particular the official residence of the Governor General of New France and its attendant buildings.

The earliest Governor General's residence was built by Charles Huault de Montmagny, the first official governor. Completed in 1648, it stood within the fortified enceinte of the largest fortress in the colony and was called 'Château Saint-Louis', after the fort on the site. The building was subsequently renovated, modified and even completely rebuilt to make it more spacious and comfortable, better suited to the governor's role in the society of New France.

It was Louis de Buade, Comte de Frontenac, who decided to reconstruct the chateau in 1694, regarding the building erected by Montmagny as outmoded, inadequate and unworthy of King Louis XIV.[2] However, Frontenac's project was ambitious and it was not completed until 1723, during the term of office of Philippe Rigaud de Vaudreuil. The chateau continued to serve as the Governor General's official residence after the British conquest of Québec in 1759. It underwent major renovations in 1808–11 and was eventually destroyed by fire in 1834.

A wealth of historical documentation has been used to study the development of the Château Saint-Louis, including building contracts, inventories, old maps and plans. Thanks to the archaeological fieldwork of 2005–07, the entire cellar of the chateau as it was in 1834 has now been uncovered.[3] Several structural components from the French regime have also been found,[4] including six rooms, two corridors, a stairwell and three privy pits. Almost all the rooms were preserved to their entire height and still contained flooring and other

DOI: 10.1179/007942309X12457508844080

features such as fireplaces, a bread oven, a built-in cupboard, air vents, and door and window jambs. A complex network of walls testifies to the building's different construction phases. Some of the excavated features pre-date the chateau, and are associated with the initial occupation of the site by Samuel de Champlain.

This paper focuses on the period from 1620–94 — from construction in the time of Champlain to the erection of the second Château Saint-Louis; it uses both archaeological and documentary evidence. It also describes briefly the reconstruction work that helped to make this residence one of the colony's most prestigious buildings by the end of the French regime.

CHAMPLAIN'S DWELLING IN FORT SAINT-LOUIS (1620–48)

HISTORICAL EVIDENCE

After establishing a settlement, or Habitation,[5] on the point of Québec in 1608 on behalf of the Compagnie de la Nouvelle-France, Champlain founded the Compagnie de Rouen et de Saint-Malo in association with Pierre du Gua de Monts and other merchants in 1613.[6] The new company, which aimed not only to pursue business interests but also to colonize the New World,[7] undertook to provide for the needs of 80 settlers and to fortify Québec. Champlain was placed in charge of the enterprise in 1619, and one year later raised a fort on the heights of Cap Diamant:

> I established this building in a very good situation upon a mountain which commanded the channel of the river St Lawrence at one of its narrowest points; though none of the shareholders of the Company had been able to appreciate the necessity for having a fortified place for the protection of the country and of their own property.[8]

The fort, known as Fort Saint-Louis, was intended to serve as a *réduit* where people could retreat for safety if the small colony was attacked. According to Champlain, the population amounted to '60 persons, all told, men, women, friars, and children'.[9] Although few historical documents offer relevant information, Champlain records that there was a dwelling in the fort.[10] The house was probably of wooden construction, and its roof angle may have been fairly steep, after the style in Normandy. In 1624[11] 'there was a very violent gale which carried the roof of Fort St Louis more than 30 feet over the ramparts, owing to its being raised too high'.[12]

In all likelihood, Champlain did not live in the dwelling in Fort Saint-Louis between 1620 and 1626, as he stayed with his wife, Hélène Boullé, and his servant at the Habitation from 1620 to 1624.[13] It is possible, however, that workmen occupied the house in the fort when Champlain returned from France in 1626:

> The fort was just as I had left it; not a thing had been done to it, as I fully expected when I went away. Nor had anything been done to the building inside, which was only begun, there being as yet only a single room in which were several households, waiting for the place to be finished. I saw a lot of work at a standstill, although, on my departure, two and a half years before, I had left a quantity of material ready, wood brought to the spot, and 1800 boards sawn for the dwelling quarters, in constructing which the workmen made great mistakes through not following the plan I had made and explained to them.[14]

In 1622, the Compagnie de Rouen et de Saint-Malo merged with the Compagnie de Montmorency; in 1625 the new company was acquired by the Duc de Ventadour. According to Champlain, the backers were more interested in profits than in colonization efforts. Nonetheless, in the interests of the colony, Champlain began to rebuild Fort Saint-Louis in 1626, for he considered it too small to protect the population in the event of an attack:

> On the other hand, I realized that the fort which I had caused to be made was very small, should necessity arise, to take in the inhabitants of the colony, together with the soldiers whom we might some day have for its defence, when it should please the king to send them; and that there would have to be room for additional building. The fort as it was had been good enough for a small number of persons; but according to the bird, the cage must be built, and now by enlarging it, it would be more comfortable. Consequently I resolved to pull it down and build it on a larger scale. [I began by] levelling it to the ground.[15]

Champlain also said that 'the materials from the demolition of the small fort helped to rebuild the larger one'.[16] It is not known, however, if a new dwelling was erected or if the old one built in 1620 was simply completed. In the year after construction work began on the new fort, Cardinal Richelieu abolished the Compagnie de Montmorency and created the Compagnie des Cent-Associés. The new company was required, among other things, to increase the number of colonists to 1,000, with equal numbers of men and women.[17] The need to build a larger fort thus became all the more urgent.

Champlain appears to have been living in the house at Fort Saint-Louis when the stronghold was captured by the Kirke brothers: 'Louis Kirke advanced to the fort to take possession of it. I wished to vacate my quarters there, but he would not hear of my doing so until I should be leaving Quebec entirely. And every kind of courtesy that he could think of he showed on me.'[18] From 1629 to 1632, the period during which they occupied the fort, the Kirkes appear to have worked on certain structures and may have improved its defences.[19] However, when Champlain retook possession in 1632, the fort seems to have been in a sorry state:

> I found the entire place left in ruins by the English. This, therefore, is to assure Your Highness that I have rebuilt the demolished ruins, enlarged the fortifications, increased the buildings, and raised two new dwellings.[20]

The 1626 fort had a double enceinte made of wood and fascines.[21] According to the plan drawn by the King's Surveyor Jean Bourdon in 1635,[22] it contained three buildings arranged in a 'U' around a courtyard inside the inner enceinte. Since this plan was made before the new governor, Montmagny, embarked on renovation work in 1637, we know that it illustrates the second fort. The key to the plan shows that one of the buildings in the inner enceinte corresponded to a house occupied by Champlain ('Le logis de monso de champlain'). The other two buildings bear the designation 'corps de logis', while the open space surrounded by the three structures is called the 'place darmes', or parade ground. Champlain's house stood on the edge of the cliff. A terrace along the rear wall overlooked the St Lawrence, providing a view of enemies coming up the river and of the Habitation situated below the fort.[23] Two doors led into the house from the courtyard, or parade ground, located in front. One of the doorways opened onto the *corps de logis* to the north.

ARCHAEOLOGICAL EVIDENCE

Three archaeological discoveries may attest to the presence of the buildings erected in the time of Champlain inside the second fort's inner enceinte (Fig. 1); their stratigraphic position associates them with the site's early occupation. All these features were investigated only partially, as they extended beyond the limits of the excavation.

The first feature consists of the corner of a stone building, of which barely two courses of masonry were preserved. Built directly on the bedrock and belonging to a structure situated on the very edge of the cliff, this might well be part of the foundations of the building called 'Le logis de monso de champlain' on Bourdon's 1635 plan. However, the feature's location in relationship to the fort's south curtain wall casts some doubt on this: the distance between the building's corner and the southern limit of the fort's inner enceinte, marked by a sharp drop in the bedrock, is too small to leave enough room for the *corps de logis* shown to the south of the courtyard on the 1635 plan.

The masonry feature discovered on the edge of the cliff is undoubtedly associated with the occupation phase pre-dating the construction of the first chateau (1620–48), since it was covered by a soil layer containing artefacts of the first half of the 17th century. This was overlain in turn by the south-east corner of the first chateau built by Montmagny in 1647–48. The fact that Montmagny positioned the corner of his chateau in exactly the same place as the earlier foundation surely shows that he knew of its existence; a building must still have been standing when the governor embarked on his construction project. Since Montmagny lived in Champlain's former house throughout his term of office before erecting his chateau,[24] the building was probably Champlain's old living quarters. It remains to be determined whether this building was started in 1620 and only completed in 1626, or was entirely rebuilt in 1626.

In 1644, Marie de l'Incarnation, the founder of the Ursuline order in Québec, said of the second Fort Saint-Louis: 'The fort is of stone, as are the houses that belong to it.'[25] Since the excavated masonry represents only a very small portion of the foundations of one of the fort structures, it does not necessarily corroborate this statement; indeed it could have supported different types of superstructure — of wood, timber framing or of stone. It is known that stone used to build the foundations was extracted from Cap Diamant, perhaps right on the site.

Features possibly associated with the *corps de logis* on the north side of the courtyard in the second fort were excavated only partially. They were almost completely overlain by the remains of a structure erected in 1648–80 which had to be left *in situ* during excavation.[26] This evidence is highly significant, consisting of a very narrow limestone wall, possibly a partition, and an unidentified masonry structure, which might be another wall or a section of paving. Since the building is presumed to extend beyond the limits of the excavation, more could be learned about it by future archaeological investigations.

The function of the building has not been determined with certainty. However, because it had an entrance-way next to one of the doors of the

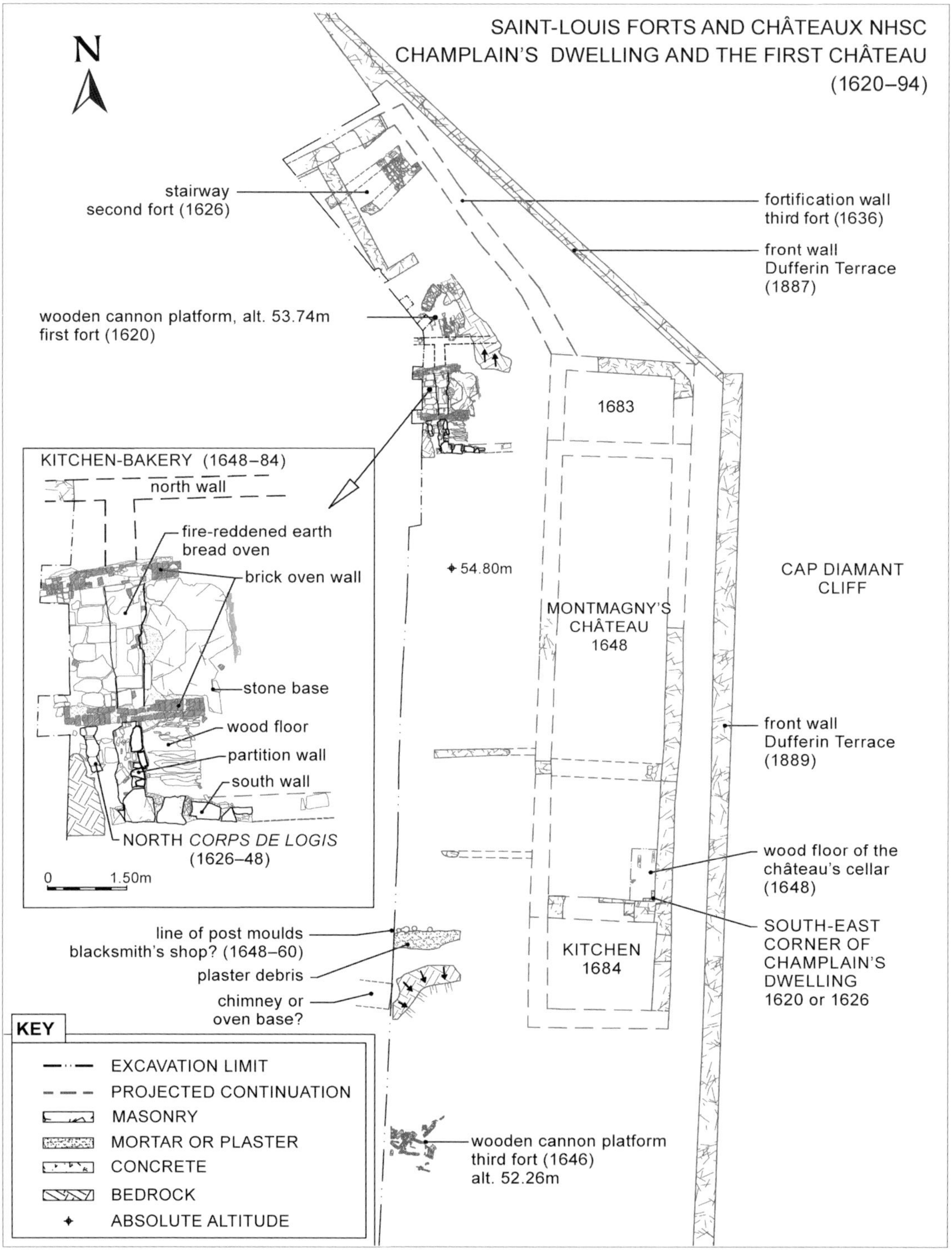

FIG. 1

Remains of the first Château Saint-Louis and its outbuildings superimposed on the remains of structures erected in the time of Champlain in Fort Saint-Louis (drawn by L. Gagnon, J. Croteau, Parks Canada, 2008-38G-04).

house on the edge of the cliff, it seems to have been used for access between the two buildings. The most plausible hypothesis is that the *corps de logis* to the north of the courtyard served as an annexe, housing accessory facilities such as a kitchen or a bread oven, with further rooms on the second floor or in the attic. Six Jesuit fathers are known to have lived at the fort with Champlain after the Kirke brothers left.[27] In 1639, when Champlain's former house was occupied by Governor Montmagny, Ursuline and Hospitaller nuns visited the fort's kitchen on a regular basis, and ate their meals there.[28] The house that served initially as the private living quarters of the founder of Québec and later as those of the first Governor of Québec, measured only 48 French feet (15.6m) long by 18 French feet (5.85m) wide.[29] It might well be asked if it was large enough to house the kitchen of Fort Saint-Louis, which may instead have been located in the *corps de logis*.

Layers of ash and clay containing charcoal associated with the *corps de logis* may indicate the presence of a fireplace. Since only a small area was excavated, the artefact assemblage recovered is fairly limited. There are few obvious traces of culinary activities, apart from table scraps in the form of bird, fish and mammal bones, which were admittedly uncovered in other contexts as well. Besides food remains, finds include a wood-splitting wedge, a copper tack, pins, balls and shot, a trinket, glass beads and wampum.

The third building, shown on the south side of the courtyard on Bourdon's 1635 plan, may have been built by the Kirke brothers. Although originally from Dieppe in Normandy, they had turned to the king of England to further their financial interests, and occupied Fort Saint-Louis on behalf of the English Crown from 1629 to 1632. It appears that they erected a building inside the fort during that period. When Champlain returned to Québec in 1632, he described the work they had undertaken as follows:

> The only building they had constructed inside was a framed one against the rampart, which they had partly thrown down on the side towards Cape Diamond, so as to gain room; and that one was not yet finished.[30]

This framed building may have been completed by Champlain and have been one of the two houses he is said to have erected in the fort on his return.

The only archaeological finds which shed any light on the building on the south side of the courtyard are a few pieces of metal slag and iron tailings found in contexts contemporary with the fort's early days, and a layer of ash and reddened schist. The layer can be associated stratigraphically with the period 1626–48, prior to the construction of the first Château Saint-Louis. Chemical analyses of soil samples from this deposit revealed that it contained an iron ball and thin fragments of iron, indicating that the metal was worked in the vicinity.[31] Although no structural evidence has been uncovered to date, these traces of ironworking may suggest that the structure forming the southern limit of the fort's courtyard housed a blacksmith's shop. The inventory drawn up by Champlain when he surrendered the fort to the Kirkes in 1629 mentions 'a smithes fordge with the appurtenances'.[32] Further excavation is needed to verify this hypothesis.

ORIGINS OF THE BUILDING LAYOUT

In all likelihood, the arrangement of the buildings in Fort Saint-Louis from 1626 was dictated by defensive considerations. According to Bourdon's plans of 1635 and 1647, the two *corps de logis* to the north and south of the courtyard were built against the fort's earth ramparts and were thus integral parts of the inner enceinte. It is also possible, however, that the U-shaped arrangement of the fort's buildings around an open space was inspired by a layout commonly found in north-west France in the 17th century. This layout, with several interdependent structures around an inner courtyard, resembles a form of architecture encountered in Perche, Normandy and Brittany, regions that Champlain visited while in France.[33] A similar layout seems to have been applied in the settlements on Saint-Croix Island and in Port-Royal, where a blacksmith's shop, a kitchen and a bakery were set up in structures other than those occupied by Champlain, Du Pont Gravé and Du Gua de Monts. It is not surprising therefore, that Champlain reproduced this architectural model at Fort Saint-Louis in Québec.

A number of similarities can also be observed between the construction materials used at the fort and in the mother country. According to A. Robitaille, 'Modest houses in Normandy had floors of hard-packed clay mixed with limestone, while more comfortable dwellings had stone or ceramic tile floors. In houses with no cellars, the stone or ceramic tile flooring was usually laid directly on the ground.'[34] However, Robitaille also explains that the European tradition of building floors directly on the ground without any crawl space gave disappointing results when it was tried in Canada by Port-Royal settlers in 1605, for it was ill-adapted to the harsh climate.

Since ceramic tiles were found in the context associated with the demolition of the building on the north side of Fort Saint-Louis' courtyard, it appears that some of the floors in one or more of the buildings erected by Champlain were tiled

FIG. 2

Artefacts from contexts associated with the structures erected in the time of Champlain and with the first chateau in Fort Saint-Louis. From left to right: 1. roof tile; 2. scored tile; 3. ordinary tile; 4. Dutch delftware tile; 5. arquebus or musket barrels showing signs of repair work (photograph, Parks Canada, 38G08R1E005).

(Fig. 2). Tiles of the same type, some of which had been scored to make them easier to break in two, were also found in contexts associated with the Habitation built by Champlain on the point of Québec.[35]

The large number of bricks found in contexts dating from the early occupation of Fort Saint-Louis indicates that some of its chimneys, fireplaces or ovens were made of this material. Flat ceramic tiles may have been used for roofing material, as in the Habitation.[36] They were not of the lugged variety which could simply be hooked in place, but of the type that had to be attached with nails. The only document which makes any mention of tiles at Québec in the time of Champlain is an order that he drew up in 1618, which lists, among other things: '10,000 curved tiles or 20,000 flat, 10,000 bricks for making an oven and chimneys.'[37] Could the flat tiles mentioned in this document have been used for roofing at Fort Saint-Louis?

The presence of these building materials in the fort may have reflected Champlain's special status in the colony. If, as Marie de l'Incarnation recorded, his house and the two other structures in the second fort's inner enceinte were made entirely of stone, they were unusual. Several studies of New France architecture have shown that structures made completely of stone were quite rare in Champlain's day; most contemporary buildings of tenant farmers, or *habitants*, were of wooden or timber-framed construction.

In any case, Champlain's dwelling at Fort Saint-Louis was special on account of its location. Situated inside the fortified enceinte atop the Québec promontory, it occupied one of the best defensive positions on the banks of the St Lawrence. From this fort Champlain could not only keep an eye on the Habitation, but also exert the tightest possible control over access to the colony's interior.

THE FIRST CHÂTEAU SAINT-LOUIS (1648–94)

CONSTRUCTION OF MONTMAGNY'S CHATEAU

After Champlain died in 1635, Charles Huault de Montmagny arrived in Québec in June of the following year with the official title of Governor.[38] Struck by the colonists' insecure situation, he soon undertook the reconstruction of Fort Saint-Louis. His primary goal was to turn the Québec trading post into a French colonial city and to provide it with an official residence for the Governor General of New France. However, Montmagny never had the opportunity to live in this residence, for he left the colony before the building was completed, living in Champlain's old house throughout his entire term of office (1636–48). Louis d'Ailleboust de Coulonge, Montmagny's successor, would be the first governor to occupy the Château Saint-Louis.

Construction work on the first chateau began in 1647. Jean Bourdon, who was in charge of the project, had Champlain's dwelling torn down so that the new building could be erected on the same spot.[39] According to the contract concluded between Bourdon and the masons responsible for the work, the latter were authorized to reuse the brick from the chimneys in Champlain's former living quarters: 'when the said building is demolished, the said Bourdon agrees and gives leave that the aforementioned may use to their advantage the bricks from the chimneys.'[40]

The governor's new residence, built entirely of stone, measured 86 French feet (27.9m) long by 24 French feet (7.8m) wide, or almost twice the size of the house in which Champlain had lived. It was to have four rooms, a cellar and, like Champlain's old house, a terrace along the rear wall, overlooking the river. Plans from 1648–85 show one large residence called a chateau, without the annexes or additional structures found in the fort in the previous period. Illustrations by Franquelin[41] and Villeneuve (Fig. 3), dating from 1683 and 1685 respectively, depict a rectangular building with just one storey and a hipped roof with dormer windows. The north wall of the chateau and the retaining wall of its rear terrace also served as parts of Fort Saint-Louis' fortification wall, now made of stone.

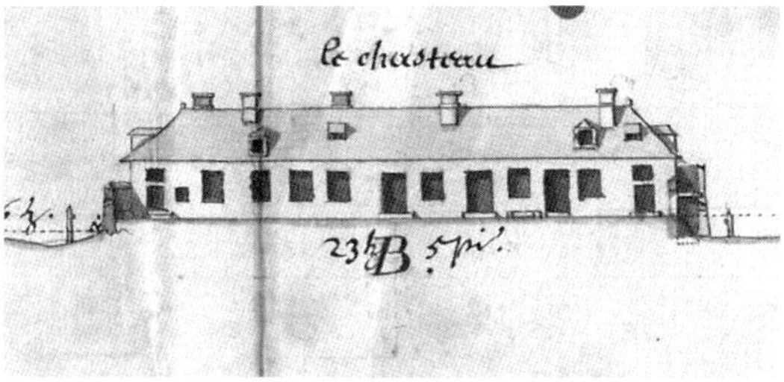

FIG. 3

View of the façade of Montmagny's chateau, after the building's expansion in 1683–84 (Robert de Villeneuve, *Coupe sur la ligne D, B, E marqué sur le plan de Québec* (detail), ANOM, FR CAOM 3DFC353C).

THE ARCHAEOLOGICAL EVIDENCE

Several archaeological discoveries have contributed to a better understanding of the spatial organization of the chateau complex during this period, adding to the information in historical documents and suggesting new interpretations. These discoveries include not only the remains of the first chateau, but also secondary buildings to the north and south of the courtyard that may have housed some of the fort's ancillary facilities in the time of Champlain.

Three stone foundation walls excavated in 2005–07 have revealed the location of the southern third of the first chateau and confirmed that it was erected on the edge of the cliff, on the same site as Champlain's house (Fig. 1). The foundations were built with limestone from the Beauport area[42] and with schist extracted from Cap Diamant.[43] The outer face of the south-east corner of the chateau's foundations was built with quoins of dressed stone.

Various types of floor tile were found in the layers associated with the occupation of the first chateau, and in deposits relating to its demolition in 1694. The same types of tile were also associated with Champlain's house. Although they could be residual, they may have been reused in Montmagny's chateau, like the brick from the chimneys in Champlain's house reused in the governor's residence, described above.

The remains of wooden flooring were uncovered more than 3m below the estimated level of the chateau's ground floor. The flooring was at least 1.40m wide and on its west side abutted the underlying bedrock, which sloped upward towards the west-facing front of the building. This discovery confirms that there was a cellar beneath the ground floor of Montmagny's chateau, as shown on the cross-section drawn by Villeneuve in 1685 (Fig. 4).

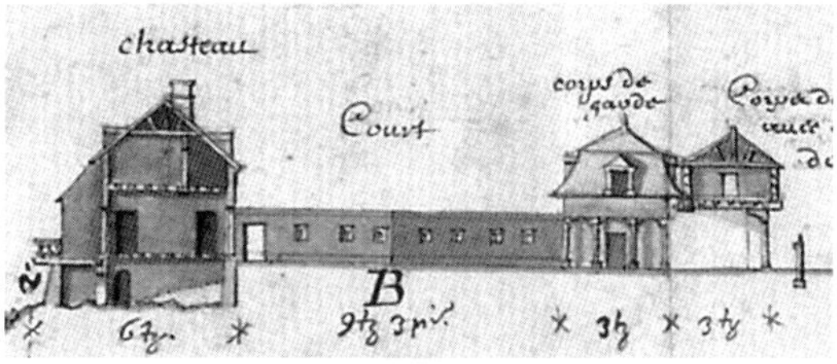

FIG. 4

Cross section of Montmagny's chateau, south view. Note the ground floor surmounted by another floor beneath the roof, the rocky outcrop in the right-hand side of the cellar and the wood floor in front of the door just to the left of the rocky outcrop (Robert de Villeneuve, *Couppe sur la ligne A, B, C marqué sur le plan de Québec le Chasteau St-Louis* (detail), ANOM, FR CAOM 3DFC352C).

According to this, the cellar had a narrow, deeper section that occupied roughly half the building, and a shallower section containing a fairly steep rocky outcrop occupying the other half. A wooden floor ran along the rear wall of the building in the deeper part of the cellar.

Few documents describe the chateau and its interior layout as it was first built; those that do exist contain little information. It has therefore been necessary to turn to documents of the 1660s to 1680s to gain some idea of the functions of the building's different rooms. According to a *procès-verbal* describing the state of the premises, prepared at the request of Governor d'Argenson in 1660,[44] the chateau appears to have had four rooms, two of which were equipped with a private chamber or closet, and a kitchen. The governor's private apartments seem to have been situated in the northern part of the building. The chateau is also said to have had a cellar that could be reached by a ladder from the kitchen.

The *procès-verbal* makes no mention of a bread oven in the kitchen, although it does say that implements for the hearth were found there. It also refers to another building housing a bread oven and various features related to a bakery:

> In another building is a low room with a chimney, in which there is now an oven, a kneading trough and a table, an oven door made of iron, as is the locking door, the windows with iron bars and shutters.[45]

Evidence for a building equipped with an oven was found during the 2005–07 fieldwork next to the chateau, on the north side of its front courtyard (Figs 1, 5). Two parallel stone walls formed the northern and southern limits of a building, inside which a large rectangular base made of flat stones was covered with a patch of fire-reddened earth displaying the characteristic horseshoe shape of a bread oven.[46] The base, which would have occupied the centre of the building, was erected against a third stone wall, possibly a partition, and had two low brick walls covered with plaster on either side. These walls may have formed the sides of the oven and supported the hood leading to the chimney. To the south of the oven, one of the rooms beside the partition wall had a wooden floor and may have been used for storing food, as indicated by the discovery of associated fragments of French stoneware containers.

The occupation layer outside the building contained many artefacts that could have been deposited from food-related activities: numerous French stoneware storage containers; a few faience plates and other containers; and several fish-hooks and pieces of shot, which may have been removed while game, wildfowl or fish were being dressed.[47] The assemblage also included many eggshell fragments and a large number of bones from mammals, game birds, poultry and fish.[48]

The archaeological evidence suggests that the building on the north side of the chateau's courtyard was probably a bakery. It does not appear on any historical plans but the 1647 construction contract for the chateau stipulated that a bakery was to be erected in the fort:

> An over 50-*thoise* section of the enceinte still has to be built, including the gallery to be made with the curtain wall, and a building must be put up to house people if necessary. Also needing to be constructed are a bakery, a prison, a cistern and a drawbridge.[49]

Ovens built within walls seem to have been fairly common in Québec in the 17th and 18th centuries, particularly in bakeries, where they were apparently always of this type.[50] Bread ovens in New France were used not only for baking bread: since they took about 24 hours to cool down, they were often employed for cooking other dishes once the bread had been removed.[51] Therefore, the building uncovered at Fort Saint-Louis might best be described as a 'kitchen-bakery'.

The stratigraphic position of the building shows that it was erected at roughly the same time as the first chateau, between 1648 and the 1660s. It overlay the remains of the *corps de logis* built on the north side of the courtyard in the time of Champlain and depicted on Bourdon's plans of 1635 and 1647. Since the *corps de logis* in the first Château Saint-Louis may have housed a kitchen, a building serving the same function may simply have been constructed in its place.

A building on the south side of the courtyard of the first chateau may also have had the same function as the *corps de logis* of Champlain's time, which appears to have housed a blacksmith's shop. The deposits associated with the older smithy were overlain by evidence for a second forge (Fig. 1). Five or six aligned postholes and associated layers to each side appeared to represent a wall within the building and internal and external occupation; a layer of plaster bordering the line of posts showed that the wall had been plastered. An organic layer to the south contained decomposed wood which may have been the remains of an internal floor. A brick feature, not excavated, was visible in the section of the excavation trench; it probably belonged to a chimney base or hearth. These remains were covered with demolition debris; a piece of framing timber and a number of brick fragments may have come from the chimney base or hearth.

Both the occupation layer associated with the building and the fill marking its abandonment contained waste typical of a blacksmith's shop:

FIG. 5

Remains of the kitchen-bakery (1648–83) (photograph, Parks Canada, 38G07R36T0024).

ashes, charcoal, metal slag, waste from casting copper alloy, iron rods, strips and shavings, and various wrought iron objects, such as nails and tool blades, either broken or repaired.[52] All of these items could indicate that a blacksmith worked nearby. The base of the fill even included the reworked barrels of two arquebuses or muskets (Fig. 2:5).[53] It seems likely, therefore, that the building housed a smithy where a craftsman not only made nails and building hardware that could have been used in the construction of the first chateau in 1647–48, but also repaired weapons, axes, knives and other everyday objects.

The forge in the southern part of the fort appears to have been demolished before 1660, when a new curtain wall was erected in this sector to provide better protection for Montmagny's chateau. This conclusion is supported by the inventory of 1660, which makes no mention of a smithy or any other building there. The inventory also records a bakery in the fort; it is unknown whether it was still in the building on the north side of the courtyard or had been moved to another part of the fort. The building housing the bakery from 1648 was certainly demolished around 1660, as its foundations were covered by a surface used from *c.* 1660 until *c.* 1680.

The chateau seems still to have been in fairly good condition nearly twelve years after its construction. Only its terrace appears to have been rebuilt after it collapsed in 1658 under the weight of Huron, Algonquin and Iroquois ambassadors who had come to hold a meeting at the chateau with three Jesuits and the acting governor, Louis d'Ailleboust.[54] From 1663 however, there is documentary evidence that repair or maintenance work was needed on the chateau. In 1669, Governor Courcelles was obliged to invest funds to maintain the building and 'prevent the entire structure from collapsing'.[55]

Of all the governors who lived in the Château Saint-Louis, it was Frontenac who complained most openly about its poor condition. From 1672, during his first term of office, he frequently denounced the building's state of disrepair. At one point he even said that he would be obliged to set up his apartments 'in the house of the Gentlemen of the Company', i.e. in the fort's guardhouse.[56]

CHANGES TO THE FIRST CHATEAU IN 1683–84

Governor de La Barre (1682–85) also complained about the chateau's terrible condition and planned in 1682 to repair the roof. A total of 7,000 cedar shingles were needed for the task.[57] In 1683 he had his private living quarters in the northern part of the chateau enlarged; in 1684 he extended the building southward in order to lay out a new kitchen with more specialized facilities. These additions can be seen on an anonymous plan from 1685 (Fig. 6). The old kitchen consisted of a single room; the new one took the form of a complex of rooms comprising a pantry, a larder, and a kitchen with a fireplace and stew stove (*potager*).

Since the governor often entertained high-ranking guests at his table, he needed servants to prepare and serve at official dinners in the chateau's grand hall. On such occasions, pantry-men or 'victuals officers' arranged food on the guests' plates in the pantry. This room was also used for storing table linen and silverware, which were placed in lockable cupboards. Since the pantry could house one or two beds, it also served as a living space for the butler or the pantry-men, who had to be available at all times to meet the personal needs of the governor and his family.

Joseph-Antoine Le Fèvre de La Barre was the first governor to live at the chateau with his wife and children.[58] Previous governors had been either single or widowed, or, like Frontenac, had not brought their families with them to New France.

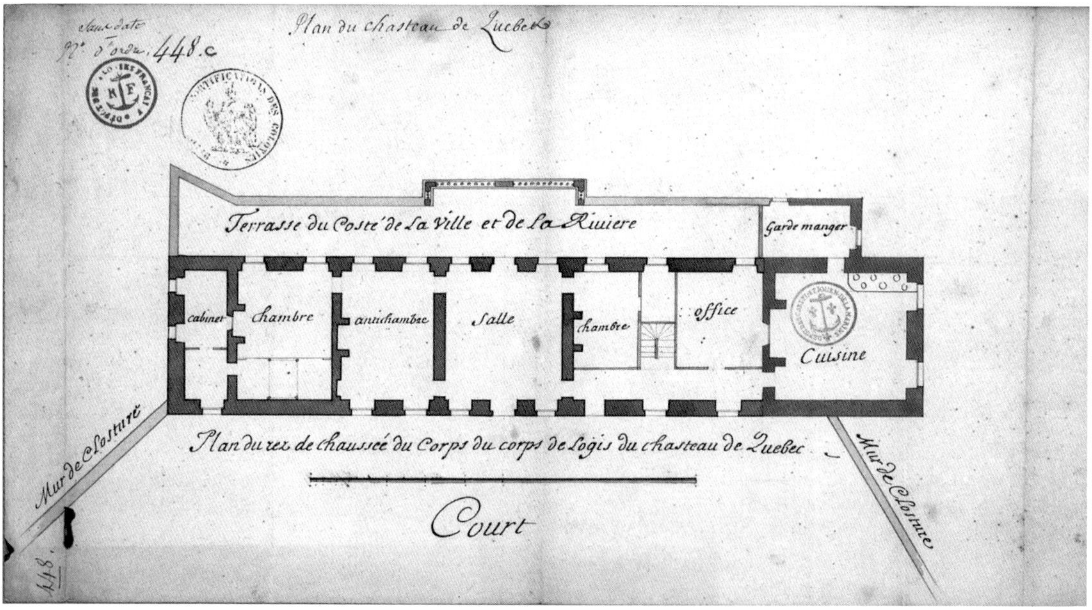

FIG. 6

Plan showing the layout of the rooms in Montmagny's chateau after the expansion work in 1683–84. The governor's living quarters are on the left, while the new culinary complex, with its kitchen, larder and pantry, is on the right. The fireplace is in the wall dividing the pantry from the rest of the complex, while the stew stove (*potager*) is visible against the rear wall in the upper right-hand corner, near the larder (Anon., *Plan du chasteau de Quebek*, ANOM, FR CAOM 3DFC448C).

La Barre may therefore have been the first governor to find the residence too small. This might explain why from 1682–84 he not only went ahead with urgent maintenance work such as repairing the roof, but also enlarged his private apartments and the chateau's kitchen by adding the pantry and larder.

Despite this expansion work, it appears that the chateau was still not large enough for the governor to fulfil all his official duties. During La Barre's term of office the Sovereign Council held its meetings in the building, much to the displeasure of Intendant de Meulles, who felt that Jean Talon's brewery would be a more appropriate venue.[59] In his view, the problem stemmed from the fact that La Barre asked the council to meet informally in his anteroom, where servants were always coming and going, and which was next to a noisy guardroom. De Meules said in 1684 that 'the governor holds audiences ... throughout the winter by the fireside, in the constant presence of his wife, children and domestics'.[60]

EVIDENCE FOR THE CHATEAU'S ENLARGEMENT

Excavation uncovered a section of the foundations of the governor's private cabinet or closet, along with the rear or east wall of the new, more spacious, kitchen. Although these foundations were built with the same stone as that used in Montmagny's original chateau, they were clearly of later date, since they abutted the walls of the original residence. The kitchen's three other foundation walls were not found; they had been demolished in 1723, when a new kitchen was laid out in the cellar. Their foundations may still lie beneath the chateau's cellar floor, which was left in place during the excavations. The materials used in the new portions of the chateau included more decorative faience tiles, which may have been used on the walls or for facing the mantelpiece of the kitchen fireplace (Fig. 2:4).[61]

The documents relating to the chateau's enlargement make no mention of a bakery in the vicinity of the residence. This comes as no surprise: the archaeological sequence shows that the bakery housed in a secondary building next to the chateau was demolished before the latter was enlarged. Since new windows were installed in the governor's apartments during the expansion work, it is unlikely that the view would have been obstructed by a building immediately in front of it.

THE LAST YEARS OF MONTMAGNY'S CHATEAU

La Barre was called back to France in 1685 and replaced by Charles-René de Brisay, Marquis de Denonville. The new governor, appointed for a term of four years, was no more satisfied than his predecessor with his residence in Québec. He wrote to the minister on several occasions to complain about the disrepair of both the fort and the chateau, stressing that the residence's frame and shingle roof were rotten and that the roof continued to leak. It can be concluded, therefore, that La Barre had undertaken only makeshift repairs.[62]

Since the chateau's interior walls were panelled[63] and its roof was covered with cedar shingles, Denonville felt that the building was at risk of catching fire, especially since all the fireplaces had to be kept burning to heat the structure in winter. To offset the risk, he suggested that the roof be rebuilt and the cedar shingles replaced with slates. However, the engineer Villeneuve proposed that the building should be completely reconstructed: 'With regard to the house and fort of Québec, I will not make any suggestions for putting everything in order, for nothing can be done that would be worthwhile.'[64] Therefore, during Frontenac's second term of office (1689–98), work was undertaken to build a second Château Saint-Louis which was not only larger and safer but also more worthy of its occupants, the Governors General of New France. Montmagny's old chateau was torn down, although parts of its foundations were reused in the new building. These foundations were still visible in the cellar of the chateau in 1834, when the residence was destroyed by fire.

MONTMAGNY'S CHATEAU: THE TRANSITION TO A PRESTIGIOUS RESIDENCE

The site of the residence that housed the colony's highest-ranking official underwent three main phases of development during the French regime, when the site was occupied successively by structures erected in the days of Champlain (1620–48), the first Château Saint-Louis (1648–94) and the second Château Saint-Louis (1694–1759). Analysis of historical documents and archaeological evidence relating to the first two phases has shown that the building pattern of the first chateau complex followed from that of earlier structures erected by Champlain. The chateau's various buildings were constructed not only in the same locations, but also according to the same spatial organization model derived from an architectural tradition of north-west France.

Champlain erected the first buildings inside Fort Saint-Louis, on the edge of Cap Diamant, with a view to founding a permanent colony that could be protected in the event of attack. Because of its strategic location and outstanding view, the house in which he originally lived and which served as the fort's main dwelling from 1626 to 1647, enabled its occupants to keep watch on the St Lawrence and thus control access to the colony's interior. As shown by Bourdon's 1635 plan, there were probably three structures in the fort's inner enceinte in Champlain's time: his living quarters and two *corps de logis*, laid out in a 'U' around a courtyard. Although the archaeological evidence is limited, it suggests that the latter two buildings could have housed, respectively, a kitchen or a bakery and a forge, as did buildings in the settlements on Saint-Croix Island and in Port-Royal. However, this does not exclude the possibility that the buildings also served to lodge soldiers or members of the general population if necessary.

Archaeological evidence shows that when Montmagny decided to replace Champlain's old house with the first Château Saint-Louis in 1647–48, he followed the same building layout. The chateau, for example, which was the first monumental building to exemplify mid-17th-century institutional architecture in New France, was raised on the same spot as Champlain's former dwelling. It also reused some of the building materials recovered from the house and offered exactly the same view, as well as a terrace along the rear wall. What is most surprising, however, is that the chateau complex had the same ancillary facilities as Champlain's fort, with its 'kitchen-bakery' and blacksmith's shop on either side of the fort's inner courtyard, and Montmagny's residence between them. Like Champlain, the governor ensured that bread could be made at the fort and that weapons and hardware could be repaired, even during a siege, although his living quarters were more elegant than those of the founder of Québec.

The first Château Saint-Louis, with its squat shape and outbuildings, was a modest structure, but it was nevertheless the most prestigious building in the colony, apart from the Ursuline Convent.[65] Following the demolition of the blacksmith's shop, no later than 1660, the residence was expanded southward by Governor La Barre in 1683–84 to incorporate a new kitchen, better suited to his needs. By then, the bakery in the immediate vicinity of the chateau had been demolished, although another one may have been constructed elsewhere in the fort.

The changes to the old chateau made by La Barre were not sufficient to turn Montmagny's outmoded building into a residence that fully satisfied the requirements of those who would succeed him as Governor General. Therefore, in 1694, the building was demolished and rebuilt by the Comte de Frontenac. A wealth of historical and archaeological evidence is available on this second chateau and could easily serve as the basis for a separate paper.

The second Château Saint-Louis was located in exactly the same place as the first one and, therefore, as Champlain's dwelling. Just as the first chateau had been built in part on the foundations of this earlier building, so the second one stood in part on the foundations of its predecessor, incorporating the kitchen built in 1684. Although Frontenac had wished for nothing less than a chateau reflecting the grandeur of Louis XIV's reign,[66] his new residence was not completed in accordance with the original plans, owing to a lack of financial support from France. The building was only finished in 1723, during the Marquis de Vaudreuil's term of office; it then incorporated changes that had been proposed by Chaussegros de Léry.[67] From this time onwards, the Château Saint-Louis at last mirrored the status of the Governor General, the king's representative in the colony. By the end of the French regime, when it boasted a paved courtyard and fortified enceinte,[68] it was a magnificent building in the French classical style, well suited to the noble class established in Canada since the 17th century. It had finally become a building worthy of the mother country and of the French capital in North America.

NOTES

[1] For the site's general location and more information on Fort Saint-Louis, see the papers by P. Cloutier and P.-G. L'Anglais, and by J. Guimont, in this volume.

[2] Cloutier and L'Anglais in this volume, Fig. 5.

[3] The Château Saint-Louis was destroyed by fire in 1834. However, when the predecessor to the present-day Dufferin Terrace, Durham Terrace, was built along the edge of Cap Diamant in 1838, all the foundation walls of the ruined chateau were left in place beneath the terrace's deck. In 1879, when a funicular was installed to transport pedestrians between the cliff top and Place Royale in Lower Town, the walls of a room in the cellar in the northern part of the chateau were incorporated into the building, providing access to the funicular beneath Dufferin Terrace.

[4] Archaeological fieldwork also uncovered structural remains associated with alterations to the chateau during the British regime; they are not discussed in this paper.

[5] The term 'Habitation' refers to the settlement founded by Champlain on the point of Québec in 1608. This point, situated in Québec's Lower Town, extends into the St Lawrence River.

[6] See Litalien & Vaugeois 2004, 367: the company was also known as the Compagnie du Canada or Compagnie de Condé. Made up of merchants from Saint-Malo and Rouen, it strove to exert 'a monopoly over trade along both sides of the St Lawrence River, from Matane westward, for a period of eleven years'. [Translation.]

[7] Delalande 1927, 18.

[8] Laverdière 1870, **5**, 991. [Translation, Biggar 1971, **5**, 8.]

[9] Laverdière 1870, **5**, 992. [Translation, Biggar 1971, **5**, 10.]

[10] No plans of this fort have been found to date.

[11] Laurent & Saint-Pierre 1982, 16.

[12] Laverdière 1870, **5**, 1055. [Translation, Biggar 1971, **5**, 116.]

[13] Robitaille 1996, 178. See also Laverdière 1870, **5**, part 2 (1620–24).

[14] Laverdière 1870, **5**, 1108. [Translation, Biggar 1971, **5**, 200–1.]

[15] Laverdière 1870, **5**, 1110. [Translation, Biggar 1971, **5**, 204.]

[16] Laverdière 1870, **5**, 1111. [Translation, Biggar 1971, **5**, 205.]

[17] Delalande 1927, 24.

[18] Laverdière 1870, **5**, 1229. [Translation, Biggar 1971, **6**, 64.]

[19] Niellon 2008, 7, and in this volume; Laurent & Saint-Pierre 1982, 26–7.

[20] Laurent & Saint-Pierre 1982, 24–5: excerpt from Biggar 1933, **6**, 378. [Translation.]

[21] See J. Guimont in this volume.

[22] Cloutier and L'Anglais in this volume, Fig. 2.

[23] Québec was founded where the St Lawrence River narrows substantially and was therefore well situated for exerting control over navigation into the interior. Since Fort Saint-Louis and its main dwelling afforded an excellent long-range view of the river, the occupants could keep an eye on the waterway and see enemies approaching at a distance. See also Bernier *et al.* 2008, 56.

[24] Laurent & Saint-Pierre 1982, 62.

[25] Marie de L'Incarnation, quoted in Laurent & Saint-Pierre 1982, 62. [Translation.]

[26] These remains were left in place for conservation and commemorative interpretation purposes.

[27] Niellon 2008, 7, and in this volume.

[28] Marie de L'Incarnation, quoted in Laurent & Saint-Pierre 1982, 62.

[29] 1 French foot = 0.3248m.

[30] Laverdière 1870, 1304–5, quoted in Robitaille 1996, 239. [Translation, Biggar 1971, **6**, 183–4.]

[31] This chemical analysis was carried out thanks to Parks Canada's Ontario Service Centre.

[32] Laverdière 1870, **5**, 1414.

[33] The settlements on Île Sainte-Croix and in Port-Royal were built on a similar layout, with their bread ovens and other accessory facilities separate from the main dwellings and arranged around an inner courtyard (Robitaille 1996, 117, 122).

[34] Robitaille 1996, 127. [Translation.]

[35] Niellon & Moussette 1985, 191–2.

[36] Niellon & Moussette 1985, 190–1.

[37] 'Estat des personnes qui doivent estre menés et entretenus en l'habitation de Québec, pour l'annéee 1619', Laverdière 1870, **5**, 973–5. [Translation, Biggar 1971, **4**, 353–6].

[38] Between 25 December 1635 and 11 June 1636, when Montmagny arrived, Champlain was temporarily replaced by his lieutenant, Marc-Antoine Bras-de-Fer de Châteaufort: Hamelin 2000.

[39] Laurent & Saint-Pierre 1982, 63.

[40] *Marché fait par Mr Bourdon avec les massons pr la maison du fort, 24 novembre 1647* (NAC, MG18, H34). [Translation.]

[41] Cloutier and L'Anglais in this volume, Fig. 3.

[42] A type of stone generally used in the 17th and early 18th centuries for facing the outside of buildings or for dressed masonry: Guimont 2006.

[43] The entire Québec promontory, including Cap Diamant, is made of schist, which was used from the time of Champlain's arrival in the first half of the 17th century. It was extracted in a number of quarries, one of which was located next to the Château Saint-Louis, at the end of Rue des Carrières (literally, 'Quarry Street'): Guimont 2006, 6; Laurent & Saint-Pierre 1982, 97.

[44] Gillet, 'Inventaire et état des lieux du fort Saint-Louis' (30 Sept. 1660), *Canadian Antiq. Numis. J.* **1**, 2nd series (Apr. 1889–90), 155, quoted in Laurent & Saint-Pierre 1982, 178–81.

[45] Gillet, 'Inventaire et état des lieux du fort Saint-Louis' (30 Sept. 1660), *Canadian Antiq. Numis. J.* **1**, 2nd series (Apr. 1889–90), 155, quoted in Laurent & Saint-Pierre 1982, 178–9. [Translation.]

[46] Dupont 1974, 28.

[47] In addition to food-related objects, this layer contained a remarkable number of small finds, some of which were trade goods: glass beads of various types, shell beads (wampum), trinkets, rosary beads, a medal, coins, pins, clasps, tacks, gun flints and shot. There were also numerous iron objects, including different types of tools (e.g. seven axe blades), as well as a large quantity of iron shavings, rods and bars and other evidence for iron-working.

[48] So far, no osteological analyses have been carried out for this context in order to identify the species represented.

[49] Bermen, 'Marchez faicts en 1646 et 47 jusque en 1648 au mois de septembre pour la construction de l'église et du fort à Québec', quoted in Roy 1901, 271, and in Laurent & Saint-Pierre 1982, 67.

[50] Rainville 1977, **1**, 66–8.

[51] Boily & Blanchette 1976, 3, 28.

[52] Paul-G. L'Anglais, pers. comm. (2008).

[53] Michel Brassard, pers. comm. (2008).

[54] Laverdière & Casgrain 1973, 236–7. Montmagny's successor, Louis d'Ailleboust de Coulonge, was still governor in 1658, although only in an acting capacity. He served as acting governor until d'Argenson arrived in the colony on 11 July 1658.

[55] 'Jugements et délibérations du Conseil Souverain', quoted in Laurent & Saint-Pierre 1982, 69. [Translation.]

[56] Laurent & Saint-Pierre 1982, 69. [Translation.]

[57] Laurent & Saint-Pierre 1982, 73.

[58] Governor Lauson also came to the colony with his son, although they were both soon granted property of their own.

[59] See the paper by D. Simoneau on the Intendant's Palace site in this volume.

[60] 'Documents des Archives du Canada, Correspondance générale', quoted by Roy 1920, 263.

[61] See the paper by P. Cloutier and P.-G. L'Anglais in this volume.

[62] Laurent & Saint-Pierre 1982, 74.

[63] According to a *procès-verbal* describing a tour of the premises by architects and contractors in 1691, the chateau's interior walls were covered with wooden planking: Laurent & Saint-Pierre 1982, 78–9.

[64] Laurent & Saint-Pierre 1982, 74. [Translation.]

[65] See Noppen *et al.* 1979, 9.

[66] Noppen *et al.* 1979, 22.

[67] Cloutier and L'Anglais in this volume, Fig. 5.

[68] The recent archaeological fieldwork on this site uncovered a section of paving made of large sandstone and limestone flagstones in the courtyard to the south of the chateau. Remains of similar paving were also found in the front courtyard, suggesting that a kind of 'driveway' may have been built to enable carriages, as well as carts laden with merchandise, to circulate more easily around the chateau. This paving was probably associated with that laid down in 1750 to link the Intendant's Palace with the Château Saint-Louis and which was mentioned by Intendant Bigot in one of his letters (*Lettre de Bigot*, 16 Oct. 1750, C11A, **96**, ff. 42–4).

BIBLIOGRAPHY

PUBLISHED SOURCES

Bernier, S. *et al.* 2008, *Québec, ville militaire, 1608–2008*, Montréal: Art Global.

Biggar, H.P. (ed.) 1971 [1922–1936], *The Works of Samuel de Champlain*, Pub. Champlain Soc., facs. edn, 6 vols, Toronto: University of Toronto Press.

Boily, L. & Blanchette, J.-F. 1976, *Les Fours à pain au Québec*, Ottawa: Musée national de l'Homme, Musées nationaux du Canada.

Delalande, J. 1927, *Le Conseil Souverain de la Nouvelle-France*, Québec: Ls-A. Proulx.

Dupont, J.-C. 1974, *Le Pain de l'habitant*, Ottawa: Leméac.

Hamelin, J. 2000, 'Huault de Montmagny, Charles', *Dictionary of Canadian Biography* <http://www.biographi.ca/> [accessed 7 Apr. 2008].

Laverdière C.-H. (abbé) 1870, *Œuvres de Champlain: publiées sous le patronage de l'Université Laval*, facs. of 2nd edn, 5 vols, Québec: Desbarats.

Laverdière, C.-H. & Casgrain, H.-R. (abbés) 1973 [1871], *Le Journal des Jésuites*, Montréal: François-Xavier.

Litalien, R. & Vaugeois, D. (eds) 2004, *Champlain, la naissance de l'Amérique française*, Sillery: Septentrion.

Niellon, F. 2008, 'Québec au temps de Champlain', in Roy & Côté 2008, 1–17.

Niellon, F. & Moussette, M. 1985, *L'Habitation de Champlain*, Collection Patrimoines, Dossiers **58**.

Noppen, L., Paulette, C. & Tremblay, M. 1979, *Québec: trois siècles d'architecture*, Montréal: Libre Expression.

Rainville, A. 1977, *Le Four à pain à Québec, aux XVIIe et XVIIIe siècles*, Collection Travail inédit **235**, 2 vols, Ottawa: Direction des Lieux et des Parcs Historiques Nationaux, Parcs Canada, Ministère des Affaires Indiennes et du Nord.

Robitaille, A. 1996, *Habiter en Nouvelle-France 1534–1648*, Beauport: Publications MNH.

Roy, C. & Côté, H. (eds) 2008, *Rêves d'Amériques: regard sur l'archéologie de la Nouvelle-France — Dreams of the Americas: Overview of New France Archaeology*, Archéologiques, hors série **2**.

Roy, P.-G. 1901, 'Bermen, "Marchez faicts en 1646 et 47 jusque en 1648 au mois de septembre pour la construction de l'église et du fort à Québec"', *Bull. Recherches hist.* **7**:9.

Roy, P.-G. 1920, 'Les familles de nos gouverneurs français', *Bull. Recherches hist.* **26**:9.

UNPUBLISHED SOURCES

Guimont, J. 2006, 'Petit guide pour l'identification des pierres de grès et de calcaire au L.H.N.C. des Forts-et-Châteaux-Saint-Louis', Québec: Parcs Canada.

Laurent, J. & Saint-Pierre, J. 1982, 'Les forts et châteaux Saint-Louis, 1620–1760', Manuscrit classé, Québec: Parcs Canada.

ABBREVIATIONS

ANOM	Archives nationales Outre-mer
LHNC	Lieu historique national du Canada — NHSC National Historic Site of Canada
NAC	National Archives of Canada

SUMMARY IN FRENCH, GERMAN, ITALIAN AND SPANISH

RÉSUMÉ

L'origine du château Saint-Louis, résidence du gouverneur de la Nouvelle-France

Les fouilles archéologiques de 2005 à 2007 sur le site du Château Saint-Louis ont mis au jour des indices de la résidence officielle des gouverneurs généraux du Canada au cours de la période coloniale. Le château a subi plusieurs changements au cours de son existence et était devenu à la fin du Régime français l'un des plus prestigieux édifices de la colonie. Les indices archéologiques montrent que le plan du château et ses bâtiments secondaires ont suivi un modèle d'organisation spatiale antérieur appliqué par Champlain en 1626, vraisemblablement dérivé d'une tradition architecturale du nord-ouest de la France.

ZUSAMMENFASSUNG

Die Ursprünge des Schlosses Saint Louis, der Residenz des Gouverneurs von Neufrankreich

Archäologische Grabungen von 2005-07 auf dem Gelände des Schlosses von Saint Louis erbrachten Nachweise der offiziellen Residenz des kanadischen Gouverneurs während der Kolonialzeit zutage. Das Schloß erfuhr mehrere Umbauten im Laufe seiner Geschichte und war am Ende der französischen Herrschaft eines der repräsentativsten Gebäude in der Kolonie. Archäologische Spuren zeigen, daß der Grundriß des Schlosses und seiner Nebengebäude dem ursprünglichen Model Champlains von 1626 folgten und offensichtlich aus der architektonischen Tradition Nordwest-Frankreichs stammten.

RIASSUNTO

Le origini del castello di Saint-Louis, residenza del governatore della Nuova Francia

Gli scavi archeologici condotti dal 2005 al 2007 nel sito del castello di Saint-Louis hanno portato alla luce i resti della residenza ufficiale dei governatori generali del Canada durante l'era coloniale. Il castello andò incontro a una serie di cambiamenti nel corso della sua esistenza e alla fine del regime francese era diventato uno degli edifici più prestigiosi della colonia. I dati archeologici mostrano che la struttura del castello e degli edifici secondari seguivano il precedente modello di organizzazione spaziale applicato da Champlain nel 1626, apparentemente derivante da una tradizione architettonica del nord-ovest della Francia.

RESUMEN

Los orígenes del Château Saint-Louis, la residencia del gobernador de Nueva Francia

Las excavaciones arqueológicas desarrolladas entre 2005 y 2007 en el yacimiento del Château Saint-Louis han descubierto la residencia oficial del Gobernador General de Canadá durante la era colonial. El castillo sufrió diversos cambios durante su existencia, habiéndose convertido ya al final del régimen francés en uno de los edificios más prestigiosos de la colonia. La evidencia arqueológica muestra que su planta y edificios de servicios derivan de un modelo de organización espacial anterior empleado por Champlain en 1626, probablemente derivado de modelos de tradición arquitectónica del noroeste de Francia.

Parcs Canada, Centre de Service du Québec, Division Patrimoine Culturel, 3 Passage du Chien d'Or, Québec (Québec), Canada G1R 4V7
[manon.goyette@pc.gc.ca]

Post-Medieval Archaeology **43/1** (2009), 140–155

Fort Saint-Louis and other 17th-century fortification works discovered recently in Québec City

By JACQUES GUIMONT

SUMMARY: Recent excavations in Québec City have greatly enriched our knowledge of the location, character and likely ordnance of its sequence of 17th-century fortifications. Champlain's first simple defence of the Habitation in Lower Town (1608–24) was intended primarily to protect the population against the Iroquois. The increasing scale and sophistication of his two successive Forts Saint-Louis on the cliff top above it (1620–26 and 1626–35), followed by the third (1636–90) and fourth (1691–94) Forts Saint-Louis, reflect the development of defences capable of engaging in European siege warfare, notably with France's eternal enemy, England.

INTRODUCTION

The city of Québec is world-renowned for its fortified enceinte; indeed, it was this feature which led to the inscription of the Historic District of Old Québec on UNESCO's prestigious World Heritage List in 1985. 'Québec City [then] became the only city north of Mexico to receive this honour, one it shares with such age-old cities as Tunis, Cairo, Damascus, Jerusalem, Rome, Florence, Cracow, and Warsaw.'[1] In fact, it is the only fortified city in North America north of Mexico City, and is also considered the cradle of French civilization on the continent.

This paper will focus solely on Québec's 17th-century fortifications. It will begin by discussing the ditch associated with the first Habitation erected by Samuel de Champlain in 1608 and then examine the development of the first three forts, all known as Fort Saint-Louis, erected on top of the city's promontory. It will also describe one of the works associated with its first fortified enceinte, the Palace Redoubt built in 1690. The last part of the paper will focus on the fourth Fort Saint-Louis, a Vauban-style work built by Governor Frontenac between 1691 and 1694. It will also discuss the city's first real rampart, erected by Josué Boisberthelot de Beaucours in 1693 — the first enceinte that was truly capable of withstanding a European-style siege.

THE FIRST DEFENCE WORKS: CHAMPLAIN'S FIRST HABITATION (1608–24)

After taking part in the unsuccessful attempt to found a settlement at Port-Royal in Acadia in 1604, Samuel de Champlain endeavoured to establish another settlement four years later. Sailing up the St Lawrence River for the second time, he weighed anchor at the foot of the promontory known as Cap Diamant, where he constructed his first Habitation. It was 3 July 1608; the city of Québec was born.

The first Habitation housed a trading post and was simply a temporary structure designed to ensure the safety of men and merchandise. Some of its defence works were fairly rudimentary. The Habitation 'was reminiscent of a medieval castle and met similar needs'.[2] It had a ditch measuring 15ft (4.87m) wide and 6ft (1.95m) deep, outside

 DOI: 10.1179/007942309X12457508844125

which were 'pointes d'esperons',[3] or salients, for cannon (Fig. 1). The post was not only surrounded by a palisade but had galleries running around the outside of its buildings from which the occupants could fire muskets and arquebuses.

A roughly 4m-long section of the Habitation's ditch was uncovered during archaeological fieldwork at Place-Royale in 1988.[4] The original width of this feature could not be determined, but its depth was 1.73–2.03m (5.32–6.25 French feet) — dimensions that correspond to those given by Champlain. Analysis in the wake of the excavation determined that the ditch had been dry.

The fieldwork also uncovered a man-made mound of earth 0.60m high, which may have been a salient for installing a piece of artillery; however, no remains of a cannon platform were found on the mound. The triangular platforms or salients of the first Habitation 'were small outworks from which cannon could be fired. They resembled the famous *boulevards* of the 15th century, erected in front of medieval enceintes to take advantage of new types of artillery that could be used for defence'.[5]

THE FIRST FORT SAINT-LOUIS (1620–26)

In order to strengthen his trading post's defences, Champlain started building a small fort on the cliff overlooking the Habitation in 1620. The top of Cap Diamant was a strategic spot commanding the St Lawrence; a fort here would also prevent the Habitation from being attacked from the rear. In Champlain's opinion it was essential 'to guard against possible dangers, seeing that, without this, there was no security in a country so far removed from all help. I established this building in a very good situation upon a mountain which commanded the channel of the river St Lawrence at one of its narrowest points'.[6]

The fort erected by Champlain from 1620 was the first Fort Saint-Louis. Historically speaking, very little is known about it, except that it was small and made of wood. To quote Br Gabriel Sagard,[7]

> The house of Kebec [is] built on the banks of a narrow part of the river . . . at the foot of a mountain, on top of which is the small wooden fort that was constructed to defend the country . . . it is very easy to take this fort and the house [the Habitation in Lower Town] without cannon, for there are neither ramparts nor walls to prevent the entire place from being captured in a surprise attack.[8]

Although the fort's dimensions are not known, a few hypotheses may be advanced about them, based on the configuration of the bedrock at the top of the cliff. Archaeologists noted a flat stretch of bedrock, or terrace, at this spot measuring

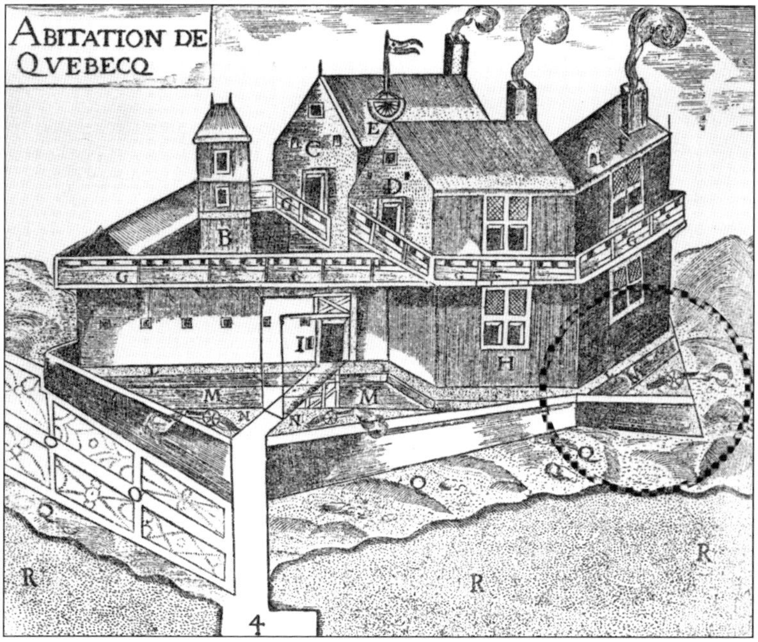

FIG. 1
'*L'Abitation de Quebecq*'.
On the right-hand side of the illustration is a 'pointe d'esperon', or salient, on which a small cannon mounted on a carriage has been installed. A portion of the ditch (marked 'M') can be seen behind the salient (detail of Laverdière 1870, **3**, 155).

c. 34.75m (*c.* 107 French feet) north–south.[9] At the southern edge of the terrace, near the cliff, the bedrock slopes sharply, dropping as much as 2.20m. It also slopes at the northern edge but the drop is smaller — about 1.00m. It can be presumed that Champlain used the natural topography of this terrace to establish the limits of his first fort's enceinte and thereby allow the site to be defended more effectively. The palisades surrounding the fort would not have served to revet earth embankments because, according to Sagard, the fort had no ramparts.

The fort's weaponry must have been minimal during this period. In 1621 Champlain asked to be sent the 'cannon, gunpowder and other munitions that the king had promised him for defending the fort'.[10] However, only a few weapons were delivered, including two wheel-lock arquebuses 5–6ft (1.62–1.95m) long, two matchlock arquebuses of the same length,[11] two bronze petards weighing 44lbs (19.9kg) each, and a few bladed weapons such as pikes and halberds.[12] Barrels of lead shot for muskets were also included in the list of weapons Champlain received, indicating that firearms of this type were available at the fort.[13] In all likelihood the muskets were matchlocks. During archaeological fieldwork in 2007, a 0.56m-long fragment of an arquebus or musket barrel, with its brass rear sight still attached, and two smaller fragments of musket barrels were found on the site of the fort.

Muskets were used with a gun fork[14] — a rest with two short prongs forming a U mounted on a 4ft- (1.30m-) long shaft. The fork was set in the ground, helping the artilleryman to adjust his aim. Two such rests were brought to light during the excavations.[15] In the 16th century gun forks were also used when firing arquebuses but they gradually fell out of use as these weapons became lighter. Hand-held arquebuses then came into use; when fired, the weapon rested against the chest.[16] From about the mid-16th century, 'the word arquebus . . . seems to have designated primarily a light, small-calibre, matchlock or wheel-lock weapon. Later models of the arquebus could thus have been fired from the shoulder without a gun fork'.[17] Although arquebuses and muskets seem to have been used side-by-side at Fort Saint-Louis, muskets requiring gun forks must have remained the more common gun.[18]

The list of weapons delivered to Québec does not mention any pieces of ordnance. Does this show that there was no artillery at the fort between 1620 and 1626? This seems unlikely, even though Champlain complained that he received only small arms.[19] There were cannon at the Habitation in Lower Town; it is possible, therefore, that they were also present at Fort Saint-Louis.

In 2007 the remains of a cannon platform associated with the first fort were found at the base of the slope at the northern end of the bedrock terrace. In front of the platform were remnants of a masonry feature 0.60–0.70m (1.85–2.15 French feet) wide, whose stones were bonded with clay rather than mortar. Clearly this work was of fairly rudimentary construction. The feature had two faces which met at an angle of slightly more than 68°. The left face, which was excavated over a length of 2.00m, continued beyond the limits of the excavation.[20] The right face extended 1.00m before joining a 1.00m-high ridge of bedrock which sloped upwards towards the south. Perhaps the bedrock at this spot served as a kind of parapet, like the masonry feature itself, whose original height cannot have exceeded 1.00m. Since the two faces of this feature formed an angle, it may have been a salient, like the ones built a few years earlier at the first Habitation (Fig. 1). Like them, it must have stood immediately in front of the palisade that rose above it, on the terrace.

The maximum inner width of the cannon platform was just over 2.00m (6.0 French feet); its maximum length was 2.80m (8.6 French feet). The platform was therefore large enough for only one piece of light artillery that would no doubt have been fired *en barbette*, or directly over the stone wall that formed the parapet. The ordnance at Port-Royal[21] and in the Habitation in Lower Town would also have been fired in this way. The light artillery installed on the platform could only have been a small-calibre, easily manoeuvrable piece, such as a perrier (also called a 'murderer'), like those mentioned in an inventory drawn up a few years later, when Québec was surrendered to the Kirke brothers in 1629 (see below). However, perriers had only a limited range since they were naval pieces which armed the decks of ships, providing mainly close-quarter defence when vessels were being boarded. Obviously the piece of artillery installed on the salient must have been used solely to cover the path leading from the Habitation to the cliff top (today's Côte de la Montagne). Indeed, it could only have fired very small-calibre projectiles which would probably not have reached the river a few hundred metres below.

The fort's north palisade must have stood immediately behind the salient. Since very little natural soil covers the bedrock on the cliff top, it would have been impossible to bed the base of the palisade in a trench; it must have been supported by other means. A concentration of stones found around the salient may have provided partial support; reinforcement could have come from struts placed inside the enceinte. The height of the palisade is unknown.

THE SECOND FORT SAINT-LOUIS: A MORE SOPHISTICATED DEFENCE WORK (1626–35)

Champlain returned to Québec in 1626. Since the first fort was still not finished, he decided to tear it down and build a new defence. In any case, the old fort was no longer big enough to accommodate Québec's population, which had grown to around 60 people:

> I realized that the fort which I had caused to be made was very small, should necessity arise, to take in the inhabitants of the colony, together with the soldiers whom we might some day have for its defence, when it should please the king to send them; and that there would have to be room for additional building. The fort as it was had been good enough for a small number of persons; but according to the bird, the cage must be built, and now by enlarging it, it would be more comfortable.[22]

The new fort was raised with fascines, earth, turf and wood. Although it had an irregular shape, Champlain declared that it was constructed 'as I had formerly seen some very good fortresses built'.[23] It now had two enceintes — an inner and an outer one.[24] To the south and north, the inner one was erected along the edges of the bedrock terrace described earlier. Its plan was probably the same as that of the first fort. The outer enceinte formed a first line of defence. The fort had thus been enlarged to the south and north, and perhaps even to the west, in the direction of the open countryside. Two bastions separated by a curtain wall also faced the countryside; beside each of them was a cannon platform or a small bastion.[25] There were also two small bastions on the edge of the cliff, on either side of the inner enceinte; they both faced the river. The plans of the second fort's two enceintes were irregular:

> [In] Upper Town ... [the] layout of Fort St Louis [was complex]. There were two parallel enceintes on the west side. Almost identical, they consisted of earth and wood ramparts. Batteries of cannons arranged in bastion shape prevented approach from the river. In its overall plan, the double enceinte was reminiscent of medieval fortification, although several elements of flank defence were evident in its design.[26] The layout of [the second] enceinte indicates that it was a *réduit*, or keep.[27]

The stakes used for the fort's two palisades also served to revet the outer faces of its earth embankments or ramparts, while fascines provided support for the inner faces. It is estimated that the inner palisade was at least 12½ French feet (4.06m) high. If the 4½ French feet (1.46m) normally prescribed for the parapet protecting the artillerymen is taken into account, the palisade's total height would have been 17ft (5.52m). In this author's view, the parapet would have been made of horizontal planking.[28]

Archaeological excavations conducted in 2005–07 investigated only part of the second Fort Saint-Louis; nevertheless they shed light on a very important aspect of the layout of its double enceinte. Consideration of the cliff top's natural topography, with a high bedrock terrace and slopes on its north and south sides, suggests that the outer enceinte stood on lower ground than the inner one. Champlain would have used the site's topography to ensure that the inner one commanded the outer,[29] the difference in height between the crests of the two enceintes being about 5 French feet (1.62m). Indeed, if the prescribed parapet height is added to the height of the fort's outer circuit, the outer palisade would have measured a total of 12 French feet (3.90m) high, or 5ft (1.62m) less than the inner palisade. In addition, an earth banquette was no doubt built in the two bastions and along the curtain wall of the outer enceinte in order to provide artillerymen with a place where they could stand when firing their muskets and arquebuses. In accordance with the width generally prescribed for this type of work, the banquette would have been three French feet (0.97m) wide (Fig. 2).

The overall plan of the second Fort Saint-Louis reveals that all parts of the enceinte were properly protected:

> The cliff served to defend the side toward the river. However, a salient was laid out so that it would be easier to watch the north-east, where an attack could be attempted from Côte de la Montagne. The second entrenchment was also well defended, as the two demi-bastions were flanked by square platforms located along the ramparts. The right platform also protected the entrance to the fort.[30]

The fact that Champlain wanted to ensure that the fort's inner line of defence would command the outer one, and that each part would

FIG. 2
Model of Fort Saint-Louis in 1635. By this time the fort had both an inner and an outer enceinte. The inner one had a command of 5 French feet over the outer one (reproduced by courtesy of the Musée de la Civilisation; model by M. Bergeron; photograph, J. Beardsell).

be properly flanked, shows that he was well acquainted with basic principles of fortification, even though he had not been trained as a military engineer. A small stone stairway, uncovered in 2005 (Fig. 3), would have led to the cannon platform or small bastion on lower ground on the north-east side of the outer enceinte. The six excavated steps and two retaining walls of the stairway were all built of limestone and shale, bonded with a mixture of mortar and clay.

The two small bastions on the edge of the cliff, on each side of the outer enceinte, could no doubt have been used for firing towards the river. What types of artillery armed them? The inventory of 21 July 1629, when Québec was surrendered to the Kirke brothers, mentioned the presence of several pieces of ordnance at the fort and the Habitation, including five brass[31] 'espoirs', of which four weighed 150lbs (68kg) and one 80lbs (36kg); two iron 'breteuls' weighing 800lbs (362kg) each; and seven perriers. The *espoir* was a 'small bronze piece that was mounted on a ship's deck for conducting raids'.[32] According to Niellon and Moussette, the *breteul* must have 'corresponded to the falconet as defined by the Edict of Blois, issued by Charles IX in 1572'.[33] It is also possible, however, that it corresponded to the demi-culverin of the early 17th century.[34]

In all likelihood the artillery pieces listed in the 1629 inventory were not of the latest models; the ordnance is likely to have been of lesser quality than that reserved for the service of the king in France. The colony's early 17th-century artillery would thus have been closely related to that used during the previous century. In any case French artillery, both on land and at sea, did not change much between 1546 and 1620. 'Apart from a few slight modifications, the ordnance employed in the days of Henri II remained in use up to the reign of Louis XIV.'[35]

The other piece of artillery listed in the 1629 inventory of the weaponry of the Habitation and the fort is the perrier. The naval perrier with 'boxes', or chargers (*pierrier à boîte*), was already in use in the 16th century. According to Furetière, it was 'a cannon employed mainly on ships when vessels were being boarded and that served to fire stones, pebbles, balls, and pieces of iron crammed

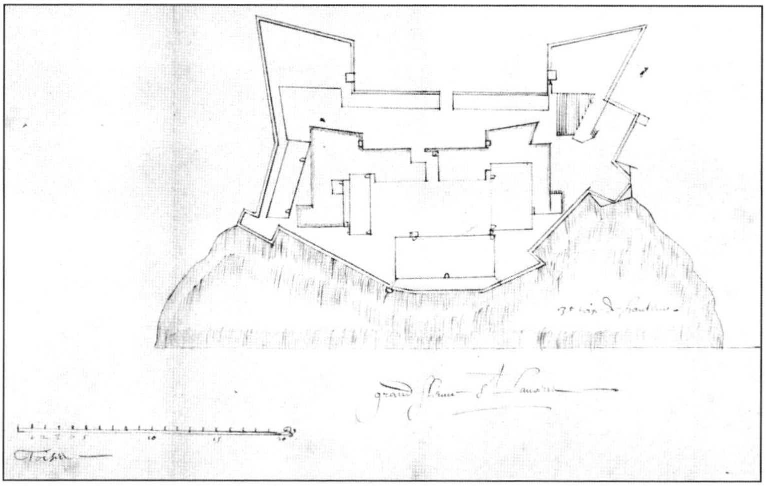

FIG. 3

Plan of Fort Saint-Louis by Jean Bourdon in 1647, during Governor Montmagny's term of office. The fort's entire south enceinte was rebuilt in 1646. The south-west bastion was completely redesigned and the platform or small bastion to the south-east was made much smaller (McGill University Library, 'Plans of the First French Settlements on the Saint Lawrence 1635–42 by Jehan Bourdon', plan 3, Montreal, 1958; facs., Université Laval, G1141 S1 B769 1958).

into removable chambers'.[36] It was also frequently employed on vessels of small tonnage. Bronze perriers were:

> ... of great service in chateaux and small places where artillery could not be employed because the terrepleins were too small and narrow to accommodate the recoil of common carriages, all necessary shot could not be fired owing to a lack of ammunition, or the artillery of the place could not be set at a sufficient angle to deliver plunging fire to where enemies were lodged, since the place under attack was very high and the enemy very close.[37]

To make them easier to manoeuvre, perriers were mounted on forked swivels. Two such swivels, described as 'greate brasse croes [weighing] 80lbs [36kg]', were listed in a deposition made by Champlain regarding the items in the fort when it was surrendered to the Kirkes in July 1629.[38] The weight of the perrier suggests that it had a more limited range than the *breteul*. The *espoir*, whose weight (150lbs, 68kg) was between that of the perrier and the *breteul*, is presumed to have had a range of *c*. 150–250m (460–770 French feet). It is known that pieces of artillery called *breteuls* were installed at the Habitation, while *espoirs* were installed at Fort Saint-Louis:

> On the following day, he [Lewis Kirke] had the English flag hoisted on one of the bastions, ordered the drums to beat to assemble the soldiers, whom he placed in order on the ramparts; he then had a salute fired from the ships as well as with the five brass guns [*espoirs*] at the fort [and] the two small falconets [*breteuls*] at the factory [Habitation].[39]

Since the range of the fort's *espoirs* — at least in the case of the four weighing 150lbs (68kg) each — was probably sufficient to reach the deep channel of the river off the city, these pieces must have been used to arm the two small bastions on the edge of the cliff. This arrangement would also have made it possible to cover the Habitation and perhaps the path leading up to the cliff top on the north-east side of the fort. These small bastions could each have accommodated two *espoirs*, mounted for greater manoeuvrability on forked swivels, in the same way as perriers.[40] The range of the fort's perriers, which weighed 80lbs (36kg), half that of the *espoirs*, was more limited; they must, therefore have been installed primarily on the platforms on each side of the bastions facing the open countryside to the west of the fortress. These two platforms could have been used for firing to the west, south and north, and would no doubt have been big enough for installing four perriers. An advantage of pieces of artillery with 'boxes', like the *espoirs* and perriers of Fort Saint-Louis, was that they could be fired more rapidly than other ordnance: 'Firing could be fairly fast because users had access to several chargers.'[41]

The construction of the second Fort Saint-Louis lasted roughly ten years, although 'most of the work seems to have been carried out between the summer of 1626 and the spring of 1627, as well as during the year 1634'.[42]

THE THIRD FORT SAINT-LOUIS: THE FIRST STONE FORTIFICATION IN UPPER TOWN (1636–90)

Charles Huault de Montmagny, the first Governor General of New France, came to Québec in 1636. As soon as he arrived at Fort Saint-Louis, he replaced the palisades of his predecessor's fort with stone revetments. Work seems to have been conducted initially in the southern part of the fort's circuit, although the configuration of that section remained unchanged during the early years of Montmagny's term of office. In 1646 the governor began refacing the south-west bastion of the outer enceinte with stone, and took the opportunity to change the design of the south front and to move the fort's entrance to the middle of the west curtain wall, facing the open countryside (Fig. 3). Champlain's old south-west platform was torn down and the small bastion to the south-east was made much smaller. The original ground plan of the north side of the enceinte was not changed during Montmagny's renovations.

A few scattered remnants of wood, discovered a short distance below the bedrock terrace in 2007, may have been part of a cannon platform in the south-east part of the fort. Although these remains were in poor condition, it was established that they had belonged to the platform's ledgers, joists and planking. Unfortunately, because the fragments were so dispersed, it was impossible to determine the original dimensions of the platform; in any case, the feature extended beyond the western limits of the excavation and was probably disturbed to the south-east, where a later trench had been dug to build a wall for the Château Saint-Louis. The layout of the ledger, joist and plank remains and the roughly 0.30m slope between their western and eastern ends, indicate that the platform must have been orientated so that its cannons fired towards the river. The platform seems to have been within the bastion shown at the south-east corner of the outer enceinte on the plan of 1647 (Fig. 3).

The artillery pieces installed on the cannon platforms of the third Fort Saint-Louis were probably of the same type as those employed in the first fort and described in the inventory of 1629. In view of their respective ranges, *espoirs* must have armed the platforms overlooking the river, while perriers would have protected the fort against attack from the south-west, west, north-west and north — in the last case, covering the road leading from Lower Town to Upper Town. As for portable weapons, both arquebuses and matchlock muskets were still used in the days of Montmagny, although muskets must have been more common.

The masonry work undertaken by the governor was not completed during his term of office. When he left for France in 1648, 'an over 50-*thoise* [96m] section of the enceinte, including the gallery to be made with the curtain wall' still had to be finished.[43]

Other renovations were carried out after Montmagny's departure. Between 1648 and 1660 the colonial authorities embarked on additional fortification work at the fort in response to the growing Iroquois threat. A new gallery or terrace was built along the rear wall of the Château Saint-Louis, probably soon after Montmagny left.[44] The stone wall that supported this terrace then became an integral part of the fort's defences. Some of the components of the enceinte proper were eliminated over the years to make way for others; for example, the north-west bastion was replaced by a *guérite*,[45] and the original ground plan of the northern part of the enceinte, which used to be *en crémaillère*[46] (i.e. a zigzag trace), was changed so that there would be only one salient angle or redan. Beside the redan was a cannon platform[47] that defended the road linking Lower Town to Upper Town. A 4.72m length of the wall that formed the right face of the redan has been uncovered. Made of limestone and slate, it had a maximum width of 1.20m (3.7 French feet) at its base and 0.90–1.00m (2.8–3.0 French feet) at its levelled-down top (Fig. 4); its preserved height was 1.85m. The ground surface behind the wall, associated with its use, lay 1.30m (4 French feet) above the base of the feature, which sat on bedrock. If 4½ft (1.6m), or the prescribed firing height, is added to this figure, the wall would originally have measured 8½ French feet (2.75m) high, except if it had covered loopholes, in which case it would have been as much as 12 feet (3.90m) high.

On the south side of the fort, the south-west bastion was completely demolished during the period 1648–60 and replaced by a 'square tower'.[48] The south curtain wall then stood on the bedrock terrace and joined the south wall of the chateau erected by Montmagny in 1648.[49] The old outer enceinte on this side of the fortress was abandoned; the north part of the inner enceinte was torn down.

Even though Governor Montmagny had wanted to build a fortress according to generally accepted principles of fortification, the fort still had an irregular ground plan and was in a sorry state in 1660. According to an inventory drawn up that year, the artillery was minimal, including only five pieces of iron cannon, one of which was 'worn out'; only one of the others had a carriage.[50] The calibre of these pieces is not known and, considering that most lacked carriages, they may

FIG. 4
Fort Saint-Louis. In the foreground is the stone stairway leading to one of the cannon platforms of the second fort, built by Champlain in 1626. This platform stood on the outer enceinte, on the north-east side of the fort. In the background is a portion of a fortification wall erected between 1648 and 1660, which was part of the fort's north enceinte (photograph, Parks Canada).

even have been in store. With regard to portable weapons, the inventory mentioned the presence of 84 muskets in the fort's storehouse — most of them 'spoiled' and the others out of commission[51] — plus 20 or 30 'musket guns'.[52] There were no longer any arquebuses in the fort's arsenal at the time; guns of this type had gone out of use in New France around 1640–50.[53]

As the fort was still in a deplorable state in 1660, additional work had to be carried out over the next ten years. The alignment of the enceinte's south wall was changed, and covered loopholes may have been installed. The south-east corner of the circuit was demolished and the wall laid out so that the river could be watched more effectively.[54] Despite this work, the defences were still far from adequate. Shortly before he was called back to France in 1681, Governor Frontenac complained that 'the fort was completely open, its walls were in ruins and it was accessible from all sides.'[55] The fortification was still not finished in 1683. Nevertheless, the south curtain wall was rebuilt in 1684, the year in which the chateau was enlarged to the south.[56] The new wall, like the old one, had several covered loopholes, behind which was an earth banquette from which muskets could be fired. According to a 1685 plan, the south enceinte wall, including the banquette and its slope, would have had a total width of about 1½ *toises* (9 French feet or 2.92m). This could not be confirmed, however, during the archaeological fieldwork as no remains of the banquette were found.

No further renovations were carried out on the fort's defences over the next few years; they remained unchanged until they were reconstructed under the new administration of Governor Frontenac between 1692 and 1694.

THE CITY'S FIRST ENCEINTE (1690)

Raids conducted in the British colonies, began in 1686 under Governor Denonville and continued three years later by Frontenac, sparked the anger of the colonies of New York and Massachusetts.

'The "Bastonnais" assembled a fleet under Sir William Phips in order to capture Acadia and its main settlement, Port-Royal. Ill-armed, Port-Royal fell with little resistance. Encouraged by his success, Phips led his fleet up the St Lawrence to Québec.'[57] Anticipating an attack by the Iroquois, Frontenac ordered that trees be cut down to build a palisade to protect the city in the winter of 1689–90. However, because of the imminent threat of Admiral Phips' fleet sailing up the river, the palisade had to be built in haste in the spring of 1690.

This line of defence, made of cedar posts 10ft (3.25m) high, protected the city on its south and west sides, and on part of its north front.[58] It was a simple palisade with no rampart, although it had an earth banquette from which muskets could be fired. A few fragmentary remains of this defence were found during excavations by Parks Canada behind the New Barracks and the Coteau de la Potasse Demi-Bastion in Artillery Park in 1995–99. The line of fortification was completed by eleven small stone redoubts placed strategically along the palisade. Their walls projected out from its front and were pierced by loopholes, allowing the entire fortification to be flanked, although in a more-or-less regular fashion. The masonry remains of the Palace Redoubt[59] were uncovered in 1998; considered with historical documents, they have made it possible to reconstruct the form of these defences. The redoubts were all pentagonal. They had two storeys of stone, standing about 18ft (5.85m) high; a third storey was made mainly of wood and is said to have been machicolated because it projected out over the lower walls (Fig. 5). The projecting part of the floor on the third storey had openings though which soldiers could fire projectiles (musket balls or grenades) vertically on the enemy. Since this storey did not have a roof, its walls must have formed a parapet over which the soldiers could fire their muskets; it would thus have been no more than 4½ft high, the prescribed firing height.[60] The flintlock replaced the old matchlock musket during the period concerned.

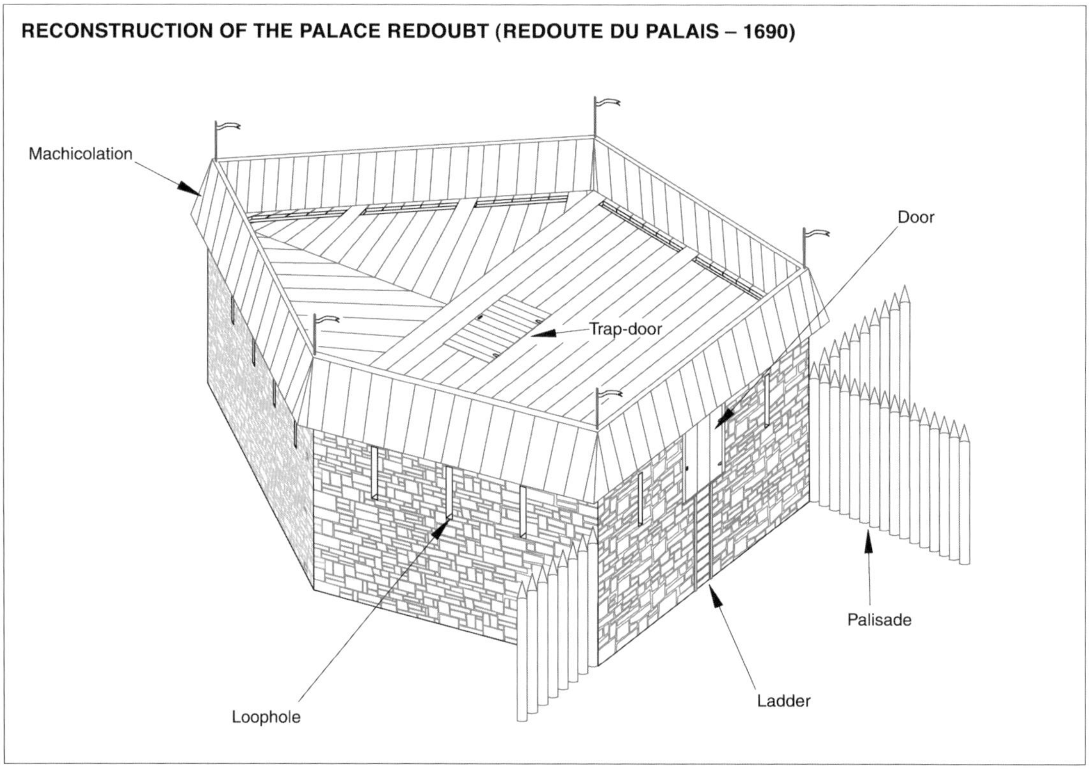

FIG. 5
Fort Saint-Louis. Isometric reconstruction of the Palace Redoubt, associated with the 1690 palisade. This redoubt was located at the south end of the palisade and overlooked the Intendant's Palace in Québec's Lower Town (drawn by F. Pellerin & J. Croteau, Parks Canada).

> Major Provost's fortification had been conceived specifically to enclose a town faced with imminent attack; at the same time it was to provide the retrenchments needed to install artillery ... In short, this fortification may be considered a natural reaction to a wish to obstruct an enemy.[61]

However, this line of defence did not prove very useful, since Phips and his men did not attack the city from the side on which it was built, but landed instead at Beauport to the north-east. Nevertheless, 'without proper ground on which to conduct a siege and faced with the prospect of dealing with the hardships of the oncoming winter, Phips decided to retreat'.[62]

THE FOURTH FORT SAINT-LOUIS: A BASTIONED VAUBAN-STYLE FORTIFICATION (1691–94)

The attack by Admiral Phips and his 'Bastonnais' brought the question of the city's fortifications to the fore once again. Governor Frontenac saw this event as a golden opportunity to convince the king to undertake the works needed to improve the city's defences. Now that Québec was surrounded by a palisade, Frontenac's next concern was to build a new cannon battery to control traffic on the river. Its construction began in 1691, even though the governor had still not received authorization from the king. The new battery had seventeen guns, and stood just south of the Château Saint-Louis.

To build this structure, Frontenac first erected a schist wall measuring about 15ft (4.87m) high; it had to be of this height because extensive earth infilling operations had to be carried out before cannon platforms could be installed there. The distance between the base of the wall and the platforms was 8ft (2.60m). When the height of the *genouillère*,[63] (usually 3 French feet, 0.97m), and the estimated height of the merlons,[64] (4 French feet, 1.30m), are also taken into account, the wall would have been at least 15ft (4.87m) high. Of course, its total height would have varied in places depending on the configuration of the underlying bedrock, since the top of the wall would have been level. The best-preserved part, uncovered during the 2006 field season, was built entirely of limestone and was roughly 1.90m high.

The cannon platforms were built with large beams supporting the joists on which the plank floor rested; numerous traces of these timbers were uncovered by Parks Canada archaeologists in 2006 (Fig. 6).[65] It was determined that the battery's cannon platforms would have been 3.00m (9.25 French feet) wide by at least 2.50m (7.70 French feet) long.[66] Behind the platforms was a *trottoir* or wooden walkway. Since the platforms were built on the lower part of the promontory, a wall had to be erected behind the battery to retain the soil overlying the bedrock further up. It was of dry-stone construction,[67] made of large blocks of schist and standing 1.25m (3.85 French feet) high at the most. Only part of it was uncovered during the excavations. The battery was armed with cannon that could fire 12lbs (0.34kg) balls; in fact, several balls of this calibre were found in association with the platforms' remains.[68]

The construction of this new battery was only the first step in the complete overhaul of Fort Saint-Louis. In 1692, Frontenac began to demolish the fort's old enceinte and raise a new wall. The new fort was almost four times larger than the previous one. The south front was moved further south to encompass eight of the seventeen cannon platforms of the Château Battery built the year before; the nine other platforms remained outside the fort. Frontenac also moved the western enclosure further west by about 100 French feet (32.50m), setting it closer to the Place d'Armes. As for the fort itself, the building estimate specified that the walls were to measure 4ft wide (1.30m) at the base and 3ft (0.98m) wide at the top. It also stipulated that the walls of the north-west bastion should be 16ft (5.20m) high and that 'the curtain wall of the entrance to the said fort should have the same slope' as the bastion.[69] On the basis of these measurements, it can be calculated that the enceinte walls would have had a batter of 6.25% (1:16). Frontenac planned to build a terreplein behind the wall and set up four cannon platforms in addition to those of the battery near the chateau. However, owing to a shortage of funds, he did not proceed with this project.

The fort's ground plan was now as follows. At the eastern end of the south front, flanking the south curtain wall, was a demi-bastion. This had one flank and one complete face which abutted the wall of the Château Battery. At its western end, the south front was completed by a bastion flanking both the south and the west curtain walls. A second bastion stood to the north-west. Thus two bastions flanked the west curtain wall, where the main entrance to the fort was situated. Owing to the configuration of the promontory, the portion of the north front to the east of the north-west bastion had only a very short curtain wall, at the end of which was a second irregularly shaped demi-bastion, whose long right face joined the north-west corner of Château Saint-Louis. The layout of the fort thus adhered perfectly to the basic tenets of flanking implemented by Sébastien Le Prestre de Vauban, the renowned military engineer. Following the renovations described here, no

FIG. 6

Fort Saint-Louis. Archaeological remains of one of the cannon platforms of the Château Battery constructed in 1691. The fortification wall built by Frontenac can be seen in front of these remains. In the upper right-hand corner is a *heurtoir*, or beam of wood that was placed on the fore part of the platform to prevent the gun from running over the edge (photograph, Parks Canada).

major changes were made to the ground plan of Fort Saint-Louis. However, the portion of the Château Battery that lay outside the enceinte was abandoned in the early 1740s — an event that signalled the decline of the fort's defensive role.

A few sections of the walls of the fourth Fort Saint-Louis were brought to light during fieldwork in 2005–07. They were situated, for the most part, on the edge of the cliff north of Château Saint-Louis. The long right face of the north-east bastion was uncovered over a distance of 13m. Although its summit was levelled in the 19th century, the wall had a preserved height of up to 3.30m or 10.8 French feet (23 courses). It was made of squared green sandstone, and its outer face had been removed during work undertaken after the time of Frontenac. Its inner face was still in place[70] and had a batter of 9% (1:11) (Fig. 7).

QUÉBEC'S FIRST RAMPART (1693)

The palisade built by Major Provost in 1690 was merely a makeshift work, erected in haste in response to a specific threat. Once the defences of Fort Saint-Louis had been completed, those of the city had to re-examined, especially on the west side, where the enemy was most likely to attack. Therefore, in 1693, the engineer Josué Boisberthelot de Beaucours undertook the construction of a true earth rampart at this spot, consisting of a parapet, banquette and terreplein. A much more regular line of defence than the palisade of 1690, 'it stretched from the Cape Diamond Redoubt at the east end to the St Simon Demi-Bastion at the other end and thus enclosed the city along its entire western front'.[71] The rampart was revetted with a wooden palisade 8ft (2.6m) high; taking into account its superior position on the slope, the maximum height of the parapet would have been 9–10ft (2.92–3.25m). The wooden stakes of the revetment were slanted to counter the pressure exerted by the earth embankment. The fortification included fraised bastions and curtain walls, with a ditch in front. The ditch measured three *toises* (18ft or 5.85m) wide in front of the bastions

FIG. 7
Fort Saint-Louis. Outer facing, made of sandstone, of a portion of the long face of the demi-bastion in the north-east part of the fort erected by Frontenac. The wall's batter is clearly visible. The central part of the wall's outer facing was rebuilt shortly after the British conquest (photograph, Parks Canada, 38G05R11T-20).

and thirteen *toises* (78ft or 25.33m) wide in front of the curtain walls. The new circuit complied with the concept of flanking that was so dear to Vauban:

> This new enceinte was the first construction at Québec that was inspired by Vauban's first system. Beaucours was explicit on this point. He clearly demonstrated his knowledge of Vauban's techniques for deciding upon the proportions to be assigned to the layout of the magistral line, such as how to calculate the length of the perpendiculars and the faces and the method to determine the size and position of the flanks and the curtain walls. ... The proposed rampart thus respected several general maxims of fortification.[72]

Some components of this large fortification were found by Parks Canada in the New Barracks sector of Artillery Park during excavations in 1995–99. These remains, which consisted of stakes, retaining posts and struts, all made of cedar, enabled the archaeologists to gain a better grasp of how the embanked palisade was put together. Even though the new enceinte was never completed, it reflected the determination of the colonial authorities to build a fortification able to withstand a siege, like the defences of fortified cities in Europe. However, it was not until 1740–50 that a stone fortification which accorded with generally accepted principles of fortification was finally built. Credit for this goes to Gaspard-Joseph Chaussegros de Léry, the most experienced military engineer of the French regime.

CONCLUSION

When Champlain built his two Habitations in Lower Town and the first two Fort Saint-Louis on the cliff top, the defence systems he applied were undeniably of medieval inspiration. Nevertheless, although he was not a military engineer, he was certainly interested in building a system which conformed to more modern principles of fortification. His main concern was defending the small colony against the Iroquois rather than the Europeans; he could not have foreseen the capture of Québec by the Kirke brothers. It was not until the second half of the 17th century, particularly after the 1660s, that concern about European enemies, whether from the British colonies of the 'American' North-East or from England itself, obliged the colonial authorities to consider building a more sophisticated defence system, adapted in particular to the military tactics and technology of these potential new adversaries. New fortification principles developed in Europe by eminent military engineers — the best known and no doubt the most prestigious of whom was Vauban — would be adopted rapidly in the young colony.

Archaeological excavations in Québec City over the past 20 years have greatly enriched our knowledge of the city's defence system by locating part of the ditch of the first Habitation of 1608, by uncovering some of the defence works associated with the little-known first two Forts Saint-Louis erected on the cliff top by Champlain, and by shedding light on improvements made by his successors. The fieldwork has also made it possible to document much more thoroughly the fortifications erected during Governor Frontenac's second term of office in the 1690s, namely the city's first palisaded enceinte (1690), the Château Battery (1691), and the first rampart raised by the engineer Josué Boisberthelot de Beaucours

(1693), whose archaeological remains reveal how it was assembled. This information has contributed significantly to our understanding of a large part of Québec City's defensive system.

These findings have enabled researchers to follow the development of fortification techniques adopted by the city during the 17th century. Initially based on principles of medieval inspiration, these techniques later incorporated modern concepts such as flanking and command, as shown by the reconstruction of Fort Saint-Louis and the establishment of a veritable fortified enceinte in the late 17th century.

NOTES

[1] *World Heritage City*, Ville de Québec, <http://www.ville.quebec.qc.ca/EN/apropos/portrait/ville_internationale/index.aspx> [accessed 26 Oct. 2008].

[2] Charbonneau *et al.* 1982, 21.

[3] Salient: 'A term used in warfare to refer to an outward projecting work of fortification in the middle of a curtain wall, in front of a door or on the edge of a river for preventing entry to a fortress' (Furetière 1690). [Translation.]

[4] Guimont 1992.

[5] Bernier *et al.* 2008, 56. [Translation.]

[6] Champlain 1632, 5. [Translation, Biggar 1971, **5**, 8.]

[7] Gabriel Sagard was a 'Recollet friar, missionary in the Huron country in 1623 and 1624, [and] first religious historian of Canada', *Dictionary of Canadian Biography*, <http://www.biographi.ca/>.

[8] Sagard 1866 [1636], 158. [Translation.]

[9] The excavations did not extend far enough west to determine the east–west dimensions of the bedrock terrace. It should be noted that Dufferin Terrace is orientated north–south.

[10] Laurent & St-Pierre 1982, 17. [Translation.]

[11] Early 17th-century arquebuses fired 1½oz balls (Favé 1862, 301, based on information provided by Diego Ufano regarding Spanish guns used in the early 17th century).

[12] Laurent & St-Pierre 1982, 17.

[13] In the early 17th century, ordinary muskets fired 2½oz balls (Favé 1862, 301, based on information provided by Diego Ufano regarding Spanish guns in use in the early 17th century).

[14] Also known as a gun rest.

[15] Only the upper metal parts of two gun forks were found, that is, the small U-shaped portion which supported the musket or arquebus stocks. The wooden shafts to which the forks were attached were not found.

[16] Favé 1862, 331.

[17] Brassard 2008. [Translation.]

[18] Michel Brassard, pers. comm., January 2008. In the early 17th century the range of muskets (93 ordinary steps of 2½ft, i.e. 232½ft (75.5m)) was greater than that of arquebuses (75 steps of 2½ft, i.e. 187½ft (61m)). (Favé 1862, 301, based on information provided by Diego Ufano regarding Spanish guns in use in the early 17th century.)

[19] Laurent & St-Pierre 1982, 18.

[20] The right and left components of a work of fortification are determined facing outward from inside the work.

[21] In 1604 Sieur Dugua de Monts dismantled the settlement at Sainte-Croix and founded another one on the other side of the Bay of Fundy in a place he called Port-Royal. However, the colonists soon abandoned the new settlement because of scurvy and the harsh climate. <http://www.histori.ca/champlain/page.do?pageID=157> [accessed 21 Apr. 2008].

[22] Laverdière 1870, **5**, 1110. [Translation, Biggar 1971, **5**, 204.]

[23] Charbonneau *et al.* 1982, 22. [Translation, Biggar 1971, **5**, 205.] Unfortunately it is not known which fortresses Champlain was referring to.

[24] Cloutier and L'Anglais in this volume, Fig. 2.

[25] Bourdon, who drew the two surviving plans of the 1635 fort, used both 'platform' and 'small bastion' to designate the works beside these two bastions.

[26] 'The principle of flanking was intended to ensure that each precise point of an enceinte was visible from another, so that no area was left unprotected' (Charbonneau *et al.* 1982, 86).

[27] Charbonneau *et al.* 1982, 22.

[28] This hypothesis is based on the reflections of Michel Bergeron, who made the scale model of the second Fort Saint-Louis. However, it is also possible that the parapet was formed simply by the upper part of the enceinte's wooden stakes and that no horizontal planking was found in the upper part of the palisade.

[29] 'Command of one work over another refers to the difference between the heights of their two crests': Lebeau 2007. [Translation.]

[30] Laurent & St-Pierre 1982, 29. [Translation.]

[31] Historically, brass was the general name used to designate all alloys of copper made with tin or zinc. The term bronze was later adopted to distinguish alloys of copper and tin (*Compact Oxford English Dictionary*, 1971, s.v. 'brass').

[32] Furetière 1690. [Translation.] The *espoir* actually corresponds to an *espingole*: 'As P. Fournier said in his *Hydrography* in 1634, these carracks usually have a capacity of 1,500–2,000 *tonneaux* ... they always carry small pieces like *espoirs* (*espingoles*; formerly called *springrales* or *espringalas*) and perriers, which they put in the tops' (Jal 1840, 213 [Translation.]). Therefore *espoirs* were small bronze pieces of naval

ordnance that were mounted on ship decks or light vessels (Michel Brassard, pers. comm. March 2008).

[33] Niellon & Moussette 1985, 93. [Translation.] The large number of artillery pieces with different calibres and weights used at this time created a great deal of confusion. The edict of 1572 was designed to regularize the situation. It specified that only six types of bronze ordnance would be cast from that time: the cannon (*canon*) (33⅓lbs), the culverin extraordinary (*grande coulevrine*) (16½lbs), the bastard culverin (*coulevrine bâtarde*) (7½lbs), the demi-culverin (*coulevrine moyenne*) (2¾lbs), the falcon (*faucon*) (1½lbs) and the falconet (*fauconneau*) (3½ quarters), the quarter being a quarter of a pound' (De Lombarès 1984, 79). However, according to Louis-Napoléon Bonaparte, calibres had already been standardized by Henri II in 1552: 'The edict of 1572 was merely a repeat of an old law that had fallen into abeyance during the civil war . . . It would be surprising indeed if artillery had been simplified and standardized during troubled times, when an effort would have been made to use everything on hand rather than to innovate' (Bonaparte 1846, 200–1. [Translation.]). The credit for bringing about the adoption of the six French calibres goes to D'Estrées, 'grand master of artillery from 1550 to 1569, who was already performing the duties of this position in 1548' (Favé 1862, 240. [Translation.]).

[34] In two documents of 1608 the demi-culverin is described as a piece of artillery weighing 600–700lbs (270–315kg), or about as much as the two pieces listed in the 1629 inventory, i.e. 800lbs (360kg) each (Denoix & Muracciole 1963, 942). The demi-culverin fired a 2½lb ball, but could also be loaded with balls weighing 2lbs 12oz (De Lombarès *et al.* 1984, 79). Another piece of the same weight as the demi-culverin also existed during this period: the falcon (*faucon*), which in the early 17th century could weigh 800lbs (Favé 1862, 299) or 600–700lbs (270–315kg; Denoix & Muracciole 1963, 942); however, it could fire only 1½lb balls. In any event, Jean-Baptiste de la Curne de Sainte-Palaye (1877, 3) defined the *breteul*, or *breteuil,* as a 'kind of canon. Culverin or falconet'.

[35] Bonaparte 1846, 203.

[36] Furetière 1690. [Translation.]

[37] Mallet 1696, 154. [Translation.] There were several models of perriers with different lengths and calibres. This type of weapon was used for defence at close-quarters since its range was very limited, barely exceeding 100m (*c.* 310 French feet or 300 English feet). 'Stones cannot be fired very effectively, not only because their velocity slows at the end of their fall, even though they are propelled at high angles, but also because they end up being scattered over a wide area; therefore they cannot be fired to advantage except over distances of 100–150m' (Piobert 1836, 211 [Translation.]).

[38] Laverdière 1870, **5**, 1414.

[39] Champlain 1632, 222. [Translation, Biggar 1971, **6**, 67.]

[40] The supports used with *espingoles* were called *chandeliers* (Boudriot 1970, 7). As for the *espoirs* mentioned by Champlain, they had 'boxes', or chargers, like the perriers. No specific references to *espingole à boîte* were found in the many works consulted in the course of this research.

[41] Boudriot 1970, 1. [Translation.]

[42] Laurent & St-Pierre 1982, 39. [Translation.]

[43] Roy 1901, 271. [Translation.]

[44] A terrace of this type already existed at the time of Champlain's second dwelling built in 1626.

[45] *Guérite* is the term used on plans of this period. In this context it did not refer to a watch turret, i.e. a small structure used for posting sentries.

[46] A work was said to be *en crémaillère* 'when a branch of it was traced in a series of several redans' (Charbonneau *et al.* 1982, 91).

[47] Laurent & St-Pierre 1982, 50.

[48] Laurent & St-Pierre 1982, app. A, 180.

[49] M. Goyette in this volume.

[50] Laurent & St-Pierre 1982, 49.

[51] Laurent & St-Pierre 1982, 181.

[52] These were probably flintlock muskets, while the others were muskets of the matchlock type. They could not have been the *fusil-mousquet* or *mousquet-fusil* invented by Vauban that had both types of firing mechanism. This type of portable weapon began to be tested in France only in 1672 (Bonnefoy 1991, **1**, 47).

[53] Bouchard 1999, 104.

[54] Laurent & St-Pierre 1982, 51.

[55] Charbonneau *et al.* 1982, 30.

[56] M. Goyette in this volume.

[57] Guimont 2002, 17. [Translation.]

[58] This enceinte was supposed to have been built by the engineer Robert de Villeneuve. However, as Villeneuve had returned to France, it was erected by François Provost, the town major of Québec. It came to be known as 'Major Provost's palisade'.

[59] A few years later, when this redoubt served as lodgings for the executioner, it was christened the *Redoute du Bourreau* (Executioner's Redoubt).

[60] Roofs were added to these redoubts in 1693. As a result, the walls on the third storey had to be pierced with loopholes.

[61] Charbonneau *et al.* 1982, 118.

[62] Charbonneau *et al.* 1982, 34.

[63] The *genouillère* was 'the portion of the interior wall of the parapet between the gun platform and the base of the embrasure' (Charbonneau *et al.* 1982, 92).

[64] The merlon was the portion of the wall between two cannon embrasures; it served to protect artillerymen from enemy fire.

[65] The species of wood used to build these platforms was not known when this paper was written.

[66] Guimont 2007, 6. This information comes from excavations conducted by Parks Canada in 1985–86 and 2006.

[67] A drystone wall is a masonry structure in which no mortar is used to bind the stones together.

[68] The range of 12lb cannon was roughly 1,700ft (550m; Favé 1863, 9; Piobert 1836, 130). They could thus fire on ships in the middle of the St Lawrence.

[69] 'Marché entre François de Lajoue et Hilaire Bernard de La Rivière et le comte de Frontenac et Monseigneur de Champigny Noroy', 28 Sept. 1692, BAnQ, greffe François Genaple. [Translation.]

[70] Part of this face was rebuilt, however, shortly after the conquest, as the wall had been damaged during the bombardment of 1759.

[71] Guimont 2002, 49. [Translation.]

[72] Charbonneau *et al.* 1982, 120.

BIBLIOGRAPHY

PUBLISHED SOURCES

Bernier, S. *et al.* 2008, *Québec: ville militaire 1608–2008*, Montréal: Art Global.

Biggar, H.P. (ed.) 1971 [1922–36], *The Works of Samuel de Champlain*, Pub. Champlain Soc. **6**, facs. edn, Toronto: University of Toronto Press.

Bonaparte, L.-N. 1846, *Études sur le passé et l'avenir de l'artillerie* **1**, facs. edn, Paris: J. Dumaine.

Bonnefoy, F. 1991, *Les Armes de Guerre Portatives en France, du début du règne de Louis XIV à la veille de la Révolution (1660–1789): de l'indépendance à la primauté* **1**, Paris: Librairie de l'Inde.

Bouchard, R. 1999, *Les Armes à Feu en Nouvelle-France*, Québec: Septentrion.

Boudriot, J. 1970, 'L'artillerie de mer de la marine française 1674–1856, C: La petite artillerie des hunes, bastingages et embarcations', *Neptunia* **100** (4th trim.), 1–8.

Champlain, S. (de) 1632, *Les Voyages de la Nouvelle France occidentale, dicte Canada faits par le Sr de Champlain, Seconde partie des voyages . . .*, facs. edn, Paris: Claude Collet.

Charbonneau, A., Desloges, Y. & Lafrance, M. 1982, *Québec ville fortifiée du XVIIe au XIXe siècle*, Éditions du Pélican/Parks Canada. [Published in English under the title *Québec the Fortified City: from the 17th to the 19th Century*, Ottawa: Supply and Services Canada.]

Clermont, N., Chapdelaine, C. & Guimont, J. (Cérane inc.) 1992, *L'Occupation Historique et Préhistorique de Place-Royale*, Québec: Publications du Québec Collection Patrimoines, Dossiers **76**.

De Lombarès, M. *et al.*1984, *Histoire de l'artillerie française*, Paris-Limoges: Charles-Lavauzelle.

Denoit, L. & Muracciole, J.-N. 1963, 'Historique de l'artillerie de la marine de ses origines à 1870', in *Mémorial de l'artillerie française*, 4th fasc. **37**, Paris: Imprimerie Nationale.

Favé, I. 1862, *Études sur le passé et l'avenir de l'artillerie, ouvrage continué à l'aide des notes de l'Empereur*, **3**. *Histoire des progrès de l'artillerie*, facs. edn, Paris: Librairie militaire J. Dumaine.

Favé, I. 1863, *Études sur le passé et l'avenir de l'artillerie, ouvrage continué sur le plan de l'Empereur*, **4**. *Histoire des progrès de l'artillerie, livre II*, facs. edn, Paris: Librairie militaire J. Dumaine.

Furetière, A. 1690, *Dictionnaire universel: contenant généralement tous les mots françois tant vieux que modernes, & les termes de toutes les sciences et des arts . . . divisé en trois tomes* **2**, La Haye: Arnout.

Guimont, J. 1992, 'L'occupation historique à Place-Royale du début du 17ième à la fin du 19ième siècle, rapport de fouilles historiques', in Clermont *et al.* 1992, 281–426.

Jal, A. 1840, *Archéologie navale* **2**, facs. edn, Paris: Arthus Bertrand.

La Curne de Sainte-Palaye, J.-B. (de) 1877, *Dictionnaire historique de l'ancien langage françois ou glossaire de la langue françoise depuis son origine jusqu'au siècle de Louis XIV* **10**, Niort: L. Favre.

Laverdière C.-H. (abbé) 1870, *Œuvres de Champlain: publiées sous le patronage de l'Université Laval*, facs. of the 2nd edn, 5 vols, Québec: Desbarats.

Lebeau, J. 2007, *Terminologie de la fortification*, <http://www.clham.org/050355.htm> [accessed 8 Feb. 2008].

Mallet, A.M. 1696, *Les Travaux de Mars ou l'art de la guerre*, La Haye: Adrian Moetjens.

Niellon, F. & Moussette, M. 1985, *L'Habitation de Champlain*, Collection Patrimoines, Dossiers **58**, Québec: Publications du Québec.

Piobert, G. 1836, *Traité d'artillerie théorique et pratique, précis de la partie élémentaire et pratique*, facs. edn, Paris: Leneveu.

Roy, P.-G. 1901, 'Bermen, "Marchez faicts en 1646 et 47 jusque en 1648 au mois de septembre pour la construction de l'église et du fort à Québec"', *Bull. de recherches historiques* **7**:9, 271.

Sagard, G. 1866 [1636], *Histoire du Canada et voyages que les frères mineurs Récollets y ont faicts pour la conversion des infidèles depuis l'an 1615* **1**, facs. edn, Paris: Librairie Tross.

UNPUBLISHED SOURCES

Brassard, M. 2008, 'Résumé des armes à feu individuelles à l'époque du fort Saint-Louis', Québec: Parks Canada.

Guimont, J. 2002, 'L'Evolution des fortifications dans le secteur du Parc de l'Artillerie, la Tenaille des Nouvelles Casernes et le demi-bastion du Coteau de la Potasse, 1690–1871', manuscrit classé, Québec: Parks Canada, Patrimoine culturel et biens immobiliers.

Guimont, J. 2007, 'L.H.N.C. des Forts-et-Châteaux-Saint-Louis: campagne de fouilles de 2006, les faits saillants', Québec: Parks Canada, Centre de services du Québec, Service du Patrimoine culturel.

Laurent, J. & St-Pierre, J. 1982, 'Les forts et châteaux Saint-Louis, 1620–1760', manuscrit classé, Québec: Parks Canada.

ABBREVIATIONS

BAnQ Bibliothèque et Archives nationales du Québec

SUMMARY IN FRENCH, GERMAN, ITALIAN AND SPANISH

RÉSUMÉ

Regards sur le fort Saint-Louis et quelques ouvrages de fortification du XVIIe siècle mis au jour récemment à Québec

De récentes fouilles à Québec ont grandement enrichi notre connaissance de la localisation, du caractère et de la probable artillerie de la série des fortifications du XVIIe siècle. La première défense simple par Champlain de l'Habitation dans la basse ville (1608–24) était destinée dans un premier temps à protéger la population contre les Iroquois. L'échelle et la sophistication croissantes des deux forts Saint-Louis successifs sur le haut de la falaise (1620–26 et 1626–35), suivis par le troisième (1636–90) et le quatrième (1691–94) forts Saint-Louis, reflètent le développement des défenses capables d'engager une guerre de siège européen, en particulier avec l'ennemi éternel de la France, l'Angleterre.

ZUSAMMENFASSUNG

Das Fort Saint Louis und andere Befestigungsanlagen des 17. Jhs, die vor kurzem in der Stadt Quebec entdeckt wurden

Jüngste Ausgrabungen in der Stadt Quebec haben unsere Kenntnis von der Lage, dem Charakter und der mutmaßlich militärischen Ausrüstung einer Folge von Befestigungen aus dem 17. Jh. außerordentlich bereichert. Champlains erste einfache Befestigungsanlagen der Unterstadt (1608–24) waren vor allem dazu bestimmt, die Bevölkerung vor den Iroquois zu beschützen. Das wachsende Größenverhältnis und die Verfeinerung der zwei aufeinanderfolgenden Forts Saint Louis auf der darübergelegenen Klippe (1620–26 und 1626–35) der ein drittes (1636–90) und viertes (1691–94) Fort folgten, lassen auf die Weiterentwicklung der Verteidigungsanlagen für den Belagerungsfall, insbesondere gegen Frankreichs Erbfeind England, schließen.

RIASSUNTO

Fort Saint-Louis e altre strutture fortificate di XVII secolo recentemente scoperte nella città di Quebec

I recenti scavi condotti nella città di Quebec hanno arricchito considerevolmente le nostre conoscenze circa l'ubicazione, la natura e il probabile materiale militare e la sua sequenza nelle fortificazioni di XVII secolo. Le prime semplici strutture difensive costruite da Champlain nell'abitato nella parte bassa della città (1608–24) avevano principalmente lo scopo di difendere la popolazione degli Irochesi. L'incremento in scala e complessità delle due successive realizzazioni di Fort Saint-Louis sulla sommità del promontorio sovrastante (1620–26 e 1626–35), seguite dalla terza (1636–90) e quarta (1691–94) edificazione di Fort Saint-Louis, riflettono lo sviluppo di strutture difensive capaci di impegnarsi in una guerra di assedio europea, specialmente contro l'eterno nemico della Francia, l'Inghilterra.

RESUMEN

El fuerte Saint-Louis y otras fortificaciones del siglo XVII descubiertas recientemente en la ciudad de Quebec

Las excavaciones arqueológicas que recientemente se han desarrollado en Quebec han enriquecido nuestro conocimiento sobre la situación, carácter y posible desarrollo de sus fortificaciones del siglo XVII. La primera defensa sencilla de Champlain en la Habitation en Cuidad Baja (1608–24) fue concebida principalmente para proteger a la población contra los iroqueses. El aumento en escala y sofisticación de ambos sucesivos fuertes Saint-Louis en lo alto del acantilado (1620–26 y 1626–35), fueron seguidos por un tercero (1636–90) y cuarto (1691–94), reflejando el desarrollo de defensas capaces de acometer campañas bélicas de tipo europeo, especialmente con Inglaterra, el enemigo eterno de Francia.

Parcs Canada, 3 Passage du Chien d'Or, C.P. 6060 Haute-Ville, Québec (Québec), Canada G1R 4V7 [jacques.guimont@pc.gc.ca]

Post-Medieval Archaeology **43/1** (2009), 156–170

The Intendant's Palace site: urbanization of Québec City's Lower Town

By RÉGINALD AUGER, DANIEL SIMONEAU *and* ALLISON BAIN

SUMMARY: Several archaeological field studies have been carried out on the Intendant's Palace site since 1982. In the first ten years, research concentrated on the 17th-century brewery, the Intendant's Palace and the King's Stores. When Université Laval's field school returned to the site in 2000, it took a holistic approach rather than focusing on specific buildings. In so doing, it documented the urban evolution of this part of Québec City, which has yielded evidence of continuous occupation since the mid-17th century.

INTRODUCTION

The Intendant's Palace site covers an entire city block at the bottom of a narrow street connecting Québec City's Upper and Lower Towns (Fig. 1). On account of its strategic location and easy access to the Saint-Charles River, the site was identified in the 17th century by Intendant Jean Talon as a suitable spot for pursuing his economic endeavours in New France. Talon's short venture into boat construction, beer brewing and potash production on the Intendant's Palace site followed a brief ownership of this piece of land by the widow of Guillaume Couillard, which in turn followed a series of small-scale Native occupations of the area during the Late Woodland period (*c.* AD 1300). Archaeological research in Place Royale, situated on the banks of the St Lawrence River to the east of the Intendant's Palace site, has also yielded evidence of Aboriginal occupation in Québec's Lower Town. In that case, the occupation involved seasonal use of a narrow beach at the foot of the Cap Diamant cliff for the purpose of fishing the river's brackish waters and hunting migratory waterfowl. The research also unearthed a Native burial containing corn remains dating back 790 years.[1] Despite the presence of Native occupation on the Intendant's Palace site, the aim of this paper is to acquaint the reader with a broad spectrum of European occupation in this part of Québec City over a period of nearly four centuries. The discussion will be limited to the evolution of the European-built environment and the presence of associated architectural and artefactual remains.

The present paper describes the results of archaeological research conducted on the Intendant's Palace site since 2000; it focuses on the evolution of its built environment as a whole. It is important to emphasize that this approach represents a departure from previous studies carried out from 1982 to 1990, which concentrated primarily on the excavation of a single building.[2] The goal of the more holistic approach adopted in 2000 was to assess how the various phases of construction identified on the site correlated with the evolution of Québec City and how each new industrial or residential feature testified to the needs of the city's changing economic environment.[3] By combining data obtained in 2007 and 2008 with previous findings, it was possible to obtain a better understanding of the principles behind the site's physical and environmental evolution.

Until recently, the Intendant's Palace site had been analysed from a diachronic perspective, which has had the merit of establishing clear

DOI: 10.1179/007942309X12457508844161

FIG. 1
The Intendant's Palace complex in Québec City's Lower Town (photograph, Pierre Lahoud).

links with the known historical chronology. Such an approach was designed to demonstrate, for example, how the brewery erected by Jean Talon was transformed into the Intendant's Palace and how, after being largely destroyed by fire, the palace was in turn converted into the King's Stores. However, when recent discoveries began to be studied in light of the older data, it soon became obvious that a synchronic approach would be more appropriate. The Intendant's Palace complex could thus be viewed as representative of the rapidly changing political and economic context of the French government in the New World.

TABLE 1
Timeline for the Intendant's Palace site.

Native occupation of the riverbank, Late Woodland	*c.* AD 1300
Official founding of Québec	1608
Jean Talon's brewery	1668–75
Building of the potash factory	1670
First Intendant's Palace	1685–1713
Construction of a palisade around the first palace	1689
Destruction of the first Intendant's Palace by fire	1713
Second Intendant's Palace	1716–75
King's Stores	1716–60
Construction of latrines in the second palace	1723
American invasion	1775
Second palace in ruins for 75 years	1775–1850
Boswell brewery	1852–1968

This new synchronic approach showed that, even though there was necessarily a chronological order to events on the Intendant's Palace site, each major change constituted a radical break with what had gone before. This discovery led to new interpretations of the site which suggested in particular that the continued choice of this location was not based on previous functions but appeared instead to depend on the environmental advantages offered by the site in the context of the colony's political and economic development. It was then possible to advance the hypothesis that the Intendant's Palace complex functioned initially as an industrial sector designed to provide the newly founded colony with essential goods such as ships, beer and potash. However, as Québec became more than simply a way station for dispatching adventurers into the continent's interior in search of fur resources, the complex gradually began to play the role of an industrial hub at the mouth of the Saint-Charles River.

The objective of this paper is to report on the various archaeological excavations that were undertaken at the site beginning in 2000 through a research programme carried out by Université Laval's field school in historical archaeology. The site's evolution is described in order to provide an interpretative framework for other studies. The reader must bear in mind that the goal of the research programme was twofold: it aimed not only to provide a new understanding of the Intendant's Palace site but to glean information from the study of its material culture and past environments that could be used in on-site exhibitions to be held during Québec City's 400th anniversary celebrations. The projected venue for the exhibitions was an interpretation centre that was to be built on the site. While designing the spaces and volumes of the future museum was the domain of the architects involved in the project, the archaeologists were responsible for acquiring an intimate understanding of the site's multiple contexts and their evolution over time in order to provide detailed contextual data for preparing the museum displays. It was decided that attention would be devoted to explaining the urban fabric of the Intendant's Palace site in order to avoid creating another Place Royale, which is more of an architectural pastiche than an accurate representation of the French regime in late 18th-century Québec.[4]

Generally speaking, archaeological research on the Intendant's Palace aimed to understand the site in its urban dimension; it sought not only to gain insight into the urbanization of this sector through the study of archaeological remains associated with its 17th- to 20th-century industrial and commercial activities, but also to document the inhabitants' foodways and health, using approaches borrowed from environmental archaeology. For this purpose, it was necessary to collect data on the evolution of both the built and natural environments and to study the site's extensive material culture.[5] The strategy adopted for recent research viewed the site as a microcosm of the city's urbanization, and involved the application of a spatial approach derived from landscape archaeology. The concept of landscape used in the course of the research corresponds, in its broadest sense, to a unifying model that includes the natural environment in which the site's industrial, colonial and urban modes of settlement evolved. Environmental factors such as geology, drainage, soils and access to the Saint-Charles River have all contributed to the characterization of the built landscape. Therefore, the historical context lies somewhere between past aesthetic considerations that influenced the decision to situate the Intendant's Palace in Lower Town and factors related to access to environmental resources — factors that can be documented through archaeological, environmental and archival investigations. It is argued that the study of landscape must include the contribution of human activities to shaping history and natural settings, since both are central to an ecosystemic approach that considers concurrently the natural and cultural dynamics within which specific procurement strategies and aesthetic representations can be identified. To demonstrate this point, this paper will present the discoveries made on the Intendant's Palace site since 2000 and analyse them in conjunction with recent information in order to assess the validity of the hypothesis that these remains shed light on both the physical and functional environment of the site at different points in time. Together, the physical and functional environments represent the global political stand taken by France towards its colony and the impact of this stand on the evolution of the city of Québec.

PREVIOUS RESEARCH ON THE SITE

Archaeological excavations were carried out on the Intendant's Palace site by Université Laval's field school from 1982 to 1990. A synthesis of the results of this fieldwork was published by Marcel Moussette in 1994.[6] As these excavations were not subject to the constraints common to salvage operations in urban archaeology, they were conducive to collaboration between field school participants and City of Québec archaeologists and ultimately led to a sustained partnership between these parties, as well as to the creation of an interpretation centre in the vaults of the second Intendant's Palace. The exhibition mounted in the centre was based on field data from the southern part of the site and focused on five different aspects of its occupation: the Talon brewery (1668–75), the first Intendant's Palace (1686–1713), the King's Stores (1716–60), a period during which the site's function is uncertain (1760–1852) and the Boswell-Dow Brewery (1852–1971).

Around 1668 Intendant Jean Talon purchased the tract of land in Lower Town that now makes up the Intendant's Palace site from the widow Couillard as part of his master plan to boost the economic development of the young colony. He decided to build a brewery on the land and, two years later, he erected a potash factory nearby. It is believed that Talon built the brewery and the potash factory on this site as a way of centralizing his commercial operations on the banks of the Saint-Charles River — operations that were not part of the governor's political responsibilities. The Intendant's decision to establish a brewery at this location stemmed from several factors. First, there was more available space here than elsewhere along the Saint-Charles, whose banks were generally quite narrow because of the proximity of the Cap Diamant cliff. Secondly, the site offered easy access to the river, which was a major factor, as breweries required considerable quantities of water.[7] In all probability, water for the brewhouse was also collected from a spring-fed well on the cliff behind the building (Fig. 2). Thirdly, the site offered the advantage of being next to a ready supply of building materials. Indeed, masons could extract schist from the adjacent cliff face, while conveniently enlarging the narrow riverside setting. However, even though Cap Diamant schist was used repeatedly in early Québec constructions, it made for poor quality construction material as it was very friable. In erecting Talon's brewery, the masons had to dig trenches down to the bedrock in order to provide a stable base for the building's foundations since the natural substrate in this area was composed of loose coarse deposits.

The brewery was shut down in 1675, making it necessary to find a new function for the large slate-roofed building. Various uses were envisioned, including Talon's proposal to convert the structure into a hospital. Intendant de Meulles, who was appointed to succeed Talon in 1683, recognized the building's potential for another industrial function and suggested it be used to house various craftsmen such as weavers, shoemakers, and hat-makers.[8] However, the Intendant needed appropriate living quarters and eventually

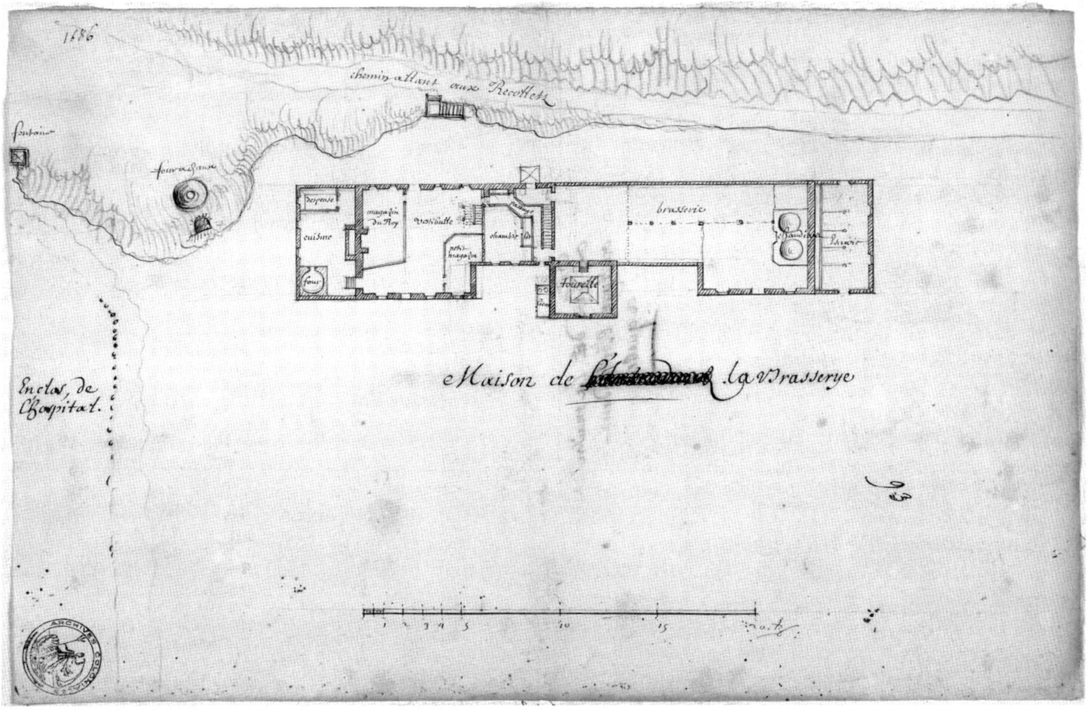

FIG. 2
Plan of Jean Talon's brewery in 1686 ('Maison de la brasserye', anon., 1686; NAC, M350-Québec/1686). North is at the bottom of the plan.

decided to take up residence in the building along with his staff. From 1684, Talon's former brewery became the official residence of the colony's intendant, and de Meulles held his first Sovereign Council meeting in the converted brewhouse in January 1689.[9] In addition to serving as the intendant's living quarters, the palace housed the King's Stores until 5 January 1713, when a fire broke out during the night and burned the building to the ground.[10]

RESEARCH SINCE 2000

The most significant changes to the landscape of the Intendant's Palace site resulted from a change in its function around 1675. All the evidence suggests that, at the turn of the 18th century, there emerged a greater need for a physical symbol of the intendant's important status in the colony.[11] Therefore, a three-storey palace was built to lodge the intendant and his personnel, reflecting a major shift from the site's initial industrial focus on shipbuilding, potash production and brewing. The new palace was suited to the intendant's administrative and commercial role, and it continued to evolve as an administrative and political centre for most of the first half of the 18th century. The building fell into British hands after the conquest of 1759 and was almost totally destroyed during the American invasion of 1775. Following the invasion, the site was initially abandoned, but it eventually began to serve various functions. James Clearihue started a bakery there in 1825, and then sold the property to the Boswell brothers in 1852. As a result of these different functions, the data set for reconstructing the sequence of events on the Intendant's Palace site is very complex. Nonetheless, it is obvious that the successive occupations reused walls that already existed on the site as foundations for new buildings.

NAVAL SHIPYARD

In 2007, Université Laval's field school unearthed an unexpected wood deposit buried in the lowermost levels of the site. Many pieces had been squared off, while others bore tool marks. Subsequent analysis of this cultural deposit by City of Québec archaeologists revealed the presence of hardwood timbers, many of which had been worked in a manner similar to pieces associated with shipbuilding.[12] It is highly likely, therefore, that this buried cultural level belonged to the naval shipyard founded by Talon in 1665 along the shores of the Saint-Charles River. Although the precise location of the shipyard is still unknown, it is presumed to have been situated in the vicinity of the Intendant's Palace site, on the small piece of land that Talon purchased from the widow Couillard.[13] The discovery of this wood deposit appears to confirm that Talon intended to develop an industrial sector which, with its shipyard, brewery and potash factory, would provide the colony with an economy that could generate its own revenue. Naval construction would have been the spearhead of this self-sustaining economy.

Few other traces remain of this ephemeral shipbuilding enterprise, with the exception of a long wall underneath the 1668 brewery, interpreted by Simoneau as the remnants of a building used at the shipyard.[14] This building, which existed prior to the brewhouse, may be the only architectural feature uncovered to date that is associated with the shipyard. It is also possible that a water basin shown in front of the Intendant's Palace on an engraving dating from 1699 may actually be a vestige of the former shipyard (Fig. 3). This basin, which provided access to the river, would have been an appropriate setting for transferring goods to the King's Stores from ships that had sailed up the Saint-Charles River. Merchants such as Aubert de La Chesnaye, who lived on the waterfront near Place Royale, made use of similar facilities.[15]

THE POTASH FACTORY

Research on this industrial facility began with a spatial approach and, as a result, the presence of the potash factory was confirmed during the first year of the archaeology programme launched on the Intendant's Palace site in 2000. A 1m-wide stone wall running in an east–west direction and supported by logs was identified as belonging in all likelihood to the north wall of the potash factory indicated on a 1686 map of the site. Although consideration was also given to the hypothesis that the wall belonged to one of several other buildings shown to the west of the first palace in an inset on a plan dated *c.* 1690, this hypothesis was eventually

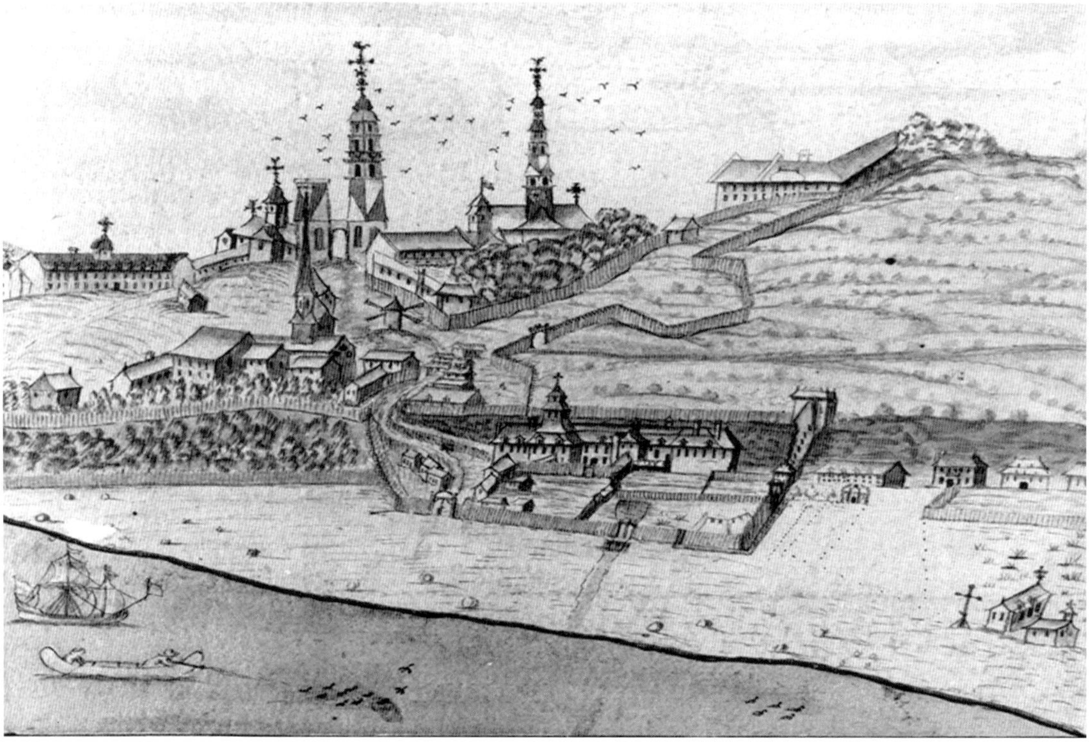

FIG. 3
Plan of the first palace compound attributed to Fonville, 1699 (*Québec veu dv Nord Ouest*; NAC, C–46450).

rejected on account of the wall's sheer size and location, both of which argued strongly for an association with the building used for potash production.[16] A bakery was also noted on the *c.* 1690 plan in the same area as the factory.[17] Therefore, the sector in the vicinity of the potash facility appears to have been used for activities that required large quantities of wood and thus posed a greater fire hazard than activities carried out elsewhere.

Potash production in New France started around 1670 on the initiative of Talon. The superintendent in charge of production claimed that the potash was of comparable quality to that made by the Muscovites and the soap as soft as that made by the Dutch.[18] Following Talon's departure from the colony, potash production slowed to the point where operations were eventually abandoned. Perhaps the fire hazard posed by this activity, which was carried out close to the palace, was sufficient reason to abandon it. Nevertheless, two lime kilns continued production in the vicinity.[19]

IDENTIFYING THE LIMITS OF THE INTENDANT'S PALACE SITE

One of the aims of the research programme initiated in 2000 was to determine the perimeter of the palace compound in order to define the space used by the French administration. Accordingly, a series of excavations were undertaken to locate fortifications known to have existed on the site, specifically a masonry curtain wall and a palisade that surrounded the first palace. Late 17th-century cartographic sources indicate a stone wall running down the cliff and joining a wooden palisade that continued northwards to a battery known as the St Nicholas Redoubt, erected on the banks of the Saint-Charles River. Québec's population was keenly aware of two sources of danger: open conflict between France and other European nations, most notably England, and attacks by local Amerindian populations. As a result, a defensive system combining stone works and a palisade was built around both Upper and Lower Towns.[20] As construction plans from 1692 suggest, a watchtower protecting the palace grounds was located at the compound's western entrance, where it marked the end of the stone wall and the beginning of the wooden palisade. A number of excavation units were therefore opened in this sector to better understand the boundaries of the Intendant's Palace complex following the abandonment of the Talon brewery.[21] However, despite the numerous historical sources that point to the presence of imposing features at the west end of the palace compound, the many occupations at the site seem to have obliterated or hidden a large portion of the compound's west wall.

The first archaeological excavations aimed at locating the stone wall that descended the cliff face were conducted at the spot most likely to contain the remains of this massive foundation.[22] However, a series of three adjoining walls built on sterile ground were unearthed at this location instead. The earliest levels associated with these walls yielded a coin from Limoges dating to 1655–1713, as well as coarse green-glazed earthenware and white French faïence. Despite its limited size, this excavation unit may have exposed structural remains associated with the watchtower located at the junction of the fortification wall and the palisade. However, it was impossible to draw any definite conclusions in this regard owing to the proliferation of massive masonry features in this very restricted space.

Another excavation unit was opened further south to locate the continuation of some of the aforementioned features, but the results were mixed.[23] Instead, these investigations revealed traces of the cork-insulated Boswell cold storage facility and a series of 19th- and 20th-century terracotta drainage pipes, as well as the original macadamed surface of Rue Vallière dating to the 19th century. Interpretation of historic plans had initially suggested that the watchtower was built squarely on the fortification wall; however, closer scrutiny of the plans revealed that the tower protruded slightly beyond the wall.[24] Moreover, it was clear from the excavations that the wall's location had been misinterpreted. It was situated perhaps several metres further east.[25]

Additional efforts to locate the original fortification wall in 2002 unearthed more remains of the Boswell brewery, as well as the foundations of 19th-century houses built on Rue Saint-Vallier.[26] In addition, traces of a layer associated with Colonel Zachariah Thompson of the Royal Engineers, who lived on this street from 1766 to 1775, were found beneath 19th- and 20th-century levels. The association of this layer with Thompson was confirmed by the discovery of creamware and pearlware ceramics in a black organic deposit that sealed another level dating from the 1760s. Colonel Zachariah Thompson's presence on Rue Saint-Vallier came to an abrupt end when this sector was heavily damaged by shelling during the 1775 American invasion.

The last excavation unit opened in order to document the stone fortification wall was positioned 22m north of the previous units. It uncovered numerous 20th-century reinforced concrete floor layers from the Boswell brewery, and considerable effort was devoted to removing the floors and metal pipes that crisscrossed the southern section of the unit.[27] However, no traces of the masonry defensive wall were located. Nonetheless, if projections of the wall's orientation are reliable, it is likely that the remains of this structure, which defined the western limit of the palace compound, are still present on the Intendant's Palace site. In fact, the wall is believed to be situated in the western part of the aforementioned excavation unit at a depth lower than that attained during the fieldwork. In spite of its size, this massive stone fortification wall is one of the most elusive features constructed on the west side of the site. It was built apparently during the 1680s when Talon's brewery became the intendant's official residence, and was extended to the shores of the Saint-Charles River in the early 1690s by means of a wooden palisade made of white cedar posts.[28]

THE PALISADE

The objective of the 2004 summer field school was to excavate the latrines built at the western end of the second palace around 1723. The project took an unexpected turn when the remains of the wooden palisade from the first palace compound were discovered instead. This feature was by far the most promising find to date, as it documented the boundary that reflects the transformation of this space into an administrative centre used by the intendants. Encircling a city the size of Québec with a palisade was a daunting task due to the limited manpower in the colony. Major François Provost initiated the palisade's construction in 1690 and the work took almost an entire decade.[29] Josué Dubois Berthelot de Beaucours took over the project in 1693 and the king's engineer Jacques Levasseur de Néré finally completed it in 1697.[30] The excavations conducted in 2004 unearthed eleven white cedar posts varying from 1.0 to 1.5m in length (Fig. 4), aligned in a 0.60m-wide trench dug into the sterile soil. The trench appears to have been backfilled immediately after the posts were installed in order to hold them solidly in place. Preservation of the posts was excellent, with the bark still intact in some instances. All the bases of the posts showed the unmistakable cut marks made by the axes used to fell the trees.

Excavation work continued on the palisade in 2005–06 with the goal of verifying its construction method and date, and determining whether more posts were situated further north.[31] The excavation unit opened in 2004 was extended northward and the sediments uncovered were sampled in order to reconstruct the site's palaeoenvironment during the late Holocene. This northern extension of the dig uncovered other worked pieces of wood, located in what may have been a ditch surrounding the palisade and deposited apparently during the dismantling of this structure.[32] Although the levels

FIG. 4

White cedar posts used in the construction of the 1690 palisade (right), and remains of the palisade on the west side of the palace compound (left) (photograph, Université Laval).

sampled in the extension were largely undisturbed, they did not yield any information on the exact date the palisade was taken down. However, this most likely occurred in the early 1720s when three-storey stone privies were added to the eastern and western ends of the second palace.

THE BOAT BASIN

Two plans dating from the late 17th century depict a small boat basin within the first palace compound. One of these, an inset dating from 1699 that appears on J.-B. Louis Franquelin's map of Québec City's Lower Town, suggests that flat-bottomed boats would have been able to move freely out of the basin at high tide through a small gate opening onto a shallow man-made canal dug from the palace enclosure to the Saint-Charles River (Fig. 3).[33] It appears that the basin was built around a natural body of water trapped between the river and the cliff, on the river's south bank. A plan drawn up by the royal engineer Villeneuve in 1692 proposed enclosing this body of water, which seems to have been a small pond, in order to create a basin that could accommodate up to 300 boats.[34] Although the plan that Villeneuve submitted to the king may have been grandiose, the basin that was actually built was probably more like the one shown in the above-mentioned inset dating from 1699.[35] The inset depicts a tiny basin and what is presumably a watercraft under construction lying nearby. A slipway of logs can also be seen just outside the entrance to the basin.

Archaeological investigations on the Intendant's Palace site have not yet yielded any traces of this late 17th-century basin, and Herzog and Nadeau have a offered plausible explanation for this state of affairs.[36] While it was once thought that the basin lay underneath the second palace, both authors now suggest that it was situated to the north-west of this building. The precise location of this rather obscure feature remains to be determined during future work on the site.

THE SECOND INTENDANT'S PALACE

Although an analysis of 18th-century plans suggested that the second palace was probably buried beneath Rue des Prairies, no attempt had been made to determine if anything remained of this impressive 1716 construction prior to the research programme launched in 2000. Therefore, one of the programme's objectives was to determine the state of preservation of the northern portion of the second palace. Built almost immediately after the fire that destroyed the first palace in 1713, the 1716 structure was similar to its predecessor in that it too served as the centre of operations for the intendant's activities, including the administration of justice and presiding over New France's Sovereign Council. However, contrary to its predecessor, it did not house the King's Stores, which continued to occupy the renovated remains of the first palace.

A majestic edifice, the second palace was considered one of the most important buildings in the colony. It was a two-storey stone structure adorned with a mansard roof covered with slates.[37] On 28 December 1725, the second palace in turn fell victim to a fire, which destroyed all but the walls and vaults. Chaussegros de Léry, the king's engineer, subsequently drew up plans for a safer, fireproof building. The new design did away with the mansard roof and extended the stone walls upward to form a third storey. Measures were also taken to reduce the risk of fire inside the structure, by covering the top floor with tiles and the apartment floors with either stone or brick. The reconstruction work went rapidly and Intendant Claude Thomas Dupuy was able to move into the renovated palace in the autumn of 1726.[38] The palace was almost completely destroyed in 1775 during the siege of Québec by American revolutionary forces, and it remained more or less abandoned until the Boswell brothers bought the land in 1852. After some refurbishing work, they established a brewery in the southern half of the building.

Four excavation units were opened to document the northern half of the second palace buried beneath Rue des Prairies. The base of the building's large east gable wall, which measured 3m wide at the bottom, was identified during the first year of the research programme.[39] Part of the west gable wall was discovered the following year.[40] Excavations at the north-west corner of the building not only revealed a thick layer of stone and mortar outside the west wall that attested to the 1775 bombardment but also provided a better understanding of the construction methods used to raise the gabled walls in the 18th century. The foundations were set directly on the bedrock following the removal of the loose overlying sedimentary deposits. This was only way to provide them with a sufficiently stable footing to support a three-storey building at this spot, which was located on the buried banks of the Saint-Charles River. The masons even took care to remove a thin peat layer during the construction work in order to erect the walls on firmer ground.

Once the two gabled walls had been located during the fieldwork, interest focused on whether any of the second palace's interior was still in place underneath Rue des Prairies, a street laid out in

1927.[41] A study of historic plans prior to the excavations showed that, during the refurbishing work by the Boswell brothers, only the southern portion of the palace had been restored. The fieldwork, for its part, demonstrated that the base of a wall running east–west and dividing the palace in two had been preserved and reused as a foundation for a 19th-century brick wall that was part of the brewery. In addition, the outlines of the vaults located at both ends of the palace were still visible in the 19th-century masonry.

A number of the excavation units opened to document the northern portion of the palace clearly illustrated the constraints of urban archaeology in Québec City. The municipal sewer system and water mains ran through the units, while electrical wiring sat in a concrete duct on top of the palace's north wall. Nevertheless, after digging through the burnt remains of two 19th-century coal storage sheds that went up in flames during a major fire in Québec City in 1845, the original ground floor of the palace and its north wall were located. The base of the wall was not reached, but the floor was found to be constructed of thick sandstone slabs set on a layer of mortar, which in turn rested on a substantial deposit of clay and sand.[42] Although the floor yielded few diagnostic artefacts, a re-examination of the 1726 plan of the palace drawn by Chaussegros de Léry showed that the portion of the floor uncovered overlapped the common room and another space whose function was not indicated.[43] Excavations further west revealed additional features, including a cross-wall and more flooring.

The discovery of the well-preserved palace floor kindled high expectations regarding the excavation of an area where the kitchen was known to have been located. Interest centred particularly on recovering 18th-century kitchen remains and utensils.[44] However, none of the artefacts recovered bore witness to culinary activities. Moreover, there was no evidence of the fire that ravaged the building in 1725. As elsewhere, the sandstone floor in the kitchen area was well preserved and, in the western part of the excavation unit, the base of the kitchen's chimney was identified. In addition to being associated with food preparation, the chimney may have served to evacuate smoke from a small wood stove installed in an office located in the north-west corner of the palace's ground floor.[45]

THE LATRINES

The contents of the latrines built in 1723 at the western end of the palace offered an unusual opportunity for documenting foodways and sanitary habits. These privies are a time capsule of life on the site during the French administration, the short-lived British military presence and the American invasion, as their contents cover the period from 1723 to 1775 and comprise exceptionally well-preserved organic remains.[46] The excavations also revealed the drainage system used to evacuate the latrines' contents toward the Saint-Charles River just to the north.[47] Although the Boswell brothers built their malthouse on top of the privies at the end of the 19th century, this construction work did not alter the overall external shape of the latrines. In fact, it conveniently sealed their contents.

These latrines, which were first used by the French, contained table scraps and other domestic refuse in their lowermost levels (Fig. 5). They also contained an abundance of French faïence and bottles, a number of small personal items and numerous plant and faunal remains.[48] Judging from the vertical distribution of the ceramics, it was suggested that the privies may have been used as a garbage pit by the British military for a short period between the conquest and the American invasion, when these installations were destroyed by shelling. The use of the palace as a barracks by the British army strongly influenced the character of the material culture in the upper levels of the latrines. Indeed, a preliminary analysis of these levels revealed a concentration of bottles and ceramics of British origin.[49]

CONCLUDING REMARKS

When investigations resumed at the Intendant's Palace site in 2000, the research programme aimed to provide a broad understanding of the palace complex. More specifically, it sought to examine the many features that could document the city's urbanization, as well as evaluate the site's potential for heritage development. Rather than focusing on a particular building and its associated material culture, efforts were invested toward understanding the site's evolution in both its natural and built environments. Excavations revealed that the urbanization of Québec City resulted from a series of human activities initially aimed at developing industries to provide goods that were essential to the development of the French colony in North America. In order to pursue this grand economic scheme, local authorities needed a number of basic infrastructures, particularly a shipyard for building and repairing boats to provide access to inland waterways and furs; a brewery to provide beer and other essential products for the inhabitants, thus limiting wine imports and fostering the use of

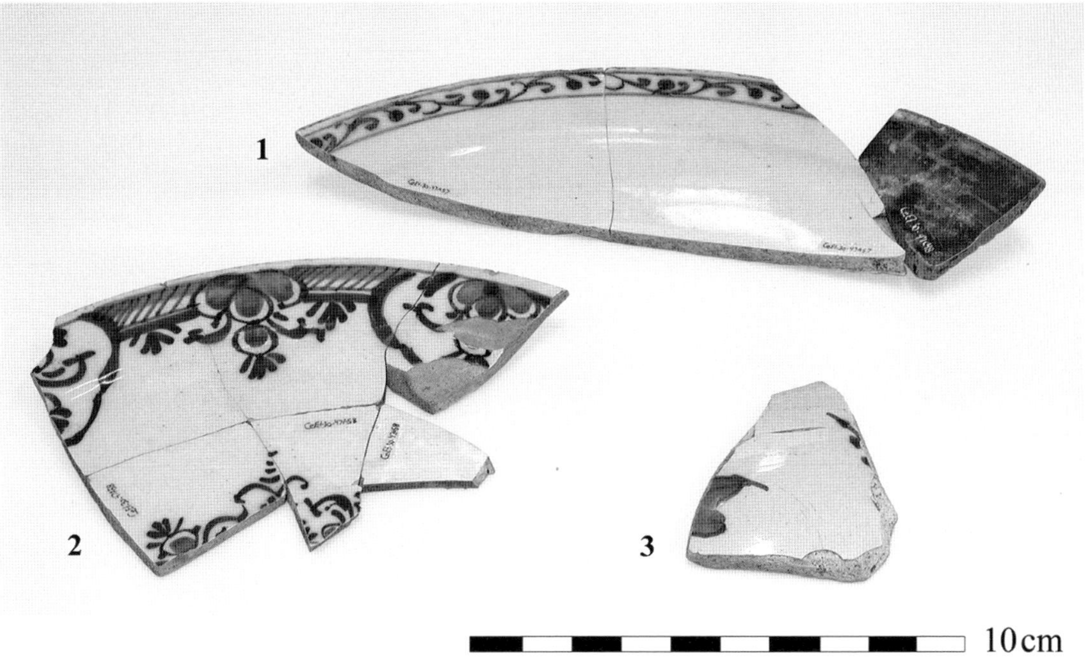

FIG. 5
Tin-glazed earthenware from the latrines: 1. Dutch delftware pancake plate, 1730–40; 2. Dutch delftware pancake plate, camaïeu decoration, 1730–40; 3. Dutch delftware with polychrome decoration (blue, green and brownish red) (photograph, Université Laval).

surplus hops and barley in the colony; and, lastly, facilities for producing potash, which was in ever-increasing demand for making bottles, soap and gunpowder, and for bleaching textiles. For all these reasons, the space that would eventually become the Intendant's Palace complex initially served as an industrial park. In fact, it was the first industrial park in Québec City's Lower Town.

Two different phases of urban development have been identified on the site. The first, dating from 1665 to 1713, involved the exploitation of an industrial and commercial venture, while the second, dating from around 1716 to 1760, was centred on the operation of a political and administrative complex. During both phases, access to water transportation was imperative. The political and administrative complex housed a monumental palace which expressed the intendant's need to distinguish himself from the governor of New France, who resided in Upper Town on the most prominent plot of land in the city. The first phase was a time of pragmatic measures when the intendants focused primarily on the colony's economic development and defence, while the second phase, which witnessed the emergence of the second palace complex, compellingly illustrates how the intendants sought to assert their role in the colony.

In this paper, the Intendant's Palace site has been described in relation to the various historical phases it went through since its initial occupation. Thanks to the research programme prepared by Bain and Moussette,[50] which sought to establish links between the site's different occupation phases, the research approach originally adopted in 2000 was rapidly fine-tuned. Archaeological fieldwork undertaken as part of the new programme led to the discovery of a small-scale Native occupation as well as traces of the shipyard, brewery and potash factory associated with the site's ephemeral early industrial development. The excavations also documented the first and the second Intendant's Palaces and their associated buildings, as well as the ultimate destruction of these structures. Lastly, they documented the Boswell brewery, which operated on the site until the 1960s.[51] Archaeological research on the Intendant's Palace site also studied the historic landscape in relation to the urban environment.[52] It showed how the natural environment was

FIG. 6

Tin-glazed earthenware and metal from the latrines: 1. English delftware chamber pot, undecorated, 1760–19th century; 2. French faïence chamber pot, undecorated, 1700–60; 3. Iron object; 4. French faïence chamber pot, undecorated, 1700–60; 5. French faïence chamber pot from Paris, camaïeu decoration (blue and black), 1720–50 (photograph, Université Laval).

transformed into a built environment, and how the latter evolved from a late 17th-century industrial complex into an administrative colonial space representing the ultimate transformation of the built environment into an entirely urban setting. On the initiative of different intendants, the site became the centre of political decision-making for New France as a whole, and the buildings erected there reflected this status. While being adapted to the local climate, they displayed a monumental architecture that was well in line with European standards of the day.

The evolution of the Intendant's Palace, as revealed through archaeological, environmental and historical research, represents a set of behaviours that are in turn reflected through various cultural manifestations, such as the need for space and the exercise of power by the colonial administrators. Its evolution is still being studied by a research team composed of material culture specialists, art historians, environmental archaeologists, physical geographers, geologists and archaeometrists.

ACKNOWLEDGEMENTS

The archaeological investigations conducted on the Intendant's Palace site by students at Université Laval's historical archaeology field school were made possible through a tripartite agreement between the Province of Québec's Ministère de la Culture, des Communications et de la Condition féminine, the City of Québec and Université Laval. Over the years, this agreement has enabled researchers to study a number of archaeological sites within the city limits and to help municipal planning services better understand the heritage resources within their territory. These municipal services must be praised for their foresight in prioritizing investments in cultural resources. The work accomplished since 1982 would not have been possible without the help of colleagues who instigated the programme, namely, Professors Marcel Moussette and Michel Fortin. Similarly, our current understanding of the site would not have been achieved without the input of specialists, too numerous to name, and of the many assiduous students who have trained with the field school since 1982. It is also important to underscore the contribution of Lise Jodoin, the conservator in charge of Université Laval's conservation laboratory, who restored all the artefacts and took the photographs illustrating this paper. A final word of recognition goes to William Moss for preparing this special issue of *Post-Medieval Archaeology* and to the revisers for their constructive comments on our work.

NOTES

[1] Clermont *et al.* 1992.

[2] Moussette 1994.

[3] Bain & Moussette 2007.

[4] A critique of this approach was presented by Auger & Moss 2001.

[5] Several graduate theses currently in preparation at Université Laval involve detailed analyses of the material culture.

[6] Moussette 1994.

[7] Guimont 1987.

[8] Moussette 1994, n. 49.

[9] Moussette 1994, 69–70.

[10] Letter from Clairembault d'Aigremont, comptroller of the marine, to the minister, 17 February 1713 (Colonial Archives, General Correspondence series, Canada; Centre des Archives d'outre-mer (France), Col. C11A 34/fols 104–5v).

[11] The office of intendant of New France was created in 1663, when King Louis XIV established a system of government, including a governor and a sovereign council, in the colony. Since the intendant was the king's representative in the colony, he had a special status which, according to historians, called for suitable living quarters. In New France, as in the provinces of the mother country, the intendant was the king's 'right-hand man'. Second in rank to the governor, the intendant controlled the colony's entire civil administration. He was responsible for the administration of justice, the police (i.e. law and order) and finance, and also devoted particular attention to settlement and economic development (agriculture, trade, industry and communications). Moreover, since he managed financial matters, he had the most sweeping powers in the colony's government. See *The Canadian Encyclopedia*, s.v. 'Intendant', <http://www.thecanadianencyclopedia.com/index.cfm?PgNm=TCE&Params=f1ARTf0004023>.

[12] Expertise on these wood pieces, stored at the Centre de conservation du Québec, was generously provided by Marc-André Bernier of Parks Canada.

[13] Brisson 1983, 28–9.

[14] See the paper by D. Simoneau on the Intendant's Palace in this volume.

[15] Rouleau *et al.* 1998.

[16] Lapointe 2001.

[17] See detail of the *c.* 1690 map of Québec viewed from the north-west, published in Noppen and Villeneuve 1984.

[18] GRHQ 1994, 69, cited in Lapointe 2001.

[19] Lapointe 2001, 6; see also *Gravure de Québec montrant le secteur du deuxième palais et le bâtiment de la potasse* (NAC, H3/340/Québec, *c.* 1721).

[20] Charbonneau *et al.* 1992, 32–8.

[21] Hare *et al.* 1987.

[22] Duchaine 2001.

[23] Eid 2003.

[24] Duchaine 2001.

[25] Eid 2003.

[26] Alberton 2005.

[27] Arpin 2005.

[28] Querrec *et al.* forthcoming.

[29] Desjardins 2006.

[30] Desjardins 2006, 68–9.

[31] Lambert & Mercier 2008; Janson 2008.

[32] Janson 2008; Lambert & Mercier 2008.

[33] The excavation of a canal of this type is mentioned in Moussette 1994, 71.

[34] The word used on the 1692 plan is *batteaux*, which refers to a kind of flat-bottomed boat similar to a rowing boat.

[35] Villeneuve's map (Centre des archives d'outre-mer (France), 03DFC439A) and J.-B. Louis Franquelin's map of Lower Town, Québec City (NAC C46450).

[36] Herzog 2005, 53–8; Nadeau 2007, 147–57.

[37] Richardson 1984.

[38] Roy 1943, 94.

[39] Dionne 2001.

[40] Gilbert 2003.

[41] Herzog 2005; Nadeau 2007; Letarte 2007.

[42] Herzog 2005, 35–6.

[43] Chaussegros de Léry, 1726, *État détaillé des travaux proposés par l'ingénieur Chaussegros de Léry pour rétablir le Palais de l'intendant, le rendre plus solide et lui assurer une meilleure protection contre l'incendie*, 28 Jan. 1726 (Colonial Archives, C11A, General Correspondence series; Canada; Centre des archives d'outre-mer (France), Coll. C11A 48/fols 9–12v).

[44] Letarte 2007.

[45] See Moussette 1983, 68 for an illustration.

[46] Gaudreau & Taschereau 2006.

[47] Janson 2008.

[48] Several field reports describe the results of the excavation of these latrines. Two ongoing Master's theses by Caroline Parent and Jacynthe Bernard focus, respectively, on the material culture and the faunal remains. The plant remains are being studied by doctoral student Julie-Anne Bouchard-Perron.

[49] Gaudreau & Taschereau 2006.

[50] Bain & Moussette 2007.

[51] Bain & Moussette 2007.

[52] See A. Bain *et al.* in this volume.

BIBLIOGRAPHY

PUBLISHED SOURCES

Alberton, L. 2005, 'Rapport d'intervention, le Palais de l'intendant: opération 40', in Alberton *et al.* 2005, 1–60.

Alberton, L., Arpin, C. & Herzog, A. 2005, *Site du Palais de l'intendant: chantier-école de l'an 2002*, Cahiers d'archéologie du CÉLAT **17**.

Arpin, C. 2005, 'Fouille archéologique dans le stationnement près de l'entrée actuelle des voûtes du palais sur la rue Vallière: opération 39 à la recherche du mur d'enceinte de la cour intérieure des palais', in Alberton *et al.* 2005, 1–88.

Auger, R. & Moss, W. 2001, 'The archaeology of physical and social transformation: high times, low tides and tourist floods on Québec City's waterfront', in Mayne & Murray 2001, 132–43.

Brisson, R. 1983, *La Charpenterie Navale à Québec sous le régime français*, coll. Edmond-de-Nevers **2,** Québec: Institut Québécois de recherche sur la culture.

Charbonneau, A., Desloges, Y. & Lafrance, M. 1992, *Québec the Fortified City: from the 17th to the 19th Century*, Ottawa: Supply and Services Canada.

Clermont, N., Chapdelaine, C. & Guimont, J. 1992, *L'Occupation historique et préhistorique de Place-Royale*, coll. Patrimoines, Dossiers **76,** Québec: Ministère des affaires culturelles.

Dionne, M.-M. 2001, 'À la recherche des vestiges du nouveau palais de l'intendant enfouis sous la rue des Prairies: l'opération 33', in Dionne *et al.* 2001, 3–46.

Dionne, M.-M., Duchaine, D.-E. & Lapointe, R. 2001, *Site du Palais de l'intendant: chantier-école de l'an 2000*, Cahiers d'archéologie du CÉLAT **9**.

Duchaine, D.-E. 2001, 'De 1693 à aujourd'hui, secteur de la rue Vallière situé à l'ouest du palais de l'intendant: l'opération 34', in Dionne *et al.* 2001, 1–44.

Eid, P. 2003, 'Le secteur de la rue Vallière à l'ouest du palais de l'intendant: opération 37', in Eid & Gilbert 2003, 1–58.

Eid, P. & Gilbert, L. 2003, *Site du Palais de l'intendant: chantier-école de l'an 2001*, Cahiers d'archéologie du CÉLAT **15**.

Gilbert, L. 2003, 'Le site du deuxième palais de l'intendant à Québec (CeEt-30, opération 36)', in Eid & Gilbert 2003, 1–59.

Guimont, J. 1987, *Le Site du premier palais de l'intendant à Québec (CeEt-30). Rapport préliminaire de la quatrième campagne de fouilles (1985)*, Rapports et mémoires de recherche du CÉLAT **8**.

Hare, J., Lafrance, M. & Ruddel, D.-T. 1987, *Histoire de la ville de Québec 1608–1871*, Montréal: Boréal Express.

Herzog, A. 2005, 'Rapport de la XIIe campagne de fouilles: l'Îlot des palais de l'Intendant CeEt-30, opération 38', in Alberton *et al.* 2005, 1–116.

Lapointe, R. 2001, 'Le bâtiment de la potasse de Québec: d'une industrie du XVIIe siècle aux industries du XXe siècle', in Dionne *et al.* 2001, 1–62.

Letarte, J. 2007, 'CeEt-30 Site de l'Îlot des palais, opération 41: à la recherche de la cuisine du second palais de l'intendant', in Letarte *et al.* 2007, 1–86.

Letarte, J., Nadeau, R. & Rochefort, F. 2007, *Site du Palais de l'intendant: chantier-école de l'an 2003*, Cahiers d'archéologie du CÉLAT **20**.

Mayne, A. & Murray, T. (eds) 2001, *The Archaeology of Urban Landscapes: Explorations in Slumland*, Cambridge: University Press.

Moussette, M. 1983, *Le Chauffage domestique au Canada des origines à l'industrialisation*, Québec: Presses de Université Laval.

Moussette, M. 1994, *Le Site du Palais de l'intendant à Québec: genèse et structuration d'un lieu urbain*, Sillery: Septentrion.

Nadeau, R. 2007, 'CeEt-30 Site de l'Îlot des palais, opération 42: le plancher du palais et le bassin', in Letarte *et al.* 2007, 89–198.

Noppen, L. & Villeneuve, R. 1984, *Le Trésor du grand siècle*, Québec: Musée du Québec.

Richardson, A.J.H. 1984, *Québec City Architects, Artisans and Builders*, Ottawa: History Division, National Museum of Man.

Rouleau, S., Cloutier, C., Fortin C. & l'Ostéothèque de Montréal inc. 1998, *L'Archéologie de la maison Aubert-de-La-Chesnaye à Québec (CeEt-46)*, Cahiers d'archéologie du CÉLAT **3**.

Roy, P.-G. 1943, *À travers les mémoires de Philippe Aubert de Gaspé*, Montréal: G. Ducharme.

UNPUBLISHED SOURCES

Bain, A. & Moussette, M. 2007, 'Îlot des Palais: programme de recherche archéologique', CÉLAT, Université Laval, INRS, Ville de Québec and Ministère de la Culture, des Communications et de la Condition féminine.

Desjardins, M.-P. 2006, 'Des premières fortifications de la ville de Québec à aujourd'hui, secteur ouest du second palais de l'Intendant. CeEt-30, opération 45', Ministère de la Culture, des Communications et de la Condition féminine, Québec.

Gaudreau, N. & Taschereau, E. 2006, 'Rapport de fouilles archéologiques: le site de l'Îlot des

Palais, CeEt-30, opération 47', Ministère de la Culture, des Communications et de la Condition féminine, Québec.

GRHQ (Groupe de recherches en histoire du Québec) 1994, 'Étude d'ensemble: sous-secteurs Maison-blanche et Côte-d'Abraham, synthèse', Québec: Service de l'Urbanisme, Ville de Québec.

Janson, R. 2008, 'Le site de l'Îlot des palais (CeEt-30), rapport préliminaire d'intervention, 2006, opération 48', Ministère de la Culture, des Communications et de la Condition féminine, Québec.

Lambert, V. & Mercier, C. 2008, 'Le site de l'Îlot des palais (CeEt-30), rapport d'intervention 2005, opération 46', Ministère de la Culture, des Communications et de la Condition féminine, Québec.

Querrec, L., Filion, L., Auger, R. & Arseneault, D. 2008, 'Archaeological and Historical Woods from Québec City, a UNESCO Heritage Site: a 342-year (1489–1830) White Cedar Tree Ring Chronology', poster presented at the Eurodendro conference in Vienna, May 2008.

Querrec, L., Filion, L., Auger, R. & Arseneault, D. forthcoming, 'Tree-Ring Analysis of White Cedar (*Thuja occidentalis L.*) Archaeological and Historical Wood in Québec City (Québec, Canada)', *Dendrochronologia*.

ABBREVIATIONS

CÉLAT	Centre interuniversitaire d' Études de recherche sur les lettres, les arts et les traditions
INRS	Institut national de la recherche scientifique

SUMMARY IN FRENCH, GERMAN, ITALIAN AND SPANISH

RÉSUMÉ

Le site du Palais de l'intendant : urbanisation de la basse ville de Québec

Plusieurs campagnes de fouilles archéologiques ont été menées sur le site du Palais de l'intendant depuis 1982 par le chantier-école de l'Université Laval. Au cours des dix premières années, les recherches ont été concentrées sur la brasserie du XVIIe siècle, le Palais de l'intendant et les Magasins du Roi. Lorsque l'Université Laval est retournée sur le site en 2000, elle a pris une approche holistique plutôt que de focaliser sur des constructions spécifiques. De cette façon, elle a documenté l'évolution urbaine de cette partie de la Cité de Québec, qui a produit des indices de l'occupation continue depuis le milieu du XVIIe siècle.

ZUSAMMENFASSUNG

Der Palast des Intendanten: die Besiedlung der Unterstadt von Quebec

Seit 1982 wurden mehrere archäologische Feldstudien im Palast des Intendanten ausgeführt. Während der ersten 10 Jahre konzentrierten sich die Untersuchungen auf die Brauerei, den Intendantenpalast, und die Läden des Königs, alle stammen aus dem 17. Jh. Als im Jahre 2000 die Feldarchäologen und die Abteilung der Universität Laval ihre Arbeit wieder aufnahmen, arbeiteten sie nach holistischer Methode und zeigten weniger Interesse an einzelnen Gebäuden. Dabei dokumentierten sie die Stadtentwicklung dieses Teils der Stadt Quebec und wiesen damit eine seit der Mitte des 17. Jhs. andauernde Besiedlung nach.

RIASSUNTO

Il sito del palazzo d'intendenza: urbanizzazione della parte bassa della città di Quebec

Dal 1982, una serie di interventi archeologici sono stati condotti nel sito del palazzo di intendenza. Per i primi dieci anni la ricerca si è concentrata sulla birreria di XVII secolo, il palazzo d'intendenza e i magazzini reali. Quando la scuola di ricerca sul campo dell'Università Laval tornò sul sito nel 2000, ebbe un approccio olistico piuttosto che concentrarsi su edifici specifici. Nel fare ciò fu documentata l'evoluzione urbanistica di questa parte della città di Quebec, raccogliendo testimonianze di un'occupazione continuativa a partire dal XVII secolo.

RESUMEN

El yacimiento del Palacio del Intendente: la urbanización de Cuidad Baja en la ciudad de Quebec

Se han desarrollado diversas campañas arqueológicas en el Palacio del Intendente desde 1982. Durante los primeros diez años la investigación se ha centrado en la fábrica de cerveza del siglo XVII, el Palacio del Intendente y los almacenes del rey. Cuando la universidad Laval regresó al yacimiento en el 2000 optó por adoptar un enfoque más global en vez de centrarse en edificios específicos. De esta manera ha podido documentar la evolución urbana en esta zona de Quebec, recuperando evidencia de ocupación ininterrumpida desde mediados del siglo XVII.

CÉLAT and Department of History, 1030 Avenue des Sciences-humaines, Université Laval, Québec (Québec), Canada G1V 0A6 (RA)
[reginald.auger@celat.ulaval.ca]

CÉLAT and Department of History, 1030 Avenue des Sciences-humaines, Université Laval, Québec (Québec), Canada G1V 0A6 (AB)
[allison.bain@hst.ulaval.ca]

Ville de Québec, Service de l'aménagement du territoire, Division du design, de l'architecture et du patrimoine, 295 boulevard Charest Est, Québec (Québec), Canada G1K 3G8 (DS)
[daniel.simoneau@ville.Québec.qc.ca]

Post-Medieval Archaeology **43/1** (2009), 171–182

The Intendant's Palace site: new insight into its physical evolution and initial occupation

By DANIEL SIMONEAU

SUMMARY: Archaeological investigations on the Intendant's Palace site in the 1980s determined the site's physical evolution and the activities pursued there since 1668. In 2006, the City of Québec and Université Laval launched another field study, which uncovered evidence not only of a prehistoric presence, but also previously unknown historic occupation pre-dating Jean Talon's brewery and possibly associated with a shipyard established by Talon next to the Saint-Charles River around 1666.

INTRODUCTION

In the spring of 2006, the City of Québec undertook an archaeological field study on the site of the Intendant's Palace, which in the late 17th and first half of the 18th century served as the official residence of the Intendant of New France. This fieldwork, which was concentrated in the southern portion of the site, had to be carried out before the construction of an archaeological museum, the Pavillon Jean Talon, intended to incorporate all the site's archaeological remains. The museum was to be a legacy of the city's 400th anniversary celebrations.

This part of the site had already been studied extensively. Throughout the 1980s it was the focus of the annual field school organized by Université Laval under the direction of Professor Marcel Moussette. This decade of intensive research culminated in many academic publications, as well as in the erection of a structure which protected the archaeological remains and made them accessible to the general public. However, it was only a temporary shelter designed to be removed when an interpretation centre could be built. Unfortunately, construction plans were not fully implemented and the site was filled with sand after the temporary shelter reached the end of its useful life. A synthesis of the knowledge acquired during the 1980s was published by Professor Moussette.[1]

The archaeological research lasted for two field seasons. In 2006 the aim was to document areas inside the first Intendant's Palace which had not previously been excavated, notably its east and west wings, as well as adjacent land, especially that along the front and rear façades. In 2007 excavations were to be carried out in the south-western part of the site, an area that had not been studied to any great extent and would be heavily affected by the construction of the projected museum. Given the scope of the task, the City of Québec decided to join forces with Université Laval to carry out the second phase of the project.

Although never completed, work on building the Pavillon Jean-Talon started in 2007 after the second archaeological field season. This inevitably entailed large-scale machine excavation around the perimeter of the first palace, which in turn required constant archaeological monitoring, leading to several emergency excavations.

The archaeological excavation and monitoring work conducted in 2006–07 yielded much new information and thus enriched the already substantial body of evidence amassed by Université Laval, resulting in the launching of a major multi-disciplinary research programme. An

DOI: 10.1179/007942309X12457508844206

in-depth discussion of the results of this programme will be presented in a future publication. Although the greatly expanded body of evidence on the southern part of the Intendant's Palace site has not yet been fully analysed, it has already confirmed conclusions drawn by Marcel Moussette and his research team and shed light on a number of unresolved questions. It is now possible to document better the occupation of the site, particularly during the earlier periods, including that associated with Jean Talon's brewery.

JEAN TALON'S BREWERY

The Intendant's Palace site lies in the northern part of Québec City's Lower Town, at the foot of a steep hill near the Saint-Charles River. The site has long offered distinct advantages, and attracted a prehistoric presence dating to *c.* AD 1300. The first Intendant's Palace was erected here in 1686; plans of the period show that it consisted of a narrow central section flanked by two wings (Fig. 1). The building was largely a product of renovation work on an earlier structure, a brewery operated by Jean Talon from 1668 to *c.* 1675.

The site had already yielded some information about the occupation associated with the brewery. Excavations by Université Laval in the 1980s located a structure whose characteristics linked it to the brewhouse. It contained a large room with a magnificent stone floor, the slope of which had been expertly calculated to allow the liquids used there to flow into a stone drain. This was identified as a malting floor,[2] where barley was left to germinate before being dried in a malting kiln (*touraille*). The remains of a kiln of this type were excavated nearby. Work by the field school also demonstrated that the walls of the brewery had been reused for the first Intendant's Palace, which stood on the site from 1686 to 1713, and even in part for the King's Stores, built on the ruins of the first palace. Construction of the stores started in 1716; the building was destroyed in 1760. In order to supplement the excavated evidence, Professor Moussette's team carried out extensive historical research on the kind of installations required by brewhouses in the 17th century.

Additional archaeological evidence on the Talon brewery was obtained in 2006, when the west wing of the palace was excavated. Until then, this area had been studied only through an exploratory trench dug in 1982; the results were rather mixed. The trench had uncovered a massive stone feature cut by a cast-iron pipe; both were identified as features associated with the industrial-scale Boswell brewery that operated on the site from the second half of the 19th century until 1970.

The excavations of 2006 were initially quite daunting; the research team was quickly confronted, in over half the area explored, with a series of overlapping features of brick and stone, dating from every phase of the site's occupation. Nonetheless, by determining the relative position of each feature in the site's structural sequence, it was possible to identify clearly those associated with Talon's brewery. A plan from 1686 has proved very useful (Fig. 2); even though it post-dates the period of operation of the brewhouse, it is the only plan known to illustrate some of its original components.

The fieldwork revealed the layout and construction of the west wing (Fig. 3). It was already known from the 1686 plan that this part of the building was divided into two sections of unequal size. The smaller one, on the western side, occupied roughly one-third of the structure and housed a stable, while the larger section took up the remaining two-thirds and housed brewing equipment, as shown by the presence of two brewing vats, or coppers, on the 1686 plan. A massive stone structure with a preserved height of up to 1.80m, built directly on the bedrock, occupied about two-thirds of the wing. This feature formed the floor of the stable; in the brewing room its complex structure supported the large copper vats. It did not extend to the south wall of the wing, leaving room for a corridor *c.* 1.10m wide. This corridor may have housed a stairway leading to a cellar situated between the stone feature and the wing's east wall; the space between the masonry structure and the east wall, measured from the surface of the masonry feature, was *c.* 3.50m wide and up to 1.80m deep.

Two circular cavities were uncovered in the stone sub-structure; the large coppers used in the brewing process would have been placed inside them. Unfortunately, the northern one had been badly damaged during the site's industrial phase, and only small portions were still in place. The southern cavity was much better preserved, with almost its entire western half more-or-less intact; the eastern half had been destroyed by the installation of the sub-structure for one of the coppers of the Boswell brewery in the early 20th century (Fig. 4). Thus two similar installations intended for the same use were built at exactly the same spot within some 250 years of each other.

The discovery of features associated with Talon's brewery provided an opportunity to examine how it compared with the kind of installation recommended nearly 100 years later in the encyclopaedia of Diderot and d'Alembert (Fig. 5).[3] For

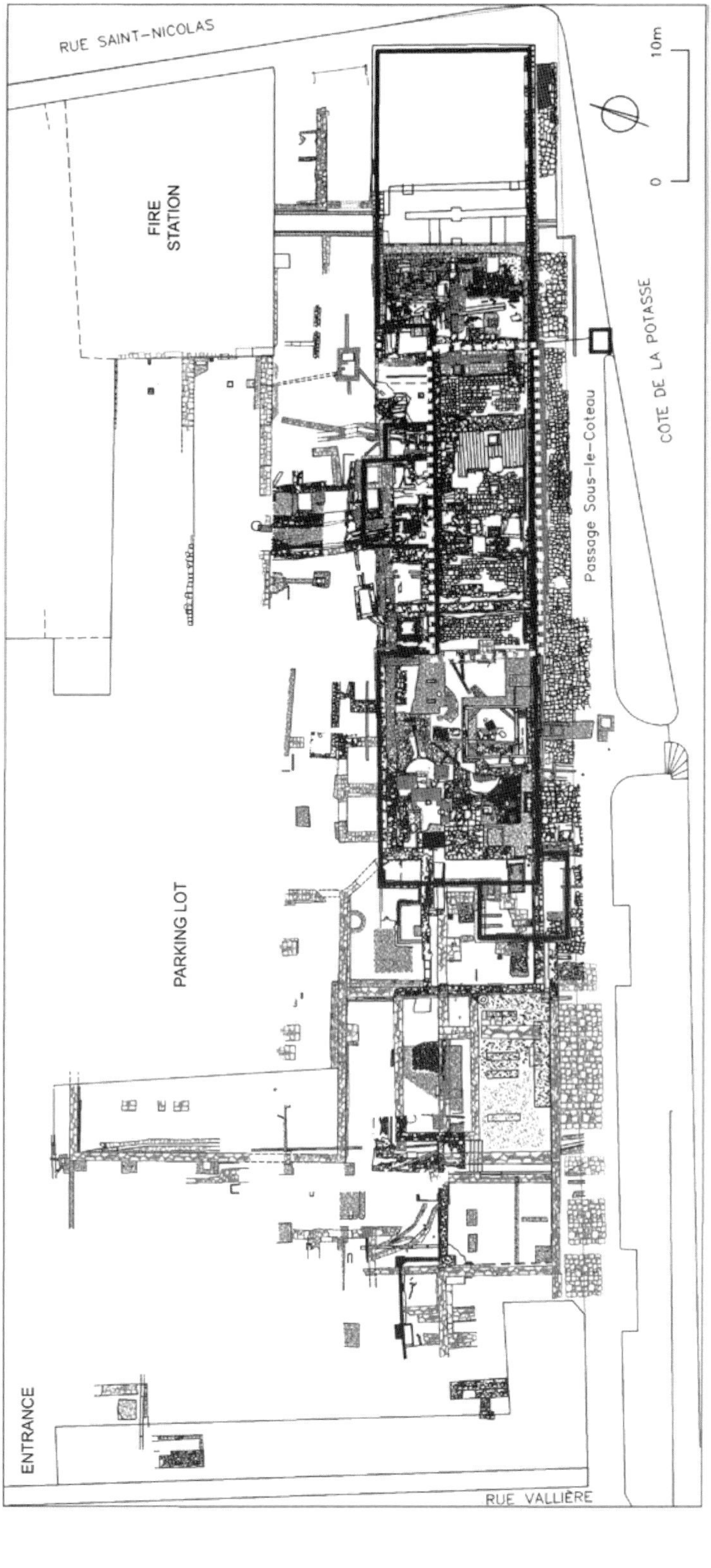

FIG. 1
Intendant's Palace site (CeEt-30): plan of known archaeological remains and the first Intendant's Palace; the broken line represents the plan of the building erected prior to the brewery (drawn by F. Pellerin & A. Nault, Ville de Québec).

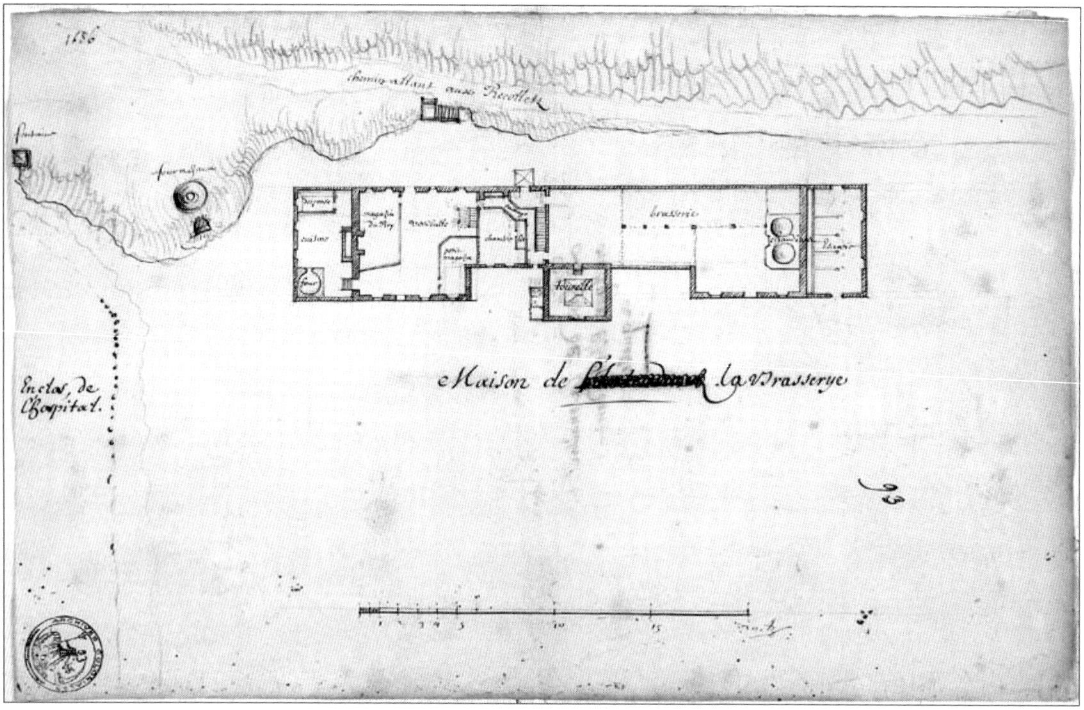

FIG. 2

Maison de la brasserye, anon., 1686 (NAC, M350-Québec/1686). North is at the bottom of the plan.

the beer fermentation process, this recommended erecting a building which contained a large stone structure with circular cavities into which copper vats could be set. Below each cavity was a chamber which left the base of the coppers exposed, as if suspended in mid-air. The chamber was connected by a small flue to a large fire-box in the form of a long, more-or-less vaulted corridor, ventilated by a chimney. The system was designed to keep the coppers at the temperature needed for the beer to ferment without exposing them directly to flames or excessive heat, which would have destroyed the ferment or bacterial culture. The vat openings were at ground-floor level; the source of heat and the flues for distributing it lay below.

Analysis of the excavated evidence demonstrated that the design of Jean Talon's brewery was very much in keeping with that recommended by Diderot and d'Alembert roughly a century later. Québec's installations may not have been avant-garde, but they were no doubt as acceptable in 1668 as they would have been in 1750. The remains consisted not only of the stone sub-structure for the coppers, but an indentation in the lower part of the side of one of the cavities, to the north-east, would have created a kind of chamber beneath the copper. Unfortunately, there were no traces of a flue leading from the chamber to a fire-box, probably because this area was very disturbed. Nevertheless, the heat source was probably on this side. The fire-box could therefore have been in the space to the east of the stone sub-structure, although no evidence for it survived. The area contained only two parallel sections of wall at an angle to the masonry structure; these may have formed a corridor leading to the coppers. Excavation in the area east of the stone feature revealed that almost all contexts pre-dating the late 18th century had been destroyed. Intendant de Meulles may have been referring to this area when he wrote in a letter to the Minister that he could easily set up a powder magazine 'in an almost finished vault, in which there were two immense fireplaces'.[4]

The sizes of the cavities in the stone sub-structure show that the copper on the north side would have had a diameter of 2.60m, while that to the south would have been larger, with a diameter of 3.00m. According to an appraisal made in 1687, while the vats were in storage on baulks of wood,[5] they were said to be made of yellow copper, to be

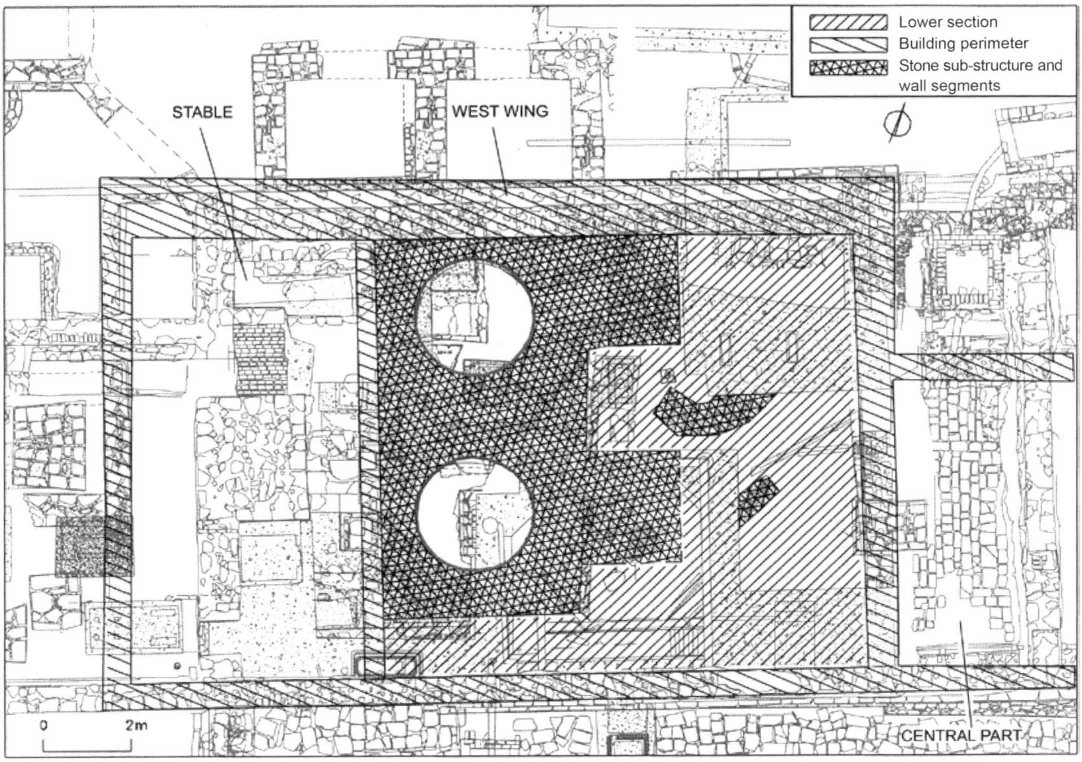

FIG. 3

Intendant's Palace site (CeEt-30): plan of archaeological remains associated with the coppers of Jean Talon's brewery (drawn by F. Pellerin & A. Nault, Ville de Québec).

quite large and to be equipped with supports, each in the form of a large circular piece of iron with projecting lugs. Their respective capacities were then estimated at about 60 and 40 *barriques*, or 13,500 and 9,000 litres. Considering their diameters, each would need to have been 1.70m deep in order to have these capacities. Even though the stone structure that supported the coppers may have been truncated, its excavated remains were still high enough to accommodate coppers of this depth.

The archaeological fieldwork also furnished information on the architectural development of the brewery. Analysis is not yet complete, but certain points are already apparent. In 2007, excavations along the façade of the west wing uncovered one of its corners, which was built with carefully laid quoins of bonded stone. The presence of quoins indicates that the façade was built of stone and reflected a concern for the structure's appearance. Excavation along the south wall in 2006 clearly identified its construction trench, as well as the new ground surface overlying the infilled trench. This surface did not undergo any changes until 1713, when fire destroyed the first Intendant's Palace. It had been thought that the western part of the building was timber-framed and the remainder of stone.[6] This was obviously not the case; there is nothing to indicate that the west wing was reconstructed before the fire, or that it was originally erected in a material other than stone. Nonetheless, historical evidence indicates that the building was made of two different construction materials, for Intendant de Meulles wrote in a letter in November 1684 that 'only eight of the thirty *toises* making up the length of the brewery were built of stone, while the rest was of timber-framed construction, which was rotten and about to collapse'.[7] It can be concluded, therefore, that the western part of the building, where the brewing coppers stood, was made of masonry, whereas the rest, including the entire narrower central section, was timber-framed. It can also be concluded that, in 1684, only a portion of the central section was

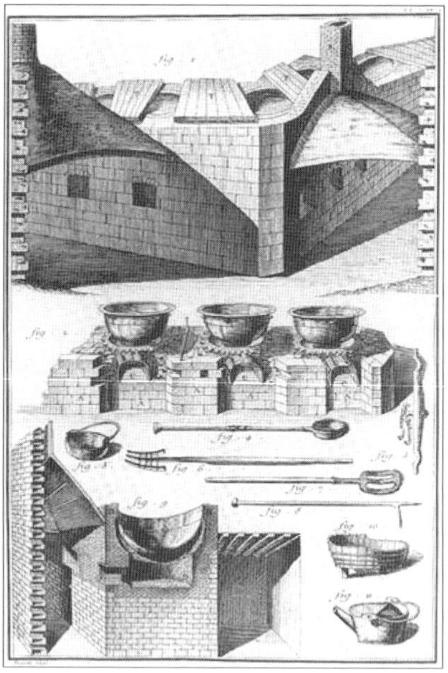

FIG. 4

Intendant's Palace site (CeEt-30): view of remains of the sub-structure for the south copper of Jean Talon's brewery, north view.

FIG. 5

Illustration of a brewery *c.* 1762 (from Diderot & d'Alembert 1969, **4**).

in a state of advanced disrepair, for de Meulles himself said that he had just restored the entire east wing up to the malting kiln, identified as a *tourelle* on the 1686 plan (Fig. 2).

The west wing's function as a brewery is now clearly established; the structure for supporting coppers inside the wing provides conclusive evidence. Moreover, since this stone sub-structure was integral with the west wing, particularly with its north wall, the wing was clearly built for brewing operations from the beginning.

INTIAL OCCUPATION OF THE SITE DURING THE HISTORIC PERIOD

During the 2006 fieldwork, the south, or rear, wall of the west wing and the central part of the brewery erected in 1668 were excavated down to bedrock. This led to the surprising discovery that the section in the west wing stood on bedrock, while that in the central wing stood on a stone foundation predating the brewhouse (Fig. 6). The different stonework of the latter could be distinguished from the brewery; moreover, it did not have a perfectly vertical face but curved slightly. Standing directly on the bedrock, the older foundation measured 0.81m high; its south face projected about 0.30m from the brewery foundation. On the south face, part of the base of the foundation extended outward over an area measuring slightly less than 2.00 × 2.00m, which formed a platform resting on bedrock; it became progressively thinner towards the edge. The purpose of this feature has not been determined, although it seems to reflect a desire to create an even ground surface.

The western limit of the earlier foundation seems to have corresponded to the position of a partition wall marking the junction between the west wing and central part of the brewery. The stonework of the lower part of this wall was similar to that of the earlier foundation and markedly different from that above, which was also laid out on a slightly different angle. It seems clear that the lower part of the partition wall formed a corner with the foundation beneath the brewery's south wall and thus represented the western foundation wall of the earlier structure. In 2007 it also became clear that the foundation beneath the south wall continued further eastward, over a total length of 24m. It was therefore exactly the same length as the central part of Talon's brewery (Fig. 1).

A SHIPYARD FOR THE INTENDANT?

Excavations in 2006 brought to light an occupation layer contemporary with the feature that pre-dated the brewery. It consisted of black and very compact clayey earth that gave off a strong odour and did not contain any artefacts except for a few pieces of wood. The layer was cut by the

FIG. 6
Intendant's Palace site (CeEt-30): view of the south wall of Jean Talon's brewery resting on an earlier foundation (photograph, S. Santerre, Ville de Québec).

construction trench for the rear wall of the brewery's west wing, showing that it pre-dated the brewhouse. The discovery was extremely important, for it pushed back the start of historic occupation on the site to an earlier date than previously thought. No documentary sources refer to the use of this site before it was officially acquired by Talon in 1668.

The excavated evidence confirmed that the building preceding the brewhouse probably had the same dimensions as the latter's central section. The earlier building evidently had no connection with beer-making, since this activity began only with the construction of the massive stone substructure for the brewing coppers, which were essential to the operation of a brewery. Furthermore, it was obvious that the earlier structure had not been reused for the brewery but had been completely replaced. What then was the function of this building measuring 24 × 8m, built before 1668? What were the activities associated with it?

Initially, consideration was given to hypotheses relating to its use by the Couillard family, who owned the site before Jean Talon. However, it soon became clear that most of the Couillards' installations were located near their house on the site where the Seminary of Québec now stands, or in their fields in the Espinay fiefdom to the north of the Saint-Charles River.[8] The most probable explanation is that our building was linked to a shipyard beside the Saint-Charles established in 1666 by Jean Talon, working in partnership with Charles Aubert de La Chesnaye.[9] This operated until 1671; it therefore coexisted for a while with the brewery. Numerous ships were built there, including vessels with a capacity of 120 *tonneaux*, with even one 300-*tonneaux* ship, *L'espérance de Québec*, launched in 1668.[10]

Since no documents relating to it have been found to date, it is difficult to determine the exact location of the shipyard. None of the property-owners on the banks of the Saint-Charles River seems to have signed a contract with Talon for its construction between 1665 and 1668. The site chosen may have been covered by a simple verbal agreement; alternatively the rental contract may have been lost. The historian Réal Brisson believes that the early shipyard was situated in exactly the same place as Talon's brewery. He bases this on an isometric illustration of Québec, made before 1670, which shows boats under repair on the banks of the Saint-Charles.[11] Other researchers also place the shipyard there.[12] An illustration of the Intendant's Palace in 1699 shows two structures which might be the frames of ships, lying next to a basin on the banks of the river, beside the palace.[13] The function of the building pre-dating the brewery therefore seems most likely to be linked with Jean Talon's shipyard, even though there is little documentary evidence to support this.

During the last week of Université Laval's 2007 field school, a very interesting layer was uncovered in the western part of the site. Lying on natural soil, it pre-dated the level associated with the gardens of the first palace. Since it consisted of very compact, dark grey to black clayey soil which emitted a very strong odour, it was identified as the same layer as that found the previous year and interpreted as contemporary with the foundation pre-dating the brewery. However, the layer found in 2007 was richer in artefacts; it was covered with wood debris, pieces of shaped wood and wood chips (Fig. 7). Université Laval students began to excavate the deposit but, at the end of the field school, the City of Québec research team took over the task. Analysis of this layer is still in its early stages; at the time of writing, the results of the specialist studies are still largely unavailable. Nonetheless, the initial results are very encouraging; they offer some support for the theory that the deposit is related to a shipyard.

It is important to recognize that 17th-century shipyards differed from those of the 18th century. Rather than being fully-fledged boatyards, they consisted of areas where shipbuilding activities took place; vessels were simply built on a beach or riverbank, without any specialized installations, particularly dry docks or slipways. A drawing of 1670 showing a shipyard in Toulon, France, clearly illustrates the rudimentary nature of this type of facility (Fig. 8). The large building complex in the background is not part of the shipyard, but belongs

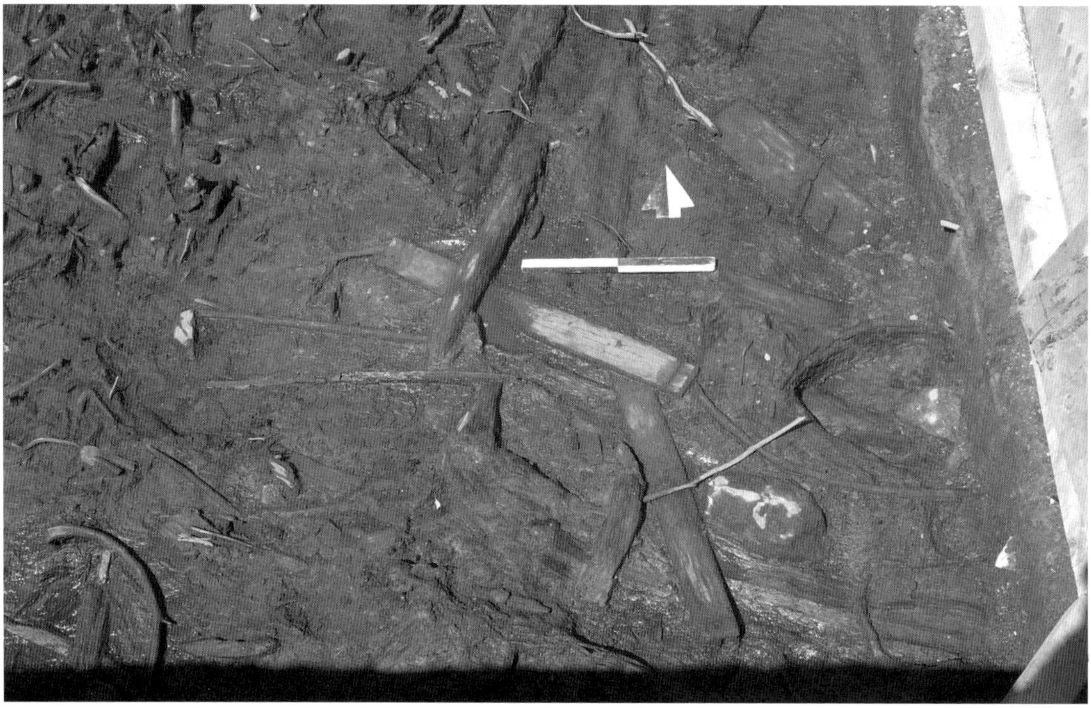

FIG. 7
Intendant's Palace site (CeEt-30): north view of the layer containing numerous pieces of wood (photograph, S. Santerre, Ville de Québec).

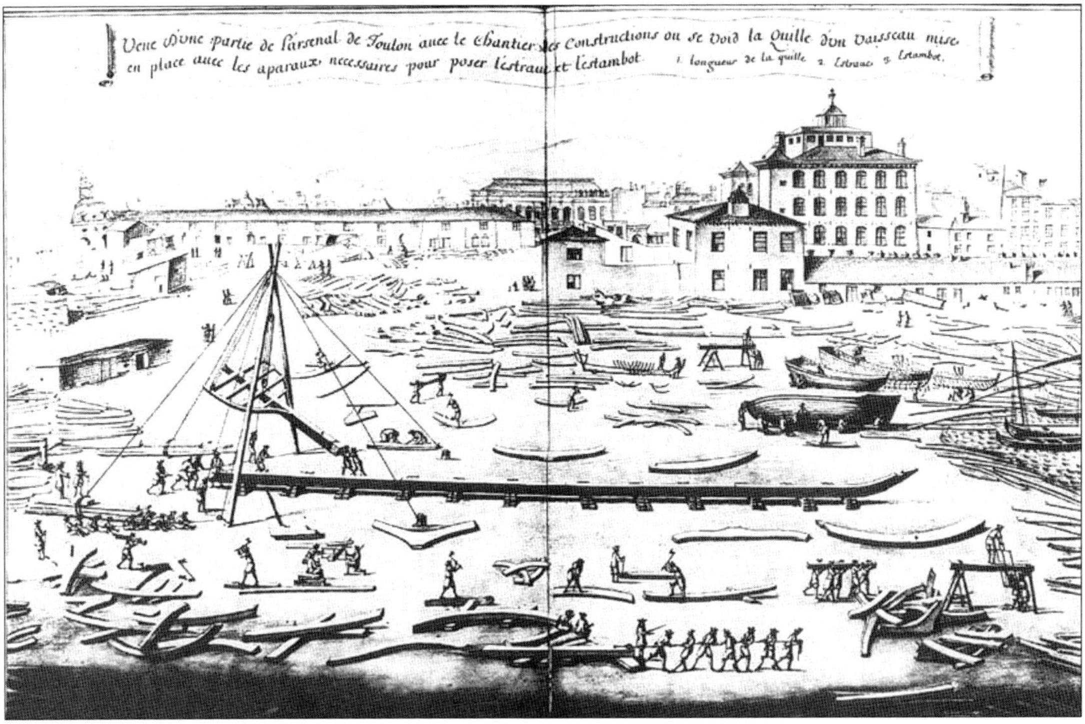

FIG. 8

Vue d'une partie de l'arsenal de Toulon avec le chantier des constructions ou se void la quille d'un vaisseau mise en place avec les aparaux pour poser l'estrave et l'estambot, Album de Colbert, 1670 (from Vergé-Franceschi & Rieth 1992).

to the city's arsenal. The only structure which may have been associated with the yard is the long rectangular building with a lean-to roof on the left; it may have resembled the building that stood on the Intendant's Palace site, on the foundations beneath the central part of Talon's brewery. The illustration shows that boat preparation and construction activities were carried out all over the beach in a very disorderly manner.

The layer unearthed in 2007, with its compact, black, strong-smelling soil and more-or-less omnipresent wood debris, displays characteristics one might expect of a site where ships were built in the days of Jean Talon.[14] Some of the timbers found in this layer were shaped like components of boats, particularly knee timbers,[15] although all had been only roughly formed.[16] One of the unworked specimens was of interest because its curved shape was of the type particularly sought after for shipbuilding. Another timber had received its final shaping and was identified as a small keelson or a piece of inner hull planking. It could have been an old timber that was replaced at some point and might therefore attest to repair and careening activities on the site.

Preliminary analysis indicates that all the pieces of wood associated with this layer are from hardwoods, namely maple, birch and ash,[17] species that could have been used for boat building. It also indicates that fibres recovered from the deposit were of hemp and flax, which could have been used for caulking, although there is no specific evidence that they served this purpose.[18] Soil analysis aimed at determining whether the layer's strong odour was due to the presence of pitch, used for caulking, was inconclusive, but did show that the soil contained traces of hydrocarbon, which could have derived from one of the components of pitch.[19] Additional analysis of the wood fragments is currently underway to determine whether they bear any traces of this kind of tar.

Several conclusions can be drawn from this information. First, the site was occupied before the construction of Jean Talon's brewery. The discovery of roughly shaped and unworked pieces of wood and numerous wood chips in a layer pre-dating the brewery indicates that the western part of the site was used for cutting and preparing wood. There is still insufficient evidence to be certain that this was a shipyard, but the shapes of some of the timbers and the possible presence of pitch and caulking material support the theory that the area was used for building ships, or at least for preparing timbers needed for shipbuilding. On the other hand, some of the species of wood found in this layer would have been suitable for barrel-making,[20] an activity which would be compatible with the operation of a brewery; in fact a collapsed barrel was uncovered among the wood debris. Even though no mention has been found of a cooperage on the site of the brewery, and the wood debris clearly pre-dates the remains associated thus far with beer-making, the possibility remains that a cooperage may once have existed at this site.

Fortunately, evidence for the pre-brewery layer has been found in a number of places around the Intendant's Palace site; investigation of these deposits may provide additional information about this early phase of occupation. The same strong-smelling dark grey to black layer with numerous wood inclusions was probably identified directly to the north of the site in the parking lot of the Maison de Lauberivière;[21] underneath Rue des Prairies, a street bordering the north side of the site; in the area to the west of Rue Vallière, a street bordering the site's west side;[22] and perhaps near an area containing the remains of a potash factory built by Jean Talon around 1670, just behind the building that used to house the Institut Maritime on the west side of Rue Vallière.[23] However, no traces of the layer have been found to the east or north-east of the palace, and although the deposit has been identified in the southern part of the site, it contained only a few small pieces of wood. This suggests that the areas with highest potential for future study are mainly to the north, north-west and west, particularly underneath Rue Vallière.

Wood chips and burned resin were also found in the 1980s beneath the malting floor of Jean Talon's brewery. At the time they were associated with the construction of the building's framework[24] but it is possible that these finds relate to occupation pre-dating the brewery. The question could be resolved by analysing the wood chips to determine whether they come from hardwoods or softwoods; softwoods alone would have been used for the building's framework.

NEW RESEARCH PERSPECTIVES

The 2006 and 2007 field seasons on the Intendant's Palace site were particularly fruitful. They not only led to the discovery of the first evidence for the site's prehistoric occupation, but also yielded much new information about its initial occupation during the historic period. Earlier work had revealed some evidence about the brewery established by Jean Talon in 1668: remains of the malting floor and part of the malting kiln had been excavated, and it was demonstrated that the brewery walls were largely reused in the exterior walls of the first Intendant's Palace. In 2006–07 evidence found in the brewery's west wing shed light on the installation of the brewing coppers and associated facilities. The wing was also shown to be of stone construction rather than being timber-framed, as was previously thought. The most surprising discovery was the unearthing of an earlier stone foundation beneath the brewery, pushing back the date of the site's initial occupation of the historic period. Construction activities, or at least some type of activity involving the cutting of wood, had taken place there.

Although it would be premature to attempt to draw definite conclusions at this stage, the most likely interpretation of these pre-brewery remains is that they belonged to a shipyard which is known to have operated on the banks of the Saint-Charles River from 1666 to 1671. Set up on the initiative of Jean Talon after he had secured the cooperation of the rich merchant Charles Aubert de La Chesnaye, this yard launched many ships, some of them very large.

More archaeological evidence will be needed to determine whether this hypothesis is correct. Fortunately, the site and its immediate surroundings contain areas that are known to be fairly undisturbed and where previous archaeological work has reported the presence of deposits similar to the pre-brewhouse layer discussed in this paper. Therefore, the chances of obtaining further relevant information look very good, with the prospect of new research perspectives opened up by the discovery of occupation preceding Jean Talon's brewery.

ACKNOWLEDGEMENTS

I wish to extend my sincere thanks to Allison Bain, William Moss, Réginald Auger and Marc-André Bernier for their constructive comments on this paper. I would also like to thank the entire field team, particularly, Marie-Hélène Daviau and Simon Santerre, without whom these archaeological discoveries would not have been made.

NOTES

[1] Moussette 1994.
[2] Guimont 1987, 92–3.
[3] Diderot & d'Alembert 1969, **4**, 'Brasserie'.
[4] *de Meulles au ministre, 12 novembre 1684*, AN, C11A, **6**, ff. 409v–411r (cited in Moussette 1994, 50). [Translation.]
[5] *Estimation par Philippe Gaultier sieur de Comporté, Pierre Soumande de Lorme, François Pachot et Jean Corbin, habitants de la Nouvelle France de certaines chaudières qui ont cy devant servy a l'usage de brasserie dans la maison communement appellée la Brasserie et a present le Palais, 30 octobre 1687*, AN Colonies, C11, **10**, f. 140 (cited in Moussette 1994, 44).
[6] Moussette 1994, 38.
[7] *de Meulles au ministre, 12 novembre 1684*, AN, C11A, **6**, ff. 409v-411r (cited in Moussette 1994, 50). [Translation.]
[8] Simoneau 2008, 35–48.
[9] Brisson 1983, 45.
[10] Brisson 1983, 217.
[11] Brisson 1983, 28.
[12] Benoît *et al.* 1988, 41–2.
[13] Inset by Fonville, 1699 (NAC, C46450).
[14] Stéphanie Wicha, Université d'Aix-Marseille 1, pers. comm. (3 Oct. 2007).
[15] A knee is a piece of artificially or naturally bent wood that is used to support structures coming together at an angle (e.g. the framing and deck timbers of a ship).
[16] Marc-André Bernier, Parks Canada, pers. comm. (8 Nov. 2007).
[17] Delwaide & Filion 2008, 3.
[18] Laflèche & Sergeant 2007.
[19] Helwig & Corbeil 2008.
[20] Marcil 2003, 39–41.
[21] Simoneau 1989, 2–10.
[22] CÉRANE 1994, 39–40.
[23] Lapointe 2000, 19–20.
[24] Guimont 1987, 85.

BIBLIOGRAPHY

PUBLISHED SOURCES

Brisson, R. 1983, *La Charpenterie navale à Québec sous le régime français*, Québec: IQRC.

Diderot, D. & d'Alembert, J. 1969, *Encyclopédie, ou dictionnaire raisonné des sciences, des arts et des métiers*, New York: Readex Microprint.

Guimont, J. 1987, *Le Site du premier palais de l'intendant à Québec: rapport préliminaire de la quatrième campagne de fouilles (1985)*, Rapports et mémoires de recherche du CÉLAT **8**.

Lapointe, R. 2000, 'Le Bâtiment de la Potasse de Québec: d'une industrie du XVIIe siècle aux industries du XXe siècle. Intervention archéologique 2000', in *Site du palais de l'intendant, chantier-école de l'an 2000*, Cahiers d'archéologie du CÉLAT **9**.

Marcil, E. R. 2003, *Les Tonneliers au Québec du XVIIe au XXe siècle*, Québec: Édition GID.

Moussette, M. 1994, *Le Site du Palais de l'intendant à Québec: genèse et structuration d'un lieu urbain*, Sillery: Éditions du Septentrion.

Simoneau, D. 2008, *Le Site du Séminaire de Québec: 140 ans de recherches archéologiques*, Cahiers d'archéologie du CÉLAT **23**, Québec: Université Laval.

Vergé-Francheschi, M. & Rieth, É. 1992, *Voiles et voiliers au temps de Louis XIV*, Paris: Du May.

UNPUBLISHED SOURCES

Benoît, J., Laroche, D. & Vallières, M. 1988, 'Étude de potentiel archéologique et historique, l'Ancien-Chantier: un faubourg en pleine évolution (1670–1870)', Québec: Ville de Québec, Service de l'Urbanisme.

CÉRANE inc. 1994, 'Surveillance archéologique des travaux souterrains de Gaz Métropolitain, arrondissement historique de la Ville de Québec', Ville de Québec.

Delwaide, A. & Filion, L. 2008, 'Évaluation du potentiel dendrochronologique de neuf pièces de bois provenant du site du Palais de l'Intendant, ville de Québec', Québec: Laboratoire de dendrochronologie, CEN, Université Laval.

Helwig, K. & Corbeil, M.-C. 2008, 'Analyse d'un échantillon de sol provenant d'une fouille au site de l'îlot des Palais', Ottawa: Laboratoire de recherche analytique, Institut canadien de conservation, Patrimoine canadien.

Laflèche, L. & Sergeant, C. 2007, 'Rapport d'analyses', Ottawa: Services analytiques, Centre de services de l'Ontario, Parcs Canada.

Simoneau, D. 1989, 'Rapport de surveillance archéologique: interventions ponctuelles 1988', Québec: Ville de Québec, Service de 'Urbanisme.

ABBREVIATIONS

AN	Archives nationales de France
CÉLAT	Centre interuniversitaire de recherche sur les lettres, les arts et les traditions
CEN	Centre d'études nordiques, Université Laval
IQRC	Institut québécois de recherche sur la culture
NAC	National Archives of Canada

SUMMARY IN FRENCH, GERMAN, ITALIAN AND SPANISH

RÉSUMÉ

L'îlot des Palais: une évolution bonifiée, une genèse repoussée

Les recherches archéologiques sur le site du Palais de l'intendant dans les années 1980 ont déterminé l'évolution physique du site et les activités qui s'y sont menées depuis 1668. En 2006, la Ville de Québec et l'Université Laval ont lancé une autre campagne de recherches, qui ont permis la mise au jour d'indices non seulement d'une présence préhistorique, mais aussi d'une occupation historique jusqu'alors inconnue, pré-datant la brasserie de Jean Talon et probablement associée à un chantier naval établi par Talon près de la rivière Saint-Charles vers 1666.

ZUSAMMENFASSUNG

Der Intendantenpalast: neue Erkenntnisse der Entwicklung und seine ursprüngliche Nutzung

Archäologische Untersuchungen des Intendantenpalastes in den 80er Jahren zeigten die physische Entwicklung und den Verlauf seiner Aktivitäten seit 1668. Im Jahre 2006 begannen die Stadt Quebec und die Universität Laval eine neue Feldstudie, die nicht nur prähistorische Zeugnisse lieferte, sondern auch Hinweise auf bisher unbekannte historische Nutzung, die vor der Zeit von Jean Talons Brauerei liegen, und möglicherweise mit einer ungefähr um 1666 von Talon errichteten Werft am Saint Charles-Fluß zusammenhängen.

RIASSUNTO

Il sito del Palazzo di Intendenza: un nuovo quadro sulla sua evoluzione fisica e sulla sua iniziale occupazione

Gli scavi archeologici condotti nel sito del Palazzo di Intendenza negli anni Ottanta del secolo scorso hanno accertato l'evoluzione fisica del sito e le attività lì condotte dal 1668. Nel 2006 la città di Quebec e l'Università Laval hanno dato il via a un altro studio sul campo, che ha portato alla luce testimonianze non solo di un insediamento preistorico, ma anche di un'occupazione di periodo storico, fino a quel momento sconosciuta, anteriore alla birreria di Jean Talon e possibilmente associata a un cantiere navale fondato da Talon nei pressi del fiume Saint-Charles intorno al 1666.

RESUMEN

El yacimiento del Palacio del Intendente: nuevos datos sobre su evolución física y ocupación inicial

Diversas campañas arqueológicas en el Palacio del Intendente en la década de los 80 determinaron la evolución física del yacimiento y las actividades allí desarrolladas desde 1668. En el 2006 la ciudad de Quebec y la universidad Laval iniciaron otro estudio de campo por el que se ha descubierto no sólo evidencia de presencia prehistórica, sino también un yacimiento histórico desconocido con anterioridad y que es anterior a la fábrica de cerveza de Jean Talon, estando posiblemente asociado con el astillero fundado por Talon junto al río Saint-Charles hacia 1666.

Ville de Québec, Service de l'aménagement du territoire, Division du design, de l'architecture et du patrimoine, 295, boulevard Charest Est, Québec (Québec), Canada G1K 3G8
[daniel.simoneau@ville.quebec.qc.ca]

Post-Medieval Archaeology **43/1** (2009), 183–197

Bugs, seeds and weeds at the Intendant's Palace: a study of an evolving landscape

By ALLISON BAIN, JULIE-ANNE BOUCHARD-PERRON, RÉGINALD AUGER *and* DANIEL SIMONEAU

SUMMARY: Used intensively from the second half of the 17th century to the British conquest in 1759, the Intendant's Palace compound accommodated the King's Stores, a brewery, a shipyard, a bakery and other facilities. The site was transformed from a natural marshy riverside to an impressive complex of buildings representing the power of the king in New France and the prestigious role of the intendant. This study in landscape change and environmental archaeology draws on recent research in archaeoentomology, archaeobotany and dendrochronology. The integration of natural, written and material data provides a better interpretation of the site.

INTRODUCTION

Other papers in this volume examine sites dating from the early occupation of Québec City, including the Cartier-Roberval Upper Fort and the Saint-Louis forts and châteaux site on the Cap Diamant cliff overlooking the city. In Lower Town citizens and enterprising merchants such as Charles Aubert de la Chesnaye, Philippe Gauthier de Comporté and, most importantly in the context of this paper, Jean Talon established themselves on or near the banks of the St Lawrence and Saint-Charles rivers. Talon was the administrator of New France and the first intendant to live in the colony. During his two brief terms of office he introduced new industries in an attempt to make the colony more self-sufficient. More significantly perhaps, Talon clearly established the role of the intendant in New France.

The Îlot des Palais, the site of his official residence on the banks of the former Saint-Charles River, was first settled in about AD 1300. Between the mid-17th century and the early 18th century the French regime dramatically transformed this landscape from a marshy riverside into one of the most important economic hubs of the colony by building a shipyard, a brewery, a potash works, the King's Stores and two successive palaces for the intendant.

As waterways linked the colonial outposts in New France and as the intendants were responsible for many provisions, ships docked frequently at the Intendant's Palace, carrying colonists and goods such as arms, building supplies, and food. Many species of European insects and weeds were imported unwittingly with the cargoes and rapidly adapted to their new environment. The King's Stores played a key role in introducing the Old World flora and fauna which eventually changed the face of the North American landscape.

This paper examines how the study of plants and insects have enhanced our understanding of the physical transformation of the Intendant's Palace compound, the daily lives of its occupants, and changes in the local fauna and flora.

THE FIRST OCCUPANTS (*c.* 1300)

The narrow band of land between the riverside and the cliff separating Upper Town from the Saint-Charles River provided a suitable location

DOI: 10.1179/007942309X12457508844242

for Native populations to fish for species adapted to brackish waters. A 1664 description of Canada by Pierre Boucher mentions the abundance of fish at low tide. Tidal activity near the Intendant's Palace probably made it easier to catch fish feeding near the shore.[1] Radiocarbon dating of a hearth and knapped stone flakes, which were found together in 2006, confirm an indigenous presence around AD 1300. The palaeoecology of the nearby Grande Place site indicates a mature cedar (*Thuja*) forest with significant stands of spruce trees. The mosses identified also suggest a damp environment.[2]

SHIPBUILDING (*c.* 1665–71)

The earliest recorded European use of the site was by the first Intendant, Jean Talon, who purchased land from the widow of Guillaume Couillard, perhaps as early as 1665.[3] Talon worked tirelessly to develop the economy of the struggling colony, bringing carpenters from France and introducing new enterprises such as shipbuilding, brewing and potash production.[4] He imported looms for weaving and encouraged the growth of hops, barley and wheat with the goal of exporting these crops or at least reducing reliance on imports from France.[5] While this economic strategy may appear to be at odds with the mercantilist system established by Jean-Baptiste Colbert, the powerful secretary of the navy under Louis XIV, Talon's aim seems to have been to increase the amount of money circulating within the local economy. Upon taking office in 1665 Talon had the forests of the colony inspected and designed a plan to export wood to France and to fellow colonies. As early as 1667 his carpenters prepared masts for export to France; timber along with items such as barrel staves was shipped to the West Indies.[6] In 1665 or 1666 he built small ships in his shipyard and later a few larger vessels. However, the governor Frontenac criticized the skill of his shipwrights; by 1671 shipbuilding effectively ceased.[7] Other shipyards followed his example in making small craft like *chaloupes*, *charois* and *barques* for local use; presumably they also refitted ocean-going vessels.[8]

In a small area excavated in 2007 logs were discovered piled on the shore ready for use in Talon's shipyard.[9] They included sugar maple (*Acer saccharum* Marsh.), birch (*Betula* sp.) and ash (*Fraxinus* sp.), whereas the species most commonly recorded for naval construction in New France are eastern white pine (*Pinus strobus* L.) and oak (*Quercus* sp.) followed by white cedar (*Thuja occidentalis* L.), cherry birch (*Betula lenta* L.), spruce (*Picea* sp.), elm (*Ulmus* sp.) and hemlock (*Tsuga* sp.).[10]

Stone foundations may have supported the shipyard's office or a shed where shipbuilders worked, although most of the shipbuilding appears to have taken place on the shore, where tar and horsehair (used to make ships watertight) and fragments of worked wood were found amongst the logs.[11]

Samples from this shipbuilding phase show that within 60 years of the colony's foundation European weed flora, including sun spurge (*Euphorbia helioscopia* L.), sowthistle (*Sonchus* spp.), hemp-nettle (*Galeopsis* sp.) black henbane (*Hyoscyamus niger* L.) and shepherd's-purse (*Capsella bursa-pastoris* (L.) Medic.), had become mixed with the native flora. These introduced weeds suggest an open landscape disturbed by human activity. Couillard's widow may already have felled the trees before selling the land to Talon, thereby providing a favourable setting for new weed species adapted to anthropogenic sediments. They rapidly dominated the indigenous flora; the few identified include sedges (*Carex* spp.), American water horehound (*Lycopus americanus* Mühl.) and vervain (*Verbena* sp.). They confirm that Talon's shipyard was located on poorly drained soils in a riverside setting.

JEAN TALON'S BREWERY (*c.* 1668–75)

As the colony spent 100,000 *livres* on imported wine and spirits, Talon devised a plan to keep some of this money in the colony by making beer from locally grown barley and wheat.[12] After he had obtained permission from Colbert, the enterprising intendant built in about 1668 a brewery alongside his shipyard (Fig. 1).

Two huge cauldrons were bought and housed in the substantial 45m-long stone brewery, which may have been erected on the foundations of an earlier building.[13] It contained two large hearths to heat the cauldrons and a tower-shaped kiln to dry barley for malt. Building materials were imported from 1667 and production began in 1670.[14] Like so many of Talon's initiatives in the New World, the brewing enterprise ended shortly after his return to France in 1675, when the governor Frontenac lifted the quotas on imported wines and spirits.[15] The brewery building was eventually sold to the king and later substantially renovated as the official residence for the intendant Jacques de Meulles.[16]

The brewery's latrines contained edible fruits and berries, including raspberries, figs, grapes,

FIG. 1
Québec from west, *c.* 1670, showing small boats in front of the brewery, marked 5 (Anon., *L'entrée de la Rivière St Laurent et la ville de Québec dans le Canada*, BNF, dépôt des cartes et plans, S.H. portf. 128, div. 6, piece 1).

small cherries and strawberries. Little hogweed (*Portulaca oleraceae* L.) and European stoneseed (*Lithospermum officinale* L.) suggest an environment like that in the shipyard. They and other weeds such as common plantain (*Plantago major* L.) and prickly lettuce (*Lactuca serriola* L.), as well as the economically important plants of cucumber (*Cucurbita* sp.) and hazelnut (*Corylus* sp.), are almost entirely European. The presence of prickly lettuce is particularly interesting as it is commonly assumed to have arrived in the region in about 1900.[17]

The ground near the brewery contained a mixture of introduced and indigenous plants. The latter included spikerush (*Eleocharis* spp.) and Pennsylvania smartweed (*Polygonum pensylvanicum* L.), whereas common chickweed (*Stellaria media* (L.) Cyrill), common nipplewort (*Lapsana communis* L.), common dandelion (*Taraxacum officinale* Weber), catnip (*Nepeta cataria* L.), coriander (*Coriandrum* sp.) and beets (*Beta* sp.) number among the introduced weeds. A drain yielded Old World species such as hops (*Humulus lupulus* L.), hemp (*Cannabis sativa* L.), lamb's-quarters (*Chenopodium album* L.) and yellow foxtail (*Setaria glauca* L.).[18] In contrast with the indigenous wood used in the shipyard, brewing accelerated the transformation of the flora by introducing European plants.

THE POTASH WORKS

In 1670 Talon set up close to the brewery a third enterprise to produce potash, which between 1685 and 1688 expanded into a larger building.[19] Potash was exported to Europe for use in the manufacture of soap and mortar. This industry provided the first settlers with additional revenue from the sale of tree stumps cleared from their land.[20]

THE FIRST INTENDANT'S PALACE (*c.* 1675–1713)

By the 1670s a building was needed in the colonial capital to accommodate the intendant and his activities and to reflect his status. De Meulles moved into the former brewery, where the King's Stores were also housed. His successor, Jean Bochart de Champigny, convinced the king to buy it and adjoining land from Talon and to upgrade the building. In 1687 no fewer than five masons were assigned to the task.[21] As it appears that Champigny felt that the funds assigned were insufficient, moneys were diverted from other colonial projects to the renovation.[22]

THE PALACE COMPLEX

This riverside setting now became an important symbol of the king in New France. The old brewery was transformed into a large multifunctional colonial building, which included storerooms, a prison with four cells, and living quarters for the intendant, his family and domestics, as well as for a few civil servants. It also contained meeting rooms for the Sovereign Council, the highest court in the colony, which was presided over by the intendant. Formal gardens were laid at the western end of what now became the palace complex or compound. A basin for up to 300 boats may also have been dredged and enclosed.

THE PALISADE

In 1690 François Provost started to enclose the complex with a wooden palisade, built in two phases.[23] Posts excavated in 2004 and 2005 were dated by dendrochronology and were, with one exception, made of *Thuya* or white cedar.[24] The Royal Engineer Robert de Villeneuve had repeatedly lobbied for a palisade to protect Québec from attack.[25] The section erected along the Saint-Charles River formed part of the defences encircling the city.[26] However, because it was built in haste, posts were often washed away by the tide.[27] At the eastern end of the complex a gate was constructed at the end of what is now Rue Saint-Nicolas to allow access to the riverfront.

The palisade helped to create a space which reflected the status and power of the intendant in the colony. In comparison with the various industries that grew in a rather organic fashion on the site during the early years of European settlement, the palisade abruptly transformed the palace by separating it from its natural riverside setting. The intendant's residence was now both integrated into the city's landscape and yet set apart in a compound which served residential and administrative functions.

A 1699 view of the Intendant's Palace (Fig. 2) shows what may have been a ditch around the north-west corner of the palisade. The botanical remains from a section of the ditch excavated in 2006 point to a number of infilling episodes. Contrary to expectations, introduced weeds usually found in open dry spaces, such as pepperweed (*Lepidium* sp.), dominated the samples studied, while local plants that favour damp settings were rather rare. Seeds from small fruits point to the disposal of domestic and human waste.

The insects found include the seed-corn beetle *Stenelophus comma,* which often lives in open, mostly sandy places near water and in cultivated fields.[28] Staphylinid beetles from the genera *Quedius* and possibly *Gyrohypnus*, both of which are found on decomposing organic remains and often close to human settlements, were also identified. The presence of rotting organic remains is suggested by *Cercyon* or water scavenger beetles, who also prefer damp environments.[29] The scarab beetle, *Trox scaber*, usually feeds on chicken feathers, dead fish and other carrion.[30]

So, the surviving insect and seed remains suggest a depositional environment close to sandy soils containing some decomposing organic remains, probably domestic rubbish or human waste. The palisade ditch was dug into the sandy riverbanks and was gradually filled, at least in part, with domestic refuse.

THE BOAT BASIN

Plans from as early as 1692 show a *bassin des bateaux*. As part of the city's fortifications, it protected merchandise delivered to the palace and the King's Stores. A similar enclosure was built on Rue Saint-Pierre for the merchant Charles Aubert de la Chesnaye.[31] If the boat basin was a vestige of the former shipyard, it would explain de Meulles' interest in securing the site for the intendants.

The vernacular term *batteau* describes the shallow, flat-bottomed vessel used for inland navigation on the North American continent. As these boats were essential in waging war, the State built most of them.[32] The basin may have also been used to store the boats by submerging them when they were not in use.[33] The engineer Jacques Levasseur de Néré proposed similar harbours in the Cul-de-Sac and Sault-au-Matelot sectors, which also allowed boats to enter at high tide.[34]

The 1692 plan — of what may only have been a proposal — shows the basin enclosed by a substantial fortification opening onto the river with a

FIG. 2

Quebec veu dv Nord Ouest with the first Intendant's Palace in the foreground, 1699 (attributed to Fonville, NAC, C-46450).

battery protecting its entrance.[35] Representations in 1699 and 1700 illustrate an irregular and rather flimsy structure apparently surrounded by stone and earth banks and a wooden palisade.[36] Originally the basin was probably a natural pond which had been adapted to accommodate boats. A plan drawn in 1709 is probably closer to reality (Fig. 3).[37] The basin represented here is aligned with the palace gardens and is pointed, perhaps following a natural feature of the shoreline (Fig. 3:5). It also illustrated proposed changes, including additional wharves and retaining walls.

Sediments from what may have been the boat basin contained water-dwelling beetles of the Elmidae family, as well as an *Aphodius* beetle from the scarab family and a ground beetle from the genus *Nebria*. This small assemblage indicates a shoreline setting and organic waste including animal dung, probably from large domesticates such as sheep, cows or horses.

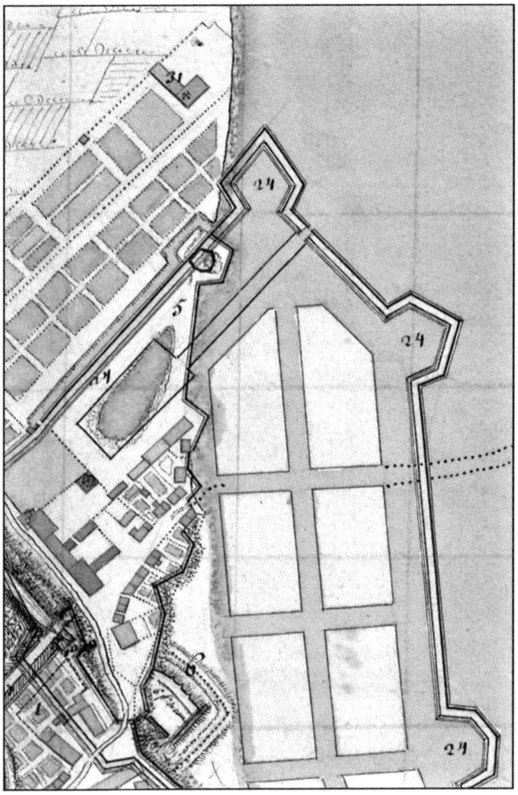

FIG. 3

Québec, Intendant's Palace: boat basin from east, 1709 (detail, Levasseur de Neré, *Plan de la Ville de Québec, 1709*, FR CAOM 3DFC375A, <http://bd.archivescanadafrance.org/acf/search-acf.xsp>).

Excavations in 2008 on another part of the site uncovered layers of compacted fine wood chips or shavings separated by sandy deposits, initially interpreted as debris and silt from the bottom of the boat basin. Although European dill (*Anethum graveolens* L.) and clover (*Trifolium* sp.) are present, the botanical content of these layers was dominated by local shrubs and trees, including needles of eastern hemlock (*Tsuga canadensis* (L.) Carr.), northern white cedar (Thuja occidentalis L.), balsam fir (*Abies balsamea* (L.) Mill) and white spruce (*Picea glauca* (Moench) Voss.), as well as seeds from birch (*Betula* sp.), alder (*Alnus* spp.), American black elderberry (*Sambucus canadensis* L.), red elderberry (*Sambucus pubens* Michx) and common ninebark (*Physocarpus opulifolius* (L.) Maxim.). As these often grow in riverside settings, they may represent the original flora close to the Saint-Charles River.[38] The weeds found have similar ecological preferences, while *Potamogeton* or pondweed, a semi-aquatic plant, point to a waterway close by.[39] As none of these weeds were retrieved from the brewery or the shipyard, a wet milieu is their most likely context.

The dominance of indigenous flora suggests that the excavated sediments date from before the construction of the boat basin, perhaps when the sector was cleared some time before 1665. The wood chips and shavings may represent debris washed down the riverbank from wood working in the shipyard. Traces of the boat basin have so far proved elusive; it will continue to be a research priority.

THE SECOND INTENDANT'S PALACE AND THE KING'S STORES (1716–60)

The first Intendant's Palace burned down in 1713 and was replaced three years later by another to the north. Another fire in 1725 led to renovations and changes in the roof design (Fig. 4). Once repaired after the 1713 fire, the first palace continued to serve as the King's Stores and also housed a bakery. Stables and other secondary buildings were built in the south-west part of the compound and formal gardens were laid out to the west of the original complex. Pehr Kalm, the eminent botanist who visited the colony in 1749, described them as large and beautiful gardens, and the Intendant's Palace as a chateau.[40]

The intendant now lived in an imposing structure suitable for his growing status, which was a considerable improvement on the first palace in the converted brewery. The new palace respected the tenets of French Classicism. It still served as the meeting-place for the Sovereign Council and as

FIG. 4
Québec, south façade of the second Intendant's Palace, 1759 (Richard Short, *A View of the Intendant's Palace*, NAC, C-19318).

the residence for the personnel who worked for the intendant and his family.

For the Jesuit missionary Pierre-François-Xavier de Charlevoix, the palace was now a 'Grand Pavilion . . . The Front towards the Garden is much pleasanter than that of the Entrance, having a View of the little River', which he contrasted favourably with its predecessor: 'It was much worse before the Fire, which some Years ago entirely destroyed this palace, for it had no Court in Front, and the Buildings stood upon the Street, which is very narrow.'[41]

The transformation of this area into a palace complex included major physical changes to the surrounding landscape. The palisade was dismantled, and the land along the shore was stabilized. Early 18th-century plans show that the space north of the palace was no longer a tranquil riverside setting; instead, the riverbank and the boat basin had been filled and a large breakwater constructed to the north along the new shoreline. A metre or more of almost sterile sandy fill with occasional mortar and brick fragments overlay some of the earliest deposits in the northern part of the site. Its relative homogeneity suggests a massive infilling in a short period of time. The archaeobotanical samples from nearby indicate a sudden decline in the number of local plants which normally grow in riverside settings.

The site had been transformed. By the early 18th century the town had grown, leaving the intendant less isolated. Whereas the first Intendant's Palace abutted the street descending from Upper Town, now visitors entered a large courtyard framed at the back by a palatial building, built according to the latest architectural style prevailing in France and reflecting better the prestige of the intendant.

THE LATRINES

Two three-storey stone latrines were built at both ends of the second palace. The western privy was excavated in 2005 and 2007.

The food remains indicate a good-quality diet dominated by pork with some beef and wild game.[42]

The privy contained at least 70 different plant species, including imported foods such as almonds (*Prunus amygdalus* Batsch), olives (*Olea europaea* L.), grapes (*Vitis vinifera* L.) and coffee beans (*Coffea arabica* L.). Other items like butternuts (*Juglans cinerea* L.) were imported from nearby regions. Indigenous fruits such as cranberries and blueberries (*Vaccinium* spp.), small cherries (*Prunus virginiana* L. and *Prunus pensylvanica* L.f.), hawthorn fruits (*Crataegus* spp.) and viburnum fruits (*Viburnum* spp.) were also identified.

The insect fauna document personal hygiene as well as diet. The consumption of cereals is reflected by the granary weevil, *Sitophilus granarius*, and *Tenebrio* species, and peas by a pea weevil, *Bruchus* sp. The flea beetle, *Phyllotreta striolata*, which attacks crucifers such as turnips, radishes and cabbage, suggest that some of these vegetables were eaten.[43] Fungus-feeding and mould-loving species indicate rotting food and infested food stores, to be expected at the time. As the two ectoparasites identified, bedbugs (*Cimex lectularius* L.) and what appear to be head lice (*Pediculus humanus humanus* L.), were common in all socioeconomic groups, their presence in the intendant's latrine is not surprising.[44]

THE KING'S STORES

The King's Stores spread from the ground floor of the first palace to occupy the entire building (Fig. 5). Burnt down again in 1719, the stores were rebuilt and remained in use until the conquest in 1759. They were excavated in the 1980s and again in 2006.[45]

The botanical remains from the earlier investigation of Room 2 (Fig. 5) were dominated by beans (*Phaseolus vulgaris* L.) and peas (*Pisum sativum* L.), but also included wheat (*Triticum aestivum* L.), barley (*Hordeum vulgare* L.), almonds, olives, and grapes (*Vitis vinifera* L.) as well as many other species.[46] Carbonized wheat, grapes and garden peas, along with a large variety of unwanted weeds and pests (Fig. 6), were found in the more recent excavations of rooms 3 and 5 (Fig. 5).

The sediments analysed from Room 3 date to around 1716. Besides the trio of peas, grapes and wheat, they contained flax, watermelon, cucumber, cannabis and a few corn kernels. The native weeds include not only those which prefer fairly open, dry landscapes with some wet areas, such as black bindweed (*Polygonum convolvulus* L.), but also others which favour a combination of both wet and dry conditions, such as the prostrate knotweed (*Polygonum aviculare* L.). This assemblage suggests that local produce and foreign imports were stored together in a damp setting.

The insect fauna from the same room include the granary weevil *Sitophilus granarius*, a serious pest of stored grains and flour worldwide (Fig. 7).[47] Other species reflecting flour and cereal storage are the yellow mealworm *Tenebrio molitor,* another tenebrionid, *Tribolium* sp., the two-banded fungus beetle *Alphitobius bifasciatus* and *Ptinus fur*, the golden spider beetle. *T. molitor* prefers feeding on moist and decaying grain and cereal products, while *A. bifasciatus*, as its name suggests, feeds generally on decaying grains and cereals, as do spider beetles.[48] Other beetles indicative of decaying and damp grains are *Cryptophagus* and the handsome fungus beetle *Mycetaea subterranea.*

Dermestes lardarius, Quedius mesomelinus and *Cercyon analis* are commonly found in historic urban contexts rich in decaying organic material. *Trox scaber*, which normally feeds on 'dry' meats or carrion, such as hoof parings or chicken feathers, may have been feeding here on dried fish or meat. Another member of the dung beetle family, *Aphodius*, points to animals working or being stalled nearby or to the disposal of related refuse in the vicinity.[49]

Whereas native weeds were found in the damp environment of Room 3, the insects appear to be almost entirely European and associated with flour or cereals, but not peas. This archaeoentomological assemblage differs markedly from the historic latrines so far studied in north-eastern America. They are usually dominated by several beetle families which reflect the organic composition of these contexts.[50] Privies are the type of structure most commonly sampled for archaeoentomological analysis, because their anaerobic conditions preserve the chitinous exoskeletons of insects. The King's Stores provide a rare opportunity to study insect remains that were *not* from a latrine. Those identified suggest that at least part of Room 3 served as a store for cereals or flour. The 1718 plan of the King's Stores shows a bakery on the ground floor (Fig. 5).[51]

However, because the few wheat grains recovered were carbonized and a damp basement is unsuitable for storing grain,[52] it is more likely that during the 1713 fire wheat and peas fell from the ground floor above. The basement was probably used to store cucumbers and other vegetables better suited to damp conditions. Spoilt or infested flour and other rubbish may have been discarded here, which would account for the high number of granary weevils.

Room 5 presents a different pattern. The native weed species suggest a damp environment, while the introduced weed species point to open anthropogenic settings. The room appears to have been poorly drained, a hypothesis corroborated

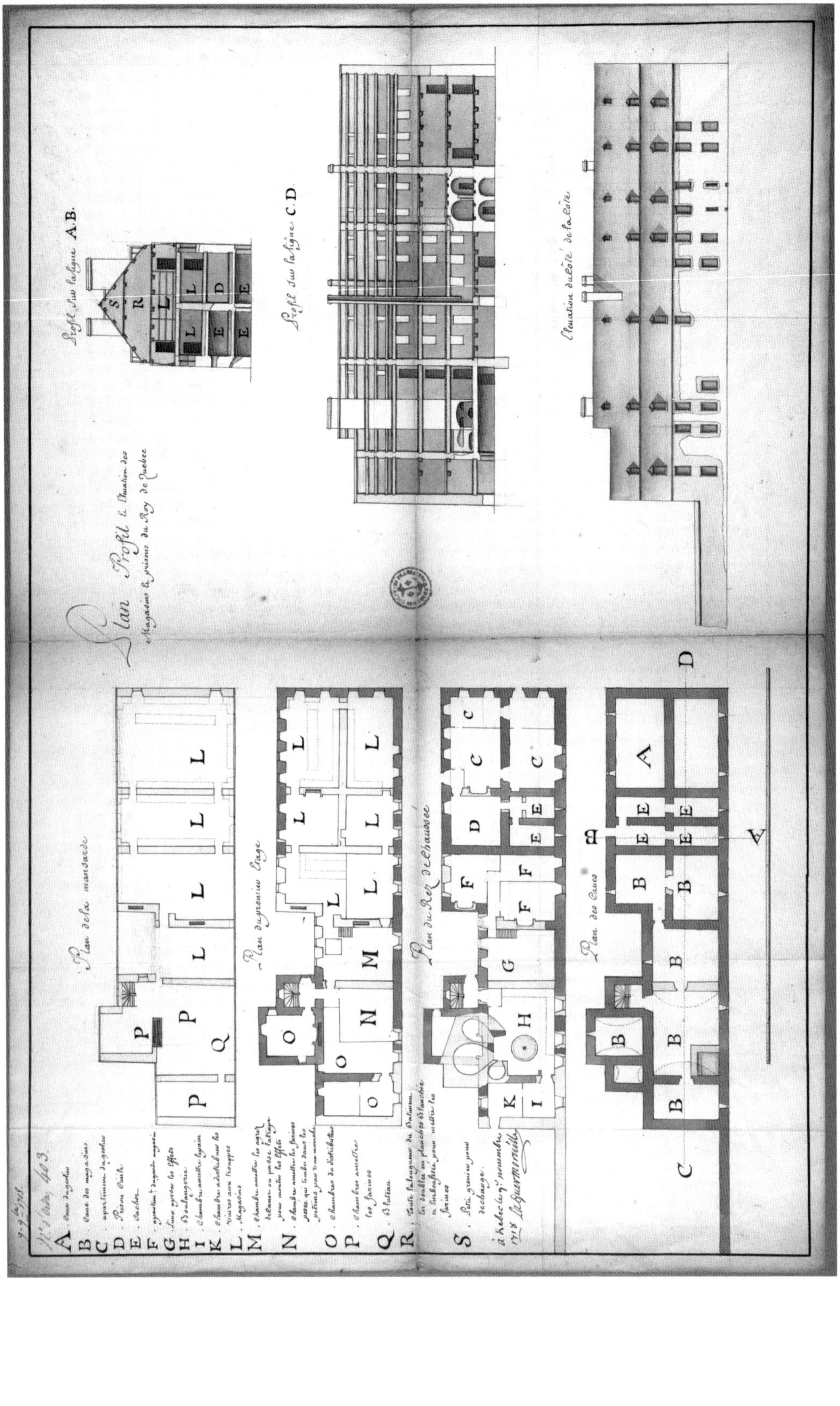

FIG. 5

Québec, the King's Stores, 1718. The basement Rooms 2–3 and 5 are indicated by the letter B and the ground-floor bakery by the letter H (Guer de Morville, *Plan Profil & Elevation des Magasins & prisons du Roy de Quebec*, ANF, Amérique septentrionale, Portf. V, no. 403B, 9 Nov. 1718).

FIG. 6
Québec, the King's Stores, Room 3: carbonized pea and wheat seeds (left); waterlogged weeds (right) (photograph, J.-A. Bouchard-Perron).

FIG. 7
Québec, the King's Stores, Room 3: granary weevil (*Sitophilus granarius* L.) (photograph, J.-A. Bouchard-Perron).

by the ostracods or small crustaceans, indicative of aquatic environments. Thousands of *Tubifex* worms were identified in the earlier study of Room 2. They live in polluted fresh water rich in organic remains, such as one would expect to find near a brewery.[53] These data confirm the interpretation of this part of the site as poorly drained and perhaps at times wet.

The beetles from Room 5 suggest it was much damper than Room 3. Despite the addition of wooden flooring in the early 18th century, Room 5 remained damp. Floor-level samples indicate grain infestation like that in Room 3. Granary weevils (*Sitophilus granarius*), grain-infesting tenebrionid beetles (*Tenebrio* sp.), spider beetles (*Ptinus* sp.) and cryptophagid beetles were common. Over forty handsome fungus beetles (*Mycetaea subterranea*) and numerous members of the *Latridius minutus* group were also identified, along with many rhizophagid species (*Henoticus* sp. and *Corticaria* or *Corticarina* sp.). They suggest that the grain and other goods stored here were in damper and mouldier conditions than in Room 3. The greater number of staphylinid and hydrophilid beetles confirms this interpretation. Several species of staphylinid beetles were recovered, including members of the subfamily Aleocharinae, *Quedius* sp., and possibly *Gyrohypnus*. A hydrophilid beetle from the genus *Helophorus* also points to a wet environment.[54]

In 1720 the Jesuit Charlevoix described a nearby hospital as built on a marsh. He claimed there was some hope of draining it, but the Saint-Charles River 'makes an Elbow in the Place, and the Waters do not easily run off, and this can never be well mended'.[55]

DISCUSSION

The transformed landscape and recent environmental analyses show that at times the Intendant's Palace site departed from the pattern of shoreline development seen elsewhere on the Québec City waterfront. Excavations of 17th-century levels at the Îlot Hunt site in Lower Town, the property of another merchant competitor of Jean Talon, Charles Aubert de la Chesnaye, also document the transition from a riverside setting, where domestic waste was discarded, to an urban environment.[56] The mixture of introduced and local weeds and grasses and of imported and cultivated foods may have come from latrines or other domestic waste thrown on the shore.[57] The insects from the Intendant's Palace point to less dumping. Whereas European species such as granary weevils, rove beetles and handsome fungus beetles are indicative of domestic refuse, the ground beetles are associated with a wet milieu, perhaps stagnant water.[58] Several other sites in Québec City show a similar pattern in the late 17th century.[59]

The palace complex documents the early industrial history of the city, with the establishment in the second half of the 17th century of a brewery, a potash works and a shipyard. As a result the shore would have been littered with their waste, exemplified by the recent excavation of compacted wood shavings. Because of industrial development and its distance from the central square of Place Royale on the St Lawrence riverfront, the Intendant's Palace site was less densely populated than other parts of Lower Town. Although residences lined the nearby Rue Saint-Nicolas and eventually the western side of the Intendant's Palace, few people lived here in comparison with elsewhere in the city. So, less domestic refuse was available to infill the shore. Construction along the Saint-Charles River started with the temporary palisade built in the early 1690s to defend the city.

The plant and insect analyses demonstrate the role the site played as a port of entry into the colony of new flora and fauna. Ships sailed up the St Lawrence Estuary to Québec to provision the colony. On a less visible scale they introduced unwanted weeds and pests. From the late 17th century foodstuffs, animals, arms, and construction materials, along with their unsuspected passengers, were unloaded and stored in the King's Stores. This warehouse provides a unique glimpse of the transformation wrought by introduced species — a process which can only be documented by environmental archaeology.

The integration of environmental data has resulted in more nuanced interpretations of some contexts, while forcing us to question others. For example, a better understanding of the damp conditions in the King's Stores together with the dietary information from the second palace's latrines provide a better understanding of the challenges facing those who managed the state warehouse and of the daily lives of some of the Lower Town's inhabitants.

The boat basin has yet to be found. The flora in the sediments, which were initially interpreted as from the bottom of the basin, suggests instead that they relate to earlier shipbuilding. Although archaeology is multi-disciplinary by nature, it is not always so in practice. The interpretations of these sediments illustrate how documentary and material evidence is insufficient and how environmental data can make a substantive contribution in reconstructing historical narratives.

The intendants of the colonial capital of Québec were powerful men who oversaw military provisioning, justice and the economy. The creation of the palace complex with its gardens, palisade and imposing architecture is a fascinating case of landscape transformation. It was not only a tightly regulated urban space serving many functions, but also a symbol of the status and power of its occupants.

CONCLUSION

The Intendant's Palace site is a complex space whose functions varied from industrial to administrative, defensive, political and domestic. They often involved concurrent and even competing interests, which tell different stories about the period between the second half of the 17th century and the British conquest in 1759. Most previous discussions of the archaeology of the palace have focused on the built environment or on the copious finds of artefacts. This paper has examined the important transformations this landscape underwent from tree and shrub clearance to the building of the second palace and the bakery in the King's Stores. The recent environmental analyses illuminate aspects of the past which would have otherwise remained unknown. By integrating data from archaeobotany, archaeoentomology and dendrochronology with the available historical documents, certain events, such as the organization of activities within the King's Stores, are now better understood. Clear answers cannot always be gleaned from maps and stratigraphic sections alone; in the case of the boat basin they still elude us.

ACKNOWLEDGEMENTS

The environmental analyses were undertaken as part of the current research agreement between the City of Québec, Université Laval and the Province of Québec's Ministère de la Culture, des Communications et de la Condition féminine. Marcel Moussette and two anonymous readers made many helpful comments on an earlier version of this paper. We thank those who worked in the field and in the laboratory for conscientiously collecting and processing samples. The paper is dedicated to our colleague, mentor and friend, Marcel Moussette, who understood long ago the importance of bugs, seeds and weeds.

APPENDIX

TABLE 1

Québec, Intendant's Palace site: list of flora identified.

Latin name	Common name
Acer saccharum Marsh.	Sugar maple
Abies balsamea (L.) Mill	Balsam fir
Alnus spp.	Alder
Anethum graveolens L.	Dill
Beta sp.	Beets
Betula lenta L.	Cherry birch
Betula sp.	Birch
Capsella bursa-pastoris (L.) Medic.	Shepherd's-purse
Cannabis sativa L.	Hemp
Carex spp.	Sedges
Chenopodium album L.	Fat hen or lamb's quarters
Coffea arabica L.	Coffee beans
Coriandrum sp.	Coriander
Corylus sp.	Hazelnut
Crataegus spp.	Hawthorn
Cucurbita sp.	Cucumber
Eleocharis spp.	Spikerush
Euphorbia helioscopia L.	Sun spurge
Fraxinus sp.	Ash
Galeopsis sp.	Hemp-nettle
Hordeum vulgare L.	Barley
Humulus lupulus L.	Common hops
Hyoscyamus niger L.	Black henbane
Juglans cinerea L.	Butternut
Lactuca serriola L.	Prickly lettuce
Lapsana communis L.	Common nipplewort
Lepidium sp.	Pepperweed
Lithospermum officinale L.	European stoneseed
Lycopus americanus Mühl.	American water horehound
Nepeta cataria L.	Catnip
Olea europaea L.	Olives
Phaseolus vulgaris L.	Common beans
Physocarpus opulifolius (L.) Maxim.	Common ninebark
Picea glauca (Moench) Voss.	White spruce
Picea sp.	Spruce
Pinus strobus L.	Eastern white pine
Pisum sativum L.	Garden peas
Plantago major L.	Common plantain
Polygonum aviculare L.	Prostrate knotweed
Polygonum convolvulus L.	Black bindweed
Polygonum pensylvanicum L.	Pennsylvania smartweed
Portulaca oleraceae L.	Little hogweed
Potamogeton sp.	Pondweed

TABLE 1 (*continued*)

Latin name	Common name	Latin name	Common name
Prunus amygdalus Batsch	Almonds	*Thuja occidentalis* L.	Northern white cedar
Prunus pensylvanica L.f.	Small cherries		
Prunus virginiana L.	Small cherries	*Trifolium* sp.	Clover
Quercus sp.	Oak	*Triticum aestivum* L.	Bread wheat
Sambucus canadensis L.	American black elderberry	*Tsuga canadensis* (L.) Carr.	Eastern hemlock
		Tsuga sp.	Hemlock
Sambucus pubens Michx	Red elderberry	*Ulmus* sp.	Elm
Setaria glauca L.	Yellow foxtail	*Vaccinium* spp.	Blueberries
Sonchus spp.	Sowthistle	*Verbena* sp.	Vervain
Stellaria media (L.) Cyrill	Common chickweed	*Viburnum* spp.	Viburnum
Taraxacum officinale Weber	Common dandelion	*Vitis vinifera* L.	Grapes

TABLE 2

Québec, Intendant's Palace site: list of insects identified.

Latin name	Common name	Latin name	Common name
PHTHIRAPTERA		**Anobiidae**	
Pediculus humanus humanus Linné+	Head lice	*Ptinus fur*	Golden spider beetle
HEMIPTERA		**Cryptophagidae**	
Cimex lectularius Linné+	Bedbug	Cryptophagus sp.	
COLEOPTERA		*Henoticus* sp.	
Nebria sp.		**Endomychidae**	
Stenelophus lecontei (Chaudoir)	Seed corn beetle	*Mycetaea subterranea* (Fabricius)+	Handsome fungus beetle
Staphylinidae		**Latridiidae**	
Aleocharinae spp.		*Latridius minutus* group	Minute fungus beetles
Quedius mesomelinus (Marsham)+		Corticaria or Corticarina sp.	
Gyrohypnus sp.		**Tenebrionidae**	
Hydrophilidae		*Tribolium* sp	
Helophorus sp.		*Alphitobius bifasciatus*	Two-banded fungus beetle (Say)
Cercyon sp.		*Tenebrio molitor* Linné+	Yellow mealworm
Scarabaeidae		*Tenebrio* sp.	
Aphodius sp.		**Bruchidae**	
Trox scaber (Linné)+		*Bruchus* sp.	Pea weevil
Elmidae		**Chrysomelidae**	
Elmidae sp.		*Phyllotreta striolata* (Fabricius)+	Striped flea beetle
Dermestidae		**Curculionidae**	
Dermestes lardarius Linné+	Larder beetle	*Sitophilus granarius* (Linné)+	Granary weevil
		+ introduced species	

NOTES

1 Boucher 1964.

2 Garneau 1997; see Filion *et al.* in this volume.

3 Brisson 1983, 27; Moussette 1994, 34.

4 *DCB*, s.v. 'Jean Talon'.

5 *DCB*, s.v. 'Jean Talon'.

6 *DCB*, s.v. 'Jean Talon'.

7 *DCB*, s.v. 'Jean Talon'.

8 Brisson 1983, 44–5.

9 See Simoneau 'Intendant's Palace' in this volume.

10 Brisson 1983, 103; Dagneau 2004; Mathieu 1971, 28.

11 See Simoneau 'Intendant's Palace' in this volume.

12 *DCB*, s.v. 'Jean Talon'.

[13] Moussette 1994, 36–7.
[14] Moussette 1994, 38.
[15] Moussette 1994, 47.
[16] *DCB*, s.v. 'Jean Talon'.
[17] Marie-Victorin 2002, 556.
[18] Fortin 1989, 28.
[19] Lapointe 2001, 6-7.
[20] *DCB*, s.v. 'Jean Talon'.
[21] Moussette 1994, 53.
[22] Moussette 1994, 53.
[23] See Auger *et al.* in this volume.
[24] See Auger *et al.* in this volume; Querrec *et al.* forthcoming.
[25] Charbonneau *et al.* 1982 for discussion.
[26] Charbonneau *et al.* 1982, 117–18.
[27] Charbonneau *et al.* 1982, 366.
[28] Lindroth 1968, 919.
[29] Smetana 1988.
[30] Vaurie 1955, 29.
[31] Simoneau, 2008; see Rouleau in this volume.
[32] Dagneau 2004.
[33] Dagneau 2004.
[34] Charbonneau *et al.* 1982, 367.
[35] Moussette 1994, 71.
[36] Herzog 2005; Nadeau 2007.
[37] Herzog 2005; Nadeau 2007, 147.
[38] Burns & Honkala 1990.
[39] Dumont 2005a; 2005b.
[40] Kalm 1977, 320.
[41] Charlevoix 1763, 24.
[42] Jacynthe Bernard, pers. comm., 2008.
[43] Bain & Lesage 1998, 715.
[44] Bain 2004.
[45] Moussette 1994; 1997. The 2006 excavations were undertaken by the City of Québec archaeologist Daniel Simoneau.
[46] Fortin 1989.
[47] Bousquet 1990, 100; Campbell *et al.* 1989.
[48] Bousquet 1990.
[49] Vaurie 1955, 29.
[50] Bain 1998; 2001; Prévost & Bain 2007.
[51] Moussette 1994, 109–10.
[52] See interpretation of Room 5 below.
[53] Fortin 1989.
[54] Smetana 1988, 19.
[55] Charlevoix 1763, 24.
[56] Bain 2001; Simoneau 2008; see papers by Cloutier and Rouleau in this volume.
[57] Fortin 2006, 136.
[58] Bain 2006, 60.
[59] Simoneau 2003, 28.

BIBLIOGRAPHY

PUBLISHED SOURCES

Alberton, L., Arpin, C. & Herzog, A. 2005, *Site du palais de l'intendant: chantier-école de l'an 2002*, Cahiers d'archéologie du CÉLAT **17**.

Bain, A. 1998, 'A seventeenth-century beetle fauna from colonial Boston', *Hist. Archaeol.* **32**:3, 38–48.

Bain, A. 2001, *Archaeoentomological and Archaeoparasitological Reconstructions at Îlot Hunt (CeEt-110): New Perspectives in Historical Archaeology (1850–1900)*, Brit. Archaeol. Rep. Int. Ser. **973**.

Bain, A. 2004, 'Irritating intimates: the archaeoentomology of lice, fleas, and bedbugs', *Northeast Hist. Archaeol.* **33**, 81–90.

Bain, A. 2006, 'Analyse archéoentomologique du site Îlot Hunt (CeEt-110) 2004', in Cloutier 2006, 158–64.

Bain, A., Chabot, J. & Moussette, M. (eds) 2007, *La Mesure du passé: contributions à la recherche en archéométrie (2000–2006)*, Brit. Archaeol. Rep. Int. Ser. **1700**.

Bain, A. & Lesage, L. 1998, 'A late seventeenth-century occurrence of *Phyllotreta striolata* (Coleoptera: Chrysomelidae) from North America', *Canadian Ent.* **130**, 715–19.

Boucher, P. 1964 [1664], *Histoire véritable et naturelle des mœurs et productions du pays de la Nouvelle-France, vulgairement dite le Canada*, Boucherville (Québec): Société historique.

Bousquet, Y. 1990, *Beetles Associated with Stored Products in Canada: an Identification Guide*, Ottawa: Agriculture Canada.

Brisson, R. 1983, *La Charpenterie navale à Québec sous le régime Français*, Québec: Institut québécois de recherche sur la culture.

Burns, R. & Honkala, B. 1990, *Silvics of North America*, Washington: US Department of Agriculture.

Campbell, J.M., Sarazin, M.J. & Lyons, D.B. 1989, *Canadian Beetles (Coleoptera) Injurious to Crops, Ornamentals, Stored Products, and Buildings*, Ottawa: Agriculture Canada.

Charbonneau, A., Desloges, Y. & Lafrance, M. 1982, *Québec the Fortified City: from the 17th to the 19th Century*, Ottawa: Parks Canada.

Charlevoix, P.-F.-X. de 1763, *Letters to the Dutchess of Lesdiguieres Giving an Account of a Voyage to Canada*, London: R. Goadby.

Cloutier, C. 2006, *Les Battures du Saint-Laurent aux XVIIe et XVIIIe siècles: un dépotoir à ciel ouvert? Le cas du site archéologique de l'îlot Hunt*, Cahiers d'archéologie du CÉLAT **19**.

Dagneau, C. 2004, 'The "batteaux plats" of New France', *Int. J. Naut. Archaeol.* **33**:2, 281–96.

Dumont, B. 2005a, *Les Niches écologiques des arbres, arbustes et conifères*, Boucherville (Québec): Bertrand Dumond.

Dumont, B. 2005b, *Les Niches écologiques des vivaces et plantes herbacées*, Boucherville (Québec): Bertrand Dumond.

Fortin, C. 1989, *Les Macrorestes végétaux du site du premier palais de l'intendant à Québec (CeEt-30)*, Sainte-Foy (Québec): CÉLAT.

Fortin, C. 2006, 'Analyse paléoethnobotanique du site de l'Îlot Hunt (CeEt-110)', in Cloutier 2006, 120–55.

Garneau, M. 1997, 'Paléoécologie d'un secteur riverain de la rivière Saint-Charles: analyse macrofossile du site archéologique de la Grande Place à Québec', *Géogr. Phys. Quat.* **51**, 211–20.

Herzog, A. 2005, 'Rapport de la XIIe campagne de fouilles: l'Îlot des palais de l'Intendant CeEt-30, opération 38', in Alberton *et al.* 2005, 1–116.

Kalm, P. 1977 [1749], *Voyage de Pehr Kalm au Canada en 1749: traduction annotée du journal de route*, Montréal: Pierre Tisseyre.

Lapointe, R. 2001, *Le Bâtiment de la potasse de Québec: d'une industrie du XVIIe siècle aux industries du XXe siècle, intervention archéologique 2000*, Cahiers d'archéologie du CÉLAT **9**.

Letarte, J., Nadeau, R. & Rochefort F. 2007, *Site du palais de l'intendant: chantier-école de l'an 2003*, Cahiers d'archéologie du CÉLAT **20**.

Lindroth, K. 1968, 'The ground beetles (Carabidae excl. Cincindelinae) of Canada and Alaska', *Opusc. Ent. Suppl.* **29**, 409–648.

Marie-Victorin, F. 2002, *Flore Laurentienne*, 3rd edn, Montréal: Gaëtan Morin.

Mathieu, J. 1971, *La Construction navale royale à Québec, 1739–1759*, Cahiers d'histoire Soc. Hist. Québec **23**.

Moussette, M. 1994, *Le Site du Palais de l'Intendant à Québec: genèse et structuration d'un lieu urbain*, Sillery: Septentrion.

Moussette, M. 1997, 'The site of the Intendant's Palace in Québec City: the changing meaning of an urban space', *Hist. Archaeol.* **30**:2, 8–21.

Nadeau, R. 2007, 'CeEt-30, site de l'Îlot des Palais, opération 42: le plancher du palais et le bassin', in Letarte *et al.* 2007, 89–198.

Prévost, M.-A. & Bain, A. 2007, 'L'implantation d'une colonie terre-neuvienne au XVIIe siècle: l'apport des analyses archéobotanique et archéoentomologique', in Bain *et al.* 2007, 205–16.

Simoneau, D. 2008, *L'Îlot Hunt, vingt ans de recherches archéologiques*, Cahiers d'archéologie du CÉLAT **23**.

Smetana, A. 1988, 'Review of the Family Hydrophilidae of Canada and Alaska (Coleoptera)', *Mem. Ent. Soc. Canada* **142**.

Vaurie, P. 1955, 'A revision of the genus *Trox* in North America (Coleoptera, Scarabaeidae)', *Bull. Amer. Mus. Natur. Hist.* **106**:1.

UNPUBLISHED SOURCES

Querrec, L. *et al.* forthcoming, 'Tree-ring Analysis of White Cedar (*Thuja occidentalis* L.): Archaeological and Historical Wood in Québec City (Québec, Canada)', *Dendrochronologia*.

Simoneau, D. 2003, 'Rapport d'interventions archéologiques, Îlot Hunt 2001–2002', Ville de Québec, Division design, architecture et patrimoine, Service de l'aménagement du territoire.

ABBREVIATIONS

ANF	Archives nationales (France)
BNF	Bibliothèque nationale de France
CÉLAT	Centre interuniversitaire de recherche sur les lettres, les arts et les traditions
DCB	*Dictionary of Canadian Biography Online*
NAC	National Archives of Canada

SUMMARY IN FRENCH, GERMAN, ITALIAN AND SPANISH

RÉSUMÉ

Insectes, graines et mauvaises herbes sur le site du Palais de l'intendant : étude d'un paysage en évolution

Utilisé intensément de la deuxième moitié du XVIIe siècle à la Conquête britannique en 1759, le site du Palais de l'intendant abritait les Magasins du Roi, une brasserie, un chantier naval, une boulangerie et autres installations. Le site a été transformé à partir de berges naturelles marécageuses en un complexe imposant de bâtiments représentant le pouvoir du roi en Nouvelle-France et le rôle prestigieux de l'intendant. Cette étude sur le changement du paysage et l'archéologie environnementale exploite les recherches récentes en archéoentomologie, archéobotanique et dendrochronologie. L'intégration de données naturelles, écrites et matérielles fournit une meilleure interprétation du site.

ZUSAMMENFASSUNG

Insekten, Samen und Kräuter am Intendantenpalast: eine Studie der Landschaftsentwicklung

Der Komplex des Intendantenpalastes, der von der zweiten Hälfte des 17. Jhs. bis zur Eroberung durch die Briten 1759 intensiv genutzt wurde, beherbergte die Läden des Königs, eine Brauerei, eine Werft, eine Bäckerei und noch andere Einrichtungen. Diese Gegend verwandelte sich von einer am Fluß gelegnen Marsch in eine beeindruckende Anlage von Gebäuden, die die Macht des Königs in Neufrankreich und die bedeutende Rolle des Intendanten repräsentierte. Diese Studie der Landschaftsgestaltung und Umweltarchäologie stützt sich auf jüngste Forschungen in der Archäoentomologie, der Archäobotanik und der Dendrochronologie. Die Verflechtung ursprünglicher, geschichtlicher und materieller Daten liefert eine präzisere Interpretation des Palastes.

RIASSUNTO

Insetti, semi ed erbacce nel Palazzo di Intendenza: uno studio del paesaggio in evoluzione

Usato intensamente dalla seconda metà del XVII secolo fino alla conquista Britannica del 1759, il complesso del Palazzo di Intendenza ospitava i magazzini reali, una birreria, un cantiere navale, un forno e altre strutture. Il sito fu trasformato da area naturale paludosa lungo il fiume in un imponente complesso di edifici che rappresentavano il potere del re nella Nuova Francia e il prestigioso ruolo del suo intendente. Questo lavoro sui cambiamenti del paesaggio e l'archeologia ambientale attinge a recenti ricerche in archeo-entomologia, archeobotanica e dendrocronologia. L'uso integrato di dati naturali, fonti scritte e materiali fornisce una migliore interpretazione di questo sito.

RESUMEN

Insectos, semillas y malas hierbas en el Palacio del Intendente: el estudio de un paisaje cambiante

Utilizado intensivamente desde la segunda mitad del siglo XVII hasta la conquista británica de 1759, el Palacio del Intendente dio cabida a los almacenes del rey, fábrica de cerveza, astillero, un horno de cocer pan y otras facilidades. El yacimiento fue transformado de rivera de río a un impresionante complejo de edificios representantes del poder real en Nueva Francia y de su intendente. Este estudio del cambio en el paisaje y arqueología medioambiental hace uso de estudios recientes en la arqueología de insectos, flora y dendrocronología. La integración de datos de material natural, escrito y objetos nos ayuda a obtener una mejor interpretación de este yacimiento.

CÉLAT and Department of History, 1030 Avenue des Sciences-humaines, Université Laval, Québec (Québec), Canada G1V 0A6
[Allison.bain@hst.ulaval.ca; julie-anne.bouchard-perron.1@ulaval.ca; réginald.auger@celat.ulaval.ca]

Ville de Québec, Service de l'aménagement du territoire, Division du design, de l'architecture et du patrimoine, 295 boulevard Charest Est, Québec (Québec), Canad, G1K 3G8
[daniel.simoneau@ville.quebec.qc.ca]

Post-Medieval Archaeology **43/1** (2009), 198–212

Québec in the time of Champlain

By FRANÇOISE NIELLON

SUMMARY: When Champlain died in 1635, the trading post he had founded in 1608 was the embryo of a permanent settlement. Vicissitudes in assigning privileges ensured that its development had been slow and halting. The artefacts found in Québec and on the farm at Cap Tourmente show that these settlements were provided mainly with goods from the hinterlands of the French ports in which the merchant companies were based. The houses on the St Lawrence were small and built in timber and cob. The expatriate craftsmen and labourers consumed a standard seaman's diet supplemented by plums supplied from France.

In 1608 Pierre Dugua de Monts, the king's lieutenant-general in New France, entrusted Sieur Champlain with the task of founding a settlement on the banks of the St Lawrence River. Dugua had known Samuel de Champlain for many years and was aware that he was well acquainted with New France. In 1603 Champlain had travelled up the St Lawrence to the La Chine Rapids and from 1604 to 1607 had lived in Acadia. He had thus already demonstrated his endurance, taste for exploration and ability to report on the discoveries made.

The settlement erected on the banks of the St Lawrence gradually began to expand beyond the ditches that surrounded it, initiating the slow process of development that led to the city of Québec. Archaeological excavations, which are still in progress, bring a particular perspective to what Champlain and his contemporaries had to say about this process, because the architectural remains, artefacts and ecofacts uncovered make its development more tangible.

THE FOUNDING OF QUÉBEC IN 1608

CHANGES AND CHALLENGES

The founding of Québec is somewhat of an enigma. It is difficult to understand how Dugua managed to convince his associates in Rouen to make another attempt to establish a permanent settlement in New France. Even though he had previously obtained an exclusive trading privilege for the colony, he had been unable to amass the financial resources needed to maintain the settlement of Port-Royal. So, in response to demands for free trade, in 1607 Sully had revoked Dugua's monopoly.

Despite this, Dugua was still determined to found a settlement in New France and persuaded the king to grant him the ways and means to defray the cost. His monopoly over trade with the 'savages' was restored on 7 January 1608, but only for a year,[1] which may explain why apparently only one group of Rouen merchants agreed to invest in the project. His aim was to establish a *Habitation* or settlement at Québec on the shores of the St Lawrence rather than in Acadia, the area previously chosen for colonization.

Dugua was familiar with the region. He had gone to Tadoussac, perhaps in 1599 but more probably in 1600, with his former comrade-in-arms and fellow Huguenot, Pierre Chauvin de Tonnetuit, who then held the St Lawrence trade monopoly. François Gravé, Sieur Dupont, who was already a regular participant in this trade network, accompanied them; the three men must have drawn up an agreement on the venture's potential costs and

 DOI: 10.1179/007942309X12457508844288

benefits. Nevertheless, it is likely that Dugua was unconvinced, for he set sail for Acadia in 1604 after obtaining a royal commission and a monopoly on trade with the Aboriginal people.

However, once Dugua reached Acadia, he could not find an appropriate site for a permanent settlement nor a reliable source of profits. The most promising opportunities were offered by fishing in the Gulf of St Lawrence and by trade along the river. A way had to be found to prevent competitors, particularly the Dutch, who had inflicted major losses on Dugua's company in 1606, from gaining access to the St Lawrence corridor. The solution was to found a settlement at Québec, where the narrowing of the river would probably make it possible to bar access upstream, which Gravé and Champlain knew held great promise. Nonetheless, Tadoussac — where the Habitation built by Chauvin in 1600 was still maintained — continued to serve as the terminus for ships. Large ocean-going vessels did not travel further upstream for another 20 years.

In the spring of 1608 Dugua and his associates sent three ships to New France, two to Tadoussac and one to Acadia. Only one of the two vessels headed for the St Lawrence is known, the *Liepvre,* a small ship from Honfleur with a capacity of about 80 *tonneaux*, on which Gravé embarked. The other ship with Samuel de Champlain on board may have been the *Levrette*,[2] a 50–60-*tonneau* vessel from Havre de Grâce.

The arrivals of both Gravé at Tadoussac and Champlain at Québec were quite eventful. Gravé was injured along with three of his men during a violent armed altercation with the crew of the *Marie*, a 150-*tonneau* ship from Saint-Vincent de Luz. Champlain uncovered a plot for his assassination, which was to be followed by taking control of the intended Québec Habitation and handing it over to the Basques. He firmly asserted his authority by sending three accomplices back to France and by executing the ringleader, whose head was displayed on a stake.

ESTABLISHMENT OF A SETTLEMENT ON THE POINT OF QUÉBEC

THE SITE

When Champlain laid anchor off the Québec point in June 1603, he described the area as:

> a narrow part of the said river of Canada . . . At these narrows . . . is a very high mountain, which slopes down on both sides: all the rest is a level and beautiful country, where there is good land covered with trees . . .; so that in my opinion, if this soil were tilled, it would be as good as ours.[3]

Five years later, he headed straight back, where 'on arrival [he] looked for a place suitable for [his] settlement, but . . . could not find any more suitable or better situated than the point of Québec'.[4]

The point is a low-lying terrace where shaly debris from Cap Diamant once accumulated and was reworked by water. A thin humus layer 50–150mm thick gradually formed on this debris, on which trees eventually grew. Over a period of nearly 2,000 years Amerindian groups occasionally camped on this rounded hillock, which descended sharply to the foreshore. Traces of their presence are rarer in the archaeological record after about AD 1200; the site was probably no longer used by *c.* 1600.

The Québec toponym is a Micmac word. In the early part of the 17th century Amerindians came there from downstream, particularly to fish eel in the autumn. They were already used to trading with Europeans. However, the St Lawrence River would soon give these traders access to native peoples much further upstream who until then had not been encountered.

Like the settlements in Sainte-Croix and Port-Royal, the Habitation at Québec served both as a defended warehouse and living quarters. The warehouse (known as the *magasin*) contained the goods offered to Amerindians at agreed meeting places. Food supplies for the Habitation's leader and workers were kept in a separate area.

THE WORK OF 1608

Dugua entrusted Champlain with the responsibility of building the outpost. However, Champlain could not have known much about setting up a settlement, apart from what he had learned from Chauvin's achievements at Tadoussac and Dugua's in Acadia. He may also still have been quite young at the time, perhaps not yet in his thirties.

In order to build the Habitation at Québec, Dugua hired eighteen men in Paris: a logger, two pit sawyers, seven carpenters, two masons, two locksmiths, two labourers, a gardener and a tailor.[5] Gravé or Dugua's associates may have hired other people in Honfleur or Rouen, along with the ships' crews, which included at least one surgeon and a few sailors who, together with the craftsmen, were to overwinter in Québec. The Habitation was to house about 30 people, including Champlain and his footman.

They were fewer than those planned for the colonization of Acadia. Sainte-Croix was intended to accommodate 80 people over the winter, while Port-Royal was to serve 40 or 50. Québec was also more modest in that its inhabitants did not include gentlemen, notables or priests. As Champlain lived there only with his men, he was unable to replicate his experience at Port-Royal, where he had founded the *Ordre du Bon Temps*, or Order of Good Cheer, which brought together an elite group of about fifteen people around J. Biencourt de Poutrincourt's table. Clearly Dugua and his associates were uncertain about the Québec Habitation's future.

Once the men arrived at the site in early July, they had to make it habitable before the winter. Champlain described the Habitation they erected:

> our quarters . . . contained three main buildings of two storeys. Each one was three fathoms [*thoizes*][6] long and two and a half wide [5.88 × 4.9m]. The warehouse was six long and three wide [11.76 × 5.88m], with a fine cellar six feet [1.82m] high. All the way round our buildings I had a gallery made, outside the second storey . . . There were also ditches fifteen feet [4.9m] wide and six [1.95m] deep, and outside these I made several salients which enclosed a part of the buildings, and there we put our cannon. In front of the building there is an open space four fathoms wide and six or seven long [7.84 × 11.76–13.72m], which abuts upon the river's bank. Round about the buildings are very good gardens, and an open place on the north side of a hundred, or a hundred and twenty, yards long and fifty or sixty wide [98–117 × 49–59m].[7]

The building complex was eventually protected by a palisade, completed in 1610. Champlain had vegetable seeds planted in the gardens, wheat and rye sown on a cleared piece of land, and wild vines transplanted to the site. His account describing the initial work on the Habitation was published in 1613, illustrated by an engraving which is both informative and enigmatic (Fig. 1).

INTERPRETATION OF THE ACCOUNT AND ILLUSTRATION (FIG. 1)

It is rather difficult to understand how the different parts of the Habitation were arranged. It was small, covering a rectangular area 8 × 10 *toises* (15.7 × 19.6m) — the same size as Dugua's at Port-Royal.[8] The three dwellings ('main buildings') seem to have been arranged in a U, leaving an open space between the façade of the warehouse A and the gable walls of the workers' accommodation C and D.

The ground-level area inside the warehouse was 72m^2. Together the three dwellings provided 90m^2, but, as they were of two storeys, their habitable floor space was about 180m^2. The warehouse cellar perhaps consisted of no more than 30m^2.

As the walkway (*promenoir* L) between the built complex and the ditch was not a *terreplein*, the cannon platforms N were built outside the ditch. These salients probably rested on the palisade that Champlain mentioned two years later, which, for some reason, were not illustrated or mentioned in the key.

The walls and roofs seem to have been covered with vertical planking, in contrast with the brick facing shown at Port-Royal. Even the chimneys at Québec look as though they were faced with vertical planks. Presumably the masons hired by Dugua built the chimneys and perhaps also installed nogging in the timber framing.

The wood fragments associated with the Habitation's initial occupation phase suggest that the timber used was white pine (*Pinus strobus*), a common local species. The chimneys may have been made of brick, about 200kg of which were recovered from the same contexts.

It is hard to determine the Habitation's orientation. The outpost was readily accessible from the south, where the ground sloped gently to the sandy river edge. Rowing boats could have been beached there and a landing stage installed. In contrast it was difficult to reach the Habitation from the east, i.e. from the point, where the ground sloped sharply and the riverbank was steep and rocky. Nevertheless, if the way in were to be flanked by cannon platforms M, the access opted for in 1608 must have been from the east.

No remains of the first Habitation were uncovered during the excavation, although some features associated with the second Habitation were identified. As later rebuilding was staged, replacing the first Habitation and as many earlier objects were found in the second Habitation's deposits, it is likely that the first was located in the same place as the second, that is under the present-day church of Notre-Dame-des-Victoires and in its vicinity towards the river.

CONSOLIDATION OF THE POST BETWEEN 1609 AND 1635

A TIME OF INSTABILITY

The written sources seem to indicate that the Habitation developed more or less in step with the ups and downs of the St Lawrence trade monopoly.

1609–13

As trade was free, Québec was used for little else than a warehouse. Champlain reported that sixteen people wintered there in 1609–10 and

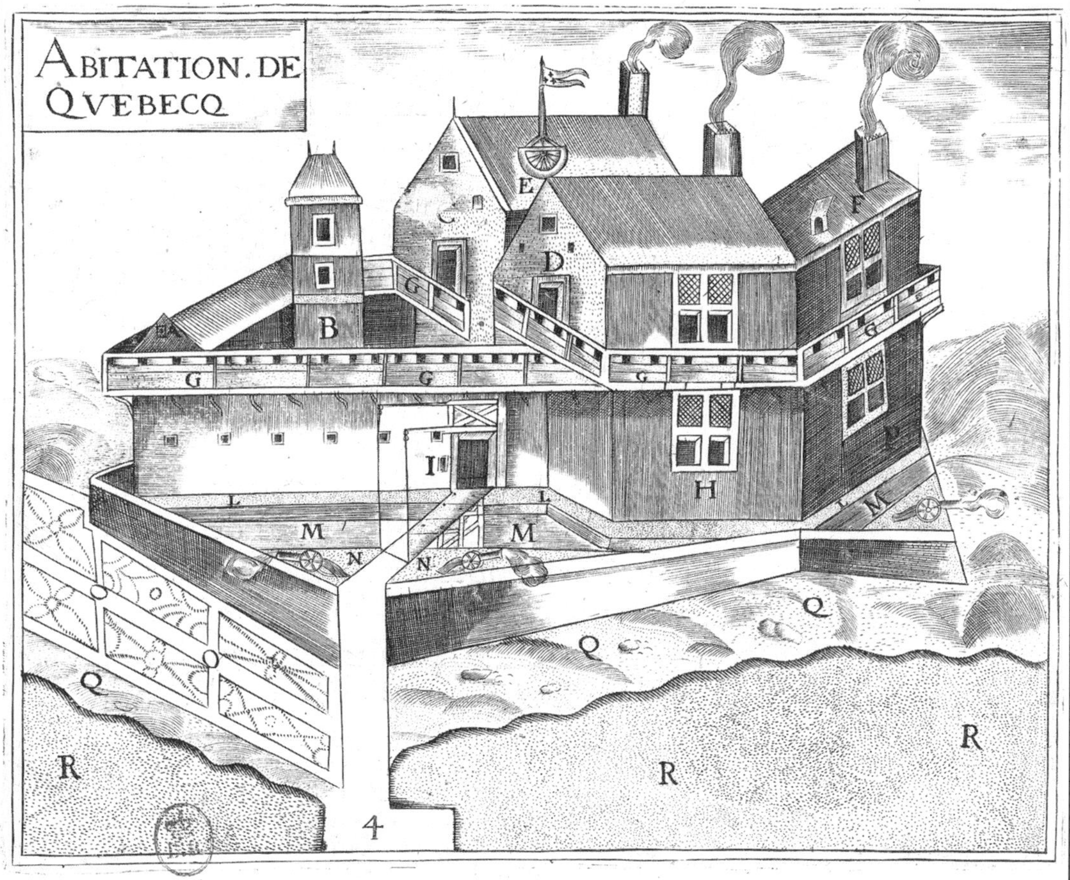
DV SIEVR DE CHAMPLAIN. 187

A Le magazin.
B Colombier.
C Corps de logis où ſont nos arm[e]s,& pour loger les ouuriers.
D Autre corps de logis pour les ouuriers.
E Cadran.
F Autre corps de logis où eſt la forge, & artiſans logés.
G Galleries tout au tour des logemens.
H Logis du ſieur de Champlain.
I La porte de l'habitation,où il y a Pont-leuis
L Promenoir autour de l'habitation contenant 10. pieds de large iuſques ſur le bort du foſſé.
M Foſſés tout autour de l'habitation.
N Plattes formes,en façon de tenailles pour mettre le canon.
O Iardin du ſieur de Champlain.
P La cuiſine.
Q Place deuant l'habitation ſur le bort de la riuiere.
R La grande riuiere de ſainct Lorens.

Aa ij

FIG. 1

Abitation de Quebecq (from Champlain 1613, 187; photograph, Bibliothèque nationale de France).

seventeen the following winter. The Habitation received only minimal maintenance and fell into disrepair.

1614–20

The reinstated trade monopoly was now managed by the second Compagnie du Canada or Compagnie de Rouen et de Saint-Malo, in which Dugua had shares. The company bought the Habitation from Dugua for 3,900 *livres* 'along with all the barques, tackle, utensils and weapons, without any exceptions'.[9] The sum paid was equal to the wages that would have been earned by a hired craftsman over 39 years or by Champlain in three and a half.

Once the outpost changed hands, the number who overwintered in Québec increased sharply; from at least 1616 it rose to 50 or 60. Champlain described the ensuing expansion:

> we enlarged our said settlement by a third at least with additional fortified buildings, because it was not sufficiently roomy . . . and we built the whole solidly with lime and sand, having found some of very good quality at a spot near the said settlement.[10]

When the Récollet fathers arrived in 1615, the associates built them a small house-chapel on a flat piece of cleared land outside the Habitation. By 1619 they erected workshops in the same area for the locksmith and the baker, because there was no longer space for them alongside the dwellings within the enclosure. The Habitation now boasted some vital auxiliary structures.

More significant was the spread of the settlement further away from the Habitation. Work began on a convent for the Récollets on the banks of the Saint-Charles River and a house was erected for Louis Hébert's family on the plateau. Hébert was well known to Dugua and his associates, as he had lived for a long time in Port-Royal. In 1617 the associates engaged him for two years to work in Québec. This time he brought his wife, three children and brother-in-law. He had a 'licence to clear, till and improve the land in the said country' and as an apothecary he promised to treat the sick.[11] At the end of his contract Hébert left the Habitation to move into the house that the company had helped him build on his 'tillage'.

In contrast with this flurry of activity elsewhere, for some reason the Habitation seems to have been poorly maintained. According to Champlain, who had been in Québec in all for only a few weeks in the preceding decade, the outpost was in a terrible state when he returned in 1620 with his young wife Hélène Boulé. He undertook repairs right away and 'in a short time the building was habitable'.[12]

At the same time Champlain obliged the company to erect a fort on the height overlooking the Habitation. This was the first of a series known as Fort Saint-Louis. It was a modest two-storey structure in wood, probably surrounded by a simple wooden palisade. The fort belonged to the king, but the company had to cover its costs.

1621–32

The trade monopoly was now operated by a company formed by the de Caëns, merchants in Rouen and Dieppe. As the associates who had formerly held the monopoly soon obtained a major share (40%) in the company, Dugua became a member. However, in 1627 the king handed New France and the trading privileges over to the Compagnie des Cents-Associés, created ad hoc; but the new arrangement did not take effect immediately.

This was a period of intense work. The rebuilding of all or part of the Habitation and Fort Saint-Louis was undertaken; the Récollet convent on the right bank of the Saint-Charles River was completed; and the Jesuit convent of Notre-Dame-des-Anges was erected on the opposite bank. Upstream of the Jesuits Hébert cleared and farmed a large piece of land granted to him in 1626 by the Viceroy of New France. Lastly, a farm was built at Cap Tourmente, about 50km downstream from Québec.

However, construction work progressed slowly on the Habitation and the fort, and the plans were only partly implemented. The buildings at Cap Tourmente were crude, and surprisingly those of the Jesuits were hardly better. In comparison the Récollet convent must have seemed opulent.

In 1628 the development of the St Lawrence colony was brought to a halt by war. The English fleet under the command of David Kirke took control of the river, preventing supplies from reaching Québec; and his men sacked the farm at Cap Tourmente. Champlain immediately 'set all hands to work to make entrenchments around the settlement [Habitation], and barricades on the ramparts of the fort which were not completed . . . These things [were] accomplished in all haste'.[13] The entire population was on a war footing. However, the efforts to protect the colony were in vain. On 20 July 1629 the keys to the Habitation and Fort Saint-Louis had to be handed over to Lewis Kirke, David's brother. Québec remained English until July 1632.

The Kirkes lived at the fort, maintaining and improving its defences. They may have used the

Habitation as a warehouse and to house some of their 200 or so men. A fire damaged the Habitation, which the French discovered on their return. The men lodged in the Jesuit and Récollet convents seem to have ransacked the premises and burned down part of a Jesuit outbuilding. In contrast, according to the Jesuits, the Hébert's property, run during the British occupation by his widow and her son-in-law G. Couillard, exuded prosperity.

1632–35

In 1632 France retook Québec, but the Compagnie des Cent-Associés left the trade monopoly in the hands of the de Caëns for a year. They came back with three Jesuits, who reoccupied their convent, where they were joined the following year by three other fathers and a few labourers. When E. de Caën departed, he left them three cows. The Jesuits' quarters at Notre-Dame-des-Anges were renovated to serve as a farm and as lodgings for their labourers. The fathers moved to Fort Saint-Louis while they waited for a presbytery to be built, which became the nucleus of their college. As the Récollets did not return to Québec for another 40 years or so, their convent deteriorated. The farm at Cap Tourmente also seems to have been abandoned. G. de Caën transferred the seigneury including the farm, which had been granted to him in 1624, to the Compagnie des Cent-Associés. However, the farm was not developed until the 1660s.

The Hébert-Couillard enclosure, established as a fief in 1626, was divided by Louis Hébert's heirs. A detailed but obscure description of the holding is in the deed of partition.[14] Apart from cultivated fields and gardens, the enclosure included at least three dwellings, a barn, a stable, a mill and a 'fountain'. As well, a brewhouse equipped with a brew kettle seems to have been attached to the courtyard side of one of the three houses. A path led to the Habitation via the *coste du sault au mathelot* (now Côte de la Montagne). On the other side another led to the hill descending to Pointe aux Lièvres (probably Côte de la Canoterie). Other deeds dating from about the same time show that buckwheat for making flat cakes, peas for making soup and barley for making beer were grown in their fields. It was almost a hamlet, where women and children lived as well men.

Champlain came back to Québec in 1633 and took up residence in Fort Saint-Louis, which at last had a garrison. F. Derré de Gand, the representative of the Compagnie des Cent-Associés, also lived there. So the fort became the colony's seat of command, even before an official governor was installed there. Champlain also started building a wooden chapel near the fort, called Notre-Dame-de-Recouvrance, in thanks for the colony's return to France. This was the first church in Upper Town.

However, most effort was devoted to renovating the Habitation. Champlain had 'work done with great energy on repairing and maintaining the buildings'. He had 'all the burned and demolished ruins rebuilt . . . and an infinite amount of debris and stone removed'. He used what was left of the main building 'to put up a new storehouse' or warehouse. This 'very fine and good' building measured 13 *toises* (25.48m) long by 22 French feet wide (7.19m) and 12 or 13 French feet (3.92 or 4.25m) high. Opposite the warehouse on the riverside, Champlain had 'a fine platform built for installing three or four cannon for firing across the river at water level'.[15] Jean Bourdon, the king's surveyor, who came to Québec the following year, drew a plan of the renovated Habitation shortly after his arrival (Fig. 2). Bourdon also drew a plan of the 'fort of Québec' that dates in all likelihood to 1635 (Fig. 3). It includes the work done by the English, which Champlain mentioned very briefly in 1630,[16] and perhaps a few later additions.

On Champlain's death on 25 December 1635, Québec had about 300 inhabitants and the Laurentian colony had finally taken shape.

THE ARCHAEOLOGY OF QUÉBEC IN CHAMPLAIN'S TIME

THE ARCHITECTURAL REMAINS

Archaeological excavations on the sites of both the Habitation and the farm at Cap Tourmente have uncovered important structural remains testifying to the development of the colony on the banks of the St Lawrence during Champlain's lifetime. Traces of structures dating in part from this period have also been found in Upper Town, on the Hébert-Couillard site and possibly at Fort Saint-Louis. However, the Saint-Charles and Notre-Dame-des-Anges convents have not yet been discovered.

The remains unearthed on the Habitation site correspond to the structures on Bourdon's plan (Fig. 2): a central block with a return wing at each end and with towers at each corner flanking the rear façade. The structural remains and associated stratigraphy point to the following construction sequence. The south wing seems to have been the warehouse began in 1614 and completed in 1621. The building of the central block, which was perpendicular to the warehouse and incorporated its western portion, was begun in 1624. However, there is no written or archaeological evidence to suggest that a north wing was built in 1624 or soon

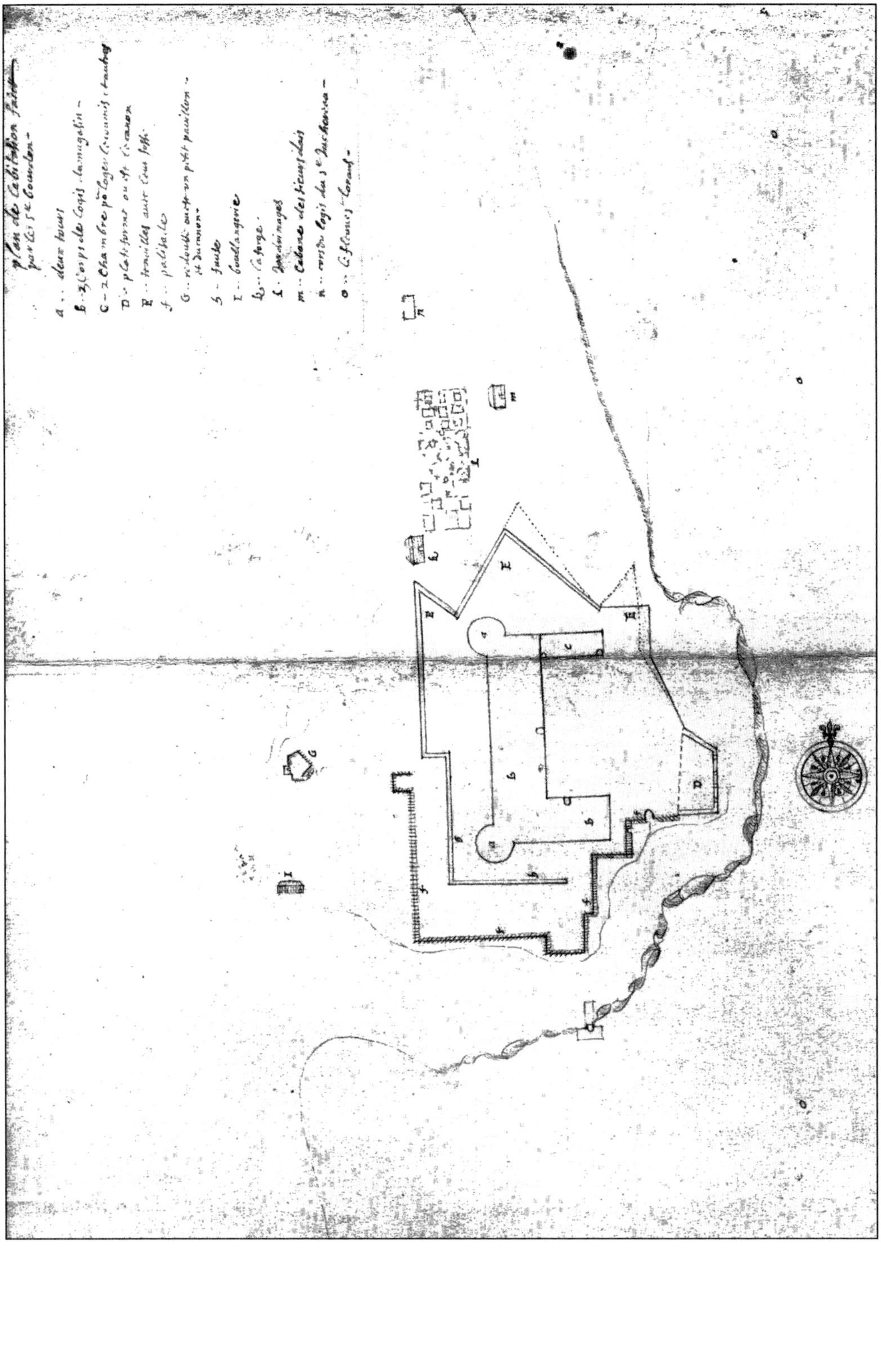

FIG. 2
Plan de labitation faict par le sr bourdon (*c.* 1634–35) (Department of Rare Books and Special Collections, McGill University Libraries, Montréal; photograph, Université Laval).

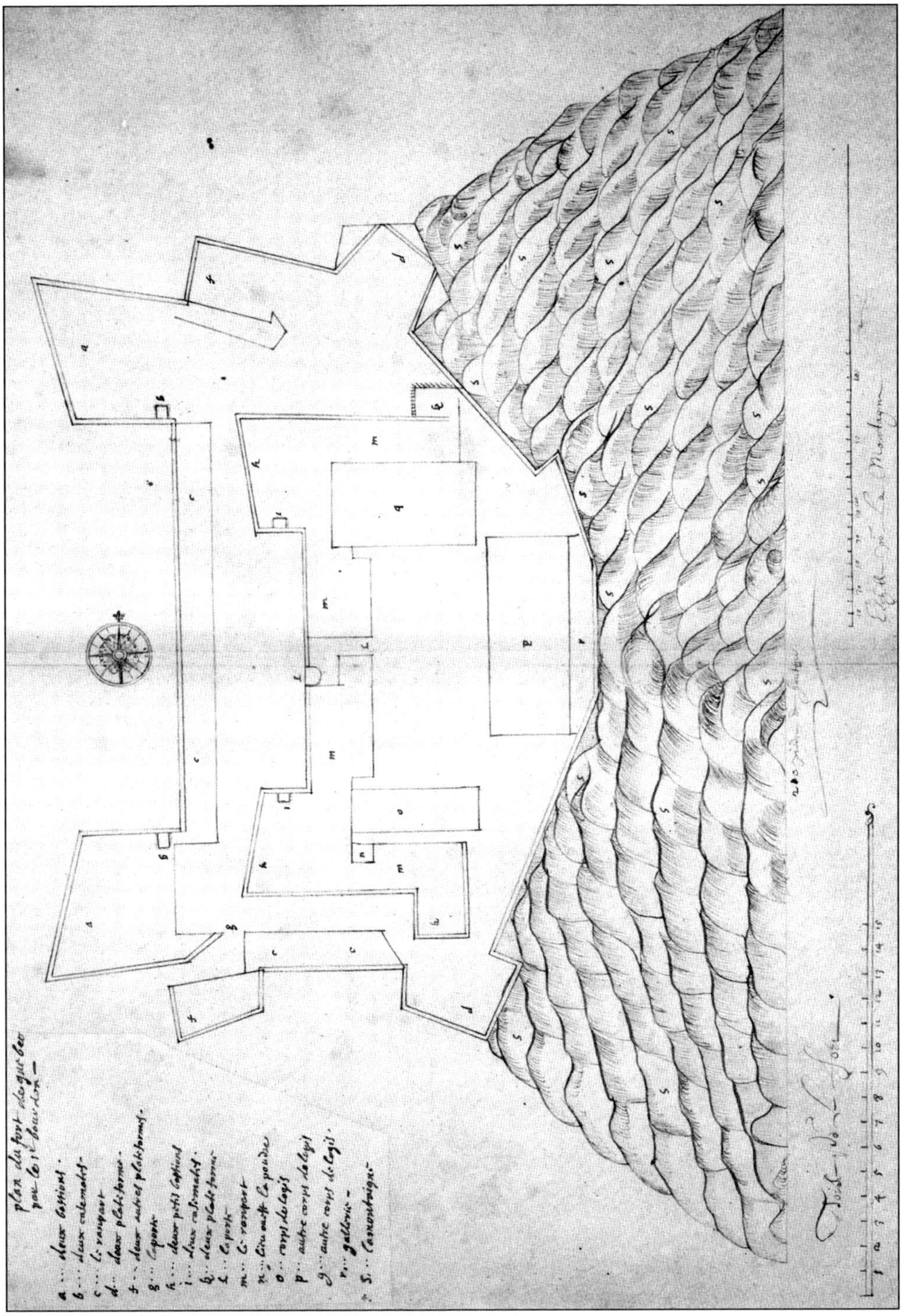

FIG. 3
Plan du fort de québec par le sr bourdon (1635) (Department of Rare Books and Special Collections, McGill University Libraries, Montréal; photograph, Université Laval).

afterwards. It may have been erected shortly before Bourdon drew his plan. Its remains were not bonded to the central block, nor was its north wall aligned with that of the central block. The stratigraphy and finds date the wing to *c.* 1675, when it would have replaced the one drawn by Bourdon. The central block and towers were made of black shale, a local stone known as *pierre du Cap* (Cape stone); the unearthed masonry stood close to 3m high in places and was about 0.65m wide (Fig. 4).

The short sections of ditch found on the site and under Place Royale could not be associated with a particular phase of the Habitation, because the stratigraphy had been truncated by later construction work. If these small ditch sections belong to the same feature, they may be the 'entrenchments' hastily dug in 1628 and still visible *c.* 1635. As the ditch would have impeded the paths from the riverbank and up the side of the hill, they must have been filled in soon afterwards.

Although only a small area was excavated at Cap Tourmente, remains of the 1626 buildings were found.[17] They were 'constructed of wood and clay after the fashion of those . . . built in the villages of Normandy'.[18] The *c.* 0.30m-deep foundation trenches were filled with blocks of pure clay. The wooden posts of the wall frames were placed at one-metre intervals in this foundation. Pisé or cob, a building material of stiff earth or clay usually containing animal hair or plant fibre, was rammed into the spaces between the posts, probably within shuttering, placed one lift on top of the other. One room had a wood floor; the others had hard-packed earth. Although the farm's barn was not found, two small outbuildings (root cellar, woodshed?) and a garden seem to have completed the settlement, which may have been surrounded by a wooden palisade. Traces of fire damage were visible throughout the site.

The Hébert-Couillard enclosure was found under the Québec Seminary. Two buildings have been successively interpreted as Couillard's house: one east of the *aile de la Procure* (procurator's wing) and the other to its west. The first was discovered by chance during repairs in 1866, when Father Laverdière recorded its plan.[19] It consisted of two adjoining structures, one about 30 × 24 English feet (9.14 × 7.31m) and the other, apparently the older of the two, 27 × 21 English feet (8.23 × 6.40m). Their foundations at least were of stone. Part of the second building was excavated in 1991 and 2002.[20] It formed a square about 19 × 17 French feet (6.21 × 5.56m), to which was later added another structure of unknown size on masonry foundations. The older part seems to have been timber-framed with a rudimentary stone foundation and a wood floor. The building to the east of the procurator's wing is also known from a description made during an appraisal in 1639 and the one to the west by a contract for an addition signed in 1653.

Houses in Champlain's time were small. The dwellings in the 1608 Habitation and on the Cap Tourmente farm measured 18 × 15 French feet (5.87 × 4.90m); the older parts of the two Hébert-Couillard buildings were only slightly larger. Their walls were timber-framed and filled with stone or cob. Walls entirely of stone were exceptional — for example, the gable wall of the house Hébert erected in 1619/20.[21] Perhaps timber framing and stone were combined in this building, as they were later in the 17th century. Although constructed in the same way, the conventual living quarters were much larger, 34 × 22 French feet (11.12 × 7.19m)

FIG. 4

The second Habitation at Québec: remains of the north-west corner (photograph, MACQ).

in the Récollet convent and 40 × 23 French feet (13.08 × 7.52m) in the Jesuits'.

THE FINDS

The material excavated at the Habitation is the main source of information on the provenance of the goods sent to Québec and on the way the colonists lived in Champlain's time. Only 30 artefacts were found at Cap Tourmente. The Hébert-Couillard assemblage extends from 1608 to 1680, beyond the period of this paper. Although few people lived there before 1629, the Fort Saint-Louis excavation may yield interesting finds, comparable with the data from the Habitation.

Most artefacts came from Normandy and the nearby Maine region. Upper Normandy was the source of some of the pottery, glassware and tobacco pipes — and probably also the glass beads and combs — which were shipped through Honfleur and Dieppe, ports from where most of the supply ships set sail each year. Other types of pottery and pins came from Lower Normandy and Maine via Rouen or more commonly Saint-Malo. However, from the early days of the colony and with increasing frequency, Québec at least also received pottery from the Saintonge, which was usually loaded in La Rochelle.

The finds are thus representative of the goods shipped from the main ports where the companies supplying Québec operated. They show that the merchants obtained their merchandise from as close as possible to the ports they used. However, none of the items are like those recovered from Basque whaling sites in Canada, which may be because the Basques only supplied Québec through merchants in La Rochelle and for a short period.

In addition to goods from the mother country, a few objects of foreign manufacture reached Québec, although by what routes is unclear. A spectacular black stoneware Martabani jar from Burma in south-east Asia was deposited between 1624 and 1632 on the ground floor of the Habitation's north-west tower (Fig. 5). Jars of this type are regularly found in the cargo of ships operated by the Dutch West India Company. The de Caëns forged close commercial ties with the Dutch, which led to Cornelius van den Bogaert becoming chief assistant clerk of the Habitation's warehouse from at least 1627 to 1629. These ties may also explain the few fragments of oriental porcelain of the same period at the Habitation and from the Hébert-Couillard site.

A less exotic but unexpected discovery is the brown salt-glazed coarse stoneware bottle of a type usually attributed to Rhenish production centres, particularly Frechen. It was made in Bouffioulx, an important Walloon pottery centre from 1610–20. The name of the maker, Ian Allers, appears on the moulded medallion on the body (Fig. 6). Although stoneware was marketed on a large scale in the Netherlands and England, it seems to have been exported in only small quantities to France, except in the north-eastern part of the country and perhaps Paris.

FIG. 5
Québec Habitation site: Martabani stoneware jar (photograph, MACQ).

Apparently some of the coarse earthenware milk pans found at Cap Tourmente were made in south-west England, i.e. north Devon/south Somerset (Fig. 7).[22] Their sandy bodies and glaze displaying a wide range of colours are unlike the pottery tempered with fine gravel and covered with an olive green glaze which was exported later in the 17th century. As the latter are thought to have entered New France via Boston and New England, the earlier variety may have followed the same route.

The artefacts and ecofacts found indicate that the principal activities on the sites examined in this paper were related to food and building. Trade and smoking are the only other activities represented by more than a few artefacts. An unusual pewter lead-alloy *escritoire* or ink stand may have been used by the Habitation's warehouse clerk to keep the outpost's books (Fig. 8:1). The brass weight

FIG. 6

Québec Habitation site: stoneware bottle from Bouffioulx, Belgium (photograph, MACQ).

FIG. 7

Cap Tourmente farm: coarse earthenware milk pan from south-west England(?). Height: 129mm; rim diam.: 290mm; base diam.: 123mm (photograph, Canadian Museum of Civilization).

from the Hébert-Couillard assemblage was once part of a series of eight cups that fitted one into the other and weighed a total of one mark or eight ounces (Fig. 8:2). It may have belonged to Louis Hébert, who was an apothecary.

The outpost's trading activities are demonstrated by the 350 glass beads from the Habitation site, although tens or hundreds of thousands must have been kept in the warehouse. They were recovered almost entirely from under the Place Royale, or the *place du Septentrion* mentioned by Champlain in 1608. It is unlikely to have been where they were traded, as it was too close to the Habitation. The beads found here, in later 17th-century contexts and on the Hébert-Couillard site, varied in shape, colour and decorative technique.

The taste for tobacco is rather surprising as smoking was then a recent European practice. The 2,000 or so fragments recovered of at least 140 pipes come mainly (126) from the ground floor of the north-west tower, which burned down in about 1632. As the different forms were probably shipped in a single box of twelve dozen, they may all date from the same period and have been made in the same place. At this time in France pipe smoking was especially popular among sailors, soldiers and craftsmen, which may explain why so many pipes were found in the Habitation.

The construction and repair of the Habitation left a large amount of debris. Some was disposed of in the construction trenches of the Habitation's central block, while the rest was used to fill and level vacant areas. It contained bevelled floor tiles, once laid in mortar to form pavements. These were probably installed only in places exposed to moisture or extreme heat. Some tiles had a deep 2–3mm scored groove to make it easier to break them in two.

The food-related artefacts consist mainly of containers for transporting or storing foodstuffs (about 48%). They include two forms which seem to have fallen into disuse in New France later on: a globular flask or costrel with one flattened side (Fig. 9:1) and a small pot intended for individual use, mistakenly called an albarello (Fig. 9:2), which may not have held food. Another example of the latter was found at Cap Tourmente. The export of stoneware from Normandy to the Channel Islands and southern England is well documented.

Tableware, especially items for individual use, and cooking pots are rare, reflecting either the period or the social group to which the users belonged. The significance of social affiliation is underscored by the Cap Tourmente assemblage and the post-mortem inventory of the effects of Louis Hébert's son, Guillaume, who belonged to a family whose status surpassed that of hired labourers.[23] Whereas no plates, porringers, goblets or even dishes were found on the Cap Tourmente farm, such objects were plentiful in Hébert's house. Since the pottery was not deemed worthy of mention, the inventoried tableware was made of pewter

FIG. 8

1. Québec Habitation: pewter lead alloy *écritoire* or ink stand (photograph, MACQ); 2. Hébert-Couillard farm: brass weight (60.4g; height: 20mm; rim diam.: 36mm; base diam.: 26mm) (photograph, Ville de Québec).

and even included a silver porringer and spoon. A spit and a grill were also listed alongside a cooking-pot, copper cauldrons of different sizes and a copper frying pan, no traces of which were found in the archaeological excavations. So, stew was not the only thing cooked in the Hébert household.

A zooarchaeological analysis of the 2,335 bone fragments from the 1608–32 period of occupation of the Habitation identified the types of meat consumed.[24] A minimum of 216 individual mammals, birds and fish were represented, not all of which were eaten. The small proportion of wild species shows that the outpost's occupants did little to reduce their dependency on the companies' annual supplies by taking advantage of the natural resources in their new environment. However, it is unlikely that the craftsmen and labourers who then resided at Québec knew how or had the inclination to use a gun, set a snare or catch a fish with a line or a net.

Nor were many wildfowl and fish present in the Cap Tourmente assemblage; mammals account for 88% of the fragments uncovered. This is in sharp contrast with the period from 1664 to 1759, when the site was the seminary's farm; mammals accounted for only 45% of the bone fragments, while birds make up 40%.[25]

The diet of the Habitation's and Cap Tourmente's residents must have been based on starchy foods. The food people ate at the time consisted mainly of cereal products (bread, biscuits and flat cakes), dried peas and salted cod or pork, simmered together in soups. The colonists drank diluted cider. An inventory drawn up by the de Caëns of the foodstuffs supplied 'to the boors [*manans*] and occupants of the settlement of Québec' from September 1627 to July 1629 lists as

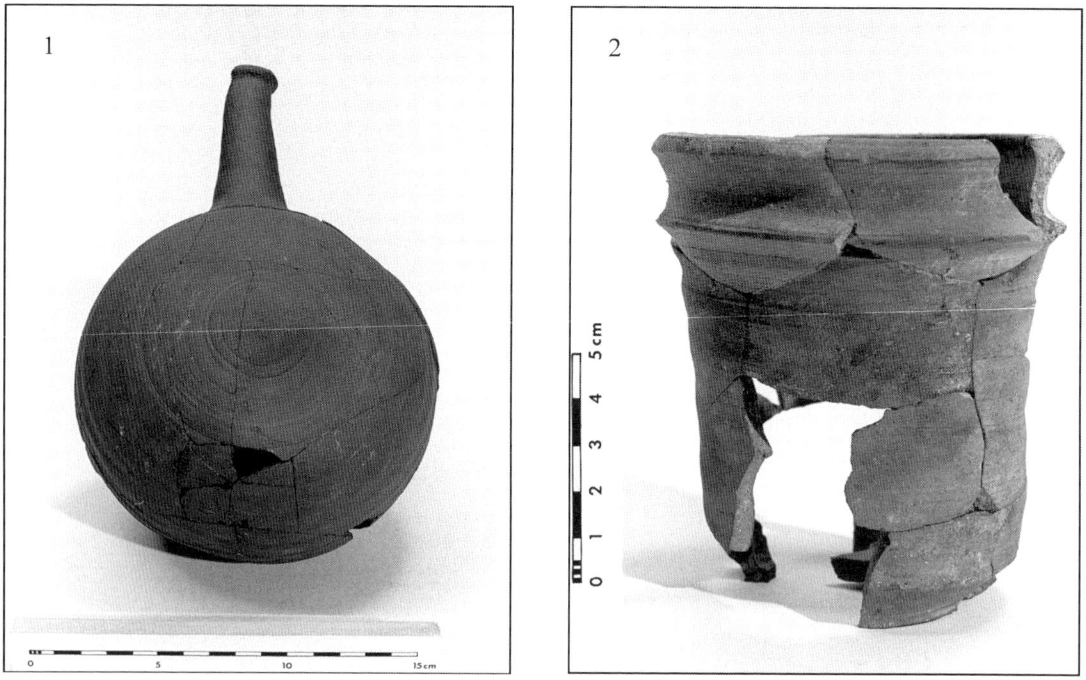

FIG. 9
Québec Habitation: 1. flask or costrel; 2. small Normandy stoneware pot (photograph, MACQ).

well corn and beans after peas, wine and beer alongside cider (*sildre*), and butter with the salted pork, butter, and plums.[26] A plum stone was recovered at Cap Tourmente, where remarkably a large quantity of broad beans was also found stored in a jar.[27]

This diet was the same as that eaten by sailors on transatlantic voyages and was the regular fare of the French lower classes. However, the craftsmen and labourers who came to Québec had probably never eaten salted cod or plums before. Their diet was rich in calories and perhaps sufficient in protein, but was poor in minerals and especially in vitamins.

The foodstuffs consumed were only partially responsible for the ravages caused by scurvy during the first winters spent in New France. Acute vitamin C deficiency is the outcome of a slow process which probably begins at birth.[28] The individuals who died had probably already suffered for a long time from its absence. Regardless of whether or not they had been to Canada, French people usually lost all their teeth before they reached middle age. This explains why the elite at places like Sainte-Croix, Port-Royal or Québec did not come down with scurvy. From childhood they must have eaten foodstuffs with a higher vitamin C content than had itinerant masons or carpenters and were thus better equipped to face the harsh climate of New France. Cold weather can only weaken a body that is already in a poor condition and unprepared for four or five months of snow and sometimes brutal cold. Vitamin C deficiency struck workers recruited from what would now be labelled an at-risk population.

It is difficult to imagine how grim life must have been in the Québec Habitation during the winter half of the year, when its residents were reduced by disease and lacked the company of women and children and even religious music to enliven their daily routine. By spring time life at the outpost must have ground to a standstill with the inhabitants anxiously awaiting news of the arrival of ships from France.

CONCLUSION

In the first quarter-century the merchant companies did not succeed in establishing a strong colony on the banks of the St Lawrence River. However, contrary to Champlain's repeated complaints, they accomplished much considering the inadequate political support and means at their disposal. When the Compagnie des Cent-Associés retook control of Québec, the layout of the future city was already in place, with commercial activities concentrated near the river and government administration in Upper Town. All that was needed to complete the urban plan was to transfer the religious communities from the Saint-Charles River to Upper Town and to eliminate agricultural activities. Indeed farming in Upper Town would soon be a thing of the past.

NOTES

[1] Le Blant & Baudry 1967, 168.
[2] Liebel 1999, 233, n. 14.
[3] Biggar 1971, **1**, 129; Champlain1973, 89–90.
[4] Biggar 1971, **2**, 24; Champlain 1973, 296.
[5] Le Blant & Baudry 1967, 154–61.
[6] 1 *toise* = 6 French feet = 1.96m.
[7] Biggar 1971, **2**, 35–6; Champlain 1973, 303–4.
[8] Champlain 1973, 227.
[9] Le Blant & Baudry 1967, 313.
[10] Biggar 1971, **3**, 172–3; Champlain 1973, 593.
[11] Le Blant & Baudry 1967, 361.
[12] Biggar 1971, **5**, 8; Champlain 1973, 990.
[13] Biggar 1971, **5**, 277; Champlain 1973, 1157.
[14] ANQQ, greffe G. Audouart, 15 Sept. 1634.
[15] Campeau 1979, 365, 378.
[16] Champlain 1973, 1304–5.
[17] Guimont 1996, 32–52.
[18] Biggar 1971, **5**, 203; Champlain 1973, 1110.
[19] ASQ, fonds Laverdière, no. 126–II; Provost 1961, 98–103.
[20] Simoneau 1996; Rouleau 2003.
[21] Champlain 1973, 1055.
[22] Duguay 1996, 72–4.
[23] ANQQ, greffe M. Piraube, 21 Oct. 1639.
[24] Rick 1985, 309–65.
[25] Guimont 1996, 222–4.
[26] ADSM, Tabellionnage de Rouen, Meubles, ser. 1, 20 Jan. 1631.
[27] Guimont 1996, 40, 56.
[28] Larocque 2005.

BIBLIOGRAPHY

PUBLISHED SOURCES

Biggar, H.P. (ed.) 1971 [1922–36], *The Works of Samuel de Champlain*, facs. edn, Toronto: University Press.

Campeau, L. 1979, *Monumenta Novæ Franciæ*, **2**. *Établissement à Québec (1616–1634)*, Québec: Presses de l'Université Laval.

Champlain, S. de 1613, *Les Voyages du Sieur de Champlain*, Paris: Jean Berjon.

Champlain, S. de 1973, *Œuvres*, Montréal: Éditions du Jour.

Duguay, G. 1996, 'Par les routes du nord: des terres cuites communes pour la ferme de Champlain', in Guimont 1996, 70–4.

Guimont, J. 1996, *La Petite-Ferme du cap Tourmente: de la ferme de Champlain aux grandes volées d'oies*, Sillery: Septentrion.

Le Blant, R. & Baudry, R. 1967, *Nouveaux documents sur Champlain et son époque*, **1**, Ottawa: Public Archives of Canada.

Liebel, J. 1999, *Pierre Dugua, sieur de Mons, fondateur de Québec*, Paris: Le Croît Vif.

Niellon, F. & Moussette, M. (eds) 1985, *L'Habitation de Champlain*, Collection Patrimoines, Dossiers **58**.

Provost, H. 1961, 'La Maison Couillard', *Cahiers Hist. Soc. hist. Québec* **13**, 98–103.

Rick, A.M. 1985, 'Étude zooarchéologique du site de l'Habitation de Champlain: périodes 1608–1632 et 1675–1700', in Niellon & Moussette 1985, 309–56.

UNPUBLISHED SOURCES

Larocque, R. 2005, 'Les Pathologies bucco-dentaires de deux époques et leurs causes: les cas comparés de Louisbourg et de l'île Sainte-Croix', Québec: AAQ 24th Annual Conference paper.

Rouleau, S. 2003, 'Recherches archéologiques: fouilles de la maison Couillard (CeEt-32)', Québec: Ville de Québec, Service de l'aménagement du territoire.

Simoneau, D. 1996, 'Recherches archéologiques dans la cour des Petits du Séminaire de Québec (CeEt-32)', Québec: Ville de Québec, Division design et patrimoine.

ABBREVIATIONS

AAQ	Association des archéologues du Québec
ADSM	Archives départementales de la Seine-Maritime, Rouen, France
ANQQ	Archives nationales du Québec à Québec
ASQ	Archives du Séminaire de Québec, Québec
MACQ	Ministère des Affaires culturelles du Québec

SUMMARY IN FRENCH, GERMAN, ITALIAN AND SPANISH

RÉSUMÉ

Québec au temps de Champlain

Quand Champlain mourut en 1635, le comptoir commercial qu'il avait fondé en 1608 constituait l'embryon de l'implantation permanente. Les vicissitudes lui ont assuré un développement lent et hésitant. Les artefacts trouvés à Québec et dans la ferme de Cap Tourmente montre que ces implantations étaient majoritairement approvisionnées avec des marchandises de l'arrière-pays des ports français dans lesquels les compagnies marchandes étaient basées. Les maisons sur le Saint-Laurent étaient de petites dimensions et construites en bois et torchis. Les artisans et les laboureurs expatriés consommaient un régime maritime standard complété par des prunes approvisionnées de France.

ZUSAMMENFASSUNG

Quebec und die Zeit Champlains

Als Champlain 1635 starb, bildete die Handelsstation, die er 1608 gegründet hatte, den Kern der dauerhaften Besiedlung. Die Unbeständigkeit beim Zugeständnis von Privilegien verursachte, daß die Entwicklung nur langsam und schleppend voran ging. Die Artefakte, die man in Quebec und auf der Farm Cap Tourmente fand zeigen, daß diese Siedlungen im wesentlichen mit Gütern aus dem Hinterland der französischen Häfen versorgt wurden, woher auch die Handelsgesellschaften stammten. Die Häuser am St Lawrence-Fluß bestanden aus kleinen Fachwerkbauten. Die eingewanderten Handwerker und Arbeiter aßen gewöhnliche Seemannskost, die durch Pflaumen aus Frankreich aufgebessert wurde.

RIASSUNTO

Il Quebec ai tempi di Champlain

Alla morte di Champlain nel 1635, l'emporio che aveva fondato nel 1608 era divenuto l'embrione di un insediamento stabile. Le vicissitudini legate all'assegnazione di privilegi garantivano che il suo sviluppo fosse stato lento e incerto. I manufatti rinvenuti in Quebec e nella fattoria di Cap Tourmente mostrano come questi insediamenti fossero principalmente provvisti di generi provenienti dall'entroterra dei porti francesi in cui avevano sede le compagnie mercantili. Le case lungo il San Lorenzo erano piccole e costruite con legno e mattoni crudi. I lavoratori e gli artigiani emigrati avevano una dieta simile a quella dei pescatori, integrata con prugne provenienti dalla Francia.

RESUMEN

Quebec en el tiempo de Champlain

Cuando Champlain murió en 1635 el pequeño núcleo comercial que había fundado en 1608 fue el embrión de un asentamiento permanente. Diversas vicisitudes a la hora de asignarle privilegios supusieron que su desarrollo fuera lento. Los materiales encontrados en Quebec y en la granja de Cap Tourmente demuestran que estos yacimientos fueron proveídos principalmente con materiales de la zona circundante a los puertos franceses donde las compañías mercantes estaban basadas. Las casas en el St Lawrence eran pequeñas y construidas de madera y tapial. Artesanos y jornaleros expatriados consumían una dieta estándar suplementada con ciruelas llegadas de Francia.

514 rue Saint-Olivier #1, Québec (Québec), Canada G1R 1H1

Post-Medieval Archaeology **43/1** (2009), 213–228

The Seminary of Québec site: from New France's earliest farm to its first religious institution

By DANIEL SIMONEAU

SUMMARY: In 1991–2002 the first full archaeological excavations were conducted on the Seminary of Québec site. Numerous studies, based mainly on historical sources, had previously established the sequence of major events and physical developments relating to it. Louis Hébert, traditionally regarded as the country's first settler, took possession of the site in 1617; structural, artefactual and environmental evidence was found relating to the Hébert-Couillard period which preceded the foundation of the seminary in 1663. Neither the houses of Guillaume Couillard and Louis Hébert nor the Petit Séminaire erected by Mgr de Laval were situated where previously thought.

INTRODUCTION

The Seminary of Québec is located on a low hill, formerly called Sault-au-Matelot, which forms part of the promontory on which the city stands. It is a large building complex that includes components dating from the time of Mgr de Laval, who founded the seminary in the 17th century (Fig. 1). The site comprises two plateaux. The first, which is the flatter and higher of the two, occupies the western portion and is bounded to the north, north-west and east by steep inclines. The second, which is much bigger, extends north and east from the foot of these inclines, and slopes very slightly towards the north-east.

THE SITE'S ORIGINAL ENVIRONMENT

Data gathered during archaeological fieldwork have provided a picture of the site's original environment. The upper plateau and the northern part of the lower one were fed by an underground spring that flowed in from the south.[1] This spring has been uncovered on a few occasions over the years, particularly on the site of the present-day Anglican Cathedral of the Holy Trinity and in the basements of the old Holt Renfrew building and Notre-Dame Basilica-Cathedral. Several 17th-century plans indicate a fountain or well and even a pond at this spot. The pond was perhaps a vestige of the palaeoenvironment which was maintained for practical reasons during the historic period. Trenches dug in 1993[2] and 1994[3] showed that there are still fairly substantial inflows of underground water in the eastern part of the lower plateau, as water appeared rapidly in the trenches when they reached a certain depth. Moreover, the presence of certain types of plant macro remains in this area showed that water had accumulated there in pools.

The plant taxa recovered from the original soil layer in the eastern part of the site demonstrate that the terrain was originally open and dotted with native shrubs, such as elder, raspberry, wild cherry, aralia and cranberry.[4] American green alder also grew in high thickets in this area, and birch seems to have been predominant.[5] Generally speaking, the site was characterized 'by the alternation of grass-covered zones with wooded areas (shrubby undergrowth) and had a number of outcropping shaly ridges. It is even likely that small, clay-bottomed ponds were found in some of the depressions between these ridges'.[6] The presence of spores and certain types of pollen indicates that

DOI: 10.1179/007942309X12457508844323

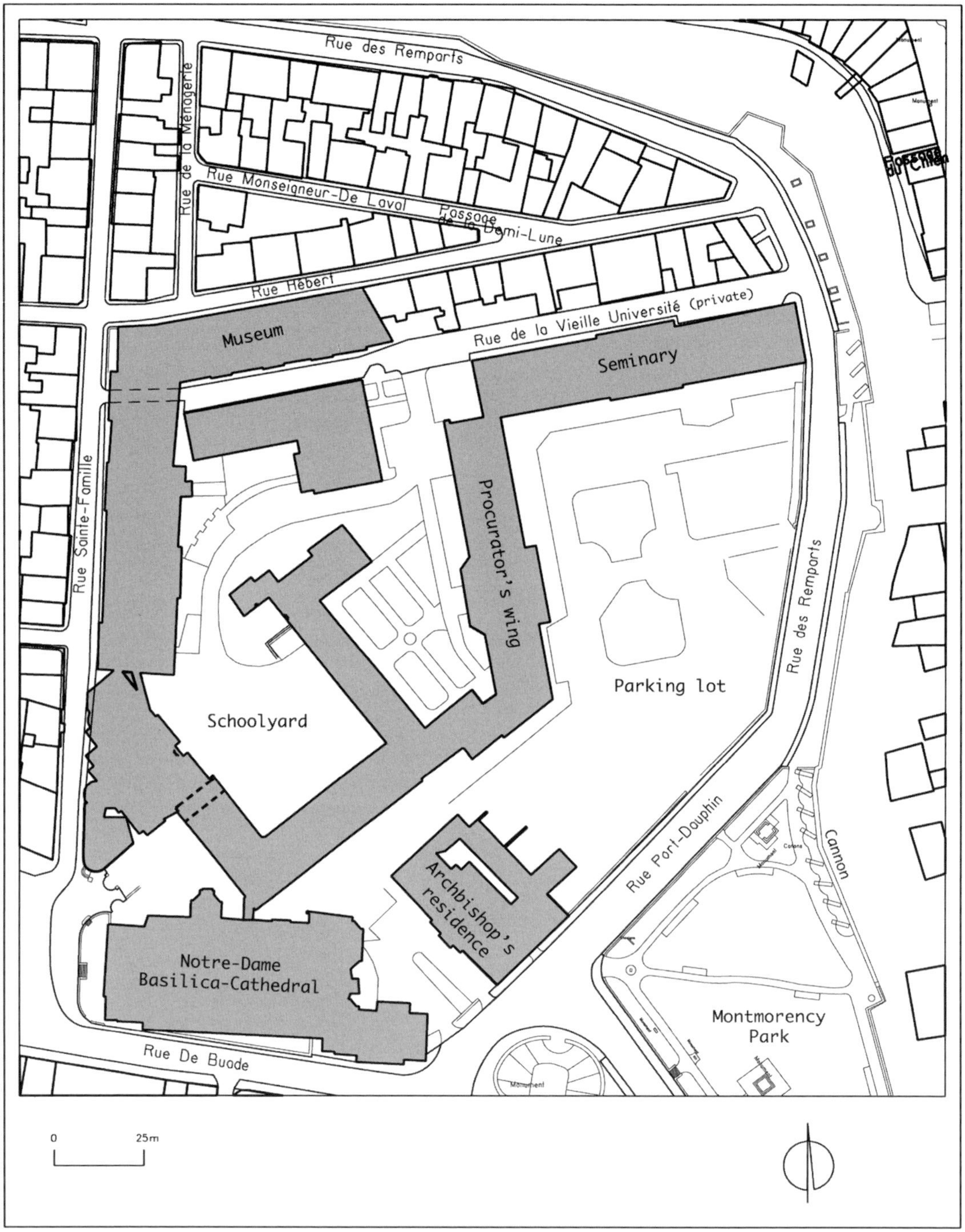

FIG. 1
Seminary of Québec site (CeEt-32): plan of the seminary complex (drawn by F. Pellerin, Ville de Québec).

this sector was shady and poorly drained. Archaeological research on the seminary site has thus made it possible to picture this area when the first French settlers visited it.

A WELL-ESTABLISHED HISTORY

Mgr de Laval was not the first owner of the land that was to become the Seminary of Québec site. Louis Hébert, traditionally known as Canada's first settler, was initially granted this property and took possession of it in 1617. He and his son-in-law Guillaume Couillard were close associates of Samuel de Champlain. The seminary site is thus deeply rooted in Canadian history. Historians began to take an interest in it very early on, and it has since been the focus of many studies.

The history of this site is extremely rich. Its occupation by the Hébert-Couillard families and the subsequent founding and development of the seminary cover more than 390 years. Various buildings and other features testify to this roughly four-century period of human occupation and development. Those that have survived to this day have witnessed momentous events in the history of New France.

The history of the seminary site has been studied for many years; studies and publications have discussed the institution's origins, exploits, misfortunes and accomplishments. They have identified the historical context in which each of its buildings was constructed and altered; every addition of new structures or change in existing ones testified to the institution's growing importance, financial health or misfortunes. However, few researchers have published their results. Those who have done so were active at different times over many years, from about 1860 to 1993; they consist mainly of Frs Azarie Couillard-Després and Noël Baillargeon, who published their findings, respectively, in 1934 and in 1972; Fr Honorius Provost, who wrote regularly on the seminary throughout the 1960s; and André Vachon, the latest researcher to take an interest in this question, who published a study in 1993. Thanks to these researchers, an official history of the seminary site and an understanding of its physical evolution have been established. However, no real synthesis of this information has ever been written.

When the findings of these authors are summarized for the period associated with the Hébert-Couillard family, the following 'official version' of its historical sequence is obtained. It will be demonstrated later in this paper that in some respects the account is questionable.

Louis Hébert landed at Québec on Saturday, 15 July 1617.[7] He was accompanied by his entire family: his wife Marie Rollet, his children and his brother-in-law Claude.[8] Even though he was under contract to work for the Compagnie des Marchands, he began to cultivate his land.[9] His property would be established as a noble landholding, the fief of Sault-au-Matelot, on 28 February 1626.[10] In the meantime, in 1621, Guillemette Hébert, Louis' daughter, married Guillaume Couillard, a carpenter in the service of the Compagnie des Marchands. At the time of their marriage the couple received half the Sault-au-Matelot fiefdom, although, according to the historian Noël Baillargeon, the gift had been granted to Guillemette alone.[11] From then on, the property would be exploited jointly by Hébert and Couillard.

Louis Hébert died on 25 January 1627 following an accident.[12] However, it was not until seven years later that his inheritance was divided up, probably in anticipation of the marriage of his son, Guillaume. On this occasion, the Couillard couple received confirmation that they would own half of the Sault-au-Matelot fiefdom, while the other half would go to Hébert's son and Guillaume Huboust, who had married Hébert's widow, Marie Rollet.[13] The land was already well developed at the time, containing not only the houses and secondary buildings of Couillard and Guillaume Huboust, but also a brewhouse with outbuildings, a mill and an associated dwelling, a barn, a stable, and several pathways and tracks.[14] It also contained a house in front of the brewhouse, 'three other buildings (one with a chimney and the two others serving, respectively, as a barn and a stable) and a "fountain"'.[15] The Couillard house stood quite close to the east façade of the present-day procurator's wing (*aile de la Procure*) of the seminary complex, near the wing's main door.[16] It was a timber-framed structure with two chimneys and was enlarged in 1653.[17]

Mgr de Laval arrived in Québec on 16 June 1659;[18] four years later he founded the Séminaire des Missions Étrangères.[19] He soon planned to acquire the fiefdom of Sault-au-Matelot, which, in addition to being very large, had the advantage of being situated beside the church of Notre-Dame-de-la-Recouvrance. Guillaume Couillard died in 1663. His widow kept the property;[20] she agreed to sell it for 8,000 *livres*;[21] the contract was signed on 10 April 1666.[22] The sale, however, was contested by Couillard's heirs, leading to an imbroglio which was not resolved until 1674.[23] This probably explains why Mgr de Laval did not undertake any major projects there. Nonetheless, he eventually set up his Petit Séminaire, using the Couillard house to lodge the students.[24] Classes began on 9 October 1668,[25] and thirteen boarders were accepted.[26] Once the title deeds were properly established, Mgr de Laval was able to proceed with the rest of his plans.

REVIEW OF THE HISTORICAL DOCUMENTS

As preparations were made for archaeological work on the seminary site, the historical data were revisited, often using new approaches and previously neglected documents. As a result, certain details have taken on greater importance and significantly supplemented the established historical sequence. It has thus been possible to expand slightly on the site's history and development, and even make certain revisions or adjustments to conclusions drawn in the past.

It can now be said that Louis Hébert probably built his house fairly rapidly. The contract binding him to the Compagnie des Marchands stipulated that, after two years in the exclusive service of the company (1619–21), he would have to rely solely on his own resources for food and other needs.[27] In 1618, however, Champlain mentioned arable land that was 'sown and filled with fine grain', which can only have been the land that Hébert was farming on the Sault-au-Matelot promontory.[28] Therefore, within barely a year of their arrival, Hébert and his family seem to have developed the land and were probably already living there. Furthermore, a reference dating from July 1620 reports that Champlain's labourers were building a stone house for Hébert; it was situated on his 'tillage'.[29] It is unlikely that this was Hébert's first house, for his contract with the Compagnie des Marchands had already expired one year earlier. The construction work in question may have been undertaken to expand the house that Hébert was already living in, but it seems more likely that it was for a new dwelling. Several researchers agree that Louis Hébert's house was transferred to his son Guillaume following the partition of Louis' property in 1634[30] and that this was the completed dilapidated house[31] that Guillaume Couillard acquired in 1644.[32] According to an appraisal of 1639, it was located near the Couillard house; it comprised two sections, one timber-framed, the other of masonry, and measured 38 × 19 French feet (12.43 × 6.21m). However, when Guillaume Hébert died in 1639, he was surely not living there, even though he owned the house, as the appraisal declared it was 'uninhabitable and unoccupiable'.[33] Indeed, the inventory of his property made one month earlier stipulated that he lived near the church. Clearly, the dwelling he occupied at that time was habitable; in fact, it was the house of his wife, Hélène Desportes, who had received it as a dowry from Champlain.[34] Considering that the structure was described as ruinous in 1639, it was probably one of the first dwellings erected on the fiefdom and was possibly her father's.

As mentioned earlier, Guillaume Couillard married Guillemette Hébert, Louis' daughter, in 1621. It is not known exactly when the couple built their house, but it is generally assumed they did so shortly after they married. A building contract for expanding the dwelling, concluded in 1653, indicates that it was to be entirely timber-framed and that the new part would measure 18 French feet (5.89m) long by exactly the same width as the original structure.[35] The contract also indicated that the house was to have two chimneys.

Although the historical sources reveal the existence of a number of buildings, paths and shared facilities, they contain almost no information about the location of these features or even about the shape and size of the plots that were handed down to Hébert's heirs when the property was divided. For example, the 1634 partition deed is almost incomprehensible in this regard, as the landmarks to which it refers are unknown. Similarly, graphic sources are not very helpful, as only two plans illustrate components of Sault-au-Matelot before it was developed by the Seminary of Québec. The first dates from 1664 and indicates, through a rough sketch, that a fountain was located there (Fig. 2).[36] The second, which dates from 1670, shows the fiefdom after it was acquired by Mgr de Laval but before the first seminary structures were erected (Fig. 3). However, the number of buildings indicated on this plan is far less than the number mentioned in the partition deed. The plan illustrates a large garden and no more than three buildings, one of which is larger than the others and can be identified as the house of the clergy. This was no doubt the house formerly occupied by the Couillards.

It is hard to paint a more precise portrait of the seminary site's occupation using the historical sources currently available. Consequently, it has become imperative to make use of new data. Archaeology has provided this precious information, which, in some cases, has called certain earlier conclusions into question.

ARCHAEOLOGY AT THE SEMINARY

Even though the discovery of masonry remains in 1866 first sparked interest in the history of the seminary, many years passed before archaeology could make its own contribution to this area of enquiry.

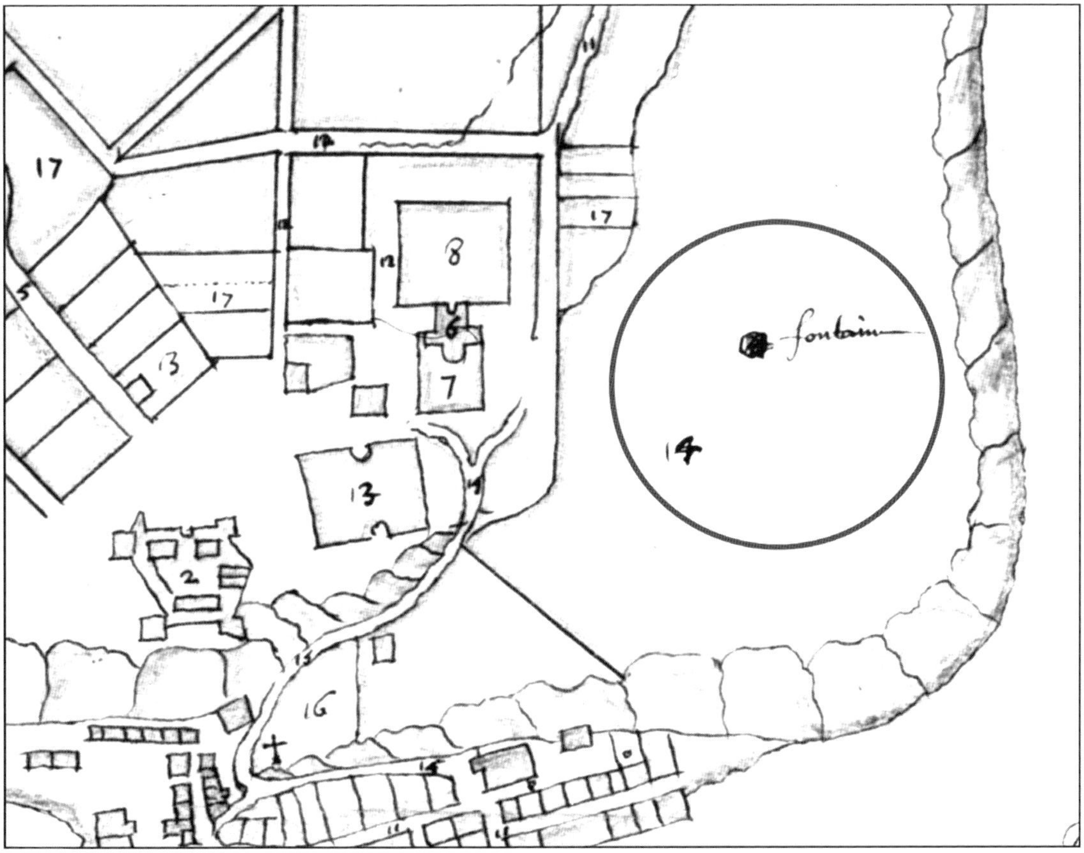

FIG. 2

Véritable plan de Québec comme il est l'an 1664 et les fortifications que l'on puisse faire, Jean Bourdon, 1664: detail (NAC, C21758).

To date, thirteen archaeological interventions have been carried out on the site; they have given rise to reports of varying scope. The research has varied from simple observation following mechanical excavation and archaeological monitoring during mechanical digging to full-scale archaeological excavations.

The first intervention was conducted in 1866 by 'occasional archaeologist' Fr C.H. Laverdière next to the main door on the east façade of the procurator's wing (Fig. 5). Another 104 years would pass before the rich archaeological heritage of the seminary site would attract new interest. The institution's buildings underwent many changes in the meantime, but none of this work was monitored for potential archaeological discoveries.

In 1970, Québec government archaeologist Michel Gaumond was called to the site when excavation beneath the corridor of the parlour wing (*aile des Parloirs*) uncovered human burials.[37] He returned the following year, but simply in an advisory capacity. In 1986, after another fifteen-year interval with no fieldwork, a series of archaeological investigations, often large, began to be undertaken on the seminary site; the main one, in 1991, involved major excavations by the City of Québec.[38] Other archaeological work was later carried out by the City, with the most recent field study taking place in 2002.[39]

All of these archaeological investigations yielded discoveries, and all of these finds, which were often surprising, shed fresh light on the seminary's history. Moreover, they soon raised questions about new and unexpected aspects of the site's occupation, particularly by the Hébert-Couillard family.

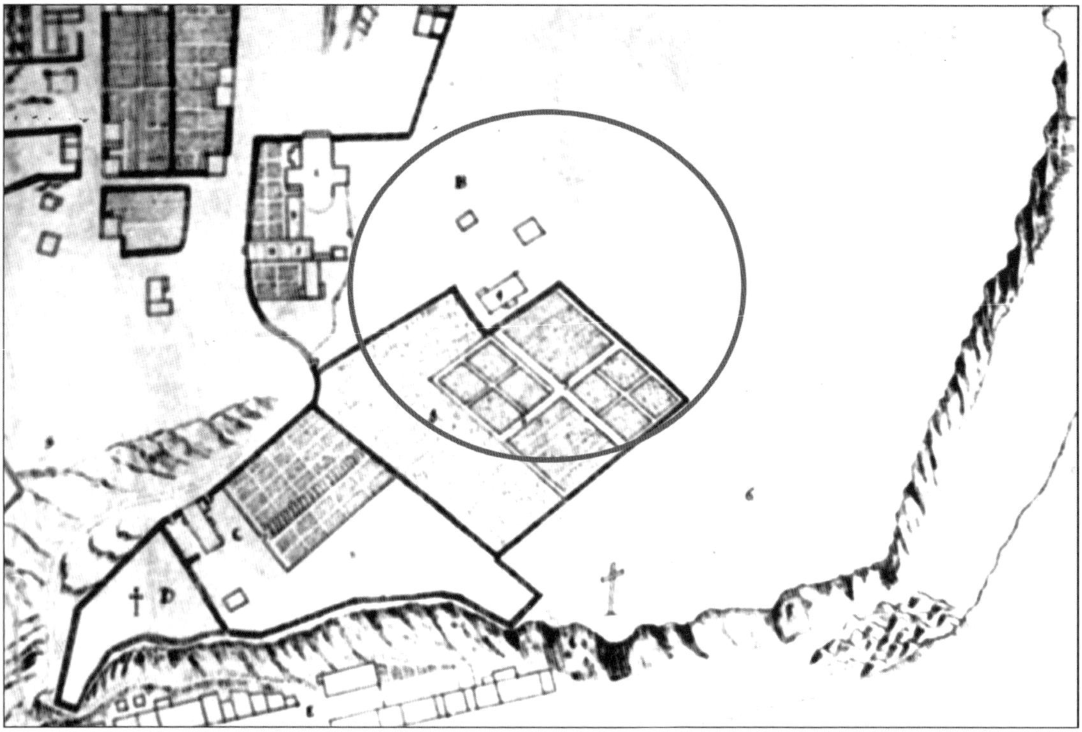

FIG. 3
La ville haute et basse de Québec en la Nouvelle-France, Vateau, 1670: detail (ASQ, tiroir 213, 29, fiche Z 3).

THE CONTRIBUTION OF ARCHAEOLOGY

Prior to the archaeological fieldwork, knowledge about the occupation of the site by the Hébert-Couillard family was very restricted; it was based on the interpretation of limited and fragmentary historical information which offered no insight into major aspects of the site's history. The contribution of archaeology has thus been crucial in filling in a number of gaps.

Credit for the first archaeological intervention on the seminary site, in 1866, goes to Fr Charles-Honoré Laverdière. He uncovered the foundations of a building beside the east façade of the procurator's wing. It was laid out on a slightly different angle from the wing (Figs 4–5), was orientated north–south, and measured roughly 17 × 7m overall. It consisted of two adjoining sections, the one to the south being a little wider than that to the north. It seems that the building had suffered the effects of age, since portions of its walls were missing. However, Fr Laverdière offered a reconstructed plan of the structure in which the missing portions were marked by dotted lines. He noted a large gap in the east wall of the building's south section, which must have marked the position of a large door since he did draw dotted lines there to indicate missing walling. The remains were identified as those of the Couillard family's house.[40] Their location corresponded fairly closely to that proposed on the basis of the 1670 plan; moreover, the fact that they consisted of two adjoining sections tallied with the known historical data, which indicated that Couillard had enlarged his house in 1653.[41] As was normal at the time, no specialized studies were conducted and nothing is known about any artefacts which may have been found.

Another 125 years would pass before archaeological fieldwork in 1991 uncovered a second building associated with this period; only part of the building's remains were uncovered during these investigations.[42] The building stood beside the west façade of the procurator's wing, precisely parallel to the structure discovered in 1866 (Fig. 5). Although it was impossible to determine the building's dimensions, since none of its corners was uncovered, it was at least noted that this also

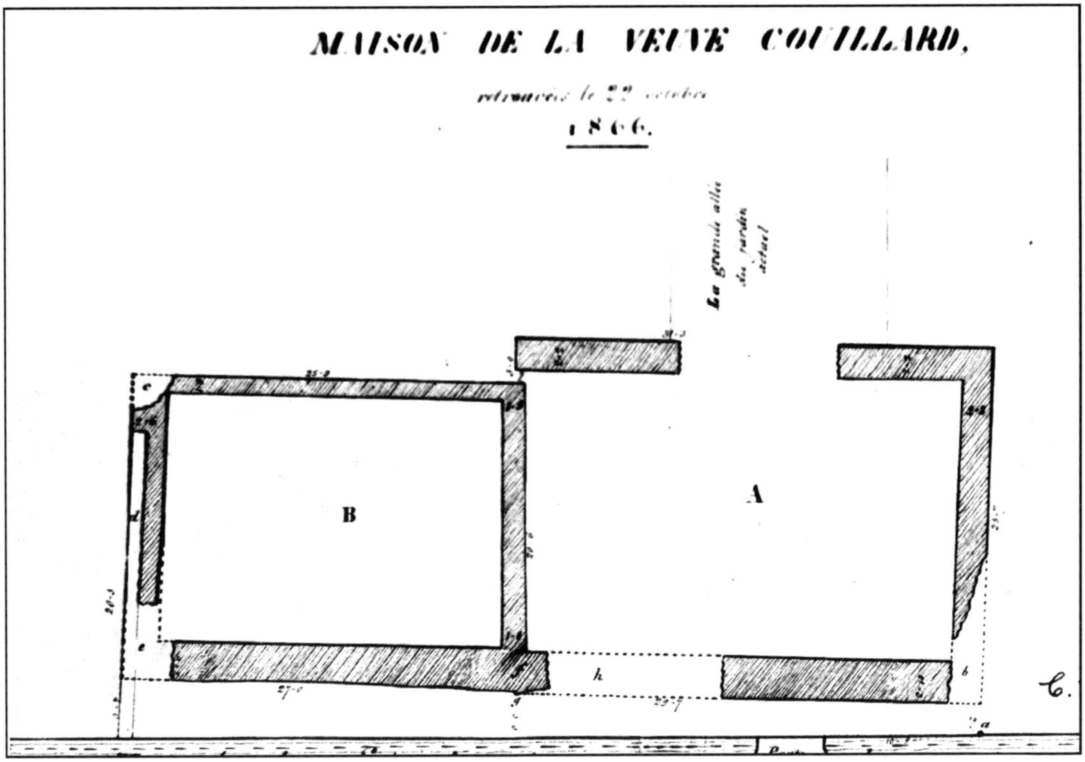

FIG. 4

Plan des fondations de la maison de la veuve Couillard retrouvées le 22 octobre 1866, C.H. Laverdière, 1866: detail (ASQ, fonds Laverdière, no. 126-II).

consisted of two adjoining sections. The south section had very crudely built foundations but enclosed traces of a wooden floor lying directly on hard-packed earth. Stones partially visible in one of the sides of the excavation trench pointed to the presence of a hearth against the north wall of this part of the building. The building's north section was of much less rudimentary construction, and the fact that it did not contain traces of a floor lying directly on the ground suggested that its floor was raised in order to create a crawl-space. These characteristics indicated that the north section was more recent than the south one. Moreover, the south section, with its floor resting on the ground, illustrated the transfer of a European architectural model to Québec without any adaptation to the latter's much harsher climate.

The 1991 fieldwork also yielded additional data on the building's immediate environment. Excavations in the south-west part of the seminary's present-day schoolyard, where the well dated by some historians to the Hébert-Couillard occupation was located, clearly demonstrated that the area was not used during the period when these families lived on the site. Therefore, this well could not be the 'fountain' mentioned in the 1634 deed of partition or shown on the plan of 1664. In fact, the 'fountain' referred to in these documents is more likely to be the one that appears on the plan of 1692 (Fig. 6), in the area where the Musée de l'Amérique française now stands.

Numerous artefacts, as well as plant and animal remains, were recovered during the excavation of the levels associated with the building found in 1991. These finds come mainly from the east side of the structure; their analysis has been very instructive. First, the collection showed that the building was occupied from roughly the end of the first quarter of the 17th century to around the end of the third quarter, and that its function was essentially domestic. It was therefore a main dwelling rather than an outbuilding or some sort of workshop. In addition, many of the objects uncovered were of high quality and thus testified to

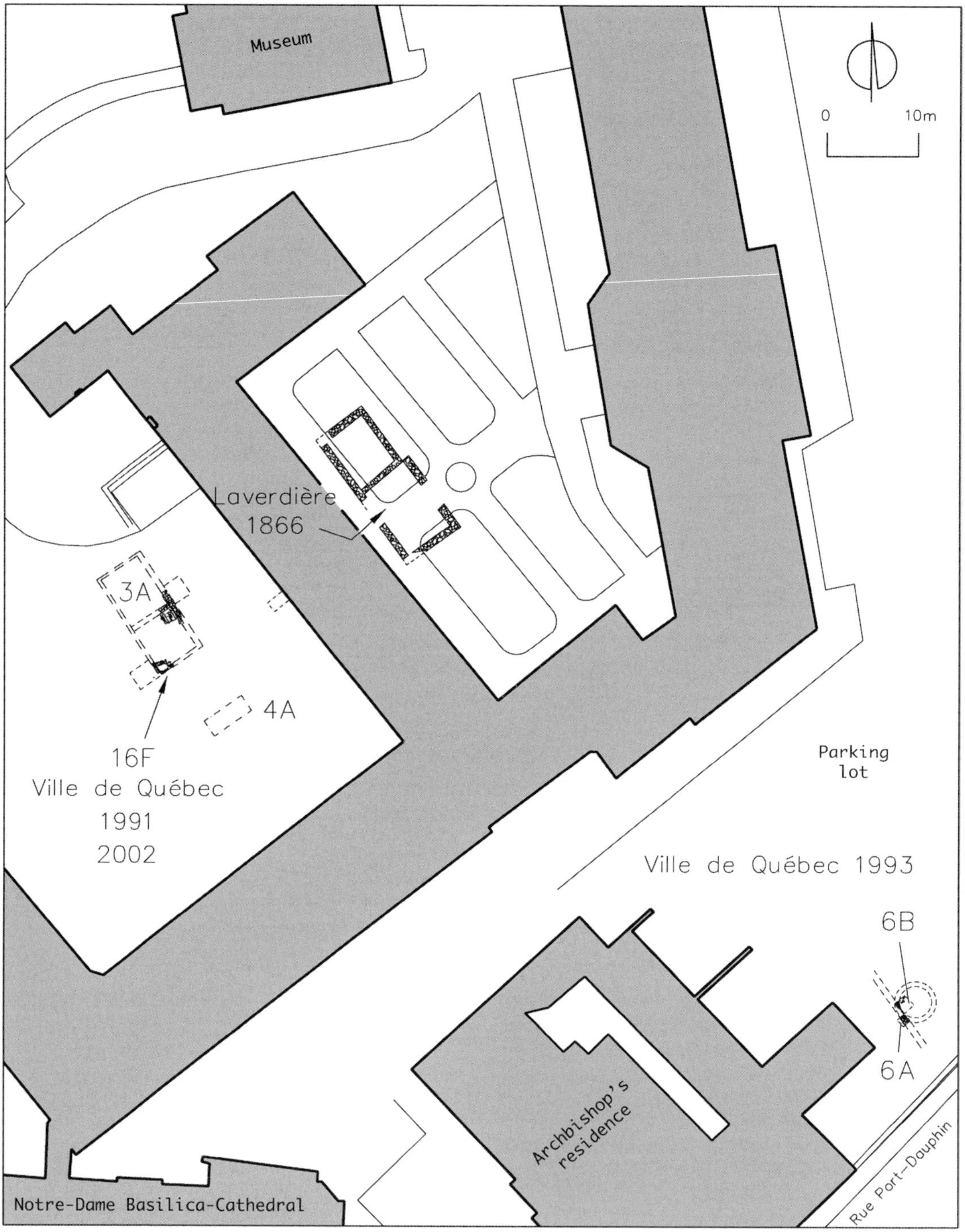

FIG. 5
Seminary of Québec site (CeEt-32): plan of known structural remains associated with the Hébert-Couillard family occupation (drawn by F. Pellerin, Ville de Québec).

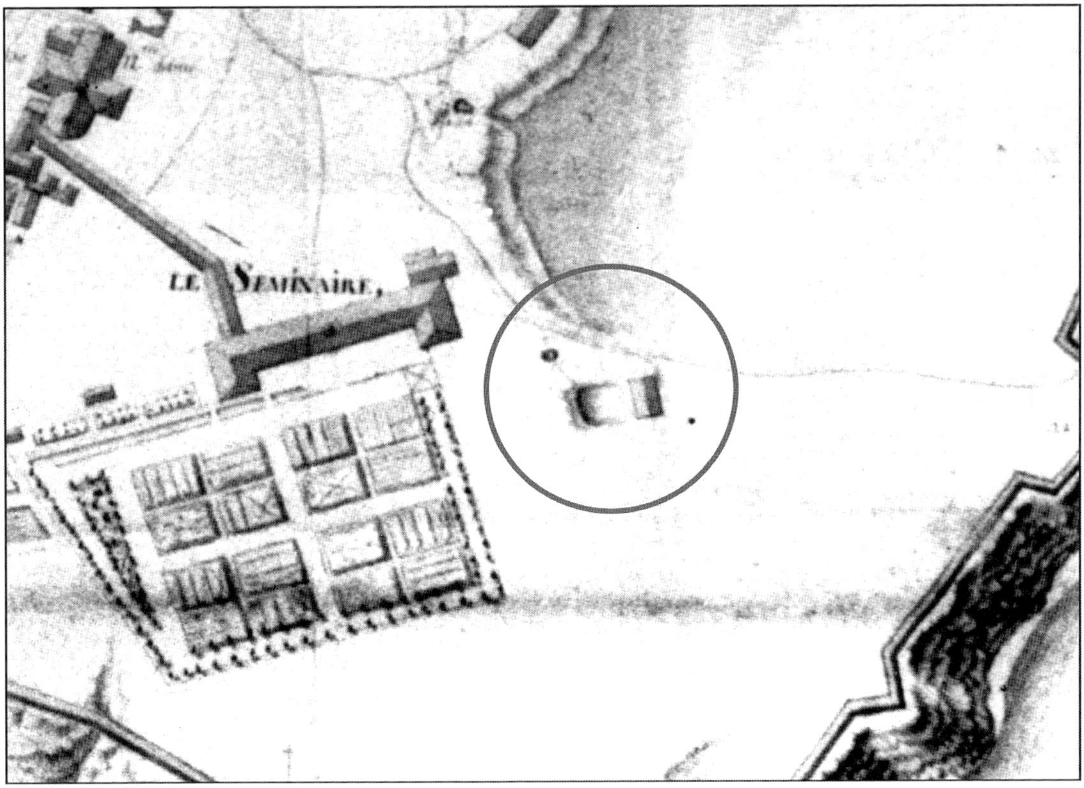

FIG. 6
Plan de la ville de Québec en la Nouvelle-France, Villeneuve, 1692: detail (ANOM).

a fairly affluent and refined standard of living. Besides objects associated with the preparation and consumption of food and beverages, the collection contained coins, hunting-related objects and items associated with sewing.[43]

Table scraps shed light on the household's daily diet,[44] which seems to have been varied and of high quality. The occupants most frequently ate pork, but also a large amount of beef; there are also indications that they ate lamb, although in much smaller quantities, as well as goose and probably chicken. This basic menu was often supplemented with game, particularly beaver, but also moose, duck, wild goose, partridge and passenger pigeon. Fish also served as a supplement, with channel catfish being eaten most often; however, sturgeon, which were abundant in the St Lawrence River, formed part of the diet as well. Interestingly, the collection contained the remains of a haddock, a type of fish which had to be imported, usually in salted or dried form. In short, the faunal remains recovered from the site showed that raising domestic animals, hunting and fishing were important means of obtaining food for the occupants of this house. The remains also revealed that hunting and fishing were probably sources of income as well — a conclusion based primarily on the presence of beaver. Lastly, some of the bones indicated that the occupants had vermin problems and had probably tried to combat them by keeping a cat.

The few plant remains indicated that the residents also ate wild berries, particularly raspberries.[45] The presence of a henbane seed, from a plant grown essentially for its powerful medicinal properties, was probably related to Louis Hébert's work as an apothecary.

Excavation just south of the dwelling also unearthed a traffic area whose well-paved surface had a clear affinity with what we would call 'macadam'. Although it was established that this surface was contemporary with the Hébert-Couillard occupation, its edges were not found and therefore its direction is unknown. Clearly, however, the occupants were concerned about the aesthetics of their surroundings; at this date one would have expected to find a path of hard-packed earth.

These discoveries changed our understanding of the occupation of the site by the Hébert and Couillard families. First, they indicated that the occupants lived comfortably and were able to surround themselves with luxury items, a finding that contradicted the long-standing image of the poor deprived colonist. Secondly, it was clear that the house was the main dwelling occupied during the Hébert-Couillard period. Moreover, the structural remains' characteristics and location made it possible to consider seriously the possibility that this building was the Couillard house. This led to a review of Fr Laverdière's interpretation of the building he had uncovered on the opposite side of the procurator's wing.

On closer examination it was noted that several characteristics of the remains unearthed by Fr Laverdière in 1866 did not correspond with the house described in the historical documents. First, the remains did not include a chimney base, an essential component of any dwelling. Secondly, the documentary evidence recorded that when the Couillard house was enlarged in 1653, the addition measured 18 French feet (5.89m) long by the same width as the original part of the dwelling. The widths of Fr Laverdière's buildings did not coincide with one another, the south section being 1m wider. Neither did their lengths correspond to those recorded. According to the documents, Louis Hébert's house had a total length of only 12.3m. The combined length of the sections of building uncovered in 1866 was much longer: 17.5m. Moreover, if the interpretation of the large gap in the east wall as a wide door is correct, this would support the interpretation of the structure as an outbuilding such as a barn. Lastly, Fr Laverdière's plan indicates what seems to be the beginning of a wall extending northward; it is therefore possible that there was a third adjoining section to the north. The feature uncovered in 1866 could therefore have been a row structure consisting of three adjoining buildings.

Thus analysis of the new data obtained by the end of fieldwork in 1991 changed our perception of the occupation of the site during the Hébert-Couillard period, and provided a new basis for studying the ways and quality of life of these families. It presented an opportunity to use new data to give consideration to the study of the spatial organization of the property during this period — an important aspect of the site's history.

The site's spatial organization was documented further during the next archaeological field study, carried out in 1993 in the car park next to Rue des Remparts.[46] Two of the trenches dug on that occasion uncovered the remains of a third structure dating from the Hébert-Couillard period (Fig. 5). This building had exactly the same orientation as the other two structures found on the site, even though it was situated much further south, bounded on one side by the car park's enclosure wall and on the other by the property attached to the archbishop's residence. The remains consisted of a stone wall; in view of the presence of a floor, it may have been a dwelling. Since none of the structure's corners was found, it was impossible to determine its dimensions. Abutting the east side of this wall was a second masonry feature, which seemed to be circular in shape and whose diameter was estimated at about 4.5m. Little information was recovered about the use of the building to which these two features belonged. Their dimensions suggest that the circular feature may have had a wooden superstructure, while the other one would have been entirely of stone.

Interestingly, analysis of the surrounding stratigraphy showed that this building was demolished well before the seminary period. Its demolition debris had been left undisturbed and, according to the archaeological evidence (mainly intact but very fragile gastropods), the walls soon enclosed a pond formed by the periodic inflow of large amounts of water. The structure was filled in naturally by a process of sedimentation over a long period.

The latest archaeological investigations to yield information on the Hébert-Couillard period were carried out in 2002, when the remains of the house uncovered in the schoolyard in 1991 were re-examined.[47] The earlier investigations had already provided strong evidence that this was the Couillard house; the conclusion was confirmed in 2002. In the latter excavation the south-west corner of the house was uncovered, along with the foundations of a small annexe abutting the west wall. The layout mirrored perfectly that shown on the plan of the Couillard house dated 1670. This new information made it possible to establish that the south section of the building measured 5.7 × 5.8m. As indicated earlier, the two sections of these structures were of equal width and the north section constituted an extension. Fragments of infill material and roughcast plaster associated with the structure showed that its south section was timber-framed, with vertical wooden wall-posts placed at intervals of over 160mm. On the outside, the spaces between the posts were infilled with a mixture of mortars which sometimes contained plant matter or pebbles. It was clear that the infill had been applied over a concentration of plant fibre, mainly grasses, suggesting that the spaces between the uprights were first packed with hay which was then covered with mortar, probably to improve the structure's insulation. A similar mortar coating over a concentration of plant fibre appears to have been applied inside the building; this seems also to have covered the framing timbers so that they would not be visible from within the house. The inner coating was better finished than that on the outside and was covered with whitewash. Therefore, the interior of the Couillard's house was white. Impressions in the fragments of infill, coupled with the scarcity of nails in the contexts excavated, suggest that the structure's timbers were fastened together mainly with wooden dowels or pegs.

These characteristics of the south, or older, part of the house show that it was different from the north one, which would have been built in 1653. Indeed, the walls of the north section were of vertical log construction, as indicated in the construction contract. In other words, no interstices were left between the upright wall members, unlike those in the older section, which we presume was built around 1620 or perhaps even earlier, as will be seen below. This sequence of building methods reflects the adaptation of a European construction model to the environment encountered in Québec.[48] Despite the structural differences between the two parts of the house, there is every reason to believe that their interior finish was identical.

A number of artefacts were found in the small annexe abutting the west wall of this house, including a brass ring that could have belonged to a young girl; gun flints and balls, all of which were unused; and a brass apothecary weight bearing an official fleur-de-lis stamp that points to an affiliation with Louis Hébert (Fig. 7:2). The presence of these objects strongly suggests that this small space was used for storage.

A CLEARER UNDERSTANDING OF THE SITE

The information obtained from the archaeological investigations on the seminary site has significantly increased our knowledge of the occupation associated with the Hébert and Couillard families. Although many parts of the site remain undocumented, our understanding now surpasses the framework previously defined by historical studies. Joint consideration of the archaeological and historical data allows a much clearer picture of the site during the Hébert-Couillard period to be presented. This is very different from that generally accepted previously and may be summarized as follows:

A house belonging to the Couillard family stood near the eastern edge of the small plateau on the Sault-au-Matelot property; its site is now occupied by the seminary's schoolyard. Artefactual, documentary and architectural evidence suggests that this dwelling was the first house of Louis Hébert and his family, which he gave to his daughter Guillemette when she married Guillaume Couillard. This conclusion is supported by the fact that Hébert built a new stone house in 1620 and gave his daughter's hand to Couillard and half of his fief to both his daughter and her husband the following year.

It is also known that the area beside the house was developed to some extent. At least part of the surface of the courtyard south of the building was paved; this may have been the property's entry-way. The zone along the east side of the house, on the edge of the plateau, was a 'high traffic' area and may have been one of the pathways that criss-crossed the property, leading to the 'fountain', for example. This 'fountain' was probably at the foot of the plateau, in the area where the museum now stands, rather than on top of the plateau as had long been thought. Lastly, the fact that numerous artefacts were found to the east of the house, while no traces of occupation were uncovered to the west, suggests that the most of the household's daily activities were carried out on the side of the dwelling that faced the river.

Several other structures also stood on the Sault-au-Matelot property: additional houses including the second dwelling of Louis Hébert, outbuildings, one or two mills and a brewhouse. At least two and perhaps three of them made up a row structure at the foot of the plateau, in front of the Couillard house. They were probably utilitarian buildings. If there really were three of them, they may correspond to a group of buildings mentioned in the documents which comprised a barn, stable and dwelling. The dwelling, referred to as the mill house, was mentioned in the partition deed of 1634.

As for the building uncovered in the parking lot next to Rue des Remparts, very little is known about it, except that it consisted of a four-sided structure, against which abutted another probably circular structure. The presence of a floor suggests that it may have been a dwelling. The data also revealed that this building was destroyed at a very early stage in the site's history and that its remains were left undisturbed and were not filled in. Almost immediately, it was occupied by a small pond at certain times of the year; eventually soil collected in it by simple sedimentation as water alternately accumulated and dried up. This pond can probably be seen to the south of the

FIG. 7

Seminary of Québec site (CeEt-32): 1. glass beads and coins; 2. small apothecary weight (60.4g; height: 20mm; diam.: 36mm at the rim, 26mm at the base). These artefacts were found in contexts associated with the occupation of the Couillard house (*c.* 1620–66).

procurator's wing on the plan drawn by Villeneuve in 1685 (Fig. 8). Indeed, part of it looks roughly circular, while the remaining part has a more or less rectangular contour.

Since this building was destroyed during the Couillard occupation and was located inside the limits of Sault-au-Matelot, it may have been the house that belonged to Guillaume Hébert. His dwelling was already a complete ruin and was deemed uninhabitable in 1639. It is generally accepted that Guillaume's house was originally owned by his father Louis and that Guillaume finally inherited it when the fiefdom was divided in 1634. The remains under the parking lot next to Rue des Remparts may therefore be those of the dwelling that Louis Hébert built in 1620. Although the archaeological data gathered to date are very limited, they support this hypothesis; indeed, Champlain stipulated that this house should be made of stone.[49] The circular feature abutting the straight section of this building may have been a dovecote, an amenity that only seigneurs were entitled to own. Therefore, the hypothesis that the remains under the parking area are associated with the Hébert house is plausible. If so, the dwelling was located in the south-east part of the fief, as Fr

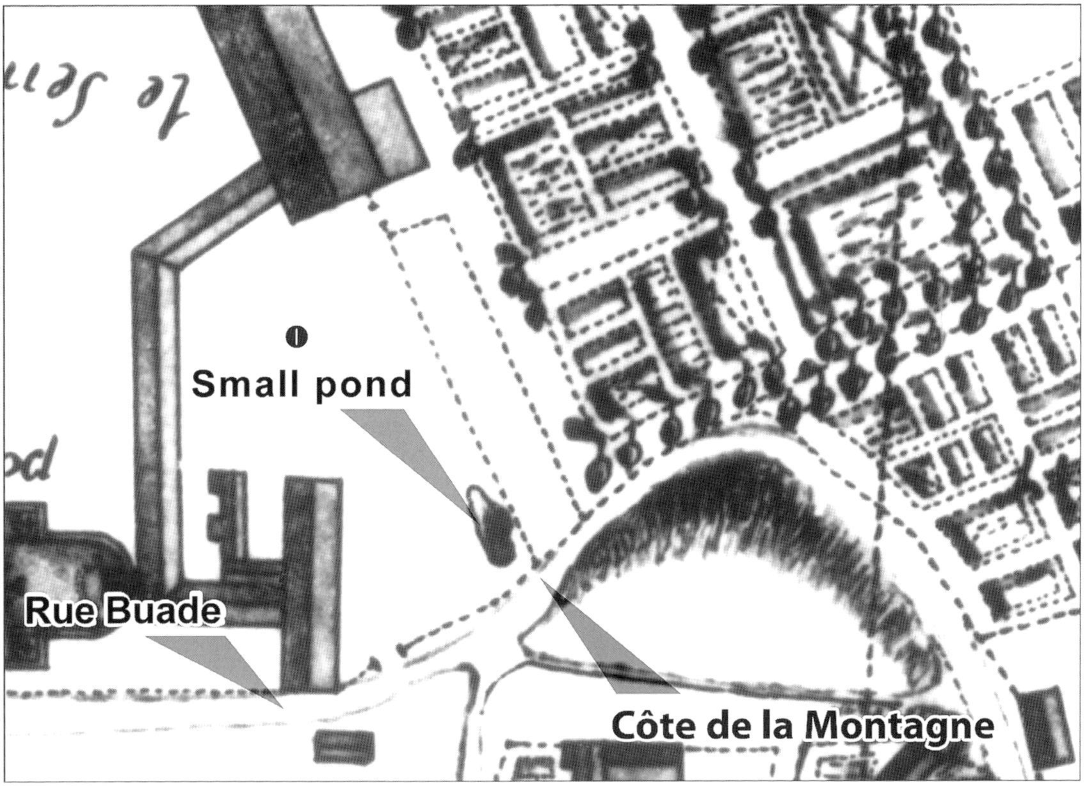

FIG. 8
Plan de la ville et Chasteau de Québec fait en 1685, Villeneuve, 1685: detail (NAC, C15797).

Laverdière believed,[50] and not in the north-east section, near the intersection of Rue des Remparts and Rue Hébert, as suggested by André Vachon.[51]

All the buildings excavated to date had exactly the same north–south orientation; at least three of them, and perhaps four, were situated in the lower part of the fief — the eastern part of the plateau now occupied by the schoolyard. The north-east part of the site, where the underground gymnasium of the Petit Séminaire is situated, was not used for any specific purpose or in a sustained manner during the Hébert-Couillard period, probably because its many rocky outcrops made it uninviting. This was also true of the area along the northern edge of the plateau, just north-east of the Couillard house.

Contrary to what was previously believed, the Couillard family enjoyed a certain affluence and were able to afford and appreciate luxury items. They also had a varied diet, including meat derived from animals they raised: primarily pork and beef, but probably lamb and various types of poultry as well. This regular fare was often supplemented with game, especially moose and beaver, but also wildfowl and fish. Therefore, the Couillards hunted, trapped and fished, and probably traded with Native people, as shown by the trade objects such as glass beads they had at their disposal. In fact, they are known to have had excellent relations with the Amerindians. The members of the family thus broke the law regarding trade with Native groups, for the Compagnie des Marchands forbade colonists to engage in such activities.

NEW RESEARCH PERSPECTIVES

The information now available on the occupation of the Seminary of Québec site by the Hébert and Couillard families can yield very positive results. However, since the original corpus of data was practically non-existent, the current store of information is still far from sufficient. Even though many aspects of the Hébert-Couillard occupation have been documented, at least partially, they still require much more study, while other aspects, such as craft and agricultural activities, have not been documented at all. For example, the Couillard house and its immediate environment have been excavated to only a limited extent and may yet yield a substantial amount of new information. The schoolyard still has archaeologically intact deposits whose potential is considered very high. This is also true of the southern part of the parking lot next to Rue des Remparts, which is an extremely promising sector that has barely been studied. It contains the remains of a structure that might correspond to the house built by Louis Hébert in 1620, and priority should be given to verifying this hypothesis. Moreover, based on what is known now, this whole section of the seminary site may have been a major occupation zone in the second and third quarters of the 17th century, and the structural remains and material culture that might be uncovered here could be among the oldest in Québec. Any discoveries of this kind would contribute significantly to our understanding of a period that remains poorly known.

Unfortunately, other parts of the site can no longer provide any information. This is the case with the area between the procurator's wing and the priests' wing (*aile des Prêtres*), now occupied by an underground parking lot, and the north part of the Rue des Remparts parking lot, where an underground gymnasium has been built. In the latter case, however, it was possible to study the area properly before all traces of past occupation were destroyed. This was not the case with the lower part of the site, behind the museum, which was disturbed substantially during renovation work in the mid-1980s. Nevertheless, the seminary site still contains a few promising sectors, particularly to the south, between the parlour wing and the property attached to the Archbishop's residence. In addition, since the fiefdom of Sault-au-Matelot extended well beyond the present-day limits of the seminary's property, several interesting sites probably survive on private properties to the north and west. This is particularly true of the backyard of 38 Rue Sainte-Famille and the area next to Rue Christie, both of which probably contain traces of the Hébert-Couillard occupation.

This paper has discussed only one of the occupation periods of the Seminary of Québec site. However, the archaeological data have also provided a much clearer picture of the site's physical and human environment in subsequent periods, particularly the seminary's early years. For example, our findings have made it possible to determine that the institution's first building, the Petit Séminaire, erected in 1675, was not located where historians had always believed. As a result, the entire sequence of the site's physical evolution has been changed, leading to a new understanding of the development of the seminary complex. This demonstrates the important contribution that archaeology can make to long-established understanding based almost entirely on the interpretation of written records. Not only has this archaeological work contributed fresh information; its value also stems from its analytical approach, which allows previous conclusions to be re-examined and enriched with new, well-founded data.

ACKNOWLEDGEMENTS

I would like to extend my thanks to Serge Rouleau for his important contribution to this project and the constructive discussions his input prompted, and to William Moss for his steadfast support of my research on the Seminary of Québec complex, a truly remarkable archaeological site. I would also like to thank the directors of this institution for their unswerving generosity in granting me access to their property.

NOTES

1 Simoneau 1996, 24–5.
2 Simoneau 1995.
3 Rouleau & Desgagné 1995.
4 Fortin 1994, 16.
5 Garneau 1994, 13–14.
6 Garneau 1994, 20. [Translation.]
7 Couillard-Després 1934, 156.
8 Couillard-Després 1934, 153.
9 Couillard-Després 1934, 154.
10 Couillard-Després 1934, 157.
11 Baillargeon 1972, 67.
12 Couillard-Després 1934, 157.
13 Couillard-Després 1934, 159.
14 Couillard-Després 1934, 162–3.
15 Vachon 1993, 63. [Translation.]
16 *Plan des fondations de la maison de la veuve Couillard retrouvées le 22 octobre 1866*, C.H. Laverdière, 1866, ASQ, fonds Laverdière, no. 126-II.
17 Vachon 1993, 64.
18 Maheux 1963, 598.
19 Maheux 1963, 591.
20 Couillard-Després 1934, 161.
21 Baillargeon 1972, 68.
22 Couillard-Després 1934, 162–3.
23 Baillargeon 1972, 70–5.
24 Couillard-Després 1934, 160.
25 Baillargeon 1972, 77.
26 Provost 1965, 8.
27 Couillard-Després 1934, 154.

[28] Giguère 1973, **2**, 616. [Translation, Biggar 1971, **3**, 205.]
[29] Giguère 1973, **3**, 988.
[30] *Partage fait entre Guill. Couillard, Guillaume Huboust et sa femme pour servir Guill. Hébert, le 15e 7bre 1634*, Duhaime, 15 Sept. 1634, ASQ, carton 6, 2.
[31] *Rapport de charpenterie pour la maison de Guillaume Hébert*, ASQ, carton 6, 33.
[32] *Vente faite par le Sr le Tardif et aues au Sr Couillart d'un corps de logis en 1644*, ASQ, carton 6, 31.
[33] *Rapport de charpenterie pour la maison de Guillaume Hébert*, ASQ, carton 6, 33. [Translation.]
[34] *Concession à Noël Morin pour sa femme*, 4 Sept. 1640, ASQ, carton 6, 9.
[35] *Marché entre Thomas Touchet et Guillaume Couillard, 3 février 1653*, greffe Guillaume Audouart, ANQQ.
[36] It could be concluded, on the basis of this plan, that this 'fountain' or well was as large as the nave of Notre-Dame-de-la-Recouvrance Church. Obviously, there is a problem with the scale of the drawing of this feature.
[37] Gaumond 1970.
[38] Simoneau 1996, 24–5.
[39] Rouleau 2003.
[40] Provost 1953.
[41] *Marché entre Thomas Touchet et Guillaume Couillard, 3 février 1653*, greffe Guillaume Audouart, ANQQ.
[42] Simoneau 1996, 24–5.
[43] Cloutier 1996.
[44] Ostéothèque 1992.
[45] Fortin 1992.
[46] Simoneau 1995.
[47] Rouleau 2003.
[48] Gauthier-Larouche 1974, 29.
[49] *Vente faite par le Sr le Tardif et aues au Sr Couillart d'un corps de logis en 1644*, ASQ, carton 6, 31.
[50] Giguère 1973, **3**, 988, n. 2.
[51] Vachon 1993, 65.

BIBLIOGRAPHY

PUBLISHED SOURCES

Baillargeon, N. 1972, *Le Séminaire de Québec sous l'épiscopat de Mgr de Laval*, Québec: Presses de l'Université Laval.

Biggar, H.P. (ed.) 1971 [1922–36], *The Works of Samuel de Champlain*, 6 vols, Toronto: University Press.

Couillard-Després, A. 1934, 'Le fief du Sault-au-Matelot', *Proc. Trans. Roy. Soc. Canada* 3 ser., **28**, 149–70.

Gauthier-Larouche, G. 1974, *Évolution de la maison rurale traditionnelle dans la région de Québec: étude ethnographique*, Québec: Presses de l'Université Laval.

Giguère, G.E. 1973, *Œuvres de Champlain*, Montréal: Éditions du Jour.

Maheux, Mgr A. 1963, 'Historique du Séminaire de Québec', *Rev. Université Laval* **17**:7, 291–599.

Provost, H. 1953, 'Au berceau du Petit Séminaire de Québec', *Bull. Recherches Hist.* **59**:1, 5–10.

Provost, H. 1965, 'Le Séminaire de Québec, terrains et constructions (1663–1700)', *Rev. Université Laval* **20**:1, 3–23.

Vachon, A. 1993, 'La Cour des Petits (Petit Séminaire de Québec)', *Les Cahiers des Dix* **48**, 63–85.

UNPUBLISHED SOURCES

Cloutier, C. 1996, 'Des Siècles piétinés: aperçu de la collection archéologique du Séminaire de Québec', Québec: Ville de Québec, Centre de développement économique et urbain, Division design et patrimoine.

Fortin, C. 1992, 'Les Marcrorestes végétaux de la cour du Séminaire de Québec', Québec: Ville de Québec, Centre de développement économique et urbain, Division design et patrimoine.

Fortin, C. 1994, 'Analyse paléoethnobotanique du site du Séminaire de Québec', Québec: Ville de Québec, Centre de développement économique et urbain, Division design et patrimoine.

Garneau, M. 1994, 'Analyses palynologiques complémentaires aux fouilles archéologiques effectuées dans la cour du Séminaire de Québec pendant l'été 1994', Québec: Ville de Québec, Centre de développement économique et urbain, Division design et patrimoine.

Gaumond, M. 1970, 'Rapport sur les sépultures trouvées le 13 août 1970 sous le corridor de l'aile des Parloirs au Séminaire de Québec', Québec: Ministère des affaires culturelles du Québec.

Ostéothèque (de Montréal) 1992, 'Analyse zooarchéologique des vestiges osseux provenant du site du Séminaire de Québec (CeEt-32)', Montréal.

Rouleau, S. 2003, 'Recherches archéologiques, fouilles de la maison Couillard et surveillance cour des Petits du Séminaire de Québec, CeEt-32', Québec: Ville de Québec, Centre de développement économique et urbain, Division design architecture et patrimoine.

Rouleau, S. & Desgagné, A. 1995, 'Recherches archéologiques, le site des Jardins du Séminaire de Québec', Québec: Ville de Québec, Centre de développement économique et urbain, Division design et patrimoine.

Simoneau, D. 1995, 'Rapport d'inventaire archéologique: les Jardins du Séminaire de Québec (CeEt-32)', Québec: Ville de Québec, Service de l'urbanisme, Division du design urbain et du patrimoine.

Simoneau, D. 1996, 'Rapport de fouilles archéologiques dans la cour des Petits du Séminaire de Québec', Québec: Ville de Québec, Centre de développement économique et urbain, Division design et patrimoine.

ABBREVIATIONS

ANF	Archives nationales de France
ANOM	Archives nationales Outre-mer
ANQQ	Archives nationales du Québec à Québec
ASQ	Archives du Séminaire de Québec
NAC	National Archives of Canada

SUMMARY IN FRENCH, GERMAN, ITALIAN AND SPANISH

RÉSUMÉ

De première ferme en Nouvelle-France à premier institut réligieux: le site du Séminaire de Québec au berceau de la ville

Entre 1991 et 2002, les premières fouilles archéologiques complètes ont été conduites sur le Séminaire du site de Québec. De nombreuses études, basées principalement sur des sources historiques, avaient préalablement établi une suite d'événements majeurs et de développements physiques qui lui étaient liés. Louis Hébert, traditionnellement considéré comme le premier colon du pays, prit possession du site en 1617; les indices structuraux, matériels and environnementaux sont liés à la période Hébert-Couillard qui a précédé la fondation du séminaire en 1663. Ni les maisons de Guillaume Couillard et de Louis Hébert, ni le Petit Séminaire érigé par Mgr de Laval ne sont situés là où on l'avait précédemment pensé.

ZUSAMMENFASSUNG

Das Quebec-Seminar: von Neufrankreichs ältester Farm bis zum ersten religiösen Institut

Auf dem Gelände des Quebec-Seminars wurde von 1991–2002 eine vollständige, archäologische Grabung durchgeführt. Zahlreiche Studien, die hauptsächlich auf historischen Quellen beruhen, haben früher die Abfolge der Begebenheiten der physischen Entwicklung bestimmt. Louis Hébert, der traditionell als der erste Siedler im Land angesehen wird, nahm das Grundstück 1617 in Besitz. Man fand aber später heraus, daß Baureste, Artefakte und Umweltproben aus der Hébert-Couillard-Periode, die der Seminargründung 1663 voranging, in Verbindung stehen. Weder die Häuser von Guillaume Couillard und Louis Hébert noch das Kleine Seminar stehen dort, wo man sie bisher vermutet hatte.

RIASSUNTO

Il sito del seminario del Quebec: dalla prima fattoria della Nuova Francia alla sua prima istituzione religiosa

Fra il 1991 e il 2002 furono condotti nel sito del seminario del Quebec i primi scavi archeologici completi. Numerosi studi, basati principalmente su fonti storiche, avevano precedentemente stabilito la sequenza degli avvenimenti più importanti e dei cambiamenti fisici ad essi relazionati. Louis Hébert, tradizionalmente considerato il primo colono del paese, prese possesso del sito nel 1617; sono stati rinvenuti resti di strutture, di artefatti e attestazioni paleo-ambientali relative al periodo Hébert-Couillard e che precedono la fondazione del seminatio nel 1663. Né la casa di Guillaume Couillard e Louis Hébert, né il Piccolo Seminario eretto da Mgr de Laval erano ubicati dove precedentemente ipotizzato.

RESUMEN

El yacimiento del seminario de Quebec: de la primera granja de Nueva Francia a su primera institución religiosa

En 1991–2002 se llevó a cabo la primera excavación arqueológica en el lugar del seminario de Quebec. Estudios previos, basados principalmente en fuentes escritas, habían establecido la principal secuencia evolutiva e histórica. Louis Hébert, tradicionalmente considerado como el primer colono del país, tomó posesión del lugar en 1617; se ha encontrado evidencia estructural, material y medioambiental relacionada con el período Hébert-Couillard que precedió la fundación del seminario en 1663, aunque ni las casas de Guillaume Couillard y Louis Hébert ni las del Petit Séminaire eregido por Mgr de Laval están situadas donde se había pensado tradicionalmente.

Ville de Québec, Service de l'aménagement du territoire, Division du design, de l'architecture et du patrimoine, édifice de la Fabrique, 295, boulevard Charest Est, Québec (Québec), Canada G1K 3G8
[daniel.simoneau@ville.quebec.qc.ca]

Post-Medieval Archaeology **43/1** (2009), 229–244

An archaeological view of the French colonial port of Québec

By SERGE ROULEAU

*SUMMARY: In this paper the remains of the first harbour front discovered on the Îlot Hunt in Québec are discussed in relation to evidence found on other sites in the city's Lower Town. These remains throw light on the nature of the French colonial port, testifying to the initiatives of its merchants and the actions of its colonial authorities. Structures built during the British regime by merchants belonging to the Lymburner family provide an example of the kind of innovative facilities that inaugurated the disappearance (*c. *1775–80) of the harbour front developed during the French colonial era.*

INTRODUCTION

This short overview is based on archaeological data from the Îlot Hunt site, which lies in Québec's Lower Town. Archaeological investigations conducted there and in the immediate vicinity have yielded discoveries which expand our understanding of the city's first harbour front. To interpret the data relating to this initial urban shoreline, the overview will draw upon all the archaeological evidence for harbour facilities under the French regime.

Located a short distance from Place Royale, Îlot Hunt is a site which throws light on the sequence of changes which took place in the Lower Town's harbour area from the 17th to the 19th centuries. The archaeological work carried out there by the Université Laval field school between 1991 and 1995, coupled with various excavations by the City of Québec, has produced a mass of valuable data about the installation of its first shoreline structures. This supplements the findings from a series of isolated excavations conducted in the city since the 1980s. Many of these projects were initiatives of the Province of Québec's Ministère de la Culture, des Communications et de la Condition féminine (MCCCFQ) and the City of Québec under the terms of a cultural property agreement between these two bodies. Further valuable evidence was recovered by fieldwork undertaken during the construction of the Musée de la civilisation in 1984–85; this project, sponsored by the Société immobilière du Québec, provided many novel insights into the evolution of the harbour area through the centuries. Lastly, excavations conducted by the provincial government since the 1970s under the auspices of the MCCCFQ at Place Royale and in Lower Town have also yielded information about Lower Town's changing harbour front.

A SINGULAR LOCATION

The local geography was instrumental in Samuel de Champlain's decision to establish a trading post at Québec in 1608. A unique topography has been formed here — on the one hand by the St Lawrence River as it flows between two steep-sided shores, and on the other by a promontory bordered on one side by the mouth of a tributary. Furthermore, the narrows of the river here constitute a meeting point between the end of the St Lawrence Estuary and the beginning of the freshwater reach extending westward.

Rising *c.* 40m from the shoreline, the promontory dominates the river flowing at its foot. A

 DOI: 10.1179/007942309X12457508844369

narrow strip of land occupies the available area extending between the cliff side and the St Lawrence to the south. On this space Lower Town grew up around a hub known as Place Royale. With time, many merchants and traders built their homes and warehouses in this area. Only the hillside road known as Côte de la Montagne provided access to Upper Town, a part of the city occupied predominantly by religious institutions.

Along the north and north-east side of the promontory, the shorelines of the St Lawrence and the Saint-Charles River meet almost at the foot of the cliff. The construction of the Intendant's Palace along the north-west side of the promontory, begun in 1688, spurred the development of a town.[1] This palace, which served as the administrative headquarters of the French colony, stood next to the Saint-Charles River estuary and Rue Saint-Nicolas, a street leading to Upper Town.

THE MARINE ENVIRONMENT

The marine conditions at Québec are also unusual.[2] Although the city is flanked by fresh water, it is subject to tides. The significant tidal range makes for an alternating tug of flow up- and down-river, exposing the broad foreshore at ebb tide. Nowadays the maximum tidal range varies from 4m to 6m. The prevailing winds are westerly, although north-easterly winds can persist during spells of bad weather. The combined impact of wind and tidal currents often makes for choppy waters; in the past they could seriously complicate the handling of small boats, hamper the manoeuvres of ocean-going ships, and make some mooring operations risky. As a rule, however, such problems would have arisen sporadically, mirroring variations in the tides and weather. The break-up of ice on the St Lawrence each spring could also have caused damage to shoreline structures, even those made of masonry.

Historically, the Québec shoreline featured a number of coves which provided rudimentary havens from the river current and temporary shelter from the wind and waves. However, the depth of the riverbed varied greatly in this stretch of the river: for example, there were deep waters off the cove known as Anse du Cul-de-Sac, whereas sites to the north generally had wide foreshores. Off Lower Town, the area exposed at low tide could easily run to more than 220m in length. In general, the foreshore consists of a layer of sand over shale, the type of rock that typifies Québec's promontory. This sand also contains considerable quantities of plant debris.[3]

The Saint-Charles River estuary was an open space which was particularly vulnerable to north-easterly winds. For example, the launching of the store ship *Canada* here in 1742 had to be postponed for fifteen days because intense winds blew from the north-east.[4] The estuary was also subject to tidal movements along the St Lawrence. The foreshore exposed at low tide could extend to more than 500m in some places; at such times the Saint-Charles was often reduced to a trickle which could be forded at a number of points. The riverbed here was mainly clayey, with some concentrations of sand.[5] As elsewhere, the foreshore was strewn with pebbles, cobbles and boulder,[6] which were gradually removed in order to improve the safety of the waters.

QUÉBEC, THE COLONY'S PORT

Throughout the French regime, Québec remained the only port city in Canada open to ocean navigation; Montréal and Trois-Rivières could only be reached by river vessels adapted to shallow waters. Being strategically positioned at the westernmost end of the St Lawrence Estuary, Québec was also the port of arrival for transatlantic shipping. From the time of its founding, the city served as the colony's administrative capital and the centre of its defence. A garrison town, the city was also the home of the representatives of the king and the church.

Like several of Europe's ports, Québec featured a number of beaching points at which vessels with shallow draughts could land. However, any seagoing ship arriving there had to moor in the roadstead — the deep part of the river off the city; the landing of passengers and cargo from such ships thus entailed using scows, boats and even river schooners.[7] Three places, referred to as 'ports', provided shoreline access to the city (Fig. 1). In the 17th and 18th centuries the word 'port' was used in both French and English to mean any naturally protected area or harbour which was well suited for the mooring of ships. Port du Cul-de-Sac, the oldest such harbour, was located in a cove of the same name, wedged between the cliff-side and a spit of land known as Pointe aux Roches. Lower Town was built on a portion of this spit, the east side of which was defined by the St Lawrence shoreline. The open, accessible stretch of this riverfront was called Port de la Basse-Ville. A third 'port' named Port Saint-Nicolas or Port Dauphin lay in the Saint-Charles Estuary, at the end of Rue Saint-Nicolas, within a stone's throw of the Intendant's Palace.

Beaching at one of these 'ports' often entailed patient, painstaking manoeuvring in response to shifts in the prevailing conditions. Although there

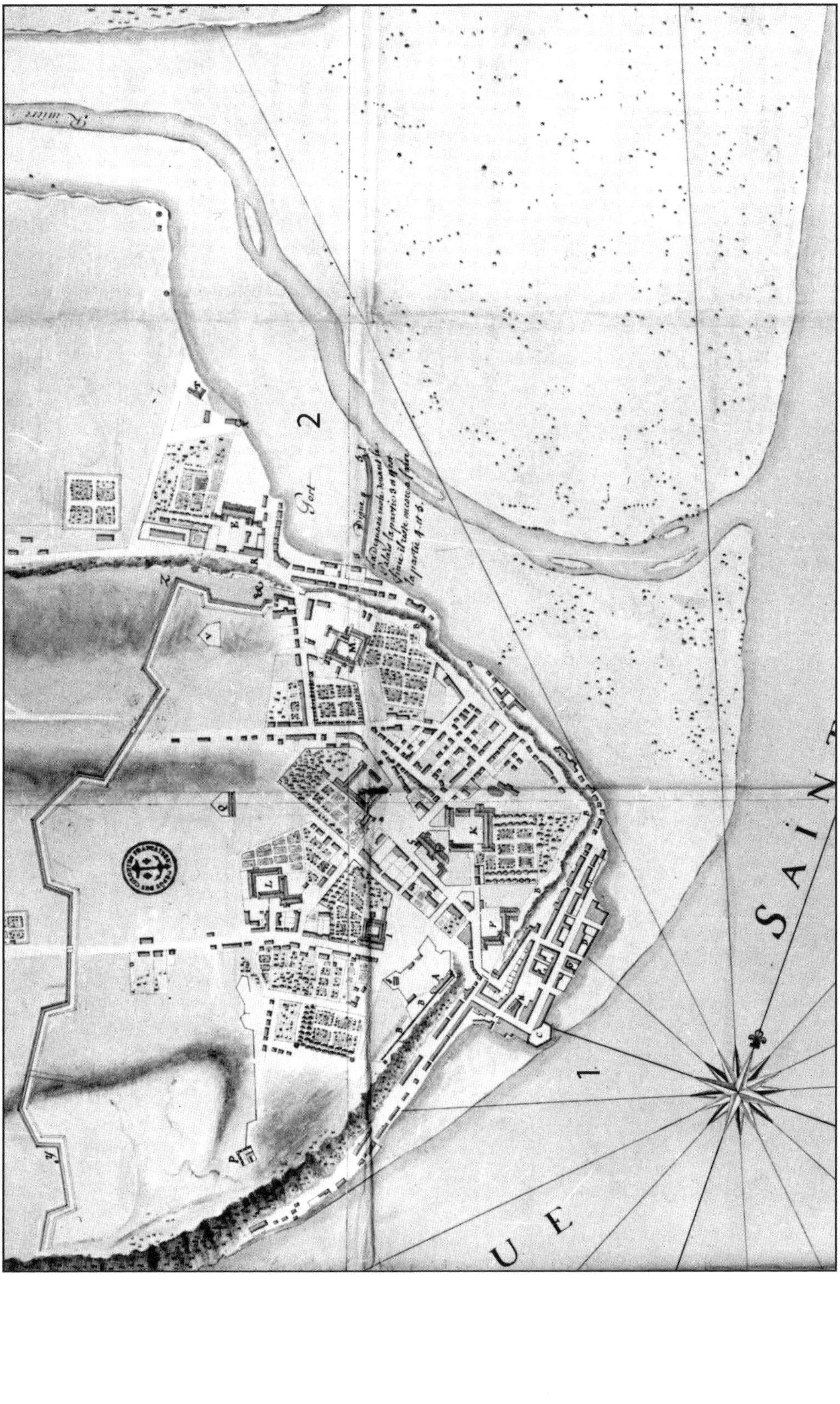

FIG. 1

Detail of a map of the city of Québec in 1733 by Chaussegros de Léry. 1. Port du Cul-de-Sac is located to the left of the Royal Battery, with the Lower Town river-front extending to the right. 2. Port Saint-Nicolas is located next to the dyke. The fleur-de-lis appearing in the compass rose points north (NAC, C-15739).

were few dangerous rocks jutting upward from the riverbed, this advantage was commonly offset by a combination of winds, waves and currents which complicated manoeuvres and made heaving to or setting sail risky. The open stretch of water alongside these three harbours lacked any natural features which could shelter vessels. Coursing off the city, the St Lawrence flowed no less than half a nautical mile (926m) to the east and three miles (5.5km) to the north and north-east. In order to ensure that the waters were deep enough, a ship or boat manoeuvring to enter one of the 'ports' also had to time its movements to coincide with the tides. As heavy ships were less manoeuvrable, they were more vulnerable to drifting towards hazards.

During the 17th century a service structure was built on the property of Charles Aubert de la Chesnaye, one of the most prosperous merchants of the time. From the 1660s he was the owner of a combined house and warehouse on Rue Sault-au-Matelot in Lower Town. It was designed to tranship cargo; its closed courtyard featured a central doorway through which wares initially landed on the nearby shoreline could be brought in. In 1687 de la Chesnaye purchased two water lots behind his house; in the following year he built a 'coffer-like frame' around them measuring 125 French feet (40.6m) long and 72 French feet (23.4m) deep.[8] The specifications on the construction plans provide clear evidence of his intention to install a cedar-pole structure 15 French feet (4.87m) high along the river front. This was to be made of sections of vertical poles set upon a sill between load-bearing uprights anchored in the ground. The structure is best described as an 'enclosure'; it was fitted with large gates in the centre of the north and south sides for 'letting in and out carts, horses and oxen'.[9] It was designed to be more solid on the north, east and south sides, which came within the tidal range. The enclosure was evidently designed to provide protection from the waves and to facilitate trans-shipment operations. Shallow-draught vessels would probably have been brought inside it, beached and unloaded. At the same time, the structure enabled its owner to make official the private character of the beaching point by preventing onlookers and passers-by from drawing too close. Finally, the erection of the enclosure also served to achieve compliance, at least ostensibly, with administrative requirements relating to the occupation and development of water lots.

Despite seven archaeological field studies conducted on this site by Université Laval in the 1990s and excavations by the City of Québec in 1987, 1990, 1991 and 2002, no remains of this facility have been uncovered. It appears that its components were destroyed, either through contact with moving ice or through the subsequent erection of buildings on the site. The existence of the enclosure is however attested both by the building contract signed before a notary and by topographical drawings (Fig. 2). In fact, a number of contemporary illustrations depict similar structures on other lots. Aubert de la Chesnaye's enclosure thus appears to have been adapted not only to the characteristics of the Lower Town beaching point but to the type and volume of cargo trans-shipped there. His commercial activities centred primarily on the fur trade; he also operated a barque for inshore navigation along the St Lawrence and was involved in the chartering of ships.[10] The enclosure also served to delimit Lower Town's first harbour front.

THE EVOLUTION OF THE LOWER TOWN HARBOUR FRONT: THE ROLE OF THE MERCHANTS AND THE CROWN

THE FIRST PERMANENT HARBOUR FRONT

Three riverside sites in Lower Town have yielded evidence relating to the formation of its first permanent harbour front at the turn of the 18th century. It is worth recalling that, under the conditions governing the acquisition of water lots, owners were required to build houses and storehouses on them within three years of taking ownership.

The owners of three water lots lying to the north of the narrow street known as Ruelle des Sœurs (today's Côte de la Montagne) built permanent structures to offset the effects of tides and to develop the area left dry at low tide (Fig. 3). In 1699 Aubert de la Chesnaye proceeded to erect a 'high wall' (*muraille*) along the two water lots behind his house.[11] On the neighbouring lot, which had once belonged to Philippe Gauthier de Comporté but had since become the property of Jean Gobin, the work of building a masonry wall was begun prior to 1707. Further to the north, the ship's carpenter Guillaume Pagé dit Carcy also built a 'high wall' in stone around 1702 in order to close off his property.[12]

The stone wall (Fig. 4) built for Aubert de la Chesnaye rose on the same site as the wooden enclosure which he had erected previously.[13] This solid masonry structure ran the entire length of the lots facing the river, just under 42m in all. On the river side the wall rose to 5.85m (18 French feet) and was sheathed with timbers, as attested by the cramp-irons uncovered at the base. To come alongside, boats had to beach at ebb tide. The archaeological evidence relating to this structure

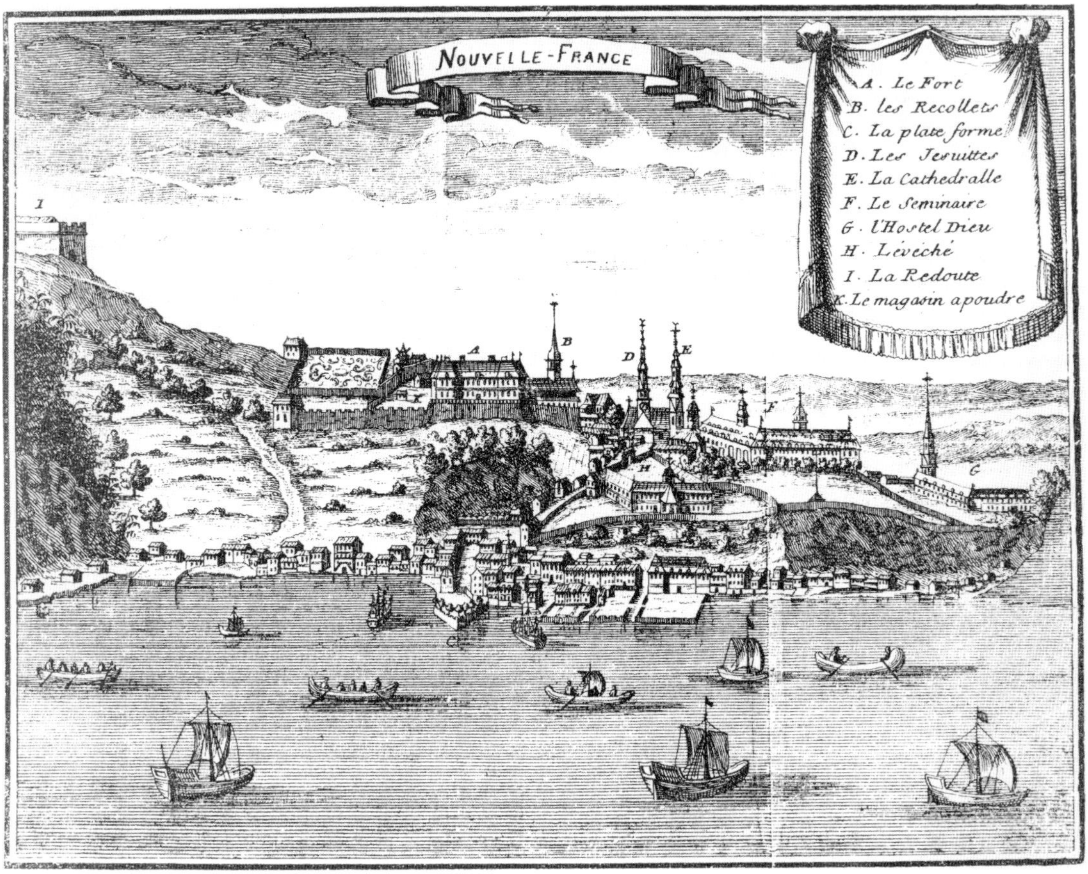

FIG. 2

View of Québec before 1700. The wooden enclosure erected behind the Aubert de la Chesnaye house can be seen on the shoreline (NAC, BK/340 Québec-1700).

shows that its height (between the upper surface of the wharf embankment and the 'high wall' proper) ranged from 1.30 to 2.30m.[14] This difference in level defies easy interpretation. One possible explanation is that work developing the embankment had not been completed before the owner's death in 1702. The excavated evidence may have brought to light the primary purpose of the 'high wall' — to counter the impact of high tides and to retain the fill which raised the level of the lot. The 'high wall' may have been an obstacle to the handling or transshipment of wares, at least along the side of the wall giving onto the river. Unfortunately, many components of the initial 'La Chesnaye wharf' had been destroyed by later work on the lot, first for building and then for repairing the Dauphine Battery.

Shortly before 1707, the building of a masonry wall on the neighbouring water lot owned by Jean Gobin was begun. On the riverside, its face measured slightly under 15m in length and abutted the north-east corner of Aubert de la Chesnaye's wall. A wall more than 17m in length ran along the north side of Gobin's lot, which bordered Rue Saint-Antoine. As on other sites, an angular structure was installed inside the north-east corner of the Gobin wharf in what was clearly an attempt to consolidate the end of the wharf which was most vulnerable to the impact of the elements at high tide. The south-east corner, which abutted the La Chesnaye lot, also underwent consolidation work with the addition of a curving structure. Finally, remains of decking were located 0.80m below the upper surface of the main wall,[15] making the difference in level considerably less than that observed on the La Chesnaye property.

Guillaume Pagé built a wall on the north side of Rue Saint-Antoine; it bounded his water lot

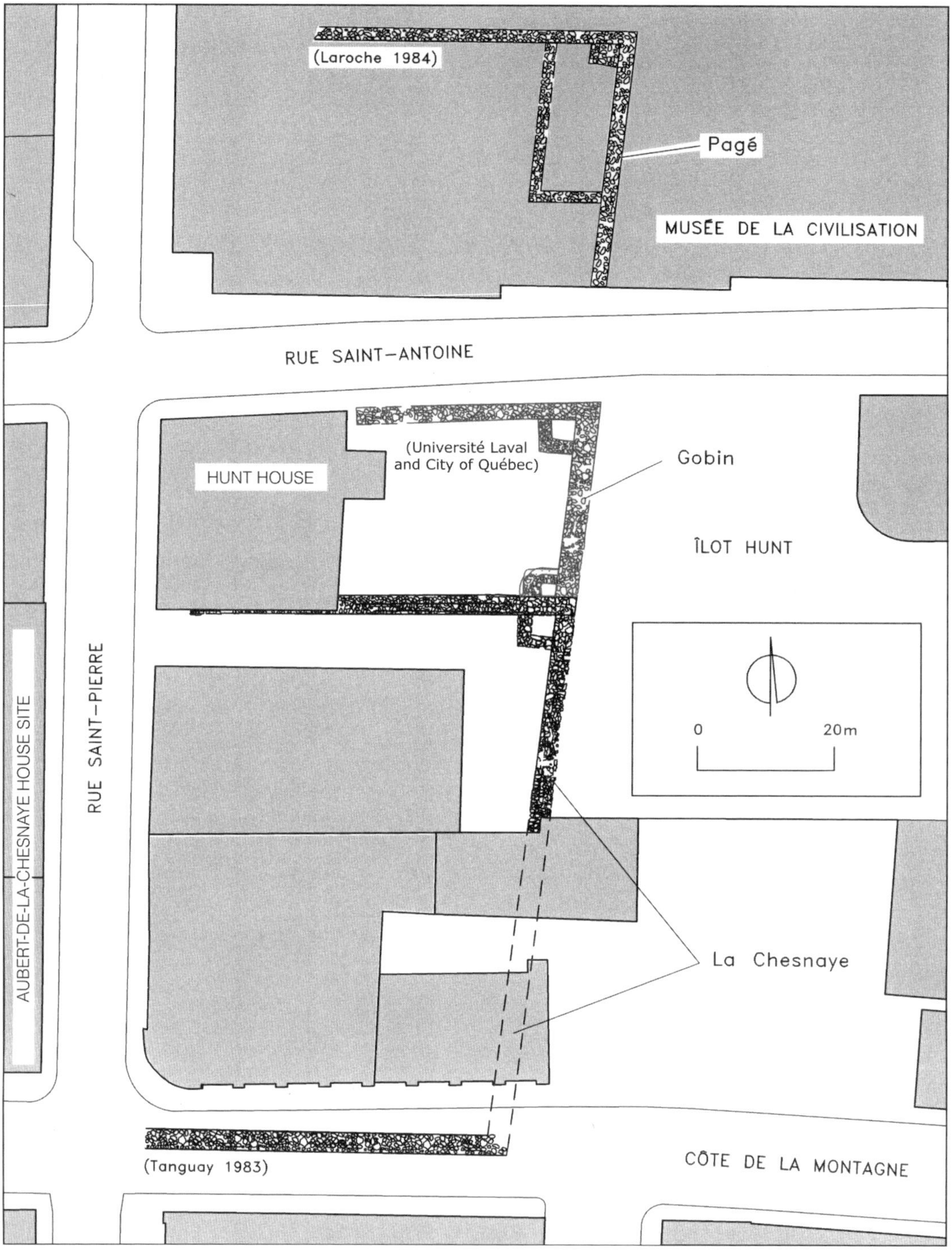

FIG. 3

Archaeological remains of Lower Town's first harbour front. Ruelle des Sœurs was later widened, becoming Côte de la Montagne (drawn by L. Grenier, F. Pellerin, Ville de Québec).

FIG. 4

Îlot Hunt site (CeEt-110): view of the remains of the high wall erected on the Gobin and Aubert de la Chesnaye properties. Part of the outer side of the wall, facing the river, was refaced during the construction of the Dauphine Battery (photograph, Ville de Québec).

at the corner of Rue Saint-Antoine and Rue Saint-Pierre. Archaeological investigation has revealed the presence of a masonry wall running *c.* 20m along the riverside, with another such wall enclosing the lot's northern flank. Masonry structures were also built into the inside corner of these two walls.[16] Finally, a stone house was erected on the Rue Saint-Pierre frontage.

These archaeological remains provide evidence of individual development projects, carried out to counter erosion on the sides of the properties concerned. The masonry structures were clearly built to shore up the land; acting as a bulwark against the 'sea', the high wall enclosed the water lots along the sides subject to rising tides. This structure also served to make official the private character of the spaces it bounded, and enabled the owners to comply with legal requirements relating to the development of water lots. On each of these properties, supplementary masonry structures were fitted into the corners of the walls in order to strengthen them; they were later converted into wells or privies.

The development of the shoreline properties appears to have been undertaken primarily to gain space along the riverside; the projects form part of a wider pattern of expansion of the Lower Town. Such encroachments on the foreshore stimulated the extension of the surrounding public streets, notably Rue Saint-Pierre to the north, and Ruelle des Sœurs and Rue Saint-Antoine to the east. The last two streets led to the shore and thus constituted points of entry into Lower Town.

Although these facilities were employed for typical harbour activities, such uses do not appear to be the reason that initially drove their construction. It is worth recalling that the term employed by the lot owners involved in drafting and signing construction contracts was 'high wall' rather than 'wharf'. As was previously noted by LaRoche,[17] the choice of these words could reflect their intention to build walls solely to secure their gains on the foreshore and to stave off the daily invasion of the tides. This interpretation appears to be borne out by the considerable difference in level between the lot surface and the east wall of the La Chesnaye property.

The individual projects carried out on these water lots ultimately resulted in the formation of a portion of Québec's first permanent shorefront (Fig. 3). On the east side of the city these walls were set out in a straight line parallel to the rivershore, with houses laid out along Rue Saint-Pierre. The building line used with the shore wall was uninterrupted, with the exception of the opening of Rue Saint-Antoine onto the shoreline.

THE EVOLUTION OF THE HARBOUR FRONT

Rumours of an armed conflict prompted the colonial authorities to build the Dauphine Battery on the properties belonging to Gobin and the de la Chesnaye family estate between 1707 and 1709 (Fig. 4). The battery covered the harbour front between Ruelle des Sœurs and Rue Saint-Antoine and stood 120m from the Royal Battery, an impressive bastion-like structure built in 1691–92 at the tip of Pointe aux Roches. Together, the two batteries at water level could have concentrated their firepower on any enemy ships manoeuvring in the roadstead.

In 1710 the Dauphine Battery featured six embrasures and a palisade.[18] Following the signing of the Treaty of Utrecht in 1713, this structure fell into disrepair, quickly suffering damage from floating ice and being stripped of its merlons at the behest of local merchants. From 1721, the colonial authorities indicated their determination to maintain the use of this site for defence by returning the battery to its original function. The major repairs undertaken on this work in 1729 by the engineer Chaussegros de Léry were still visible at the time of the archaeological fieldwork, notably the use of green sandstone in the exterior facing. The brick left cheek of an embrasure was also brought to light in 2002.[19] On the occasion of new upgrading work in 1745 the battery was expanded northward, beyond the property of Guillaume Pagé up to the wharf of merchant Nicolas Boisseau. Access to the shore from Rue Saint-Antoine was nevertheless preserved.

As the result of additional grants of water lots around 1750, merchants were able to pursue further the expansion of the harbour front begun in the early 18th century. The archaeological evidence relating to this area, which today lies between Rue Saint-Antoine and Rue de la Barricade, was recovered in 1984–85 during construction work on the Musée de la civilisation, a project of the Société immobilière du Québec. This work, carried out under the direction of Daniel LaRoche, has documented the process whereby various property owners appropriated space from the foreshore as they set up houses fronting onto Rue Saint-Pierre, with their courtyards and wharves.[20]

The pattern of lot development was similar to that established in the early 18th century. As a rule, each property owner began by setting out a wall around the perimeter of his lot, and then erected a house fronting onto Rue Saint-Pierre that was accompanied by sheds in the courtyard. In documents signed before a notary, owners occasionally included specific provisions concerning the establishment of a wharf on the river side of their property. The use of these facilities for harbour activities is confirmed by the presence of anchoring rings and sheds. On several occasions, owners concluded agreements that allowed a common structure to be erected on adjoining lots. Taken together, these individual development projects on the foreshore again fostered the formation of a straight harbour front stretching from Rue Saint-Antoine to Pointe à Carcy (today's Rue de la Barricade). This wave of property allotment spurred the development of a harbour front offering a better fit with the surrounding urban fabric and Rue Saint-Pierre (Fig. 5).

The excavation of these wharves has shed light on the different construction techniques used in these properties; some were masonry structures whilst others had wooden components. Buttresses installed on the inner side of the stone wharves show that river-borne pressures were anticipated. That said, the positioning of three buttresses against the outside of the Boisseau wharf soon after its construction testifies to the difficulties of an environment that was not conducive to the survival of this type of structure.

Archaeological research also led to the exceptional discovery of the remains of eight boats abandoned on the foreshore prior to the construction of these wharves; they had been covered by fill deposited as the properties were developed. These vessels, consisting of five flat-bottomed boats (*batteaux plats*) and three keeled ones, are a unique group of examples of the service vessels used at Québec and in New France. LaRoche has provided a valuable account of some of them in a recent article.[21]

During the Seven Years War a battery was built on these wharves; work began on the docks belonging to the merchants Levasseur, Imbert and Estèbe in the summer of 1757. The north-east end of the harbour front was particularly sought-after because it gave a wider range of artillery fire out over the north and north-east sectors of the roadstead.

PORT DE LA BASSE-VILLE

In the early 18th century Québec's harbour landscape was shaped by the construction of a straight

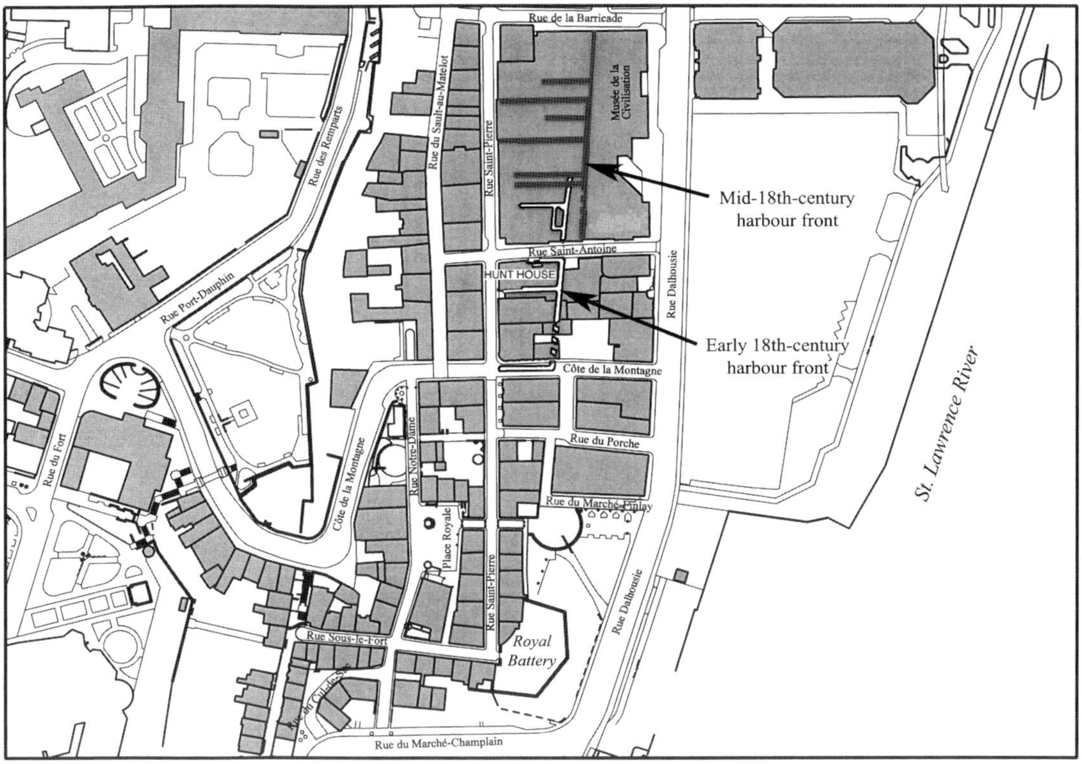

FIG. 5
Location of 18th-century archaeological remains of the Lower Town harbour front (drawn by L. Grenier, Ville de Québec).

line of masonry walls running parallel to the river, intersected here and there by streets that led down to openings onto the foreshore. Apart from the sector occupied by the Royal Battery, which had been constructed in 1692, the first linear harbour front resulted from a series of individual developments on the lots granted along the upper limits of the foreshore. The collective result of these shoreline projects was a continuous line of masonry walls giving onto the river (Fig. 5).

The siting of cannon batteries near the river provided an additional impetus to the development of the Lower Town harbour front. A front measuring *c.* 99m was achieved by constructing the Dauphine Battery on river-shore properties in 1707 and by the subsequent extension of this defence northward to the Boisseau lot in 1745. Evidence of mixed use, with harbour activities taking place despite the presence of military works, has been recovered.[22] Nevertheless, it is surprising to see how much space was occupied by the cannon batteries along the Lower Town's harbour front; depending on the year, they took up from 43% to over 50% of the harbour area in the early 18th century.

The novel feature of the first private shoreline developments, both residential and harbour-side, is their dual use. This appears to have grown directly from customary practices in Lower Town, where merchants used their homes to store goods for sale: their characteristic multifunctionality may have served as a model for subsequent building projects on shoreline properties. The evidence relating to this period suggests that the property owners began by erecting a wall to enclose the lot that had been granted to them, and then built a house fronting onto Rue Saint-Pierre, supplemented by sheds to the rear. Once such urban development had been undertaken, attention could be directed to using the river side of properties for harbour activities. The data from this first wave of development indicate a degree of ambivalence as to the intended end-use of the structures erected. In contrast, building projects conducted in the mid-18th century show a shift in the approach adopted by property owners, who sometimes mentioned a wharf on their water lot. The combined use of these sites for harbour facilities and domestic occupation has been confirmed by archaeological remains, which have also shown that the residential function continued to figure prominently in the use of shore properties. This was a vital component in the dynamic surrounding the appropriation of shoreline space throughout the French regime.

The harbour structures consisted of facilities for berthing ships and for trans-shipping and storing cargo. They varied according to the nature and volume of the goods transferred, the constraints specific to the river, and the ships and boats involved. These facilities constituted a link between land and marine transport. As objects of archaeological analysis, their remains provide insight into the facilities established to meet the commercial requirements of their owners. The remains of the Lower Town harbour front indicate that infrastructure was developed as a direct outgrowth of private lots. The wharves could only be accessed by shallow-draught service vessels, and then only by coordinating harbour activities with the movements of the tides. Beaching therefore had to be timed just before the onset of ebb tide. A comparison of archaeological data for early 18th-century shore-front facilities with those from the middle of the same century has brought to light the stronger integration of harbour activities during the latter period. As will be seen below, the trend toward the exclusive use of this space for harbour activities would become apparent in the infrastructure built in the late 18th century.

In the morphology of the Lower Town harbour, the formation of a linear front stands out as an evolving process. In LaRoche's view, the development of a straight-lined front was based on a European rather than a North American model.[23] This kind of layout was similar to that seen in several small European ports and even at Louisbourg, a city founded in 1719 in the neighbouring colony of Île Royale (today's Cape Breton Island, Nova Scotia), which boasted a major seaport opening onto the Atlantic. A comparison of the harbour infrastructure established in Québec and Louisbourg brings out differences in the ways in which harbour space was developed, despite the fact that both cities boasted a linear front. The side of Louisbourg facing the roadstead was fitted out with a linear wharf that meshed closely with the surrounding urban fabric.[24] In contrast with Québec, the design of the *Quay de Louisbourg* followed from a decision by the colonial authorities that its construction should fit with a broader urban planning scheme aimed at stabilizing shoreline erosion and developing a public space along the harbour front. The wharf consisted of a masonry wall a little more than 2m thick, covered with a timber facing protecting it against the elements. The case of Québec was very different, as the construction of wharves had been undertaken entirely by shoreline lot owners. There was, moreover, no question of allowing free movement along the river-front, for each of the properties on which these wharves had been built also featured a courtyard wall which formed an effective obstacle to traffic. Furthermore, the city ports fronted onto bodies of water that differed considerably from each other. The Louisbourg harbour was located at the head of a bay whose entrance provided protection from the ocean's waves. Rising alongside a major waterway, Québec was more exposed to the river's shifts in weather, tides and currents, not to mention the rigours of winter in the St Lawrence Valley. Moreover, the long foreshores were virtually inaccessible to boats at ebb tide. Finally, Louisbourg's defences were judiciously sited at distinct strategic locations around the rim of the bay and did not constitute a major hindrance to the harbour facilities. In contrast, the defensive structures of Québec's harbour were erected on the wharves of the merchants who owned and occupied shoreline properties. In short, considerations of urban planning, defence and commercial function in the two colonial cities were very different.

PORT SAINT-NICOLAS

Port Saint-Nicolas was a beaching point opposite Rue Saint-Nicolas in the part of the city associated with the Intendant's Palace. The development of a town in this area during the second quarter of the 18th century spurred the emergence of marine activities, including shipbuilding by private interests, as well as careening and refitting work.[25] In particular, shipbuilding operations on the shores of the Saint-Charles River were begun by Intendant Talon and the merchant Aubert de La Chesnaye between 1666 and 1671. Beaching conditions improved considerably following the construction of a dyke to protect this 'port' from winds and waves;[26] the structure was built in response to violent autumn winds.[27] Construction work directed by the engineer Chaussegros de Léry took place between 1733 and 1735; shipbuilding operations close to the 'Palace dyke' got underway in 1736.

The dyke was a long structure in dry masonry measuring about 10m wide and an estimated 160m long. It was erected on the foreshore of the Saint-Charles River, starting at the upper shoreline and extending to the riverbed further to the north

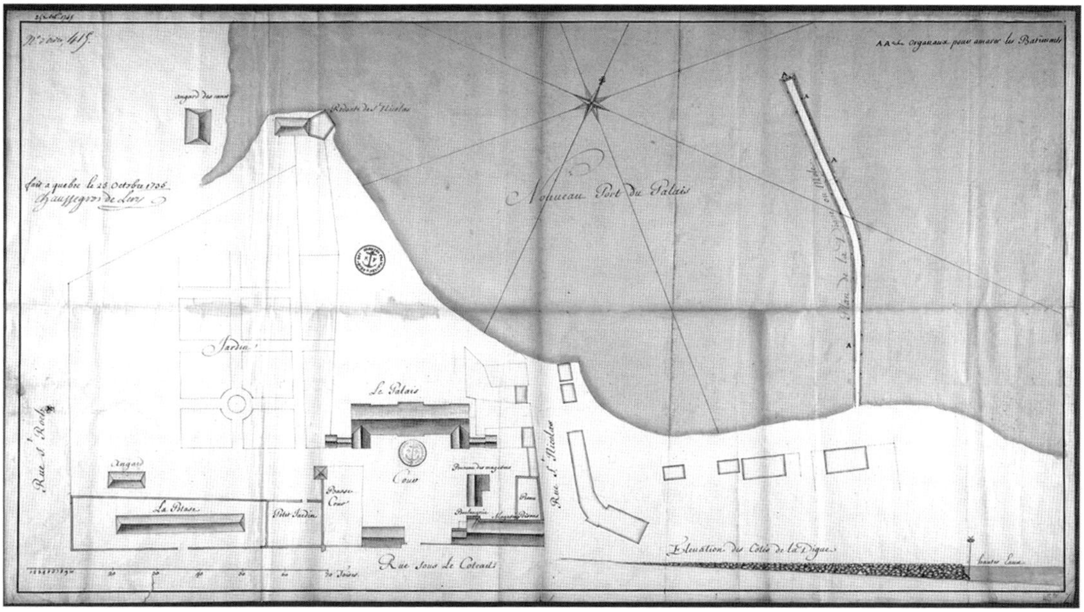

FIG. 6
The Intendant's Palace and outbuildings, along with the outline of the dyke, in 1733, by Chaussegros de Léry (NAC, C-21774).

(Fig. 6); it enclosed a space covering more than 200m to the north and east of the Saint-Charles Estuary's shoreline perimeter. Its sides were fitted with mooring rings for boats which drew alongside. A portion of the dyke was uncovered during roadworks in 1983;[28] the structure had two long parallel masonry faces, the eastern one taking the form of a stone embankment 3.84m wide. Outsized river boulders and hefty rock fragments were used in its construction.

Once completed, the dyke helped to improve the safety of Port Saint-Nicolas by providing a haven for boats. About 20 years after its construction, the structure was cited by its engineer, de Léry, as an example of efficacy and solidity.[29] A large-scale work, it remained a fixture of Québec harbour until the end of the first decade of the 19th century.

In 1739 the siting of the royal shipyard in this sector entailed the occupation of a considerable portion of the shore to the west of the dyke, accentuating the industrial character of the area. The shipyard, only a stone's throw from the Intendant's Palace, enhanced the presence of the Crown at Port Saint-Nicolas with the addition of various structures including a berthing block, a double-spur wharf, boat-sheds and workshops. Beginning in 1742, a series of transformations were carried out with a view to adapting the existing infrastructure to provide for the maintenance and wintering of the king's ships.[30] However, the users of the shipyard were quickly confronted with the natural constraints of this sector, whose long foreshore and shallow waters compromised the safety of large ships when they were launched. Shipbuilding operations were thus transferred to Port du Cul-de-Sac in 1748. From that time on, Port Saint-Nicolas was used primarily for harbour activities, including the maintenance or sheltering of boats.[31]

The royal shipyard site was the scene of various archaeological projects conducted by the City of Québec, specifically a survey undertaken in 1988 and major excavations in 1989 and 1997.[32] The remains dating to around 1742–43 testify to two contrasting architectural visions of the royal shipyard then current in the colony: one an empirical perspective that drew on local practices, the other a view shaped by new conceptions originating in the mother country.[33]

PORT DU CUL-DE-SAC

From the time of the founding of Québec, the natural beach at Cul-de-Sac was used as a beaching point for boats. It was a choice location for the careening or refitting of ships, owing to the proximity of deep waters and the presence of a uniform and generally hospitable river-bed. Nestled within a small cove, Cul-de-Sac was much sought after as a place for wintering small vessels. As well, damaged ships were often taken to this harbour which, according to the historian Réal Brisson, served as a ship hospital/shipyard for the colony.[34] The large stones on the foreshore were removed around 1712 to improve the safety of the harbour's waters. Finally, this 'port' was used as a place for building small vessels by ship's carpenters and workmen living in the vicinity.

With the establishment of the king's shipyard in *c.* 1747–48, structures were installed in the western portion of the cove. Over the succeeding years the shipyard was fitted out with wharves, construction docks, workshops, offices, a large forge and a boat-shed measuring 300 French feet (97.5m) in length.[35] Whereas this 'port' had previously been used for harbour operations, the focus of its activities now shifted to work associated with the king's shipyard.

The harbour activities conducted at Cul-de-Sac did not lead to the construction of many facilities. The structures that were built in the sector stemmed primarily from the establishment of the royal shipyard. As archaeological work could only be undertaken in the streets nearby, little information concerning the Cul-de-Sac sector has been found. Despite today's office buildings, the site of this 'port' offers some archaeological potential: beneath today's car parks and public roads there may lie harbour-related facilities and a number of royal shipyard structures. It is thought that a little over 65% of the Port du Cul-de-Sac archaeological site could survive below unoccupied spaces.

THE DISAPPEARANCE OF THE FRENCH COLONIAL PORT

During the first years of the British regime, few modifications were made to the city's harbour facilities. Even though a number of repairs and projects were carried out by local merchants, the Lower Town's harbour front remained, on the whole, very similar to the one established under the French regime. The infrastructure associated with the Cul-de-Sac royal shipyard and near the Intendant's Palace was retained and used by the new colonial authorities. One of the first modifications made to the French harbour was to remove the cannon batteries shortly after the transfer of Canada to the British Crown under the 1763 Treaty of Paris. These defence works were soon converted into commercial wharves.

A number of new large-scale projects were gradually implemented in the Lower Town harbour after 1770. The trend was to extend wharves into the river towards deep water. One example of the facilities characterizing the new British colonial port is to be found in the wharves of merchants of the Lymburner family, erected on the site of the former Pointe à Carcy. A portion of the Lymburner harbour complex was the site of archaeological excavations conducted by the City of Québec during construction work to convert the former fire station into the Ex Machina centre, near Rue Dalhousie, in 1995–96.[36]

Adam Lymburner, a native of Kilmarnock, Scotland, arrived in Québec around 1772. He had come to the city in order to take over the commercial activities of his brother John, who had died recently. He eventually formed a company with his other brother, Mathew, and a nephew, John Crawford. Their business dealings centred on the fur trade and fishing off Labrador. From 1795, Mathew Lymburner continued his commercial activities as a partner in the firm known as Lymburner and Crawford.

Transformations at the former Pointe à Carcy were begun after 1780 with the creation of a basin at the north end of the harbour front. To this end, a 57m-long wharf was built on a water lot owned by Robert Wilcox. Lying 34m from previously existing facilities, this new wharf gave shape to a basin whose entrance opened onto the river. The east end of the wharf was excavated during archaeological work in 1996. The structure consisted of coffers built of medium-sized round logs, held together with wooden pegs, which retained a fill of earth and boulders.

Upon assuming ownership of these facilities, Mathew Lymburner carried out a series of improvements. The first, built prior to 1799, was designed to protect the basin entrance and to extend the former Wilcox wharf south-east into the river (Fig. 7). Subsequently, another construction pointing north-east was added at the basin entrance; the completed structure was thus Y-shaped. The south-east component of these additions proved to be of particular interest in both design and location.

The archaeological remains uncovered testify to a massive, carefully executed structure. The rectangular wharf measured 26m in length and 10m in width. Each side rose upon a 2m-wide dry masonry foundation. Its outer face was sheathed in timbers, held in place by tie-beams set into the foundation (Fig. 8). Finally, a spacious, two-storey warehouse, also in stone, was erected on the wharf; a portion of it stood as late as 1875.

The Lymburners' harbour facilities constituted an innovative complex located upon the water lots of the former Pointe à Carcy, which were left dry at low tide. These constructions marked

FIG. 7
Harbour infrastructure of the Lymburner family (CeEt-536): the Y-shaped structure erected along the north side of the basin. Detail of a map drawn by William Hall in 1804. North is at the top (NAC, NMC-19308).

a break with the type of development seen in Québec's Lower Town under the French regime. The basin and wharves were not built to reclaim ground but to extend a harbour structure into the river, thereby shortening the waiting times between tides. The siting of the wharf at the basin entrance was clearly designed to improve its protection and, much as with a breakwater, to facilitate the entrance of boats. The addition of another wharf on a north-east tangent was evidently designed to provide a range of alternatives regarding the protection and mooring of boats in accordance with shifts in tides, winds and waves. These facilities were exclusively dedicated to harbour activities, in contrast with the practice under the French regime, in which residential and harbour functions were combined.

Quite remarkably, the Lymburner wharves remained in active use for more than 50 years, testifying to the financial wherewithal of the owners and their firms. The longevity of these wharves, located as they were in an environment subjected to the daily impact of tides and the annual spring break-up of the ice, no doubt owes much to the quality of the work of the late 18th-century builders.

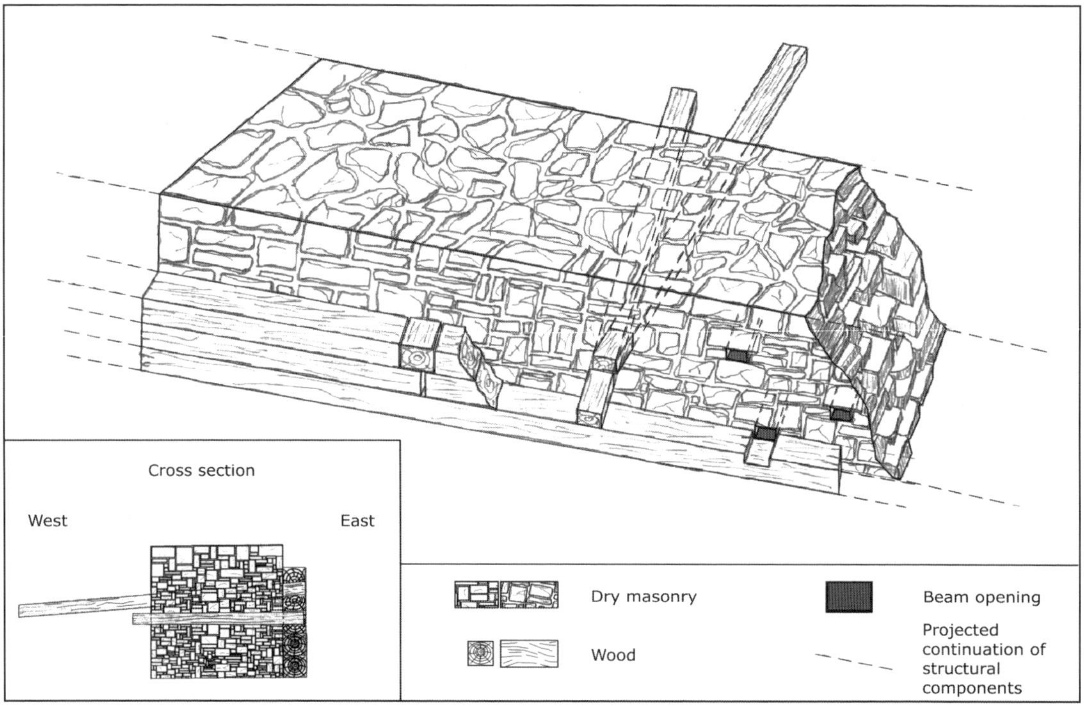

FIG. 8

Harbour infrastructures of the Lymburner family (CeEt-536): archaeological remains of a portion of the south side of the Lymburner wharf located in front of the basin entrance. This dry masonry feature, 2.4m wide, was faced with timbers (drawn by B. Fiset, F. Pellerin, Ville de Québec).

CONCLUSION

Of the three areas of the French colonial port, the Lower Town merchant quarter was home to the greatest number of harbour developments. The Cul-de-Sac site boasted numerous natural advantages, and was preserved largely intact. The Port Saint-Nicolas sector was, from 1733, the site of a few developments, chief of which remains the establishment of a dyke to improve the protection afforded to this beaching point.

The Lower Town 'port' facilities were the outcome of initiatives undertaken by river-shore property owners. The basic dynamic driving these developments was the need for residential space capable of accommodating commercial and harbour activities. The structures built in the early 18th century served, to a certain extent, to formalize the city front, which assumed a straight line running parallel to the river. The masonry structures erected during this period, intersected here and there by the openings of streets onto the river-shore, shaped the harbour environment of this French colonial city of the North American interior. Subsequent grants of water lots in the mid-18th century carried forward this trend.

The French colonial port gradually disappeared during the last decades of the 18th century, although several components survived until the beginning of the following one. After the port became British, the batteries were quickly supplanted by wharves, and the new harbour facilities were henceforth orientated toward satisfying the requirements of a new economy.

ACKNOWLEDGEMENTS

I would like to thank William Moss and Daniel Simoneau, of the City of Québec, as well as Allison Bain and Réginald Auger, both of Université Laval, for their support during the drafting of this paper.

NOTES

[1] Moussette & Moss 2008, 26.

[2] These paragraphs concerning the marine environment are designed to highlight the main aspects likely

to have had a direct impact in the past on ships, boats and river-shore infrastructure. Statistics in relation to these factors have been kept to a minimum.

[3] Simoneau 2003, 27–8.
[4] Mathieu 1971, 18.
[5] SAAC & Laroche 1990.
[6] Mathieu 1971, 18.
[7] Proulx 1984, 45–6.
[8] ANQQ, greffe Gilles Rageot, 8 Aug. 1688.
[9] ANQQ, greffe Gilles Rageot, 8 Aug. 1688.
[10] Zoltvany 1969.
[11] ANQQ, greffe François Genaple, 4 June 1699.
[12] LaRoche 1986, 52.
[13] ANQQ, greffe François Genaple, 4 June 1699.
[14] Simoneau 2003, 68.
[15] Simoneau 2003, 69.
[16] LaRoche 1986, 258.
[17] LaRoche 1986, 289.
[18] Simoneau 2003, 41.
[19] Simoneau 2003, 82.
[20] LaRoche 1986.
[21] LaRoche 2008, 222.
[22] Simoneau 2003, 69.
[23] LaRoche 1986, 290.
[24] Lavoie 1965, 5.
[25] Brisson 1983, 45, 58.
[26] Charbonneau *et al.* 1982, 370.
[27] Brisson 1983, 45.
[28] Giroux 1984, 13–14.
[29] Charbonneau *et al.* 1982, 373.
[30] Loewen & Cloutier 2003, 39–40.
[31] Brisson 1983, 45.
[32] GRHQR 1989; SAAC & Laroche 1990; Cloutier 1998.
[33] Loewen & Cloutier 2003.
[34] Brisson 1983, 58.
[35] Mathieu 1971, 22.
[36] Rouleau 1997.

BIBLIOGRAPHY

PUBLISHED SOURCES

Brisson, R. 1983, *La Charpenterie navale à Québec sous le régime français*, Collection Edmond-de-Nevers **2**, Québec: Institut québécois de recherche sur la culture.

Charbonneau, A., Desloges, Y. & Lafrance, M. 1982, *Québec ville fortifiée du XVIIe au XIXe siècle*, Éditions du Pélican/Parcs Canada. [Published in English under the title *Québec the Fortified City: from the 17th to the 19th Century*, Ottawa: Supply & Services Canada.]

LaRoche, D. 2008, 'Au gré des vents et marées à Québec! Embarcations naviguant sur le fleuve Saint-Laurent au XVIIIe siècle: tradition ou adaptation?', in Roy & Côté 2008, 221–42.

Loewen, B. & Cloutier, C. 2003, 'Le Chantier naval royal à Québec et le savoir maritime au XVIIIe siècle', in Roy *et al.* 2003, 23–42.

Mathieu, J. 1971, *La Construction navale royale à Québec*, Cahiers d'Histoire **23**.

Moussette, M. & Moss, W. 2008, 'Québec, ville coloniale et porte atlantique du nouveau monde: un point de vue archéologique', in Roy & Côté 2008, 18–37.

Proulx, G. 1984, *Entre France et Nouvelle-France*, LaPrairie (Québec): Marcel Broquet.

Roy, C., Bélisle, J., Bernier, M.-A. & Loewen, B. (eds) 2003, *Mer et monde: Questions d'archéologie maritime*, Archéologiques, hors série **1**.

Roy, C. & Côté, H. (eds) 2008, *Rêves d'Amériques: regard sur l'archéologie de la Nouvelle-France — Dreams of the Americas: Overview of New France Archaeology*, Archéologiques, hors série **2**.

Zoltvany, Y.F. 1969, 'Aubert de La Chesnaye, Charles', in *Dictionnaire biographique du Canada* **2**, Québec: Université Laval, 27–36.

UNPUBLISHED SOURCES

Cloutier, C. 1998, 'Place de la gare, rapport d'interventions archéologiques', Québec: Ville de Québec, Division design et patrimoine.

Giroux, P. 1984, 'Rapport de surveillance archéologique Sous-secteurs Ancien Chantier et Saint-Paul', Québec: Ville de Québec, Division du Vieux-Québec et du Patrimoine.

GRHQR 1989, 'Inventaire archéologique Place de la gare et les environs', Québec: Ville de Québec, Division du Vieux-Québec et du Patrimoine.

LaRoche, D. 1986, 'La surveillance et le sauvetage des vestiges archéologiques au musée de la civilisation à Québec', 4 vols, Québec: Société immobilière du Québec.

Lavoie, R. 1965, 'Quai de Louisbourg I: étude sur sa construction, son usage et son histoire, de 1716 à 1760', Parcs Canada. [Republished in 1972 with an English addition by R. Cox, in the series Travail inédit **195**, Ottawa: Parcs Canada, Direction des lieux et parcs historiques nationaux.]

Rouleau, S. 1997, 'Rapport de recherches archéologiques: les installations portuaires des marchands Lymburner, Monro et Bell (CeEt-536)', Québec: Ville de Québec, Division design et patrimoine.

SAAC & LaRoche, D. 1990, 'Recherches archéologiques: la Place René-Lévesque', Québec: Ville de Québec, Division du Vieux-Québec et du Patrimoine.

Simoneau, D. 2003, 'Rapport d'interventions archéologiques: l'Ilot Hunt 2001–2002', Québec:

Ville de Québec, Division design, architecture et patrimoine.

ABBREVIATIONS

ANQQ	Archives nationales du Québec à Québec
AAQ	Association des archéologues du Québec
GRHQR	Groupe de Recherches en Histoire du Québec Rural Inc.
MCCCFQ	Ministère de la Culture, des Communications et de la Condition féminine
NAC	National Archives of Canada (Ottawa)
SAAC	Société Archéologique de l'Ancien Chantier

SUMMARY IN FRENCH, GERMAN, ITALIAN AND SPANISH

RÉSUMÉ

Un regard archéologique sur le port colonial français de Québec

Dans cet article, les vestiges de la première devanture portuaire découverte à l'Îlot Hunt à Québec sont étudiés en relation avec les indices trouvés sur d'autres sites de la basse ville de la cité. Ces vestiges jettent la lumière sur la nature du port colonial français, témoignant des initiatives de ses marchands et des actions de ses autorités coloniales. Les structures construites au cours du régime britannique par des marchands de la famille Lymburner fournissent un exemple des infrastructures innovantes qui inaugurent la disparition (vers 1775–80) du port développé au cours de la période coloniale française.

ZUSAMMENFASSUNG

Eine archäologische Betrachtung des französischen Hafens Quebec

In dieser Arbeit werden die Reste der ersten Hafenfront, die auf der Îlot Hunt in Quebec gefunden wurden, im Zusammenhang mit anderen Überresten in der Unterstadt behandelt. Diese Überreste werfen ein Licht auf die Natur des französischen Kolonialhafens und zeugen von der Initiative der Kaufleute und den Handlungen der kolonialen Behörden. Bauten, die unter dem britischen Regime von zur Lymburner-Familie gehörigen Kaufleuten gebaut wurden, sind Zeugen neuartiger Einrichtungen, die das Verschwinden (ca. 1775–80) der alten Hafenfront aus der französischen Kolonialzeit einläuteten.

RIASSUNTO

Una prospettiva archeologica del porto coloniale francese di Quebec

Questo contributo discute i resti del primo fronte del porto, scoperti a Îlot Hunt nella città di Quebec, in relazione a quanto emerso in altri siti nella parte bassa della città. Questi resti gettano luce sulla natura del porto coloniale francese, testimoniando le iniziative dei suoi mercanti e le azioni delle autorità coloniali. Le strutture costruite durante il regime britannico dai mercanti della famiglia Lymburner forniscono un esempio del tipo di strutture innovative che portano alla scomparsa del fronte del porto (c. 1775–80) sviluppato durante il periodo dell'era coloniale francese.

RESUMEN

Un enfoque arqueológico del puerto colonial francés de Quebec

En este artículo se consideran los restos del primer puerto descubierto en el Îlot Hunt en Quebec en relación con evidencia derivada de otros yacimientos en la Cuidad Baja de la ciudad. Dichos restos nos informan sobre el tipo y carácter del puerto colonial francés, sobre las iniciativas de sus comerciantes y sobre las acciones de las primeras autoridades coloniales. Las estructuras construidas durante el período británico por comerciantes de la familia Lymburner son un ejemplo del tipo de facilidades innovadoras que marcaron la desaparición (*c.* 1775-80) de la primera línea del puerto creada durante la era colonial francesa.

Ville de Québec, Service de l'aménagement du territoire, Division du design, de l'architecture et du patrimoine, édifice de la Fabrique, 295, boulevard Charest Est, Québec (Québec), Canada G1K 3G8 [serge.rouleau@ville.quebec.qc.ca]

Post-Medieval Archaeology **43/1** (2009), 245–257

The foreshore of the St Lawrence at the Îlot Hunt site in the 17th and 18th centuries: an open dump?

By CÉLINE CLOUTIER

SUMMARY: This paper investigates the state of the St Lawrence riverbanks along Québec's Lower Town in the 17th and 18th centuries. A detailed study of archaeological collections was undertaken to evaluate the impact of Euro-Québécois occupation on this natural environment. Soil samples were used to study plant macroremains, insects and parasites from the ancient shores. At first glance the data seem to indicate that the beaches were used as a dumping ground during the period. However, the study of these remains gives a more nuanced picture, testifying to the area's many public and private roles and the diverse interests it served.

INTRODUCTION

Québec was founded on the shores of the St Lawrence, one of the mightiest navigable waterways in North America, and the city's riverside setting played a determining role in its development and population growth. A seaport sheltered from winds and powerful waves, and favoured by tides that allowed vessels to drop anchor in deep water, Québec became the commercial hub of the colony during the French regime and continued to play an important mercantile role under English rule. Despite the narrowness of the shore, hemmed in between the river and the cliffs, merchants and businessmen involved in maritime and port activities, and in trade and commerce with the colony's interior and the motherland, elected to live in this part of Québec's Lower Town, particularly in and around Place Royale. This concentration of dwellings became the city's main residential quarter in the 17th and 18th centuries.

In 1659 Charles Aubert de La Chesnaye, whose business activities placed him among the principal players on the colony's economic scene in the second half of the 17th century, began building an imposing residence in this area, at the northern tip of the Point of Québec. The archaeological site that bears his name is so called not just because of his status, but also because of the quantity and quality of the remains associated with his property.

From an archaeological and historical viewpoint, the Îlot Hunt cannot be dissociated from the Aubert de La Chesnaye site, since it comprises shore lots that formed an eastward extension of the properties belonging to the illustrious merchant and his neighbour, Gauthier de Comporté. They were both experienced businessmen who exploited these lots, granted to them in 1687.[1] The development of Îlot Hunt was closely linked to the advantages and constraints of an exceptional natural environment. Initially, the site had sandy beaches; it soon became part of the port facilities which have been a feature of Québec's waterfront since the settlement's earliest days. Thanks to nearly fifteen years of research and many scientific reports, this archaeological site is now known to encompass the remains of numerous structures, including dwellings, wharves, military works, warehouses, workshops, commercial buildings, outbuildings and sanitary facilities. A research report prepared by Daniel Simoneau for the City of Québec[2] shows how these remains, associated with domestic, commercial and military occupation,

DOI: 10.1179/007942309X12457508844404

along with port- and craft-related activities, testify to the site's physical evolution from the 17th century to the present day.

In the 1600s, the port of Québec was a natural harbour in which the largest vessels of the day could drop anchor. Ships' cargoes were transferred by boat and dinghy to the shore, where sandy flats bordering the shore lots made it easy to land these small craft, laden with merchandise. It took a great deal of costly work to make a waterfront lot profitable. Since the port area was constricted between the shoreline and the cliffs, property owners could expand their operations only by gaining land from the river by extensive landfill. In 1688 Charles Aubert de La Chesnaye began such work by building a wooden enclosure on one of the shore lots he owned in front of his prestigious residence. The enclosure was equipped with gates through which horses, oxen and carts could pass, and, at high tide, it presumably facilitated the transportation of merchandise to the shore in small boats. In 1699, the enclosure was replaced by an impressive masonry wharf. This was transformed into part of a defensive work known as the first Dauphine Battery in 1709, when a British attack on Québec seemed imminent.[3] A second advanced work was begun in 1757 following a new declaration of war with Britain. Archaeological research has clearly shown that this second Dauphine Battery was never completed; the only elements constructed were the foundations and a façade wall along Rue Saint-Antoine (Fig. 1).[4]

After the British conquest, the old port facilities remained unchanged for almost a quarter of a century. Then improvements became necessary to keep pace with two developments: ships with greater tonnage were required to supply England with newly available products such as wheat, potash and lumber, and at the same time maritime traffic increased as a result of growing trade activity. These developments were reflected in a rapid succession of structures of various forms that advanced into the river. For example, three new wharves were built at Îlot Hunt within less than 30 years. At this time, many port cities were more or less simultaneously affected by changes in international trade and, prompted by economic considerations, they enlarged their docksides through

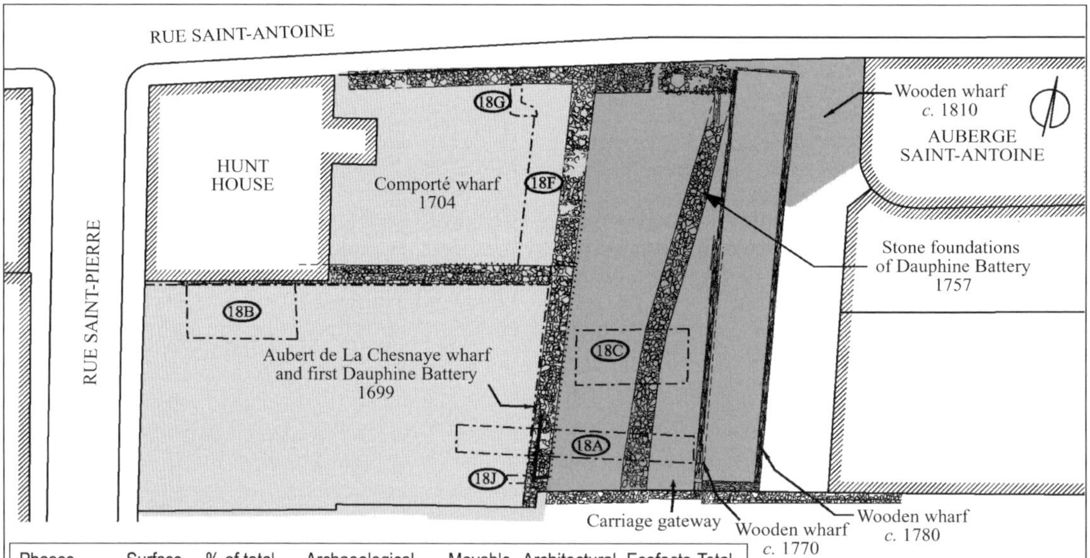

Phases studied	Surface area (m²)	% of total surface area	Archaeological excavations	Movable	Architectural	Ecofacts	Total
Phase 1 17th century	792.68	60.96	Detailed excavation and monitoring	876	898	1,077	2,851
Phase 2 18th century	507.59	39.01	Detailed excavation and monitoring	3,480	294	136	3,910
Total	1,300.27	100	Beach level	4,356	1,192	1,213	6,761

-·-·- Limits of excavation units (detailed excavation)

0 10m

Plan No. 00007a32.dgn

FIG. 1

The Îlot Hunt archaeological site (plan, Ville de Québec).

massive landfill operations. Numerous archaeological projects have centred on the analysis of these man-made spaces and the impressive landfill schemes required to develop ports and build wharves, particularly on sites in New York, Philadelphia, Boston and Baltimore[5] and, here in Québec, at the Musée de la civilisation and the Bell and Hunt sites.[6] The transformation of the landscape as the city encroached on the river has been documented at Îlot Hunt. The most recent archaeological work on this site, carried out in 2001 by the City of Québec's design, architecture and heritage service, made it possible to reach the level of the ancient foreshore.[7] This was apparently the first time that a natural environment buried for centuries under immense loads of fill was specifically targeted for a material culture study. This study, rendered particularly interesting by the palaeoenvironmental approach that was taken, sought to assess the state of the ancient foreshore when it was first used by Europeans, and to determine how conditions changed with the construction and expansion of commercial, defensive and port facilities in the 17th and 18th centuries. Research into the condition of the ancient beach represents something quite new. As well as shedding light on the state of the shore and the changes in its condition over the periods studied, this investigation has provided an opportunity to compare the kind of natural beach sediments found there before the arrival of Europeans with the deposits that began to pollute the strand as it was used increasingly throughout the 17th and 18th centuries. This paper will look at how this research might answer the question of whether the foreshore was truly an open dump, as has been suggested both by written sources and by the quantity of material uncovered there.

ARCHAEOLOGICAL PERSPECTIVES AND CONTEXTS

Today much interdisciplinary research is focused on ecosystems, the fundamental ecological units that involve all living things on earth, along with their habitats and their interdependence. Basing their work on a range of sciences, researchers and interest groups are more concerned than ever with conserving and protecting natural environments and landscapes. The earth's ecological heritage is multi-faceted and those concerned about it are motivated by numerous interests. There are widespread signs of fear of a disruption in the balance between natural resources and humans' ability to control them — and thus control their own destiny. Ultimately, this amounts to fear of extinction, since humans are part of the threatened ecosystem, but, at the same time, it reflects an emerging awareness of responsibility for the future of the planet.

Archaeology is also caught up in this current.[8] By treating the city as an ecosystem — as part of a natural environment that it both exploits and depends on — researchers can look at the relationship humans have maintained with their natural habitat in the past and present, and thus study how the development of inhabited spaces has been affected by the changing density and growth of human populations. Such new perspectives make it possible to broaden our research horizons and construct different working hypotheses. Environmental archaeology is increasingly used in urban environments, and the fact that it calls on diverse disciplines like zooarchaeology and microbiology makes it well suited to an approach based on ecosystems.[9] Taking this approach, the palaeoenvironmental study of the Îlot Hunt foreshore has placed the site in a broader urban context, providing a suitable framework for investigating the state of the foreshore at the time of the first European occupation in the 17th century, and for examining the ways in which this evolved in the 18th century as the population grew and port activities intensified.

Research conducted both by historians and archaeologists over the past decade into various written sources, including regulations, edicts and orders, suggests that the town's vacant spaces were in a deplorable state.[10] According to these documents, the streets, alleys and beaches were cluttered with household waste, table scraps, animal carcasses, muck, filth, straw and manure, resulting not only from the concentration of people but also from the presence of live animals and the accumulation of their remains after butchering. Despite numerous prohibitions, animals wandered freely about the town in the 17th and 18th centuries, producing considerable quantities of refuse. Waste from butchered animals was left to accumulate in the streets. In the hope that the tides would eliminate some of the garbage generated by the town, the authorities asked residents to take their household waste and butchering refuse to the banks of the Saint-Charles or the St Lawrence.[11] In 1694 carters were hired to collect refuse and transport it to one of the rivers every week, except in winter, when the state of the streets made this impossible. In the first half of the 18th century, documents indicate that the mounds of garbage on the beaches had reached such proportions that they impeded the landing of rowboats and other small craft.

Thus, according to written sources, the beaches were the final destination of all kinds of waste in the 17th and 18th centuries. It is therefore easy to imagine that the urban environment in

Lower Town, especially near the St Lawrence and the Saint-Charles, left much to be desired — and to infer that large accumulations of garbage dating from this period remain buried there today. There must have been considerable pollution from human and animal sources. But what was the actual condition of the banks of the St Lawrence in the 17th and 18th centuries? The following sections explore the question of how archaeological research on the foreshore area of Îlot Hunt may help to evaluate the true extent of domestic and other pollution of the river's shores, described by some as a vast open dump right up to the early 20th century.

METHODOLOGY

For the purposes of this study, two chronological phases were chosen, both associated with projects that advanced the shoreline and enclosed sections of the former beach when wharves or defensive works were built. The first dates to the 17th century, particularly its latter part, when a portion of the beach was enclosed by the waterfront facilities constructed by Aubert de La Chesnaye. The second dates to the 18th century, when the environment of this sector of the port underwent infilling for construction projects (Fig. 1). The material culture was studied against the backdrop of these developments; in order to reveal changes in public hygiene, the artefact assemblages from the two centuries were compared. The objects represented were listed by building a directory file for the collection with the help of a computerized database, tabulated on an Excel spreadsheet. This quantitative approach highlighted the representativeness and identity of the objects; it was chosen in preference to a qualitative approach based on functional categories, which would have been more suitable for characterizing the lifestyles and living conditions of a social group or household, but seemed less appropriate for answering the palaeoenvironmental research questions posed here, mainly because the artefacts and ecofacts were not discovered *in situ*. The qualitative approach is used here only for a discussion of certain particularities shown by the objects found in the shore environment and of the ways in which these remains changed over the periods under consideration.

THE FORESHORE IN THE 17TH CENTURY

The 17th-century deposits were sealed below waterfront structures built by Charles Aubert de La Chesnaye in 1699[12] and Gauthier de Comporté around 1704,[13] and thus contain contexts dating from before the turn of the century. They covered 792.68m^2, or 60.96% of the area which had been the subject of detailed excavation and archaeological monitoring (Fig. 1). The layers studied had an average depth of 0.34m; they sloped down slightly to the east and north.[14] They consisted of black sand containing a great concentration of organic material (branches, bark, wood chips, straw and hay),[15] representing river sediments which accumulated in a small cove as tides ebbed and flowed, isolated from the rest of the late 17th-century foreshore. In all, 2,851 artefacts and ecofacts were found on the beach in these two areas (Fig. 1), showing that it was used freely as a dump. Table 1 summarizes the principal categories of object found.

MOVABLE OBJECTS

Movable goods make up 31% of the assemblage. Apart from pipe fragments and glass beads, there were 234 ceramic objects and 28 fragments of glass; many of the last were oxidized and leached by water. The domestic rubbish also included broken tools, pieces of fabric and the remains of footwear, brooms and faggots. The remains were similar to the domestic garbage found in the town's yards, streets, alleys and gardens, where waste would have been left before being collected and hauled to the beaches.

Exactly what proportion of the movable objects should be regarded as garbage dumped on the beach is uncertain. Many of the finds are related to hunting and fishing, and to various activities connected to trade and commerce, all of which took place on the site. Such objects are represented by gunflints and lead shot, which may be associated with hunting small game in this area, and by hooks, which could have been used for line fishing from the shore or for commercial fishing. Glass beads, scraps of copper and the remains of a clasp knife represent trade goods that were much prized by Amerindians in the contact period (Fig. 2). A collection of 88 wound wire-headed pins, all of the same size, might also be trade goods. Certain remains, such as quartz and chert flakes and a partly carved stone pipe, probably made by an Amerindian, indicate that the site was used by Aboriginal groups. Fragments of birch bark items were also found in this context (Fig. 3) and, although it is difficult to identify with certainty the objects represented, they seem to have been containers, bags or baskets laced with strips of birch bark. One of these fragments is heavier than the others and might be associated with the remains of a birch bark canoe. Lumps of resin, which

TABLE 1

Distribution of objects from the 17th-century beach level of the Îlot Hunt site.

MOVABLE	ARCHITECTURAL	ECOFACTS
31% (876 objects)	**31% (898 objects)**	**38% (1,077 objects)**
Ceramic: 324 objects including **90** pipes and fragments. **Glass: 141** objects including **113** trade beads. **Metal:** **192** lead shot; **88** wound wire-headed pins; copper scraps, buttons, keg tap, coins, bale seal, scissors, knife, fish hooks, saw blade. **Other inorganic material:** Stone pipe, chess piece, flakes of chert, flint and quartz, gunflint. **Organic material:** Bone and shell beads, brooms, buttons, tool handle, clasp knife handle, 40 shoes, fragmentary barrels, residues of fur, feathers, threads, fabric, oakum, resin, birchbark containers.	**500** planks or pieces of milled wood. **149** nails. **97** fragments of window glass. **78** roofing slates. **28** bricks and tiles. Hinge, pintle, metal scrap.	**944** vertebrate bones. **19** shells, etc. **114** plant remains.

have also been categorized as movable objects, may have been used to caulk birch bark canoes, since this was common practice at the time. Coins, a bale seal and barrel fragments may have served in the course of commercial transactions. The 90 pipes and pipe fragments, gaming pieces, buttons and other small items are typical of the objects left accidentally by people passing through open urban spaces. Falling from a pocket or someone's fingers, these objects may simply have been lost and abandoned *in situ*; they need not necessarily be considered as town rubbish.

The layer under study was also characterized by numerous leather remains; 404 fragments were discovered, scattered across the entire area. About 40 shoes for men, women and children are represented. Most are ordinary, sturdy peasant shoes, many of them well worn and repaired; some may date from before the 17th century. It seems likely that these remains came from one or more of the cobblers' workshops operating nearby.[17] Tanners had set up business in Québec and the surrounding area by the last third of the 17th century; they processed the skins of cows, oxen, seals, does and stags, and supplied the makers of leather goods. By the end of the 17th century, 20 cobblers worked in the city region, most of them in Lower Town and concentrated around Place Royale.[18] Such an accumulation of footwear is not unique to the foreshore zone of Îlot Hunt; the beach levels of neighbouring archaeological sites are also characterized by a scatter of shoes and shoe fragments.[19] Being waterlogged, these beach environments in Québec's Lower Town tend to preserve organic material. A similar situation comes from London, England, where around 1,500 shoes dating from the period AD 1100–1450 were recovered in the late 1980s by the Museum of London's Department of Urban Archaeology from waterlogged deposits along the north shore of the Thames, providing material for a major typological study of medieval footwear.[20] In Québec's Lower Town, it is quite possible that the accumulation of shoes on the shore resulted from large-scale dumping of waste from one or more cobblers working nearby. After the great fire that ravaged Lower Town in 1682, there would have been a great deal of such waste to dispose of in the sector.[21]

Natural organic material included water- or air-borne chaff (twigs, hay and straw), carried to the beach by the movement of winds and tides, as well as debris from activities associated with this environment, such as small game hunting (feathers and fur) or caulking light boats (resin, oakum, hemp and flax).

ARCHITECTURAL OBJECTS

Architectural objects account for 31% of the collection. In this category there are 500 fragments of worked wood (shingles, planks, sheathing, stakes and wood chips), 149 wrought nails, 78 fragments of roofing slates, 97 pieces of window glass, 28 fragments of brick, 3 coarse earthenware sheathing tiles, 18 chunks of limestone and a few pieces of building hardware. There are several possible explanations for the large quantity of building materials on the beach. Pieces of lumber are cumbersome, and at the time it would have been easy to dispose of them in public places and open, empty areas. Wood may have also accumulated when floating debris was washed up on the shore; in any case, the natural contours of the cove would have encouraged floating wood to collect there. The most likely explanation, however, is that the worked wood was deposited on the beach when Aubert de La Chesnaye's house was renovated in 1679, or when his wooden enclosure was demolished around 1699.

ECOFACTS

A number of ecofacts were recovered. Of these, 88% consist of vertebrate bones and 11% are plant specimens, while only 2% are shells. The vertebrate bones that make up the bulk of these finds are large pieces representing the by-products of butchering. Such food refuse on the river's shores is no doubt attributable to the density of the population around the nearby wharves and to activities at the small outdoor market in Place Royale. The bone remains have not yet been studied. In 1689, the town of Québec and its suburbs had a human population of about 1,700 inhabitants living in 239 dwellings, while the animal population is estimated at 713. This figure includes 52 horses, 295 head of cattle, 180 sheep and 186 pigs, but does not take into account small farmyard animals and household animals like dogs and cats.[22]

A negligible quantity of shells — only 2% of all ecofacts — was found at this level of the beach. This material consisted of snail shells and the valves of molluscs such as oysters and clams. The rarity of shells suggests that they may have been salvaged and used for other purposes. Large amounts of shell are sometimes observed in old road beds, and it may be supposed that this material was used to fill holes and ruts, help dry out muddy surfaces and provide grit for better traction on Québec's steep, winding streets. Seashells were also collected by Amerindians to make jewellery and trinkets. Finally, oyster shells served as containers in which ink was diluted.[23]

MACROREMAINS

Catherine Fortin's study of the site's plant macroremains links the ways the shores were occupied to changes in the natural environment and its flora. She compared the relative abundance of plants from the natural environment — that is, indigenous plants and introduced weeds — with those originating in the cultural environment. The latter, related to domestic occupation of the area by Europeans, were transported to the beach as waste from food preparation and from privies, whose contents were emptied periodically. The results of the macroremains study confirm that the foreshore sector delimited by the La Chesnaye and Comporté wharves was polluted in the 17th century; its assemblages are dominated by macroremains associated with human excrement, table scraps and kitchen refuse. The concentration of waste can be related to the proximity of sources of contamination on higher ground — in particular the privies at the Aubert de La Chesnaye house. The privies' contents were analysed in 1995; they were remarkably similar to the assemblages discussed here. The distribution of macroremains on the beach indicates that the source of the waste was inland rather than near the water, since the proportion of faecal matter diminished with distance from the privies located higher up. The presence of remains related to luxury food, such as almonds, walnuts and olives, within the walls of the La Chesnaye wharf provides further evidence that this sector was polluted by privies belonging to rich merchants living in the neighbourhood. The macroremains also testify to intercontinental trade, since they include fragments of imported fruit, as well as seeds for growing flax, hemp and tobacco. The seeds may have fallen here when merchandise was unloaded from boats.[24]

ARCHAEOENTOMOLOGICAL REMAINS

The results of the archaeoentomological analysis carried out for this period by Allison Bain identified 45 types of beetles belonging to seven different families. The species represented are typical of those normally found in a beach environment which was evolving as the proportion of natural and cultural components changed. Most of the species are associated with damp shore environments containing stagnant water and decaying organic matter such as manure, compost, wood, bark, moss, plants and stored food goods. Beetles living on the fungi that grow in these decomposing environments were also identified.[25]

THE FORESHORE IN THE 18TH CENTURY

The sector studied for this period lies between the river and the La Chesnaye and Comporté wharves, and covers 507.59m², or 39.01% of the total surface area of the Îlot Hunt site (Fig. 1). The beach levels in this sector are generally characterized by a blackish crumbly sand; in contrast with the sand in the previous period, this consists primarily of mineral matter, the organic material being only a few wood chips.[26] According to Daniel Simoneau, who excavated the site, this environmental change is probably a consequence of new port regulations prohibiting the dumping of garbage on the shore, a practice that had interfered with unloading merchandise from boats. From 1711, a harbourmaster ensured that these regulations were respected.[27] In 1739, for similar reasons, the authorities issued new edicts forbidding people from leaving refuse on the beaches.[28]

In all, the late 18th-century levels yielded 3,910 artefacts and ecofacts, distributed over an area of 507.59m^2 — some 200m^2 less than the area studied for the 17th century. The finds include 3,480 movable and 294 architectural objects (89% and 8% of the assemblage); ecofacts (shells and vertebrate bones) account for only 3%. It is clear that the profile of this assemblage is quite different from that of the previous period. A summary table (Table 2) shows the main categories of object.

MOVABLE OBJECTS

The large number of movable objects characterizing this environment is probably accidental, since it includes 2,204 small, headed pins (Fig. 4), which, in all likelihood, were deposited here when a crate of merchandise fell to the beach. A similar occurrence may also explain the presence of 168 personal accessories — small objects and trinkets, including buttons, cufflinks, belt and shoe buckles, shoe irons, fastenings, rings, small chains, brass wire, thimbles, tacks, snuffers and a Jew's harp, most of which were made of brass (Fig. 5). Although

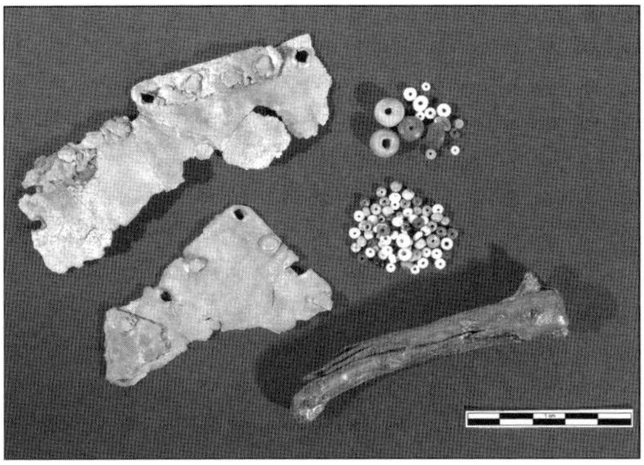

FIG. 2

Îlot Hunt site (CeEt-110), Québec City: 17th-century scraps of copper, glass beads, clasp knife (photograph, Ville de Québec).

FIG. 3

Îlot Hunt site (CeEt-110), Québec City: 17th-century birch bark containers (photograph, Ville de Québec).

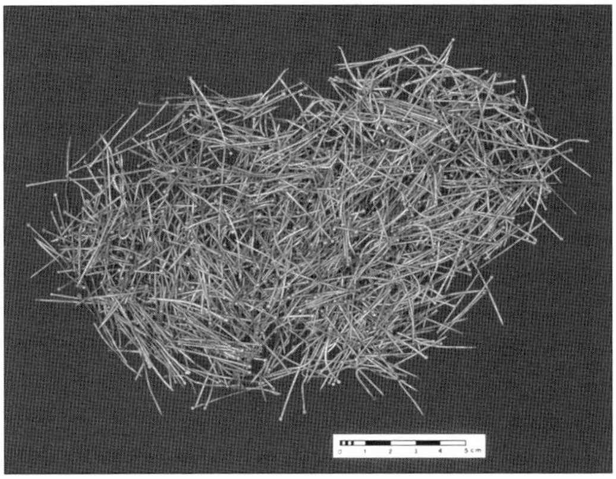

FIG. 4

Îlot Hunt site (CeEt-110), Québec City: 18th-century pins (photograph, Ville de Québec).

FIG. 5

Îlot Hunt site (CeEt-110), Québec City: 18th-century brass shank buttons and cufflinks with decorative motifs (photograph, Ville de Québec).

TABLE 2

Distribution of objects from the 18th-century beach level of the Îlot Hunt site.

MOVABLE	ARCHITECTURAL	ECOFACTS
89% (3,480 objects)	**8% (294 objects)**	**3% (147 objects)**
Ceramic: 968 objects including **99** pipes and fragments. **Glass: 72** objects. **Metal: 2,426** small brass objects, including **2,204** small, headed pins and **168** small objects, **1** cannon ball, **2** musket balls, **15** barrel hoops, **2** hooks, **1** tool handle, **1** bale seal, etc. **Other inorganic and organic material**: 1 marble, 1 chert flake, 2 flint flakes, 5 shoes.	**180** nails. **2** hinges, 1 pintle, 6 pieces of hardware. **41** bricks. **4** roof slates. **19** tiles. **51** fragments of window glass.	**136** vertebrate bones. **7** shells.

it is normal to find such accessories in vacant lots, the large quantity discovered on the Hunt site is at present unique in Québec; it is probable that, like the pins, they were all deposited on the beach at one moment in the last decades of the 18th century, perhaps when a crate of merchandise slipped from someone's hands. These items should therefore be dissociated from domestic refuse dumped on the beach; they reflect instead the site's economic function. The commercial activities that once took place on the wharves are also reflected in the tokens, bale seals, barrel hoops and coins found among the movable objects. Two tinkling cones, scraps of copper and flakes of chert and flint should be classified as trade goods, and probably date from the previous period. They are the only trade goods present; there are no artefacts associated with hunting or fishing. Ceramic and glass objects, represented by sherds or very fragmented items characteristic of the kind of garbage disposed of in vacant spaces (yards, streets, alleys and gardens), make up about a third of the catalogued objects, that is 1,040 of the 3,480 movable objects in the collection. The 1,040 glass and ceramic items accumulated over the course of the 18th century contrast with the 465 objects of the same sort in the 17th century.

ARCHITECTURAL OBJECTS

Architectural objects account for only 8% of the 18th-century assemblage, compared with 31% of the earlier collection. They include 180 wrought nails, 41 bricks, 19 coarse earthenware tiles, 51 window glass fragments, a few pieces of slate, and various items of building hardware. The homogeneous nature of the material and the French origins of the bricks, tiles and roofing slates suggest that these objects come from a single dwelling — no doubt one of those reduced to rubble during the bombardment preceding Québec's fall to the British. The attacks destroyed most of the houses in Place Royale, including the home of Jean Mailloux which stood on the Hunt site, and the residential and commercial compound built by Aubert de La Chesnaye immediately to the west of the site. By this time most of the houses were constructed of stone; when this area of Lower Town was reduced to ruins and the colony was crushed, the rubble that remained proved indispensable to rebuilding efforts. The relative lack of building materials in the late 18th-century beach levels indicates that materials were salvaged from the ruins for the intense reconstruction activities that followed the Seven Years War.

ECOFACTS

The ecofacts from this period include only 136 vertebrate bones representing kitchen garbage, compared with 944 specimens in the previous period. Considering that in 1698 Québec and its suburbs had a population of 1,700, while in 1795 there were 7,162 inhabitants, a third of them living in this area of Lower Town,[29] it is difficult to explain the decline in food remains from 38% in the 17th century to 3% in the 18th. Concerns about rats, the enemies of ports, may have discouraged people from leaving their food garbage on the shore and led them to dispose of it elsewhere, for example in privies. Only seven mollusc valves were found in the 18th-century deposits; as mentioned above, shell remains may have been put to other uses.

MACROREMAINS

The analysis of the macroremains indicates a reduction both in plants that colonize empty spaces and in plant remains usually associated with the contents of privies. According to the study carried out by Catherine Fortin, it appears that the 18th-century beach soil was less contaminated than the 17th-century land colonized from the river. The quantity of macroremains originating from domestic waste, particularly in the north-eastern section of the site, is more closely comparable to the remains found on the town's street levels in the same period. The contrast with the 17th-century assemblage may result in part from the deposition of the later material closer to the water's edge, but it may also reflect 18th-century improvements to the sanitation of the area. The study of the macroremains also reveals a massive invasion of non-indigenous ruderal plants, most of which would be considered undesirable weeds, reflecting an increase in goods transported from Europe.[30]

ARCHAEOENTOMOLOGICAL REMAINS

The study of archaeoentomological remains shows that the great majority of insects identified from this period belong to species living in stagnant water near organic deposits. Allison Bain's research revealed only eighteen kinds of insect, compared to 45 for the previous period. One of these, the rove beetle, is generally found in plant litter and composted material close to water. The assemblage includes weevils that live on wood, and grain weevils known for infesting stored cereals. Certain of the insects identified are associated with the growth of fungi on stored foodstuffs and would thus have originated in storage areas before the goods fell onto the beach or were thrown there.

CONCLUSION

This study of the beach levels on the Îlot Hunt site in the 17th and 18th centuries is a reminder that waste management is a phenomenon that dates back to the earliest cities. Urban pollution has long been considered a threat to a community's health; it spurred the earliest developments in public hygiene in industrialized Western cities. Concerns about urban pollution were voiced from the very beginnings of the modern city. In the 17th, 18th and 19th centuries, there was a preoccupation with urban garbage; contemporary written sources painted a picture of citizens living in the midst of waste heaps of every description. The regulations of these centuries would lead one to believe that private sanitary facilities were largely deficient and that open urban spaces were contaminated with all sorts of garbage. It was implied that people's mentality and habits were the root cause of the revolting filth in which everyday life took place. However, this picture has been shown to be somewhat more nuanced by historians interested in cultural and social history, as well as by recent archaeological research.

The research discussed here confirms that the river's shore at Îlot Hunt was used to dispose of various kinds of refuse at the end of the 17th century. The area received the contents of emptied privies, the carcasses of butchered animals, building materials, plant matter and domestic garbage. It seems, however, that this refuse originated from the shore's immediate surroundings. The macroremains were probably left on the beach when the Aubert de La Chesnaye privies were cleaned out, while the large quantities of worked wood may have been dumped there when the merchant's wooden enclosure (built in 1688) was demolished to make way for the wharf constructed in 1699. On the other hand, although the vertebrate bones have not yet been analysed, they clearly make up a considerable proportion of the refuse from the site, and may have come from the neighbourhood.

It is difficult to estimate the quantity of domestic waste among the movable objects found on the beach. Of the 876 objects in this category, only 234 are ceramic items, 28 glass containers and 40 shoes. The largest group of movable objects consists of items that testify to the way this exceptional natural environment was used before the arrival of Europeans and shortly thereafter. Numerous small objects are evidence of Amerindians staying there; others testify to the first contacts between the Aboriginal people and the French colonists, and still others reflect activities such as trade, exchange and commerce, as well as hunting and fishing, all of which could have taken place on the shore. The results of the present research project suggest that, in general, the waste left deliberately on the foreshore area of Îlot Hunt came from the immediate vicinity and, more specifically, from the wealthy merchants living nearby.

In the 18th century the proportion of rubbish left on the site diminished considerably. Apart from the 1,040 ceramic and glass objects representing domestic waste deliberately dumped on the beach, there was far less refuse coming from outside the area. The lack of organic material, the decline in building materials and ecofacts, and the relatively large number of movable objects, contrast with the late 17th-century refuse. The exceptional increase in small imported objects is fortuitous, since they must all have been dropped by accident at the same time; they bear witness to the growing intensity of commercial activities on the site. A massive invasion of non-native ruderal plants, whose percentage among the macroremains tripled between the 17th and 18th century, is also indicative of the increased circulation of merchandise imported from Europe. The decrease in food waste and faecal matter, which had contaminated the Îlot Hunt site in the previous century, might be the outcome of improvements in urban sanitation in this area. The results of the archaeoentomological analysis support this possibility, since the number of insects identified from the 18th century is much lower.

Other factors may explain the changing character of the foreshore environment. As land was gained from the river to construct port facilities, the form of the cove was modified, the shoreline was advanced into the deeper riverbed and, in the second half of the 18th century, more and more lots were converted into private properties — lots which up to the Seven Years War had been shared with public interests. These factors, along with the action of tides and currents, may have contributed to the changes noted in the shore's condition. On the other hand, the gradual construction of large masonry structures to the north and south of the site and the building of wharves in rapid succession downstream, as well as the infilling required for these projects, will probably have resulted in the accumulation of greater concentrations of waste, just as the construction of Aubert de La Chesnaye's enclosure and wharf had when they isolated part of the beach in the 17th century.

Previous archaeological studies in Québec City have thrown some light on the question of urban hygiene. They have shown that in the 17th and 18th centuries the private sanitary facilities at Place Royale and on the Aubert de la Chesnaye site conformed in every respect to the edicts issued by the authorities of New France. In fact, these facilities generally respected the principles of hygiene espoused by the wealthier classes in French society at the time.[31] The results of archaeological studies of 19th-century urban hygiene in Québec's Lower Town have indicated that the inhabitants of the Saint-Roch quarter, as well as those of Îlot Hunt, were able to maintain a certain level of public health, despite crowding, promiscuity, insalubrity and disease — problems decried in contemporary written sources because they had devastating effects on people's daily lives.[32] The measures taken to improve hygiene, from the construction of sanitary facilities to the upkeep of people's surroundings, were in every case the result of private initiatives.

In Québec major urban hygiene problems did not arise until the early 19th century, a period marked by the unprecedented development of shipyards and the economic prosperity that ensued, alongside the growth of new, densely populated city quarters and a massive influx of immigrants. At this point the difficulties of maintaining thoroughfares and the problems of filth and infectious diseases obliged the municipal authorities to adopt a more enlightened approach and take an interest in public health. In the struggle against pollution, it was no doubt fear that eventually inspired the general population and, above all, the authorities of the 19th century to support a public hygiene campaign.

Îlot Hunt, located in a port area with a particular flora and fauna, was a point at which individuals, nations, cultures and languages converged, a place through which food, produce and merchandise flowed and where interests and conflicts were intensified. For over four centuries, Îlot Hunt reflected the influence of various populations and contacts, and fulfilled several purposes. It has also been a place where animals, plants, parasites and diseases have passed. Despite the site's vulnerability, urban pollution from human and animal sources at Îlot Hunt in the 17th and 18th centuries did not reach the proportions described in official colonial documents, which sound much like documents from the Middle Ages onward dealing with urban waste in large cities in France.

ACKNOWLEDGEMENTS

The present study was made possible with the help of many people. My thanks go in particular to biologist Catherine Fortin, who conducted the palaeoethnobotanical analysis, and to Allison Bain, Professor of Archaeology at Université Laval, who studied the entomological remains from this waterfront. I am grateful to Jean-Pierre Chrétien, curator with the Archaeological Survey of Canada at the Canadian Museum of Civilization, who organized the study of the footwear collection from Îlot Hunt, and researcher Keltie Mierins, who carried out the study. Finally, I would like to thank the members of the review committee for their careful reading of the text.

NOTES

[1] The place name Îlot Hunt no longer exists. Named after James Hunt, one of the influential owners of this city block in the 19th century, the site is today occupied by the Auberge Saint-Antoine.

[2] Simoneau 2003, 1–183.

[3] Simoneau 2003, 4.

[4] Simoneau 2003, 117.

[5] Geismar 1987, 30–5; Huey 1984, 15–37; Weber 1988, 14.

[6] LaRoche 1986, 1–338; Le Groupe Harcart inc. 1989, 1–105.
[7] Simoneau 2003.
[8] L'Anglais 1994.
[9] Several recent studies have taken this innovative approach. Examples include Goyette 2000; Bain 1999.
[10] L'Anglais 1996, 9–15; Cloutier 1996, 17–24.
[11] L'Anglais 1996, 11.
[12] Simoneau 2003, 27.
[13] Daniel Simoneau, July 2004, pers. comm.
[14] Simoneau 2003, 27.
[15] The foreshore levels associated with Québec's earliest days consisted of orangey sand containing a few household artefacts of European origin. Simoneau 2003, 24–6.
[16] Simoneau 2003, 25.
[17] The collection was restored and given to the Archaeological Survey of Canada at the Canadian Museum of Civilization for detailed study.
[18] This information is taken from Bluteau *et al.* 1980.
[19] Simoneau 2003, 29.
[20] Grew & de Neergaard 1988, 1–143.
[21] Hare *et al.* 1987, 64.
[22] Hare *et al.* 1987, 81.
[23] Diderot & D'Alembert 1966–7, **24**, 'Dessin'.
[24] Fortin 1998; 2005.
[25] Bain 2005.
[26] Simoneau 2003, 119, 146–7.
[27] Simoneau 2003, 102.
[28] Simoneau 2003, 102.
[29] Hare *et al.* 1987, 81, 325. In 1795, 2,512 of Québec's 7,162 inhabitants lived in Lower Town.
[30] Fortin 2005.
[31] Cloutier 1996, 17–24.
[32] The discovery of twelve privies in the Saint-Roch suburb shows that such sanitary facilities were set up in the back yards of workers' homes in the 19th century, contrary to evidence from written sources, which report a lack of such facilities in this quarter. A study of the density and distribution of waste in a few of the back yards associated with the same group of houses also indicates that the people living there in the 19th century were conscious of the importance of a certain level of sanitation. That the residents in this sector of the city were able to find ways of meeting their public hygiene needs is demonstrated by the concentration of waste along the sides and at the back of their yards, as well as by a steady reduction in the amount of garbage left in vacant spaces in the course of the 19th century. On this subject, see Cloutier 2004 (Chapter 3); Goyette 2000 discusses the structural evolution of sanitary facilities at Îlot Hunt in the 19th century and considers the way they reflect appropriate behaviour adopted by the population in regard to public hygiene. For Îlot Hunt see also Bain's 1999 research on insects and parasites found in soil samples of *c.* 1850–1900, which shows that the craftsmen and workers living on this site knew how to keep their surroundings healthy, contrary to the very different picture painted in official discourse.

BIBLIOGRAPHY

PUBLISHED SOURCES

Bluteau, M.-A. *et al.* 1980, *Les Cordonniers, artisans du cuir*, Montréal: Boréal Express.

Cloutier, C. 1996, 'Hygiène privée, transferts culturels et mécanisation: le cas des latrines du site Aubert-de-La-Chesnaye à Québec', in Pothier 1996, 17–24.

Cloutier, C. 2004, *De la Stratification archéologique à la stratification sociale: hygiène urbaine et conditions de vie de six familles ouvrières du faubourg Saint-Roch à Québec au XIXe siècle*, Cahiers d'archéologie du CÉLAT **16**.

Diderot, D. & D'Alembert, J. 1966–67 [1751–80], *Encyclopédie, ou dictionnaire raisonné des sciences, des arts et des métiers*, facs. of 1st edn, 35 vols, Stuttgart-Bad Cannstatt: Frommann.

Fortin, C. 1998, 'Analyse paléoethnobotanique du site Aubert-de-La-Chesnaye', in Moss 1998, 299–378.

Geismar, J.H. 1987, 'Digging into a seaport's past', *Archaeology* **40**:1, 30–5.

Goyette, M. 2000, *Des Vestiges d'une arrière-cour à l'histoire de l'hygiène publique à Québec au XIXe siècle: la troisième campagne de fouilles archéologiques à l'îlot Hunt*, Cahiers d'archéologie du CÉLAT **6**.

Grew, F. & de Neergaard, M. 1988, *Shoes and Pattens: Medieval Finds from Excavations in London*, London: HMSO.

Hare, J., Lafrance, M., & Thiery-Ruddel, D. 1987, *Histoire de la ville de Québec, 1608–1871*, Montréal: Boréal.

Huey, P.R. 1984, 'Old Slip and Cruger's wharf at New York: an archaeological perspective of the colonial American waterfront', *Hist. Archaeol.* **18**:1, 15–37.

L'Anglais, P.-G. 1994, *La Recherche archéologique en milieu urbain: d'une archéologie dans la ville vers une archéologie de la ville*, Cahiers du CÉLAT, hors série **6**.

L'Anglais, P.-G. 1996, 'L'Hygiène urbaine à Québec au temps de la Nouvelle-France', in Pothier 1996, 9–15.

Moss, W. (ed.) 1998, *L'Archéologie de la maison Aubert-de-la-Chesnaye à Québec*, Cahiers d'archéologie du CÉLAT **3**.

Pothier, L. (ed.) 1996, *L'Eau, l'hygiène publique et les infrastructures*, Mémoires vives, Montréal: Groupe P.G.V.

UNPUBLISHED SOURCES

Bain, A. 1999, 'Archaeoentomological and Archaeoparasitological Reconstructions at Îlot Hunt (CeEt-110): New Perspectives in Historical Archaeology (1850–1900)', PhD thesis, Université Laval.

Bain, A. 2005, 'Analyse archéoentomologique du site Îlot Hunt (CeEt-110) 2004', Université Laval.

Fortin, C. 2005, 'Analyse paléoethnobotanique du site de l'îlot Hunt (site CeEt-110) aux XVIIe et XVIIIe siècles à Québec', Ville de Québec, Service de l'aménagement du territoire, Division du design, de l'architecture et du patrimoine.

LaRoche, D. 1986, 'La surveillance et le sauvetage des vestiges archéologiques au Musée de la civilisation à Québec', Société immobilière du Québec.

Le Groupe Harcart Inc. 1989, 'Inventaire archéologique, îlots Bell et Hunt', Ville de Québec, Service de l'urbanisme, Division du Vieux-Québec et du patrimoine.

Simoneau, D. 2003, 'Rapport d'interventions archéologiques, îlot Hunt, 2001–2002', Service de l'aménagement du territoire, Division design, architecture et patrimoine, Ville de Québec.

Weber, C. 1988, 'Philadelphia's Early Waterfront: the Hertz Lot Excavation', Philadelphia Historical Commission, paper presented at the CNEHA, Québec.

ABBREVIATIONS

CÉLAT	Centre interuniversitaire de recherche sur les lettres, les arts et les traditions
CNEHA	Council for Northeast Historical Archaeology
HMSO	Her Majesty's Stationery Office

SUMMARY IN FRENCH, GERMAN, ITALIAN AND SPANISH

RÉSUMÉ

Les battures du Saint-Laurent sur le site de l'îlot Hunt aux XVIIe et XVIIIe siècles : un dépotoir à ciel ouvert ?

Cet article étudie l'état des berges du Saint-Laurent le long de la basse ville de Québec aux XVIIe et XVIIIe siècles. Une étude détaillée des collections archéologiques a été menée pour évaluer l'impact de l'occupation euro-québécoise sur l'environnement naturel. Des échantillons de sol ont été utilisés pour étudier les macrorestes des plantes, les insectes et les parasites des anciennes rives. Au premier coup d'œil, les données semblent indiquer que les plages étaient utilisées comme un lieu de décharge au cours de cette période. Cependant l'étude de ces restes donne une image plus nuancée, témoignant des nombreux rôles publics et privés de la zone et des intérêts divers qu'elle a servis.

ZUSAMMENFASSUNG

Das Küstenvorland des St Lawrence-Flusses auf dem Îlot Hunt-Gelände im 17. und 18. Jh: eine offene Abfallhalde?

Diese Arbeit untersucht den Zustand des St Lawrence-Ufers entlang Quebecs Unterstadt im 17. und 18. Jh. Eine detaillierte Studie der archäologischen Fundsammlungen wurde erstellt, um den Einfluß der Europäischen Bevölkerung in Quebec auf diese natürliche Umgebung zu bewerten. Bodenproben wurden benutzt, um die Makroreste von Pflanzen, Insekten und Parasiten der alten Ufer zu bestimmen. Auf den ersten Blick scheint es, daß die Ufer in dieser Zeit als Abfallplätze benutzt wurden. Eine genauere Studie dieser Abfälle jedoch gibt dem Bild mehr Zwischentöne, die auf die vielen öffentlichen und privaten Verwendungen, die den verschiedensten Interessen dienten, hinweisen.

RIASSUNTO

La zona intercotidale del fiume San Lorenzo e il sito di Îlot Hunt nel XVII e XVIII secolo: una discarica a cielo aperto?

Questa ricerca si incentra sulle condizioni delle sponde del fiume San Lorenzo nel tratto della città bassa di Quebec durante il XVII e il XVIII secolo. È stato intrapreso uno studio dettagliato del materiale archeologico per valutare l'impatto della popolazione europea del Quebec su quest'ambiente naturale. Sono stati usati campioni di suolo per studiare i macroresti di piante, insetti e parassiti delle antiche rive. Da un primo approccio, i dati sembrano indicare che le rive fossero usate in questo periodo come discariche. In ogni caso, lo studio di questi resti fornisce un'immagine più sfumata, testimoniando le diverse funzioni pubbliche e private dell'area e i diversi scopi a cui serviva.

RESUMEN

La playa del St Lawrence en el Îlot Hunt durante los siglos XVII y XVIII: ¿un basurero a cielo abierto?

Este artículo investiga el estado de las riberas del río St Lawrence en la Ciudad Baja en Quebec durante los siglos XVII y XVIII. Se ha desarrollado un detallado estudio arqueológico para determinar el impacto de la ocupación europea y

Quebecquiana en este tipo de medio natural, tomándose muestras de tierra para estudiar los restos de plantas (macros), insectos y parásitos de las riberas antiguas. A primera vista los resultados parecen indicar que las playas se utilizaron como basureros durante dicho período, aunque el panorama ofrecido por tal estudio en mucho más matizado, constatándose las numerosas funciones públicas y privadas que tenía dicha zona y los diversos intereses que servía.

Ville de Québec, Service de l'aménagement du territoire, Division du design, de l'architecture et du patrimoine, Édifice de la fabrique, 295, boulevard Charest Est, Québec (Québec), Canada G1K 3G8 [celine.cloutier@ville.quebec.qc.ca]